LBJ

A Life

Irwin Unger

Debi Unger

John Wiley & Sons, Inc.
New York • Chichester • Weinheim • Brisbane • Singapore • Toronto

In Loving Memory of
Paul Goodman (1934–1995)
Mary Weisstein (1905–1999)

Credits: All photographs courtesy of LBJ Library Collection: pages 279, 280, Johnson Family Photo; page 281, *Austin Statesman*; page 284 top right, Mr. Frank Muto; page 284 bottom, Cecil Stoughton; page 285 and page 287 top, Yoichi R. Okamoto; page 286 top, page 287 bottom, page 288, Frank Wolfe; page 286 bottom, Mike Geissinger.

This book is printed on acid-free paper. ∞

Published by John Wiley & Sons, Inc.
Published simultaneously in Canada

This publication is designed to provide accurate and authoritative information in regard to the subject matter covered. It is sold with the understanding that the publisher is not engaged in rendering professional services. If professional advice or other expert assistance is required, the services of a competent professional person should be sought.

Library of Congress Cataloging-in-Publication Data:

Unger, Irwin
    LBJ : a life / Irwin Unger, Debi Unger.
        p.   cm.
    Includes bibliographical references and index.
    ISBN 0-471-17602-8 (alk. paper)
    1. Johnson, Lyndon B. (Lyndon Baines), 1908–1973. 2. Presidents—United States Biography. 3. United States—Politics and government—1963–1969. I. Unger, Debi. II. Title.
    E847.U59   1999
    973.923'092—dc21
    [B]   99-22475

Printed in the United States of America

10 9 8 7 6 5 4 3

Contents

Acknowledgments

Authors are needy people who require much help, comfort, and support. Happily, we have received these from many people. At the LBJ Library, Linda Seelke was always generous with her informed and skillful aid, and Philip Scott, the photo archivist, came to our rescue when time was short. Other librarians and archivists who helped us include Rosemarie O'Leary of the Mercantile Library of New York; Ann Fotiades of the CBS Archives; John Broders of the *Texas Monthly*; and Joan Lager, Kelly Booker, Wanda Wykoff, and Robert Stewart, all of the Asbury Park Library. We also wish to thank the staffs of the Elmer Bobst Library at New York University and of the New York Public Library for all the friendly services they provided.

Many friends, by listening, criticizing, contributing documents and memories, and making our lives pleasanter during the years of the book's genesis, deserve our gratitude. We particularly wish to thank David Burner, Bernard Weisberger, Ralph Dannheiser, Dr. Edith Jacobs, Dr. Solomon Farhie, Ellen Farhie, Dr. Paul Ehrlich, Lillian Z. Cohen, Elaine Blume, Joyce and Anthony Infante, Kim Kamaris, Howard S. Sussman, Phyllis and Jerry Reich, Libby and Arnold Friedman, and Norma and David Schechner.

We are more than usually grateful to Hana Lane, our editor at John Wiley. Her faith, her praise, and her skill have sustained us through many gritty places and immeasurably improved the book. We also would like to thank John Simko, Wiley's associate managing editor, who ably helped in the production of the book. William Drennan's painstaking work as copyeditor was rigorous and indispensable.

Finally, once again, we thank our agent, Alexander Hoyt. Alex's good humor, optimism, and hard work on our behalf have been necessary for our sanity and an essential pillar of our joint enterprise. May he keep up the good work!

Irwin Unger
Debi Unger

CHAPTER 1

Beginnings

LYNDON JOHNSON WAS A SON of the Texas Hill Country. A broad band of terrain just west of the Gulf of Mexico coastal plain, it is a beautiful region of rolling hills covered with cedar, Spanish oak, bald cypress, and cottonwood. During the fall, sumac and maple turn the hills bright red; during the spring, the fields and roadsides are blanketed with bluebonnets, Indian paintbrush, daisies, poppies, and buttercups. The land still supports white-tailed deer, wild turkeys, opossums, raccoons, and armadillos. Its original fauna included mountain lions, black bears, and gray wolves, even bison. "It is a place for dreams," writes Bill Porterfield.[1]

Geologists call the Hill Country the Edwards Plateau. It is a raised former sea floor, and its soil, except in a few river valleys, is a thin layer over a limestone base. Its rainfall is erratic. At times the land succumbs to drought; at times it is struck by "gullywashers," cloudbursts that send walls of water down the rain channels with destructive force. The plateau marks the start of the West. Its people do not raise cotton—or not very much—or sorghum, as in East Texas; they herd cattle, hunt, and grow peaches and plums. Stonewall, where Lyndon Johnson was born, was at a crossroads of East and West, a site that blurred a strong identification with either section. Acknowledging this hybrid origin, Johnson once referred to himself as a "cross between a Baptist preacher and a cowboy."[2]

Although Lyndon Johnson lived in Washington more than half of his adult life, he was deeply attached to his place of birth. "In almost every action that Johnson . . . [took] as President," claims journalist Hugh

Sidey, "there is a strand which can be clearly followed back to his home in Texas. As a branding iron sears flesh, the memories of . . . the Texas Hill Country etched themselves on Lyndon Johnson's cortex."[3] When he left the presidency in 1969, he returned to his ranch on the Pedernales River, a mile away from the tiny farmhouse where he was born. It was there that he died four years later, and after a formal state funeral in the nation's capital, was buried on its cherished river's banks.

If Johnson loved the Hill Country, he also loved Texas. His state was a more abstract concept than the rolling hills of the Edwards Plateau, but it was tightly entwined with his family's history. The first Johnson ancestor to reach Texas was his great-great-uncle John Wheeler Bunton, who arrived in 1833 while Texas was still a state of the Mexican Republic. Bunton played an important role in the Texas war of independence as both a soldier and a legislator. But he did not die at the Alamo, as Lyndon and his father claimed; he died in bed. The first direct Johnson forebear to reach Texas was his great-grandfather Robert Holmes Bunton, who came from Tennessee in 1858 and fought for the Confederacy in the Civil War. His daughter, Eliza Bunton, would be Lyndon's paternal grandmother.

The Buntons were the first in Texas, but the Johnsons were first in the Hill Country. In 1846 Jesse Johnson moved from Georgia to Lockhart, Caldwell County, in East Texas, where he acquired 330 acres of land and a respectable amount of other property. Somehow Jesse lost it all, and when he died in 1856, his ten children were left without an inheritance. Without money or chattels, his son, Sam Ealy Sr., Johnson's grandfather, joined forces with brothers Tom and Andrew and set out for Blanco County, farther west, determined to make their own fortunes.

The Johnson brothers settled along the Pedernales River near what would become Johnson City—named for a nephew who had surveyed the land—and made good money raising cattle. Then came stints as Confederate soldiers in the Civil War. At one point Sam Sr. reportedly risked his life by carrying a wounded comrade from the battlefield on his own back. The Johnson brothers came back to the Hill Country after the war and resumed ranching. In December 1867 Sam married Eliza Bunton. The Johnson boys were among the pioneers of the "long drives" of the post–Civil War Cattle Kingdom era and became wealthy guiding their herds of Texas longhorns north up the Chisholm Trail to sell at railhead in Abilene. In 1871 Tom Johnson was reported to be the second richest man in Blanco County.

But then their fortunes, like their father's, turned. By 1870 the cattle market was glutted and the price per head at Abilene plunged. The next year they lost all their land. In 1877 Tom Johnson, who never married, drowned under never-explained circumstances in the Brazos River. Sam Sr., a father of nine, struggled to support his wife and family. After a few unsuccessful attempts at farming in other parts of Texas, he moved back to the Hill Country. Here, proud Eliza sold her last remaining wedding presents, her silver-mounted carriage and her two Thoroughbreds, to make a down payment on land on the Pedernales. This tract stayed in the family until her death.

The Johnsons never made a go of agriculture, and Lyndon's later devotion to husbandry on his ranch seems like an attempt to revise the family past. Although Sam Sr. now had a permanent farm, he remained relatively poor for the rest of his life. Farming in the Hill Country was hard. When the first settlers arrived they found green grass and gentle hills, suggesting fertile ground. But in fact, as we have seen, the soil was thin and the region afflicted with alternating periods of heavy rains and long droughts.

Lyndon's father, Sam Ealy Jr., the fifth child and the first son of Sam and Eliza Bunton, was ten when the family moved to the Pedernales farm. Called "Little Sam" to distinguish him from his father, he had a good mind, loved school, and hoped to continue his studies. But acquiring an education was hard for farmers' sons, who were needed at home to help out, and he had to finish high school by studying on his own and passing a special state examination that gave him a diploma and a license to teach school. He would always remember with pride his test scores of 100 percent in U.S. and Texas history.

Three years of teaching made Little Sam yearn to be a lawyer. Finding it impossible to rustle up enough money for law school, he went back to the farm, where he waited for something better to come along. In 1904 he learned that a seat in the Texas legislature from his county was vacant. He ran for it and won.

It didn't take long for him to realize that politicking was more stimulating than farming. Sam Ealy Jr.'s politics were a special brand. Sam Sr., his father, had been swept up in the revolt of Texas small farmers against the dominance of the planter-business elite during the 1890s, a time when cotton was a ruinous six cents a pound and the railroads had them by the throat. Sam Sr. became a Populist and ran on the People's Party ticket for the state legislature in 1892. He was defeated, but Populism did not die in Texas. Four years later the "respectable classes" mounted a vicious campaign against another Populist challenge, a campaign that resembled the tactics of the Ku Klux Klan during Reconstruction. Thereafter, the People's Party quickly deflated, leaving Texas a one-party state but leaving the predominant Democrats with a residue of anti-elite insurgency.

Lyndon Johnson's father, like his grandfather, was a defender of the "common man." Elected to the state legislature in 1904 as a Democrat, Sam Ealy Jr. opposed the "interests," the trusts, and big business. He supported an eight-hour day for railroad laborers, pure-food legislation, and municipal regulation of utility rates. He also attacked the Ku Klux Klan on the floor of the Texas House of Representatives at a time when many of its members were Klan sympathizers. "My father," said Lyndon, "was a liberal, progressive fella that dealt in helping the poor."[4]

His forebears' political lives deeply influenced the future president. Johnson was born with politics in his blood. His great-great-uncle John Wheeler Bunton signed the Texas Declaration of Independence, helped write the new Lone Star Republic's constitution, sat in the first Texas Congress, and voted for the bill establishing the Texas Rangers. His mother's father, Joseph Wilson Baines, was a former Texas secretary of state and member of the state legislature. Sam Ealy Johnson Jr. would serve five terms in the Texas state legislature. On the day of his birth, LBJ would later recount, his grandfather Sam Ealy Sr., himself a failed office-seeker, rode through the Texas Hill Country announcing, "A United States Senator was born this morning!"[5]

Lyndon's immediate political heritage was populistic. Some of his earliest memories were of listening to his grandfather "talk about the plight of the tenant farmer, the necessity for the worker to have protection for bargaining. . . ."[6] LBJ never repudiated his family's political credo, though he often suspended it in practice. Lyndon Johnson, wrote George Reedy, his later aide and presidential press secretary, felt an enduring passion "to make life easier for those who had to struggle up from the bottom. His interpretation of what was required might be open to question but not his desire to act."[7]

Johnson's political legacy is congruent with his gut suspicion of intellectual and cultural elites, though ego more than principle, resentment more than morals, may have been at its heart. "The men of ideas think little of me," he confided to biographer Doris Kearns many years later; "they despise me."[8] Toward people with patrician backgrounds and better education, he displayed an excruciating ambivalence. He was convinced that education was the only escape from poverty and secretly admired intellectuals and Ivy League blue bloods. But he was also jealous of those who never had to fight for their credentials, their cultivation, and their privileges. "My daddy always told me," Lyndon later confessed, "that if I brushed up against the grindstone of life, I'd come away with far more polish that I could ever get at Harvard or Yale. I wanted to believe him, but somehow I never could."[9] His "betters" brought out the boor in Johnson. He often went out of his way to be boastful, churlish, and abusive with well-educated or cultivated men. He sometimes acted crudely in their presence, as if trying to reduce them to his own level and muffle his feelings of inferiority. His friends ignored his tasteless behavior; his enemies condemned him for it.

Yet Johnson's politics did not include typical Populistic rancor against businessmen and the merely rich. Despite his sympathies for the underdog, his father had associated with some of the lobbyists who collected around the Texas legislature and found a patron in Roy Miller, the jovial representative of Texas Gulf Sulphur and a member of the fabulously rich King family. Johnson himself never had difficulty getting along with millionaires, especially the rough-hewn, self-made kind. His friends included Texas oil tycoons, railroad magnates, TV executives, and Henry Ford II of the motorcar giant. Nor did it interfere with his own urgent quest for wealth. Johnson made himself a millionaire through adroit manipulation of the business system, yet he never ceased to identify with the men and women of common clay.

Johnson's parents met when Rebekah Baines was teaching elocution and working as a stringer for an Austin newspaper. At her father's suggestion she interviewed the young Texas legislator Sam Ealy Johnson Jr. and found him "dashing and dynamic." He in turn was delighted to find "a girl who really liked politics."[10] Their dates often consisted of listening to admired political orators, including the populist hero William Jennings Bryan. Having just been spurned by a local sweetheart, Sam was determined not to let this beautiful and intelligent woman get away. After a whirlwind courtship, they were married on August 27, 1907.

Rebekah Baines considered her family superior to the Johnsons. A college graduate with fine features and genteel demeanor, she looked and acted like an aristocrat. Once past that first, fine careless rapture, she came to feel that she had married beneath her. She discovered, she told her son, that his "daddy was not a man to discuss higher things." He was "vulgar and ignorant." He liked to "sit up half the night with his friends, drinking beer, telling stories, and playing dominoes."[11] She not only disapproved of her husband's habits; she also disdained his forebears, comparing them unfavorably with her own. She agreed with her husband's aunt, who often said: "The Baineses have the brains and the Johnsons have the guts."[12]

Sam and Rebekah moved into a small four-room cabin upstream from his father's land. Although by Hill Country standards the house was far from squalid, it was still a comedown for a refined young woman who remembered her spacious and charming childhood home. Sam painted the house bright yellow to cheer her up, but that failed to do the job. Rebekah was unsuited to the rigors of farm life. Farm work was hard not only for the men, but also for their wives. The women did their chores without the help of gas or electricity. They heated the water drawn from outside wells in cast iron kettles over wood stoves. They washed their clothes in zinc tubs, scouring away the ubiquitous farm filth on metal scrub boards with harsh, homemade soap. They cooked on wood-fired ranges that had to be continually stoked with logs and chips. They fed the chickens and cattle, grew their own vegetables, and then canned and preserved them for the coming winters. The workday seemed long even for rural women accustomed to this drudgery, but for Rebekah, who had no experience in homemaking and who admitted that she "never liked country life and its inconveniences . . . ,"[13] it was interminable. She sometimes felt overwhelmed. "I was confronted," she wrote in her memoir, "not only by the problem of adjustment to a completely opposite personality, but also to a strange and new way of life. . . ." It was not, she added, "the charming fairy tale of which I had so long dreamed."[14]

The birth of her son on Thursday, August 27, 1908, a year after her marriage, helped reconcile Rebekah to her less than satisfactory spouse and surroundings. As the first Baines grandchild, he was the object of much attention and affection throughout her family. The Lone Star State teemed with maternal and paternal LBJ relatives. Lyndon's prolific eight great-grandparents produced hundreds of Texas-based descendants, many of whom lived close enough to visit. His relatives provided the emotional nourishment that Lyndon would need until the day he died. And besides, he hated to let go of anyone in his past, family or friend. Typically, when he signed the Elementary and Secondary Education Act at the site of his first schoolhouse in Texas, he brought back from California his first teacher, Kate Deadrich Loney, to witness the ceremony.

His very personal political style was based on a familial model. He incorporated his staffs into extended families of which he was the sheltering, generous, and exacting patriarch, always alert to their achievements and loyalties, and acutely sensitive to their feelings for him. At times, however, he was the demanding parent, pushing his staff beyond their limits. Historian Paul Conkin calls him the "big daddy of American politics."[15]

All his relatives were pleased with his looks; he had black curls, dark eyes, and white skin and resembled Eliza, his handsome paternal grandmother. The baby earned the regard of all who met him for, in his mother's words, "he was bright and bonny, a happy, winsome child, who made friends easily, ate and slept as he should, and woke with a laugh instead of a wail."[16] But best of all, he was precocious. Rebekah couldn't wait to start teaching him. At two she gave him A-B-C blocks and taught him the alphabet. At three he could recite the Mother Goose rhymes and poems from Longfellow and Tennyson. She spent long hours telling him stories from the Bible, from history, and from mythology. By four he could spell "Grandpa," "Dan" (his horse), and "cat," and could read a little.

When Lyndon was two he had to share his parents' formerly undivided attention with his new sister Rebekah. Then, two years later, came Josepha. His only brother, Sam Houston, was born in 1914 when he was six, and a third sister, Lucia, arrived in 1916. Oldest siblings always feel displaced no matter how hard parents try to compensate. Although LBJ seemed to adjust, he could not help feeling exiled from paradise. One early memory reveals his subconscious dismay. He is playing ball with his sister Rebekah, while Josepha is behind them crying in her crib. As he throws the ball, his pregnant mother goes to comfort the baby, and the ball hits her in the middle of her stomach, causing her to lose her balance and fall down. Lyndon, as most of us would perceive, did not want another rival, but he also understood he must not harm his sibling-to-be. "I was terrified at . . . what I'd done," recalled LBJ. "I was certain that her belly would pop just like a balloon." His mother later admitted that she was afraid the baby had been damaged but "at the time she said nothing of her fear; she immediately gathered me up into her arms and held me until I finally stopped crying."[17]

The little boy had other means of deflecting attention from his siblings. Though warned that he would get lost or hurt, he ran away from home several times. His parents usually found him at Grandfather Johnson's or at the schoolhouse, but there were times when he hid in the fields, refusing to reveal himself when his parents called his name. "He wanted attention," said Jesse Lambert, the Johnsons' hired help. "He would run away and run away, and the minute his mother would turn her back, he would run away again, and it was all to get attention."[18] As he got older, he began to wander off to more distant relatives, often meandering half a mile before someone spotted him and brought him back to his mother.

Mothers are usually the most important people in the lives of young children, and Rebekah assuredly was the guiding light for little Lyndon. Her life in a rural farmhouse often plunged her into despair. She counted on her firstborn son to make up for all the frustrations she had to endure—her anger at her husband's failures and his drinking, her own lack of achievements, and the straitened circumstances in which she lived. She died in 1958, before he became president, but his successes gave her great joy. His election to Congress, she wrote him, had already made up for her previous disappointments. "You have always justified my expectations, my hopes, my dreams . . . my darling boy, my devoted son, my strength and comfort."[19] As his Senate accomplishments grew, so did her gratitude and pride. "Naturally, I love all my children," she said, "but Lyndon was the first, and to me he was the greatest marvel in the world. I had always dreamed of a career for myself, but Lyndon was career enough for me."[20]

Her son, at least outwardly, returned the devotion. "My dear mother," he wrote, "the end of another busy day brought me a letter from you. Your letters always give me more strength, renewed courage and that bulldog tenacity so essential to the success of any man."[21] At times he seemed a mama's boy. In this respect he was very much like Franklin Delano Roosevelt, the commanding leader who would be his sponsor and his model. To the modern sensibility their relationship seems to verge on the incestuous. When Lyndon's father was away on business, he sometimes slept in the same bed with his mother, who, as Johnson told Doris Kearns, first scrubbed his hands and face and "then tucked me in between the cool, white sheets." Lyndon would watch as she brushed her hair and washed her face, throat, and arms from a basin. Then she would get into bed with him and read him the classics or tell him stories about her girlhood. In the first grade his choice of a poem in a school recital was "I'd Rather Be Mama's Boy." In college, in an editorial for the San Marcos *College Star*, he extolled mother love as incomparable. "Our best description of it," he wrote on May 9, 1930, "is that of all types of earthly love, it most nearly approaches the divine."[22] As Sigmund Freud has noted, "A man who has been the indisputable favorite of his mother keeps for life the feeling of a conqueror, that confidence of success that often induces real success."[23] Certainly, his mother's fervent love contributed to his achievements. LBJ recalled how his mother made him feel "big and important" and made him believe he "could do anything in the whole world."[24]

But Rebekah's love was not cost-free. From an early age she tried to stage-mother his life. If he didn't do his lessons, she would read them aloud at breakfast, and Johnson, a captive audience, would be forced to absorb the day's assignment. She would walk him to school, reading to him on the way. Johnson told reporter Isabelle Shelton in 1964 that on one occasion she "stayed all night with me working on plane geometry. . . ." Mother and son did not go to sleep until just before his eight-o'clock class. "And I just did make it," Johnson admitted. "I mean I just made a passing grade."[25] But it didn't stop there. She made him take college entrance exams even though he didn't want to, and even in college, when home for visits, she helped him on "everything." She would be "helping me now if she was here," he told Shelton, "and she'd be telling me what not to say in some of these speeches. . . ."[26]

If he felt gratitude, he also felt smothered. When he recited poems as a little boy, he remembered that the moment he was done, "she'd take me in her arms and hug me so hard I sometimes thought I'd be strangled to death."[27] More damaging was her inconsistency. She set impossible goals for her son and was annoyed when he failed to achieve them. Rebekah's love was conditional. Her behavior toward her son vacillated between doting affection when he pleased her and total rejection when he failed her. At seven or eight, when he resisted the violin and dancing lessons she had signed him up for, she refused to acknowledge his presence. "For days after I quit those lessons," he told Doris Kearns, "she walked around the house pretending I was dead. And then to make it worse, I had to watch her being especially warm and nice to my father and sisters."[28]

Rebekah again froze him out when he decided initially not to go to college. Her displeasure with him in this case lasted for months. Extreme inconsistency of parental love creates lasting anxieties. The victim fears that love depends on performance and resents being loved for his deeds, not himself. It left its mark on the adult Lyndon Johnson. For his entire life he had an insatiable need for attention, affection, and approval. Rebekah's qualities as well as her failings certainly influenced all his relationships with women. His wife, Lady Bird, in many ways served a maternal role. She helped him "on everything," he boasted, just the words he used about his mother. "Bird can still write the best speech of anybody in the family. Her judgment is better on reading something and giving it analysis. . . . She's always got the most discerning observations."[29] In the years just before he died, he formed a close relationship with Doris Kearns, who helped him write his presidential memoirs. He told her that her "intelligence, grace and strong will" resembled his mother's.[30]

Lyndon's bond to his mother did not preclude a powerful tie to his father. His beloved paternal grandfather was probably the first important male in his life. But he died when Lyndon was only seven, and the little boy turned to his father for comfort and for a masculine role model. Sam Ealy Jr. was a receptive target. Ninety years ago mothers often asserted ownership of their small sons by dressing them as girls and letting their hair grow long. One day, when Lyndon was four or five and Rebekah was in church, Sam Johnson took a large scissors and cut off all Lyndon's curls. It was about this time that Lyndon began to imitate his father, picking up his earthy, picturesque speech in contrast to his mother's refined diction. He was often restless in school, bursting at the seams to be doing things with his father. He loved to hear Sam Ealy Jr. talking politics on the porch at night with his cronies. "I wanted to copy my father always, emulate him, do the things he did," he later revealed. "He loved the outdoors and I grew to love the outdoors. He loved political life and public service. I followed him as a child and participated in it."[31] Johnson's friend Otto Crider said that Lyndon lavishly admired his father, calling him a "great man." He told Otto that he wanted to become "just like my daddy, getting pensions for old people."[32] It is significant that later in life he gravitated toward father figures. Although his relationship with older men inevitably had opportunistic aspects, he sincerely admired, even loved, Alvin Wirtz, Sam Rayburn, Richard Russell, and Franklin Roosevelt. People who met him after his Texas years often thought his mother's influence grossly inflated. A friend of his early Washington years, Virginia Foster Durr, thought the "crazy stuff about his mother being the dominating influence in his life" was "so exaggerated."[33] It is telling that his aides remember being assigned to write dutiful letters to her in their boss's name.

Sam Ealy Johnson Jr. shared his exciting political life with his son. In 1918, after a ten-year break to repair the family's fortunes, he decided to run once again for the legislature. This time he had the ten-year-old Lyndon's help in handing out campaign literature, stuffing envelopes, licking stamps, and hand delivering the material himself. Sam took his oldest son with him on campaign trips through the countryside. "We drove in the Model T Ford," Lyndon later recalled, "from farm to farm, up and down the valley, stopping at every door. My father . . . would bring the neighbors up to date on local gossip, talk about the crops and the bills he'd introduced." Campaigning was the happiest time in his father's life, and Lyndon remembered that he himself "wished it would go on forever."[34] Sam won reelection in 1918 and stayed in the Texas legislature until 1924. Once back in the political swim, he often took Lyndon with him to the state capitol to see the legislature in session. Johnson remembered sitting in the gallery for long stretches of time watching the politicians bustling about on the floor. "I heard my father pleading for seven-months school and for building little red school-houses," he said. "I heard him pleading for a way to get the farmers out of the mud. I heard him pleading for a rural route that would bring us our mail during the week."[35]

Lyndon adopted much of his father's political style. Sam Ealy Jr. took good care of his constituents. He helped to get pensions for elderly veterans or their widows, sometimes traveling to San Antonio or Houston to locate the necessary documents. He induced the legislature to appropriate $2 million for seed and feed during a serious drought, making Texas one of the first states to grant relief in times of natural catastrophe. "If there was some legislation to be passed," recalled Stell Gliddon, a newspaper editor and postmaster of Johnson City, "it was always to . . . Sam that people went, and he was always there to do it."[36] Some of Lyndon Johnson's famous mannerisms were those of his father. Sam was tactile, touching all those he conversed with. "He would get right up to you, nose to nose, and take a firm hold," said future Texas Congressman Wright Patman, who had shared a desk with "Little Sam" in the state legislature. And they resembled one another physically. Sam Ealy Jr. was a tall man with smooth, dark hair and a strong chin. He bears an uncanny resemblance to his adult son. "They looked alike, they walked the same," noted Patman.[37]

But his relationship with his father was as full of ambivalence as his relationship with his mother. Lyndon's younger brother, Sam Houston, felt that he himself was his father's favorite and that "there was a kind of tension" between Lyndon and Sam Ealy, "a sort of competition that frequently occurs between a father and the oldest son."[38] Sam Houston describes a mind game between the nine-year-old Lyndon and his father. The Johnson house was not well heated, and at night Sam Jr. would ask Sam Houston to get into his bed to contribute his body warmth. Like a puppy, the three-year-old would oblige, only to hear his older brother, after their father had fallen asleep, call to the little boy to come back to warm *his* bed.

Like Rebekah, Sam Jr. was very ambitious for his oldest son. He would wake Lyndon up every morning by shaking his feet and scolding, "Get up, Lyndon. Every boy in town's got a two-hour head start on you."[39] And his father was almost as cruel as his mother when it came to Lyndon's reluctance to go to college. At one point he told his wife in a voice loud enough for his son to hear: "That boy's just not college material."[40]

Though his father was capable of great warmth, he was also very moody. Cordial and captivating one minute, Sam Jr. could be angry and sarcastic the next. In addition, he was an old-fashioned patriarch who wanted things done his way, and when thwarted revealed a bad temper. Some of his tantrums terrified Lyndon, who remembers that his father would beat him with a razor strap. Lyndon also objected to his father's drinking. As a young adolescent he and some friends stood outside the saloon yelling for their fathers to leave. Embarrassed by his son's conduct, Sam offered him a quarter to go away, but the boy would not back down.

Johnson's stormy and ambivalent relations with his parents would in many ways foreshadow his later interactions with his friends, his staff, and his superiors and, when he was president, toward both his supporters and his opponents. He was generous and affectionate when the spirit moved him or when he perceived someone in need. He paid for hospital bills, warm clothing, and home repairs for friends and staff. He was especially generous to childhood pals. During the Depression he bought Ben Crider "the best suit of clothes" he "ever owned in his life," and signed a bunch of blank checks that Crider could use to pay expenses in those hard times.[41] He would spring for luxuries for friends on impulse. Years later, he unexpectedly gave George Reedy an expensive Lincoln automobile as a gift. But like his mother's, his price was high. He needed to be in control of everybody's behavior and expected a level of allegiance and gratitude often impossible to fulfill. He would also emulate his mother by freezing out the people who displeased him. He had wide mood swings like his father, changes that bordered on the pathological. People often observed him oscillate between grandiosity and gloom in amazingly short intervals. And even though he became president, the most powerful figure in the world, he would always question his worth.

When Lyndon was five, his father, who liked rural life and farming no more than his wife did, moved the family to Johnson City, the seat of Blanco County. Here he took up real estate and cattle dealing.

The Johnson family lived in a small frame house that LBJ later lovingly restored. The town had a population of only three or four hundred and lacked electricity, piped-in water, and a sewage system. It did not have a rail connection to the rest of the state; goods, people, and mail arrived and departed by horse, wagon, and buggy until autos came into wide use. The town boasted a courthouse, a café, three grocery stores, a barbershop, a blacksmith shop, a bank, and a post office. For a time it had a saloon, though many of the townspeople were prohibitionists and in 1916 voted to close it. All these establishments were lined up along a one-block street. The community had a combined elementary and high school building where Rebekah taught poetry and public speaking.

It had three Protestant churches, and these were the centers of social as well as religious life.

The Johnsons, like most other families, used an outhouse for nature's urges and a pump-activated well for water. But if living conditions in Johnson City were only a modest advance over the farm's in a physical sense, the Johnsons were less isolated than they had been. Though Lyndon's mother would have preferred a real city with some cultural life, she kept busy editing a weekly newspaper, the *Record-Courier*, and taking care of her family. She also joined the local temperance society, a move intended, perhaps, to defy her husband.

Lyndon's introduction to formal education began before the move to Johnson City and was a by-product of his wanderlust. Across the field from the Johnsons' farm was the play area for the one-room Junction School. The age for starting school in Texas was five, but at four the ever-sociable Lyndon began to toddle off to the playground at recess when he heard the sounds of play. He could not be stopped. In desperation, his mother persuaded the teacher, Kate Deadrich, to permit him to enroll. Although ahead of his age mentally, he was still childish emotionally. When it came his turn to read aloud, he would only do so by sitting on Miss Deadrich's lap. He had completed a primer and a reader when whooping cough cut short his first year of school.

Johnson remained the youngest in his grade in his new elementary school, after the move to Johnson City. Yet his native talent and intelligence, as well as his mother's close supervision of his schoolwork, helped him surpass his older classmates scholastically. He got mostly A's. His peers thought he was brilliant. "The boys his age just wasn't his class mentally," said his friend Ben Crider, Otto's brother.[42] Yet Johnson's mind, even at five, was mostly on politics. In the first grade he was already passing out campaign literature and listening attentively when his father and friends discussed affairs of government. "I'd just sit there," LBJ reminisced, "and eat it up."[43]

In other ways, his youth was similar to that of other Texas boys of his class and location. His first close friend was Huisso, a Mexican American boy who lived across the fields from the Johnsons. "We raced our horses together," Lyndon recalled, "when we were both just learning to ride."[44] According to Kittie Clyde Ross, Lyndon's cousin by marriage, the Johnson City kids "played all sorts of things that children play and fussed, squabbled, all the other things that kids do."[45] Lyndon had a succession of dogs, the first named "Bigham Young." When one of his hunting dogs, "Evelyn," had a litter of puppies, Johnson put up a sign in the barbershop: "See me first for hound pups, Lyndon B. Johnson." And he managed to sell all of them. He had lots of assigned farm chores—gathering eggs, putting logs in the wood box, slopping the pigs. Like Tom Sawyer, he sometimes managed to coax his siblings and friends to do them for him by passing out cookies as rewards. He often went "varmint hunting" with his friends,[46] but despite his later Texas macho image, never wanted to kill the foxes, squirrels, and rabbits. Once, when taunted by his father about his "cowardice," he killed a rabbit and then promptly vomited. Lyndon picked cotton, built fences, and herded goats for twenty-five cents a day at other farms and ranches nearby. Like other rural boys in these years, he played marbles and baseball and went swimming in the "Baptizin' hole" with his friends. But he was easily bored and always wanted to find something else to do.

At age ten Lyndon started a business of his own shining shoes, getting his mother to run an ad for him in the local paper. His business premises was the town barbershop across from the courthouse, the center of political talk and gossip. Only one daily big-city newspaper was delivered to all of Johnson City, and it came to the barbershop. Lyndon was the first to read it, running from school to the barber's as fast as possible to peruse the paper from front to back, sitting in the barber's chair. He then narrated the news to the customers, often with his own comments on its significance. At dinner, his father would pose questions of contemporary interest to his family, guests, and friends, and after dinner the family would engage in debates. When his father came back from Austin with the *Congressional Record*, Lyndon carried it around ostentatiously wherever he went.

Sam could not avoid the problems of the family farm even while serving in the legislature. His mother, Eliza Bunton, died in 1917, two years after her husband, Sam Sr., leaving the 433 Johnson acres in Stonewall to her eight children collectively. Dividing up the farm eight ways was clearly unrealistic, and in 1919 Sam decided to buy out his siblings, mortgaging all his other assets, and eventually taking on a very large debt. The family moved to the farm. He expected to repay this debt by raising cotton, but by the time the first crop came in, cotton was selling at less than eight cents per pound. In 1922, ruined financially, he had to sell the farm and move back to Johnson City. The family was saved from complete bankruptcy by the intervention of Sam's brothers Tom and George, who paid some of the back interest and who made sure the Johnson children would not be deprived.

His father's misfortune profoundly affected Lyndon. "The experts . . . tell us," he declared, "that one of the necessities for children is the feeling of security in their formative years. I know that as a farm boy I did not feel secure, and . . . I decided I was not going to be the victim of a system which would allow the price of a commodity like cotton to drop from 40 cents to six cents and destroy the homes of people like my own family."[47] The family was never dirt poor, but the Johnsons' fortunes had gyrated wildly. Each of his grandfathers made a fortune early in life and then lost it, bequeathing to their children and grandchildren the burdensome family myth of vanished wealth. The family's economic hardships while Lyndon was a child not only reinforced his sympathy for the needy but also undoubtedly bolstered the urge to get rich that marked his later career.

Sam's economic difficulties impaired his health and morale. He spent weeks at a time in bed, getting up only to sign the business papers that foreclosed his remaining property. In 1924 he gave up his seat in the legislature. The following year he got a government job—foreman of a highway-grading crew resurfacing the rough parts of the Austin–Fredericksburg Road, which he himself had proudly sponsored as a legislator. During this period Sam began to drink heavily. His personal and economic collapse affected his wife's pride and her own mental health. "There was nothing mother hated more," LBJ told his biographer Doris Kearns, "than seeing my daddy drink. . . . When she got upset, she blamed our money problems on my father's drinking. And then she cried a lot."[48] Much of her time was spent writing poetry and fantasizing about the past, to the neglect of her home and children.

These years were emotionally difficult for Lyndon. In his early adolescence, suffering all the upheavals of puberty, he had lost his most important male role models. His beloved grandfather had died a few years before, and now his father seemed no longer worthy of respect. Sam's failure to live up to family responsibilities compelled his son to take his place. Lyndon felt bitter at the new family burdens, sometimes resenting his brothers and sisters, sometimes bullying them, sometimes manipulating them. His sister Rebekah remembered him as bossy. "He thought he was papa," she said.[49] The paternal role, both the nurturing and the coercive sides, stayed with him his entire life and influenced all his political relationships.

These were also his high school years, and though his mind was not often on his schoolwork, he managed to get A's and B's. Given his family's bent, it is no surprise that his favorite academic subjects were history and government. These interests was reinforced by the lively teaching of Mr. Scott Klett, the school district superintendent, who taught high school "civics" on the side. Klett, at one point, divided his small class into two sides, pro and con, and let them debate the issue of the United

States joining the League of Nations. Lyndon, by choice, was on the pro-League side.

Known as a prodigious talker and a big joker, Lyndon became president of his senior class and graduated second in a class of six. His mother described him as a "popular, fun-loving teen-ager."[50] Rebekah exaggerated both his popularity and his merriment. If these were his characteristics at times during his adolescence, his need to be noticed, if anything, had increased with the years. He hated to lose in sports or in a fight with another boy, and when he did, he ran home through the streets crying, a peculiar mode of behavior for a boy in his teens. "All anyone had to do was touch Lyndon, and he let out a wail you could hear all over town," said Emmette Redford. "He wanted attention. He wanted everyone to know someone had injured him. He wanted everyone to feel sorry for him."[51] But Redford liked him in spite of this and thought most others did, too. He was "personable and outgoing," he later said.[52] His appearance was also intended to attract notice. He was the only boy of his age who wore a bow tie and slicked back his hair. In his senior year he sported the only straw boater in Johnson City and a spiffy summer suit.

In high school Lyndon's closest friends were the Crider and Redford boys. His first girlfriend was classmate Kittie Clyde Ross. She and Lyndon went on picnics beside the Pedernales and attended Johnson City women's club socials, where ice cream and cake were the standard fare. They also marched in temperance parades in town and went to silent movies in the makeshift town theater above an office building. Reminiscing many years later about their relationship, both remembered they did not kiss, then considered a daring act by adolescents. Though Sam Ealy was personally popular, his drinking in a temperance town and his reputation for not paying his bills to the local merchants made him suspect to the prosperous, respectable Rosses, and they took steps to abort their daughter's relationship with Lyndon. When, at her parents' behest, Kittie turned down Lyndon's invitation to go to the annual Johnson City–Fredericksburg baseball game and picnic, he never asked her out again. But he did not forget her. Johnson was a sentimentalist who reveled in nostalgia and enjoyed seeking out old friends from childhood and youth. In January 1965 he invited Kittie and her husband to his inauguration, flew with them from Austin to Washington on *Air Force One*, and then saw to it that they had a good time at the inaugural festivities.

If his relations with the respectable Kittie seem proper and innocent, he was not a prig. During his high school years, much to the chagrin of his mother, Lyndon began to act boisterous and aggressive like many other adolescent boys. There were episodes of furtive drinking and reckless driving and a growing interest in sex. At one point Lyndon borrowed his father's car and went off to carouse with some friends. He drove the car into a ditch, badly denting its fenders. Too frightened to face his dad, he ran away to some cousins in Robstown, near the gulf, and got a job in a cotton ginning establishment. When Sam learned where his son was, he promised to forgive him, and sent Walter Crider, another Crider friend, to bring him back. As Lyndon remembered it, his mother did not overlook the accident. Instead of scolding him, however, she withdrew, staring at him, whenever she saw him, with a baleful eye.

As he later said, his teenage preoccupations never eclipsed his interest in current affairs. While his father was still in office, Lyndon campaigned for other Democratic candidates, placing election posters in the local shop windows. In school he was a member of the debating team, winning his first argument, on whether Texas should be divided into a number of states. In his senior year, he and his partner won the debating championship of Blanco County, but did not make the statewide finals. The skinny, six-foot-tall young man was also the valedictorian at his graduation.

Lyndon bitterly disappointed his parents when, after graduation, he announced that he was sick of school, tired of being a "sissy," and, unlike the rest of his classmates, would not go on to college. Rebekah reprimanded him with "a terrible knifelike voice," and when that failed to persuade him, shut him out completely. At the dinner table she spoke only to her husband and her younger children, ignoring Lyndon's very existence. "We'd been such close companions," he recalled sadly, "and boom, she'd abandoned me."[53] Lyndon was hurt by her anger, but he could not, at that point, face four more years of school.

Lyndon finally yielded to his mother's pressure but then faced another delay in starting college. Johnson City High School, a two-story stone structure housing eleven classes in five rooms, was not accredited. Like similarly situated applicants from Johnson City High to Southwest Texas State Teachers College at San Marcos, he would have to take six weeks of intensive remedial courses and then pass entrance exams in three subjects, including math. In August or September 1924 Lyndon registered at San Marcos for the preparatory curriculum (the "subcollege"). It is not clear what occurred that fall. Probably he engaged in personal civil disobedience. He either did not attend classes, dropped out completely, or failed one or more of the exams. Whatever happened, he returned home in disgrace, and began making plans to go to California with some noncollege-bound buddies from town, Walter and Otto Crider, who had bought a Model T Ford and planned to join their older brother, Ben who lived in Tehachapi and promised to find them jobs in the cement factory where he worked.

Sam Jr. objected strenuously to Lyndon's scheme, but the rebellious adolescent was determined to go. Waiting until his father was out of town on business, Lyndon grabbed his already packed suitcase from under the bed and notified his companions that he was ready to leave. "In less than ten minutes," according to Lyndon's younger brother, "they . . . filled the gas tank, and zoomed out of town. . . ." Three hours later, when Sam Jr. returned, he erupted in fury. "Cranking the phone as if it were an ice-cream machine, he called the sheriff of nearly every county between Johnson City and El Paso . . . asking them to arrest his runaway son. . . . " Lyndon outsmarted his father by asking his companions to sleep during the day and drive by night "while the sheriffs were snoring away."[54]

Lyndon and his friends managed to make it to California, after a ten-day journey in the renovated Model T they called *The Covered Wagon*. There, only two of the boys got work in the cement factory; the other two, including Lyndon, became farm laborers, harvesting grapes and other fruit. Lyndon later fascinated listeners with colorful descriptions of his near starvation and "the grapes he picked, the dishes he washed, and the cars he fixed."[55] It is not clear how much fruit the future president actually removed from the vines for sale. But the grapes proved useful in any case. As he wrote his brother, he was sick of "eating warm grapes for breakfast, lunch and supper."[56] After a few weeks of this wretchedness, he called his cousin Tom Martin, a lawyer in San Bernardino, to ask for a job.

The round-faced, paunchy attorney, son of Johnson's Uncle Clarence whose house is now part of the Johnson ranch, gave Lyndon and his friend John Koeniger jobs as clerks in his office, and promised to train them as lawyers. California, like Texas, required passing a bar examination, but nearby Nevada did not. If Lyndon and John worked hard, Martin promised, he would see to it that his friends in the neighboring state got the young men admitted to the Nevada bar. Lyndon was delighted at the opportunity to become a lawyer. This seemed to be his first real chance to become independent, make good money, and be somebody his parents could respect, even if he did not have a college education. He applied himself to his new job with the energy and dedication that was lacking in high school. He spent his spare time reading the law books in Martin's office. "Lyndon wanted to be a lawyer," said Koeniger, "wanted it very badly."[57]

Unfortunately, Tom Martin had serious character flaws. He had bolted to California after a scandal in San Antonio forced him to resign as police chief. He was married with a child, but when his wife departed for Texas on a visit, Martin invited his girlfriend, a Hollywood actress named Lotte Dempsey, to stay with him in San Bernardino. While Martin and Lotte partied and romanced with all their might, Lyndon and Koeniger tried to run the office by themselves. When they found themselves paying Martin's bills out of their own pockets, they began to have second thoughts about the whole enterprise. Then the seventeen-year-old Lyndon found out he would not be able to practice law in Nevada until he was twenty-one. To make matters worse, Nevada was making it difficult to get a law license without a college diploma. That fall of 1925 Lyndon decided to ride back to Texas with his Uncle Clarence Martin, who was returning from California after driving his son's wife and child back from their visit.

So Lyndon returned home in his uncle's Buick, but not as an emotionally secure, financially independent adult. He was still under the wing of his family, and was broke and disillusioned. His friends and neighbors noticed the change. "Before he went to California, he was just a happy-go-lucky boy," said a neighbor. "When he came back, well . . . I saw what disappointment had done." It was on the drive back, he told Doris Kearns, that he decided to become a politician, thinking it would both gain the respect of his father and recapture his mother's love. If he could "build great power and gain high office" his mother "would never be disappointed" in him again.[58]

Whatever splendid resolutions he made on the trip back, Lyndon did not immediately buckle down when he arrived home. Instead, he joined a road-building crew near Johnson City, where he scooped up sand and gravel, swung a pick and shovel, pushed wheelbarrows, and drove a tractor. He also resumed his semidelinquent behavior after hours, taking up with an older, wilder group of boys who drank moonshine whiskey, showed off for the girls, and played mischievous pranks. He wrecked his father's car again and this time ran away to an uncle in San Antonio. Then one Saturday night he came home from a dance that had ended in a bloody fight with both a bruised nose and an arrest citation for disorderly conduct. His mother sat on the edge of his bed, weeping copiously. "To think that my eldest born would turn out like this," lamented Rebekah.[59]

Finally, one winter evening in 1927, Lyndon returned home from his road work cold, wet, and exhausted. "[A]ll right," he said to his mother, "I'm sick of working just with my hands and I'm ready to try and make it with my brain. Mother, if you and Daddy will get me into college, I'll go as soon as I can."[60] Rebekah dashed to the phone and made arrangements for him to be admitted to Southwest Texas State Teachers College, pending satisfactory completion of the preparatory course in the "subcollege."

One week later Lyndon hitchhiked to San Marcos to take his entrance examinations. He had now been out of school for almost three years. As part of the admissions process he submitted a paper on current affairs. It easily qualified as evidence of his language ability. In fact, the head of the English Department at San Marcos remembered it as so well written that she could hardly "believe that a boy so young could have had such a wide grasp of politics."[61] It was the math he was worried about, since he had scraped by in high school only with the tutoring of his cousin Ava. His mother now flew to his rescue, arriving in San Marcos like an angel of mercy. Johnson would never forget her help on his exams. "She came to San Marcos," he recalled, "and stayed up with me the entire night before the math exam, drilling me over and over until it finally got into my head."[62] He passed all of his entrance exams. He would enter college on March 21, 1927, the start of the spring semester.

Lyndon was on his way. His years of childhood and adolescent rebellion were over.

CHAPTER 2

College

L BJ WOULD BE ASHAMED of his education and compare it unfavorably with that of other contemporary political leaders. But it was the best he could manage. The University of Texas at Austin, just forty miles away, was too academically rigorous for the poorly prepared young man, who had danced his way through high school and had not given a thought to book learning since graduation. San Marcos, moreover, was only forty-five dollars a year, and its curriculum, geared to teacher education, suited his needs. He intended to teach before he embarked on his projected political career.

When Johnson arrived at San Marcos in March 1927, the school had just graduated its first fully accredited class. With most of its fifty-six professors holding master's degrees, it was considered average in educational quality among teacher's colleges. There were no dormitories; the students lived in boardinghouses or found other private accommodations. They walked to their classes on dirt paths in back of residents' yards. The largest building then (and now) was Old Main, a red brick turreted castle, perched on a hill, which could be seen for ten miles across the plain. There was also a gym, a demonstration farm, and some laboratories. The library, whose floors were always in danger of caving in, had only twenty-one thousand volumes, fewer than some contemporary big-city high schools. The most attractive feature of the campus was a strip of land along the San Marcos River, where the water fed by artesian wells was crystalline and a comfortable seventy degrees all year. On the banks were picnic tables and a bathhouse. An island in the river featured a dancing area and a bandstand.

Most of the seven hundred students came from the area's farms and such small neighboring cities as Kyle, Martindale, Lockart, and Seguin. They were predominantly of British or German stock. There were, even in those days, a few Mexican American students, but there were no blacks; Texas schools were still segregated. Since women outnumbered men three to one, the males were requested to date more than one woman at a time. All the students were required to attend weekly chapel. The rules governing social behavior were strict. There were enforced curfews; women had to wear their skirts below their knees and could not ride alone in cars with men. When using the swimming pool they were required to wear stockings, though, as one coed of this era later noted, they often managed to lose one or both while in the water. Social activities consisted of parties and dances and swimming and picnicking on the river. The Williams drugstore downtown was a popular gathering place, as was the Palace Theater.

Now that Johnson was in college, he was determined to get his teaching degree with dispatch. In an editorial he wrote for the *College Star* in his freshman year, Lyndon declared that to accomplish one's goals and achieve success "one should . . . train the mind to concentrate upon the essentials and discard the frivolous and unimportant."[1] He did his first two years without a break, attending summer sessions two years in a row. He majored in history and prepared to teach in both elementary and high school.

Despite his resolve, Lyndon was often unhappy during his freshman and sophomore years, displaying the erratic emotional streak that tormented his entire life. There were times when he felt like dropping out, and in one instance wrote Ben Crider, still in California, that he would like to quit and return to the Golden State. Could Ben get him a job there? He was always short of money, he explained, and was embarrassed to go to class in his shabby clothes. Rebekah wrote to Ben asking him to persuade Lyndon to stay. Crider responded by sending his friend a hundred dollars to "help keep him in school."[2]

Lyndon's classes failed to satisfy his active imagination, and he was often bored. He had never developed self-discipline or good study habits in high school and was not a good student. A college friend, Ella SoRelle, remembered that Lyndon "focused his energies where he was most interested and let everything else go at whatever luck he could luck out with."[3] Even Rebekah's help in correcting and criticizing written work he mailed her did not help too much. Though he made some A's in education and history, he barely scraped through with enough credits and passing grades to get the sophomore standing required for a temporary teaching certificate.

.   Lyndon was often homesick and lonely for his family and found it difficult to make friends. Much has been made of Johnson's outstanding ability to size up the political currents in whatever environment he was exposed to, but in his first years at college he was insecure and unpopular. Always skilled at cultivating and impressing his elders, he was awkward with his peers. His teachers would always remember him with fondness and respect. But in his attempts to win the friendship of his fellow students, he tried too hard. He talked too intensely and too incessantly. His boasting about his ancestors, his IQ, and his grades annoyed his acquaintances, and they nicknamed him "Bull." The humor column of the *College Star* offered this definition of the term: "Bull: Greek philosophy in which Lyndon Johnson has an M.B. degree."[4]

His roommate in these early years was another young man named Johnson (no relation), the well-liked football hero Alfred ("Boody") Johnson, who had been dating Lyndon's cousin Margaret. They soon became fast friends, spent much of their free time together, and were known as "Johnson and Johnson." Boody belonged to Beta Sigma, the social fraternity at the college dominated by athletes and referred to by nonmembers as B.S. or "the Black Stars." The Beta Sigmas also controlled student politics on campus. Lyndon yearned to join and hoped that his roommate's connection would give him entrée. He tried outfor the baseball team to achieve status as an athlete, but he was uncoordinated, and the coach turned him down. Boody apparently proposed the younger Johnson for membership anyway, but one of the other Black Stars, Frank Arnold, who was competing with Lyndon over a girl, blackballed him. The rejection rankled, and he resolved to get even.

Like many other San Marcos students, LBJ had to earn all of his tuition and living expenses. For a time he picked up garbage on the college grounds for fifteen dollars a month. Then he worked as a janitor in the science building. Shortly after that he induced San Marcos president Cecil E. Evans, who knew Rebekah and Sam, to hire him as an assistant in his own office for $37.50 a month. This was a prototype of Johnson's philosophy of self-advancement. "He once said to me," reminisced Lyndon's roommate, "the way you get ahead in this world, you get close to those that are the heads of things. Like President Evans, for example.' And before long he was working as a clerk in Prexy's office."[5]

Evans was the brother of Hiram W. Evans, grand kleagle of the Texas Ku Klux Klan during its heyday in the early 1920s. A decent, moderately liberal man, he disapproved of his brother's doings, though the town of San Marcos itself was a Klan stronghold. A somewhat aloof man, to everyone's surprise he opened up to his young assistant. Lyndon did secretarial work and carried messages from Evans to other faculty members. He also ran errands for the Evans family, bringing the president his morning newspaper and carrying Mrs. Evans's groceries. Boody already lived in one of the two rooms above the Evans's garage, and the "Prexy" let Lyndon move into the other. Evans did not charge them rent but expected them to paint the wooden structure and do odd chores for him. According to Boody, they "painted that garage three times in two years, and Prexy once said that it might not be the best-painted garage in San Marcos, but it was the most painted garage there."[6]

LBJ quickly ingratiated himself with Evans. The president had no son of his own and was pleased by the young man's diligence and devotion. Buttering up Evans was undoubtedly opportunistic at first, but Lyndon soon came to regard the older man as a surrogate father and found his affection a welcome balm. Lyndon placed a desk for himself right outside Evans's office and, using his native political instincts, began to act as his receptionist as well. Before long people regarded him as their channel to the president. Evans, in turn, began to have long conversations with his new aide and found that he knew a great deal about the workings of Texas politics, more so than most of his own colleagues. Lyndon, for his part, was always delighted to tell stories about the legislators he knew and speculate about what was going on in Austin and Washington.

Evans soon considered the young man an informal political adviser. Several San Marcos professors remembered that he helped draft Evans's political correspondence and prepared reports to agencies with control over the college and its finances. Evans took his assistant with him to lobby at the state capitol. Later Evans teased him, saying, "I could hardly tell who was president of the school—you or me."[7] Even after Lyndon left San Marcos he kept in touch with Evans and exchanged letters with him until the older man died.

At college Johnson enjoyed best his extracurricular activities—debating and journalism. The faculty adviser to the debating team was Professor of Government Howard M. Greene, an unconventional man with a populist philosophy. The teacher at San Marcos who influenced Johnson the most, Greene was deeply interested in politics and was unusually knowledgeable about current events and trends. Although Lyndon was on the debating team only one year, Greene listened to him, advised him, and argued with him throughout his entire college career. He, too, eventually became a lifelong friend.

Lyndon's involvement in journalism was even more intense. He joined the staffs of the college newspaper, the *College Star*, and the year-book, the *Pedagog*. He edited the *Star* for a summer. The newspaper post was not only a mark of prestige, it also provided an outlet for his ideas. It even furnished him a small salary. In his first summer session he became editor in chief.

Most of the articles and columns under his byline were on subjects that appealed to an unsophisticated patriotic Texas college student in the 1920s—prudence, courage, responsibility, honesty, the importance of the U.S. Constitution, the Battle of San Jacinto, and love for one's parents. His Thanksgiving column in 1927 mused about the joys of "eating Mother's turkey and basking in her smiles and talking politics with Dad."[8] Lyndon was clearly a fine student journalist. He "had exceptionally good judgment of what was appropriate," commented Academic Dean Alfred H. Nolle, "there was no need to censor, to edit, any of Lyndon Johnson's writing."[9] It is not surprising: Rebekah, the journalist, critiqued all her son's written work.

It was during this momentous first year at San Marcos that Johnson fell seriously in love and wanted to get married. The young woman was Carol Davis, daughter of a prosperous wholesale grocer who was also the former mayor of San Marcos. Carol was two years older than Lyndon, an honor student who had already graduated from college. She was an attractive girl, "very beautiful, tall and blonde, with dark blue eyes," in Lyndon's memory.[10] But she was quite shy. In an environment where co-eds outnumbered their male counterparts three to one, she had not had many dates, much less a significant suitor.

Lyndon was a nice-looking young man. Tall, dark, with a pleasant smile, he could be charming when he put his mind to it. Carol was flattered by his attention. Cynics have noted that she was rich and depict Lyndon as a fortune-hunter, but he seemed genuinely smitten. Carol, for her part, worried that they did not have much in common. She liked music and theater, while he appeared to be mostly interested in politics. She was placid, cultivated, and well-read. He was impulsive, unpolished, and unliterary. But, as she told biographer Robert Caro, "we were very interested in one another."[11]

The two young people soon began to talk about marriage. Although Rebekah and Sam approved, Carol's father, A. L. Davis, was appalled. He didn't want his precious daughter to marry a sophomore in college with no money and uncertain prospects. "I won't let you," he thundered. "I won't have my daughter marrying into that no-account Johnson family. . . . None of them will ever amount to a damn."[12] Years later, during

Lyndon's first campaign for Congress, Davis would denounce him for his liberal stand in favor of public power.

Lyndon worked hard at overcoming Davis's objections, playing from his strength—his interest in politics. In 1928 the Democrats were holding their presidential nominating convention in Houston. Showing samples of his work on the *College Star*, Lyndon got himself a press pass as a student reporter. He also used his father's political connections to wangle some tickets and persuaded Carol and her father to come with him. For Lyndon the convention was a peak event. He probably heard Franklin Delano Roosevelt's eloquent nominating speech for Al Smith. But as a courtship device it was a bust. Carol was not as fascinated by the political hurly-burly as her suitor was. In fact, the convention probably highlighted her differences with Lyndon.

Lyndon's precarious financial situation was even more damaging to his marital chances. He was willing to take jobs at San Marcos to earn money, but he also liked to splurge on himself, his sisters, and his girlfriend, and by now he was deeply in debt for his educational and living expenses. With President Evans's approval he decided to drop out of school for a year to make enough money to finish college. During the summer of 1928 he had made friends with W. T. Donaho, superintendent of schools in Cotulla, Texas, who himself had come to the San Marcos summer session to earn more credits. LBJ talked him into giving him a job teaching seventh and eighth grades at a salary of $125 a month, starting that fall. At the same time he got Carol a teaching job in Pearsall, thirty-three miles away, so he could visit her on weekends.

In September 1928 Lyndon, in his newly purchased Model A Ford, drove to Cotulla to start his new job. Located sixty miles above the Mexican border in the hot, dry, treeless Nueces Plains of south-central Texas, the town was a knot of buildings and stores on the fringe of a highway. Its population was three thousand, three quarters of whom were Mexican Americans who lived on the eastern side of the Missouri-Pacific tracks. Lyndon was assigned to teach at the all-"Mexican" Wellhausen school. Since few accredited teachers were willing to come to this part of Texas, Johnson was also appointed principal.

Johnson tackled his new duties with the same energy and enthusiasm he had displayed in his cousin Tom Martin's law office. The job charged him up. For the first time in his life he had gotten a respectable position without family pull, and as a additional boost to his confidence he was now in charge, an authority figure, looked up to and respected. He also knew that if he impressed Donaho he could get better jobs in the future. He devoted himself totally to his responsibilities. Besides the teaching itself, these included administering college correspondence courses and coaching in a nearby high school.

Johnson was a strict teacher who punished his students for talking, giggling, and kidding around in class. He was there to teach them, and they were there to learn. None of the previous teachers had really cared if their Mexican American students learned anything. But Johnson was dedicated to enriching their lives. "I was determined," he told Doris Kearns, "to spark something inside them, to fill their souls with ambition and interest and belief in the future."[13] He also insisted that they speak English in school at all times, even on the playground. Boys who broke the rule were spanked; girls were scolded. He taught his students the chauvinistic version of Texas history and the Mexican War that was then the standard curriculum in Texas schools. Recent critics have charged that he had no respect for his students' own cultural traditions. But they forget that this was 1928 and that Johnson's assimilationist attitudes represented the contemporary liberal view: If foreign-speaking students learned English and adopted American ways and values they could succeed in the United States. One of his former pupils, Daniel Garcia, target of a Johnson school time paddling, reminisced on the *I've Got a Secret* TV show in 1964 that Johnson continually told them that this country provided "great liberties and opportunities for everybody, and that any individual by studying hard . . . would possibly be able to become president of the United States."[14]

And Lyndon was compassionate as well as tough with the children. After learning that his students often came to school without breakfast, he started a lunch program that served nutritious hot food. This experience may have inspired the food stamp programs of his later career. Noticing that students at the local "Anglo" school had access to extracurricular activities and sports equipment while his own pupils had neither, he got the school board to contribute volleyballs and softballs, nets and bats, and spent part of his first paycheck purchasing other equipment. The new principal also organized volleyball, basketball, and baseball teams and arranged for competition with other schools. The teachers at Wellhausen had been doing as little as they could get away with. During recess, students fended for themselves on a bare dirt lot while their teachers smoked in the lounge. Johnson ordered the teachers to spend recess with the students, supervising activities. He started spelling bees and organized a literary society and a debating team. The Cotulla experience buried itself deep in Johnson's soul. Wilbur Cohen, later Johnson's secretary of health, education, and welfare, described how LBJ talked constantly about the year he spent in Cotulla. Cohen believed that "it motivated him on the education bills, on his nondiscrimination, on civil rights and a great many basic ideas that were developed during his presidency. . . . [W]hen he saw those hungry children digging into garbage, it was the first time he had really seen grinding poverty."[15]

At the end of the term the school board asked him to remain, but he turned them down to return to his own education at San Marcos. The superintendent gave him his hoped-for enthusiastic recommendation. He had also finished between twelve and eighteen credits worth of correspondence courses, which shortened the time for his degree. Professionally, the year was a resounding success.

By now, however, his romance was on the rocks. In spite of his hectic schedule, Johnson took time during the school year to drive to Pearsall to see Carol every evening she was free. But it was clear that they were growing apart. Johnson himself began to have qualms about their personality and cultural differences. He told his Cotulla landlady that his girlfriend loved opera, "but I'd rather sit down on an old log with a farmer and talk."[16] The number of evenings that Carol was "free" grew fewer; she had found another boyfriend in Pearsall, Harold Smith, who apparently was more acceptable to her parents. Despite his reservations, Lyndon formally proposed marriage, but so did Smith. Finally, the word reached Johnson, still teaching in Cotulla, that Carol would marry his rival. Lyndon was undoubtedly hurt by this rejection, but no one will ever know how much it bothered him. We do know he was very pleased when, seven years later, she came to hear his opening speech in his first congressional campaign and voted for him despite her father's opposition.

In June 1929 it was a more mature and experienced Johnson who returned to San Marcos to finish his college work. Notwithstanding the unfortunate romance, he had gained a lot of confidence in his teaching and administrative abilities from his year at Cotulla. What he wanted now more than ever was to get his degree so his adult life could begin. He planned to graduate after the 1930 summer session and signed up for as many credits as he could in each of his remaining terms. During his last three semesters he took courses in areas where his interests lay, but did not get good grades. Not that he lacked ability. Professor Howard Greene called him "clearly the best student in government and politics I ever had the pleasure of teaching."[17] "He had too many irons in the fire," was the way Dean Alfred Nolle explained the mediocre results.[18] Grades aside, he did reach his goal on time, graduating with a B⁻ average.

During this last stint at college, LBJ also got involved with campus politics. His old nemeses, the Black Stars, had begun to arouse resentment among the unaffiliated young men, particularly the bookish non-athletes. Before Johnson left for Cotulla they had organized a secret society, which they called the White Stars. Johnson asked to join when he came back to San Marcos and at first was turned down, possibly on the grounds that it was a clandestine society and Johnson was incapable of keeping quiet. A few weeks later some friends resubmitted his name, and this time he was accepted.

At the time of its creation the White Stars had no specific program. As one of the founders later explained, "We formed it . . . to tell you the truth . . . because it was hard for anyone who wasn't a Black Star to get a date with the pretty girls."[19] It is unclear whether it was Johnson's idea or not, but in the fall of 1929 the White Stars nominated a slate of candidates for campus office. It was certainly his suggestion that the White Stars run his handsome, well-liked friend Willard Deason for senior class president against the Black Stars' nominee, the popular football and track star Dick Spinn.

Now they needed an issue, and it is likely that Johnson was the one who found it. Part of each student's tuition was an all-inclusive fee that underwrote extracurricular activities. The student council, made up mostly of Black Stars, gave the largest share to the athletic teams. Using the slogan "Brains Are Just as Important as Brawn," the White Stars demanded that a greater share of the funds be given to nonathletic activities, including debate and drama. This issue especially pleased the women students, whose activities usually received the smallest share of the money. But Johnson also tried to capitalize on the jealousies felt by most of the nonathlete males toward the popular and powerful jocks. He instinctively understood the resentment of have-nots toward haves.

No White Star took this election more seriously than Johnson. The most active campaigner, he spent all his free evenings canvassing in the students' boardinghouses. He talked to every student he could accost, using a style that lasted all of his life. "His greatest forte," said Johnson's loyal lifelong friend Willard Deason, "was to look a man in the eye and do a convincing job of selling him his viewpoint. In one-on-one salesmanship, Lyndon was the best."[20]

Even with this issue and Lyndon's unceasing electioneering, the White Stars were far from victory. On election eve they were sure they had lost. But Lyndon would not give up. All night long he worked, talking to students. "It's the kind of thing," said Deason, that " . . . Lyndon did later in the Senate when he was majority leader. Until the last vote was committed, you couldn't get him to stop."[21] And sure enough, when the votes were tallied in the morning, Deason beat Spinn by eight votes.

In an election four months later the White Stars put up another candidate and won again, and this time Lyndon won the seat he had held earlier on the Student Academic Council. The White Stars had learned how to manipulate the loosely run campus elections and before long controlled most of the student electoral offices. Lyndon's friendship with President Evans also probably contributed to the White Stars' success, and they ended up with the choicest student jobs in the library and the college offices.

Forty years later LBJ returned to San Marcos and reminisced with his former professors about his first foray into political activity. By then he had retired from the presidency and had a serious heart condition. The sick old man was compensating for his lost youth and strength by harsh overstatement:

> The freshmen, the sophomores and me—we had a majority. We gave to the Band, the Dramatic Club, the debaters and we started electing the Gaillardians [prettiest girls on campus], and we were still doing it when I left. . . . It was a pretty vicious operation for a while. They [the Black Stars] lost everything. . . . It was my first real big dictat—Hitlerized—operation, and I broke their back good. And it stayed broke for a good long time.[22]

Whether or not Johnson was really as powerful or Machiavellian as he claimed, by 1930 he had become identified as the number one campus politician at San Marcos, and his activities and tactics set the tone for his future political career. He was not only skilled at getting votes, but also at advertising his every triumph. He knew what he wanted. "Politics is a science," Lyndon said to a fellow student, "and if you work hard enough at it, you can be president. I'm going to be president."[23]

When San Marcos students were interviewed many years later, they remembered with passion the gangly, energetic, loquacious young man dashing around, campaigning for votes. Some of his San Marcos supporters, including Bill Deason, worked for Johnson for much of their political careers and were well rewarded. But others carried the old resentments for decades. He was probably subject to more insults and scorn in the yearbook than any other student. Still, many agreed with Ella SoRelle, editor of the *Pedagog*, who campaigned for Johnson many years after college. "He was very capable, had a lot of energy, and had the ambition to do things that other people didn't."[24]

The summer before graduation Johnson became involved in real politics. Former Texas governor Pat Neff, who had been appointed in the spring of 1930 to fill out the unexpired term of the newly deceased state railroad commissioner, was running for the full term. Neff had given Sam a badly needed job as a state bus inspector in San Marcos, enabling Sam, Rebekah, and the two youngest children to live near Lyndon and his sister Rebekah, who was now attending the college, too. Sam's position depended on Neff's reelection, and Lyndon threw himself into the canvass.

The campaign gave LBJ his first public speaking opportunity. Neff was expected to appear in mid-July at an annual political barbecue and picnic in the neighboring town of Henly. Lyndon accompanied his parents to the festivities. In the audience was Johnson family friend Welly Hopkins, a liberal and an influential lawyer from Austin who was serving in the Texas House of Representatives and was now running for the State Senate. The crowd patiently listened to many speakers in the sweltering heat, and then it was Neff's turn. But he was nowhere to be found. Neither was his rival Gregory Hatcher, but Hatcher at least had sent a substitute. Who would defend Neff against the Hatcher partisan's attack? The assault seemed to consist mostly of allegations that Neff did not like fishing or hunting, but the audience seemed to take these charges seriously. When it was clear that Neff was not coming and had sent no proxy, Sam pushed Lyndon up to the platform. Grateful, he would later explain, that Neff had given his "daddy a job when he needed it,"[25] Lyndon rose to the task with great aplomb, giving what an impressed picnicgoer called "an enthusiastic, arm-swinging defense of Pat as governor and railroad commissioner—a completely extemporaneous and spontaneous speech of approximately ten to fifteen minutes."[26]

Hopkins, too, was impressed and asked Lyndon to help in his own campaign. This would encompass six counties, and Lyndon would have principal charge of Hays and Blanco. During the three weeks left till the election Lyndon was on the campaign trail whenever he could find some time from classes, often bringing with him some of his fellow White Stars to help. He used the college mimeograph to print Hopkins literature and organized many rallies throughout the district, dragooning as many people as possible into attending. He carried with him to these rallies a traveling claque that yelled enthusiastically when Hopkins' name was mentioned and applauded exuberantly when he spoke. On weekends he went to outlying areas to talk to individual farmers and ranchers. LBJ even persuaded the politically neutral Evans to let him hold a huge rally in the auditorium at Old Main and then induced the president to sit on the platform.

Hopkins won and credited Johnson with his victory. "He did a magnificent job for me," Hopkins told an interviewer.[27] After LBJ's graduation later that summer Hopkins took his helper with him on a victory trip to Mexico.

August 17, 1930, graduation day, was another triumphant occasion that summer for the Johnson family. Sam and Rebekah were particularly pleased to note that President Evans reserved his choicest praise for their son Lyndon among all the graduates. As the lanky, loose-jointed, twenty-two-year-old approached the dais, Evans smiled. Then the president handed Johnson his diploma, saying, "Here's a young man who has so abundantly demonstrated his worth that I predict for him great things in the years ahead."[28] Sam smiled, and Rebekah cried with joy. Their son had certainly proved his abilities. Now what he needed was a paying job.

Late summer of 1930 was a hard time to find a job for anyone, let alone a beginner. On October 29, 1929, the stock market crashed, ushering in the Great Depression. By the time Lyndon got his Bachelor of Science degree, six million people were out of work, and teaching opportunities were as scarce as jobs in the business sector. Teachers with seniority were being laid off as school districts all over the country cut their budgets. Significantly, President Evans had given a speech to the graduating class called "All Dressed Up and No Place to Go."[29] Johnson had already decided that he preferred politics to teaching, but the Depression had slashed government jobs as well.

When LBJ needed something in the past his family had always come through. They did so again. His father's brother George Johnson was chairman of the history department at Sam Houston High School in Houston. Uncle George had promised to give his nephew a place to live and help him get a teaching position at his school, but at the beginning of the 1930 fall term there were no vacancies. The one job available was in public speaking at the high school in Pearsall, the scene of Lyndon's romantic downfall. The superintendent there knew him from his courtship of Carol Davis and was willing to appoint him as teacher and vice principal of the high school at a salary of $1,530 a year. In early September Lyndon drove back to South Texas to begin the fall term. He was at Pearsall only a month when the good news came from Uncle George: a vacancy had occurred in Sam Houston High School's speech department, and they were prepared to hire him immediately.

Johnson arrived at Sam Houston to find that he would be teaching commercial geography and arithmetic as well as public speaking, and coaching the debating team besides. When Principal William Moyes noted that the team had never won the city championship, Johnson quickly assured him that this year the prize would be theirs. Not knowing Johnson, Moyes put this promise down to youthful enthusiasm. But although the young man was moonlighting in the evening to earn extra money by teaching the Dale Carnegie method to businessmen, he was prepared to expend his last drop of energy to produce a successful debating team.

Lyndon was a good classroom teacher. Ella SoRelle once sat in on one of his evening classes and found him "very enthusiastic."[30] But he was far more interested in his debate team coaching. Every day after school he interviewed students until he found the most talented speakers for both the boys' and the girls' teams. He finally selected Margaret Epley, Evelyn Reed, Luther Jones, and Gene Latimer. He then drilled them hard, compelling them to repeat their recitations over and over until they were "perfect." Johnson replaced the declamatory style they had been learning with a more conversational approach. "Act like you're talking to those folks. Look one of them in the eye and then move on and look another one in the eye," he advised.[31] Gene Latimer believed that this style explained why Johnson would later be so effective in small groups, if not on TV. The coach set up practice debates all over Texas, driving the students to the sites himself in his Model A, finding them overnight accommodations with either family or friends. The team practiced even as they drove to the next stop, recalled Latimer, but however arduous, they were days to treasure and remember with Lyndon playing "daddy," leading the singing and the joking as the miles passed. Johnson got the rest of the school to treat his debaters like football heroes, with pep rallies and dances in their honor.

Both teams won the city and district championships, but the girls were eliminated in the first rounds of the state contest. Meanwhile, Latimer and Jones advanced to the state finals in Austin in early May. Johnson was dismayed when they lost the Texas championship by one vote, According to Latimer, "it killed him, made him sick at his stomach," and he threw up in the men's room.[32] Yet he quickly put the defeat aside and did not blame his debaters for the result. Overall the experience was a good one. Latimer and Jones remained friends of Johnson's for life and later worked for him in Washington. LBJ himself got a new contract and a raise, despite the Houston School Board's efforts to cut costs.

In the fall of 1931, Lyndon came back to Sam Houston High School for his second year of teaching. He was a conscientious and successful teacher, staying up nights to grade papers so the students would get them back the next day. The students considered him a strict disciplinarian, but they respected and liked him. Many tried to change their schedules to take his speech class, and enrollment shot up from 60 to 110 in his first year.

Still, as he told anyone who would listen, he did not want to stay in education. Politics was still his first love, and even a full load of teaching and coaching could not stop him. He spent time in Austin lobbying for the Houston teachers and helped convince the legislature to tax cigarettes to provide the teachers with a pay raise. His political savvy impressed even the professionals. Bill Kittrell, the campaign manager for a previous lieutenant governor, said that everyone in Austin was talking about Johnson's political talents. "[T]his kid teaching school in Houston . . . knew more about politics than anyone else in the area."[33]

Johnson's big political chance came in the middle of the 1931 fall term, when plans for the new debating season were just getting under way. The Republican representative to Congress from the Fourteenth District, which included San Antonio and part of the Hill Country, had just died, leaving a vacancy to be decided by a special election barely two weeks away. The national Democratic leadership desperately wanted this seat to bolster their shaky majority in the House of Representatives. The Democratic candidate was conservative Richard Kleberg, heir to the King Ranch, reputed to be the largest cattle ranch in the world. Kleberg won handily on November 24.

It is not clear whether Lyndon, busy with his classes and his debating team, actually participated in Kleberg's winning campaign. In any case, Lyndon's political friends told Kleberg about his accomplishments, his familiarity with the Fourteenth District's constituents, and his extraordinary skills in personal political contact. The congressman-elect, they urged, should hire this young political phenomenon as his personal secretary. In fact, according to Boody Johnson, it was Sam Ealy—who had talked the reluctant Kleberg into accepting the nomination in the first place—who, after Kleberg's victory, induced the new-minted congressman to take Lyndon on as his secretary. In any case, Kleberg telephoned Johnson at the high school to set up an interview in his office. A thrilled Lyndon dashed off to Corpus Cristi, accompanied by his father, and impressed Kleberg, who immediately gave him the job as administrative aide. He would start in less than two weeks when Congress convened for its new session. Kleberg called Principal Moyes to arrange for a leave of absence.

As Johnson prepared to leave for Washington, the *Houston Post-Dispatch* gave him a fond farewell: "Young Johnson . . . [during] his first year as debate coach at Sam Houston, turned out a winning team. . . . Himself an orator of much ability, Johnson coached with a contagious enthusiasm which made him a favorite, not only with his own pupils, but with the entire school."[34] It was a fitting send-off.

CHAPTER 3

Congressional Secretary

J OHNSON WAS BOTH EXCITED AND ANXIOUS at the prospect of leaving Texas. He was finally leaving home to "meet the adventure" of his future. He was also somewhat sad. "I felt grownup," he told Doris Kearns, "but my mind kept ranging backward in time. I saw myself skipping down the road to my grandfather's house. I remembered the many nights I had stood in the doorway listening to my father's political talks. I remembered the evenings with my mother when my daddy was away."[1] For many years he had boasted that he was going to have an important political career, that he would even be president someday. Now his big talk would be put to the test.

Cardboard suitcase in hand, Lyndon Johnson arrived in the nation's capital on December 7, 1931, to begin a political career that would last thirty-eight years. He and Congressman-elect Kleberg had traveled together by train, Lyndon getting his first taste of luxury in the Pullman car they shared. The first night in Washington, they both stayed in Kleberg's suite at the expensive, red-carpeted Mayflower Hotel on Connecticut Avenue, but this was the last taste of high living for LBJ for a long time. Ahead was the hard work, intense discipline, and austerity that would ensure him a good start in his career.

LBJ quickly found himself a room on Capitol Hill in the shabby old Dodge Hotel. It was in the subbasement, the area that the hotel reserved for seventy-five government workers. The room, which he shared, cost twenty dollars a month, and even at that price was too expensive for what was provided: no windows, two single beds, a bathroom that served all the tenants and was at the end of the long hall, and overhead steam pipes that hammered incessantly at night during the winter. Lyndon ate his lunch in the House and Senate dining rooms and his dinner in the company of fellow government employees at Child's or the All States Restaurant, two cheap eateries nearby. He liked chili—and hot, too hot for most of the office staff.

Despite its tacky accommodations, the Dodge was a good place to live for a young man eager to climb the ladder in Washington. The hotel was only a few blocks north of the domed Capitol and the Senate and House Office Buildings, and the congressional aides and secretaries who lived below street level constituted an invaluable intelligence corps on national politics. Johnson had not yet put his clothes in the bureau when he went out into the hall to see what was going on. "Networking" as a term had not yet been coined, but this was precisely what he did, wandering up and down the passageway meeting people, knocking on doors, shaking hands, and exchanging life histories. These clerks knew what was happening on the Hill and the reasons behind the events. They knew which congressmen had drinking problems, which led irregular sex lives, and most important, who among them had real power. Johnson was determined to learn all these things and learn them fast. Every meal and every stroll became an opportunity for him to question, to examine, to clarify, to argue—in short, to add to his storehouse of political information. While Johnson lived there the Dodge was a "permanent debating society," said fellow resident Arthur Perry, "with Lyndon as the focal point."[2]

Johnson subordinated everything else to his desire to learn about life in the capital. Late evenings he went through the Washington papers, along with the *New York Times*, the *Wall Street Journal*, and local Texas dailies. He also perused government pamphlets, committee reports, and each day's *Congressional Record*. When his crowd went to a Washington Senators baseball game "Lyndon would go along because he didn't want to be left behind," Arthur Perry said. "But he didn't give a hoot about the game. He would keep on arguing politics through every inning."[3] Then, as later, he seemed uninterested in any other human activity except where it intersected politics. "He had the most narrow vision of anyone you can imagine," said his Dodge roommate, Robert Jackson of Corpus Christi. "Sports, entertainment, movies—he couldn't have cared less."[4]

There was one exception: women. Gene Latimer, Johnson's Houston debating team student, now also on Kleberg's staff, remembered Lyndon's penchant for "pretty faces and figures" without much attention to "what was behind those faces."[5] But during the three years he spent as a congressional secretary—as later—he pursued even romance sporadically. "He was quite a ladies' man when he would go on a spree," a friend noted, "but his work was his love."[6]

Part of Johnson's game plan in these early Washington days was getting to know influential Texans in the nation's capital. Early on he and Kleberg paid their respects to the two Texas senators, Morris Sheppard and Tom Connally. Neither was particularly interested in befriending a junior congressman's young secretary, nor did the other Texas congressmen care to bother with a mere aide. One exception was Congressman Wright Patman, who had served in the Texas legislature with Sam Johnson and had met the young Lyndon when he accompanied his father to Austin. "Lyndon dropped into my office almost every day," recalled Patman. "He seemed especially interested in the fight I had started to impeach Hoover's Secretary of the Treasury, Andrew Mellon, on a serious conflict-of-interest charge. . . ." Other things that Lyndon enjoyed talking about, Patman recalled, were "the dirty political fighting that was part of Texas electioneering, and . . . the earlier-day doings in local politics."[7]

Another responsive Texas congressman was Sam Rayburn, of the House Commerce Committee, who also remembered his old colleague Sam Johnson from the Texas House and quickly took to Lyndon when he came around to say hello. The veteran Rayburn, a powerful figure in the House, was a very lonely man whose three-month marriage to a woman he loved for nine years before he got up the nerve to propose had failed. After the marital debacle, Rayburn had moved into two rooms in a shabby apartment house near Dupont Circle and never changed his lodgings again. Rayburn soon established a father-son relationship with Lyndon, whose talent at bringing out paternal feelings in older men had already proved useful. Lyndon listened carefully to what Rayburn said and asked intelligent questions. One day when Lyndon failed to appear at Kleberg's office, Rayburn began to worry, assuming that the young dynamo must be sick. He was right; Johnson had pneumonia and could not get out of bed. When Lyndon finally awoke that evening, the first thing he saw was Rayburn sleeping in a chair next to his bed with cigarette ashes covering the front of his suit. Johnson asked him why he was there and Rayburn told him that "maybe Sam Johnson's boy didn't have anybody who cared whether he was sick or not."[8] He had come to find out how he was.

When in 1934 Johnson married Claudia Taylor, a Texas girl, the friendship got even closer, with Rayburn becoming practically a member of the family. Just chosen majority whip in the election of 1932, the Texas congressman was an especially important friend because savvy Washington knew he was rising fast.

Another Texas associate was Roy Miller, the Texas Gulf Sulphur lobbyist his father had known. Though Kleberg scarcely needed financial assistance, Miller kept the congressman's office "stocked with fine whiskey."[9] He often visited the office and, in Kleberg's absence, took his staff out to dinner. According to Gene Latimer, Miller and Lyndon were good friends.

Before long Lyndon understood Washington as well as he had Texas. "This skinny boy," said Arthur Perry, Tom Connally's secretary, "was as green as anybody could be, but within a few months he knew how to operate in Washington better than some who had been here twenty years before him."[10] He managed to get his name in the newspapers by sending out notices about various events in Texas. These took the form: "It was announced today by Lyndon B. Johnson, Secretary to Congressman Kleberg . . ."[11] Robert Jackson, aide to another Texas congressman, was impressed by his "absolutely incredible restless energy." Politics was everything, and there was never enough time for it. Lyndon could not sit through a movie. "We'd no sooner get there than he'd get up and leave," Jackson remembered.[12] At the Child's cafeteria, where he and other congressional aides ate their meals, he would rush to the head of the line, dash with his tray to the table, and gobble down his food.

Serving as Kleberg's secretary proved to be far more work than Lyndon ever imagined. He quickly discovered that his playboy boss was no more serious about politics than he had been about the affairs of the vast King Ranch, which had suffered from neglect until the congressman's younger brother put it back on its feet. In Washington, after taking Johnson around to introduce him to his influential friends, Kleberg left the running of his office to his assistant. In fact, Kleberg practically never came to room 258 in the old House Office Building, preferring to spend his time playing golf at the Burning Tree Country Club. Nevertheless, when Kleberg ran for a full term in 1932, with Johnson as his campaign manager, he was handily reelected.

The 1932 elections launched a national political revolution. In this year of the catastrophic Depression, the Democratic presidential candidate, Franklin Delano Roosevelt, pledged to involve the federal government in national planning and regulation of utilities and the stock market and vowed to increase aid to the unemployed. Promising a "new deal," a new political hand, for the American people to play, Roosevelt and the Democrats swamped Hoover and the Republicans. FDR took 282 counties that had never voted Democratic before.

During the long interregnum between the old administration and the new, the economy deteriorated further. By inauguration day, March 4, 1933, the jobless rate hovered close to a quarter of the entire labor force, a historic high. Practically every bank in the country had been closed or placed under restriction by state decree to keep them from defaulting and obliterating the life savings of millions. The nation was in crisis, the worst since secession of the South seventy years before.

Johnson was standing and cheering at the East Portico of the Capitol on the chilly, damp day that Roosevelt was sworn in. He listened as FDR told the country that "the only thing we have to fear is fear itself." The new president proposed a program of federal public works, measures to redistribute population from the cities to the country, to inflate the prices of agricultural produce, to end home and farm foreclosure, and to tighten federal regulation of banking and stock speculation. The inaugural address made Johnson a supporter of future New Deal programs. He would be caught up in the exhilarating political climate that the New Deal ushered in, and Roosevelt would become his new hero and "first daddy."

Kleberg's constituents were as hard hit by the Depression as any in the country. The Fourteenth Congressional district extended from the Hill Country to Corpus Christi and included half a million residents, twice as many as most districts in the state. Its population, though largely agricultural, was very diverse, including ranchers with large cattle spreads and poor farmers, many of whom actually lived in the district's small cities and towns. It also included the servicemen and veterans associated with Fort Sam Houston, the nation's biggest army post; Mexican Americans in San Antonio; and gulf fishermen. The volume of mail from Kleberg's constituents was larger than in most districts and covered an exceptional range of interests. Farmers wrote to ask about rural-route mail delivery; businessmen sought to get road paving contracts at military bases. With the country deep in the Depression, job-seeking letters from constituents, received by every congressman, soared. There was also a flood of letters asking for simple relief to pay for food, shoes, rent. To complicate matters further, Kleberg's predecessor had been sick for more than a year and fallen far behind in his constituent work.

Lyndon quickly realized that he had to run the congressman and the district as well as the office. This was a daunting job for an unsophisticated, untrained novice. When he first entered room 258, what he saw were giant, overflowing gray sacks of mail that needed to be answered. "I felt," he remembered, "I was going to be buried."[13] And to make things worse, he could not type. That would have to be done by his one assistant, Estelle Harbin, a twenty-eight-year-old secretary from Corpus

Christi. Kleberg could not be bothered to read his mail, dictate replies, or do any office work at all.

Johnson began to tackle the mail, with Harbin's assistance, working seven days a week from sunup through midnight. He dictated scores of letters and wrote out in longhand others he wanted sent. These he corrected over and over. Other congressional secretaries remember that no matter what time they arrived or left their offices, the light in room 258 was always burning. Kleberg had given him *carte blanche*, so Johnson simply answered the letters without clearing them with the congressman, even writing to Kleberg's mother. Since he was then too short of time to write to his own mother, his assistants began to write in his name to Rebekah.*

Once the backlog was out of the way, Johnson responded to each letter the day it arrived. When Harbin left to return to Texas, he brought to Washington his two prize Sam Houston debaters, Luther Jones and Gene Latimer, to assist in answering the correspondence. The pay was not very good, but Johnson worked them just as hard as when he coached the debating team, using their competitive instincts to squeeze the last ounce of effort out of them. "He'd say 'Gene,'" Latimer recalled, "'it seems L. E.'s a little faster than you today.' And I'd work faster."[15] Lyndon showed his assistants exactly what he wanted in each letter when they first began. Soon Jones and Latimer knew his preferences. "He'd just make a few comments," Jones told Merle Miller. "Johnson would tell me: 'Say yes, say no . . . butter him up.'"[16] Kleberg saw few of the letters. Occasionally, just to impress the congressman with his industry, Johnson would dump a batch of outgoing mail on Kleberg's desk to be signed. Usually, however, he just copied his boss's signature and sent them out.

In addition to the mail, Johnson took on almost all the congressman's official chores. He answered the telephone calls, sometimes claiming he was Kleberg himself to expedite matters. He gave out patronage jobs. He was Kleberg's contact man with federal agencies. He built up and reinforced political support for Kleberg in the Fourteenth District, taking time to go back to Texas to listen to the complaints of constituents and then to act on his promises. He cultivated and maintained relationships with other congressmen. And when he became more familiar with the job, he began to advise Kleberg on policy, plying him with memoranda, and pressuring him to vote favorably on New Deal programs.

---

*Gene Latimer declares it was *he* who composed most of the letters that Congressman Johnson supposedly wrote home to he mother; Johnson did not have the time. Latimer takes special issue with Doris Kearns, who made much psychologically of these letters. She was "absolutely out of her mind," Latimer notes.[14]

Much of the business of the Fourteenth District involved Depression-struck farmers and ranchers, and many of Johnson's communications were with the Department of Agriculture. Kleberg, himself, had been named to the House Agricultural Committee and was deeply involved with the hearings on the major new agriculture bill, the Agricultural Adjustment Act (AAA) of 1933. The New Deal's attempt to solve the acute farm crisis, the AAA sought to raise farm prices and farmers' purchasing power by eliminating surpluses. Growers of seven basic commodities, including cotton, corn, rice, wheat, and dairy products, who agreed to curtail their production would be reimbursed from the proceeds of a special tax levied on the processors of these products. The administration assumed the decrease in farm output would curb the precipitous price slide and ultimately raise farm income. Meanwhile, the reimbursements by themselves would lift farm income.

Johnson's populist memories of his own father's farming disaster still seared his brain, and he yearned to see the bill pass. The mail from the Fourteenth District, moreover, supported the AAA thirty to one. Practically all the liberal congressmen were supporting it as well. The wealthy Kleberg, who had no communication with his constituents in any case, was prepared to vote against it, claiming it was "socialistic." When Kleberg refused to change his vote, Johnson threatened to quit. If the congressman voted against AAA, he told his boss, he himself would be ashamed to face the people of the Fourteenth District. According to Russell Morton Brown, a Rhode Islander whom Lyndon hired to help with Kleberg's correspondence, LBJ said: "I just can't stay, because I feel that I'd be betraying the folks at home just as much as you are." Besides, he told Kleberg, the AAA would pass anyway and the congressman would "stand out like a traitor to the country" if he was "one of the few Democrats who vote[d] against the president, and against this legislation."[17] Apparently this was the decisive argument. Kleberg voted "yea" on the bill.

Kleberg also voted for the National Industrial Recovery Act (NIRA) to restore industrial prosperity and reduce unemployment through industrywide codes of "fair competition" that would limit output and fix prices. LBJ nagged Kleberg into voting "yes" on other New Deal measures, including Social Security, which Kleberg also thought was "socialistic."

Once the AAA was law, Johnson actively used it to help Kleberg's constituents. Roosevelt personally awarded the first check for plowed-under cotton to a farmer from Nueces County in the Fourteenth District. But even payments for reducing crops were not enough for the South Texas farmers. Many hoped to refinance their mortgages through the Federal Land Bank but had run out of collateral. By October 1933 sixty-seven farms in the Fourteenth District were due to be foreclosed, but the agency, swamped by thousands of applications from all over the country, was moving at a snail's pace.

Johnson got the Federal Land Bank to expedite the applications from the Fourteenth District by setting up a meeting in Corpus Christi with W. I. Myers, a high-ranking official of the Farm Credit Administration, the bank's parent body, who just happened to be a friend of Kleberg. Myers brought with him A. C. Williams, the president of the Federal Land Bank's Houston office. Johnson induced everybody to agree to his proposal: The farmers would promise a third of their crops to the mortgage companies, the government would agree to accelerate and liberalize mortgage refinancing, and the banks would consent to accept the terms and take down the foreclosure notices. All told, under Johnson's management, Kleberg's office, according to the journalist William S. White, "began to run up an extraordinary record in the matter of taking care of the homefolks."[18]

Whether Johnson at the time grasped the theoretical complexities of New Deal programs is not clear, although, to be honest, neither did contemporary economists or later historians. But he intrinsically understood that supporting and implementing these new policies was one of the best ways to help his fellow Texans. Many years later he reminisced about the New Deal. "Today some say that the New Deal was an experiment," he told participants in a Jefferson–Jackson Day dinner in 1963. "Some say it was a 'failure.' Some say that it became 'outmoded' and 'obsolete.' But I say that the philosophy of government which helps people to help themselves against depression, against unemployment, against old age will never be outmoded or obsolete in civilized society."[19]

Johnson also found patronage jobs for the homefolks. The New Deal created new programs, which in turn spawned new bureaucracies to manage these programs. The number of federal jobs swelled to unprecedented levels. Although the senior congressmen had their pick of the prize positions to offer, there were now many lowly ones that needed to be filled—in government mailrooms and galleries, at the Library of Congress, the Department of Agriculture, and the Treasury Department. Similar state jobs were also being created in Texas. The salaries for these positions were paltry, but during the Depression they were lifesavers for those fortunate enough to land them.

LBJ lassooed whatever jobs he could for needy fellow Texans. Many fellow White Stars would be forever grateful to Johnson for the work he got them when they graduated from San Marcos and found there were no teaching positions to be had. Johnson's populism and his own fear of poverty engendered sympathy with the unemployed. But he understood that he was creating a nucleus of loyal friends forever in his debt. Such dedicated supporters were indispensable to a man planning to make politics his life's work.

Johnson worked just as hard as a patronage broker as he did as a letter writer. He sometimes spent hours on the phone for one job, persuading his listener to call someone else who knew the official who knew another official in charge of hiring. His aggressive techniques sometimes provoked resentment, but he also earned the gratitude he sought. As White Star Ernest Morgan put it: "I was very appreciative of what Lyndon Johnson did for me." Another admitted he attached himself to Johnson "because I wanted to go up with him."[20]

Besides doing much of Kleberg's work, Johnson squeezed out the time to join the "Little Congress." Formed in 1919 to give congressional staff members practice in public speaking and training in parliamentary procedures, by the time Johnson arrived in Washington, it was on its last legs. Most of the new secretaries ignored it, and its members consisted mainly of old-timers among congressional aides who used it primarily as a social club. Despite its decline, Lyndon's friend Arthur Perry thought that joining and running it would be a good way to get to know people.

To become Little Congress Speaker Johnson had to overcome its rule that officers were chosen by seniority. He had to persuade newer staff members—primarily those working for Democrats who had come to Washington in the Roosevelt landslide—to both join the Little Congress and to vote for him. Johnson approached the task in his usual systematic way. First he nailed down the support of five of his friends. Then he and his clique collared every legislative assistant on the Hill. Since everyone on the payroll of Congress was eligible for membership, Gene Latimer lined up employees of the congressional post office. About two hundred new people showed up at the Cannon House Office Building for the relevant meeting, and before the evening was out, Lyndon B. Johnson was the new Speaker.

Johnson began his Little Congress speakership by calling weekly meetings instead of monthly ones. As promised, he arranged for debates by prominent politicians, sponsored policy discussions, and held mock votes on pending congressional legislation. Soon after he took over as Speaker, more than two hundred people were attending the weekly meetings. Johnson milked the Little Congress for whatever publicity he could get. He told the press that the mock votes were important to cover because congressional aides were attuned to the feelings of their bosses. Once the newspapers started covering meetings, more and more prominent speakers agreed to appear.

At one point Johnson invited Huey Long, the flamboyant Louisiana senator who would later challenge Roosevelt and the New Deal with his own more radical "Share the Wealth" program. The "Kingfish" came, trailing hordes of reporters and newsreel cameras. Another memorable Little Congress occasion was a three-day trip to New York on which Mayor Fiorello LaGuardia, a former congressman himself, gave the Washington visitors the key to the city and took them all to Radio City Music Hall.

The Little Congress provided Johnson with vast opportunities for self-advertisement. He sent newspaper clippings and photographs concerned with the Little Congress's doings back to his friends and family in San Marcos and Johnson City. The need for fresh speakers gave him a reason to visit important politicians. "Once he got in to see somebody," recalled Latimer, ". . . [Johnson] being the way he was, would make them remember him."[21]

During the summer of 1934 Maury Maverick ran for the House in the new Twentieth District in Texas, a split-off from the Fourteenth that included liberal San Antonio. A defender of the underprivileged and a member of the American Civil Liberties Union, Maverick was a utopian radical whose politics echoed his family name. Maverick considered Johnson "the brightest secretary in Washington" and was impressed with his efficiency and his "ready entrée into all of the government departments."[22] He asked Lyndon to manage his primary campaign. Unopposed in the Fourteenth District primary, Kleberg agreed to let his aide take a short leave of absence to help Maverick.

The candidate consulted Johnson on every phase of his campaign. Lyndon wrote brochures and advertising and did extensive campaigning among Mexican Americans in San Antonio. He delighted the crowds by his unabashed embracing and body contact, unusual actions for an "Anglo" politician. The June primary was close: Maverick won, but not by the necessary plurality. A second primary, in August, was scheduled. Though besmirched by rumors of "buying the Mexican vote," Maverick's rerun campaign was successful. After victory, he gratefully sent Johnson his photograph, inscribed: "To Lyndon Johnson who got me started."[23]

By 1934 it was obvious that Lyndon Johnson was going places in politics. It was not quite certain, however, where. Although he began to take more and more credit for his own work, he was still a lowly congressional secretary. As he looked around, he saw that many of the leading politicians had law degrees. His clerk Luther Jones had just been admitted to Georgetown University Law School. Perhaps becoming a lawyer would be advantageous for him, too?

In September 1934 Johnson began evening law classes at Georgetown.† It did not work out. He had never had patience for studying hard. His restless, action-oriented personality was incompatible with the drudgery and memorization required of a first-year law student, and he was soon weary of the interminable cases he had to read and bored by the historical or philosophical reasoning behind specific principles of law. Law school for Lyndon, Jones commented, "was too slow, it was unemotional, he thought it was a lot of crap, briefing all those cases." Finally, after a few weeks of torture, he dropped out with what he called a B.A.—for "Brief Attendance."[24]

In the busy summer of 1934 Johnson's life would change. During the August heat, he was in Austin to see his father at the Texas Railroad Commission office. Sam was proud to introduce his promising son to Eugenia Boehringer, an attractive office secretary. Sam may have been hoping for a romantic match, but "Gene," as she was called, already had a boyfriend. She promised to get Lyndon a date with a friend the next time he was in the state capital, however, and that August, when Lyndon was again in town, she came through. The arranged date was actually with another secretary, but when Johnson came by to pick her up, Claudia "Lady Bird" Taylor, Gene's best friend, was in the office as well. Gene made the introductions, and Johnson invited both young women to join him for a drink. But it was Claudia who impressed him. In fact, in his usual overcharged way, he decided on the spot to marry Lady Bird.

Claudia was the daughter of Thomas Jefferson Taylor, a poor Alabama dirt farmer who had moved to Karnack in East Texas determined to prove to the family of the woman he loved that he would amount to something. Starting as a grocer, he had branched out into successful cotton ginning, farming, and catfish exporting, and made good money. With his new fortune Taylor bought an antebellum mansion called the "Brick House" with the first indoor plumbing in the area and a fireplace in every room. Lady Bird would describe her childhood home as "totally part of the Old South," both in the "look of the land—pine trees, rolling hills—and the economy which was cotton, principally."[25]

Taylor married Minnie Lee Patillo, the aristocratic granddaughter of a Confederate officer who could trace his ancestry back to medieval Scotland.‡ The patrician Patillos had objected to the romance and

---

†Apparently LBJ also was registered for a brief time at Washington College of Law.

‡The name sounds Latin, either Spanish or Italian, but according to Lady Bird's distant cousin "Cato" Patillo, it was originally the Scottish Pattulloch, and changed to Patillo when Robert Pattulloch, a Scot, became an officer in the French Army centuries before.[26]

conveyed their disapproval to their daughter. Accustomed to having her own way, the headstrong young woman disregarded their advice and eloped with him.

Taylor got more than he bargained for. His wife was a suffragist and an integrationist, positions that conventional, small-town Karnack thought bizarre. A cultivated woman, she had numerous health problems, including severe headaches and intensely painful rheumatism. By all accounts her moods were as changeable as southern summer weather, culminating finally in a nervous breakdown, which sent her to the Kellogg Sanitarium in Battle Creek, Michigan, to seek a cure.

Despite her infirmities, Minnie Taylor managed to find the time and energy to have three children. Her first son, Thomas Jefferson III, was born in 1901; her second, Anthony, four years later. Then in 1912, three days before Christmas, the thirty-nine-year-old Minnie gave birth to a daughter. Christened Claudia Alta Taylor, the baby was brought up by black nursemaids. A few days after her birth, one of the nannies said: "She's as pretty as a little lady bird."[27] Though she tried hard, Claudia could never get rid of the nickname, and Lyndon, in particular, loved it: their initials would be the same once she married him.

When Lady Bird was five, her mother had a miscarriage and contracted blood poisoning. She died a month later, leaving Claudia in the hands of her frail, spinster sister, thirty-nine-year-old Aunt Effie Patillo. Benevolent, refined, and otherworldly, Aunt Effie knew nothing about the practical aspects of raising a child, but she did share her sister's interest in culture and education. She made certain that Lady Bird continued to read her mother's books. She also loved flowers and took her niece into the meadows and woods to search for the first blossoms of dogwood and to teach her how to identify trees. Her aunt's nature lessons became an important part of the little girl's personality, endowing her with a lifelong sensitivity to landscape and the out-of-doors.

After graduation from high school, Lady Bird moved to Dallas with Aunt Effie to attend St. Mary's Episcopal School for Girls. It was at St. Mary's that she met Eugenia Boehringer, who became her best friend and who tutored the motherless girl in dressing, dancing, and dating. Eugenia also persuaded her to come with her to the University of Texas to finish the last two years of college.

At Austin Lady Bird, who was well liked, tried to overcome her lifelong diffidence. She began dating, and became a reporter for the *Daily Texan* and the publicity manager of the University of Texas Sports Association. Though teaching in Alaska or Hawaii appealed to her, she decided that reporters "had more exciting things happen to them" than teachers and settled on journalism.[28]

Lyndon had met Lady Bird just after she graduated from the university. She was in Austin that fateful day to interview Hugo Kuehne, an architect, whom her father wanted to renovate the Brick House. Sometime that day Lyndon asked Lady Bird to have breakfast with him the next morning in the coffee shop of the Driskill Hotel, which fortuitously was next door to Kuehne's office. The young woman was a bit overwhelmed by Johnson's approach, experiencing what she described as a "sort of queer moth-and-flame feeling."[29] She was not sure she would accept his invitation, but in the end came anyway. "I dare say I was going all the time," Lady Bird later admitted, "but just telling myself I wasn't going."[30]

From that moment on, her fate was sealed. She and Lyndon breakfasted on grits, steak, and eggs and then went for a drive around the countryside in a leather-fitted Ford roadster convertible belonging to the King Ranch. In the car, Lyndon talked for hours to his captive date, describing every member of his family and reviewing his life history. He told Lady Bird his salary and the amount of insurance he carried; he described his work as a congressional secretary and his ambitions for the future. At the end of this extraordinary narration, he asked Lady Bird to marry him. He had known her less than a day. "I was so surprised I couldn't believe it," she said. "I thought it was some kind of joke."[31] She was too taken aback to answer his proposal. His campaign that day resembled the bombardment tactics he later used so effectively to get reluctant senators to vote his way.

Though it was certainly too early in their relationship to think of marriage, Lady Bird did not want to lose him. Lyndon Johnson was quite an extraordinary young man. She had inherited a small fortune from her mother, and she worried that he might be after her money. She told him she would hate it if he went into politics. But she hoped he was sincerely attracted to her, and in any case, love might actually grow through the years. At the outset "I thought he was quite a repulsive young man," she confessed. "But then I realized he was handsome and charming and terribly bright. . . . I was terrifically interested and a little bit scared, not wanting to let him go and not at all sure I wanted to have any closer relationship."[32]

She need not have worried about scaring him away; he had no intention of giving her up. In the short time he had remaining in Texas, he gave her no opportunity to think twice. He determined, he said, to "keep her mind completely on me until the moment I had to leave for Washington. . . ."[33] He took her to meet his parents in San Marcos and then to the luxurious King Ranch, where Johnson was well liked by his employer's parents for single-handedly keeping their son in Congress. At the ranch, *grande dame* Alice Gertrudis King Kleberg, the congressman's mother, took Lady Bird aside and advised her to marry the young bureaucrat. When it was time to return to Washington, Johnson wangled an invitation to the Brick House to meet his beloved's father. T. J. Taylor needed little convincing. "My husband liked Lyndon from the first," said Ruth Taylor, T. J.'s third wife. "Both were much alike. Both were big men physically. Both were work-minded and always in a hurry." After dinner Taylor told his daughter: "You've been bringing home a lot of boys. This time, you've brought a man."[34]

Johnson did not let up on his marital campaign once he got back to Washington. He barraged his beloved with letters and phone calls every day, and "dedicated to these daily letters," recalled Gene Latimer, "the same meticulous detail he gave to every top-drawer project."[35] The letters have the manic energy of Lyndon on a high. One reads: "My dear Bird . . . I'm ambitious, proud, energetic, and very madly in love with you. . . . I want to see people—want to drive through the throngs. . . . I'm bubbling over with them. . . ."[36] It was difficult to avoid being flattered by the deluge of attention and devotion that Johnson poured into his courtship. How could this impassioned crusade fail to invoke the desired answer? "I don't think," Gene Latimer later said, "Lady Bird ever had a chance once he set eyes on her."[37]

Though Lady Bird continued to evade, Johnson gradually wore her down to the point where he could see she was weakening. Now that she was more favorably inclined, he was impatient to make her commit herself. What better way than to set a date for the wedding? Scarcely six weeks had passed since he left her when Johnson raced back from Washington to Karnack in his Ford nonstop. No sooner had he gotten out of the car than he said, "Let's get married. Not next year, after you've done over the house, but about two weeks from now, or right away." Scared at how little she knew him, she again demurred. But then, when he was not around, she missed him terribly. "It was embarrassing to admit," she confessed, "that so much could happen in such a short time. Here was this man I barely knew talking about marriage and I was seriously considering the idea."[38]

Lyndon talked her into going to Austin three hundred miles away to look at rings. There she picked out an engagement ring but refused to let him buy a matching wedding band. While he was in Corpus Christi on business, however, Lady Bird revealed her true state of mind by buying a trousseau. But then she decided to ask Aunt Effie's advice. Effie urged delay. How could her niece rush into marriage with a stranger she had known for only two months? "If he loves you as much as he says he does," counseled Effie, "he will wait for you."[39]

Back at the Brick House, her father snorted at his sister-in-law's caution. "If you wait until Aunt Effie is ready, you will never marry anyone," he said.[40] Still uncertain, Lady Bird decided to go to Austin to speak to Gene Boehringer, first packing her trousseau in a suitcase. Instinctively recognizing that she had capitulated, Lyndon insisted on driving her to the Texas capital, and as soon as they were on the road, gave his passenger an ultimatum. "If you say no, it just proves that you don't love me enough to dare to marry me. We either do it now or we never will."[41] Lady Bird continued to resist, but she did not protest as he turned the car toward San Antonio, where he intended to tie the knot in a lovely Episcopal church on St. Mark's Square.

Lyndon had alerted his San Antonio friend Dan Quill to his plans. Quill had worked for Johnson in political campaigns and was not surprised to hear his friend say: "Lady Bird and I want to be married at eight o'clock tonight at St. Mark's Episcopal Church. Fix everything up."[42] Using his influence at City Hall to bypass the rules, Quill managed to get an immediate marriage license and to persuade the Reverend Arthur R. McKinstry to perform the service. McKinstry was reluctant to marry them at first, claiming he needed to explain to them the seriousness of marriage, but Quill reminded the minister that he had received a mailing permit for his church bulletin at a reduced rate. Quill also arranged for a reception at the St. Anthony Hotel.

Lyndon and Lady Bird reached St. Mark's without the bride actually having said yes and without a ring; the groom had forgotten to stop for one. Ever helpful, Quill rushed across the street to Sears, reappearing at the church with a dozen rings of assorted sizes. Lady Bird picked one that fit, and the marriage was on. Quill then made them a wedding present of the $2.50 ring. In the commotion, the marriage license was left behind, not to be found until Quill discovered it accidentally in the San Antonio Courthouse twenty years later. As the newly married couple walked out of St. Mark's, McKinstry was heard mumbling, "I hope that marriage lasts."[43]

Lyndon and Lady Bird spent their wedding night at the Plaza Hotel and then departed for Monterrey for their Mexican honeymoon. Before they left, they called their respective parents to inform them of the momentous events. Rebekah was very disappointed that she had not been there, but wrote warm letters to Lady Bird and her impetuous son, bestowing her blessings. Lady Bird also called Gene Boehringer. "Lyndon and I committed matrimony last night," she told her friend.[44]

LBJ had acquired the wife he needed to help him to the top. This sounds calculating to a generation that cherishes unsullied romantic love, but it does not warrant cynicism. Countless generations of poor but talented young men have pursued and won well-born young women. It is a more venerable theme than "all for love." Both his grandfather and his father had married up. Though their wives had not been so much richer — Rebekah, after all, had been poor — they were better educated, more refined, and from a higher social class. Many up-and-coming but unpolished men marry women whose gentility complements their roughness. Lyndon admired Lady Bird's "ideals, intelligence, and refinement." These were the qualities that he found attractive in women at this point. And, as he said, she was "the prettiest girl I ever saw."[45]

The unhappy, complaining Rebekah had proved a disappointment to Sam, but Lady Bird fulfilled LBJ's fondest expectations. She rose to every occasion: She was calm, masked her inner feelings, and never complained. She became a skilled housekeeper and cook, though she had to learn from scratch. All her life, before Lyndon, she had had servants. Before marriage, "I had never swept a floor," she said, "and I certainly had never cooked."[46] She became an expert financial manager and a successful hostess, attributes essential to a rising politician's ultimate success. She always sought ways to improve herself. She put up with Lyndon's many impositions on her. She endured his immaturity, his vulgarity, his intrusiveness, and his egotism, often at her expense. She would also accept his philandering, knowing that he would always come back to her.

Did she love him? In many ways, her husband and her father were alike. They were both tall, hardworking, and driven. They were both crude, capable, and outwardly strong. She admired her husband's ambition and his energy. She considered him "remarkable."[47] Through the years of her marriage, she realized that Lyndon respected her, was grateful to her, and was dependent on her. According to Paul Conkin, she "basked finally in his political success, shared his enormous power and used some of it to further her own goals, and enjoyed his exuberance and his overwhelming acts of kindness and affection."[48]

But whatever deal Lady Bird had made for herself, it was now on to Washington and the great world of politics.

CHAPTER 4

Young Bureaucrat

THE JOHNSONS' FIRST LODGING in Washington when they arrived after their honeymoon was an "upstairs" room at the same dumpy Dodge Hotel where Lyndon had stayed when he first came to the capital. It was not a suitable residence for a married couple, and they soon rented a furnished two-room apartment, with a roll-away bed in the living room, on Kalorama Road, a street in what was then a shabby neighborhood. To Lyndon the new quarters must have seemed spacious.

Lady Bird, of course, was accustomed to nicer living arrangements, and like Rebekah, after *her* marriage, would have many adjustments to make. Besides sharing a small apartment with a husband she barely knew, she would have to cope with her new role as a hardworking housewife on a limited budget. Kleberg had given his aide a raise as a wedding present, but after Lyndon deducted $100 a month for personal expenses, his wife had little more than $200 left to pay the rent, buy food and other necessities, and put aside $18.75 a month for a government savings bond. The young woman who never had to worry about money before found herself mastering the arts of bargain-hunting and penny-pinching.

To learn the basics of cooking, Lady Bird bought herself a Fannie Farmer cookbook and, at her first dinner party—for Congressman Maury Maverick and his wife, Terrell—kept it open on the stove. The ham and the lemon pie she served on that occasion were very good, according to Mrs. Maverick, but the rice was pasty. Terrell Maverick remembered the charm of her hostess, who managed to disguise her obvious nervousness with a warm smile. Sam Rayburn was another early visitor to Kalorama

Road. Lady Bird learned to make the black-eyed peas, chili, and corn-bread that Rayburn had eaten on his boyhood Texas farm. Rayburn soon felt so much at ease with the young married couple that he often came for breakfast as well as dinner and made their apartment his refuge.

The goodwill of Maverick and Rayburn would prove valuable to Lyndon even sooner than expected. Johnson was tired of being just a congressional secretary; he wanted to be a legislator in his own right. Moreover, by June 1935, six months after his marriage, he was experiencing tensions with Kleberg over New Deal reform programs. To make matters worse, the congressman's wife, Mamie, a fearful, neurotic woman, had turned against him. For a time she had doted on Lyndon and sought his personal advice when Kleberg betrayed her with another woman. During the spring of 1932, away from Washington, she wrote the young aide asking for news of her husband and signing herself "your other mother."[1]

For unknown reasons, love changed to hate. Mamie apparently resented that the congressman had given Johnson the job of paying the family bills and restraining her when she exceeded the funds available. She also became suspicious of Johnson's ambitions and deduced that he was after her husband's congressional seat. There may have been something more deeply buried as well. The tone of her surviving letters to him hints at a physical attraction that may or may not have been consummated, but surely would have made relations between Lyndon and his boss uncomfortable. In any event, it seems clear that Mamie persuaded Kleberg to let Lyndon go.

Johnson turned to Rayburn and Maverick and asked for help in finding another job. He could not have chosen a more auspicious moment. June 26, 1935, marked the creation of the National Youth Administration (NYA), an agency of the Works Progress Administration (WPA). Designed to provide public works jobs for the unemployed, the WPA did a fine job with the adult jobless but did little for the young. In 1935 the Bureau of Statistics revealed that almost four million young men and women between sixteen and twenty-five needed jobs or education. Some of these would be forced to drop out of high school or college because their families could not afford to keep them in school.

To aid these young people, FDR created the NYA by Executive Order 7068. The NYA would seek meaningful part-time employment for those still in high school, college, and graduate school so they could continue their training and gain constructive work experience. The agency would also help those who had finished their schooling find full-time jobs. Finally, it would provide counseling, placement, and job training services for all young people.

Chosen to head the NYA was the hardworking and intense Aubrey Williams, an Alabama editor and passionate southern reformer whose populist faith would reinforce LBJ's own. Johnson admired Williams extravagantly, declared Elizabeth Goldschmidt, a Johnson friend, then working for the WPA. Williams was "very radical in his beliefs, homegrown radicalism," and "Lyndon was that way too," she noted.[2] The program itself would be run by state administrators through forty-eight state NYA offices. Johnson asked Maverick and Rayburn to use their influence to get him appointed Texas director. Though someone else had actually been named and already sworn in, Johnson's influential friends got FDR to reverse himself and name Johnson instead. A few days short of his twenty-seventh birthday, Lyndon Johnson became head of the Texas NYA, the youngest state director in the country. Kleberg agreed to hire Lyndon's brother Sam to take his place as congressional secretary.

The young federal official faced a challenging task. In early August 1935, at a White House briefing, FDR told his new NYA administrators: "We have given you fifty million dollars. We are going to get action." FDR asked Johnson to remain for a while after the ceremony and informed him of Maverick's and Rayburn's efforts in getting him appointed. Johnson, aware that the president had singled him out, later said that from that time on Roosevelt "always kinda petted me."[3]

The new job meant that Johnson and Lady Bird would be moving back to Austin, a change Lady Bird felt was like going "to heaven."[4] In the Texas capital, they rented a house on San Gabriel Street from Robert Montgomery, a committed New Dealer and professor of economics at the University of Texas. Montgomery would serve as entrée to an active liberal Austin social circle much given to fervent discussion of the exciting political currents of the day.

On August 15, 1935, LBJ opened the headquarters of the Texas NYA, with two San Marcos alumni—Jesse Kellam and Willard Deason—and childhood friends Sherman Birdwell and Ben Crider as his assistants and next-in-command. Talking passionately about how the NYA could "keep youngsters in school and provide work and employment for those who had been forced out of school," Johnson sold other former White Stars on joining his Austin office as well.[5] Johnson knew that an ordinarily conscientious staff was not sufficient. He would require his aides' total loyalty and commitment.

Funding was a major NYA problem from the outset. Fifty million dollars was in reality very little, considering the number of needy American youths. The initial state allocations were small, and each of the state directors had to compete fiercely with the others for shares. Five days after he opened the Austin office, Johnson went to Washington for a meeting with Williams and the other state directors. Fortunately he impressed Williams sufficiently to get Texas more than its original allotment. Even so, there was never enough money to go around.

Race, too, was a problem. The South was still deep in the miasmic era of Jim Crow, and the rest of the United States, though free of legal segregation, was profoundly racist. Under Williams, the national NYA tried to be color-blind. It sought, for example, to create biracial advisory panels, a move ahead of its day. In this area Johnson played a canny game. He was remarkably free of traditional southern bigotry, but he understood that he could wreck the entire Texas program if he challenged the entrenched racial mores of the time and place by setting up an integrated panel. Instead, he created a separate black advisory board and convinced black leaders to join it.

And Johnson did try to ensure that blacks received fully equal though separate benefits. The student aid program included all the black colleges. In fact, an even larger proportion of black than white college students received aid. Blacks were also hired for road improvement and construction jobs, though usually kept in separate crews from whites. Throughout the program Johnson walked a tightrope, publicly downplaying black projects, discounting his meetings with black college officials, and not publicizing his appearances at black schools. He managed to reassure both the national board that he was fulfilling their directives and the white community that their customs were not being violated.

Though the scheme perpetuated segregation, most black Texans were convinced that it was unavoidable and were pleased with the practical results of the program. Frank Horne (singer Lena Horne's uncle) worked for the NYA and "he kept talking about this guy in Texas who was really something . . . " reminisced Robert C. Weaver, later Johnson's secretary of housing and urban development. "That's when I first heard about Lyndon Johnson. As far as most federal agencies were concerned, the Negroes weren't even considered, but this guy in Texas was giving them and the Mexican Americans a fair break that made quite an impression on me."[6] In later years the black community remembered favorably Johnson's work in the NYA on their behalf.

Surprisingly, Johnson did less for Mexican Americans than for blacks. In Texas they represented about 12 percent of the population and were often desperately poor. Johnson's personal history demonstrates his sympathies for the state's Hispanic population. He was disturbed by the sight of Mexican American children ransacking garbage cans and chewing on the grapefruit rinds they fished out. Yet he apparently believed that they needed less help from the NYA than others. This was because they were, in his view, sustained by a quasi-feudal system as near-peons to large landowners. However deplorable, he felt their status protected them against the worst of the depressed free labor market.

Since the Texas NYA office opened in the middle of August and classes were due to start in less than a month, Johnson faced an early deadline. There could be no delay in enrolling and orienting school administrators to manage the work-study appropriations. Less pressing but equally important, Johnson had to design and launch work projects that would furnish part-time employment to the jobless young people of Texas. This meant finding public and private individuals and institutions to sponsor the work projects and provide the supervision, materials, and housing for them. He would have to personally persuade hundreds of administrators of hospitals, libraries, recreational facilities, universities, and schools of the program's worthiness.

The young bureaucrat soon put his formidable persuasive powers to use cultivating well-placed Texans and buttering up newspaper editors all over the Lone Star State for favorable attention and publicity for himself and the programs. When his carefully picked workforce showed up early on opening day, Johnson was already on the job, the telephone receiver glued to his ear. Johnson gave marching orders to his staff: "Put them to work; get them in school."[7] That would be the battle cry for the rest of Johnson's NYA administration tour of duty.

Keeping young men and women in school was another specific responsibility of the NYA, and Johnson went about it in his usual hyperactive way. The activities of the Texas NYA in the student area were broad-ranging. Some of the seventy-five thousand Texas students who stayed in college were eventually put to work under NYA programs as document catalogers, research and laboratory assistants, and student counselors. At Baylor University, sociology majors counseled almost eighteen hundred Waco public school dropouts, all of whom, except one, apparently stayed in school. Many high school students did physical work, repairing and building schools, libraries, gyms, and swimming pools. Female students often bound and restored books, sewed clothing, and served lunches in school cafeterias.

As NYA director, Johnson cooked up the idea of relocating Civilian Conservation Corps (CCC) camps, where city boys worked on outdoor projects, near colleges so that CCC members could take courses while they worked. When none of his higher-ups responded to this suggestion, he sent it to FDR himself. It was soon adopted and implemented in Texas and other states. Lyndon picked the minds of friends from his past for suggestions about innovative programs. President Evans of San

Marcos State suggested freshman centers for high school graduates who had to supplement the family income and could not afford to attend college even with part-time NYA employment. Using teachers paid by NYA funds, students could take one or two tuition-free courses at twenty of these centers situated throughout Texas in small cities as well as large ones. These centers were prototypes of the community and junior colleges that eventually gave many students, despite mediocre grades and low incomes, access to higher education in every state.

Another NYA program specifically aided rural youth. These young farm people were brought to college campuses and given a four-month vocational course to help them better their lives back home. Young men were taught animal husbandry, improved dairy farming methods, and how to repair farm machinery. Farm girls were taught more efficient methods of canning and sewing. Those young men who did not want to return to the farm were taught useful urban occupations such as plumbing, automobile mechanics, and carpentry. Women were taught secretarial skills. The *Dallas Journal* observed that the government had never been interested in helping isolated rural families before. The youth "from the forks of the creeks," it noted, "deserve some chance in life. And the NYA is going to give them that chance."[8]

Some of the Texas NYA's most imaginative projects were in the area of "works progress" for unemployed youth. Building on the inspired idea of a friend, Johnson proposed that NYA construct "roadside parks" along the highways. These would provide tired truck drivers, exhausted travelers, and homeless migrants with safe places to rest or sleep. The Texas Highway Department contributed materials, trucks, and supervisory personnel, farmers often gave up small parcels of land along the road, and the NYA was able to put to work building rest stops many blacks and Mexican Americans who could not afford to stay in school. The young men cleared and paved the land and constructed benches, picnic tables, and barbecue pits for motorists. Other states soon copied this idea.

Under Johnson, the NYA helped restore La Villita, the old Mexican center of San Antonio. The district had become a noisome, decrepit slum, yet it was a significant fragment of Texas history, and for years Maury Maverick, then mayor of San Antonio, had yearned to restore it to its original state. With federal and local money and NYA labor the old shacks were turned into dwellings, stores, and handicraft shops. La Villita became the core of the redevelopment that helped turn Old San Antonio into a major tourist magnet.

One of the most compassionate Texas NYA projects targeted young, single Mexican American and black women. NYA set up camps in rural areas where the women were given dental and medical checkups, fed nourishing food, and taught English grammar and conversational proficiency, nutrition and cooking, sewing and vocational skills. Many who came to the camp were ailing, undernourished, and depressed or anxious. After spending eight weeks in this program, they often regained their health and were able to cope with their lives successfully. "I know of no other two months," said one of the camp teachers, "in which the investment of time has shown as much visible profit. . . ."[9]

Johnson worked as hard as NYA administrator as he had as Kleberg's secretary. As Jesse Kellam later reported, "He drove himself and either drove or led those who worked with him and for him at a hard clip. More nights than not, we asked the building in which we were housed would they please leave the lights on another hour. . . . Many, many times he had the building manager agree to leave the lights on until midnight. . . . The building manager finally complained to the building owner."[10] Lady Bird did not take part directly in the office work, but she often provided meals and a refuge for Lyndon's subordinates. Johnson would invite colleagues home for dinner at all hours, and Lady Bird would whip up a quick meal for the hungry public servants. Kellam remembered that Lady Bird "could cook round steak and make creamy gravy that was out of this world."[11]

The NYA experience stamped itself firmly on Johnson's political perspective. Here was proof that activist government could rescue people from calamity and at the same time add to the permanent amenities of American life. Harry Ransom, then an Austin newspaper reporter, later claimed that the NYA experience convinced Johnson that the federal government could be more effective than the states. Moreover, there is a line, though an interrupted one, connecting NYA programs and those of the Johnson Great Society. The strongest carryover is with the future Job Corps, but roadside rest stops and the La Villita project were precursors of Great Society programs for highway beautification and landmark preservation.

New Dealers were pleased with the work of the Texas NYA. Aubrey Williams thought Johnson was accomplishing more than any other state director and sent people from other states to Texas for inspiration. Johnson, he said, "did a beautiful job . . . one of the very best in the country. He fought for those kids to get them all he could, he even fought me to get things and money for them."[12] Eleanor Roosevelt, too, was a Johnson partisan. In 1936 she came to Austin to see what this highly touted young director was doing. She inspected NYA headquarters, visited a training program for sewing machine operators and a roadside park near

Austin, and talked with college officials and NYA recipients. She left Texas profoundly impressed.

The NYA is a good example of the two sides of Lyndon Baines Johnson. One was deeply compassionate and caring, especially in areas that involved the young and the have-nots. But the other, just as strong, was the one that asked, "What will this do for my image and my career? Who can I impress and how can I best publicize my accomplishments?" Johnson clearly considered the NYA post merely a step on the ladder that would take him back to Washington. He was conscious that the thirty thousand or more young people he put on NYA payrolls—who called him "Lyn" and believed they owed their salvation to him—would deliver the votes when the time came. His old college friend Willard Deason would later observe that Johnson's political machine in Texas "all went back to that NYA."[13]

But Johnson wasn't only concerned about the future voters; there were also the people at the top. Johnson courted important men and women in Texas and in Washington, both to help his NYA projects and to augment his own political prestige. Headquartered in Austin, the state capital, he had a chance to meet most of the state's influential leaders, many of whom knew his father and were inclined to show friendship toward the son.

One of the Texans Johnson particularly cultivated was the amiable state senator Alvin Wirtz, now a powerful public utilities lawyer and Austin businessman. A dapper and distinguished-looking man, Wirtz had served in the Texas Senate when Sam Jr. was in the lower house and so had known Lyndon as a child. Mary Rather, who would join Johnson's staff in the 1940s and stay through the White House years, remembered often seeing Lyndon in Wirtz's office at Powell, Wirtz, Rauhut, and Gideon in the early 1930s, seeking advice from the senator. Later, as Kleberg's congressional secretary, Johnson would support Wirtz's plans for a series of dams under the aegis of the Lower Colorado River Authority (LCRA), a "little TVA" on the Lower Colorado River, a stream that flowed from Austin to the gulf. As chairman of the Texas NYA Advisory Committee, Wirtz often met with Johnson to talk over NYA business. Johnson was always at his best, friendly and deferential, and Wirtz, who was childless, soon began to think of the younger man, much as Rayburn did, as a son or a nephew.

Johnson also made sure he got the attention of FDR himself. Eleanor Roosevelt often praised the Texas NYA director to her husband, but Johnson was not satisfied with this indirect contact. When he heard that the president was coming to Dallas to visit the Texas Centennial Exposition, he rounded up some of his NYA workers, positioning them in a straight line at a point along Roosevelt's automobile route. Each held his shovel vertically, in "present arms" style, to the passing presidential motorcade. As Roosevelt went by, Johnson conspicuously stepped in front of the men and saluted. The delighted president waved and laughed.

February 23, 1937, was another big day for LBJ. In Houston to acquaint the Kansas NYA director with the Texas program, he caught sight of the headline in the *Houston Post* lying on a park bench: "Congressman James P. Buchanan of Brenham Dies." The conservative "Buck" Buchanan represented the Tenth Congressional District, which included both Austin and Johnson City. LBJ knew this was his big chance. Buchanan would now be replaced in a special election. It would be a "sudden death" contest: No matter how many people ran, the candidate who got the largest number of votes would go to Congress; no majority was required. Johnson had long seen the House of Representatives as the next stepping-stone in his national political career, but congressional seats from Texas, where the voters tended to return incumbents to Washington over and over, were hard to come by. Old Buck, for instance—who had himself won his seat in a special election—had stayed in office for twenty-four years. In solid Democratic Texas, the winner of an election could expect to be in Congress for life.

Now, miraculously, the seat Johnson was most eligible for was vacant. "I just couldn't keep my mind on [my Kansas visitor]," Johnson told Doris Kearns. "I kept thinking that this was my district and this was my chance. The day seemed endless. . . . And I had to pretend total interest in everything we were seeing and doing. . . . I thought I'd explode from all the excitement bottled up inside."[14] When his colleague finally left, LBJ dashed back to Austin. First, he asked Lady Bird for her approval. Then he called Alvin Wirtz. Wirtz at first was dubious despite his warm personal regard for Lyndon. He needed favors from the federal government for his Lower Colorado project and did not want to back a losing candidate and incur the enmity of the future congressman from his district. There were, moreover, already at least nine better-known people interested in running, including Buchanan's widow. Mrs. Buchanan was politically naive and very shy, but as the congressman's widow she would be a sentimental favorite. Another formidable opponent would be C. N. Avery, Buchanan's campaign manager and secretary.

Fortunately, Wirtz soon recognized that the politically skilled and persuasive Johnson, with his Washington contacts, his knowledge of the workings of Executive agencies, and his talent for cutting through red tape, might be just the man to get the Lower Colorado project funded.

He agreed to support Johnson. He would advise him on his campaign, help prepare speeches, and contact local Democratic politicians, though he was still not sure that his young friend could win. In Washington Johnson's urge to run produced dismay. Tommy Corcoran, one of Roosevelt's inner circle of brilliant young bill-drafters and congressional managers, recalled Aubrey Williams coming to him in a sweat to ask the president to dissuade the young Texan from running. "He's my whole youth program in Texas and if he quits I have no program down there."[15]

One major obstacle was money. At a meeting with Johnson, Wirtz estimated that it would cost at least ten thousand dollars to mount a campaign. Lady Bird, who was present, watched her husband's face fall as he contemplated the size of the sum. She asked Wirtz if LBJ had *any* chance of winning. A small one, Wirtz said. Lady Bird called Karnack and asked her father, who held her mother's inheritance in trust for her, for a ten-thousand-dollar advance, to be sent immediately. "I was on the other end of the phone," Johnson told Doris Kearns, "my heart pumping the whole time." Shocked by the amount, Taylor asked whether a smaller sum would do. When Lady Bird said no, her father promised to wire the money as soon as he could. "I was at the bank at 9 a.m. the next morning," remembered LBJ, "and there it was."[16] Mrs. Johnson saved the deposit slip as a treasured souvenir until the paper disintegrated.

LBJ now had to consider when to announce his candidacy. It would be discourteous to throw his hat in the ring before Congressman Buchanan's funeral on Friday, February 26. Avery, who told the *Austin American* that he would not run if Mrs. Buchanan did, also said she would have her own announcement to make on Monday. Like the others in the race, Johnson did not want to offend the widow by jumping the gun, yet he knew that the sooner he announced, the greater his advantage. Wirtz would not advise him on this matter, so Johnson sought out the one person who could. He drove the fifty miles to the Hill Country on icy roads to consult with his father, who lay sick in bed, eight months away from dying of a heart condition. "Don't go waiting on her," Sam told his son. "You go on ahead and announce right away. The minute Mrs. Buchanan knows she's got opposition, she won't get in."[17] That night, back in Austin, Lyndon told reporters he would run for Congress, whether or not Mrs. Buchanan entered the race. And the crafty old politician was right: the widow withdrew when she learned that Johnson had beaten her to the punch.

Johnson now had to differentiate himself from the eight remaining other candidates, most of whom were also Roosevelt-supporting Democrats. His advisers, including Wirtz and campaign manager Claude

Wild, told him he had to wholeheartedly support FDR. This meant a strong defense of Roosevelt's plan to reorganize the Supreme Court.

The Court issue was controversial and divisive. The Court's invalidation in 1935 and 1936 of the NIRA and the AAA, two of the heavyweight New Deal recovery programs, had dismayed Roosevelt. He now anticipated that it would soon strike down the major New Deal Social Security measures as well. The "nine old men" were barriers to social progress, and he must find a way around them. Since a constitutional amendment to reduce the Court's power was clearly too unwieldy and slow, FDR proposed to increase by statute the number of existing judges from nine to fifteen, one for each justice over seventy who would not resign. FDR, of course, hoped to create a New Deal majority on the Court, but justified his "Court packing" scheme on the grounds that younger judges would make the highest federal court more efficient.

The proposal scheme aroused opposition from virtually every ideological quarter. FDR's conservative enemies accused him of seeking to stifle the one branch of government that would stand up to him; other critics denounced the threat to traditional constitutional restraints. Some liberals charged that in the future a right-wing president might pack the Court to undermine established civil liberties protections. In the end Roosevelt would lose his Court reform battle and fritter away a great deal of precious political capital in the process. Yet the plan had its supporters, too. Many voters whose lives had improved under the New Deal idolized the president and thought he could do no wrong. These included many of the voters of the Tenth Congressional District in Texas to whom Johnson would have to appeal. Johnson's strategy was to defend FDR's Supreme Court program before any of his campaign rivals had thought it through.

He quickly went on record in favor of the "court-packing" plan, calling it the "unpacking" plan. He began to refer to his Democratic opponents as "the Eight in the Dark," implying that their devotion to the president was less than constant. Johnson's entire campaign strategy called for identification with Roosevelt. He plastered posters throughout the district proclaiming: "A VOTE FOR JOHNSON IS A VOTE FOR ROOSEVELT'S PROGRAM." Another read: "Support the Man Who—Stands with the President and for the People; Has Helped Hundreds of Farmers and Working Men; Understands Departmental Routine of Washington; Will Carry Colorado and Brazos Projects Through; Capably Administered His Part of the Roosevelt Program for Texas."[18]

Consciously imitating FDR's popular "fireside chats," Johnson turned to the radio for help. When his first radio talk seemed too stiff, he adopted the folksy and friendly delivery of Roosevelt, albeit with a Texas twist. Although at least four or five of the other Democratic candidates supported both Roosevelt and his Supreme Court plan, Johnson had been the first to do so. He promised not to evade the issue. He would not be "out in the woodshed practicing to duck."[19] By emphasizing his position earlier and more loudly, enthusiastically, and continually than the others, he convinced voters that he was the most courageous pro-Roosevelt, pro–New Deal candidate.

The candidate's focus attracted national attention to Tenth District politics. This election would be the closest thing to a referendum on the president's court reform proposal, and before long the press wire services and national radio commentators such as Walter Winchell and Lowell Thomas began to pay attention. Johnson himself was fully aware of the glare of national publicity. In a speech at San Marcos, he declared that the nation's eyes were riveted on this special election. "This national issue, which you will vote on," he announced, "is commanding the keen attention of the people throughout the country."[20]

The election was scheduled for April 10 and, despite his early start, Johnson had an uphill fight. In the last month, Johnson, nicknamed the "Blanco Blitz," was a tireless campaigner. He told Lady Bird not to let him in the house "when there's daylight and keep the screen [door] locked until dark."[21] He hit every Tenth District city and town, making more than two hundred speeches and holding elaborate barbecues. He walked the streets, shaking the hands of everyone he met, and entered stores and cafés asking for votes. The district was mostly rural, and Johnson had to spend a great deal of time traveling on its small, dusty back roads. He often stopped his car at filling stations, some with only one pump, to talk to customers gassing up, and parked alongside the road to talk to farmers working in the fields. In these country places he stressed both his rural upbringing and his support of Roosevelt's farm policies. Lady Bird did not actually campaign with her husband this time, a fact that she regretted in later years, but she licked envelopes, called up voters, and bolstered Lyndon's spirits. Rebekah phoned all her friends to make sure they voted.

LBJ also campaigned among black voters. Although some of his advisers warned against it, in an unpublicized meeting he conferred with the leaders of the Austin black community about how they could mutually help one another. If he won, he told them, he would try to enforce their voting rights and work for additional social programs that would benefit them. A participant that night later declared that from that meeting on blacks always voted for Johnson.

Even in this first campaign there were rumors that LBJ was playing dirty. One story asserted that he got federal officials to let him personally hand out AAA checks to farmers. Fund raiser Ed Clark, Governor Jimmy Allred's secretary of state, himself claimed he solicited funds from state employees by telling them that the governor wanted them to give to the Johnson campaign. But all Texas campaigns of that era were freewheeling donnybrooks where politicians bent the rules and seldom applauded their opponents' honesty.

Perhaps it was the mounds of barbecue and the towering stacks of cold pancakes he ate on the campaign trail, perhaps it was his lack of sleep, or perhaps it was the strain of overwork in general, but Johnson developed such severe stomach pains in the week before the election that he almost fainted. Still he kept going. On April 8 he finally collapsed at a meeting in Austin. His appendix had almost burst by the time his friends rushed him to the hospital for an emergency appendectomy. Johnson's opponents charged that the illness was imaginary, a trick to win the sympathies of the voters. Fortunately, Johnson had the presence of mind to insist that the physician brother of State Senator Houghton Brownlee, one of his rivals, assist at the operation, to prove that it had actually happened. But had it been an emergency? "Seems to me," said a Johnson campaign worker, "Lyndon had been complaining about that appendix for some time. But this sure was a good time to have it out—at least as far as the publicity was concerned." But his campaign manager defended him. "There wasn't any fake about it," declared Claude Wild. "He was sick."[22] On the other hand, his misery did not keep him from campaigning from his sickbed. A steady stream of well-wishers and supporters came by Brackenridge Hospital to see the horizontal candidate. Certain that the visitors themselves initiated the parade, the doctor urged Lady Bird to "stop it." "Stop it, Doctor?" she responded. "He's promoting this."[23]

Whether a campaign stratagem or not, the appendectomy undoubtedly brought out a sympathy vote. Listening to the final returns from his hospital bed, Johnson learned that he had won 8,280 votes of the 30,000 cast, 3,000 more than his closest opponent. The "Blanco Blitz" had carried his own county by 688 to 82, but even in Austin, a city he thought he could not take, he managed to win big. His victory made the front pages of many major newspapers, including the *New York Times*. "Youthful Lyndon B. Johnson who shouted his advocacy of President Roosevelt's court reorganization all over the Tenth Texas District was elected today . . . " said the *Times* article of April 11. "[H]e happily received reports of an emphatic victory over eight opponents and said he considered the result a vote of confidence in Mr. Roosevelt and his program."[24]

A picture of him taken at the hospital the day after his victory shows him flanked by two nurses. He looks weak, his face is thin and unshaven, and he has dark rings under his eyes. But around his pillowed head is a necklace of congratulatory telegrams, and his smile is triumphant.

Rebekah, of course, was thrilled by the victory. "My dear Lyndon," she wrote,

> To me your election not alone gratifies my pride as a mother in a splendid and satisfying son and delights me with the realization of the joy you must feel in your success, but in a measure it compensates me for the heartache and disappointment I experienced as a child when my dear father lost the race you just won. . . . Today my faith is restored. How happy it would have made my precious and noble father to know that the first-born of his first-born would achieve the position he desired. It makes me happy to have you carry on the ideals and principles so cherished by that great and good man. I gave you his name. I commend you to his example. You have always justified my expectations, my darling boy, my devoted son, my strength and comfort. . . . Always remember that I love you and am behind you in all that comes to you. . . .[25]

It was a letter that disclosed part of the inner sources of Johnson's ambition.

The new congressman was chafing to get up and rush off to Washington, but he was forced to stay in the hospital for two weeks after his operation. During that time he managed to do a small amount of work, mostly answering letters and telegrams from both his friends and his former opponents.

Anybody who ever wrote to Johnson got an answer. He was particularly industrious in replying to his opponents, whose goodwill and backing he might need in the future. Johnson found it hard to tolerate political enemies and perpetually hoped there was some way to win them over. His pride never intruded if he thought he had a chance to make friends with an opponent. Disarming his rivals was both personal and practical. He desperately wanted to be liked by as many people as possible. But he also wanted to ensure that he would win the next election down the road—in this case, the regular primary eighteen months away, when he would have to win 51 percent of the vote.

In a typical move, he wrote Avery that neither of them had won or lost. It had been a victory for President Roosevelt. Johnson repeated these sentiments in one form or another to all of his Roosevelt-supporting rivals. To disarm the antagonistic Mayor Tom Miller of Austin, who was planning to visit Washington, he asked his brother Sam, now Congressman Kleberg's secretary, to escort him around town. With his

friends and supporters, Johnson was even more fulsome. He told undeclared Johnson supporter Texas governor James Allred, who had worked
with him on the state NYA: "Jimmy, I couldn't have made it without
you."[26]

Johnson's campaign impressed Roosevelt. By this time the Supreme
Court had reversed itself and upheld several New Deal programs, including the watershed Wagner Labor Relations Act. Moreover, Justice
Willis Van Devanter, an elderly conservative, had decided to retire, freeing a place for a liberal justice. Roosevelt might have dropped his Court
campaign at this point and got on with the rest of the New Deal, but
foolishly he resolved to seek revenge by campaigning against his Court-
packing opponents in the upcoming Democratic primaries.

In the middle of this battle FDR went off on the presidential yacht
for a fishing vacation in the Gulf of Mexico. While cruising through the
tropical waters he learned about Lyndon Johnson's victory and told Governor Allred to bring the newly elected Congressman to meet him when
he docked in Galveston at the end of his holiday.

Though fully recovered from his operation, LBJ was still gaunt and
tired. Naturally skinny, he had lost several pounds while sick and had not
yet gained them back. But he could not pass up a meeting with the president, and he rushed out to purchase a new black suit. It hung on him
like a scarecrow. On May 11 he and Governor Allred met FDR when he
stepped ashore in a blaze of flashbulbs.

Johnson had, of course, met the president before, but was not a close
friend. Now he greeted FDR as if he had known him all his life, asking
questions about his wife and family, about his vacation, and chatting
with him about his luck in fishing for tarpon. Amused by Johnson's
cheekiness, FDR asked Lyndon to join him at the dockside ceremonies
and afterward rode with him in his car to the railroad station. By the
time they arrived at the train depot, he and FDR were "old friends."

The brief encounter would affect Johnson's congressional career.
Knowing that both Franklin and his kinsman Teddy Roosevelt had served
as assistant secretary of the navy, the congressman-elect casually mentioned to the president his own fascination with naval power and his support for a big navy. He had been inspired by the Roosevelts' example, he
added. LBJ got more than he bargained for. Johnson wanted to serve on
the House Agriculture Committee and told the president. FDR responded that he thought the Naval Affairs Committee, the precursor of
the House Armed Services Committee, was a better opportunity for a
young man, and that he could always use someone to help him out with
naval matters in Congress. "He told me what committee I should go on,"

Johnson reminisced. "Hitler was going to take over the world. [Vice President] Garner was against some cruisers. He [Roosevelt] wanted somebody from Texas that would vote for a strong Navy."[27] If he needed any help, the president said, he should call "Tommy," and gave him Corcoran's home telephone number.[28]

Lyndon flew to Washington on May 12 to be sworn in and take up his new duties. His parents saw him off, but his father, healthy six years earlier when Lyndon first left Texas as Kleberg's secretary, was now dangerously ill. As Lyndon bent over to kiss his father, Sam Jr. told him the following:

> Measure each vote you cast by this standard: Is this vote in the benefit of people? What does this do for human beings? How have I helped the lame and the halt and the ignorant and the diseased? See if this vote is generally for humanity. . . .

And as a final piece of advice: "Now you get up there, support FDR all the way, never shimmy and give 'em hell."[29]

Lyndon valued his father's counsel; it had helped his career on more than one occasion. But Sam Ealy Johnson Jr. would not live long enough to give his son much more advice. LBJ would have to rely on his other political "daddies." Now he had caught the eye of another daddy — this time the most important one in the country. Tommy Corcoran himself was amazed with how fast Lyndon had made an ally of FDR. "That was all it took—one train ride," Corcoran declared.[30] Johnson would gain access through Roosevelt's favor to the president's inner circle — other older men, other paternal figures who would also help him climb.

But his real father was fading quickly. In July, Sam had another massive heart attack and was taken to the Scott and White Clinic in Temple, Texas, where he was placed in an oxygen tent. Doctors informed the family that he would never recover. When his son came to visit him during the congressional recess in September, Sam wanted to sign out against medical advice. Lyndon tried to argue him into staying at the clinic, which was better equipped to deal with his needs than the local doctor. But Sam insisted that his son take him home. "I want to be in the part of the world I love best, where people know when you are sick, care when you die, and love you when you live."[31]

Sam preferred Johnson City, but Lyndon brought him back to his own house on Happy Hollow Lane in Austin. He got his father a radio so the patient could keep up with the news. Together they listened to Roosevelt endorse the need for a national minimum wage, calling for a special session of Congress to consider it in November. Sam's last wish was to be well enough to sit in the gallery and watch his son perform as a member of Congress. It was not to be. On October 23 he died in Austin.

The funeral was held the next day. Sam was taken to the small Johnson family burial grounds on the banks of the Pedernales, across the road from the house where he had first brought Rebekah as a bride and where his son was born in 1908. This spot was on the only property left from the original Johnson Ranch, which Sam had clung to so tenaciously. Governor Allred, riding behind the hearse, was amazed at the number of people who came to the ceremony.

Rebekah stayed in Johnson City for only a short time after the funeral. She soon moved to a small house in Austin, which Lyndon helped her buy. Sam left virtually no estate to his family. In fact, Lyndon had to pay off his father's debts. But he did transmit a complex legacy to his son that was even more important than property: a lifelong sympathy for the underdog, and the political skill to turn his yearnings into political reality.

He would now try to put his heritage to good use on a national stage.

CHAPTER 5

New Deal Congressman

O N MAY 13, 1937, the twenty-eight-year-old Lyndon Johnson was sworn in as a member of Congress by Speaker of the House William B. Bankhead. As the press photographers snapped away, the venerable Bankhead, his hand on Johnson's shoulder, informed reporters that the new representative was the youngest member of Congress. LBJ would serve as representative from the Tenth District for six successive terms.

As usual, LBJ wasted no time in getting started. Appointed to the Naval Affairs Committee through FDR's influence, he perceived his task as twofold: unswerving dedication to the voters of his district, and advancement of his own political career. Closely connected with the second was conciliating the enemies he had made during the campaign, a process he had already begun. To Polk Shelton, whom Johnson had smeared as a shyster who defended criminals and racketeers, he now wrote: "I hope you will always feel that my efforts are at your disposal. Whatever service I may be able to render will be cheerfully and gladly done."[1] A less ambitious man might have been embarrassed to write so fulsomely to a man who had been his bitter enemy the previous week. But LBJ was already looking ahead to the regular election and intended to do whatever was necessary to build support.

As soon as his newly hired aides, Sherman Birdwell, a classmate at San Marcos, and Carroll Keach, a campaign staffer, arrived in Washington, he was ready to go to work. Although it was Saturday afternoon and his aides had just made the long drive from Texas, the three men went straight to Johnson's temporary office, room 118 in the Old House Office Building, to begin answering Tenth District mail.

Responding to constituents would be an arduous task, for Johnson had decreed that all letters be answered immediately, whether they came from rich or poor, and no matter what their substance. Signed replies to correspondents, he believed, was the best way to give the voters the feeling "they had a close personal relationship, a close personal rapport with their Congressman."[2] As he anticipated, this response would translate into votes in the coming campaigns.

LBJ almost literally worked his fingers to the bone, developing a rash on his hand that cracked the skin and caused bleeding. When signing the mail, he had to wrap a small towel around his right hand so the letters would not be bloodstained. Gene Latimer, working with the Federal Housing Administration during the day, came in evenings and weekends to help out. Johnson soon persuaded him to work full-time. A year later he had a breakdown and resigned, but he would join the congressman's staff again during the war and remain with him with interruptions for more than three decades. Birdwell, too, could not take the strain and was sent back to Texas to work for the NYA. John Koeniger, the friend who had shared his ambition to be a lawyer in California, joined the office in 1938. Other friends pitched in, many leaving when the frantic pace became too much for them. Herbert Henderson, an NYA researcher and writer, wrote Johnson's speeches. When brother Sam was fired by Kleberg, Johnson hired him to become his office greeter. In 1939 Johnson brought in John B. Connally, the model-handsome former student-body president at the University of Texas, and Walter Jenkins, a UT senior. Except for his wartime service years, Jenkins would stay with Johnson into his presidency and become an indispensable coordinator and protector. Bill Moyers, a later aide, would say that Johnson owed more to Jenkins than to anyone else except Lady Bird. Most of the staff lived, as had LBJ, at the cut-rate Dodge Hotel.

Lady Bird was not spared from work. One of her jobs was to memorize the names of every precinct captain in the Tenth District. Another was to keep a scrapbook of Johnson's newspaper clippings. She also gave guided tours of Washington attractions, including the Capitol, the Smithsonian Institution, and Mount Vernon, to Tenth District visitors, and bought a movie camera to take pictures that Johnson could use in future campaigns. The congressman's dutiful wife toiled unceasingly in her husband's behalf. "Lyndon was always prodding me to . . . learn more, work harder," she said. "He always expects more of you than you think you are really mentally or physically capable of putting out. It is really very stimulating. It is also very tiring."[3]

The frantic pace paid off. No congressman got more for his constituents than Johnson. In a profile written for the *Dallas Times-Herald* in 1964, Leslie Carpenter, a Texas journalist and husband of Liz Carpenter, Lady Bird's press secretary, told of one man who had written to Johnson about a Veterans Administration claim that had been lying around for five years and who, after receiving four letters in a row from LBJ, finally received his money. "I never saw anything like it," said the veteran. "Why, I'd vote for that fellow for president."[4]

More impressive than such petty constituent service was his success in getting a disproportionate share of federal money for the Tenth District. Johnson funneled millions of dollars to Hill Country cotton farmers to make up for collapsing prices and for farm-to-market roads to enable them to move their crops. Austin got money from the Works Progress Administration (WPA), a New Deal agency, for an addition to City Hall, for a new wing on the municipal hospital, for new streetlights, and for a new building for the airport. During his first years in Congress, Smithville High School got a grandstand for its football field, Elgin received a new Federal Building, Johnson City got a new school, and the college at San Marcos added new classroom buildings. In 1938 Johnson procured 135 paved farm-to-market roads for Travis County. His biggest coup, however, was inducing federal officials to award the first New Deal public housing project to the city of Austin.

The feat required Johnson's relentless enterprise. On a visit to the state capital soon after the election, the new congressman got his first glimpse of urban slums and was horrified. Fortunately there was a remedy at hand, the new U.S. Housing Authority (USHA), with $500 million to lend to builders of low-cost housing. Johnson wasted no time in grabbing some of the new housing subsidy money for his constituents, including blacks and Mexican Americans, though these, bowing to the mores of the day, were segregated. In December he went before the Austin City Council to plead with its members to apply for USHA aid. With the consent of the council and the help of Alvin Wirtz, Johnson set up the Austin Housing Authority, which applied to the USHA for $714,000 to tear down substandard houses in Austin's slums and replace them with garden apartments.

The campaign paid off. Austin, New York, and New Orleans were the first three cities to receive federal housing aid. Public funds helped build Chalmer's Courts for whites, Santa Rita Courts for Latinos, and Rosewood Courts for blacks. Austin was much smaller than the other two cities, and its choice was testimony to the man who represented it in Congress. "There was this first-term congressman," explained economist Leon Keyserling, then deputy administrator of the USHA, "who was so on his toes and so active and so overwhelming that he was up and down our corridors all the time. . . . It was his go-getterness that got the first project for Austin."[5] "He got more projects and more money for his district than anyone else," concluded Tommy Corcoran. "He was the best Congressman for a district that *ever was*."[6]

Johnson did not ignore the local business community in his quest for support. His rescue of the Marshall Ford Dam during his first year in office would delight the district's business interests and put him into contact with powerful men who would guide and nurture his career almost to the presidency itself.

The dam was part of the Lower Colorado River Authority (LCRA), a state project designed to control flooding and provide electric power for a strip of Texas running northwest to southeast through the Austin region. Alvin Wirtz and Congressman Buchanan had secured federal support, and the Bureau of Reclamation (BOR) had started the dam in 1936 at a projected cost of $10 million. The contract for the dam had been awarded to the small, ambitious central Texas construction company of Brown and Root, headed by Herman and George Brown, friends of Wirtz. At the time of Johnson's election the dam was only half completed, and in danger of staying that way for lack of an essential authorization by Congress. The order to proceed with the project had come informally from FDR himself as a birthday favor to Congressman Buchanan, and the comptroller general's office had noticed the irregularity. Buchanan, however, had convinced the bureaucrats to advance the first half of the monies, $5 million, while awaiting the expected congressional authorization the following year and the remaining $5 million. Meanwhile, Brown and Root had begun the project on spec, laying out large sums on equipment. Matters soon got worse. Construction was well under way when the BOR discovered that the dam was on state-owned, not federal land, and that it could not legally continue the project. The land might have been deeded by Texas to the federal government, but as part of the Lower Colorado River Authority this was forbidden.

Construction could proceed only if Congress passed a special bill authorizing both the project and the BOR's existing construction contracts with Brown and Root and appropriated the promised additional $5 million in funds. At the beginning of 1937 the extra funding did not seem in doubt, since Buchanan was chairman of the House Appropriations Committee. But by the spring Buchanan was dead, Herman

Brown had already invested $1.5 million in early construction costs and was running out of money, and young Congressman Johnson had no clout with the Appropriations Committee. To get the mess cleared up, he would have to call in the chips he had with Corcoran and Roosevelt. If the contract was not confirmed, Brown and Root might well go bankrupt.

Meanwhile, the House Rivers and Harbors Committee, headed by Joseph Mansfield of Texas, was scheduled to report on the dam at the end of May, fewer than two weeks after Johnson arrived in Washington. Mansfield's committee report was favorable, authorizing the project and validating the existing contracts with Brown and Root. But before Congress approved the measure, rumors began to circulate that cast further doubt on the dam's legality. It looked as if Congress might order an investigation of the project and leave the Browns holding the very expensive bag. Johnson had Roosevelt's promise from his Texas visit that if he needed anything he should call Corcoran, and that is what he did. Corcoran went to Roosevelt, who said, "Give the kid the dam."[7] The bill might have gotten through Congress anyway, but FDR's support made its passage a certainty.

What remained was the matter of the second $5 million appropriation, which was itself running into difficulty. The money was supposed to come from federal relief funds administered by WPA director Harry Hopkins. Hopkins, however, felt that the project violated the terms of relief appropriations and threatened to stop the disbursement. Johnson again went to Corcoran and William Douglas of the Securities and Exchange Commission, who pulled various strings and contacted the President's son James Roosevelt, who made a number of telephone calls. On July 22, 1937, Johnson, Wirtz, and the directors of the LCRA went to the White House, where Johnson was handed a check for $5 million by Jimmy Roosevelt, who said his father was "happy to do this for your Congressman."[8] The headline in the *Austin American* declared, "Johnson Awarded Five Million to Finish Colorado Work."[9] The project, renamed the Mansfield Dam, would now finally be completed.

The dam affair solidified Johnson's reputation in the business community. Wirtz, for one, felt that Johnson had vindicated his election support. The Browns, of course, were also pleased and soon came to expect further help to secure changes in the contract and new appropriations. Johnson at first was reluctant to do additional favors for the Brown brothers, but soon concluded that helping Brown and Root was also helping to create jobs for the people of Texas.

His work for the Browns would ripen into a personal friendship, though it never led to agreement on political philosophy. Johnson particularly differed with Herman Brown, a "rugged individualist," who hated government regulations, despised paying taxes, worried that the New Deal would lead to socialism, and was suspicious of modern social trends. What Herman Brown and Johnson had in common was an appreciation of the practical. They were both pragmatists. "Basically, Lyndon was more . . . practical than people understand," George Brown explained. "You get right down to the nut-cutting, he was practical. He was for the Niggers, he was for labor, he was for the little boys, but by God . . . he was as practical as anyone."[10]

The Browns became Johnson's financial patrons. Herman Brown had not contributed to Johnson's first election campaign in 1937, but he assured the young politician that he would not have to worry from then on about funding his campaigns. And not only would the Browns contribute to Johnson's campaign coffers, so would their lawyers, their bankers, their insurance brokers, and any other businessmen with whom they had influence. For his part, Johnson used whatever leverage he had in Washington to expedite Brown and Root projects.

Johnson had few scruples about accepting campaign contributions from any source, but he avoided taking money for his personal use. The temptation must have been strong. In the early years of his political career he had crushing financial obligations: supporting his widowed mother and siblings, repaying his father's debts, maintaining living quarters in both Austin and Washington, and paying the cost of transportation to and from his district. Though chronically short of funds, he never accepted personal financial help from his wealthy friends. Paul Conkin attributes this to "pride, a prudent awareness of political risk, and conventional moral standards."[11] Yet to say that he did not profit personally from his political position would be naive. In later years, when he became a wealthy man, it was primarily through the help of his rich friends. In 1939, for instance, Charles Marsh, publisher of the two Austin dailies, the *American* and the *Statesman*, offered to sell him a piece of real estate in Austin worth far more than the $12,000 he asked for. Lady Bird borrowed money from her father to clinch the deal, since Johnson's congressional salary of $10,000 a year could not be stretched to cover the price.

Yet Johnson was fastidious about which favors he accepted. In 1940 Marsh offered Johnson a partnership, worth at least $750,000, in an oil business with Sid Richardson, a major oil, gas, and pipelines promoter. Marsh told Johnson that he would not have to make any down payment and could finance it out of future earnings. Johnson turned it down after thinking about it for a week. It would destroy him in politics, he concluded, if the public knew he was involved in the oil business.

Viewed in broad perspective, it must be said that many of Johnson's initiatives were two-sided, benefiting his district's business interests and its ordinary voters simultaneously. One such project was Johnson's effort to bring electricity to rural areas of the Tenth.

LBJ had already helped to secure the completion of four Texas dams that produced hydroelectric power. But the only beneficiaries were towns-people. Privately owned Texas Power and Light refused to serve thinly occupied locations, claiming that costs of constructing power lines were much too high relative to prospective customers and financial returns.

The consequences for many rural people were deplorable. Most Texas farm families did without the labor-saving refrigerators, washing machines, electric irons, and toasters that city folk already took for granted. Johnson never forgot his mother's struggle to get through the day's laundry chores without electricity. Without power, moreover, farmers could not use electric milking machines, electric pumps, electric grinders for feed, or electric shearing machines. Hill Country farm families had little diversion when the daylight ended and their chores were through. Smoky, dim, dangerous kerosene lamps made reading difficult. Rural folk were also generally without radios (battery-operated portable radios did not appear until the 1950s), though even the poorest people in the cities now had radios in their homes.

In May 1935 Roosevelt signed an executive order creating the Rural Electrification Administration (REA) to bring electricity to rural areas not served by private utilities. The REA would lend, at low interest rates, the money needed to build electric lines in rural areas, with priority given to farmers' electrical cooperatives and publicly owned electrical utilities. The REA expected to be paid back, however, and insisted that areas served meet a minimum population density requirement of three subscribers for each mile of power line.

The population rules dismayed members of the newly established Pedernales Electrical Cooperative (PEC); the Tenth District was not a densely populated region. But Johnson was determined to bring electricity to the rural Hill Country. First he recruited as many people as cooperative members as he could. Many farmers, remembering their exploitation in the previous century by the railroads, were suspicious of the new scheme. Some were barely aware of the new appliances that could make their lives easier. Johnson traveled through the district extolling the miracle of electricity, describing to even the most skeptical farm families the benefits of the new labor-saving devices, both at home and in the field, and assuring them that joining the cooperative would prevent their victimization by a "power trust" in the future. Through his persuasive talents the PEC became the largest electrical cooperative in the country.

But Johnson still did not have enough coop members, and John Carmody, the new REA administrator, was adamant about applying the density rules. Johnson persisted. Armed with detailed figures on costs, consumer usage, and power requirements, and carrying a big picture of the Buchanan Dam, Johnson got Corcoran to get him an interview with the president. The selling job worked. Roosevelt called Carmody, asking him to explain the density requirements. When Carmody was done, FDR told him to approve the loan in spite of the rules. "I'll gamble on those folks," he told the REA head. "They'll catch up to that density problem because they breed pretty fast."[12]

In September 1937 the REA informed the PEC in Johnson City of their approval of a loan of more than $1 million. Johnson was present at the happy announcement and made it clear that the decision was more than just a political victory. "Within a few months," he said, "[women] can lay aside their corrugated washboards and let their red hot cookstoves cool off while they iron on a hot August afternoon. The farmer who has been dragging water out of a well with a bucket all his life can not only get himself an electric pump to do the work, but he will have power he can afford to buy to run it."[13]

When the lights finally went on, people all over the Hill Country were enormously grateful to Johnson. Farm couples named their newborns for the man who brought them electric power. Edgar Heimer, a Hill Country farmer, told friends he named his baby daughter "for Lyndon Johnson because he has put electricity in our homes and has done so much for us working people."[14] Yet the dirt farmers of the Tenth were not the only beneficiaries. When the PEC awarded the $800,000 for the transmission line, Brown and Root got the contract. In the wake of the REA success FDR proposed that Johnson head the agency nationally. He refused; he was more interested in staying in Congress.

Johnson worked in other ways to help his poorer constituents. During his first term, the administration pushed a new law setting a minimum wage of forty cents an hour. Businessmen were incensed. The proposed Fair Labor Standards Act undermined property rights, they insisted; they should have a right to pay their employees what they wanted. Johnson's fellow Texan Vice President Garner, who owned pecan groves in South Texas and was paying his Mexican workers only a dime an hour, fought the measure, as did most of the Texas congressional delegation. Bottled up in the House Labor Committee by the conservatives, the act looked dead on arrival. At this point Johnson joined Rayburn, Maverick, and other liberal and moderate congressmen to force it to the floor for a vote. Warned that the bill smacked of "socialism" and that his support might wreck his career, he voted "aye" nonetheless. Defeated in its first House vote, the Fair Labor Standards Act finally passed the House in June 1938.

Johnson's record on blacks in these first congressional years is ambiguous. The South had a history of demagogues who blatantly manipulated white racism to procure votes. Two of the worst, Theodore Bilbo and John Rankin of Mississippi, were powerful members of Congress when Johnson arrived. The new congressman had nothing but contempt for vote-seeking race-baiters, scornfully accusing them of "niggering it" or "talking Nigra"—southern expressions describing politicians who fed racial tensions for political advantage. Most Dixie politicians of the era "talked Nigra" at least at times in their careers. Johnson never did, and he would later bring a southern audience to its feet with cheers when he denounced the practices of some of his colleagues.

Still, he operated within the southern mores of the day. To many white politicians from Dixie, even "separate but equal," the begrudging standard for government treatment of blacks established by the Supreme Court in 1896, was a sham. They had no intention of giving blacks equal consideration in public benefits. Not so with Johnson. When he discovered that government agencies were making loans only to white farmers to purchase seed and equipment, he protested vigorously. Many black farmers, he told the federal agencies, were just as good risks as whites, and some of them were even better. After raising what he called "unshirted Hell," he got the bureaucrats to approve black farmers' applications. This act by a southern politician was unprecedented. "He was the first man in Congress from the South," declared Milo Perkins, assistant administrator of the Farm Security Administration, "ever to go to bat for the Negro farmer."[15]

Yet Johnson was unwilling to be a racial Don Quixote. As a member of the House, he tended to vote the way other Texans voted on civil rights, supporting the principle of states' rights, and voting against antipoll-tax and antilynching laws. He deplored the poll tax as a device to disfranchise blacks, but unlike Maury Maverick, the maverick liberal from San Antonio who believed in "crashing against the wall if necessary," he would not vote for a measure abolishing it in federal elections.[16] The votes, he said, simply were not there. Instead, he favored a constitutional amendment to strike it down, ostensibly because that would avoid the stigma of stretching the Constitution.* All the while, however, he

---

*Of course, this was the way, in 1964, that the poll tax was actually abolished.

declared that he was not biased and supported equal opportunities. It would not be until the mid-1950s, when attitudes all over the country had changed, that his timid record on blacks and civil rights would significantly alter.

Some of Johnson's early racial caution derived from Sam Rayburn. Johnson's affection for Rayburn was boundless. When Lyndon returned to Washington as a freshman representative, he walked into the Democratic leader's office and kissed him on his bald head as he sat at his desk.

Rayburn was always ready to give Johnson advice. He told his protégé to be silent on the House floor until he knew what was really going on around him. "Also remember," he cautioned, "don't get involved with broad issues, because you have to get reelected; and if you get into the big issues, the voters will think you aren't taking care of your district's problems."[17] And, of course, Johnson faced reelection to the regular full term almost immediately. In this case, Rayburn's advice was not needed. On November 8, 1938, Johnson was returned without any opposition for the full two-year term of the Seventy-sixth Congress.

In the early years Johnson generally went along with Rayburn, earning his mentor's praise. "Mr. Sam" was impressed with Johnson's talent and his ability to work hard. "I think Lyndon is one of the finest young men I have seen come to Congress," Rayburn wrote Alvin Wirtz in 1938. "If the District will exercise the good judgment to keep him here, he will grow in wisdom and influence as the years come and go."[18] Yet occasionally mentor and protégé had their differences. Johnson was "a damn independent boy; independent as a hog on ice," Rayburn once wrote.[19]

Most of the other House members were aware of Johnson's special relationship with Rayburn. When Garner was Speaker, during the Prohibition era, he established what he called his "Board of Education," where favored congressmen would come after work to discuss House business and "strike a blow for liberty" with a few drinks. Mr. Sam kept up the tradition when Garner went to the Senate. Most of the men who attended the Board of Education were congressional leaders, such as William Bankhead of Alabama, Adolph Sabath of Illinois, and John McCormack of Massachusetts. Lyndon Johnson was the only freshman congressman.

Johnson was careful to cultivate friendships with his elders until he was able to establish his own power base. This was the means he had used since his days at San Marcos to acquire and consolidate power, and it always worked for him. But who besides Rayburn could help him in his rise through Congress? The other likely candidate was Carl Vinson, chairman of the House Naval Affairs Committee.

Vinson, a physically unprepossessing lawyer from Milledgeville, Georgia, whose passion for the navy earned him the nickname "Admiral," had been in Congress twenty-five years before Johnson arrived. A tyrant who enjoyed chewing on ten-cent cigars, Vinson insisted on strict seniority. The newest members of the committee were called "Ensign," those who showed promise "Commander," and those who had finally made the grade, "Captain." The other new congressman assigned to Naval Affairs was Democrat Warren Magnuson from Washington, whose district included the Seattle Navy Yard. At the first committee hearing, Magnuson and Johnson asked administration witnesses many questions. When the meeting was over Vinson asked to see the young members in his office and told them that he thought they were nice young men. "I'm sure you have the interest of the navy at heart," he lectured them. "But we have a rule in the committee. We call it seniority. Each of you is entitled to ask only one question this whole year, and two next year."[20]

Magnuson and Johnson quickly learned that it was important not to provoke Vinson. He would remember people who displeased him years later and see to it that the naval installation they wanted for their district, or some other favor, never got approved. The two young congressmen amused Vinson by telling him gossip and dirty jokes and made themselves more available than the older members to travel around the country on special committee tasks. It is not known whether Vinson called Johnson "Ensign," "Commander," or "Captain" in these years, but his colleagues on the committee agree that Vinson liked the young Texan. "We could get around him easily after the first few years," recalled Magnuson, "Lyndon more easily than I because he used me as a straight man and he had the southern group."[21]

As a junior member of Naval Affairs, Johnson had little power and initially could get little navy patronage for his own district. As World War II loomed, however, the government decided it would be faster to negotiate defense contracts directly with designated firms than go through the lengthy process of competitive bids. This placed politics directly in the equation. Johnson sat in on the discussions of the Naval Affairs Committee on building a new air base to train naval recruits. He conveyed the information to Brown and Root, who received a very profitable contract to build the Corpus Christi Naval Air Station, a base that provided new jobs for almost nine thousand people.

To the end of his career in the House, Johnson remained a pothole congressman, occupied primarily with helping his district. In late 1941 he proposed a bill to combine the National Youth Administration and the Civilian Conservation Corps into one agency to train young men for factory war work. Two years later he sponsored a bill out of the Naval Affairs Committee that would have made mandatory the drafting of any war worker whose absentee record seemed excessive. These two minor bills aside, he avoided sponsorship of national legislation. Johnson was also reluctant to speak on the floor of Congress, perhaps recognizing that he lacked talent for formal public address.

Johnson was unquestionably a New Dealer in these years. He voted for virtually every bill that Roosevelt favored and was often one of the few representatives from the South who did. Joseph Rauh Jr., later a Johnson adversary, remembered him as "one of FDR's young, bright guys on the hill."[22] For a while, Johnson attended the weekly meetings of the "Mavericks," a group of liberal congressmen organized by his old friend Maury Maverick, to fight for progressive causes. But at the same time Johnson tried to avoid alienating conservatives. Actually, Maverick's own case spoke eloquently for caution; his fiery liberalism was his political downfall. When in 1938 he ran for reelection in San Antonio, the large ranchers and other conservative elements in his district ganged up to defeat him. Maverick's fate traumatized the younger man. When friends urged him to act more liberal, he would respond: "Just remember our old friend Maury Maverick, [who] isn't here anymore. Maury got too far ahead of his people and I'm not going to do that."[23] People on the right felt he was probably more sympathetic to them than he admitted, but so did his friends on the left. "I was never sure," wrote Helen Gahagan Douglas, his liberal congressional colleague from California, "whether some of Lyndon Johnson's votes were cast out of conviction or out of judging what Texas politics required. . . . He was willing to make the compromises necessary . . . to stay in Congress."[24]

For someone as impatient as Johnson, the seniority protocols of Congress were particularly galling. Everyone knew that Johnson aimed at higher office than representative, but to get there he would have to abide by the rules no matter how infuriating and time-consuming they seemed. Yet he was always on the lookout for ways to advance himself. Naval Affairs became a more important assignment as the United States was inexorably drawn into the World War II, but Johnson remained unhappy with Vinson's rigid application of the seniority rules. The one House committee where a junior member might make a mark was the all-powerful Appropriations Committee, which doled out money for government programs. Appropriations was divided into thirteen subcommittees, encompassing the entire sphere of government operations. The subcommittees were small, and a junior member would have a chance to shine.

In 1938 a vacancy opened up on Appropriations. And this was not just any vacancy, but the seat traditionally "given" to Texas. Johnson wanted it very badly, but Representative George Mahon also wanted it and had first choice. The decision would be made by the Texas delegates, who would listen to the counsel of Rayburn, their senior member. Everyone knew how much Rayburn liked Johnson, but Mahon recalled that he wasn't worried about the outcome. "Rayburn followed the rules," Mahon later recalled. "I was the senior Texan who wanted the spot. I was in line for it."[25] Mahon indeed got it, and Johnson had to wait a little longer.

While waiting his turn, Johnson cultivated other contacts through the active social life that he and Lady Bird took part in. Johnson was a gregarious man. Through his entire career he made friends wholesale and tried to maintain at least a superficial relationship with everyone who passed through his life. No matter how casual the relationship, he deployed his charm, along with flattery and attention, and often gave gifts. Everyone on his vast list got a Christmas card, and the number of autographed pictures he gave out during his life is impossible to calculate. Johnson conscientiously kept in touch with his Texas friends from the old NYA days as well as state Democratic Party functionaries and local newspapermen.

But the Johnsons were closer to a prestigious circle of politicians in Washington. These were people he met when he first arrived as a freshman congressmen, many of them introduced to him by Tommy Corcoran. Aside from Corcoran and his friend New Dealer Benjamin V. Cohen, the leading figures in this circle were Senator Hugo L. Black of Alabama, named to the U.S. Supreme Court in 1937; William O. Douglas of the Securities and Exchange Commission, named to the Court in 1939; and Harold L. Ickes, secretary of the interior. The younger men in the group included Montanan James H. Rowe, a member of FDR's staff; Tennessean Abe Fortas, a Yale Law School graduate and Douglas's assistant at the SEC; Arthur Goldschmidt, from San Antonio and nicknamed "Tex," who worked for Ickes at the Interior Department; and Eliot Janeway, a business writer for the Henry Luce publications *Time*, *Life*, and *Fortune*. Some of the others, mainly New Deal liberals from the South, included Hill Country native Welly Hopkins, chief counsel to the United Mine Workers (UMW); Tom C. Clark, from Dallas, special assistant in the Justice Department; and Alabamians Clifford and Virginia Durr, he a commissioner on the Federal Communications Commission, she a sister-in-law of Senator Black. When Alvin Wirtz became Under Secretary of the Interior through the intercession of Maury Maverick,

Wirtz, too, joined the circle. Many years later Virginia Durr told an interviewer that while Lyndon "wasn't cold-blooded in that he only cultivated people who could help him," he "was going after something. . . ."[26] Many of these bright people would remain LBJ's friends and associates for life.

The Johnsons were closest to the Goldschmidts, the Fortases, and the Rowes, neighbors living in small rented houses in Georgetown, a section of Washington that had been a black slum until New Dealers began to "gentrify" it in the thirties. Though they lived in another part of Washington, the Johnsons quickly became part of the crowd. In the manner of young married couples everywhere in these years, they cooked casual dinners for each other and entertained at backyard barbecues. Weekends were more formal, with parties at the Blacks' on the Potomac in Alexandria; at the Ickes's farm in Olney, Maryland; or at the Durrs' place on Seminary Hill in Virginia. At the time the Johnsons lived in a small one-bedroom apartment on Connecticut Avenue, but they repaid the invitations by holding Sunday afternoon cocktail parties.

At first the other group members liked Johnson primarily for his diligence on the job and his political skills. "He was close to Rayburn," explained Fortas, "and an ever widening coterie of friends on the Hill and he helped us. He ran errands for us. . . . He was very useful to us."[27] But Johnson was also entertaining, kidding around at their gatherings, telling tales of Texas, and sometimes even playing harmless but elaborate practical jokes. The Georgetown folk were soon complaining that their lives were colorless if he was gone for a few days. "There was never a dull moment around him," declared Fortas.[28] And the women were attracted to his southern charm and his casual affection. Virginia Durr remembered that he "put his arm around all the girls." "He was fun," said Elizabeth Rowe. "He could take a group of people and just lift them up."[29]

Women sometimes liked Johnson too much. Even in the 1930s it was assumed that male politicians "fooled around." They were surrounded by aides, many of them women. Female staffers sometimes fell in love with their bosses. Election campaigns, moreover, attracted female volunteers who contributed their services out of admiration for the candidate. They sometimes defined their services broadly. Lyndon Johnson was not a man to turn down the adoration of attractive women, and in the course of his political career he met hundreds who were infatuated with him or at least tried to convince him they were. Just as he boasted about his conquests at San Marcos State, so he bragged about his amorous triumphs in the more sophisticated and prestigious circles in which he now traveled. But given Johnson's talent for exaggeration and his flair for drama, it is hard to say how far these casual relationships actually went.

Yet behind the smoke there was certainly some fire. From his earliest years in Congress, Lyndon was known as a skirt-chaser. A friend from these days described his collection of women as a harem. Nancy Dickerson, a television journalist for NBC, herself rumored to have been one of Johnson's sexual partners, said she had been told "firsthand" about these affairs. Some of these stories she thought were "plausible, others simply not true."[30] One that was more than just plausible was a romance in the 1940s with a female colleague, California congresswoman Helen Gahagan Douglas, wife of actor Melvyn Douglas, and herself a former actress. A Texas friend of Lyndon's who worked in Washington at the time said that the relationship was an "open scandal." The congressman would "park his car in front of the house, night after night after night and then would get up in the morning and drive off at 6:30. . . ."[31]

One bit of evidence about Johnson's proclivities comes from his office aide Walter Jenkins, a man deeply loyal to Johnson. One day Jenkins was driving with Congressman Johnson around the Tenth District, and the congressman startled the self-confessed "innocent young lad." He said, Jenkins reported, "he didn't see anything wrong with people having sex outside of marriage. . . ." When his young aide asked his boss, "Wouldn't that bother you in your family?," Johnson answered, "Not really."[32]

One woman clearly stood out from the rest of his partners. Alice Glass was mistress and then wife of publisher Charles Marsh, who supported Johnson in his first campaign and who would continue to help his career. Marsh had become enthralled by politics and wanted to become a significant player. According to Walter Jenkins, he was "extremely erratic," a "crackpot,"[33] and Johnson did not think much of his political instincts. But he understood his usefulness as a patron and friend and flattered him by asking his advice about political strategy and other matters, although he rarely took it.

In 1931 Marsh was living in Austin and hobnobbing with the state legislators when he met Alice Glass, a tall, willowy twenty-year-old secretary to the representative from her hometown of Marlin, Texas. He became so smitten with the young woman that a few weeks later he left his wife and children and took Alice East with him. Alice had two children with Marsh, but she refused for years to make the relationship legal, claiming that she did not believe in marriage.

To please his mistress, Marsh purchased eight hundred acres in Culpepper, Virginia, in the foothills of the Blue Ridge Mountains, where he constructed a large house called Longlea. Alice furnished the mansion with antiques, Impressionist paintings, and costly French rugs.[†] She was fascinated not only by politicians but also by intellectuals and cultural celebrities, and she sought to establish a European-style salon in the Virginia hills. She also fancied herself a reformer and had a burning desire to help people in need, sending money, for instance, to help Jews fleeing Hitler and making Longlea a place of temporary refuge for them. One of her beneficiaries was Erich Leinsdorf, later conductor of the Boston Symphony Orchestra, whose status as a "permanent resident" of the United States Johnson facilitated at the request of Marsh and Alice. Johnson, in fact, was active in finding permanent visas for many Jewish refugees during these years of peril when few nations, including the United States, would lift a finger to save people fleeing Nazi anti-Semitism. Working with Jim Novy, an Austin Jewish businessman, in 1938 he helped bring some forty Jews to Texas from Nazi-threatened Austria and Poland. In 1940 he collaborated with Novy and Jesse Kellam, his successor as head of the Texas NYA, to get phony passports for Jews to Latin America, and then brought them to Texas to stay in NYA camps, though this was illegal.

Invited to Longlea shortly after their arrival in Washington, Lyndon and Lady Bird were both overwhelmed. They had never seen such an opulent lifestyle. Champagne, Alice's favorite drink, was served at breakfast and dinner; meals were prepared by a gourmet chef and served by a former Prussian cavalryman. Guests at Longlea could amuse themselves with fox hunting. There was a swimming pool built from native stone that the mistress of the house herself frequently used on hot afternoons. Neither of the Johnsons was worldly enough not to be taken in by it all.

Lyndon was bowled over by Alice Glass. He had never met a woman like this before. She was striking in appearance; knew much about the arts; had refined tastes in food and dress; and had acquired polish from world travel. One of the continuing tensions between Johnson and Lady Bird sprang from Lyndon's constant attempts to make her more glamorous and more cosmopolitan. Lady Bird switched to high heels for her husband's sake and wore the brighter colors that LBJ favored, but she would never be as fashionable, as stunning, as worldly-wise, as he liked.

[†]Alice's daughter took issue with LBJ biographer Robert Caro's description of Longlea. We have used her data rather than his. See Diana Marsh's letter to the editor of *Atlantic*, March 1983.

Lady Bird herself was aware of the difference between herself and her rival. She later recalled the elegant dresses Alice wore and remarked how dowdy her own seemed by comparison.

Alice was initially impressed by Johnson's efficiency in expediting Leinsdorf's legal residence. She admired Johnson's letter on Leinsdorf's behalf, which had noted that the United States "had a holy mission to provide a peaceful haven for musical geniuses . . . from persecution and racial bias."[34] Johnson also evoked Alice's admiration by his professed idealism. According to her sister, Mary Louise Glass Young, she believed that Johnson was "going to save the world." Alice acted as his tutor, giving him advice on what clothes to buy, which side of his face to be photographed on, and other matters of style. She tried to reform his table manners, but that was a lost cause. She read him poetry, particularly Edna St. Vincent Millay, and guests at Longlea observed the usually fidgety young man sitting quietly, listening to the words and the sound of her deep, melodious voice. Endlessly craving love and attention, Lyndon would have found her hard to resist even without all the glamorous trappings of Longlea.

There is good evidence that the relationship developed into physical intimacy. Normally given to boasting about his romantic escapades, Lyndon had nothing to say on the subject of Alice Glass. But after interviewing Alice's sister, cousin, and regulars at Longlea, Robert Caro concluded that the two of them did indeed have a full-blown, long-term love affair. Alice apparently confided in her sister and cousin, telling them that Lyndon was the love of her life. But they both admit that Johnson and Glass were so discreet that they would never have known if they had not been told. "I had seen them both many times at Longlea," said her cousin, "and I never knew."[35] That the relationship was special in some way is attested to by its duration. Even after he retired as president, Alice wrote letters to "dearest Lyndon."[36]

Marsh, it seems, discovered his mistress's infidelity through his aide John Connally. Lyndon had, in case of an emergency, entrusted Connally with the phone number of a New York trysting place where he and Alice had gone one weekend. Not privy to the affair, Connally had given it to Marsh when he innocently asked to contact Johnson. We do not know exactly what ensued when Marsh called the love nest in New York, but the following Monday, when Lyndon came to the office he chided Connally, "Man, you almost ruined me."[37]

It is hard to know what Lady Bird thought about her husband's liaisons, crushes, and extramarital affairs. She remained a dutiful wife, carrying out her domestic as well as political duties with efficiency, intelligence, and dignity, with no outward sign that anything was wrong. According to Dickerson, Lady Bird knew that "LBJ's love for her superseded any sexual desire or even sexual relationship. In her realm she had no peers; she knew it, he knew it and so did everybody else."[38] In any case, he always came back to her. Expediency undoubtedly played a role here; until Ronald Reagan, no divorced man had ever became president. But even if Lyndon had had lesser political ambitions, he had been too strongly influenced by his mother's religious ideas about morals and marriage to be able to take such a radical step as getting a divorce. And Lyndon needed the special qualities that Lady Bird possessed—stability and permanence. For this restless, driven man, she represented the refuge he had not had since he was the adored only child at his mother's knee. In his own fashion, he sincerely loved her. But he also exploited her. She had to be prepared to entertain guests on five minutes' notice. He "worked her to death," in the hyperbole of Virginia Durr.[39]

Meanwhile, in the period of his deepest attachment to Alice Glass, Johnson was unhappy about a lot of other things. Lady Bird detested the need to move from a Washington apartment during the session to the rented house in Austin, kept to maintain political connections with his home district. The toing-and-froing was made all the more onerous by the need to cram their car with all their household possessions each time Congress recessed or convened. Lady Bird wished she had duplicate sets of pots and pans and linens in each place so she would not have to haul them back and forth. "I feel like a weary octopus," she complained to a friend."[40] Finally, this usually patient woman could bear it no longer. Breaking in on a meeting Johnson was having with Connally, she informed her husband that she had found the perfect Washington house to buy. Barely acknowledging his wife, Johnson immediately went back to the conversation with his aide. In a rare display of temper, Lady Bird screamed at Lyndon: "I want that house! Every woman wants a home of her own, and all I have to look forward to is the next election!" Then she stormed out of the room. Johnson was puzzled at this outburst; he had never seen his wife like this. What did Connally think he should do? Connally advised him to buy the house.[41]

As the election of 1940 neared, Johnson realized he would have no difficulty being reelected. His Tenth District constituents felt comfortable with him in Washington looking out for them. Before the New Deal wound down, he had managed to obtain seventy million dollars in federal projects for his district. The Naval Affairs Committee and the day-to-day chores of a congressman no longer satisfied him, however, and triggered a bout of depression. He wanted to move on and move up, but could not see how it could be accomplished. Then, unexpectedly, things began to look up.

In 1940, Vice President Garner, assuming that Roosevelt would not run for a third term, announced that he would like the job. Garner and FDR had been constantly at odds since the election of 1936. A patrician of inherited wealth, FDR was a liberal New Yorker; Garner, a self-made man, was a conservative southern "Bourbon." Early in his political career "Cactus Jack" had seemed a populist with compassion for the underdog. By the time he became vice president, however, his banks, ranches, and orchards were worth millions, and he had become a champion of big business. Garner complained about the huge New Deal expenditures and resulting federal budget deficits. He also denounced Roosevelt's Court-packing plan as unconstitutional. Things became so heated between the nation's two top officials that they saw each other only when strictly necessary and said unprintable things about each other in private.

By now many southern businessmen, though their breed had been Democrats since the Civil War, had defected from FDR. Rallying behind Garner, they had helped defeat various new Roosevelt proposals. In March 1939 *Time* publicized the split with a cover story on Garner that identified him as the man behind the "Undeclared War" with Roosevelt. New Dealers, the article noted, considered him a "symbol of sabotage" and "a prairie politician whose archaic notions, plus popular veneration for long public service . . . make him the leader of reaction against six years of enlightened reform."[42]

In July 1939 the powerful, hotheaded labor leader John L. Lewis aggravated the quarrel by publicly calling Garner a "labor-baiting, poker-playing, whiskey-drinking, evil old man." Garner's friends told him to ignore the insults, but the vice president was outraged. Catcus Jack demanded that the twenty-three members of the Texas congressional delegation meet and unanimously absolve him of the charges. Rayburn called the meeting. Knowing full well that rumors of hard drinking would undermine the vice president politically, FDR and his aides called on Johnson to quash the resolution when the delegation assembled. "*Everybody* called him," reported Tommy Corcoran. "There wasn't any doubt about what the Old Man [i.e., FDR] wanted."[43] Lyndon now found himself torn between his two most important political patrons— Rayburn and Roosevelt. He did not hesitate for long. Alone among the delegates, he refused to sign the statement declaring Garner neither a heavy drinker nor an enemy of labor, on the grounds that the allegations were true. Mr. Sam took Lyndon aside privately to talk to him, but he stood firm. As the story is recounted in several biographies, Rayburn said:

"Lyndon, I'm looking you right in the eye." And Lyndon countered: "And I'm looking you right back in the eye."[44] In the end the Texas delegation issued a watered-down resolution that did not disavow the part about liquor and labor, merely stating that Lewis's attack was "unwarranted and unjustified."

Johnson had embarrassed Rayburn in front of the entire Texas delegation. But Johnson managed to make political capital of the situation with his White House Daddy. His account of the debate in the Texas delegation and of his refusal to go along with his colleagues pleased the president, and he chuckled as he, in turn, told it to others. Roosevelt was now surer than ever that Lyndon Johnson was his man in Texas.

CHAPTER 6

Rehearsal for the Senate

NINETEEN FORTY WAS A FRIGHTENING YEAR for the democratic world. It opened with the ominously quiet "phony war" in Europe, but by spring Norway, Denmark, Belgium, France, Greece, Yugoslavia, and the Netherlands had joined defeated Poland under the Nazi boot, and Britain had been ejected from the Continent, its army barely escaping at Dunkirk. By the summer, badly weakened by the loss of men and equipment, Britain was reeling under massive pounding by Luftwaffe bombers seeking to soften it up for invasion. In East Asia, meanwhile, Germany and Italy's new Axis partner, Japan, now three years into its brutal Chinese venture, had begun to threaten Indochina and the East Indies, two European colonies made vulnerable by the German victories over France and the Netherlands.

How should the United States respond to these advances by the aggressors? A majority of Americans supported Roosevelt's "interventionist" policies of aid to Britain and the other Axis victims, and his preparedness programs to ready America for attack if it should come. But isolationism remained strong. Millions of citizens, especially in the heartland, were dubious of policies that could embroil the nation in a bloody and expensive foreign war. World War I had been enough. That experience, they said, had taught us the price and the futility of foreign intervention.

During the often bitter debate between the isolationist and the interventionist sides, Johnson was an interventionist. At first, fearful of offending his numerous German American constituents, he soft-pedaled

American intrusion in Europe's affairs. But he could not resist the blandishments of Alvin Wirtz, a dedicated interventionist, and more important, could not defy FDR, who had long ceased to believe it possible for America to ignore the foreign aggressors. By mid-1941 Johnson was firmly in the interventionist camp. For the rest of his life he would accept the credo that resisting "aggressors," lest they be encouraged, must be a first principle of American foreign policy.

From the beginning of his first term in Congress Johnson had voted for the preparedness measures favored by the administration. In his second term he voted against an amendment blocking the fortification of strategically located Guam, supported the final passage of a bill increasing the size of the navy, and helped defeat an amendment cutting appropriations for more combat aircraft and for army expansion. On June 30, 1940, he joined with other interventionists to revise the Neutrality Acts, which restricted the shipment of arms to the anti-Nazi nations. In the fall of 1940 he voted for the Burke-Wadsworth conscription bill, establishing a military draft for young men, the first conscription bill ever passed in peacetime.

Johnson supported enlarged military outlays for other reasons besides interventionist convictions. It was also good politics in his district, promising lucrative contracts for firms such as Brown and Root and jobs for constituents. One especially juicy plum was a contract for constructing the Corpus Christi Naval Air Station, on which Brown and Root had placed a bid. The president and his advisers moved mountains to get a generous contract for the Texas construction firm on the theory that it would protect Johnson against his Texas enemies and so strengthen the president in a vital state. Tommy Corcoran would later remember, "We all helped Brown and Root bid on the contract. . . . We advised them how to bid, what to offer, who to talk to and all the rest of it."[1] In the end the firm won an agreement for an initial federal outlay of more than twenty-four million dollars, one of the most generous at the time.

The major domestic political issue in 1940 was whether FDR would seek a third term as president. Roosevelt had convinced himself that the survival of the New Deal, besides the well-being of the nation during the international crisis, made continuity of leadership essential. Yet breaking the two-term precedent continued to bother him, and he decided that the only way to remove all doubts about Democrat preferences would be to extract a unanimous party draft. As the deadline for announcing his candidacy approached, the only man who stood in his way was Vice President Garner, who despised Roosevelt and the New Deal and who craved the nomination for himself. In December 1939, with Roosevelt still publicly undecided, Cactus Jack had formally announced his own intention to seek the Democratic presidential nomination.

Clearly FDR had to weaken Garner before the Chicago convention, and this required heading him off in his home state. "Garner has to be sent home permanently to . . . Uvalde," Roosevelt told some intimate advisers.[2] To strengthen his supporters in Texas, in January the president appointed Johnson's old mentor Alvin Wirtz as under secretary of the interior. Wirtz, FDR hoped, would help prevent the Texas Democrats at their convention, set for May 28, from committing the state delegation to Chicago to his rival.

Johnson was a Roosevelt loyalist, of course, but by now, with prosperity returning, the New Deal was losing its appeal to Texans, and he knew his support for FDR would exact a price. The contest between the nation's two highest elected officials was even more threatening to Sam Rayburn. Mr. Sam was torn between his loyalty to his fellow Texan and to his president and worried besides that if he picked the wrong man he would jeopardize his chances to become Speaker of the House. Rayburn soon came up with a compromise proposal: The Texas delegation would go to Chicago with one third voting for Roosevelt, one third for Garner, and the last third pledged to vote for Garner only on the first ballot. Rayburn's scheme competed with a "Harmony Resolution" concocted by Wirtz, Johnson, and Mayor Tom Miller of Austin, condemning the stop Roosevelt movement and pledging Texas Democrats to reject the Rayburn proposal totally. In the Democratic precinct conventions only a minority of the delegates approved the Harmony Resolution.

Roosevelt was upset at the possibility that he might be embarrassed at the Texas state convention. Not wishing to advertise his disagreements with his vice president, however, he rejected suggestions that he use his charm on oilman Myron Blalock, head of the Texas Democratic Party, to get him to approve the Harmony Resolution. He did agree to send a conciliatory telegram, to be signed by Sam Rayburn, to Blalock and Wirtz accepting Garner as a first-round favorite-son candidate. In exchange, the Garner supporters would "insist that state convention approve and acclaim [the] administration record and will refuse to be a party to any stop Roosevelt movement."[3]

Believing Johnson a greater political force in Texas than he actually was, FDR suggested that Johnson sign the telegram as well. Rayburn, though favoring the contents of the telegram, was angry at having to share equal billing with a very junior congressman, even one he regarded as his protégé, and rejected this proposal. Johnson and Wirtz continued to push for the joint meeting, and Mr. Sam reconsidered. He did not want to hurt Garner in Texas, but neither did he want to incur FDR's permanent hostility. On April 29, a beaming Johnson and a frowning Rayburn went to the White House to formally present the telegram to the president and release copies of it to the media. Johnson had now chosen between two of his mentors, and his choice had been the one with more power. But it was not just power in the abstract. Though he had been a congressman for a relatively short time, he already had far-reaching designs. Sticking with Rayburn meant at best taking the slow path through the House, one that depended on strict seniority. Roosevelt's political clout would be more useful on the national stage and running for the Senate.

The Texas Democratic state convention met on May 28, and after a three-hour riot that resulted in blood, broken furniture, and torn clothing, voted to accept the compromise. The delegates named Garner the favorite-son candidate, repudiated a "stop Roosevelt" strategy, and named Wirtz to the national convention's platform committee, with Rayburn as head and Johnson as vice chairman of the Texas delegation.

Rayburn's resistance to Johnson's maneuvering caused FDR to distrust Mr. Sam's loyalty and turn to LBJ, instead, as the "acknowledged New Deal spokesman in the Lone Star State."[4] Rayburn in turn remained cool toward Lyndon for a time, but his paternal feelings for the young congressman and his wife soon revived, and the breach was at least superficially healed. Lyndon, for his part, tried to repair the friendship by supporting Rayburn for the vice presidential nomination after FDR had been chosen on the first ballot at Chicago in July. With the energy of his first White Star election, Johnson beat the bushes for Texas delegates for Rayburn, unfortunately finding one dead in his hotel bed, and others almost as indisposed from too much alcohol. Rayburn got eighty-eight out of ninety-five votes in the Texas caucus, but it was too late. By that time FDR had decided he wanted Secretary of Agriculture Henry A. Wallace as his running mate and had asked the reluctant but dependable Rayburn to second the nomination. But Mr. Sam soon got a better reward. On September 15, Speaker of the House William Bankhead suddenly died, and Rayburn, who had coveted the Speaker's post for years, succeeded him by unanimous vote, with FDR's support.

Roosevelt had reason to be apprehensive about the outcome of the election itself. Not only was there the controversial third term, but also New Deal policies were under increasing attack from both right and left. The GOP opposition, moreover, promised to be formidable. The public was charmed by Republican nominee Wendell Willkie, a boyish, Lincolnesque liberal with an unruly lock of hair over his forehead. Some early polls showed Roosevelt only three and a half points ahead of his challenger.

And FDR was concerned about more than his own political fate; he feared the Republicans would win control of the House, though that required a fifty-seat gain. Unfortunately, many of the Democratic candidates were hard pressed for campaign funds, a plight that quiet, gentlemanly Patrick Henry Drewry, chairman of the Democratic Congressional Campaign Committee, seemed unable to relieve. Something would have to be done.

Rayburn would have been the logical choice as party fund-raiser. His position in Congress gave him enormous potential for soliciting campaign contributions on a national level. In addition, the newly rich Texas oil millionaires, who needed Congress's support to retain the existing oil depletion allowance, represented a large pool of money waiting to be tapped, and most of them were on good terms with Rayburn. Unfortunately, Mr. Sam was not good at political begging.

Enter Lyndon Johnson. Amazingly, during the whole Garner-Roosevelt fight in Texas, Johnson was able to stay on good terms with the vice president and his friends. Johnson's knack for convincing people that he was on their side was one of his greatest talents as a politician. It eased the way in many a political deal and often got Johnson out of a tight spot.

At this point Johnson told Pat Drewry that he would be glad to help raise money and would like to be secretary of the Democratic National Committee. On October 1 Drewry sent a letter to Roosevelt expressing his approval of Johnson's offer. "I believe," he wrote, "that Mr. Johnson can do some very good work in this position. . . ." LBJ had written to Roosevelt himself, telling him he had seen Drewry and that "certainly the job is there to be done." He apologized for his "youth and inexperience" but assured the president that he could ask him "for anything at any time."[5]

By now Rayburn was on the verge of panic. Republican campaign coffers were overflowing, and what little money the Democrats had raised would have to be used for the presidential race. The situation in Illinois, Indiana, and Missouri seemed particularly bad, with the Democrats in danger of losing twenty House seats in those three states alone. Rayburn and House Democratic leader John W. McCormack went to Roosevelt to see what they could do about rescuing the campaign. The congressmen recommended that Johnson be put in charge immediately, official position as secretary or no. "Sold," replied FDR. "That was my idea, too. That boy has got what's needed."[6]

Lyndon went to work using all his awesome energy. It was now October 14, and the election was only three weeks off. With his usual exuberance, Johnson procured an office on E Street in downtown Washington, stocked it with furniture, rustled up a staff from his congressional office, and installed the most important equipment of all: six telephones. He dispatched to each of his Democratic congressional colleagues a questionnaire asking how many votes they had received in 1938 and whether their present opponent was stronger than their previous one. What "type of campaign" was the candidate's opponent conducting and what was the "principal issue he is raising?" he asked.[7] What help did the congressmen most need? Unsurprisingly, most mentioned their shortage of funds first. A reply from Representative John F. Hunter of Ohio's Ninth Congressional District was most succinct. The number one need was financial assistance. "There is no two," he stated.[8] With the mailing sent, Johnson phoned Democrats around the country to determine political conditions in their region. He then drew up lists of the most threatened Democratic congressmen. Seventy-seven of these seemed to have the best chance of winning if they received substantial campaign contributions.

While Johnson was collecting information, he was also collecting money, raising more than forty-five thousand dollars the first week. Marsh and the Brown brothers were glad to help. Enlisting the services of Rayburn, Johnson tapped every source he had in Texas, including many oilmen and businessmen who disliked Roosevelt and would not contribute to his campaign but who cherished the oil depletion allowance. Besides reminding them of the Democrats' tender regard for oil depletion, Johnson pointed out that war seemed unavoidable, and war would bring expansion of the nation's defense program. With a Republican-controlled House, Texas industry and business might lose billions of dollars' worth of contracts. Although the maximum donation allowed per contributor by law was five thousand dollars, many that came in following this appeal were in cash to evade the rules. Much of the money came from Texas, but LBJ was also able to raise some from New York, particularly from Jewish groups, according to Jim Rowe.

Johnson offered moral support as well as money to the Democratic candidates. As one of his letters noted, "I want to see you *win*. In order to help you and others of our party out in the frontline trenches, I am devoting my entire time in an attempt to coordinate and expedite assistance to you from this end."[9] Listing his address and telephone number on all mail that left his office, he noted that he was available for advice at all hours. He also induced prominent New Deal leaders, cabinet members, and out-of-state speakers to campaign in districts where their voices would carry the most weight, providing them with data so they would seem well acquainted with the candidates. Under Johnson's speakers program, Florida senator Claude Pepper, a champion of the wages and hours bill, campaigned in Washington State, where labor was important; Representative Rudolph G. Tenerowicz delivered speeches in Polish where there were large numbers of Polish voters; Frank Serri journeyed to precincts where the voters were largely Italian; Arthur Mitchell, a black congressman from Chicago and well regarded as an orator, helped out where he was needed. Most impressive of all the campaigners was New York's mayor, Fiorello LaGuardia. LaGuardia could speak seven languages and was a human melting pot all by himself.

Not every congressman got what he wanted. Johnson practiced triage. Some whose elections were really doubtful got nothing, but others got even got more than they asked for. Most of the recipients were profoundly thankful. Representative Charles McLaughlin wrote Johnson from Nebraska: "I am glad you are where you are."[10] In his usual way, Johnson was merging party service with personal advantage. "He was really trying," said Jim Rowe, "to build a power base as a new congressman."[11] This was the Johnson approach: help others and you help yourself as well.

On November 5, election night, Roosevelt hooked up a private telephone line from his mother's house in Hyde Park to Johnson's office in Washington. The president and the congressman maintained constant communication through the evening until at last it was over. The results were worth the long wait. Roosevelt won thirty-eight states with twenty-seven million popular votes compared to ten states and twenty-two million for Willkie. Equally important to Johnson, the party did well in the House. Fearing a loss of fifty House seats, the Democrats in fact gained five.

Many credited Johnson with the congressional success. Journalist Robert Allen wrote to Rayburn two days after the election that Johnson's work "was one of the few really good jobs done in the campaign. . . . Lyndon performed miracles. . . ."[12] FDR himself wrote Johnson on November 25, thanking him for his superb job in the campaign. "I am still getting letters," wrote the president, "telling me of your fine cooperation in every way, and the results speak for themselves."[13]

In addition to Roosevelt's gratitude, Johnson had won friends in the House and now had the beginnings of his congressional power base. The Seventy-seventh Congress would contain about "thirty or forty people that figured they owed their seat in the House to Lyndon Johnson," declared his friend from NYA days Ray Roberts. "Whenever he called on them, he could count on this group being for whatever he wanted."[14]

Now that the elections were over, Johnson became restless again. It was hard to go back to the ordinary daily routine of Congress after the exhilarating crisis atmosphere of the campaign. But he was bothered by more than the dull routine. He still could not see how he would ever become a senator. The two men representing Texas in the upper chamber, Tom Connally and Morris Sheppard, were popular throughout the state and could count on being elected for "life" if they so chose. Sheppard, who went to the Senate in 1912, told his friends that he hoped to serve in Congress longer than any other man in history. He never got the chance. In April 1941, at age sixty-five, he suffered an intracranial hemorrhage and died. Johnson's aide Walter Jenkins was the first to hear the news and called his boss to tell him. Johnson immediately got on the phone. "I'm sure he started calling Alvin Wirtz and others," Jenkins recalled, "he must have decided immediately that he *wanted* to run, but it took a while to decide that he *would*. He was a very careful studier, deciding whether he had a chance or not."[15]

Sheppard's death was indeed Johnson's golden opportunity. The senator's term had only two more years to run, but the Democrat who won the special election to succeed him would have the inside track for the full term the following year. Another advantage was that a special election would not force LBJ to give up his House seat, as would a regular contest. Johnson already had a network of political supporters and could count on ample financial assistance from his wealthy friends.

But Johnson was aware of several drawbacks to running as well. He was well known in only two election districts: his own, the Tenth, and the Fourteenth, where he had served Kleberg as congressional secretary. He was a cipher in the others. Through his NYA work he had gotten to know many state and local officials, but his Texas contacts were not as good as he would have liked. Several of the many candidates for the Sheppard Senate seat, including Congressman Martin Dies, chairman of the House Committee on Un-American Activities, and Gerald Mann, Texas attorney general, were much better known by the public. Fortunately, most of the ultimately twenty-plus other candidates formed a roster of political grotesques—a surgeon who advertised a youth-preserving goat-gland tonic over his radio station in Del Rio; a producer of "Crazy Crystal Water," a laxative on the discredited list of the U.S. Pure Food and Drug Administration; an advocate of a *five*-ocean navy; a former bootlegger; a self-confessed kidnapper; and a Baptist minister who wanted a return to Prohibition. Still, when the weaker candidates dropped out Johnson would be left to contend with Dies and Mann.

There was one other possible serious candidate: popular, handsome, folksy Governor Wilbert Lee O'Daniel, known as "Pass the Biscuits, Pappy," after his flour company's advertising slogan. If O'Daniel had thrown his hat into the ring, the other two serious contenders might have stayed out. But at first the governor denied interest. Then Pappy appointed eighty-six-year-old Andrew Jackson Houston, last surviving son of Sam Houston, as interim Senator.* Obviously Houston was only a stopgap, and the move suggested strongly that O'Daniel might run himself for the remaining term.

Political observers thought Martin Dies would be the hardest candidate to beat. A defender of "Americanism" at a time when the war in Europe was generating patriotic anxiety, Dies had made his reputation as chairman of the House Un-American Activities Committee, investigating Communists and subversive activities. A determined competitor who despised the New Deal, he had the backing of many wealthy businessmen who appreciated his "patriotism." Roosevelt wanted to make sure Dies was defeated. The other leading candidate, liberal Gerald Mann of Sulphur Springs, was a hero to many in his home state. The thirty-four-year-old graduate of Southern Methodist University was a two-time all-conference quarterback who worked his way through Harvard Law School by serving as pastor of a Congregational church. After returning to Texas he practiced law and served in the state government until 1938, when he became state attorney general, a position he used to successfully and diligently prosecute antitrust violators, loan sharks, and usurious finance companies. Mann considered himself a New Dealer and might have had the blessing of the president if FDR had not personally preferred Johnson.

Just before announcing his candidacy, Johnson delivered a speech to a joint session of Texas's state legislature on San Jacinto Day, April 21. Instead of the ritual commemorative talk on Sam Houston, his address, probably written with White House assistance, was about preparedness. The country, he said, had to place preparation for war above all other matters, and there was very little time. "We don't know, in days, hours, weeks, and months, when this hurricane may come to us." It was a mistake to fight "among ourselves" because "we lose something that all the gold at Fort Knox, Kentucky, can't buy back." "With every second wasted, we rush one step nearer universal disaster." Johnson declared his support for the state's legitimate interest groups, but all must subordinate

---

*He served less than a month, dying of pancreatic cancer two days before the scheduled special election for senator.

their concerns to those of the nation at large. "The security of the whole country is above that of any single group—labor, capital, or farmer."[16]

After the speech, Johnson went to see O'Daniel to smoke out his plans. The governor assured him he had no intention of running; he was too much of a Texas country boy to survive in Washington. Johnson was pleased and returned immediately to Washington to speak to FDR, bringing with him a copy of the statement he had written on the plane declaring his intention to run for senator. FDR recommended that he read the announcement right away from the steps of the White House just before he held his own press conference. A few minutes later Johnson appeared before supporters outside the West Wing of the White House and told them he would make the run with the president's blessing. Sheppard had "fought the good fight for democracy" and he would do so, too, "under the banner of Roosevelt and unity." He pledged that his "long and consistent record of support of our President" would "be continued no matter what trials may face it."[17]

At the presidential press conference that followed, reporters asked FDR whether he was supporting Johnson for the Senate. Roosevelt responded in his usual sly way. "First," he said, "it is up to the people of Texas to elect the man they want as their Senator. Second, everybody knows that I cannot enter a primary election." But "Third, to be truthful," he declared, "all I can say is Lyndon Johnson is a very old, old friend of mine." At this, both he and the assembled journalists laughed.[18] The *Dallas Morning News*, which ran the story the next day, commented that "it is generally admitted that the administration has picked . . . [Johnson] for the one purpose of defeating" Dies.[19]

As a good-luck token, Johnson kicked off his campaign on May 3 in San Marcos, as he had when he ran for Buchanan's House seat. His theme, he told six thousand supporters, was "Roosevelt and Unity." The campaign banners and bumper stickers read "Franklin D. and Lyndon B." As the band from Austin High School, sent courtesy of Mayor Miller, accompanied LBJ, the candidate paraded to the college auditorium with the brim of his hat tilted up the way FDR wore his own. A huge, blown-up photograph, prominently displayed in the auditorium—and at all campaign stops thereafter—showed the young congressman shaking hands with his presidential mentor at the meeting in Galveston. The candidate's talk emphasized his agreement with the New Deal and with Roosevelt's interventionist and preparedness positions. In a line that got the most applause—and one he repeated as his showstopper throughout the campaign—he declared: "If the day ever comes when my vote must be cast to send your boy to the trenches, that day Lyndon Johnson will leave his Senate seat and go with him."[20]

Dies opened his campaign at Greenville with insinuations about a secret army of subversives "much larger than the United States army," obedient to either Stalin or Hitler, and financed with "ten million dollars a year." Mann, speaking at Sulphur Springs, promised unstinting aid to embattled Britain, higher pensions for the elderly, an "unbeatable" United States Army, and an extensive FBI probe of suspected Communists that would make the House Un-American Activities Committee effort look feeble. Both men said they supported Roosevelt, though Dies insisted that he was not a "yes-man," like Johnson.[21]

Johnson may have had the president's benediction, but at the start, that was all he had. Poll results on May 4, before O'Daniel had made his intentions clear, were very disheartening: O'Daniel, 32.8 percent; Mann, 28.2 percent; and Dies, 27.9. Johnson was last, with 9.3 percent.

When Johnson showed the figures to his House colleague Hale Boggs, the Louisianan expressed surprise that he was bothering to run at all. But Johnson hoped that the president's support would make the difference. And apparently so did FDR. In a May 17 column in the *Dallas News* Joseph Alsop and Robert Kintner noted that Roosevelt, "although overburdened with the huge war effort and facing the gravest decision in this country's history," maintained "a personal interest in the campaign of his protégé, Representative Lyndon B. Johnson. . . ."[22] The White House pushed every button to get Johnson nominated and elected. Aide Jim Rowe had orders to make sure the candidate was designated as the source of all federal spending in Texas. Roosevelt told Rowe, "Whatever Johnson wants in terms of projects to be announced, whatever the government can do, they will do it."[23] No federal projects were to be approved for Texas unless Lyndon Johnson was informed. To suggest that the representative from Texas and FDR were in constant communication, the White House also made available for newspaper publication letters and telegrams to Johnson. Nor did administration support end with the president. Alvin Wirtz resigned as under secretary of the interior to be Johnson's campaign manager, and other liberals in the capital promised to give Johnson whatever support he needed. With all the help from Washington, Johnson had good reason to be optimistic.

Then the blow fell. On May 19, a month after Johnson's San Jacinto Day speech, O'Daniel announced that he would run for the Senate. A peerless campaigner, the governor had begun his career as a salesman for the Light Crust Flour Company, becoming a radio personality by accident when the regular announcer was unavailable to read the company's advertisement on the air and O'Daniel stepped in. By 1938 his was the most popular daily radio show in Texas, a favorite of both men and women.

Until his run for governor he had been so indifferent to politics that he hadn't even bothered to pay his voter's poll tax. But he proved to be a consummate campaigner—in a Texas mode. The golden-voiced Pappy traveled with his hillbilly band and his whole family, including sons Micky-Wickey and Patty Boy, and daughter Molly. At campaign barbecues he served well-aged Texas beef and beans along with his biscuits. O'Daniel talked about the Golden Rule and the Ten Commandments, quoted from the Bible, and promised to apply religious principles to clean up politics. In 1938 he had defeated eleven other candidates combined without a runoff and was reelected two years later with an even bigger vote.

But in the end Pappy was not the formidable opponent everyone expected. He had promised not to campaign until the legislature adjourned and, through the good work of Wirtz and other Johnson partisans, the session was dragged out for weeks beyond its normal term. The governor could not leave Austin to tour the state and had to send his children as his stand-ins. For Pappy's rural and small-town followers this would not do. Not that O'Daniel did not score some political hits. At his announcement rally in Waco, he poked fun at Johnson's connection with the president. "You know," he told his audience, "that feller Lyndon Johnson is so friendly with the President they tell me he can just walk into the White House and fry his breakfast eggs on the White House stove."[24] But he also knew that many Texans revered Roosevelt and were grateful to Johnson for getting them federal jobs and programs. Instead of skewering the president, he attacked the men around him as a "gang of back-slapping, pie-eating, pussy-footing professional politicians who couldn't run a peanut stand."[25] When *he* got to Washington he would help FDR himself, although he would not be a "yes-man." O'Daniel also made radio talks from the governor's mansion that courageously pledged him to support "widows, orphans, low taxes, the Ten Commandments, and the Golden Rule."[26] Finally, on June 2, Pappy was released from captivity in Austin and started his dazzling road show. It was still not too late.

Johnson replied directly to O'Daniel's attacks on his White House connections. Yes, he was a "yes-man for everything that is American. I'm a yes-man for everything that will aid in the defense of the Republic. I am a yes-man to the Commander in Chief, as every good soldier should be in time of war and national emergency."[27] He asked his audiences whether they really thought that such men as Rayburn, Tom Connally, and Secretary of State Cordell Hull could not "manage a peanut stand." And he reminded his listeners of the recent federal projects, including lucrative WPA ventures, he had brought to Texas.

Many of Lyndon's speeches actually addressed the issues that a U.S. senator would be forced to deal with. Besides preparedness and national defense, he supported the expansion of the Social Security system with payments starting at age sixty, recommended federal maternal and child care, and championed full parity prices for farm products. He repeated his admonitions to labor and business that they cooperate in a time of emergency, and he advised working people not to strike when the nation faced war. And to make sure that people knew he was not just a political clone of FDR, he opposed federal control of oil production and defended the oil-depletion allowance.

But Lyndon was scared. He became so disheartened at the thought of losing that he suffered what aide Harold Young referred to as "nervous exhaustion."[28] Once more during a stressful campaign, he ended up in the hospital, this time with what was described as a throat infection and pneumonia. In fact, whatever the physical manifestations, this breakdown, like others, betrayed a psychological fragility that would last his whole life. Anxiety and pessimism were never far from his emotional surface. Even in the midst of triumph, he feared disaster. Mary Rather, who knew Lyndon when he was a skinny visitor to Alvin Wirtz's law office and went with him to the White House as secretary, insisted that he "never, *ever* thought he would win in every race he had."[29] One may consider this a learned response to the vicissitudes of his family's fortunes. But it may also have derived from a mood disorder inherent in his makeup, perhaps a mild version of a bipolar illness called cyclothymic disorder.[†]

Be that as it may, Johnson was convinced at this point that his hospitalization would further damage his campaign. But he was in luck. During his stay in the hospital Texas was drenched by heavy spring rains, and his competitors canceled many of their appearances until the weather improved. Meanwhile, John Connally and Alvin Wirtz substituted for Johnson on the speakers' circuit whenever they could. To keep his name in the limelight, the campaign committee plastered Johnson's name on highway billboards, a new technique at that time.

[†]Our suggestion here has been informed by conversations with Dr. Edith Jacobs of Buffalo, New York, a practicing clinical psychologist.

The makeshifts seemed to work. By the time Johnson was on his feet again, his standings in the polls had improved. Throughout the rest of the campaign, however, he looked terrible, rarely sleeping, barely eating, and totally convinced that he would lose. Lady Bird's homemade movies of the period reveal her husband as a haggard man, looking ten years older than when he first announced for the Senate.

As the campaign continued, Johnson and his advisers tried to beat O'Daniel with his own tactics, prompting *Time* to label the campaign the "biggest carnival in American politics."[30] They hired two bands, hillbilly and jazz, and featured two singers, a 275-pound woman billed as "the Kate Smith of the South" and who sang "Dixie" and "The Eyes of Texas Are Upon You," and a thinner, shapelier one who rendered "I Want to Be a Cowboy's Sweetheart" and other Texas favorites. After the singing the Johnson aides presented an American history pageant, crediting FDR with saving the country from total collapse but warning that now the United States faced ruin again in the person of Adolf Hitler. As disaster came closer, the players declaimed, FDR would need "a man who loves his country, who loves the people. . . . This man is Lyndon Johnson."[31] At this point Lyndon walked out on the platform with his white Stetson, brim rolled up, to give his speech.

Politics costs money, and this campaign proved more costly than most. Aside from the usual outlays for staff salaries and newspaper and radio ads, Johnson hired a private airplane for efficiency and convenience, an uncommon tactic in the early 1940s. And then to jazz up his rallies, he established a lottery to award defense stamps and bonds to lucky members of his audiences. Ostensibly the motive was patriotic, but few Depression-scarred Americans would pass up the chance to win money this easy way. And then on election day, of course, there was the time-honored Texas tradition of actually purchasing blocks of votes.

Estimates of Johnson's 1941 Senate campaign expenditures vary, from the under $30,000 listed on the official report to the Texas secretary of state, to the $250,000 estimated by *Life* magazine, to the $500,000 suggested by a friend of Wirtz. "Observers," declared the *New York Times*, "believe that more money was spent in Mr. Johnson's behalf than in any previous statewide campaign."[32] Whatever the actual figures, Johnson had no trouble getting the money to keep the campaign in high gear down to the wire. Most of it came from Brown and Root. Johnson admitted as much many years later to biographer Ronnie Dugger. The campaign, he acknowledged, was "Brown and Root funded."[33]

Even before Johnson's confession many people had become aware of Brown and Root's dubious role in supplying funds for the canvass. In

1942, almost a year after the campaign, the Internal Revenue Service began to audit the books of Brown and Root on unconnected matters. IRS agents were startled to discover enormous employee bonuses and attorneys' fees paid just before or during the campaign. These sums were probably channeled back to local Johnson campaign managers. Although the payments were in cash, making it difficult to check, the IRS obtained enough affidavits to prove that at least $150,000 of laundered funds found their way into Johnson's campaign coffers. Just as the IRS was on the brink of bringing criminal charges against Brown and Root, Johnson and Wirtz went to see Roosevelt. In the end, Brown and Root avoided indictment but had to pay penalties of more than $370,000 in back taxes.

The money, the energy, and the support of Roosevelt gave Johnson an enormous push. On June 26 the *Houston Post* showed him with 43 percent of the vote over O'Daniel's 22 percent, with Mann and Dies far behind. Since this was an election where a simple majority would win, the news buoyed the Johnson camp.

A last-ditch effort by O'Daniel to win over Roosevelt voters backfired. The governor had written to Roosevelt proposing that he create a separate Texas army and navy to contribute to the nation's defense. Roosevelt tactfully replied that he was reluctant to inflict on Texas a greater proportion of national defense costs than was its due. Since FDR had used the salutation "My Dear Governor," O'Daniel used it to show that the president was a close friend. But LBJ rebutted this before a crowd of four thousand in Houston when he pulled out of his pocket a telegram from FDR saying that he intended his letter to O'Daniel to be "merely courteous" and he was trying to avoid "calling the scheme preposterous, which it undoubtedly is."[34] The crowd roared with laughter.

On election day, the early reports were so promising that it seemed as if grandfather Sam Ealy Sr.'s prophesy on the day of Lyndon's birth was coming true sooner than anyone expected. Later in the evening the results seemed even better, and when the county political bosses asked Johnson whether they should report their votes, he told them to go ahead. By the following morning the banner headline in the *Houston Post* read: "JOHNSON WITH 5152 VOTE LEAD, APPEARS ELECTED." Soon after, the Texas Election Bureau, an affiliate of the *Dallas News*, proclaimed Johnson the next U.S. senator. With a 15,000-vote lead and only about the same number still uncounted, it would be a miracle if he lost. The only person not celebrating was Wirtz, who worried because O'Daniel had refused to concede and knew that votes could be "changed."

LBJ had made a fatal mistake by tallying his total too early. As soon as the O'Daniel managers knew how wide a lead they had to overcome, they made sure they found the votes. Stealing votes was easy in those days, and in Texas it was endemic. Everyone knew there were certain precincts in which the county judge waited for his instructions to report the totals to the Election Bureau.

The mechanics of this special election encouraged fraud. Paper ballots were issued, with Republicans and Democrats listed in special columns. Customarily the voters, mostly Democrats, simply scratched out the names of those in their own party they did not want, leaving the candidate of their choice unmarked. On this occasion, however, in one Johnson county, ten thousand votes had been voided because the voters had neglected to cross out the names of the opposition party candidates, including the Republican, Independent, and Communist nominees. This accorded with the law but had seldom been applied. The local election officials had used their own discretion to decide whether to count the votes. Piles of Johnson votes were thrown out in other places as well.

Complicating the murky situation was the intrusion of Lieutenant Governor Coke Stevenson's big-money supporters, many of them brewers and distillers. The thinking of these men was rather convoluted. In anticipation of war, military bases were being established all over Texas, furnishing the liquor manufacturers with a vast potential new market for their products. Unfortunately, O'Daniel had just asked the Texas legislature to pass a bill prohibiting the sale of alcohol within ten miles of a military installation. If O'Daniel went off to Washington, Stevenson, a "wet," would become governor and the "dry" bill would be defeated. As Austin mayor Tom Miller told Charles Marsh two days before the election, Lyndon had a lead, but the "gambling, horse racing and whiskey-beer combination will throw behind O'Daniel to get him out of the state."[35]

The Johnson forces miscalculated. They had devoted special attention during the campaign to the South Texas counties where "bloc" voting—boss-controlled, cash-on-the-line voting—was the norm. They had succeeded in outbidding the O'Daniel people. Convinced that the results were a certainty, Connally contacted the South Texas leaders and told them to report their district results. Meanwhile, Johnson's opponents were rallying to overturn the probable outcome. On the evening of election day the pro-Stevenson people, after a confab at the Driskill Hotel, had fanned out over the state, concentrating on the South Texas counties. Election officials soon began to receive "late" returns mostly from the Rio Grande Valley, where Dies had done particularly well. The "new" votes came in for O'Daniel, with Dies receiving a much smaller proportion of these than in the earlier count. Many people thought it strange that Dies's new percentage would have been so much smaller. Former governor Allred called Johnson headquarters and complained that the pro-Stevenson people were stealing the election in South Texas.

When it was all over, O'Daniel won by 1,311 votes. The victor himself probably had little to do with any illegalities. "It wasn't O'Daniel that beat Johnson," declared a Johnson campaign worker. "It was Coke Stevenson and the fact that a lot of people wanted him to be governor that had the greatest force on the election." "I don't know what they did," he added, "but whatever it was, apparently it was effective."[36]

Many Johnson supporters wanted him to contest the results, but LBJ refused to be a "crybaby." Several journalists, including Drew Pearson and Walter Winchell, remarked on the obvious irregularities of this contest. But in the end, nothing was done. Johnson was reluctant to approve a probe, knowing it would probably lead to an examination of his campaign finances and the role of Brown and Root. He had also committed some voting improprieties of his own, particularly in Hispanic South Texas. Johnson advised his staff to "go back to work." "There'll be another ball game to play someday."[37]

The disappointing results produced a memorable meeting with FDR. When Johnson got back to Washington, Roosevelt asked to see him. The president was annoyed by the outcome and scolded his candidate. According to Jim Rowe, FDR told Johnson: "Lyndon, up in New York the first thing they taught us was to sit on the ballot boxes."[38]

But however different the outcome might have been, Johnson prepared to return to his House seat to work once more for FDR, this time mostly on the war effort. He had learned a lesson, however: he would never be cheated out of an election again!

CHAPTER 7

Time Out for War

L YNDON JOHNSON COULD CONSOLE HIMSELF that he still had his seat in the House and the regular election for the Senate was only a year away. Returning to Congress still suffering from the aftermath of tonsillitis, he tried to present a cheerful face. Lady Bird described his demeanor when he left Texas as debonair, but she knew "just how much nerve and effort it took to keep up that appearance."[1] But this was one of the gloomiest times in his life. "I felt terribly rejected, and I began to think about leaving politics and going home to make money," he told Doris Kearns.[2]

During the spring and summer of 1941 the United States edged ever closer to war. Step by inexorable step, the country was becoming a full-scale belligerent in the European carnage. Yet despite Roosevelt's actions and the push of world events, the isolationists in Congress remained stubbornly opposed to intervention and capable of frustrating administration policies. In late summer the House faced the prospect either of extending the required term of military service under the Selective Training and Service Act or sending the draftees home after their first year. The possibility of bringing the boys home appealed to many isolationists, for whom the preparedness movement seemed a self-fulfilling process leading to war. If something were not done, the million men inducted under the 1940 law would be discharged, and the United States would lose its military capability in a time of crisis. For the administration it seemed indispensable to get the term of service stretched.

Johnson, as we saw, was an interventionist. He was also something broader: an internationalist. He himself had little contact with the world outside the United States. He had never crossed the ocean; his cultural environment was parochial. But the southern influence was powerful: few southern leaders, from a section that relied on international markets for its cotton, had illusions about insulating the United States from the rest of the world. He was also a Roosevelt man; what the president wanted was good enough for him. At Rayburn's behest, Johnson assisted majority whip Pat Boland in polling the House Democrats. The results were not promising. Many opposed any draft extension and were seconded by numerous Republicans. Rayburn appealed to Johnson to help get his fellow Democrats to accept a compromise proposal of a maximum thirty months of service.

On August 8, 1941, Lyndon Johnson gave, as his first major speech in the House, a defense of extending the draft act. The issue, he said, involved freedom or slavery; there was no way of getting around it. "Texas boys," he declared, "prefer service now to slavery later." Some people, he admitted, endorsed appeasement of the dictators, but, he added, "there is a 100 percent record of destruction and death in every attempt toward appeasement of the Axis powers."[3]

Johnson also helped the House leaders with direct appeals to the individual members, learning about buttonholing from Rayburn, who had perfected the art. As one House member described Rayburn's technique: "There he stands, his left hand on your right shoulder, holding your coat button, looking at you out of honest eyes that reflect the sincerest emotions."[4] When the roll call was taken, the military service extension passed, 203 to 202. A single vote had kept the U.S. Army intact four months before Pearl Harbor! "Lyndon Johnson," Carl Vinson later declared, "had as much to do with winning that victory as any man in the Congress of the United States at that time."[5]

Later that month Roosevelt asked Johnson to be the keynote speaker at the Young Democrats Convention in Louisville, Kentucky, where he himself would speak following the congressman. Johnson told the YDs that they were all fighters "in the heat of democracy's battle against the Nazi world." They should be as zealous in the cause of democracy as young Nazis were in the cause of fascism. The congressman listened attentively when Roosevelt followed, chastising the "appeasers and compromisers who contend for treaties with forces that make a mockery of treaties."[6]

The isolationist-interventionist struggle preceding Pearl Harbor would make a lasting impression on the congressman. Johnson had been too young to take much notice of World War I. But now, as a mature man, he was immersed in his country's public affairs. His political mentors and allies saw World War II as a struggle to the death between democracy and fascism. They were contemptuous of appeasers like Neville Chamberlain, who sold out Czechoslovakia at Munich, and they hated and feared the new breed of authoritarian dictators. LBJ's foreign policy views came directly from his perceptions of World War II. As he later told Doris Kearns, he had learned "two things" from World War II—that war came from "a lust for power on the part of a few evil leaders" and from "weakness on the part of the people whose love for peace too often displays a lack of courage that serves as an open invitation to all the aggressors of the world."[7] He would apply—or misapply—these lessons in Asia during his own term as president.

The international situation worsened as 1941 wore on. In September a German submarine fired two torpedoes at the USS *Greer*, patrolling in the waters around Iceland to protect convoys carrying American war matériel to Britain. Though the ship was not sunk, Roosevelt ordered the navy to "shoot on sight" at any hostile vessel on the North Atlantic sea lanes. In October FDR appealed to Congress to cancel the "crippling provisions" of the Neutrality Act of 1939. This bill had revoked the earlier arms embargo on belligerents but required that purchasers of munitions pay cash and transport them in their own ships ("cash and carry"). FDR wanted Congress to allow American ships to transport munitions cargoes to Britain and carry guns for self-protection when they entered combat zones. Still gripped by isolationism, Congress refused to grant this request until public opinion, inflamed by a German submarine attack on the USS *Kearny* and the sinking of the USS *Reuben James* with the loss of a hundred men, forced its hand. On November 13 the House repealed the onerous restrictions of the 1939 measure by the close vote of 212 to 194, with Johnson voting for repeal.

By this time news from the Pacific had become truly alarming. In late November America's negotiations with Japan over its brutal war of conquest in China had broken down, and intelligence sources revealed that the Japanese military were planning a massive invasion of Thailand and other aggressive acts in East Asia. On December 7, while Japanese envoys held discussions with the State Department in Washington, the Japanese Navy, without warning, attacked the U.S. naval base at Pearl Harbor, Hawaii, killing twenty-four hundred Americans and destroying or severely damaging nineteen ships, including all the battleships of the Pacific Fleet. On the day following the "date which will live in infamy," Roosevelt delivered his solemn war message to Congress. That afternoon Johnson, along with all but one House member, voted to approve the resolution for war with Japan.

Johnson had been commissioned in 1940 as a lieutenant commander in the Naval Reserve. An hour after he voted for war, he requested
that Admiral Chester Nimitz put him on active duty. "Until this war is
won, and the evil forces of dictators are crushed," he wrote a friend ten
days after Pearl Harbor, "Americans will have no time for politics."[8]

Like so many other aspects of Johnson's life, his armed services career is a subject of controversy. Some of his biographers have seen it as
an honorable interlude in Johnson's life. Others have depicted everything he did while in the service as shabby and self-seeking. The truth
falls in the middle.

To his credit, he was the first congressman to don a uniform in World
War II. Surrendering his congressional salary of ten thousand dollars a
year, he drew only a lieutenant commander's pay of three thousand dollars annually for as long as he served. Johnson was a patriot who believed
"national interest" overrode other considerations. He also felt a duty to
provide an example for other young men and to honor his campaign
promises. But he was not compelled to do any of these things; many
other colleagues remained in Congress for the duration of the war. In addition, he might legitimately have claimed the sort of medical disabilities
that would have kept an ordinary citizen from military service.

The deed, however, was obviously not pure patriotism. It was also a
calculated career move, and he sought to squeeze maximum political
capital from it. When the media expressed interest in the congressman's
enlistment, he happily accommodated them. On December 16 a Paramount newsreel crew spent an hour filming the young legislator clearing
his desk and reporting for duty to the Navy Department. Nor did Johnson resign his Congressional seat; instead, he left an unsalaried Lady
Bird in charge of the Washington office. Though he could not anticipate
it, he was also spared the four grueling years the Pacific war lasted. Unlike ordinary sailors, his length of service would be mercifully shortened
when, in July 1942, President Roosevelt insisted that all congressmen
serving in the military come back to Washington.

The navy assigned Johnson, along with aide John Connally, another
navy reserve officer, to the office of the United States–New Zealand
Command in the Twelfth Naval District, San Francisco. This was the
navy's way of finding a safe and nonstrategic job for an officer with no
training and no experience. Despite the attractions of the City on the
Bay, LBJ was disgusted with what he considered the meaninglessness of
his assignment. Some young men would have been happy to spend the
war in a beautiful locale out of harm's way, but not the driven, fidgety
young congressman, who knew the assignment was mere paper-shuffling

to appease the navy and the New Zealanders. "I didn't buy this blue uniform," he grumbled, "just to get it shiny sitting on a chair. No, sir, I want action."[9]

Johnson soon got the navy to use his "live wire"[10] talents to deal with labor problems in naval shipyards and war production plants in Texas, California, and Washington State. Though better than his previous job, this meant returning to the West Coast to set up training procedures and deal with manpower bottlenecks. Lyndon remained unhappy. He wanted to go overseas. Many who knew him thought this desire more political than patriotic. One of Roosevelt's aides who saw him during this period described LBJ as the "energetic and intelligent Texas congressman who wants for the sake of his political future to get into a danger zone, though he realizes his talents are best suited for handling speakers and public relations."[11] In his yearning for action, he resembled other politically ambitious enlistees who recognized that military glory would add luster to their reputations and look good in future campaigns.

In April Johnson wangled a meeting with President Roosevelt to complain about his posting. Fortunately for Johnson, the president had already devised a way to deal with politicians serving in the military who had no training: overseas inspection tours. The Texas congressman, FDR said, should go to Australia on a fact-finding mission. The assignment would bring FDR a two-for-one return. Not only would he get Lyndon out of his hair; he also might find out more about what was actually happening in the South Pacific.

The region was in dangerous turmoil. The Japanese had invaded the Philippines soon after Pearl Harbor, and in March 1942 the president had ordered General Douglas MacArthur, the American commander, to leave for Australia, abandoning his troops to a hopeless rearguard action. Once in Australia, MacArthur was to prepare plans to roll back the Japanese conquests and destroy their military might. By now Washington had agreed to make Europe the first priority, but it was essential not to fall too far behind in the Pacific. The area was unfamiliar to most Americans, yet thousands of soldiers and countless tons of equipment had already been sent there without much information about needs. Johnson would be making a firsthand report to Roosevelt about what difficulties American troops were actually facing and what additional equipment and supplies were necessary to avoid defeat.

Johnson would later modestly describe himself as "a very low-ranking set of eyes and ears" for FDR.[12] But Air Corps lieutenant colonel Samuel E. Anderson, on a similar mission for the War Department General Staff, later described Johnson's task as investigating the "overall problem of what our combat forces were trying to overcome in the Southwest Pacific. . . . His mission . . . was to be able to return to the president with the kind of information he needed to cut through conflicting reports from the SWPC and to carry out his planning with a clearly objective analysis of the situation in that theater."[13]

Before leaving for Australia, LBJ had to decide about filing for the November 1942 congressional election. Would he try to beat O'Daniel in the regular race for the Senate, or would he run again for the House? The *Dallas Morning News* ran a story claiming that the Roosevelt administration wanted Johnson to oust O'Daniel and that some people were circulating a petition to put LBJ on the primary ballot. Charles Marsh urged Johnson to run. But Lady Bird felt that Lyndon simply "could not win," and Alvin Wirtz agreed. "A live Congressman" was "better than a dead Senator," he noted.[14] Acting on their orders, apparently, aide John Connally filed Johnson's application for reelection to the House. "I felt," said Connally, that "he had a right to be reelected to his congressional seat without question."[15] On the filing date, Johnson was far away and had no idea which application had been registered. Although some thought that Johnson could have beaten O'Daniel this time, in fact, Jimmy Allred lost a very tight race to "Pappy."

Meanwhile, Lady Bird continued to run the Washington office, trying to handle the fifteen to twenty letters a day Lyndon had told her she must answer, taking typing and shorthand classes to be more efficient. The job was made more difficult by the absence of Gene Latimer, who had also joined the navy and who was stationed in Chicago. Since Lyndon had renounced his congressman's pay, Lady Bird rented her house for a hundred dollars a month, for a while sharing a fifty-dollar-a-month apartment with Nellie Connally, John's wife.

By the middle of May Johnson was on his way to the South Pacific. His fact-finding mission included stops in Palmyra, Canton Island, New Caledonia, and New Zealand as well as Australia. What he found was discouraging. The United States, to be properly equipped and fight effectively, would need more of everything. He was appalled, moreover, that the Australians and the Americans wasted so much time bickering that no one seemed to know what was happening, that decisions were incompetently made if at all, and that MacArthur's military headquarters was so far from the actual front in the islands to the north that the general was out of touch with his lieutenants. On the way to Australia, Johnson met Anderson and his colleague Lieutenant Colonel Francis R. Stevens, both of whom were on their way to Australia and New Guinea. The three men became good friends and decided they would stick together, carrying out their assignments "almost as a team."[16]

On May 25, after reaching Southwest Pacific Command headquarters in Melbourne, they went to see MacArthur. The general, happy to accommodate a friend of the president, gave Johnson and his companions a complete briefing that emphasized the shortages in the Pacific theater and the unreadiness of the Australians to defend themselves. Anderson, Stevens, and Johnson appreciated the general's candor.

Two weeks later, when Anderson, a pilot, decided to accompany a bombing mission on the Japanese base at Lae in New Guinea, Johnson and Stevens decided to go along. General William Marquat, assigned to the visitors from MacArthur's staff, tried to dissuade Johnson. But he was adamant. He was in the Pacific, he said, "to see personally . . . just what conditions were like and I cannot find out what they *are* like if I don't go along on this mission."[17] Unable to deter the congressman and his two fellow investigators, Marquat advised General Martin F. Scanlon at the Seven-Mile Drome airfield near Port Moresby to arrange for the three men to accompany the mission.

Scanlon's impression of Johnson, the first congressman to visit the godforsaken Port Moresby, was that of an "affable, nice person . . . who was doing a job and making very little fuss about it." But Port Moresby was dangerous, since the Japanese were bombing the place "at least two or three nights a week, plus day raids and strafing attacks by Zeros that would shoot anything that moved at our base." The tailgunner on the plane that Johnson eventually boarded described the missions as "suicide."[18]

On June 9 Johnson boarded a B-26 Marauder medium bomber called the *Wabash Cannonball*. Just before it took off, however, he got off to urinate, and Colonel Stevens took his place, refusing to give it back. Johnson then joined the crew of the *Heckling Hare*. Over Lae, Japanese Zeros attacked. Saburo Sakai, Japan's most famous ace whose sixty-two kills was a record, fired his wing cannon at the *Wabash Cannonball*, sending the plane into the Pacific, leaving no survivors. Meanwhile, the *Heckling Hare* lost the use of its right engine and dropped out of formation. Under attack by a formation of eight Zeros and hit in wings and fuselage, the crippled plane limped back to base.

Johnson was composed through all of this. According to the tailgunner, Lillis Walker, the distinguished passenger seemed to act "as if we were on a sight-seeing tour." Walker was amazed. "Bullets were singing through the plane all about us," Walker remembered, "and we were being hit by those cannon shells and he was—well, just calm, and watching everything." As he got off the plane at Port Moresby, Johnson thanked the crew, told them it had been very interesting, and walked away. "We were flabbergasted," recalled the tailgunner. "He was cool as ice."[19]

Johnson and Anderson sent word to MacArthur's headquarters that they intended to leave for home on June 18. That morning the general called the men into his office and told them he was awarding them Silver Stars, the Army's third-highest medal. Stevens would get the Distinguished Service Cross posthumously. MacArthur's citation stated that Johnson had volunteered as an observer to "obtain personal knowledge of combat conditions . . . over hostile positions in New Guinea" and had "evidenced marked coolness in spite of the hazard involved." Johnson's "gallant action," he added, "enabled him to obtain and return with valuable information."[20]

MacArthur's words make it clear that the award had political motives. After all, Johnson was an observer and a passenger on the plane, not a member of the crew, none of whom was awarded a medal, and furthermore, he had been advised against going on the mission. On the other hand, he had gone out of his way to provide accurate firsthand observations about combat for his report to the president, and he did acquit himself bravely in a perilous situation. Johnson himself hesitated to accept the honor and drafted a letter to the adjutant general at the War Department in Washington that questioned whether he had a right to the decoration, considering the "inconsequential part" he played. Apparently, the letter was never sent, and in the end he decided to keep the Silver Star. Johnson proudly wore the ribbon that went with the medal for the rest of his life.

He also kept a diary, something he apparently had never done before and never did again. In it he recorded some private observations, obviously not meant for official release. On an island garrisoned by eleven hundred soldiers Johnson wrote: "Army food lousy. Army management about as bad. Inadequate defense. No radar detector system. . . . Only 1 woman on island. . . . 60 years old. . . . Only intercourse—social." After the *Wabash Cannonball* went down, Johnson observed plaintively that he "couldn't get my mind off Steve [Francis Stevens]. . . ."[21]

On other occasions he talked about someone named "Miss Jesus," confessing that he had thought of her "all day" at one point and "plenty" on another.[22] James Rowe was convinced LBJ was "fooling around" in Australia. When Johnson came back Rowe was invited to see some movies he took on his trip. One showed a "very pretty woman in a park," and when Lady Bird asked who it was, Lyndon whispered, "I'm not going to tell her. . . ."[23]

Whether he deserved the medal or not, Johnson accomplished some things on his Pacific mission. He helped bridge the gap between American and Australian officers by talking the racist Australians into accepting black U.S. soldiers. He recommended the replacement of General George H. Brett by General George C. Kenny, mollifying MacArthur and calming relations with the air force. Johnson also eased several logistical problems that facilitated the naval victory at Midway in June 1942, the turning point in the Pacific war. Above all, for good or ill, he helped temper the administration's Europe-first priority and expedited shipments of gasoline, bombs, and ammunition, as well as food and clothing, to American soldiers in Australia.

On July 1, 1942, Roosevelt asked all members of Congress to leave military service and resume their political duties. Johnson returned to Washington by July 15. The seven-month stint, from San Francisco to the South Pacific, made up Johnson's entire military experience, but he was able to capitalize on it for the rest of his political career. In November 1942 he was reelected to Congress from the Tenth District without opposition.

Some of his future opponents would disparage his military service. In 1944 Buck Taylor, his opponent in the Democratic primary, denounced him for "his failure to keep his promises to serve his country in the trenches beside the good soldiers he helped to send to those trenches." In 1946 rival Hardy Hollers denounced him for his self-seeking behavior in the war. In Hollers's view, he went to the Pacific "with a camera in one hand and leading his publicity man with the other." Hollers also chided Johnson for using FDR's July 1 directive as "an excuse to return to an air-cooled fox-hole in Washington" instead of a real one on the combat zone.[24]

Johnson undoubtedly inflated his wartime service. He would describe making his way through the jungles of New Guinea and "the horrors" he had encountered fighting "the Japs in the Pacific."[25] As time went on his stories became more overblown, and by the time he ran for president he had become the hero of the Pacific war. Yet Johnson was not alone in embellishing his military career as a campaign tactic. After World War II, John F. Kennedy and Wisconsin senator Joe McCarthy would stretch their war records for political advantage. It is surely part of the political game to build up your assets, whatever they may be, and to tear down your opponent's. In these slugfests Johnson would both give and receive.

Back in Washington, thirty pounds lighter after a bout with fever picked up on the trip, Johnson shared his findings with the president. Johnson criticized the indecisiveness and incompetence of some of the top military brass, stressed the importance of cutting red tape, and emphasized the need for superior equipment and leadership. "We are going to have to move quickly," he told FDR, "to coordinate dive bombers and domestic politics, tanks and military strategy, ships and the will of the people. Management and manpower are going to have to be closely woven into a smoothly functioning machine devoid of departmental squabbles and petty jealousies." He had harsh words for the planes the navy was flying. "I'd just as soon try to weather a storm riding on the tail of a box-kite," he said, "as I would to face the fighting Jap Zero with one of those navy PBY crates some of those boys are now flying."[26] Despite his complaints, he appreciated the American servicemen in the Pacific, commending their "courage and guts and fighting spirit."[27]

Back in Washington, Johnson began attending Rayburn's Board of Education gatherings again. There he met Senator Harry Truman of Missouri, a new member who headed a special Senate watchdog committee overseeing the war production program. The idea of heading a similar committee in the House appealed to LBJ and he broached the subject with Rayburn. The Speaker turned him down, but Johnson managed to talk Carl Vinson into letting him chair a five-man subcommittee that would look into the navy's procurement program and its conduct of naval warfare. To keep Johnson's activities within limits, Vinson gave him a very small budget. Johnson cleverly sidestepped his lack of funds by hiring only Naval Reserve officers to staff his committee. In effect, the navy itself would pay his personnel. On the advice of his friend William O. Douglas, now a U.S. Supreme Court justice, he hired as subcommittee counsel a first-rate lawyer, Donald C. Cook. Cook remained a close ally for more than twenty years.

The subcommittee's work involved overseeing the effectiveness and working conditions of the navy's procurement program and its utilization of personnel in onshore facilities. It looked as well into naval draft deferments, the disposal of surplus naval property, and naval aviation training. Johnson's subcommittee never attracted the public attention that Truman's committee received, but it did establish a reputation for impartiality and comprehensiveness in its investigations.

The congressman threw himself into the subcommittee work in his usual frenetic way and ended up working harder than any of his staff. As chairman, Johnson met the top officers in the navy. These men, in his view, were frequently arrogant, patronizing, and rude toward their juniors, unsystematic, uncreative, ill-informed, and anti-Semitic. The contact made him forever distrustful of high-ranking military officers, and he would always believe that American foreign policy was better carried out by politicians and statesmen than by military men.

The subcommittee was often critical of the navy. One report rebuked it for wasting four thousand enlisted men on Washington desk jobs. Another criticized the service for giving Standard Oil excessively favorable terms in leasing its oil reserves at Elk Hills Field in California. This document forced the department to rewrite the contract, saving the government millions of dollars.

Johnson also looked into absenteeism in defense work. In 1943 he submitted an amendment to a House bill requiring private contractors for the navy to report inexcusably and frequently absent men to their draft boards, making them subject to immediate military call-up. The bill died in the Rules Committee, though a similar piece of legislation, known as the "Work or Fight" bill, came up again in 1945. Johnson supported this measure, much to the anger of labor leaders who accused him of "selling out to the war profiteers." He defended himself by claiming that most war workers were hardworking and patriotic, but "the loafer, the inexcusable absentee, the slacker,"[28] was in fact helping the enemy and deserved no pity. The Work or Fight bill was modified after the CIO complained that antiunion employers could use it against union men, particularly if they went on strike. Yet LBJ's endorsement remained in the memories of many labor leaders, who would show their anger against Johnson in the 1948 Senate election. But Johnson didn't hesitate to criticize business as well. "Selfish groups are fighting," he declared at a graduation speech in San Marcos, "over the question of what patents will be used, where the plants will be built, what character of basic raw materials will be utilized and behind it all, who will get control of industry and get the profits after the war?"[29]

Johnson struck a blow for principle by his vote against the oil companies in 1943. The oil industry wanted a price increase of at least twenty-five cents a barrel on crude oil, a rise favored by the wartime fuels administrator. The director of the Office of Price Administration (OPA), Chester Bowles, thought the increase inflationary, however, and asked Congress to defeat a bill permitting it. The Senate had already agreed to an increase of thirty-five cents a barrel, and when the measure came to the House, Texan Sam Rayburn supported the increase, convinced, he said, that the country would become deficient in fuel supplies unless the oil industry was encouraged to increase production. Believing that if Congress permitted one industry to raise its prices others would follow and inflation would get out of hand, Johnson voted against it. As he told Paul Porter, a New Deal administrator and lawyer, approving an increase would have bothered his conscience while soldiers were dying in battle. The price rise, he explained, "would have pyramided the cost of fuel and its derivative products and would probably have added billions" to war costs. Porter told Merle Miller that "many commentators," knowing the power of the Texas oil interests, thought that Lyndon Johnson was signing his "political death warrant."[30]

Where Johnson saw no conflict between patriotism and profit, where he could help his wealthy Texas friends without jeopardizing the war effort, he was happy to oblige. He was especially helpful to the Brown brothers. The construction contract they obtained, with Johnson's aid, for the Corpus Christi Naval Air Training Base escalated into a one-hundred-million-dollar project sprawling over twenty thousand acres in three Texas counties. The firm's business exploded during the war so that it became one of the biggest construction companies in the country. Brown and Root soon branched out into oil and gas production and the building of destroyer escorts, ultimately launching hundreds of new ships in their yards. Johnson's help mainly consisted of keeping Brown and Root informed of upcoming federal projects and making timely phone calls to war agencies.

Johnson himself found ways to take material advantage of the booming wartime economy. It was hard for LBJ, with his financial anxieties, his continuing family obligations, and his small congressional salary, not to want his share of war-created affluence. Moreover, he craved an independent source of income so he could remain free of "special interests." And if he failed to advance politically, he wanted to have a business that would compensate him psychologically, as well as financially, for his disappointments. But he was very conscious of what his constituents thought and tried not to offend them. As we have seen, at one point he turned down an exceptionally generous offer from Charles March to go into the oil business.

Lady Bird, too, had her reasons for wanting a business besides politics. She hoped to have a family, but by 1942 had had three miscarriages. Now she was looking for something productive to do in case she could never bear a child. When LBJ returned from the South Pacific, the Johnsons tried to buy a small Texas newspaper as a "mom and pop" enterprise, with Lady Bird as editor and himself as advertising salesman. The project fell through, apparently because Lady Bird thought the paper too expensive and too far from his district. Searching for a way to achieve monetary security without compromising himself politically, and hoping to find something for Lady Bird to do, he consulted Alvin Wirtz.

Already alert to the problem, Wirtz had been conferring with another Austin lawyer, Fagan Dickson. Johnson had "presidential possibilities," Wirtz told Dickson, and that meant "we've got to do something to make Lyndon financially independent" so he would not be "dependent on others for favors."[31] The solution they came up with was the purchase of a radio station in Johnson's district that had come on the market.

Station KTBC in Austin had done poorly during its five years of existence, and in 1942, though radio in general was prospering, it was still losing money. The owners, who included Robert B. Anderson, later a member of President Eisenhower's cabinet, had requested permission from the Federal Communications Commission (FCC), regulator of radio stations, to broadcast around the clock. Currently they were assigned a frequency that they shared with the Texas A & M College station, eighty miles from Austin. This arrangement made them a "sundowner," a station required to stop broadcasting when the sun set, as early as 5:00 P.M. during the winter. Such limited hours severely hampered KTBC's ability to attract advertising and precluded affiliation with a national network.

Politics undoubtedly influenced the FCC decision regarding KTBC. At least since the 1920s the media had been dominated by conservatives, and the New Deal appointees on the FCC were unhappy about continuing right-wing control of sources of information. But the agency, during these flourishing years of radio, also had to deal with a severe dearth of broadcasting wavelengths, and there was little room open on the dial. The Anderson group, unable to get the FCC to extend either the hours or the power of KTBC, lost interest in the station and tried to sell it to a highly conservative oilman, James M. West, who also owned the Austin *Daily Tribune*, a newspaper bitterly opposed to Roosevelt and all his social legislation. West agreed to buy the station, contingent on FCC consent to the sale. In 1940 the FCC answered the sale application by revoking KTBC's license on the grounds of "false and fraudulent statements and representations" about their financing. In addition, since West owned a newspaper, he was open to the charge of trying to dominate the media in Austin. The matter dragged on until West died in 1942, leaving the "insider's right" to his sons, Wesley and James, and another Republican Austin businessman, E. G. Kingsbery.

Kingsbery was on the verge of submitting yet another application to the FCC to permit the sale when Lyndon Johnson, tipped off by Wirtz, got word to the businessman that he wanted to see him. Though Kingsbery was not a Johnson supporter, the congressman had tried to make friends by getting his son John accepted as a student at Annapolis. "He knew," Kingsbery told Ronnie Dugger, "there were two ways through to me, my family and money, and of those, the most important was my family."[32] Johnson asked him to give him his option to buy KTBC, subject to

FCC approval. Kingsbery explained that he had only half the insider's right; the other half was owned by the West brothers. But to discharge his debt to Johnson for his son's appointment at Annapolis, he would give his half option to LBJ and recommend to the Wests that they give him theirs.

With half of the license right in his possession, Johnson then had to persuade the West brothers, with whom he had no leverage except Kingsbery's recommendation, to give him the other. Johnson was afraid that with his reputation as a liberal, the Wests would balk. He asked George Brown to be his front, but Brown refused, believing Johnson should do it himself. Just before Christmas the Wests and Johnson got together, apparently at the Wests' ranch in Llano. In his usual persuasive fashion, Johnson was able to talk them into giving him and Lady Bird the option, pending FCC approval. "I didn't *like* Lyndon Johnson [before the meeting]," Wesley West told a friend, "but by God I went over there, and he's a pretty good fellow."[33] West later explained to Dugger that he really had no interest in buying the station and felt sorry for the owners who were losing so much money. Nothing illicit seems to have occurred at the Houston meeting; in the end it was Lyndon's talent for cajolery that did the trick.

The next step was contacting the Anderson group to agree on a mutually satisfactory price. Lyndon, of course, had no extra funds of his own, refused to accept money from any of his wealthy friends, and did not want to be charged with using his political connections to enrich himself. In addition, one FCC requirement for the management of a radio station was the ability of the owner to oversee its operations full-time. Johnson could not devote all his time to running a radio station, but his wife could. Lady Bird also had some capital, reporting her net worth in 1943 as $64,332, part of which was cash from her mother's estate and part some Alabama real estate left to her by an uncle.

With KTBC running at a deficit and in hock to banks all over Austin, a great deal of capital would be needed to get the station in the black, and although the station's equipment was worth $30,000, expenses the previous year had been more than $34,000. Lady Bird was prepared to offer the Anderson group $17,500, which they accepted, mostly to be done with it. It helped, moreover, that the sellers believed that Lady Bird would probably succeed in getting FCC approval. In early 1943 the FCC approved Lady Bird's application to buy KTBC.

Johnson's critics have made much of the fact that it took Lady Bird little more than three weeks to get FCC approval, while its previous owners had been stalled for years. LBJ continued to deny that he had any role whatsoever in facilitating its authorization, nor with its later expansion into television. The *Wall Street Journal* agreed with his contention: "FCC public records show not a single intervention by Representative, Senator, Vice President or President Johnson in quest of a favor for his wife's company."[34] In fact, however, it is difficult to believe that a political operator like Lyndon Johnson did not have some influence in getting the FCC to approve the sale of KTBC to his wife. Yet a good case can also be made that it was done for reasons having more to do with the FCC's aversion to the sale of a potentially profitable and influential radio station to a conservative newspaper publisher than to crass political wire pulling. The knowledge that tried-and-true liberals like the Johnsons wanted it may have been sufficient for the FCC to make its decision without LBJ having to intercede overtly. Not only was the head of the FCC a zealous New Dealer, but so were most of the commission members, including Clifford Durr, who saw the Johnsons socially. Lady Bird had actually consulted Durr on the wisdom of this venture. Durr advised her that if she could "get that station on its feet and get it well managed, it ought to be a very good investment." He would always insist that the application was made solely by Lady Bird, that "there wasn't any skulduggery . . . at the FCC," and that "Lyndon never had a thing to do with it."[35]

With the FCC's approval, Lady Bird moved back to Texas to make KTBC a paying proposition. She chose Lyndon's old friend from the NYA, Jesse Kellam, to be the station manager, but she herself put in long hours and hard work on the station. An old friend remembered Lady Bird sitting at the dining-room table surrounded by books and papers, going through the station's accounts. The consensus among the Johnson friends and colleagues was that she was a very shrewd businesswoman. Leonard Marks, the attorney for the station, who stressed that "it was her station—don't let anybody tell you to the contrary," admired Lady Bird for her ability to "read a balance sheet the way a truck driver reads a map."[36]

Lady Bird's hard work paid off, and by August the station had actually made a profit of $18, the first on its upward trend. There is no denying, however, that Lyndon also helped make it a success. If Johnson had little or nothing to do with the original FCC application and approval, he now showed the same enthusiasm for advancing the station as his political career. Once Lady Bird's ownership was in the bag, Johnson went to New York to ask William Paley, president of CBS, for network affiliation. Paley turned the matter over to Frank Stanton, who looked at a map and concluded that although Austin was in the middle, it would not conflict with CBS's existing stations in Dallas or in San Antonio. It probably did not hurt that once KTBC joined CBS the network would also acquire a congressional connection. A few months later, Alvin Wirtz helped Lady Bird write an application to the FCC for an extension of the station's transmitting power from 250 to 1,000 watts and permission to broadcast for twenty-four hours a day. The FCC permitted this move a month later and also approved a new frequency, 590, which KTBC would no longer have to share and which would enable listeners in thirty-eight surrounding counties in central Texas to hear it without interference.

Johnson aggressively solicited advertising for KTBC, contacting the key people in clothing stores, car dealerships, printing companies, banks, a hotel, a funeral home, and a sporting goods store in the Austin area. It was he who initiated the policy of having station employees drop by retail advertisers' stores and price items while telling the shop owner: "I've heard about this at KTBC."[37] Some of his political supporters were happy to roust up prospective advertisers. Other advertisers believed that if they bought time on a station belonging to a congressman they were in line for possible political favors. Austin lawyer Ed Clark, who wanted leverage in Washington, was particularly helpful to the station. Among others, Clark got Howard E. Butt, who owned a statewide chain of grocery stores, to advertise on the station, and arranged for General Electric to sponsor a newscast. Johnson's assistant Walter Jenkins was also dogged in pursuing advertisers.

KTBC would become the seed of a small Johnson communications empire and the core of the Johnson family fortune. In 1952 the Johnsons would acquire an FCC license for a TV station to be affiliated with KTBC. The FCC assigned KTBC-TV a VHF channel, one of those on the limited regular dial of American TV receivers and hence immensely valuable. By early 1956 the radio and TV assets of the family were worth more than $1.5 million. Three years later they were valued at $1 million more.

It is hard to believe that influence did not play an important part in the TV transaction. Austin, a city of 130,000 in the 1950s, was assigned only a single VHF channel, giving the Johnson station a virtual monopoly in the community, while other cities of comparable size got several competing channels or were in areas where out-of-town stations could be clearly received. KTBC-TV's monopoly continued through the fifties and enabled the station to charge considerably more for advertising time than comparable stations elsewhere. Johnson was also able to induce all three networks to make the station their affiliate.

In 1959 Ronnie Dugger asked Johnson whether his interest in an enterprise closely regulated by the federal government was not a conflict of interest. Johnson denied it, repeating that the station was owned by his wife and "eleven or twelve others." Lady Bird, he noted, had a journalism degree and "she felt this was the way she wanted to invest her money." Not only that, he had never cast a vote in Congress on any controversy involving the media. Johnson also denied that he got profitable advertising from firms with government contracts. "I have never received any funds or cast any votes in connection with it," he told Dugger.[38] In truth, however, Johnson at times micromanaged the station and almost certainly used his influence to expand the family communications holdings, Texas Broadcasting, to include stations in Waco and several smaller towns.

KTBC greatly improved the Johnsons' cash flow. They purchased a triplex apartment building in Austin, living in one apartment while renting out a second to John Connally and the other to Walter Jenkins. Johnson listed this place on Dillman Street as his primary residence until he bought his ranch on the banks of the Pedernales River in 1951. He plowed back proceeds from the stations to build their profitability and made many new investments.

KTBC radio and KTBC-TV not only built the Johnsons' fortune, they also enabled them to comfortably support themselves and the children they would at last be able to have. By 1943 Lady Bird was finally carrying a pregnancy to term and expected their first child in March 1944. On March 19, their daughter Lynda Bird—the name a combination of her father's first name and her mother's nickname—was born in Washington, D.C. Johnson immediately called Sam Rayburn and then informed his staff and friends. President Roosevelt sent the baby a book about Roosevelt's dog Fala, inscribed: "From the master—to the pup."[39]

All told, the period after Lyndon's return from the navy was a good time for the Johnsons. Lady Bird was especially happy with the events of these years. "We bought a home in '42," she later said, "and had a child in '44 and another child in '47, so the forties were good years."[40] Lady Bird was emphasizing her domestic life, and indeed her family brought her satisfaction. She "enjoyed" her children, she later said, "and we had good times together." But she would always put her public life first. Many years later she admitted that the care and feeding of Lyndon was her top priority. "I'd probably get a C, or even a C⁻ as a mother," she admitted.[41] A neighbor, observing at the time that neither Lyndon nor Lady Bird spent much time with their children, and that various Johnson staff members did double duty as baby-sitters, said, "the little Johnson girls are being raised by a committee."[42] Still, we must not dismiss the

Johnsons' joys in parenthood. Lady Bird saw to the children's education and summer camps. Lyndon nagged Lynda when he felt she had gained too much weight and forbade her to eat any more candy. Once, in a severe rainstorm, he drove out into the Virginia countryside to buy a beagle puppy for Luci and named it Little Beagle Johnson, duplicating once again the LBJ pattern in family members' initials.

Good though these years had been to the Johnsons as a family, Lyndon himself remained discontented. Money and domestic comfort were all very well, but they did not satisfy his need for recognition, for influence, and for power. He had been denied the next step in his climb, the Senate. He would not be denied again.

CHAPTER 8

"Landslide Lyndon"

B Y THE END OF THE DECADE Lyndon felt that his career was in the doldrums. Actually, the political blahs had begun for him as early as 1944, when Roosevelt ran for a fourth term. Tied to FDR and identified as a "New Deal liberal," he suffered when the president's popularity began to wane and his programs came under ever more damaging attack. In Texas, especially, by the middle of the war, the New Deal label had become a liability.

Though he still considered himself a New Dealer and felt honorbound to help the president in his bid for a fourth term, Johnson did not want to go down with the ship if it sank. Instead, he sought a middle position for himself. He stayed committed to liberal welfare programs and supported economic regulations to cope with wartime and postwar needs, but he became less friendly to organized labor, less sensitive to racial discrimination, and took on the Cold War anticommunism then growing among the public and the nation's leaders. It was a politician's response to changing times. The New Deal had helped rescue the country from the Depression. But new times required new responses.

In May 1944, at the state convention in Austin, Johnson found himself once again seeking compromise between the conservative and the liberal factions of the Texas Democrats. The issue was whether the Texas Democrats would support Roosevelt for a fourth term. Johnson quickly became a target for the conservative "regulars" who, among the nicer epithets, called him a "yes-man" and "Roosevelt's pin-up boy." When the regulars defeated a motion by Wirtz to instruct the Texas presidential electors to vote for the candidate with the largest popular vote in November, the liberals, including Wirtz and Johnson, bolted the Senate chamber and regrouped in another room. Yet Johnson surprised the seceders by his warning that they should not "go off half-cocked" and that it was important to "give every Democrat and every so-called Democrat another opportunity to say whether he expects to vote for the party nominee."[1]

Meanwhile, the regulars had targeted Rayburn and Johnson as the two most important Texas representatives to beat in the primaries. Johnson's conservative rival was Buck Taylor, an anti–New Deal supporter of states' rights. Taylor ran a particularly dirty campaign, accusing Johnson of being too friendly to blacks, and blanketing the Tenth District with handbills and postcards charging that his rival intended to wreck the "white primary" that effectively disfranchised black voters. In the end LBJ managed to stave off the threat, defeating Taylor by more than two to one and carrying nine of the ten counties in his district. Rayburn also won, though by a smaller margin.

Faced with the primary fight at home, Johnson was unable to attend the presidential convention in Chicago on July 19. Texas sent two delegations—the regulars, staunchly pledged to Harry Byrd, a pro-states' rights, segregationist senator from Virginia, and the liberals, just as firmly committed to FDR. The Credentials Committee decided to seat both groups and to distribute half the forty-eight votes to each side. On the roll call vote, the twenty-four liberals voted for Roosevelt, as did twelve regulars. The other twelve voted for Byrd. Despite the Texas split, Roosevelt had no trouble winning the renomination for a fourth term. In a move to shift the party more to the center, Roosevelt dropped ultraliberal and idiosyncratic vice president Henry A. Wallace and picked Senator Harry S. Truman from Missouri as his running mate. In November Roosevelt received more than 800,000 votes in Texas, still a member in good standing of the "Solid South." Republican Thomas E. Dewey got 191,000, with Byrd third, with 135,000.[2]

In January 1945 Franklin Roosevelt was inaugurated for the fourth time. Ailing and fatigued, the president had to remain seated while delivering his opening address to the new Congress. In February FDR was off to the important international conference at Yalta with Josef Stalin and Winston Churchill, and when he returned, he was obviously a very sick man. Observing the president at his March 1 talk to Congress on the results of the conference, Rayburn told close friends that FDR was dying. On April 12, while in Warm Springs, Georgia, to regain his strength, Roosevelt expired from a cerebral hemorrhage.

Johnson, who heard the news while in Rayburn's office, was devastated. *New York Times* reporter William S. White ran into him in the Capitol corridor and found his friend with tears in his eyes, his jaw shaking. "He was just like a daddy to me always," he told White. The next day the *Times* published a story by White describing how Lyndon Johnson, a leading member of FDR's "Young Guard," had responded to the catastrophe. "There are plenty of us left here," Johnson said, "to try to block and run interference, as he had taught us, but the man who carried the ball is gone—gone." It was Roosevelt, Johnson declared, who had first inspired him to seek public office, as he had "thousands of other young men all over the country."

The published story contained a paragraph that, one critic has claimed, shows Johnson distancing himself from the president, subconsciously, perhaps, seeking to protect his political future in a more conservative atmosphere:

They called the President a dictator and some of us they called "yes men." Sure, I yessed him plenty of times—because I thought he was right—and I'm not sorry for a single "yes" I ever gave. I have seen the President in all kinds of moods—at breakfast, at lunch, at dinner—and never once did in my five terms here did he ever ask me to vote a certain way, or even suggest it. And when I voted against him—as I have plenty of times—he never said a word.[3]

In reality these were the words of an admiring son who must assert some independence of his father. What else was in his subconscious mind at that time is not clear. But eleven years later, on the seventy-fourth anniversary of Roosevelt's birth, Johnson eulogized his mentor on the floor of the Senate:

We are still too close to the period which is inescapably associated with his name to have historical perspective. But even at this range, it is apparent to every American that he was one of the giants of all time. . . . As one who was closely associated with our late President, I will never forget the meaning of his leadership to our country. . . . The verdict of history is still to be written. But however the book is finally closed, the last line must say that Franklin D. Roosevelt was a man capable of facing the terrible problems of terrible times.[4]

Roosevelt's death, however painful, did not orphan LBJ totally. He still had mentors. Rayburn would serve as father figure. There was also Alvin Wirtz. Yet neither would fill the role as well and as effectively as FDR, and LBJ would continue to seek powerful older men to guide and help him.

Harry S. Truman would not be a daddy to LBJ, although in the beginning Lyndon made overtures. Shortly after becoming president,

Truman addressed a joint session of Congress. Acquainted with Truman from the Board of Education, Lyndon him sent a warm personal message. "Those of us who know you so well were so proud of you today," Johnson wrote.[5] Truman responded, but there was no further personal contact for a long time. The first Christmas Truman was in the White House, Johnson sent him a Texas-grown turkey with an extravagantly friendly letter. The president said he appreciated it and thanked him for his gift and the lovely note, but there was no follow-up. According to Clark Clifford, at the time Truman's White House counsel, the new president was fond of LBJ. They were similar in some ways, both coming from farming communities, both "pragmatic liberals from a populist tradition, seeking concrete results," and both spurning "the empty symbolism they associated with more ideological liberals."[6] But Truman had neither the personality nor the inclination to be a father figure to anyone except his daughter, Margaret.

In any case, Truman was too liberal for most Texans. In 1946 Texas voters elected Beaufort Jester, a conservative Democrat, to succeed the retiring Coke Stevenson as governor. Jester was a law-and-order man who supported bills in the Texas legislature to prevent strikes in public utilities and to exempt workers from having to join a union as a precondition of work (a "right to work" law). He also took the lead in rallying other southern governors in their opposition to Truman's civil rights programs. Jester's regime confirmed Lyndon's sense that he would have to move right if he wanted to survive politically. As Allan Shivers, governor of Texas from 1949 to 1957, noted: "Johnson began to take that turn because he saw that shift in power from the Roosevelt era on to a more conservative approach to politics."[7]

Signaling the change was Johnson's vote for the Taft-Hartley Act in 1947. Introduced as retaliation against unions following a wave of crippling nationwide strikes, this measure banned the closed shop, allowed employers to sue unions for broken contracts or damages inflicted during strikes, authorized a government-imposed cooling-off period of eighty days for any strike imperiling national health or safety, compelled unions to publish their financial statements, and required union leaders to swear that they were not members of the Communist Party. After twelve years of riding high under the Wagner Act, organized labor would now be on the defensive.

Liberals, radicals, union leaders, and union members were all dismayed at the harsh new law. Sam Rayburn, who feared unions had become too powerful, believed it was too punitive. But Johnson supported it and voted with the majority of House members to override Truman's veto of the measure in June 1947.

Clearly, an antiunion position was a political winner at this point. Whether as part of the South or the West, Texas was a freewheeling, individualistic state. Still dependent on the extractive industries and agriculture, it lacked the large semiskilled factory workforce that formed the backbone of organized labor. The Depression and the New Deal had made Texans more liberal, but now that the great economic crisis was past, they had reverted to their normal suspicion of "labor agitators." But in truth Johnson may have favored the Taft-Hartley Act for more than politically expedient reasons. He was now a member of the business class and had become comfortable financially. Unions threatened his own financial standing. An instance of this occurred at the end of 1945, when the Communications Workers of America called a strike against KTBC. Johnson feared that strikers would damage the expensive transmission equipment at the radio station, as they had at other places in Texas on similar occasions. To prevent sabotage, he called for help from friends who had just returned from the war, including J. J. (Jake) Pickle; Merrill Connally, younger brother of John; and Joe Kilgore, a decorated combat pilot and later congressman. Wearing their uniforms and carrying revolvers, these veterans guarded the station until the threat was over and then stayed on to become active in Johnson's campaign organization in the 1948 Senate race.

Johnson's stand against Truman's progressive civil rights program also earned him liberal condemnation during the late forties. In 1948, when Truman asked Congress for federal legislation against lynching, repeal of the discriminatory poll tax, and for a Fair Employment Practices Commission, Johnson argued that the proposals usurped state powers and should be rejected. Yet ultimately it was Johnson's Taft-Hartley stand that, in the eyes of liberals, located him as a conservative on the political spectrum during these early postwar years and for long after most people had forgotten what the law was. "I think that this vote on Taft-Hartley," declared Hank Brown, a Texas labor leader, "hurt him all through his lifetime. Ever since then, whenever people were evaluating him, as late as 1960 when he was vying for the presidency, the one thing that people would always use against him when they lacked anything else was that he was one of those that gutted us in 1947."[8]

And yet in the milieu of Texas politics in the late 1940s Johnson was a liberal—a pragmatic liberal. However skeptical of unions, his drift rightward was tempered by his continued disapproval of large corporations and entrenched business interests. "We ought to call them PPP," he said of one such group: "Powerful petroleum, powerful power companies, and powerful packers."[9] He also continued to defend activist government. In 1946 he proposed a twelve-point farm program that included the electrification of every farm, an all-embracing conservation program, low farm interest rates, the continuation of government-sponsored crop insurance, continuation of the school lunch program, an honest appraisal of crop distribution problems, and an all-weather road to every farm. LBJ also championed all but the most radical welfare programs and favored liberal positions such as higher old-age pensions, conservation legislation, and international control of atomic energy.

Johnson never lost his faith in education as the way to elevate the economic and social standing of the people or ceased to believe that the government must intervene to make sure this advancement took place. When the Senate in 1948 considered a bill to subsidize the salaries of public school teachers, Johnson was very vocal in his support, although Texas big business opposed it for fear that the federal government would insist on too much control of local schools. "The same folks who are screaming federal control today," Johnson said in July 1948, "screamed state control a few years ago when Jim Ferguson* proposed state aid to the little red schoolhouse. Jim put it across and called it the egalitarian principle. That very same principle is used in federal aid."[10]

Johnson was also concerned about public health, particularly universal access to health care facilities. For him this meant making rural practice more attractive to physicians who would otherwise be lured to wealthy urban areas. "Let us have the courage to spend but a small fraction of war's cost in order that men may live a fuller, more complete life," he said in support of a 1946 public health bill.[11]

In 1946 the Texas regulars put up another, stronger candidate against Johnson in the primary election. A fiercely antiunion District Court judge, Hardy Hollers, attacked Johnson wherever he seemed vulnerable. Hollers dismissed Johnson's role in the electrification of rural homes. He ridiculed Johnson's war record, claiming that *he* was the true veteran. One of Hollers's more damaging charges was that Johnson had done little as a congressman, had in fact not sponsored one significant national bill in his nine years in the House.

But the most serious of Hollers's charges was that Lyndon had enriched himself in office, an accusation made more believable by Johnson's recently changed financial status. Jake Pickle remembers that Johnson complained that his opponents did not dispute his regard for the voters or his compassion; what they stressed was that he had gotten rich

---

*"Farmer Jim" Ferguson was governor of Texas from 1914 to 1917. A populist, he was particularly anxious to improve rural education.

in office.[12] Johnson offered evidence that he said disproved the allegations, including Lady Bird's business records, and an itemization of his own assets. During the campaign he invited one audience to come up to the speaker's platform and look at his personal records. It is not clear whether the voters believed him about his finances, but in the end he defeated Hollers, seven to three.

This election, however, marked a turning point. For the rest of his life Johnson would be on the defensive about the source of his fortune. His reputation as a selfless tribune of the people would be permanently tarnished by the rumors that were never, even after his death, laid to rest. Lady Bird called it a watershed. "It was the first time we had ugly things said about us," she said in an interview. "We ceased to be the young shining knight."[13]

By 1946 the United States faced difficult foreign policy decisions. Axis defeat had left two superpowers dominant in the world, each representing different political and economic principles, each convinced of its own virtue, and each suspicious of the other's intentions. Though history would confirm the superior humanity and staying power of democratic capitalism, the struggle would take an enormous toll of mankind's energies for more than forty years. What made the Cold War so worrisome was that unlike all previous troubled eras, the very existence of civilization seemed at stake. If the two superpowers failed to keep their suspicions and fears in check, nuclear weapons could incinerate the bulk of mankind and eradicate the achievements of millennia. Millions around the world hoped that the United Nations would serve as an agent of international harmony and collective security, but few realists believed that it would be able to settle the deep issues between the United States and the Soviet Union.

The Cold War was a divisive force in postwar America. Many who thought the Soviet Union heroic in its struggle against Hitler and had favored American-Soviet cooperation during World War II now believed, according to 1946 polls, that the USSR was no longer to be trusted. Its domination of Poland, Hungary, Czechoslovakia, and other countries in its sphere of influence expressed expansionist designs and its intention of eventually taking over the entire world. While worrying about Soviet aggression abroad, many Americans also feared Communist inroads at home and supported measures to uncover and repress pro-Soviet and Marxist views. A portion of the liberal community, accepting the necessity for coexistence with the Communist nations and unimpressed by the likelihood of Communist internal subversion, deplored the postwar Red scare. But many Democratic voters, including Catholics, Southerners, and reformed leftists, felt as threatened as the most rock-ribbed Republicans. President Harry Truman was a "Cold War liberal," who, partly to ward off attacks by Republicans, promised to rid the government of Communists and "fellow travelers." Truman feared repression of free speech and dissent, but his Federal Employee Loyalty Program and his prosecution of top American Communist Party leaders for advocating violent overthrow of the American government encouraged the panicky response to the supposed Communist internal menace.

Truman's anti-Communist foreign policies were driven by a succession of crises. In 1946 civil war between the pro-American Nationalists and the Soviet-supported Communists engulfed China. The latter group, under Mao Tse-tung, soon had the upper hand, and it seemed likely that the most populous nation on earth would shortly join the world Communist camp. Then, in early 1947, the new secretary of state, George Marshall, learned that Britain, still not recovered from the war and in serious economic difficulties, intended to abandon its support of Western interests in Greece and Turkey where Communist pressures, internal or external, threatened to ensure Soviet dominance. To check Communist advance in the two Mediterranean nations, Truman proposed four hundred million dollars in aid. In his message of March 12, 1947, he announced that the United States would protect the Free World against Communist aggressors in Europe. In what came to called the Truman Doctrine, he declared that America would "support free peoples who are resisting attempted subjugation by armed minorities or by outside pressures."[14]

Lyndon Johnson, his rightward drift in domestic affairs notwithstanding, was still an internationalist. He supported the Truman Doctrine and helped push the appropriation through the House over the opposition of the isolationist bloc. His speech on the House floor arguing for adoption of the Truman Doctrine was a rerun of the debates preceding World War II and another precursor of the arguments he would use to defend his policies in Vietnam. He personally wanted to avoid war, he said, but the issue was one of "calculated risks."

Whether Communist or Fascist, or simply a pistol-packing racketeer [he declared], the one thing a bully fully understands is force, and the one thing he fears is courage. In making this assertion, I disavow the demagoguery of a jingo. I repudiate the tactics of a warmonger. I want peace. But human experience teaches me that if I let a bully of my community make me travel back streets to avoid a fight, I merely postpone the evil day. Soon he will try to chase me out of my house. We have fought two world wars because of our failure to take a position in time. . . .[15]

Johnson also supported the Marshall Plan to prop up the devastated economies of France, Germany, Italy, and other West European nations, to overcome the despair and disillusionment that played into Communist hands. He was not deterred by the enormous seventeen-billion-dollar tab. It was sensible to "expend money on peace," he declared. "With it, there was hope, not certainty, without it, there was no hope."[16] Massive aid to Western Europe would "keep Stalin from overrunning the world."[17]

It was in this second session of the 80th Congress that Johnson felt that time was really running out for his career. He had been in the House ten years and was no longer advancing politically; in fact, he seemed to be slipping. He was now actually less well known by his fellow House members than in the days when he was FDR's protégé. His pal Warren Magnuson had already become a senator, and several other members of the Texas delegation were moving faster than he toward important committee chairmanships. The House Committee on Naval Affairs had been merged with the Military Affairs Committee into the Armed Services Committee in 1946. Carl Vinson, a friend, would be the new chairman, but the committee also consisted of six Democratic members with more seniority than Johnson; he would no longer rank third, but ninth. On top of this, in 1946 the Republicans won a majority in the House for the first time since 1928. Even assuming restored Democratic control, to become chairman of Armed Services himself might take another ten years. The seniority system was too fixed to hope for anything sooner.

Hovering over these political ponderings was the fear of mortality. Heart disease ran in Johnson's family and had killed its victims at relatively young ages. His father had died twelve days after his sixtieth birthday; his Uncle George died at fifty-seven; and his Uncle Tom, still alive at sixty-five, had already suffered two heart attacks. "I'm not gonna live to be but sixty," Johnson would intone mournfully. When friends suggested that if he stayed in the House he might eventually be Speaker, he responded: "Too slow. Too slow."[18]

The family legend that his grandfather had predicted his new grandson would be a senator also affected his mood. According to the family album compiled by Rebekah, Sam Ealy Sr. had actually written that he had "a mighty fine grandson, smart as you find them," and that he expected him to "be United States Senator before he is forty."[19] That expectation haunted him as he neared his fortieth birthday in 1948.

Fortunately, 1948 was a Senate election year in Texas, and Johnson would get another opportunity to run. Since this was a regular election, by Texas law he would have to give up his safe House seat to try for the higher position. Pappy O'Daniel, whose term was ending in 1948, had become a figure of ridicule in both Washington and Texas for his attacks on Democratic leaders, for his isolationism, and for his obsession with a Communist conspiracy in the United States extreme even for those times. His biggest fans, the rural voters who used to cheer him without reservation, were now pelting him with rotten eggs and tomatoes. Johnson would probably have little difficulty this time in beating O'Daniel in the primary should Pappy decide to run.

But the other side of the ledger was much more discouraging. According to the polls, if either popular governor Beaufort Jester or former governor Coke Stevenson decided to try for the Senate, Johnson would be at a disadvantage. Though Stevenson claimed he had no desire to be a senator and was "not fitted for the Washington pattern,"[20] on January 1, 1948, he announced during a Cotton Bowl game break that he intended to run for senator.

Meanwhile, Johnson was agonizing over his own decision. He later told Doris Kearns that "at first I just could not bear the thought of losing everything."[21] Fearing defeat in the Senate race and feeling dissatisfied with his career and his prospects in the House, he thought he might just leave Washington altogether. For a time he fantasized that he would go back to teaching while his wife continued to run the radio station, and told supporters that he would announce his retirement early in 1948.

Coke Robert Stevenson, his rival, named for a Confederate veteran who helped "redeem" Texas from the Scalawags and Carpetbaggers during Reconstruction, was born in a log cabin in West-Central Texas in 1888. So extreme was his childhood poverty that he did not have enough clothes to "dust a fiddle,"[22] and he dug irrigation ditches at age ten and worked as a cowhand at twelve to earn money for his family. In 1913, through self-study, Stevenson passed the state bar examination and hung up his lawyer's shingle. He soon owned an investment company, a hardware company, and a cattle loan firm, and became president of a hotel and of a bank. His political career followed the same surging pattern. After a term as a county judge, he served in the Texas House and became Speaker in 1933. He was elected lieutenant governor in 1938, and when Pappy O'Daniel went to Washington in 1941, Stevenson became governor.

Opponents called him "Calculating Coke" because he approached everything with the utmost premeditation, unwilling to move until he had figured out all the angles. Stevenson promised to be a daunting opponent. A laconic cowboy type whose personality appealed to Texans, he had balanced the state's books during his tenure as governor, and Texas now enjoyed a cash surplus. To run against him, as Jake Pickle noted, was "a very tricky thing to do." With money piling up in the state treasury, Stevenson could "be the taciturn, wise, careful, prudent, successful public servant. . . . Coke was a hard campaigner to beat because he'd been in the governor's office just riding the waves."[23] Stevenson, moreover, was known all over Texas; Johnson counted in only one congressional district.

There was also the matter of ideology. LBJ was still associated with the New Deal, newspapers referring to him as a Roosevelt favorite, and Texas was demonstrably tired of progressive reform. Stevenson's conservative credentials were impeccable. While governor he had appointed right-wing regents to the state university, favored segregated schools, and was dedicated to "the complete destruction of the communist movement in this country."[24]

Johnson's hopes were raised shortly after Stevenson's announcement, however, by the entrance into the primary of another conservative, George E. B. Peddy, a fifty-six-year-old Houston lawyer and former state legislator. Peddy and Stevenson held similar negative opinions about Truman's proposed civil rights legislation. Peddy would certainly drain off some of Stevenson's votes in conservative East Texas. Even if Stevenson beat all the other candidates, which some polls said was likely, he might not get a majority in the primary, and a runoff would have to be held.

A Belden poll in March 1948 showing Stevenson's initial lead over Johnson down from four to one to three to one was encouraging, as was another Belden poll revealing that congressional experience was preferred over gubernatorial experience in electing a senator. This second survey clearly favored Johnson, but the reality was that he would lose to Stevenson unless everything broke in his favor.

Johnson agonized about whether to run until his staff and his friends could no longer stand the strain. To end the indecision, they held a meeting on May 11 in LBJ's backyard in Austin. There the arguments flew back and forth, with Johnson providing all of the negatives. "We talked and talked," said one of the participants, "trying to prove to him that he could beat Stevenson. We taunted him; we sweet-talked him. We tried every argument any of us could think of."[25] Johnson could not be persuaded and finally went to bed.

The next day, another group came to see Johnson. These were people he had known from his National Youth Administration days and his 1941 campaign, many of whom were still working for the government.

"They told me," reminisced Johnson, "I had been the cause of their taking an interest in public affairs and working for better government. They said that gave me a certain obligation toward them. They asked me, quietly and without any argument, to change my mind about the Senate race."[26] Encouraged by his old associates, Johnson telephoned a few Texas newspaper editors, all of whom said they would support him if he ran. A few warned, however, that he probably could not defeat Stevenson. "Well," Johnson remembered thinking, "it's probably the easiest way to end my career."[27]

Johnson finally announced his candidacy at a news conference in the penthouse of the Driskill Hotel. He would have been a senator seven years earlier if it had been an honest election, he told the reporters, and he would have run the following year if the war had not intervened. On May 22, dressed all in white, Johnson made his first campaign speech, from the bandstand in Woolridge Park in Austin. Tossing his expensive Stetson in the air, he announced: "I throw my hat in the ring." The theme of his campaign would be peace, preparedness, and progress, "three bold signposts on the road we should travel toward a better tomorrow." Under the progress heading he intended to protect the public from both "selfish labor and selfish capital," and he would promote price supports, blacktop roads, electrified homes, and soil and water conservation for farmers; higher teachers' salaries; cost of living adjustments in old age assistance; and more hospitals, doctors, and nurses. These programs and ideas were the residues of the New Deal that most Texans still generally supported. But Johnson also tried to accommodate the postwar conservative mood in Texas. He endorsed the Taft-Hartley Act with "utmost enthusiasm," denounced many of the social programs he would later incorporate into his Great Society, and proclaimed his support for states' rights, the age-old southern shibboleth to protect Dixie's minority status in the nation. White Southerners deeply resented Truman's attempt to reverse racial traditions and attitudes spanning many generations, and Johnson played to their prejudices. He had never allied himself with the congressional segregationist bloc, but he now declared Truman's plan a "farce and a sham—an effort to set up a police state in the guise of liberty." He had voted against appropriations for the Fair Employment Practices Commission, he told his audience, to protect personal liberty. "If a man can tell you whom you must hire," explained Johnson, "he can tell you whom you can't hire."[28]

The speech was received without great enthusiasm from the audience and was barely mentioned in the newspapers. Johnson recognized that something dramatic was needed to juice up the campaign.

Even before he announced for the Senate, Johnson had been feeling ill and complaining about the abdominal pains and nausea that had usually accompanied kidney stones in the past. By the time he made his opening campaign speech, he needed painkillers to get through the evening. Most of his friends and staff knew that he often felt ill in times of stress or crisis and attributed his current malaise to the strain of opening his campaign. But his pains were not psychosomatic; they were getting worse, and soon he was running a fever. Undaunted, he continued to drive around the Texas panhandle making campaign speeches, dripping with perspiration from his fevers and doubled up with pain between his appearances before his public.

He refused to see a doctor, knowing in advance that they would prescribe an operation to remove the stone. Recovery time for the procedure could be six weeks and Johnson would be out of action for most of the campaign, almost certainly assuring his defeat and the end of his political career. But it finally became clear even to the stubborn candidate that he could not go on, and he was hospitalized in Dallas. Now Johnson was concerned about telling the press. Connally must tell reporters that he was in the hospital overnight for tests and would be out the next day, he insisted. "That's ridiculous," Connally exclaimed. "You can't have a candidate for the United States Senate . . . enter the hospital and interrupt his schedule and not tell the press."[29] Connally told the newspapers the truth. Johnson threatened to quit the campaign and call the press right then and there to tell them. Furious at his protégé, he gave him the silent treatment for a time.

Lady Bird calmed her husband down. There was a possibility that an operation might not prove necessary. Dr. Gershom J. Thompson, the head of urology at the Mayo Clinic in Rochester, Minnesota, was successfully removing urethral stones through cystoscopic manipulation, shortening the recovery time considerably. Besides, Dr. James Cain, Alvin Wirtz's son-in-law and an old Austin friend, was at Mayo and would help with the procedures. The famous woman pilot Jacqueline Cochran had been apprised of the situation by Johnson's friends and was willing to fly Johnson to Minnesota in her Lockheed Electra.

At first the Mayo doctors tried to dislodge the stone by driving Johnson over bumpy roads. When that failed, they used the cystoscope technique and were successful. Though restless and contentious, Johnson recovered quickly and left Rochester to return to the campaign in a week. The medical staff was as relieved as Johnson at his departure.

Johnson now had to make up for two weeks of lost time. Having studied the campaign tactics of Peddy and Stevenson while his own candidate was in the hospital, Wirtz found out that neither was planning an extensive campaign or large expenditures of energy and money. Stevenson, who knew he had a solid bloc of votes, was slowly touring the state in an old car, and Peddy had scheduled few personal appearances. Johnson must make himself as visible as possible in the shortest time possible.

It was Connally who conceived of campaigning by helicopter, and it was a brilliant idea. The chopper, navigated by a skilled Bell Aircraft pilot, was nicknamed the *Johnson City Windmill,* and it caused a colossal stir as it ratcheted through the sky, "Lyndon Johnson for U.S. Senator" painted on both sides of its fuselage. As he circled a landing spot, Johnson would yell over the powerful loudspeaker, "This is Lyndon Johnson, your next United States senator, and I'll land in just a minute. I want to shake hands with all of you."[30] For people in the small towns of Texas who had never before encountered a helicopter or, for that matter, a candidate for U.S. senator, this was an unforgettable sight.

Johnson made good use of his helicopter, scheduling as many as thirty stops a day. At places too small to alight, where a resident had written a letter to the congressman, Johnson would broadcast a standard spiel from the air, greeting his correspondent by name and apologizing for not being able to land. But he would be certain to add: "I'm up here thinking of you and appreciate your kind letter and comments. I just want you to be sure and tell your friends to vote for me at election time."[31] Sometimes he would make unscheduled landings, particularly where he saw groups of men working, or places where the press might be.

Unfortunately, the substance of the campaign was not as impressive as its trimmings. Aside from who was more anti-Communist and whether Johnson had missed three crucial House votes on HUAC, public issues were ignored. Johnson's "peace, preparedness, and progress" was a rather conventional and uninspired program, but Stevenson, who had said in his announcement for the Senate that he would run solely on his record, seemed to take no public positions at all. One issue that surfaced was Johnson's vote for the Taft-Hartley Act. On June 22, the Texas American Federation of Labor, holding its annual convention at Fort Worth, endorsed Coke Stevenson. Johnson immediately charged that Texas labor had made a secret deal with the former governor: a senatorial endorsement for a promise to vote for repeal of the law. Calculating that the conservative Stevenson was actually more antilabor than he, he challenged Stevenson to make his true position public. Stevenson was reluctant to take a public stand on Taft-Hartley. He privately supported it, but he realized that the labor vote was valuable and did not want to antagonize it. He said nothing, and Lyndon continued to hammer away on his opponent's refusal to commit himself.

By the end of May, political pulse-takers generally conceded that the race was really between Stevenson and Johnson. Stevenson attacked Johnson on his support of federal aid to education, then considered a fairly radical notion, but Johnson fought back. "A man who would oppose federal aid," he said, "would hamstring our great colleges . . . our leading universities and most of our fine religious institutions, all of which, for years, have participated in cooperative federal aid programs."[32] Johnson also endorsed civil rights in principle. When asked by liberal Galveston banker Walter Hall about his feelings toward civil rights, Johnson replied: "Whatever is necessary to see that a human being, black or white, gets educated or gets the vote, that's got to be done."[33] Stevenson coupled Johnson with left-wing congressman "Vito Marcantonio of the Harlem District," claiming that they voted together on many issues. Capitalizing on mounting anti-Communist hysteria, each side tried to brand his opponent a friend of the Reds.

In reality, not all of labor or the left was opposed to Johnson. All through the campaign he received contributions from liberals in Washington and New York. Whatever Johnson felt he had to say on the stump, and notwithstanding his vote for Taft-Hartley, liberals knew that Stevenson, in fact, was far more conservative on the issues than LBJ. One of Lyndon's advisers told him to take heart, since many actual trade union members were for him even if some of their leaders were not.

July 24 was primary day, and when it was over, none of the candidates was pleased. Stevenson, with 477,077 votes, received 40 percent of the total; Johnson got 405,617, or 34 percent; and Peddy took 20 percent, with 237,195. The two leading candidates would now have to face another month of campaigning in the hot Texas summer.

Up for grabs, obviously, were Peddy's 237,195 supporters, and the Johnson strategists immediately targeted them for capture. They also decided to go after the cities, where Johnson had done poorly, winning only Austin. Here they would not be able to use the helicopter, an effective weapon in rural areas but slower than a regular plane in getting from city to city.

Though the runoff was only one month away, both candidates flew to Washington the day after the election. LBJ came to attend President Truman's "Turnip Day" congressional session,[†] called ostensibly to remedy the inaction of the "do-nothing" 80th Congress but actually to embarrass

---

†Truman applied this label to the special session of the conservative Congress that he called during the 1948 presidential campaign. The term, he said, applied to July 26, which in his home state of Missouri was called Turnip Day. Expecting the Republican-dominated Congress to reject his program, he hoped to embarrass his opponents—and did.

the Republicans. Stevenson made the trip to counter his image as a Texas provincial. To make up for his perceived deficiencies in foreign policy, he met with Secretary of Defense James Forrestal; Robert Lovett of the State Department; and Texas senator Tom Connally, chairman of the Committee on Foreign Relations. LBJ made sure that he conferred with all the people Stevenson did and, in addition, got Forrestal to promise new defense contracts to Consolidated Aircraft in Fort Worth, a move expected to expand the Fort Worth workforce by three thousand workers.

Before returning home, Stevenson held a press conference. He was used to Texas reporters who never asked embarrassing questions, but now he was up against some tough-minded types, including Drew Pearson's assistant Jack Anderson, a man well disposed to Johnson. Anderson mentioned that he had read through the files carefully and had found no statement by Stevenson on the Taft-Hartley Act. "A lot of Texans still say they don't know where you stand on the act, Governor," Anderson noted. Stevenson ducked and weaved, claiming that without his notes on what he had said at home on the subject he could not answer. Pearson followed this grilling with a column that reported that "Ex-Governor Coke Stevenson of Texas . . . on a recent trip to Washington evaded more issues and dodged more questions than any recent performer in a city noted for question dodging."[34] Though Stevenson later publicly supported the controversial labor bill, his stand got buried in all the dirt flying back and forth between the candidates.

As the runoff neared, the Texas newspapers weighed in. The pro-Stevenson *Dallas News* said that Johnson had tried to be "all things to all men," and listed some of the "diverse political personalities" in LBJ's camp, including various New Dealers, anti–New Dealers, left-wingers, business moguls, and corporation lawyers. It accused him of being the "New Dealingest New Dealer around Washington" at one time and of now trumpeting his "support of the Taft-Hartley Act. . . ."[35] Charles Marsh's *Austin American* countered by reviewing Stevenson's limited background and experience. The former governor failed to understand that the two world wars had introduced "new complexities in American life." His "devotion to his ingrained philosophy" had cut him off from recent ideas and produced a "sketchy and inadequate contact with national affairs and world conditions." In spite of Stevenson's record of public service, he had been "denied the training and background to meet the acute problems facing Congress in the world of today. . . ."[36]

The runoff day was Saturday, August 28, and by that evening the Texas Election Bureau was issuing reports of an extraordinary neck-and-neck race in which the differences were measured in only hundreds or even scores of votes. First Stevenson was ahead by a few hundred votes, then Johnson, then Stevenson again. On Monday, August 30, Stevenson was up a minuscule 119 votes. But 400 ballots were still out. By September 2, Stevenson seemed to be leading by 351 votes. But there were still some counties in Southwest Texas, near the Mexican border, where votes were still being certified.

Three of these counties—Jim Wells, Zapata, and Duval—were controlled by political boss George ("Duke of Duval") Parr, who always delivered lopsided vote totals for his candidates. Parr's father had regularly laughed off charges that he bribed Mexican Americans to vote for the family political machine. George himself had spent almost ten months in jail for income tax evasion, bribery, and the extortion of protection money. He had no particular political convictions. It was power and patronage that concerned him.

Parr was still angry at Stevenson for turning down a patronage request when he was governor, and when the votes in Parr's counties finally came in, they included the correction of a "mistake" from a ballot box in Alice, Duval County, in Precinct 13, that shifted 200 votes from Stevenson to Johnson. These votes put Johnson over the top. When the dust had cleared, the Texas State Democratic convention declared that Johnson had won the primary by 87 votes.

It is impossible to penetrate through the layers of truths, half-truths, and lies to determine what really happened in Duval. To this day the facts remain murky. It does seem clear, however, that both sides committed fraud. The number of votes stolen by the Stevenson forces has been glossed over in most biographies of Johnson. But they were substantial. Sam Houston Johnson says that LBJ's friends were warned in advance about their opponents' plan to use a "graveyard vote."[37] Others had similar evidence about Stevenson's hanky-panky. The fact that Johnson actually ended up with more votes than Stevenson is attributable more to luck than to anything else. So many votes were up for grabs that even a skilled mathematician in this precomputer age would have had trouble deciding how many actual votes to steal.

Stevenson challenged the results. He could have made an appeal to the Texas Supreme Court, which would then have impounded all the ballots. Instead, he contacted an old friend, the conservative federal judge T. Whitfield Davidson, who promptly issued an injunction to keep Johnson's name off the November ballot and ordered U.S. commissioners to investigate election fraud in the three suspect counties. Johnson's lawyers, headed by ex-governor Allred, countercharged that election irregularities had taken place in Brown, Dallas, Galveston, Harris, and Jack Counties, which, if corrected, would substantially decrease Stevenson's vote. They cited 480 votes in Stevenson's favor as erroneous in Brown County alone. Judge Davidson suggested they go fifty-fifty and put both men's names on the fall general election ballot, but Johnson would not accept this compromise.

At this point, citing *"prima facie* showing of fraud," Judge Davidson ordered an immediate investigation of the vote in Parr's counties. Luis Salas, election judge for Box 13, admitted that the votes had been tampered with, and some of the evidence was already missing. There were obviously more revelations to come.

Just at the moment when Johnson's political future seemed gloomiest, he got another break. His friend Washington lawyer Abe Fortas was in Dallas at that very moment working on an antitrust case. Though Fortas had the flu and was very busy, he came to Fort Worth, where Johnson and his supporters briefed him about the situation. Since time was extremely short, Fortas said, they should ask the Circuit Court for a simple stay of the injunction and take the chance of losing there. Then, if they lost in the Circuit Court, they could take it to the U.S. Supreme Court, where it would be heard by Justice Hugo Black, a liberal and the senior justice on the Court for the area that included Texas.

The plan worked. Allred went to New Orleans, to the Fifth Circuit Court of Appeals, where Judge J. C. Hutcheson refused to dismiss Davidson's restraining order on the grounds that he, as an individual, had no right to overrule another judge. The next step was Black, who set a hearing for September 28, permitting Stevenson enough time to gather his legal team together.

Johnson fortunately had the support of the national Democratic leadership. Truman's attorney general, Tom Clark, first considered a federal investigation and then decided that his office had no authority to check returns in a state election. The Texas senatorial contest was, however, important to Truman, who was seeking election in 1948 for president in his own right. Many liberals had deserted him for Henry A. Wallace, running on the Progressive Party ticket. States rights' Democrats would vote for Strom Thurmond of South Carolina on the ticket of the new Dixiecrat Party, organized on July 14. Stevenson, of course, was an ideological Dixiecrat and was supported by Dixiecrat loyalists. Though skeptical of Johnson personally, Truman considered LBJ, a middle-of-the road Democrat, crucial in holding Texas in the Democratic column in the November election.

In the thick of this mess, Truman's campaign train pulled into Texas. Johnson climbed aboard to show his support for the president, and Truman, reciprocating, with Lyndon at his side, told the crowds at all the whistle-stop towns to vote for Johnson for senator. In between the trainside rallies, LBJ filled Truman in on how the primary dispute was proceeding.

Undoubtedly influence was brought to bear on Black. Tommy Corcoran and Attorney General Tom Clark probably spoke to the justice. Perhaps the early friendly connections between Congressman Johnson and Senator Black played their part. On September 28 Justice Black decided in favor of Johnson. In his opinion he sharply criticized Judge Davidson. "It would be a drastic break with the past," Black said, "which I can't believe Congress ever intended to permit, for a federal judge to go into the business of conducting what is to every intent and purpose a contest of an election in the state."[38] When Stevenson petitioned the Supreme Court to reconsider Black's stay of the injunction, it refused. Johnson was now the official Democratic candidate for senator.

In those days of a Democratic "Solid South," the fall general election was a formality. An irate Stevenson threw his support to Republican oilman George Porter a few days after Black's ruling, calling Johnson the "counterfeit nominee."[39] But Johnson won by better than two to one in November, carrying all but nine counties, mostly those that normally voted Republican. At the age of forty and a few months, Johnson was U.S. senator-elect from Texas.

How much did Johnson actually know about what had gone on during the vote counting? His attorney in Austin, Don Thomas, told Fortas's biographer Bruce Allen Murphy that LBJ "knew less about the facts of the election than anyone." Thomas maintained that "till the day he died he never *wanted* to know. He was really afraid someone did something wrong."[40] But the last word on who really won the 1948 primary was summed up by a Johnson campaign manager the day the results were announced: "Well, they were stealing in East Texas," drawled the Johnson man. "We were stealing in South Texas. So God only knows who really won the election. . . . But today, God was on our side by eighty-seven votes."[41] Unfortunately God exacted a price: Hereafter LBJ would be known to the ill-disposed as "Landslide Lyndon."

CHAPTER 9

Freshman Senator

O N JANUARY 3, 1949, realizing his lifelong dream, Lyndon Johnson
was sworn in as a U.S. senator. In 1952 he would become party
whip, two years later Senate minority leader, and two years after that,
Senate majority leader. Barely surviving election, his political morale
touching rock bottom the previous year, Johnson would travel farther
and faster than almost any politician on record. Six of his fellow freshmen Senate Democrats—Hubert Humphrey of Minnesota, Estes Kefauver of Tennessee, Paul Douglas of Illinois, Clinton Anderson of New Mexico, Russell Long of Louisiana, and Robert S. Kerr of Oklahoma—were
exceptionally talented leaders and would themselves have extraordinary
careers. But none ever achieved as much in the Senate as Johnson.

To leap past these able men required the political skills Lyndon had
been honing for years. Fortunately, these were more easily put to work in
the Senate, with 96 members,* than in the House, with 435. Fortunately, too, his election to the Senate lifted him out of the depression
and lethargy that characterized his last term in the House. Happily, as
well, he no longer had to worry about money, thanks to the success of his
wife's Texas broadcasting company. And to cap it all, with the birth of
their second daughter, Luci Baines, in 1947, the Johnson family was
complete. Now all that formidable Johnson energy and ambition could
again be rallied to further his political career.

---

*At this time there were only forty-eight states; Hawaii and Alaska were still territories.

His immediate task was to expand and solidify his Texas base so he could make the Senate a job for life. "Almost exactly one-half of the people who voted in the Democratic primary," Johnson said, "didn't want me for their senator. My big job is to get them to change their minds about me."[1] This was a complicated job involving not only larger numbers of people but also often diametrically opposing interests on opposite ends of the huge area that made up his home state.

To handle the geometrical increase in phone calls and letters, Johnson needed a larger staff working harder than ever. The Senate sergeant at arms usually awarded freshman senators three-room suites; the four-room suites were reserved for senior members. Johnson was stuck with a three-roomer, but LBJ managed to talk Senator Carl Hayden, head of the Rules and Administration Committee, into assigning him another, detached room elsewhere in the Senate Office Building. Freshmen usually had three telephone lines; Johnson wangled a fourth. Soon his staff of twenty, presided over by John Connally, was working full blast, handling 70 visitors, 650 letters, and 500 telephone calls a day.

As usual, Johnson drove his staff hard. His personal secretary, Mary Rather, rode to the Capitol every morning with him. "He'd pick me up on Connecticut Avenue," she later said, "and by the time . . . we reached the office he had outlined a whole day's work for me and had given me orders for the others that kept them jumping all day long, too."[2]

As he had in the House, LBJ kept himself informed on all issues that affected his constituents. This required cultivating the senators who mattered and learning how the upper chamber worked and who controlled it. It is unclear whether national power was his goal when he first entered the Senate, but he was careful to court the senior Republicans and Southern Democrats who made up the loose conservative coalition that had been informally created in opposition to FDR's 1937 Court-packing plan. By 1949 these men held the real power in the upper chamber. Johnson had to ingratiate himself with these leaders, particularly his southern colleagues, or remain ineffectual. But he also had to avoid a strictly regional reputation that could limit his ability to rise.

As we saw, Johnson was not comfortable with the South's regressive racial position. He accepted Jim Crow and black disfranchisement only as long as it was politically unavoidable. In any case, he made sure that while he preserved cordial relations with the southern bloc, he was still his own man. Archliberal Hubert Humphrey said that Johnson was "a Texan, enjoying the benefits of southern hospitality, southern power, southern support, but [he] carefully avoided the liabilities of being clearly labeled a southerner."[3] Humphrey admitted that he and his liberal friends were "very suspicious" of Johnson at the beginning of his Senate career. But the first impression did not last. They soon came to feel that "he was a lot more liberal than he ever acted."[4] Truman himself, though he chafed at Johnson's refusal to support many of his domestic programs, told Estes Kefauver that he was glad that he "and Lyndon are not permanently lined up with that [southern] crowd."[5] Truman enjoyed Senator Johnson's company and made him one of the small group of Democratic leaders he invited on all-day Potomac River cruises on the presidential yacht. There the eight or so pols in the usual party played poker—never LBJ's favorite game—talked politics, and reminisced about people and past conventions.

Though now in the Senate, Johnson continued to cultivate his connections in the House. Sam Rayburn was now Speaker, and he and Johnson maintained their close relationship. If LBJ did not appear at the "Board of Education" social hour by 5:00 P.M., Rayburn would call his office and, without identifying himself, snap, "Tell Lyndon I'm waiting for him,"[6] and hang up.

But Johnson knew he also needed a powerful patron in his own wing of the Capitol. He rejected the Senate majority leader Scott W. Lucas of Illinois as too ineffectual, an estimate proven correct when Lucas was defeated for reelection to the Senate in 1950. With his usual sure political instinct, Johnson decided that the best bet was the influential Richard B. Russell of Georgia. Though the junior senator from that state, Russell was leader of the southern bloc, composed of Senate members from the eleven states of the former Confederacy. When the Democrats regained control of the Senate in 1949, Russell became the second-ranking, but actually the most powerful, member of the Senate Armed Services Committee.

Johnson realized that Russell would be courted by others and that he would have to impress him decisively and quickly. One way was to establish a working relationship with him. "I knew," Johnson admitted, "there was only one way to see Russell every day and that was to get a seat on his committee. Without that we'd most likely be passing acquaintances and nothing more."[7] Having served on the House Armed Services Committee, it seemed appropriate to ask the Senate Democratic Steering Committee leaders for an equivalent Senate assignment. They granted him his wish. His second placement was on the Interstate and Foreign Commerce Committee, an important influence on the Federal Communications Commission, the agency that regulated broadcasting. With his committee assignments secured, Johnson began the task of constructing a father-son relationship with a man whose disposition and personality were as unlike his own as any man's could be.

Richard Brevard Russell was a reserved southern patrician with impeccable manners and refined tastes who shunned publicity and self-promotion. A lifelong bachelor, he dressed somberly and worked long hours in a minimally decorated office, with no emblems of power or wealth on display. Though Johnson could not redo himself completely to win Russell's favor, he did try to subdue his flamboyance in Russell's presence. With his innate skill in appealing to older and more powerful men, Johnson made himself a conscientious and deferential disciple of Russell. "Johnson learned to observe amenities with Senator Russell," declared William Jorden, onetime assistant to the Georgia senator. He would barge right into the offices of the other senators, barely saying hello. But when he visited Russell he "always sent in a note from the outer office to say he would like to come in."[8] Sometimes Johnson's desire to cultivate Russell backfired. With no interest in sports himself, he forced himself to accompany the Georgia senator to Washington baseball games. Unfortunately, he could not relax and enjoy the game, but insisted on discussing politics through all nine innings. To avoid the painful experience, Russell soon gave up going to the ballpark.

Their shared devotion to politics bonded Johnson to Russell. As time went on, Russell became ever more conservative, and the philosophical and political positions of the two men grew farther apart. But when Johnson first came to the Senate, they held many of the same political views. Both were committed to rural progressivism and supported farmers' loans, rural electrification, and vocational education. Most important of all, they both championed a strong national defense.

Johnson established the same sort of personal relationship with Russell as he had with Mr. Sam. The Georgian had no family; the Senate was his whole life. Johnson, though married and a father, was as willing to work long and hard as his senior. Often the two men would have dinner together across the street from the Capitol when the day was done. Johnson recognized that on Sundays, with Congress adjourned and the buildings closed, Russell had nowhere to go. He came to the rescue with invitations to the Johnson home, where the lonely bachelor was always welcome for breakfast and lunch, and where he could read the Sunday newspapers. Soon Russell was eating many of his weekend meals with the Johnsons, and Lynda and Luci were calling him "Uncle Dick." "He was my mentor," Johnson told Kearns, "and I wanted to take care of him."[9]

Russell's friendship helped Johnson establish solid connections with almost a dozen other prominent southern and western Senators who held key committee positions. He worked hard to make himself useful to them, and they, in turn, appreciated Johnson's phenomenal diligence. He soon became indispensable to them.

Johnson's desire for Russell's approval and friendship was offset by his wish to keep his options open and avoid being identified too closely with the southern bloc. Thus, when Russell called together the first meeting of the Southern Caucus of the Eight-first Congress, Johnson, along with Estes Kefauver, failed to appear. Kefauver, of course, was a deep-dyed maverick, so his absence was not surprising. But Johnson's truancy puzzled his fellow Southerners. In fact, this was how Johnson chose to demonstrate the limits of his southern affiliation. Editor Michael Janeway, son of Johnson's old friend Eliot, described his action as "treading lightly."[10]

Shortly after his nonattendance at the Southern Caucus, Johnson faced another test of sectional political loyalty. This one involved civil rights and the filibuster rule.

As we saw, in 1948 Truman had proposed what for the time was a bold new civil rights program. His unforeseen election victory that November encouraged the hopes of civil rights supporters in Congress that concrete legislation could now be passed. What stood in the way was a Senate filibuster, a surefire way in the past to foil civil rights legislation. Senate Rule 22, normally adopted intact as the first order of business when the Senate convened, allowed for "cloture," limits on debate for pending legislation. But this required a two-thirds vote and did not apply to consideration of a new bill. The inability to invoke cloture for debate on the introduction of new measures and the difficulty of achieving the two-thirds vote in any case served to abort liberal legislation and every attempt to modify the southern racial regime.

When the Eighty-first Congress convened, civil rights advocates proposed that the cloture rule be modified so that only three-fifths of the Senate would be needed to prevent unlimited debate. The administration proposed additionally that cloture be applicable to debate on motions to consider a bill. But Southerners, long accustomed to obstructing legislation they did not like, were not about to give up that privilege.

The cloture controversy posed a serious dilemma for Johnson. A Senator for fewer than two months, but already ambitious to acquire national standing, he faced a decision that threatened to tie him squarely to one side or the other. He also knew he could not evade the issue, not if he wanted to continue his relationship with Russell, who emphatically opposed liberalizing the cloture rule. Johnson's strategy was to make his maiden speech on the Senate floor in opposition to cloture, pleasing his southern colleagues, yet at the same time placating the other side.

He identified the filibuster with free speech. "It is my conviction," he said, "that the right of unlimited debate here in the Senate is an essential safeguard in our American system of representative government. . . ." Yet he sought to distance himself from southern racial mores.

Perhaps no prejudice is so contagious or so dangerous [he declaimed] as the unreasoning prejudice against men because of their birth, the color of their skin, or their ancestral background. Racial prejudice is dangerous because it is a disease of the majority, endangering minority groups. . . .

For those who would keep any group in our nation in bondage, I have no sympathy or tolerance. Some may feel moved to deny this group or that the homes, the education, the employment which every American has a right to expect, but I am not one of those. My faith in my fellow man is too great to permit me to waste away my lifetime with hatred of any group.

He opposed poll taxes and lynching, he declared, but felt the *states* should take action in those matters. He pointed out that lynchings were "virtually nonexistent" in Texas and that the present governor had recommended that the state's poll tax be repealed. One way to stop prejudice was through the schools. "I do not concede to federal law an obligation which I think rightfully belongs to education and which education alone can discharge."[11]

It was a brilliant speech, covering all the points Johnson hoped to make. It certainly pleased Russell and the Southern Caucus. But despite his intentions, it pleased most of his liberal friends back home less. Though James Allred liked it, few others did. Liberal Galveston banker Walter Hall chastised him: "I'm sorry you think more of your right to talk without limit than of another man's right to vote."[12] Another wrote: "Have the courage to defend your own convictions, Mr. Johnson, and you'll gather more votes than you will by aligning yourself with the old die-hards of the South." Many blacks were furious. The Houston branch of the NAACP sent him a telegram:

THE NEGROES WHO SENT YOU TO CONGRESS ARE ASHAMED TO KNOW THAT YOU HAVE STOOD ON THE FLOOR AGAINST THEM TODAY. DO NOT FORGET THAT YOU WENT TO WASHINGTON BY A SMALL MAJORITY VOTE AND THAT WAS BECAUSE OF THE NEGRO VOTE. THERE WILL BE ANOTHER ELECTION AND WE WILL BE REMEMBERING WHAT YOU HAD TO SAY TODAY.

Johnson replied in what the Houston NAACP people thought was an inadequate manner, and a group of blacks came to Washington to protest. The visit was inconclusive, and neither side was satisfied. Other NAACP chapters condemned Johnson for his stand, and many individual black voters wrote directly to the senator. He said he was sorry to have offended them. "It has been a matter of profound regret to me," he told one correspondent, "that many Negro citizens of Texas have viewed my speech in the Senate as an affront to them. I did not and would not make a speech in that spirit."[13]

The speech reflected the split in Johnson's political personality at the time. When it came to individual rights, especially when the injustice seemed egregious, he acted as a liberal. In 1949, for example, when the local undertaker in Three Rivers, Texas, refused to handle the interment for Felix Longoria, a Mexican American soldier killed in the Philippines in World War II, Johnson intervened and arranged to have the war hero buried at Arlington National Cemetery. He and Lady Bird then attended the burial ceremony. Though bigots accused him of pandering to Hispanic voters, the senator had been truly offended by the prejudice of the funeral director. As Johnson wrote a friend, he had "just followed the dictates of [his] heart in this."[14] Clearly he was torn between his liberal personal inclinations and his need to retain his political base in Texas and impress the southern Senate power brokers.

In the end, the liberals' bid to limit southern filibustering failed, though Johnson's speech had little to do with the outcome. The same powerful combination of Southerners and northern Republican conservatives that had blocked much progressive domestic legislation managed to postpone further consideration of a civil rights bill until 1957.

Through his first senatorial term Johnson supported the southern bloc on most race issues. Two months after his anticloture speech, he voted in favor of an amendment to the District of Columbia home rule bill upholding segregation in public accommodations. The following year he joined his southern colleagues in opposing another Fair Employment Practices Commission bill under consideration in the Senate.

A firm believer in the importance of political timing, Johnson would not be able to resolve his inner division on civil rights until the midfifties, when he began to see that the "issue had reached a point" where action was necessary. Then, as majority leader, he represented a much larger and more liberal constituency and was no longer beholden to the southern satraps in the Senate.

Shadowing his first few months as senator was the threat that Coke Stevenson would ask for an investigation of the 1948 primary. This would be politically dangerous. Johnson could not afford to lose the confidence of the senators in power. Fortunately, in the summer of 1949, when the Senate Rules Committee considered Stevenson's charges, they threw them out. He had thus passed the first test. Yet the slim margin of victory in 1948 remained to haunt him in this early phase of his Senate career.

Johnson not only had to placate the Senate elders, he also had to avoid offending the powerful oil and gas companies, the dominant industries in Texas. His lack of solid ties to the major petroleum companies was partly responsible for his poor showing in 1948. But pleasing the oil and gas magnates unfortunately meant further estranging consumer-oriented liberals.

The conflict surfaced early in 1949 when Oklahoma senator Robert Kerr introduced a bill to exempt some natural gas prices from regulation by the Federal Power Commission (FPC), which, under the Natural Gas Act of 1938, had control over such prices. Kerr was a brawny teetotaling Baptist Sunday schoolteacher, born in a log cabin in Oklahoma Indian Territory. A man with a razor-sharp mind and a wicked tongue, he shared many interests with Johnson. The two men would often be observed huddled together discussing ranch problems and actually arranging cattle and horse trades. Kerr was also the founder and principal stockholder of Kerr-McGee, one of the largest gas and oil corporations in America, and was in a position to get even richer if the bill passed and prices rose, as expected. Liberals opposed the measure as inflationary and harmful to urban consumers. Columnist Doris Fleeson called the Kerr bill "pro-interest, anti-consumer legislation of the type that Democrats for twenty years have successfully identified exclusively with the GOP."[15]

Operating under the same oil-state pressures as other Texans, Sam Rayburn helped to get the Kerr measure passed in the House. Johnson tried to stay in the background, but he lobbied for the bill among his Senate colleagues; made a short, favorable speech; and generally assisted in its passage. In the end, the president vetoed it, quoting liberal freshman senator Paul Douglas's words on the economic damage it would wreak on big-city consumers. Johnson's actions, however, gratified the oil and gas people and disgusted the liberals. Douglas, however, forgave him, later saying he understood why his colleague from Texas voted the way he did. The oilmen and gasmen "were powerful and strong, and no one could rise in Texas politics . . . if they opposed them." Johnson had to struggle against "his native tendencies, his Roosevelt idealism," explained Douglas, "faced with the hard facts of power politics and economic power. . ."[16]

If the progressives were miffed by Johnson's stand on the Kerr bill, they were infuriated by his actions in the Leland Olds controversy. A passionate left-of-center supporter of tough government utility regulation, Olds was a Roosevelt appointee to the FPC, where he had saved consumers millions of dollars through utility rate reductions and was a hero to public power advocates and assorted liberals.

Since he could be counted on to take a vigorous, proconsumer approach to oil and gas pricing, the oil and gas interests sought to quash his reappointment as head of the FPC when Truman proposed it in 1949. Olds had other enemies besides the oil interests. Many members of this conservative-leaning Congress, Democrats as well as Republicans, considered Olds a holdover from the Roosevelt era and a man who had, during the 1930s, been drawn to far-left causes and organizations. Walter Jenkins later called Olds an "abrasive sort of guy" and not "an old-time patriotic American in the old day sense."[17]

Majority leader Scott Lucas knew Senate confirmation was unlikely and warned Truman not to make the reappointment. When Truman ignored Lucas's advice, Lucas asked the Commerce Committee to appoint a special subcommittee to hold confirmation hearings. Commerce Committee chairman Edwin C. Johnson of Colorado, a vehement anti-Communist and a Truman foe, appointed LBJ chairman of the subcommittee.

The pressures on Johnson to block the nomination were intense. Johnson knew that the oil and gas industry was watching him closely. Meanwhile, mail was pouring in from Texas, most of it against the nominee. At the same time, Abe Fortas, now practicing law privately in Washington, was giving Johnson behind-the-scenes advice and providing him with information and evidence detrimental to Olds.[†] It was perhaps inevitable that Johnson would oppose the nomination, but his persecution of Olds before the subcommittee resembled Joseph McCarthy's future inquisitorial tactics. "He was not just against him," recalled James Rowe, "he was saying he was a Commie. . . . He got this damn Commie thing and he ran it into the ground for no reason anybody could see . . ."[18]

During the subcommittee hearings, Johnson concentrated on Olds's service in the field of public utility regulation, stressing his own disagreement with Olds's philosophy. He himself was a friend of public power, but he considered Olds an extremist. He referred to him as one who "has pursued a meandering but relentless course toward nationalization of the nation's fundamental power industries."[19] Other witnesses Red-baited Olds's early career as editor of the radical *Federated Press*. One congressman brought to the hearings fifty-four articles that Olds had written in the 1920s attacking the churches and ridiculing "the symbols of patriotism and loyalty such as the Fourth of July." Worse than that, however, according to the congressman, the nominee had "advocated

---

[†]Fortas, earlier a lieutenant of Secretary of the Interior Harold L. Ickes, had come to dislike Olds when he opposed Ickes's attempt to gain control for his department of the government's power role.

public ownership . . . [and had] reserved applause for Lenin and Lenin's system. . . ."[20] In rebuttal, Olds admitted he had been a radical in his youth, but never a Communist. Johnson was careful to tell his committee that Olds had never been a "member of the Communist Party" and was not "disloyal to the United States."[21] But the damage was done. When the vote was called, the seven-member subcommittee unanimously recommended against Olds's reappointment.

When the confirmation hearings moved to the Senate floor, Johnson went into high gear. He was now in the national spotlight and it inspired his worst grandstanding instincts. The record of Leland Olds, Johnson declaimed, "is an uninterrupted tale of bias, prejudice, and hostility, directed against the industry over which he seeks now to assume the powers of life and death." Olds had never been willing to look at the "industry's side of the regulatory picture." Though Olds was not a Communist, "the line he followed, the phrases he used, the causes he espoused, resemble the party line today. . . ."[22] That was not the most important reason to reject Olds, however. It was the course he had taken "toward confiscation and public ownership. . . ."[23] The Senate turned down the nomination, fifty-three to fifteen.

Johnson's actions on the Olds subcommittee were clearly lamentable. In later years the liberal Washington lawyer Joe Rauh called Johnson's tactics a preview of McCarthyism. But it is unfair to ascribe them entirely to subservience to the oil and gas industry. Johnson always gave the oilmen a respectful hearing. During the 1950s he was in touch with powerful independent oil tycoon Clint Murchison, a conservative Republican whose freely offered advice on foreign and domestic policy placed him to the right of John Birch Society founder Robert Welch. Johnson humored Murchison about the oil depletion allowance, about the threat of domestic communism, and about aid to Franco in Spain, but avoided committing himself to any of Murchison's pet causes. Less than most other Texas politicians was he a captive of the petroleum interests. His later counsel and speechwriter Harry McPherson claimed that Johnson was never a "believer in an ideological sense" in the 27 ½ percent tax allowance that the oil and gas magnates of Texas treasured. But he had concluded that "you simply could not oppose . . . [it] and stay alive as a political figure in Texas."[24]

The senator walked a constant tightrope between the demands of the nation and of his state. Neither in the Olds confirmation hearings nor in his later support for eliminating federal regulations on natural gas, retaining the oil producers' depletion allowance, and confirming the states' rights to their tidelands was Johnson acting only for the tycoons. He saw the prosperity of the oil and gas producers as essential to the ordinary citizens of Texas. Thousands in the Lone Star State were dependent on the health of its largest and richest industry. Liberal senator Richard L. Neuberger of Oregon defended Johnson in the *New Republic*, comparing his actions to those of Paul Douglas or Hubert Humphrey in "forcing special taxes on oleomargarine in the interests of dairy farmers."[25]

World events and the emerging Cold War gave Johnson his next opportunity to make his mark in the Senate. Johnson was never fully comfortable with foreign policy issues. He had taken interventionist-internationalist stands in the House during the debates preceding World War II and just after. But here he had been following the lead of mentor FDR. Generally, Johnson appeared to understand the aspirations of common people overseas, especially in the Third World; they seemed very much like poor farmers in Texas. But he would never be at ease with world leaders, men of superior education whose agendas were so foreign to his experience. Unsure of himself in events beyond the oceans, he would often rely on the experts or take refuge in formulas that seemed to have worked in the past. As representative from the Tenth District he could avoid foreign policy; as senator from Texas he could not.

During Johnson's first Senate term momentous events rocked the existing world order and deeply disturbed Americans. In 1949 the United States, Canada, France, West Germany, Britain, Italy, and several other European countries—responding to perceived Soviet belligerence—established the North Atlantic Treaty Organization, obligating the signers to mutual defense against any aggressor in Europe or North America. In that same year, in China, the American-supported anti-Communist government of Chiang Kai-shek fell to the forces of Mao Tse-tung and the Communists. Chiang and his regime fled the mainland to Taiwan, where they established themselves as a government in exile pledged someday to return to control in Peking. Though Truman refused to recognize the new Communist People's Republic on the mainland and prevented it from joining the United Nations, conservatives blamed him for "losing" China.

In June of the following year, Communist troops from North Korea, apparently with the approval of the Soviet Union, crossed the thirty-eighth parallel and invaded South Korea. Like most others of his generation, believing unchecked aggression the cause of World War II, Truman refused to repeat the mistakes of Great Britain and France at Munich. If the North Koreans were not challenged, it "would mean a third world war, just as similar incidents had brought on the second world war."[26] Taking advantage of the temporary absence of the Soviet representative, the United States won the support of the UN Security Council for a resolution demanding a cease-fire and the withdrawal of the attacking forces from South Korea and asking member nations to provide aid to the South Koreans. Three years of a costly, frustrating Asian land war followed under the guise of a UN "police action." Supported initially by the public, before it ended most Americans loathed it, and it had become a political poison pill to the party in power. It was an uncanny preview of Vietnam.

As much influenced by the lessons of Munich as was his commander in chief, Johnson dashed off a letter to the president shortly after the American intervention, praising his action as giving "a new and noble meaning to freedom. . . ."[27] He followed this up with a speech to the Senate on July 12 in which he warned his colleagues that "the name 'Korea' must not be added to the record of infamy and indecision recorded on the scroll of 'Too Little, Too Late,'" and exhorted them to approve the military expenditures necessary to win.[28]

Johnson supported postwar military preparedness, hammering away at this theme even before the invasion of South Korea. He also remembered that during World War II Truman had garnered headlines and won his 1944 vice-presidential slot through his chairmanship of the Senate committee that monitored military spending. And Johnson himself had similar success during the war, though with less acclaim, with his own five-man naval watchdog subcommittee. Now, with Russell's approval, he urged the Senate to establish a subcommittee to oversee the Korean conflict. Russell told Johnson he could not promise that he would be chairman, since a senior Armed Services Committee member, Millard Tydings of Maryland, facing Joseph McCarthy's innuendoes that he was soft on communism, also wanted the job. When Tydings withdrew, however, Johnson got the position. On July 17 he became chairman of the Senate Preparedness Investigating Subcommittee and a participant in the highest level of military decision-making.

Politically savvy observers understood the careerist goals of the new job. "Because an obscure senator named Harry Truman," wrote columnist Doris Fleeson, "parlayed an innocuous resolution for similar policing of World War II into the Presidency of the United States, unusual interest attaches both to the [Johnson] subcommittee plans and to the personality of its chairman."[29] The job was certainly an attention-getter. By 1951 the *New York Times* and the *Saturday Evening Post* had published major articles on Johnson, and *Newsweek* of December 3, 1951, featured watchdog in chief Lyndon Johnson on its cover.

Johnson claimed that the subcommittee would be nonpartisan. It would leave "politics . . . at the subcommittee-room door," work hard, and not "Monday-morning quarterback." The subcommittee was "not created to tell the generals and admirals how to fight the battles, but rather to make sure that they and the men fighting under them have what they need to win those battles."[30] But however scrupulous his professed principles, there was never any doubt that Johnson would run the subcommittee to serve his country's needs and his political career at the same time.

Johnson entertained serious doubts about Truman's conduct of the Korean War. As if criticizing his own later response to Vietnam, he thought the president should have fully mobilized the nation and imposed World War II–type controls to fight the North Korean enemy. He denounced what he called the administration's "siesta psychology." Our refusal to face the fact that "we are in a war" he dismissed as "adolescent nonsense."[31] Johnson sharply criticized Secretary of Defense Louis A. Johnson, the first witness before his subcommittee, for cutting the military budget just before the North Korean invasion. Shortly after, Truman replaced Louis Johnson with General George C. Marshall, a former secretary of state.

The Johnson subcommittee's first investigation targeted the Munitions Board, which oversaw military procurement and production, directed industrial mobilization, and supervised strategic and critical matériel stockpiling. It discovered that the government was trying to mobilize for Korea and demobilize from World War II at the same time. While the need for rubber soared, for instance, the Munitions Board was trying to sell strategic World War II synthetic rubber plants to private investors. "We believe," said a subcommittee report, "that there is sufficient organizational ability and imagination in this country to prevent the Government from buying and selling the same commodity at approximately the same time."[32]

All in all, the subcommittee prepared more than forty carefully researched, unanimously approved reports dealing with all phases of war preparation and uncovering multiple instances of waste, corruption, and stupidity by civilian and military bureaucrats alike. It can be credited with saving American taxpayers millions of dollars. Many congressional observers thought it remarkable that all the reports were unanimous, considering the range of political philosophy. Wayne Morse, a Republican member of the subcommittee, praised his chairman for his "courage, fearlessness, absolute fairness, and impartiality. . . ."[33] The work of the Preparedness Investigating Subcommittee is an instance of Johnson's ability to create consensus on a position.

During Johnson's first months as subcommittee chairman, several leading Senate Democrats, including Scott Lucas, went down to defeat in the off-year elections, reducing the administration's Senate majority by five seats. Most of the southern bloc survived, and they joined with Westerners to nominate conservative Arizonan Ernest McFarland as majority leader. Meanwhile, Oklahoman Bob Kerr talked his friend Lyndon Johnson into campaigning for Democratic whip and then persuaded Russell to support him. At first Johnson was lukewarm; a whip did not have much power of his own. But he soon realized that McFarland was old and not too bright and as whip he, Johnson, might be next in line. Besides, to be given a leadership position after so close an election was in some way a vindication. On January 2, 1951, the Senate elected Ernest McFarland majority leader and Lyndon Johnson—by acclamation— majority whip. In a mere two years, the freshman senator from Texas had risen to the number two position in the Senate hierarchy.

Military matters continued to engage Johnson even after becoming party whip. He continued to muckrake the administration's conduct of the Korean War, garnering headlines for each new exposé. Unfortunately, he was competing for public attention with Senator Estes Kefauver's Senate Crime Subcommittee. Kefauver's exposés were far more sensational and colorful than Johnson's, and the Tennessean easily won the battle of the headlines.

Johnson continued to work hard at other assignments. In April, when Truman removed General Douglas MacArthur from command in Korea for insubordination, Johnson, as a member of the Armed Services Committee, participated in the Senate Foreign Relations Committee hearings, occasionally alternating as chairman with Senator Russell.

Surprisingly, Johnson supported Truman's dismissal of MacArthur for advocating the blockade and bombing of Red China and the use of Nationalist troops to end the stalemate in Korea. He himself was one with his Texas constituents in bellicose anticommunism, and the general after all had only suggested ways to confront Communist aggression in the Far East more effectively. But Johnson opposed a military independent of civilian control and publicly said so. More than most citizens, Texans had been seduced by the stagy, melodramatic commander and were, moreover, striking out against the Korean impasse. The response to his MacArthur stand was overwhelmingly negative. He tried to placate irate constituents by praising MacArthur but refused to back down on the dismissal itself. During the Senate hearings he helped to show how little the general knew about the world outside East Asia and how little he cared about other American foreign policy goals. One of his chief points was that MacArthur's proposals threatened to escalate Korea into a third world war. Korea and the MacArthur incident were full of potential lessons for Johnson: the uncertainties of a land war in Asia, the need to rein in the military, the danger of triggering a wider war if military targets were not limited. Some he would learn; others he would not.

As his reputation in the Senate expanded, Johnson slowly and subtly shifted his political focus from Texas to the nation. Many new senators hope to achieve national prominence, but few pursue the goal with the same zeal as Johnson did.

And yet as his perspectives expanded, his emotional ties to the Hill Country grew stronger. In 1951 he exchanged his home in Johnson City for the 245 acres on the Pedernales River owned by his aging aunt, Frank [sic] Johnson Martin, widow of Clarence and mother of Tom, who needed a decent place to stay in her declining years. The house on the property was a "wreck," practically uninhabitable,[34] when Johnson bought it. It looked "like a haunted house in a Charles Addams cartoon . . ." Lady Bird later said.[35] But it was located less than a half mile from where Lyndon was born and where he had gone to school.

By 1952, through Lady Bird's diligent efforts, the residence would become livable. Frugal as ever, Mrs. Johnson bought an entire household of furniture secondhand from a lady in Washington for three hundred dollars. The Johnsons upgraded the house and grounds through the years, and constructed a swimming pool in 1955 and a guest house in 1956. More improvements followed, and the Ranch was soon one of the finest spreads in the county. It is still a successful working ranch, visited each year by thousands of tourists and by 4-H clubs and school groups who examine the operation and listen to lectures on ranching methods given by the foreman. Eventually the government built a landing strip in back of the house for dignitaries visiting by plane.

The Ranch met many of Lyndon Johnson's needs. It became a refuge from the battlefields of politics. As Lady Bird explained, it was a place to "recharge the battery of both body and spirit."[36] The past was always a powerful force in Johnson's life, and the LBJ Ranch satisfied his urge to reclaim it, even if in edited form. It also became Johnson's stage, the place where he could play to the full the Texas rancher with his wide-brimmed Stetson, tooled boots, and lavish informal Southwestern hospitality. And it became his passionate hobby. He planted many varieties of grasses, flowers, and crops. With the aid of A. W. Moursund, a savvy businessman and close friend, he bought prize cattle to stock his "spread." Johnson took his rancher role very seriously. One of the "real tragedies of his life," Walter Jenkins insisted, was when a prize bull, bought for ten thousand dollars to service his prize heifers, jumped the fence and irrevocably damaged his essential servicing equipment. John-son could never forget that he had to feed the animal for the rest of his life "without any production from him."[37]

His deepening attachment to the Hill Country made Johnson's friendship with Alvin Wirtz more important than ever. Wirtz was John-son's most trusted political adviser on Texas matters. As he had from the beginning of his career, he counted on Wirtz to keep things straight in the Lone Star State. In 1951 Wirtz was only sixty-three, and even though he joked to his friends about collecting Social Security, he expected to continue with both his law firm and his political activities for many years. It was not to be. In October, while attending a University of Texas football game, the irreplaceable Wirtz died of a heart attack. Edward Clark, later Johnson's Ambassador to Australia, gave the eulogy and in it mentioned how important Wirtz's counsel had been to Johnson's career. "He could tell Lyndon something was silly," Clark said. "No one could do that now. He molded him"[38]

Johnson would sorely miss Wirtz in many ways for the rest of his life. But for the immediate present he faced getting through the tangled elec-toral politics of 1952 in Texas without him. Wirtz usually handled John-son's political relations at home. Now the senator would have to do it by himself, and the task promised to be trickier than ever.

The special problem this time was Texas Governor Allan Shivers, a spokesman for the Dixiecrats and the oil tycoons. Good-looking, oppor-tunistic, money-hungry, and conservative, Shivers was lieutenant gover-nor when Beaufort Jester died of a heart attack. Succeeding to the state house, he lost no time consolidating his state power before the more lib-eral politicians, like Wirtz and Maury Maverick, could undermine him. Soon after taking office, Shivers purged party workers suspected of dis-loyalty or of not subscribing to his political philosophy. "Every active po-litical enemy of mine," he warned, "should expect, and receive, the works."[39] Shivers had already helped defeat veteran senator Tom Con-nally by inducing his conservative attorney general, Price Daniel, to op-pose him in the primary for the 1952 election. Johnson now feared that Shivers would take the majority of the Texas Democrats into the Repub-lican camp in November 1952. He also worried that the governor was personally interested in his Senate seat in 1954.

An important issue in the 1952 campaign was "tidelands" or off-shore oil—the underwater oil reserves on the Atlantic and Pacific conti-nental shelves—that the coastal oil-producing states, particularly Texas, Louisiana, and California, wanted to take back from federal control. The oil companies, calculating that state ownership would yield them larger profits than federal regulation and leasing, energetically supported their claims.

In 1945 Truman declared the whole continental shelf federal property and the next year vetoed a quitclaim bill giving it to the states. In 1947 the U.S. Supreme Court ruled that the United States had "paramount rights" to the oil extending "seaward three nautical miles" off California. Twice after that, Congress passed quitclaim bills for the other tidelands states, and Truman vetoed them on the grounds that they would simply be an unconditional gift "of the offshore resources of the country to the three states at the expense of the other forty-five." Them was fightin' words in Texas, Louisiana, and California, and some Texans actually mused about seceding from the Union. The conservative coalition in Congress supported states' rights, and the issue was sure to come up again.

In 1952 the question was whether the Democratic presidential candidate would adopt Truman's position. If he did, Rayburn and Johnson worried, Shivers and his supporters would bolt the party. At the state convention in May, Shivers managed to defeat a demand by liberals that all delegates to the national convention pledge to support the party nominee for president. He intended, he announced, to "keep the Democratic Party out of the hands of the ultraliberals, left-wing self-seekers."[40] Johnson deplored the Shiverites' disloyalty but he was fearful of Shivers's appeal if he ran for the Senate in 1954 and sought to appease the governor.

In July two groups of Texas politicians came to Chicago for the Democratic presidential nominating convention, the "Shivercrats" and the "Mavericks," each consisting of forty-two congressional district delegates, twenty delegates at large, and sixty-two alternates, representing the two ends of the state political spectrum. As in 1944, each delegation demanded to be seated. Rayburn wanted to seat the Mavericks, but Johnson tried to persuade him to seat Shivers's people instead. Rayburn said he would seat them only if Shivers promised to support the Democratic nominee no matter who it should be, but Shivers would make no firm commitment. Johnson now arranged a behind-the-scenes deal with Senator Earl Clements of Kentucky, chairman of the convention's Credentials Committee. Clements agreed to seat the Shivercrats on the grounds that they had not walked out on opening day, when the convention had passed a resolution binding all the delegates to a loyalty pledge. That they had stayed seemed to indicate that they would adhere to the pledge.

At this point Johnson faced another dilemma. His House mentor Rayburn and his Senate mentor Russell disagreed over the nominee for president. Rayburn supported liberal governor Adlai Stevenson of Illinois as "a combination of Woodrow Wilson and Franklin Roosevelt rolled up into one."[41] Russell was himself a serious candidate, actually running second to Kefauver in the preconvention delegate count, ahead of Stevenson. Johnson actively worked for his Georgia mentor, and the Texas delegation voted for Russell each time. More than loyalty was involved. Johnson and Russell had made a deal. LBJ would push hard to get Russell the presidential nomination, but if that fell through Russell would then use his influence to have Johnson selected as the second man on the ticket.

On the second ballot, the three candidates—Kefauver, Stevenson, and Russell—had not changed position. Then Truman stepped in, flying to Chicago to make sure the party voted for his handpicked candidate, Stevenson. Finally, on the third ballot, the governor of Illinois went over the top. Rayburn and Russell then went to Stevenson, hoping to influence him to choose LBJ as his running mate. Both Stevenson and Truman wanted a Southerner to balance the ticket and win back the 1948 Dixiecrat vote, but neither wanted Johnson, whose party voting record was not dependable. Instead, they chose a sharecropper's son, a personable and relatively liberal senator, John Sparkman of Alabama, whose loyalty seemed unshakable.

Soon after the convention, Shivers visited Stevenson in Illinois to press him on the tidelands oil question. Against Johnson's advice, Shivers asked Stevenson point-blank what his position was. The candidate, just as candidly, said he supported the Supreme Court decision and federal ownership and would veto any bill that attempted to impose state ownership. Shivers, having been renominated for governor and feeling politically secure, denounced Stevenson and the Democrats and urged his fellow party members in Texas to vote for the Republican nominee, General Dwight Eisenhower.

Johnson was in a quandary. He feared Shivers's displeasure as well as the wrath of his own business friends if he supported the national Democratic ticket. Moreover, Johnson himself did not like Stevenson's stand on the tidelands issue and was not personally comfortable with the patrician, intellectual Princeton-educated Stevenson. Yet Johnson was a party loyalist and felt honor-bound to support the candidate.

In the end he worked diligently with Rayburn and others in the fall of 1952 to keep the party together. In his endorsement of Stevenson on August 28, Johnson said: "The fact that Governor Stevenson is wrong on [the tidelands] issue does not automatically make General Eisenhower right on all other issues. Texans once left the Democratic Party to help the Republicans elect Herbert Hoover. Our people suffered many years because of this desertion. . . ."[42]

Grateful for Johnson's support, Stevenson asked him to introduce him when he came to campaign in Texas. Johnson hurried to Shivers to ask his advice. Would it hurt him in the future if he presented Stevenson at the rally in Fort Worth on October 17? Shivers told him to go ahead and promised to protect him politically even if he did so. Many of his friends and supporters thought it would be disastrous to come out so publicly for the Democratic candidate and urged Johnson to reconsider. He refused. "The Democratic Party is best for Texas and the South and the nation," he declared. "It's a firm conviction with me and I can't go against my convictions."[43]

In the end, Johnson supported Stevenson publicly, but his heart was not in it. Yet many observers believed that he did more than his share for the Stevenson-Sparkman ticket. "Johnson was roundly criticized by a lot of the liberals," Sam Rayburn's friend D. B. Hardeman said, "because he didn't take a more aggressive part in supporting Stevenson, but I never did go for that. Johnson introduced him in Fort Worth and was on the platform with him in Dallas and that wasn't easy. Except for one state-wide official, everybody else endorsed Eisenhower or ran for cover. They went to the hospital or they went to the mountains of New Mexico. They scattered like quail."[44] Rayburn himself publicly declared that Lyndon did everything he could for the campaign.

Stevenson lost big in November. Aside from Eisenhower's enormous personal popularity, many voters blamed the Democrats for the stalemate in Korea. In Texas, however, Stevenson lost by less than the national average. In the state elections, Price Daniel became junior senator, and Shivers was reelected for the second of his three terms. Johnson had once more successfully negotiated the treacherous shoals of Texas politics. He could now turn back to the national scene and resume his quest for power in the Senate.

CHAPTER 10

Minority Leader

T HE MOST IMPORTANT POLITICAL RESULT of the 1952 election for LBJ
was the defeat of Senator McFarland by Phoenix department-store
scion Barry M. Goldwater. With the Democrats narrowly losing both
houses of Congress, the top Senate party position was now minority
leader, and McFarland's loss meant the spot was available. McFarland
himself believed LBJ deserved the job. He once joked to Johnson in the
course of a party strategy meeting, "Damn it, Lyndon, you ought to have
my job—you know a helluva lot more about it than I do."[1]

McFarland's compliment undoubtedly echoed Johnson's own feelings, and in any case the vacancy activated his engine of ambition. By
one account, the very night of the Eisenhower landslide LBJ was on the
phone making calls to fellow senators asking for their help in getting the
post. One of his first calls was to Richard Russell, to whom he proposed
an unusual arrangement. If the older man wanted the minority leader
job, Johnson would do "all the legwork and water carrying."[2] Russell was
not interested. A senior member of both the Armed Services and Appropriations Committees and de facto head of the southern bloc, he preferred to wield power through his major chairmanships. Instead, the
Georgian agreed to support LBJ, as Johnson anticipated he would.

Johnson started his campaign for the post by enlisting the help of
Bobby Gene Baker, a smart, brash young man from Pickens, South
Carolina. Starting as a Senate page in his teens, Baker had learned
to navigate his way around Congress in an amazingly short time. In
1951, at the age of twenty-three, he became chief page for the Senate

Democrats. Baker's tactics, he confessed, were "to outpolitic the politicians," and to "sell, not only myself but the products of others." When Lyndon Johnson first became a senator in 1948, he had telephoned Bobby Baker and told him: "I understand you know where the bodies are buried in the Senate. I'd appreciate it if you'd come to my office and talk with me."[3]

Bobby came to see him, and the two men established a political relationship based on mutual advantage. When Johnson became minority leader, he promoted Baker to assistant secretary to the minority Democrats. In this position Baker kept tabs on everything going on in the Senate, and his intelligence, in both senses, was indispensable to his boss. Practically all the Senate Democrats, except a few fastidious liberals, trusted the young go-getter and provided him with bits of useful information that he relayed to LBJ. As time passed, with Baker's help, Johnson built up a valuable cache of information about his colleagues, which he used to advantage. Working together, Baker and Johnson were usually able to figure out accurately which senators would vote for a specific bill, when to bring it to the floor, and when to schedule a vote. Johnson's feelings for Baker went beyond professional gratitude. The young man became a family friend who at times escorted Luci and Linda to the Washington Zoo. To some extent Bobby was the son Johnson never had. Writing in February 1953 to express sympathy for Baker following his mother's stroke, the senator remarked: "I hope she knows how much we all love you."[4] No doubt this was a conventional sentiment, but it expressed sincere affection. And Bobby returned the favor. Senator Johnson, he wrote columnist Stewart Alsop, was "the greatest leader the Senate has ever had."[5]

But for the present, Baker's task was to help LBJ round up enough votes for the Senate leadership post. In calls to Democratic senators, Johnson and his sidekick emphasized Russell's support and Johnson's logical succession to the job as former party whip. Baker warned conservative Southerners that if not Johnson it might well be the liberal Minnesotan Hubert Humphrey. One of Johnson's phone calls, made practically at dawn the morning after the election, went to the newly elected senator from Massachusetts, John F. Kennedy. Johnson congratulated Kennedy on his surprise victory over Henry Cabot Lodge and said nothing about the leadership job, but Kennedy grasped the real reason behind the call and was impressed by LBJ's energy. "The guy must never sleep," he exclaimed.[6]

It was as the man in the middle—neither southern nor western, neither far right nor left—that Johnson beat out other Senate Democrats for minority leader. One last call to Governor Shivers was in order, however. Did Shivers intend to oppose him for the Senate seat in 1954? Johnson asked. He did not want to assume leadership of his party if he was going to be defeated in a year and a half, when his term ended. Shivers assured him he planned to stay in Austin and advised him to go ahead. "You'll do a great job and be a great service to the country. . . ."[7]

The last hurdle was the most liberal group of senators, men who disliked Johnson's stand on tidelands oil and civil rights and felt he could not be counted on any longer to support progressive measures. They preferred seventy-six-year-old Jim Murray of Montana, a dyed-in-the-wool New Deal–Fair Deal senator since 1934. Hubert Humphrey, possibly the Senate's most combative liberal, was one of Murray's chief supporters, and Johnson sought to change his mind. As minority leader he would consult Humphrey, he promised. And Hubert might also be next in line for a seat on the coveted Foreign Relations Committee. Humphrey did not bite; in the Democratic Senate caucus on January 2, 1953, he voted for Murray. But then, when it was clear that Johnson had all but sewed it up, he moved to make it unanimous for LBJ. The next day the *New York Times* reported that "Senator Lyndon B. Johnson of Texas, whose position is about half-way between the right-wing Southerners and the 'regular' Northern Democrats, was the unanimous choice of the Democrats for their leader."[8]

Humphrey's opposition did not alienate Johnson. Instead, Johnson cultivated the young Minnesotan. As Humphrey later told Doris Kearns, Johnson "wanted someone in the liberal ranks for information and help."[9] The personalities of the two men were widely dissimilar. Humphrey was ebullient, warm, open, and almost guileless. Johnson could be warm and ebullient at times, but guileless? At this point, moreover, they seemed far apart on many issues. But there was a basis for cooperation and friendship. Humphrey remembered that Johnson told him: "You and I can get along fine. I know we don't agree on a number of things, but at least we can get along."[10] Humphrey's sense of humor, and even more his appreciation of Johnson's, helped. LBJ often complained that liberals were humorless, "never as unhappy as when happy, or so happy as when unhappy." Humphrey did not fit that description. Humphrey, in turn, felt he "was getting more than giving." Johnson coached Humphrey on how the Senate functioned, suggested he get to know some of the southern conservatives, showed him how to achieve legislative success through compromise, and advised him to get Muriel, his wife, to make friends with the other Senate wives. Johnson urged Humphrey to become a "liberal doer" instead of a "liberal talker." The

Minnesota senator soon came to justify some of Johnson's illiberal actions as political realism and to defend him to skeptics in the liberal camp.[11]

Johnson became minority leader at a time when the Democrats were deeply rent by arguments among big-city liberals, Trumanites, and Dixiecrats, all fighting for control. Johnson worked to establish a new center under his own leadership and to transform the party into an instrument of purposeful, effective action. This required that the moderates be merged into one centrist core, without the ideologues on both extremes, and the North-South split be bridged by focusing on issues such as Social Security, farm legislation, minimum wage, housing, and rural electrification, on which both sections could agree.

When applied, his strategy often outraged liberals. In their 1952 national platform, under pressure from civil rights groups hoping to skirt the towering cloture hurdle to racial change, the Democrats had endorsed revising the Senate rules of debate at the opening of a new Congress when a simple majority, rather than the two-thirds needed for cloture, was sufficient. In January 1953, soon after Johnson became minority leader, the Senate liberals made their move to fulfill the party's recent promise. Whatever his personal feelings about race, Johnson was certain that the white South was not ready for major racial change and would defend to the death its chief parliamentary defense against federal civil rights legislation. Any move to revise the rules, moreover, would throw the Senate into turmoil and wreck his legislative plans. Allying himself with conservative majority leader Robert A. Taft of Ohio, Johnson succeeded in stopping the Senate liberals' effort and earned their disdain. As Joe Rauh later fumed: "Johnson's first act as minority leader was to help Taft wreck a proposal made in support of the Democratic platform of 1952!"[12]

Johnson set about becoming an effective leader in a systematic way. To be completely informed on every detail of the issues, he set up research staffs for each of his roles—Democratic leader, senator from Texas, and chairman of the Democratic Policy Committee. These staffs supplemented the information from Bobby Baker on how each of the Democratic senators felt and how they were likely to vote.

At this point he did not mind the Democrats' minority status in the Senate. It would give him breathing space to pull the party together without having to advance initiatives that might exacerbate conflict. He also did not mind deferring to Eisenhower. It was traditional, of course, for the party out of power to attack the incumbent president, but everybody seemed to "like Ike," including many Texas Democratic voters. "Throughout that first year as minority leader," said Gerald Siegel, lawyer and Democratic Policy Committee counsel, "Johnson picked his positions carefully. He recognized that we had a very popular president at that time . . . and that the worst thing that could happen for the Democrats was to get bloodied and lose a lot of skirmishes with him in the Senate."[13] Accordingly, a subordinate clause in LBJ's formula for success was that the minority party should not be obstructionist, but fight for a positive program that served a broad public. "There are two courses open to a minority party," the minority leader told his fellow Democrats at the Jefferson–Jackson Day Dinner. "It can indulge in the politics of partisanship, or it can remain true to the politics of responsibility."[14] Sam Rayburn, dethroned as Speaker by the Republican sweep in 1952, believed that Johnson's tactics were in the best interests of the country and was prepared to follow suit on his side of Congress.

Johnson formulated guidelines for his politics of responsibility and tried to make Senate Democrats observe them. His most important rule was that an issue or a piece of legislation must be considered solely on its merits without reference to its political origins. On matters involving national security he would expect the Democrats to cooperate willingly with the administration. He hoped to avoid *ad hominem* arguments and name-calling as political maneuvers. These precepts would, in his opinion, be good for the country; he also knew they would be good for his reputation. In his own mind, by now, the two goals were not far apart.

Johnson not only courted the White House, he also courted the Republican congressional leadership. Maintaining friendly relations with the opposition's top people was a practice he had followed from the time he became a senator. In his early Senate days he had cultivated the Republican minority leader, the partisan Kenneth Wherry of Nebraska. Wherry said that Johnson was the Democrat he preferred doing business with. When Wherry died Johnson made fast friends with Styles Bridges of New Hampshire. Bridges fought him on the floor of the Senate, but the two got together for drinks when the formal political business of the day was over. The new Senate majority leader, Robert A. Taft, son of the former president and four-time seeker of the presidency himself, was harder to win over, but Johnson even managed to soften him up a little, and they worked together in the few months that remained until Taft's death of cancer. Johnson was then able to work effectively with William F. Knowland of California, who succeeded Taft. The pattern of cultivating Republican leaders would continue into his presidency. His friendship with Senator Everett Dirksen of Illinois would yield historic dividends.

Johnson's success as minority leader was based in part on luck and in part on his organizational skills and sure political instincts. The divided

Democrats were willing to bestow authority on the man who knew how to use power and was eager to do so. Virtually everything he did received the assent of his fellow Democratic senators.

One of Johnson's first moves was to revise the hidebound tradition of seniority in committee assignments. Senate committees were controlled by southern conservatives, who had, in effect, been "elected for life." Their near-permanence kept newly elected senators from getting important or interesting assignments. Johnson, as a freshman, had used pull to secure important committee places, but other newcomers, with less influence, spent years on the District of Columbia or Post Office and Civil Service Committees or similar dead-end, low-profile spots. Johnson thought that each senator should have at least one good committee appointment.

As usual, his motives were both principled and personal. He really believed it valuable for newcomers to plunge right in with meaningful committee jobs. But since he ultimately controlled the appointments, such an arrangement would also make him patron of all the younger members and so expedite his legislative goals. And there was a further advantage: revising the system would weaken the conservative southern stranglehold on policy and give Johnson more room to maneuver.

Before taking this radical step, Johnson consulted with Richard Russell, who indicated that he was sympathetic to the change. With Russell's approval in his pocket, LBJ visited the other senior men and one by one got their okay as well. Once achieved, the rules change produced significant results: Hubert Humphrey and newly elected Mike Mansfield went to Foreign Relations; John F. Kennedy to Labor and Public Welfare; Henry Jackson to Interior; and Herbert Lehman to Banking and Currency. The younger men, especially, appreciated what Johnson had done for them. "I want to take time," wrote Wyoming senator Gale McGee in 1958, "to convey to you my deep personal appreciation for the committee assignments. Because of these appointments we freshmen have no alibis if by the end of this session we have failed to produce. . . . Your action has given to us . . . individually and collectively both the responsibility and opportunity to write a constructive record."[15]

During Johnson's years as minority leader major events at home and abroad cried out for attention. In the spring and summer of 1953 the long-festering issue of Joe McCarthy's anticommunist crusade came to a head in the riveting Army-McCarthy hearings. In May 1954 the U.S. Supreme Court handed down the landmark desegregation decision *Brown v. Board of Education of Topeka.* Abroad, the Korean War ended and the French pulled out of Indochina after a decade of struggling against Communist efforts to conquer and unify Vietnam under their rule. Lyndon Johnson's career would intersect with all these events.

Most urgent in the mid-fifties was the civil rights issue. The *Brown* decision reversed the "separate but equal" doctrine that had applied to the nation's public facilities since *Plessy v. Ferguson* in 1896 and directed that black students be admitted to public schools on a nondiscriminatory basis. The decision was the beginning of the end for the post–Civil War Jim Crow regime that had made a mockery of American political equality.

Johnson had mixed feelings about *Brown*. In a letter to a Texas constituent he wrote that the Court's ruling had been based on "criteria other than law and equity." There would, he predicted, be "a long gap between a Supreme Court decision and action to enforce a decision and within that gap I believe we can find the necessary elbow room."[16] Johnson was personally sympathetic to the decision, but worried about how it would affect him and his balancing act to keep both his Senate seat and his leadership position. "It's the most significant Supreme Court decision in a hundred years," Lyndon told Bobby Baker after dinner one night shortly after *Brown* was announced, "but it's likely to play hell with my leadership role." The Dixiecrats and a lot of his constituents would be on him "like stink on shit" if he didn't "stand up and bray against the Supreme Court decision." But if he *did* "bray like a jackass, the red hots and senators with big minority blocs in the East and North" would "gut shoot me."[17] Given the times and his constituency, Johnson would have to perform an elaborate dance on civil rights.

Johnson could dodge civil rights for the moment, but he could not duck the tidelands oil issue. There was no question which way Johnson would vote on the Submerged Lands Act of 1953. This was the bill, sure to get Eisenhower's signature, that nullified previous Supreme Court decisions upholding federal control of the offshore oil reserves of the seaboard states. Under the act the states would own the lands underwater to a maximum distance of three miles from shore. The usually pro-Eisenhower *New York Times* vehemently denounced it as "one of the greatest and surely the most unjustified give-away programs in all the history of the United States."[18] Many senators, particularly northern liberals and those from noncoastal states, also opposed it, with Oregon's Wayne Morse setting a record for Senate filibusters with more than twenty-two hours of continuous talking to defeat the bill. But Johnson, the Texan, supported it, though, as minority leader, he was not very active in getting it passed and so was able to avoid open estrangement from his northern Democratic colleagues. On May 5, 1953, the bill passed, fifty-six to thirty-five, and Eisenhower signed it as expected.

July 1953 was a month replete with happenings that demanded Johnson's attention. On the twenty-sixth American, Korean, and Chinese delegates signed a truce at Panmunjom, ending the Korean fighting. Johnson was not enthusiastic about how the war had ended. An armistice that "merely releases aggressive armies to attack elsewhere would be a fraud," he warned.[19] On the thirty-first, "Mr. Republican," the majority leader, Robert A. Taft, died of cancer. With tears in his eyes, Johnson told the Senate that "No more honorable man has ever sat as a Senate leader for any party. I have lost one of the best friends I ever had."[20] The minority leader certainly exaggerated the depth of his friendship with Taft, but the two men had shared a love for the Senate and respected each other's integrity.

Senate Republicans replaced Taft as majority leader with California newspaper publisher William F. Knowland. A large man, bull-like in appearance and personality, Knowland was an uncompromising conservative who supported Joe McCarthy's Red-baiting tactics and hoped to use American military power to get mainland China back for Chiang Kai-shek. Fortunately for the Democrats, Knowland, unlike Taft, could not compete with Johnson's political expertise and natural talent for maneuver.

A political moderate himself, Eisenhower often found Johnson and Rayburn more sympathetic to his programs than the new majority leader and began inviting the two Democrats to the White House before dinner to talk policy over drinks and hors d'oeuvres. "My friendship with Johnson," Eisenhower later wrote, "came of a birth state in common* and long personal acquaintance. We had our differences, especially in domestic and economic policy. . . . Yet when put in perspective, he was far more helpful than obstructive in furthering the recommendations I sent to Congress. The amount of legislative accomplishment that had been achieved during the six years that I had to work with an opposition Congress led in the Senate by Lyndon Johnson was impressive. For this I was grateful and frequently told him so."[21] Eisenhower's approval and friendship added to Johnson's prestige, and he was soon regarded, though only the minority leader, as the most powerful man in the Senate.

On one important foreign policy issue, however, Johnson and the president did not agree. The Bricker Amendment sought to deflate the foreign policy prerogatives of the president by limiting his power to negotiate any treaty with a foreign nation that might restrict American sov-

---

*Eisenhower had been born in Denison, Texas, in 1890.

ereignty. Its author was Senator John Bricker, a neoisolationist, ultraconservative former governor of Ohio. Like many of his ideological group, Bricker believed that Roosevelt had betrayed the United States to the Soviets at Yalta and that Truman had usurped congressional power by entangling the country in Korea. The amendment would prevent future "Yaltas" and other "sellouts" to the Communists and also block the United States from approving liberal United Nations measures, such as Mrs. Roosevelt's "Covenant on Human Rights."

Though sponsored by a right-wing Republican and meant to repudiate Roosevelt and Harry Truman, enough Democrats supported the amendment to provide the two-thirds needed for sending it to the states for ratification. Judging from the deluge of pro-amendment letters and telegrams to the president and members of Congress, the public, too, endorsed it. But the Bricker Amendment also had its spirited adversaries. Liberals and internationalists believed it would wreck American foreign policy, and Americans for Democratic Action, the League of Women Voters, the American Bar Association's Section on International and Comparative Law, the *New York Times*, and the *Washington Post* attacked it fervently. Its most important opponents, however, were Eisenhower, who deplored its infringement of executive authority, and Secretary of State John Foster Dulles, who believed it would hamstring American foreign policy and endanger peace and U.S. security.

With their president attacking it as a "stupid, blind violation of the Constitution by stupid, blind isolationists,"[22] the Republicans soon came up with a revised version. This measure failed on the Senate floor. Then Walter George, one of the most respected of the southern conservative Democrats, proposed a substitute that eliminated the possibility of local control of American foreign policy, but subjected all international agreements to Senate ratification. Eisenhower did not like the new amendment any better than the old.

Johnson had worked with George to find a compromise and supported the George alternative publicly. In private, however, he had begun to have serious doubts about the whole effort to limit the president's treaty-making powers. "It's the worst bill I can think of," Johnson said. "It ties the president's hands and I'm not just talking about Ike. It will be the bane of every president we elect. . . ."[23] Congress accepted the George substitute and then proceeded to vote on it. On February 26, 1954, sixty senators including Johnson voted in favor, thirty-one against—one vote short of the two-thirds required. Some historians think that Johnson contrived to have it fail. If true, it is ironic. Like Oedipus, Johnson was unwittingly sowing the seeds of his own destruction years later during the trials of the Vietnam War.

Whether Americans enjoyed their nation's world responsibilities or not, during the fifties they would be drawn more and more into foreign affairs. And Lyndon Johnson, whether he liked it or not, would also be forced to take foreign policy stands. How could he find positions that would simultaneously be compatible with his opinions, avoid political risk, and yet make him seem informed, competent, and in control? His formula was overall support for Eisenhower, seasoned with a pinch of hard-line anticommunism when necessary, and a dollop of criticism that would not endanger bipartisan foreign policy cooperation.

The fifties would present many challenges to Johnson's prudent approach. In Guatemala, Jacobo Arbenz, a Communist sympathizer, took power in 1950 and began to attack "Yanqui" imperialism and expropriate American-owned property. In 1954 Arbenz began to import Czechoslovakian-made arms. That March, the Organization of American States approved a Dulles-sponsored resolution declaring "solidarity for the preservation of political integrity of the American States against international communism," and the U.S. Navy began stopping foreign vessels off the coast of Guatemala to search for contraband. In June a CIA-sponsored invasion of the Central American country led by a former Guatemalan Army colonel toppled Arbenz from power.

To demonstrate his support of the administration's Guatemala policy, Johnson introduced a Senate resolution announcing what some would call the "Johnson Doctrine." While denying that the United States intended "interference in the domestic affairs of any American state," the resolution labeled "Communist Penetration of the Western Hemisphere . . . intolerable" and called for American intervention to end the "beachhead in the Americas."[24] The Senate approved Johnson's resolution, sixty-nine to one. Eisenhower and Dulles were grateful.

Meanwhile, far more important events were taking place in French Indochina. This witches' brew of nationalism, communism, imperialism, pride, stupidity, greed, and rage would plague the United States for two decades and cast a shadow over the most momentous years of Johnson's career.

Johnson's introduction to the Vietnam morass came in March 1954, when Eisenhower called a meeting of congressional leaders to discuss the disquieting situation in Southeast Asia. After World War II the former French Indochina had been divided into three quasi-independent states—Vietnam, Cambodia, and Laos—within a continuing "French Union." In Vietnam, the coastal region along the South China Sea, the Viet Minh, nationalist-Marxist insurgents under Ho Chi Minh, refused to accept colonial subordination to France and had risen in rebellion.

The French appealed to the Americans for help, and the Truman administration, determined to keep France in NATO and worried about Communist influence in the region, began to subsidize the French effort to defeat the Viet Minh. By the time Eisenhower took office the United States was supplying the French with arms and providing them with air force technicians. Despite American aid, in late March 1954 the French were on the brink of losing Vietnam and asked the United States for direct military intervention. Johnson had been hearing from constituents that the United States should avoid involvement in "Indo-China." According to newly hired aide Booth Mooney, every incoming letter to the senator on the subject "strongly opposes our sending any troops into that area."[25] Johnson soon announced that he was firmly against direct American military intervention.

For its part, the administration, though undecided, was reluctant to cut and run. On April 3 Secretary of State Dulles held a secret bipartisan meeting with Admiral Arthur Radford, head of the Joint Chiefs of Staff, and several members of the House and Senate Armed Services Committees, including Johnson and Russell. Dulles asked the congressional participants to endorse a blank-check resolution authorizing the president to take whatever action was necessary to prevent the French from losing Vietnam, with the understanding that it would involve possible use of United States airpower and seapower in the Pacific. To goad the congressmen and senators, Dulles invoked the domino theory: If one pro-Western Asian nation fell to the Communists, the others would quickly follow in sequence. But Russell, backed by Johnson, and speaking for the others, rejected the no-strings proposal. Johnson said that the Republicans had blamed the Truman administration for the Korean War and that before Congress considered such a resolution on Vietnam it should be given the full facts in the case. He then asked Dulles whether any U.S. allies had been consulted; the secretary answered no. Russell and Johnson then offered an alternative, three-point plan: Any American intervention in Southeast Asia must be buttressed by cooperation with the British Commonwealth and Vietnam's neighbors, must require that the French remain as combatants in the war, and must avoid any implication that the United States wished to preserve French colonialism. The proposal quickly died.

At the end of April, Dulles went to the Geneva Conference, where he and representatives of Great Britain, France, Communist China, the Soviet Union, Vietnam, Laos, and Cambodia discussed the future of Indochina. The conference agreed to divide Vietnam at the seventeenth parallel, with a five-kilometer demilitarized zone (DMZ) on either side.

North of this would be the domain of the Viet Minh; south of it, that of the French Union forces. Free elections would be a prerequisite to re-unification of Vietnam in the future. Believing the United States should dissociate itself from the partition plan and that the Communists would surely win the elections, Dulles left the conference early in disgust and returned to Washington.

Johnson thought Dulles should have stayed. Annoyed by the secretary of state's actions, he sharply criticized him in an address at the annual Jefferson–Jackson Day dinner in early May. Until this time, Johnson had defended the president on world issues and had tried to keep his fellow Democrats from attacking him. His restraint had led to charges that he was "soft on the Republicans." This speech, his first major foreign policy address as minority leader, earned him many political kudos and a front-page headline in the *New York Times*. In retrospect, it was full of ironies.

The minority leader warned the president that the Democrats would not provide unquestioning bipartisan support for Republican foreign policy. The administration, Johnson declared, had put the United States in an extremely vulnerable position:

> What is American policy on Indo-China? All of us have listened to the dismal series of reversals and confusions and alarms and excursions which have emerged from Washington over the past few weeks. It is apparent only that American foreign policy has never in all its history suffered such a stunning reversal. We have been caught bluffing by our enemies. Our friends and Allies are frightened and wondering, as we do, where we are headed. We stand in clear danger of being left naked and alone in a hostile world. Only a few days ago we observed our final humiliation in the spectacle of an American Secretary of State backtracking . . . from the conference at Geneva. And yet, a few weeks before, while in Berlin, he had told his own people that Geneva was the world's best hope. . . . This picture of our country needlessly weakened in the world today is so painful that we should turn our eyes from abroad and look homeward.[26]

On May 8, the day following this speech, the French Union forces, after a seven-week siege, surrendered to the Viet Minh at Dienbienphu, ending French rule in Indochina. In July the opposing parties signed the final Geneva Agreements, providing for the withdrawal of all French troops, partition of Vietnam into South and North pending future elections, prohibition of foreign bases in Indochina, and the formation of the International Control Commission to supervise the promised elections. The United States did not sign the accord but promised to comply with its terms.

The other great public concern in 1954 was what to do about Senator Joe McCarthy and the "ism" he had spawned. Back in February 1950, looking for a good issue to ensure his uncertain reelection, the Wisconsin Republican had charged that there were 205 card-carrying Communists working for the State Department. Whether true or not, the assertion was a dangerous trip wire. The United States was already in the grip of an overheated "Red" scare, and millions of citizens believed his charges. A May 1950 poll showed that 48 percent of Americans had confidence in the Wisconsin senator; only 28 percent thought him dangerous or a liar.

Though only one source of the anti-Communist panic, McCarthy soon became the vortex of the whole swirling witch-hunt mood that overwhelmed the nation's common sense. Thousands of Americans, many innocent of any far-left connections, were hounded and harassed; many lost their jobs and reputations. The intellectual and political life of the nation was poisoned as creative and original people ran for cover to avoid charges and accusations. For a time McCarthy seemed untouchable, and even President Eisenhower, who despised him, tried to avoid a confrontation.

Johnson privately thought McCarthy a "sonofabitch"[27] and "a loud-mouthed drunk,"[28] but was not sure how to stop him. When, in 1953, columnist Drew Pearson asked him to condemn McCarthy's charges that Pearson was a Communist, Johnson refused. LBJ was not a civil liberties crusader. He had supported all the loyalty and antisubversion legislation passed by Congress since World War II, partly in response to his Texas constituency's anticommunism and partly from his own concern with Soviet might. He did not believe America was riddled with Communists, however, and detested McCarthy for his attacks on the loyalty of the Democratic Party and his disrespect for Congress.

In addition, Johnson was beginning to feel growing pressure from his friends and advisers to actively dispute him. His friend journalist William White said he never advised Lyndon what to do until he got "very, very upset about McCarthy." "I though he was destroying civil liberties in this country," said White. He appealed to Johnson to "do something about this damned fellow."[29] But how could the man be stopped? Until the timing was right, Johnson concluded, little could be done. And in any case, the Democrats, their motives suspect, should probably not be his executioners. "Lyndon kept saying," Hubert Humphrey recalled to biographer Merle Miller, "that we had to wait until McCarthy began attacking the more conservative, the respected . . . [leaders] of what you might call the old school."[30]

But Johnson had actually begun to formulate some anti-McCarthy plans by early 1953 and had told some reporters off the record that he thought a bipartisan committee should be appointed to deal with the McCarthy problem. It should consist of "the very best men we have," he said, "men who are above reproach, the wisest men I know in the Senate and the best judges. . . . With the men I'd pick, the Senate would accept their judgment and that would be the end of it."[31]

The McCarthy affair finally came to a head in early 1954. By now the Wisconsin senator had alienated many supporters by his arrogance and reckless irresponsibility. He was now attacking three presumed bastions of patriotism—his own Grand Old Party, the CIA, and the U.S. Army. In January McCarthy learned that the army had given Major Irving Peress, an army dentist, first a promotion and then an honorable discharge, although Peress had refused to answer a loyalty questionnaire when he was first inducted in 1952. Charging the army with "disgraceful coddling of Communists," McCarthy began an investigation of the army's loyalty practices, calling both Peress and General Ralph W. Zwicker before his subcommittee. When McCarthy asked Zwicker for the names of the officers involved in Peress's promotion and discharge, the highly decorated officer refused to comply. McCarthy screamed at Zwicker that he was "not fit to wear that uniform" and did not have "the brains of a five-year-old."[32] The country was shocked at this name-calling, and many former McCarthy supporters were astounded by his attack on a war hero.

The army struck back by revealing that the Wisconsin senator and his aide Roy Cohn had sought preferential treatment for G. David Schine, a former McCarthy assistant and good friend of Cohn's, who had recently been drafted. Charges and countercharges were soon flying, and Congress decided to investigate the matter before McCarthy's own subcommittee. Expecting the Wisconsin senator to be a primary witness, it replaced him temporarily as chairman with Senator Karl Mundt of South Dakota.

By allowing the proceedings to be televised, McCarthy caused his own downfall. With his TV connections, Johnson understood the power of the visual image on the national imagination and thought that the scowling, heavily bearded, coarse-talking senator would repel the television audience. Even before the hearings were scheduled, he presciently told Democratic Senator John McClellan of Arkansas, a member of the subcommittee, that no matter what other concessions the Democrats made to McCarthy, they should demand full television coverage. The hearings lasted eight weeks and mesmerized the nation. McCarthy came across as a scowling villain who bullied witnesses, frequently contradicted himself, and interrupted constantly with groundless points of order. Johnson was correct: television effectively destroyed McCarthy's career.

Six weeks after the hearings ended, Republican senator Ralph Flanders of Vermont called on the Senate to censure McCarthy for bringing that body into "disrepute." Even before the censure resolution, Johnson had been studying records to find out how senators who had broken the rules had been dealt with in the past. On August 3 the Senate, by a vote of seventy-five to twelve, authorized the establishment of a bipartisan six-man "select" committee. Knowland opposed the whole idea, but conferred with Johnson on whom to include on the panel. To deflect possible McCarthyite Red-baiting and charges of partisan politics, Johnson chose conservative Democrats known to be fair: John Stennis of Mississippi, Ed Johnson of Colorado, and Sam Ervin Jr. of North Carolina, all former judges. Though he had no official say in the choice of Republicans, he maneuvered successfully to get his preference for the committee chair, Senator Flanders, selected.

The committee report recommended that McCarthy be "condemned," not censured, for his brutal treatment of General Zwicker and for conduct that brought the "Senate into dishonor and disrepute." When the condemnation resolution was brought to the Senate for action, Johnson kept it from becoming a party issue. Each of his Democratic colleagues, he noted, ought to vote his conscience so that McCarthy could never charge them with vilifying him on partisan grounds. Just before the final vote, Johnson made a statement on the Senate floor about his own feelings. "In my mind," he said, "there is only one issue here—morality and conduct. Each of us must decide whether we approve or disapprove of certain actions as standard for senatorial integrity." In criticizing McCarthy's attacks on the select committee, Johnson said that the Wisconsin senator's words "do not belong in the pages of the *Congressional Record*. They would be more fittingly inscribed on the wall of a men's room."[33] In the end, every Democratic senator except John F. Kennedy, absent supposedly with back trouble, voted to condemn the Wisconsin senator. The final count was sixty-seven to twenty-two.

Many observers gave Johnson credit for the result. Paul Douglas, a true-blue liberal often skeptical of Johnson, noted how the minority leader had effectively rounded up the votes of the southern "mossbacks." "He was magnificent in that fight," Douglas declared, "just magnificent."[34] Bobby Baker later asserted that "with his parliamentary genius," Johnson "brought an end to McCarthyism."[35] Johnson's success against McCarthy pleased the liberals and led to the first public whispers that Johnson was presidential material. Joe McCarthy remained in the Senate for three more years until his death in 1957, but his political effectiveness, despite the continued loyalty of his most ardent supporters, was destroyed.

Through late 1953 and into early 1954, while dealing with the Bricker Amendment, the upheaval in Indochina, and the McCarthy problem, Johnson worried about his own political future. His Senate term, painfully won by eighty-seven votes, was up in November 1954, with the all-important Democratic primary scheduled for July. If he won conclusively this time, he could, barring unforseen circumstances, expect to be senator for life. Elections always worried him and he still felt vulnerable, complaining that he was "called a Dixiecrat in Washington and a Communist in Texas."[36] Johnson remembered the prediction of a federal judge that whoever won the Johnson-Stevenson contest would be a one-term senator. He also knew that a flock of candidates were itching to run against him.

Hoping to improve his reelection odds, during the fall of 1953 he embarked on what he described as a "nonpolitical tour," visiting every major Texas city, "pressing the flesh" of more than 225,000 voters, and making more than 200 speeches. Besides shaking hands and talking, Johnson met with local Democratic leaders in many of the cities and puffed his importance as minority leader. He tried to justify to them why he and Rayburn had cooperated so fully with President Eisenhower. "Some people say I've been petticoatin' around with Eisenhower," he noted. "Well, that's not true. . . . I want to make absolutely sure that the Communists don't play one branch of the government against the other, or one party against the other as happened in the Korean War. . . . The danger is they'll think we're fat and fifty and fighting among ourselves about free enterprise and socialism and all that. . . . If you're in an airplane flying somewhere, you don't run up to the cockpit and attack the pilot. Mr. Eisenhower is the only President we've got."[37]

Whether all Texas Democrats bought this explanation did not matter; by the time the tour was over, no one wanted to run against Johnson. Yet Johnson, always the pessimist, could not relax. When Dudley T. Dougherty, an eccentric, cowboy-attired, long-sideburned freshman in the Texas State legislature, declared his candidacy in February 1954, Johnson concluded he would have to scramble.

A millionaire oilman-rancher, Dougherty had supported Adlai Stevenson in 1952, contributing a large sum of money to his presidential campaign. Now, having decided that most Texans were really conservative, Dougherty declared he was an isolationist and that the United States should quit the United Nations at once and immediately break off diplomatic relations with the Soviet Union. His economic policies called for a return to the gold standard. He also accused Truman and Roosevelt of being secret members of the Communist Party, called Eleanor Roosevelt an "old witch," and branded Johnson a Communist as well. His slogan was: "Clean the Godless Communists out of the State Department." Coke Stevenson, seeking revenge for 1948, agreed to manage Dougherty's campaign.

Dougherty's campaign began with a twenty-nine-hour radio and television blitz in which the rancher revealed himself as a blunderer and a bore. He soon called off two other planned telethons. Instead, to put some excitement into his campaign, he raced around Texas in a shiny red fire engine, bells clanging loudly. He delivered his speeches from the rear of the fire truck, ranting about "Reds" and attacking Johnson as soft on communism and tough on labor, ineffectual as a Senate leader, and devious in his amassing of personal wealth. To undermine LBJ's liberal support, meanwhile, he passed around a letter from oil tycoon H. Roy Cullen stating that Johnson had promised to "vote right on conservative matters." In this document Cullen insisted that the senator's record would show he was "more conservative than most Republicans would be." Maury Maverick had seen the letter and feared that if photostated and placed in newspapers around the state, "it would play hell with Lyndon."[38]

A poll back in November-December had shown a decent Johnson approval rating among Texas voters. But the senator and his staff aimed higher than a modest victory in the July primary. As a memo of early 1954, probably from George Reedy, noted, they hoped for the "reelection of Lyndon Johnson by the largest vote in the history of Texas." Such a result, it stated, would improve Johnson's ability to get things done for Texas. But more was involved. A big win would also "place Senator Johnson in a strong position for the Democratic National Convention in 1956."[39] This coy remark is one of the earliest suggestions that Johnson had been bitten by the presidential bug. When *Time* magazine in June 1953 had mentioned him as a possible candidate in 1956, he denied any interest. He intended to stay in the Senate, he declared. Yet obviously the bug had bitten, though perhaps the itch was not yet severe.

Johnson decided not to take to the personal campaign trail in Texas and made only one speech in the state before the primary. Jimmy Allred and his friends would do the local legwork. Meanwhile, the senator's Washington office distributed a stream of bulletins describing his pressing work in Washington and the difficulties if he had to come home and campaign.

Though appearing relaxed and confident, Johnson worried about Dougherty's charges. Johnson won back some union support when he helped defeat a harsh antilabor measure reported out by the Senate Labor Committee that made the original Taft-Hartley Act seem benign. The move, which the *New Republic* called "chang[ing] sides while standing still,"[40] pleased the liberals, who opposed the revision, and the Southerners, who were perfectly satisfied with the earlier law. In gratitude, organized labor in Texas made significant contributions to Johnson's campaign fund.

As for Dougherty's charge of feeble Senate leadership, Johnson felt his high card was to show how skilled he was in managing legislation. His office prepared material demonstrating how many times Johnson had gotten most or all of his fellow party members to vote the same way on such bills as the proposed Taft-Hartley revision, the measures granting statehood to Alaska and Hawaii, and the adding of an antimonopoly amendment to the administration's small-business bill. But this was an easy claim to refute. The ever-critical *New Republic* left-handedly complimented him when it advised William Knowland to "study the Johnson formula":

> The Johnson system [the magazine's article stated] is to avoid rows and antagonize as few people as possible. That approach carried over into the Senate has meant that Lyndon Johnson doesn't get into a fight for a fight's sake. . . .
>
> But Johnson is like a fire chief who doesn't turn on the siren unless he can save the house. When he thinks he can't win, he sits on the side looking for another weak spot where a successful attack might be launched. . . .[41]

In the middle of the primary fight Johnson became entangled in a Senate battle to revise the Atomic Energy Act of 1946 to permit private enterprise to participate in the development of civilian atomic power. This change provoked the heated opposition of Democratic liberals, who traditionally supported public power. Upset as well over the administration's agreement with a private firm, Dixon-Yates, to supply energy to the Tennessee Valley Authority, an icon of the public power principle, they sought to filibuster the bill to death. Johnson favored public power himself but feared that a filibuster would divide the Democrats and weaken the walls against invoking cloture. He tried to keep as aloof as possible from the fight.

On July 25, the day of the Texas primary, while the Senate was holding round-the-clock sessions on the atomic energy bill, the teletype reported that Johnson had beaten Dougherty, 875,000 to 350,000. The results were announced on the floor of the Senate. After expressions of congratulations and praise from his colleagues, Johnson proposed a "gentlemen's agreement," limiting debate on the pending bill, the very action that Knowland so ardently desired. Emphasizing moderation and responsibility, he told the Senate:

> Through many decades, my party has been the truly responsible party. These are times that call for reasonable action by reasonable parties made up of reasonable men. . . .
> [This was] the hour for each of us to search our hearts and souls and ask the question "Are we exercising the responsibility of which we are capable?"

Democratic senator Albert Gore of Tennessee, one of the leaders of the opposition, backed down, and most of the other liberals, except the now partyless, former Republican senator from Oregon, Wayne Morse, followed. The filibuster ended.

The following day, after a twelve-and-a-half hour speech by Morse, the Senate passed the atomic energy bill. In the House it lost a number of public-interest amendments the Senate liberals had managed to add. In another instance of his successful balancing act between liberal and conservative factions, Johnson successfully fought to get the disputed portions reinstated, adding some credit to his depleted liberal bank account.

Now Johnson could concentrate on the upcoming congressional elections in November. As the Democratic nominee, his own Senate race was pro forma, but he wanted to assure Democratic control of the Senate. In the Eighty-third Congress there were forty-eight Republicans and forty-seven Democrats, with Wayne Morse listed as an independent. Nineteen Democrats, including Hubert Humphrey, were up for reelection, and, in this time of acute Red scare, many of them were worried that they would be smashed by the Republicans for being "soft on Communism." With Johnson's approval, Humphrey, in a move that would later embarrass him, sponsored a bill to outlaw the Communist Party, deny it prerogatives, privileges, and immunities, and subject Communists to criminal penalties under the Internal Security Act. The other eighteen Senate Democratic candidates demanded cosponsorship of the bill as well. Though Attorney General Herbert Brownell considered several of its provisions unconstitutional, no Democratic senator felt he could vote against it, and it passed, eighty to zero.

By this time the election was heating up. The Republicans wanted a weapon of their own and asked Eisenhower, who had vowed to abstain from publicly attacking Democrats, for help in their campaigns. The president did not want to jeopardize bipartisan support for his programs by sniping at the opposition, but when early fall polls revealed that the Democrats might win, he decided to campaign for the party. Eventually Eisenhower made more than two hundred speeches in ninety-five cities, warning against the "cold war of partisan politics" that would erupt if the Republicans lost control of Congress.

Johnson felt he had to answer the president, but how could he avoid a rupture with the administration? He and Rayburn worked on a response that would target the Republicans but leave Eisenhower untouched. At a rally for Humphrey in Minnesota on October 23, Johnson read a telegram to the president that called Eisenhower's statements an "unwarranted and unjust attack" on Democrats who had "done so much to cooperate with [his] administration." Eisenhower, they noted, had been placed in his "position of rigid, unswerving partisanship" by "the frantic pleas" of his "political advisers." But Johnson hastened to assure the president that there would "be no cold war conducted" against him when the Democrats regained control of Congress.[42] The statement successfully defused a potent Republican campaign bomb and at the same time cautioned the Democratic candidates against publicly maligning a popular president. Eisenhower did not raise the issue of partisan politics for the rest of the campaign.

On November 3 the Democrats won a substantial victory in the House. The party count in the Senate remained unchanged from the previous Congress: forty-eight to forty-seven. This time, however, independent Wayne Morse of Oregon agreed to vote as a Democrat if Johnson gave him a seat on the Foreign Relations Committee. With a two-vote edge the Democrats now became the Senate's majority party. At age forty-six, only six years after his election to the Senate, Johnson would become the youngest Senate majority leader in history.

CHAPTER 11

Majority Leader

E VEN BEFORE THE DEAL with Morse that made him majority leader, Johnson announced he would continue to cooperate with the administration. At a press conference on November 6 he used an expression he would trot out many times in the future to characterize the spirit of nonpartisan accommodation he valued. His daddy, he told the reporters, would gather the family around the table when there was a decision to be made and quote Isaiah: "Come now, let us reason together."[1] As majority leader he would abide by that admonition, he said.

Yet times were changing, and Johnson gradually edged back toward the New Deal policies he had embraced when he first came to Congress. His course correction would culminate in the Great Society programs of 1964–68, but in 1955, to preserve the fragile unity of the Senate Democrats and to accommodate his wafer-thin majority in the Eighty-fourth Congress, he was still taking modest steps that lagged behind Truman's Fair Deal agenda. At times, when he felt particularly vulnerable, he even turned back to the safe conservative position. Taken together, during the mid-fifties, he was not ready to move much ahead of the country as a whole. Johnson always insisted that the timing for action be right and that programs be enactable when brought to a vote. Some liberals recognized what he was doing and praised him openly. "I think Johnson is as liberal as he can be," said Senator Richard Neuberger of Oregon, "and still continue as the effective leader of the Senators who sit on the Democratic aisle. . . ." Neuberger could not understand why Johnson was expected to maintain a perfect record "when his liberal critics are not themselves bent double with . . . decorations for bravery under heavy fire."[2]

Other liberals agreed. Humphrey later remembered how, citing education, public works, minimum wage, and other issues, he tried to convince his fellow liberals in these years that "on the basic things that we need around here Johnson is with us. . . ."[3] Harry McPherson, a fellow Texan who first met Senator Johnson when he came to work as counsel for the Senate Democratic Policy Committee in 1956, believed the Majority Leader "the most progressive senior public official [from Texas] on the scene." Even the small group of committed liberals associated with the *Texas Observer*, said McPherson—the "Dugger crowd"—considered him a possible "instrument for good."[4]

Yet many liberal Democrats remained unhappy with LBJ's performance. They disliked his cautious pace, his penchant for compromise, and his rapport with the Republican president. After Ike's State of the Union address on January 6, 1955, Johnson had announced typically: "The president correctly states a Democratic premise when he says that the general good should be our yardstick on every great issue of our time." The Democrats, he promised, would "consider his program in that spirit."[5] This was precisely the approach the liberals deplored. They wanted aggressive partisan action, not cool reason, and for the rest of his political career they would never be satisfied with his achievements, always insisting he had fallen short.

In the Senate the new session opened with another push by liberals, led by New York's Herbert Lehman, to change Rule 22 to make cloture easier to invoke. Humphrey feared that a cloture fight at the beginning of the new Congress would weaken Johnson's position as leader and attended the liberals' strategy meeting, two days before the session opened, determined to prevent the battle from occurring. Fortunately for Johnson, the Minnesotan convinced his liberal colleagues to abandon their assault on filibusters. There was a better, less disruptive, route to follow, including letting Lyndon Johnson see what he could accomplish with his fellow Southerners.

But Johnson had little time to savor this victory or his formal election as majority leader on January 5. He had been suffering from severe backaches since December and been unable to attend the Democratic National Committee Meeting in New Orleans where Paul Butler, a volatile, combative liberal, hostile to both Johnson and Rayburn, had been chosen as Democratic national chairman. Now the backaches were even worse, and while listening to Eisenhower's State of the Union message, Johnson writhed in pain. On January 18 he finally yielded to his doctor's advice and went to the Mayo Clinic. It was a kidney stone and required an invasive operation. Johnson spent eleven days in Rochester, Minnesota, and then almost two weeks at the Ranch, recovering. Two months after the operation, still in pain and his entire trunk encased in a steel brace, he was back on the floor of the Senate ready to do battle.

At stake was a tax cut bill submitted by Sam Rayburn in part because he was tired of going along with Eisenhower just to maintain bipartisanship. Eisenhower called it "fiscally irresponsible," claiming that it threatened his budget. Johnson believed this was not an important enough issue on which to buck the president, but at the same time he wanted to save his old friend "Mr. Sam" from disgrace. The Senate Finance Committee had already rejected the Rayburn proposal by a vote of nine to six, though it had narrowly squeaked through on straight party lines in the House as a whole. Johnson tried to come up with a compromise that would sustain the substance of the tax cut without alienating the Senate's fiscal conservatives and preserve some semblance of Rayburn's prestige.

The compromise, supported by the Senate Democratic Policy Committee, called for a modest $20 reduction in the taxes of heads of households and an additional $10 for each dependent other than a spouse. This would benefit mostly low-income families. The new bill would also maintain unaltered the excise and corporation taxes that the president wanted, but they would be carried forward until July 1957, a period of two years rather than one. In addition, the Johnson-sponsored bill would close many tax loopholes for corporations, businessmen, and wealthy taxpayers. Secretary of the Treasury George Humphrey was vehemently opposed to the new measure, calling it "silly" as well as "irresponsible" and "political." Johnson responded that Humphrey was aiming to be "the best big business Secretary since Andrew Mellon,"[6] a reference to the millionaire treasury secretary who epitomized the Republican–big business alliance of the 1920s. The Johnson measure was apparently also too liberal for the Southern Democrats, and they joined the Republicans to defeat it, fifty to forty-four. At this point the relationship between Rayburn and Johnson began to alter; the younger man would now become the senior partner in the friendship.

The income tax fight was Johnson's first major action as majority leader, and LBJ, in defending Rayburn, had been defeated by being too open about what he wanted. He had also left no room for further compromise. From now on he would retreat to his technique of working behind the scenes, not disclosing what he really favored, and leaving plenty of room to maneuver. There were no more substantial political setbacks the rest of the year, though the liberals continued to complain that the Senate majority leader was settling for only partial victories.

One instance of the half-a-loaf strategy was Johnson's approach to the Reciprocal Trade Agreements Act, extending by three years the president's power to cut tariffs without congressional approval in return for trade concessions by foreign nations. Reiterating Roosevelt's prewar reciprocal trade policy, the bill reminded fifties liberals of the great days of the New Deal. But Americans had become increasingly protectionist in the postwar years. The House had passed the bill by only a one-vote margin after Rayburn invited twenty Democratic freshmen members to breakfast and commanded them to support the bill. Johnson employed two strategies to ensure that at least some trade agreement was passed: obfuscation and compromise. To disarm and mislead the protectionists, he constantly complained to reporters that the trade acts were in "deep trouble." He also added some protectionist measures, including one against Japanese textile imports, so that his Southern colleagues would be more likely to vote for it. The Johnson strategy worked. The bill passed, seventy-five to thirteen.

Johnson got little credit from the left. The liberals felt the compromise bill was too protectionist. In June, Americans for Democratic Action (ADA) criticized Democratic congressional leadership in general for "affably acquiescing in the Republican assault upon liberalism," and Lyndon Johnson in particular for using the "pretext of 'party unity' to avoid action on liberal legislation."[7]

ADA's attack came shortly after Johnson had worked around the clock to get through two measures that were more liberal than his southern colleagues would have liked. One was an increase in the minimum wage, which Congress had set at 75 cents an hour in 1949. The president agreed to raise it to 90 cents. Organized labor wanted to hike it to $1.25. Liberals also wanted minimum wage coverage extended to hundreds of thousands of workers in the retail and service trades. Johnson's compromise was an increase to $1.00 and no extension of coverage. The Southern Democrats went along and the bill was passed.

On the other measure—construction of federally subsidized public housing units—even the most outspoken liberals conceded that Johnson had been effective since they had believed it a lost cause. Just the previous year, the Republicans had enacted so many restrictions on the public housing program that it seemed virtually dead. Johnson was determined to see that the program not only stayed alive but was expanded.

Johnson encouraged the Senate Banking Committee to report a bill authored by Alabama Senator John Sparkman authorizing the construction of at least 100,000 public housing units a year for four years. Johnson had already appointed a strong supporter of public housing, liberal Senator Mike Monroney of Oklahoma, to a vacancy on the Senate Banking Committee, which had jurisdiction over the Housing Subcommittee. To counter Sparkman's measure, Eisenhower induced Senator Homer Capehart of Indiana to amend the bill to reduce the number of units by almost two-thirds, to thirty-five thousand. The Republicans, anticipating southern Democratic support, were certain that the Capehart amendment would win. The Indiana senator crowed to LBJ: "Lyndon, this is one time I've really got you. I'm going to rub your nose in it."[8] LBJ thought otherwise. Staying up all night to work on his southern colleagues, he and Bobby Baker rounded up every senator they could find. The vote was scheduled for June 7.

Every vote was needed, and to make the roll call, Humphrey flew back from Minneapolis. But the planes were stacked up in the fog near Washington and couldn't land. Johnson stalled in the Senate as long as he could, finally calling the airport control tower and insisting that they land the senator's plane immediately. Alerted to the emergency, the Capitol police picked the senator up when he deplaned and raced him back to the Senate in time. Humphrey's vote was not needed. The Capehart amendment failed, thirty-eight to forty-four. Then Johnson got the Sparkman bill through, sixty to twenty-five, with southern conservatives voting in favor. Paul Douglas, the progressive senator from Illinois, usually skeptical of Johnson, was pleased. "I didn't think you could do it," he told LBJ, "and I will never know *how* you did it, but you did it, and I'm grateful."[9]

The next item on the Democratic agenda was liberalization of the Social Security Act, supported by both Johnson and Rayburn. The bill proposed lowering from sixty-five to sixty-two the age at which women would be entitled to benefits as retired workers, as widows of men covered by Social Security, or as wives of retired workers. It also provided old age and survivors benefits for workers, beginning at fifty, who became totally disabled before reaching retirement age. The bill passed in August 1956.

At the end of June *Newsweek* featured a long article on LBJ headlined "The Texan Who is Jolting Washington" and declaring that "he puts his imprint on every new law." The article described how on one day the previous week, the Senate had confirmed an ambassador and a Federal Trade Commissioner and passed ninety bills in the astonishing time of four hours and forty-three minutes. This record-breaking feat was accomplished, the article said, by the dynamism of Johnson's leadership and his disdain for the protracted debates that used to be the Senate's trademark. "Now Johnson," *Newsweek* continued, "has emerged not only as top man of the Senate, in fact as well as title, but as the dominant force in Congress. Some of his colleagues think he has more influence over the legislative branch than anyone since Uncle Joe Cannon, once a czar of the House, and more power in contemporary Washington than anyone except the President."[10]

How did he do it? Political columnists Evans and Novak described what they called the "Johnson System," consisting of the Johnson Procedure and the Johnson Network. Flexibility was the most important part of the Procedure. Figure out what the Senate was likely to agree to on any major piece of legislation and then move as briskly as possible to minimize debate. Now, to corral the votes, the Johnson Network went into action. Made up of congenial senators, of Bobby Baker and his staff, and of Rayburn and the Texas congressional delegation, it kept him apprised of doings in both Houses, counted heads, and calculated who still needed to be persuaded and whose votes needed to be switched. Johnson himself contributed to this system of intelligence, continually querying and quizzing his fellow senators wherever he could buttonhole them.

Johnson used the Senate clerks tactically to get his legislation through. On the Senate floor, when he had enough votes in place, he would twirl his finger around and around briskly, and the clerks would call the roll quickly. If his staff was still rounding up stray senators whose votes were important, LBJ would display his palm down and the roll call would be slowed accordingly. Another ploy was manipulating attendance on the floor, making sure that key senators were present or absent at any given time. Doris Kearns reports Johnson setting up a special lunch on the other side of town for a senator whose absence he desired at a two o'clock vote.

Johnson shamelessly courted the votes he wanted. Hubert Humphrey described the difference between LBJ and Scott Lucas, his predecessor as Democratic Senate leader. When Lucas wanted to talk to Senator Humphrey, a secretary would call and ask if he could come around to Lucas's office at some particular hour. When Johnson wanted to see the senator from Minnesota, he would call and ask when *he* could come to Humphrey's office to talk.

There was another key element in the process of manipulating Congress—the face-to-face physical manipulation of recalcitrants and irresolutes that became famous as the "Johnson Treatment." Johnson would get as physically close as he could manage to his targets, literally grabbing them by their lapels and poking them in the chest for emphasis.

He would drop his head and then cock it to the side so that he could get it under his captive's face. As Harry McPherson noted, "his very massiveness and bigness . . . [had] an almost inevitable force to it."[11] And his voice, alternately wheedling and threatening, laced with homespun expressions and cornpone humor, would drown out any verbal objections. *Washington Post* editor Ben Bradlee likened Johnson in this mode to a St. Bernard who "licked your face for an hour, [and] had pawed you all over."[12] He compared the experience to visiting the zoo. Mary McGrory called the "full treatment" a "rather overwhelming experience . . . an incredibly potent mixture of persuasion, badgering, flattery, threats, reminders of past favors and future advantages."[13] It was Hubert Humphrey, however, who described the process most vividly: "He'd come on just like a tidal wave sweeping all over the place. He went through walls. He'd come through a door, and he'd take the whole room over. Just like that. . . . He was not delicate. . . . He was not a ballet dancer. He was a downfield blocker and a running fullback *all at the same time.*"[14]

Even downfield blockers have to rest. But LBJ would not or could not stop, even though his doctors warned him repeatedly about his health. He had never taken the time to recuperate from his kidney stone operation, and by the end of June 1955 was driving himself harder than ever. He did not take time off for lunch, and missed many dinners, coming home most of the time at ten or eleven at night. When he did eat, it was junk food and empty calories, upping his weight to 225, more poundage than he had ever carried before. He was also smoking up to three packs of cigarettes a day and drinking more than usual.

On June 18 Johnson and George Smathers, the smooth-operating, elegantly dressed senator from Florida, drove out to visit George Brown on his horse country estate in Middleburg, Virginia, forty miles from Washington. In the car, Lyndon had what he thought was a severe attack of indigestion and asked driver Norman Edwards to stop so that he could get a Coke. The drink did not help, but he got through the rest of the day. By the next morning he said he felt better, and after the weekend he went right back to his overloaded Senate schedule. He wanted to finish Senate business early in the summer and was working harder than ever on the remaining legislation, taking, as William White noted in the *New York Times*, "the unusual step of keeping in close personal touch with the clerks and technicians of the Senate committees to keep them going full tilt."[15]

Johnson was proud of his record and boasted later in the year that 30 percent more bills had been passed in this session than in the last, and in much less time. "Furthermore," he noted, "this Senate session tackled important and highly controversial legislation—minimum wage, public housing, upper Colorado River project, long-range trade program. No one of these bills took longer than three days to pass."[16]

On Friday, July 1, Sam Rayburn, sharing a late dinner with his friend after a particularly busy day, noticed the raw, red skin blotches and the deep, dark circles under Johnson's eyes, and told him to take it easy. Johnson promised him he would when the Senate adjourned. He had arranged to spend the July Fourth weekend at George Brown's and asked Norman Edwards to pick him up at 5:00 P.M. on Saturday. Lady Bird was scheduled to join him on Sunday. As soon as he got into the car, he complained that the air was stifling and told Norman to turn on the air conditioning full blast. Again, he needed a Coke to help his nausea. By the time he reached Middleburg, his chest hurt "as though there were two hundred pounds on it." New Mexico senator Clint Anderson, a recovered heart attack victim, was already at Brown's estate.[17] By now suspecting something worse than indigestion, LBJ asked him what his symptoms meant, particularly the pain shooting up his left arm. Anderson told him he was probably having a heart attack. All the local doctors were attending the horse show, but they finally located one, who diagnosed a coronary occlusion when he arrived and ordered him to the hospital immediately.

An ambulance rushed Johnson to Bethesda Naval Hospital, where he was carried in on a stretcher and brought to a private room to await the doctors. Here Lady Bird and Walter Jenkins were waiting. Lady Bird had already called Dr. Jim Cain in Dallas and asked him to fly to Washington to help coordinate the medical team. While smoking one last cigarette, the patient gave Lady Bird his money clip and told Jenkins that his will and extra money were in his office desk. He remembered that his tailor was making two suits for him, a brown and a blue. "Tell him to go ahead with the blue," he told Lady Bird; he would need it "no matter what happens."[18] Jenkins recalled that Lady Bird was calm, though she must have been under excruciating strain. "Honey, everything will be all right," she told her husband.[19] The New York Times the following day reported the official diagnosis as a "moderately severe heart attack" with "his condition at present . . . considered serious."[20] For the first time in his adult life Johnson could not think about politics; staying alive came first.

But once out of danger, LBJ reverted. He was soon restless and making extravagant demands. Politics remained very much on his mind, and he listened to news programs against the advice of his physicians, switching from station to station and yelling colorful curses at commentators he did not like. Visitors, including Eisenhower and Vice President Nixon, streamed into and out of the sickroom.

Rebekah Johnson made the first plane trip of her life to visit her ailing son and amused the hospital staff and reporters by telling anecdotes, some highly exaggerated, about her oldest boy. Lady Bird moved into the adjoining room and stayed with him the entire time he was hospitalized. "Lyndon wanted me around twenty-four hours a day," she said. "He wanted me to laugh a lot and always to wear lipstick."[21] But if demanding, her husband was appropriately grateful. "Every time I lifted my hand," Johnson recalled fondly, "she would be there." Meanwhile, Lady Bird turned her room into an office, requesting key staff members be on call, and answering the letters that poured in from all over the country. She was the model of patience and serenity, but the costs were high. "When this is over," she said at one point, "I want to go off by myself and cry."[22]

His heart attack replenished a deep pool of fatalism in Johnson's personality. It confirmed his family history of early mortality and reinforced his conviction that time was running out. Back in 1946, when he had been advised to remain in the House and eventually become Speaker, he had intoned, "Too slow. Too slow." That phrase, or that feeling, would become a theme running through much of Johnson's public life. It was important to cram as much into the time left as possible. There would be few second chances.

Johnson was soon running the Senate by remote control, although whip Earle Clements had supposedly taken over the Majority Leader's post while he was in the hospital. Information from an assistant secretary of state enabled Johnson to respond before anyone else to President Eisenhower's Geneva Summit "Open Skies" proposal of arms verification through aerial photographic reconnaissance. Johnson got Clements to read his statement of praise for the proposal on the Senate floor, scooping William Knowland and all the other congressional leaders, and garnering almost as many headlines as the president.

Finally, on August 7, having suffered "no complications," Johnson left the hospital, expecting to be back in the Senate in January when the second congressional session began. The convalescent returned home, where he held court in a large reclining chair, informing visitors, both friends and newspapermen, of his daily doctors' reports, his meal-by-meal calorie intake, his nap- and bedtimes, and other bits of personal data. During the early weeks of recuperation Lady Bird consulted Johnson's doctors about his future. Should he remain in the Senate? Should he continue as majority leader? Would it shorten his life to continue in politics? Dr. Cain, the old family friend, advised against retirement. Politics "was what he knew; it was what he liked," and there was "no evidence that continuing on working with a degree of moderation . . . would shorten his life a bit."[23]

On his forty-seventh birthday, August 27, the doctors permitted Johnson to return to the Ranch for the rest of his recovery period. Lady Bird called Mary Rather, who had left the senator's staff and returned to Texas, to come help out with the mail and visitors. Lady Bird quickly installed a swimming pool so that her husband could get exercise. Dr. Willis Hurst, his chief cardiologist, visited the Ranch several times, and Johnson tried to follow his advice. He stopped smoking, substituting chewing gum and low-calorie candy for the weed. Eating regularly and giving up his beloved chicken-fried steak and fried potatoes, he got his weight down to 175 pounds. He slowed his pace and tried hard not to get angry over trifles. He told a reporter that he had "thrown away the whip." He began to read books, something he confessed to not doing since he left college, and to listen to music. He took more of an interest in his daughters, now eleven and eight, and made small talk with his wife. He told *Newsweek* that his heart attack saved his life. "It . . . taught me to appreciate some things a busy man sometimes almost forgets. . . . Essentially, it all means, I guess, that I'm learning all over how to live."[24] He followed the doctors' medical advice—for a time. He became calorie-conscious. He became a "cantaloupe nut" and a devotee of tapioca made with artificial sweetener.[25] At the end of July Juanita Roberts, one of the senator's secretaries, wrote him from Washington about "the new flavored Jell-O." "The *Black Cherry*," she assured him, was "a delightful flavor."[26] He exercised more. He took long walks to cousin Oriole's place down the road a convenient mile away, insisting that visitors come along. He played with Lucy's beagle. He became more philosophical. Walter Jenkins believed he was less likely to fly off the handle at little things after his heart attack than before. But he was also frequently depressed, an emotional response that often follows a heart attack but that reinforced his natural tendencies. It was during one of these times that he mournfully told a visitor that he would have to retire when his term ended in 1960 and would never be president. Though he welcomed the nurturing attention of women, he also felt suffocated by the solicitous contingent at the Ranch. "I'm a man surrounded by women who won't let me alone," he wrote his secretary Dorothy Philips in mid-September.[27]

During his enforced exile Johnson was kept current on Washington and Senate matters by Bobby Baker, who wrote several long newsy, gossipy letters, and visited the Ranch with his wife, Dorothy, in early November. Meanwhile, the senator's staff labored to keep him in the news and in the public's eye. The convalescent gave a number of press conferences carefully scripted by his aides. Booth Mooney advised Johnson to describe the plus side of his healing stay at the Ranch. The senator could not "emphasize too often the value of the reflective thinking" he was "having an opportunity to do." It would, he should say, "inevitably effect for the better" his "future work."[28] George Reedy coached Johnson on what to tell Mark Sullivan of *Sports Illustrated* to show that he had become a baseball fan while watching television during his illness. "Explain . . . " wrote Reedy—as totally ignorant of the Great American Pastime as LBJ—"that when you were lying in bed in the hospital you became attracted to the baseball games as one of the most relaxing forms of entertainment on television." "It would be a mistake," Reedy added, "to pick any favorite team or make any predictions about who will win the pennant."[29]

Johnson gradually eased himself back onto the conveyor belt and in fact began to plan for an expanded political future. Stonewall, Texas, soon became a pilgrimage site for a stream of Democratic leaders. In late September Adlai Stevenson and Rayburn came to see the wounded leader and in an outdoor press conference in the front yard the convalescent demonstrated his recovery by stealing the show and controlling the conversation. By this time Johnson had set up the agenda for the next congressional session. Underlying all the renewed motion was a sense that, despite his heart attack, Lyndon Johnson was slated for higher things than Senate majority leader.

LBJ's widening perspective became apparent on November 19, when, for the first time, he announced a specific legislative program of his own. The occasion was a Democratic fund-raising dinner in Whitney, in the heart of the Hill Country. At the stalwart-packed, ten-dollar-a-plate turkey dinner at the local armory, Johnson presented his New Dealish "Program with a Heart" with an unusual eloquence. The verve of his delivery demonstrated a renewed physical vigor, but the impact of the speech went beyond this. Whether we ascribe the shift to the philosophical mellowing of a life-threatening health crisis or to presidential ambitions, Johnson had returned to his old, more palatable role of populist tribune. Bobby Baker, after reading the press reports of the speech, joked that LBJ sounded as if he had "become more liberal than [Herbert] Lehman," ADA's favorite senator.[30]

The thirteen points of the Whitney program included enhanced Social Security benefits, tax revisions to help low-income groups, funding for medical research and for more hospitals, stepped-up school construction, new federal housing programs, water resource development, road construction, and farm price subsidies. Johnson also proposed supplementary unemployment insurance, surplus food grants, disaster insurance, amended immigration and naturalization laws, and a constitutional amendment to eliminate the poll tax. Tacked on was a proposal to end controls on natural gas prices, a true Texas issue.

Leading Democrats were enthusiastic about the Johnson plan. Objecting only to the proposed decontrol of natural gas prices as harmful to consumers, Humphrey praised Johnson for a "very fine batting average—twelve hits in thirteen times at bat." The poll tax repeal scheme, for one, would give the "long civil rights struggle some forward action. . . ."[31] The party's purist left remained skeptical, however. Joseph Rauh, national chairman of ADA, sneered at what he called a collection of "slogans and promises" and commented that he couldn't tell the difference between "Eisenhower moderation versus Johnson moderation, if indeed there is a difference."[32] But the LBJ camp considered attacks like Rauh's a plus. Rauh was "the craziest bastard in this country," Bobby Baker wrote the senator, and it was "a blessing to you that such a fool is opposed to your leadership."[33]

Johnson's renewed physical strength was confirmed by an exhaustive medical examination in December. The six doctors who tested and probed him were pleased with the "rapid rate of his recovery." The good news, however, was accompanied by a warning: Johnson must delegate responsibilities to his staff, carefully balance his time between work and rest, and take many short vacations throughout the year. Late in the year the Johnsons went to California, where the senator gave a speech to the annual American Hotel Association meeting and Lady Bird and the girls visited Disneyland. On New Year's Day, he announced that he was ready to come back as Majority Leader and that farm aid would be his first priority.

On opening day, January 3, Johnson was greeted by a loud round of applause when he appeared on the Senate floor. "You don't know," he told his colleagues, "how glad I am to stand at this desk again."[34] At first he tried to follow doctors' orders and take it easy. He came to work about ten, took a two-hour nap in the afternoon, and carried his electrocardiogram with him in his wallet, to be available to medical personnel in case of another heart attack. He also enlisted new people to help him, including James Wilson, a Texas lawyer, and his old New Deal friend, James H. Rowe. When Rowe said he could only give one day a week, Johnson pleaded with him for more. "You know I am going to die," he said tearfully to Rowe, "and you don't care." Noting the "great performance," Rowe finally gave in, saying, "oh, goddamn it, all right,"[35] and agreed to work full-time. During the session Rowe and fellow lawyers Abe Fortas and Clark Clifford would meet once a month at Johnson's house to discuss strategy.

Johnson forgot most of his good medical intentions, however, as soon as the Senate got down to work on the Harris-Fulbright bill, the proposal to lift federal controls over natural gas prices. The bill sought to bypass a U.S. Supreme Court decision giving the Federal Power Commission authority to regulate gas prices at the wellhead. However concerned with his national image, Johnson could not let the bill die. Liberals were vehement in their opposition, charging the oil and gas tycoons with highway robbery. In actual fact, the split was as much sectional as ideological, with Northerners and Midwesterners, without oil themselves and dependent on Gulf Coast fuel, most antagonistic to ending federal controls.

Johnson thought he had enough votes to win, particularly among the Republicans; Eisenhower had promised to sign the bill. At the last moment, the small, owlish, meticulously honest Republican senator from South Dakota, Francis Case, rose on the Senate floor to announce that an oil company lobbyist had offered him $2,500 to vote for the bill. He would now have to change his vote to "No." Despite the Case affair, the bill passed fifty-three to thirty-eight, but Eisenhower, deeply disturbed by the improprieties, vetoed it a month later. Unfortunately for Johnson, the president's veto furnished the liberals with more ammunition and stiffened their resolve that they not "be asked much longer to repress their own desires in behalf of party harmony."[36]

Johnson would disappoint the liberals again with his position on the Gore Federal Highway Bill of 1956. This measure authorized billions of dollars from gasoline tax revenues for a giant interstate highway system. It would be the foundation of the limited-access road system that knits the country together today. The issue was whether highway workers should be paid according to the provisions of the 1931 Davis-Bacon Act, guaranteeing high wages on federal construction projects. Burned by his early experiences with organized labor at the family radio station, Johnson objected to Davis-Bacon. The unions considered it vital, and a showdown loomed. United Auto Workers lobbyist Robert Oliver, Johnson's friend and fellow Texan, begged Johnson, for the sake of his national political future, to dodge the vote on this bill if he could not vote in favor. When Johnson balked, Oliver enlisted the help of Bobby Baker. The three concocted a plan. Johnson had a longstanding appointment for a checkup at the Mayo Clinic. Instead of leaving late in the afternoon on the day of the vote, he would leave at ten in the morning. With Johnson in the air on the way to Minnesota, the Senate passed the Gore bill, forty-two to thirty-seven, with the Bacon-Davis amendment intact. Unfortunately, it remained clear that Johnson had ducked, and the advanced liberals had another reason to attack him.

These same enemies found it harder to fault Johnson for his stand on the "Southern Manifesto," the anti-*Brown* v. *Topeka* statement its proponents called the *Declaration of Constitutional Principles*. By now the conservative South had recovered from the initial shock of the school desegregation decision. Racists and assorted social conservatives were threatening massive resistance, and White Citizens' Councils, "uptown Ku Klux Klans," were using economic intimidation to weaken the opponents of Jim Crow. The March 1956 Manifesto pledged use of "all lawful means" to frustrate the Supreme Court decision. The justices, it declared, "undertook to exercise their naked judicial power and substituted their personal political and social ideas for the established law of the land." The Court was helping to destroy "the amicable relations between the white and Negro races" that had been built up "through ninety years of patient effort by the good people of both races," and was sowing the seeds of "hatred and suspicion" where previously there had been "friendship and understanding."[37] Signed by nineteen senators and eighty-one representatives, its endorsers included even relatively liberal Southerners such as John Sparkman, Lister Hill, George Smathers, and William Fulbright.

Only three southern senators—Gore and Kefauver, both from Tennessee, and Lyndon Johnson—refused to sign the Manifesto. Johnson understood his refusal might hurt him. "The Dixiecrats and a lot of my people at home," he told Bobby Baker, "will be on me like stink on shit if I don't stand up and bray against the Supreme Court decision." "I'm not gonna sign that Southern manifesto," Johnson promised Baker, "[but] I'm gonna have to do a lot of fancy tap-dancing to survive."[38] Johnson understood that signing the document might jeopardize his chances for a presidential bid. But he also feared that the manifesto would undermine party unity, the unity he had worked so hard to preserve since becoming majority leader. Fortunately, the move worked out well for him. Liberals such as Neuberger of Oregon hailed Johnson's action as "one of the most courageous acts of political valor I have ever seen."[39] Yet at the same time southern senators did not hold it against him. They understood that as Senate leader, he "had to work with all sides" in Congress, declared Mississippi's John Stennis. "Of course we wanted him to sign it, but at the same time we recognized that he wasn't just a senator from Texas, he was a leader and had a different responsibility. . . ."[40]

Despite his principled stand on desegregation, liberals found cause for further complaint when Johnson, with Humphrey's approval, killed the civil rights bill that Eisenhower sent to Congress just before it recessed for the presidential nominating conventions. Johnson did not even want to consider the merits of the bill four days before the session ended while other significant legislation was pending. "I am not going to take the responsibility, and have the blood on my hands," he declared, "for killing the Social Security bill." He believed that if the civil rights bill reached the floor, it would bring "all legislation to a halt, as it always has."[41] He also did not want a North-South split in the Democratic party in a presidential election year, a result Russell predicted if Johnson persisted in allowing the bill to come to the floor.

Johnson sought to position himself in the middle of the civil rights spectrum. He supported a constitutional amendment to abolish the poll tax. He also opposed several conservative measures to limit the power of the federal courts in racial matters. Humphrey considered this action "a major civil liberties fight" and was impressed by Johnson's "masterful display of strategy" in defeating "all those bills at one fell swoop."[42] Speaking of this period, the columnist William White, who often served as Johnson's mouthpiece, contends that LBJ was by now disgusted by "generations of congressional demagoguery on the whole civil rights question" on both sides. He believed that civil rights advocates proposed bills "so extreme in their scope and so blind to the infinite human complications of this tragic issue" that they could never pass or, if enacted, could never be implemented. The anti-civil-rights people, on the other hand, "stood upon equally demagogic barricades in proud 'resistance.'" These people on both sides hindered the passage of important legislation such as rural electrification, public relief, and housing, for "always Topic A would intrude."[43]

Nevertheless, LBJ promised a skeptical Senator Clinton Anderson, the most ardent civil rights advocate outside the true-blue liberal bloc, that he would make sure a civil rights bill was passed in 1957. He kept his promise. But that remained in the future, and meanwhile the liberals, who could not realistically have hoped for passage of the bill in such a short time, had another reason to be disappointed.

The controversy over civil rights obscured Johnson's accomplishments in 1956. He did not get all that he wanted. Federal aid to depressed areas, immigration reform, and a public power bill died in the House, and Eisenhower vetoed the omnibus farm bill. On the other hand, just before the session ended, the Senate passed a housing bill, a flood-insurance bill, and a foreign aid appropriations bill. Also, in April, the Upper Colorado Project Act, authorizing $760 million for a large Reclamation Bureau multipurpose water project, became law. And on March 24, on the same page that the New York Times reported Johnson as under attack by the ADA for bringing the Democratic Party "to its lowest point in twenty-five years," it also reported his fight for the liberalization of Social Security benefits and his attack on the Eisenhower administration for "ignoring the needs of our senior citizens."[44]

At issue in this last matter was an amendment to the Social Security Act, passed by the House in 1955, that allowed permanently disabled workers to retire with full benefits at fifty rather than sixty-five. This change would have altered the system from one that merely covered retirement and survivor's benefits to one providing for an increasing range of social welfare assistance. The American Medical Association (AMA) was convinced that this would lead to "socialized medicine," a pejorative term for federal health insurance. Eisenhower agreed with this assessment and went on record as opposed. Senators in states where the AMA was powerful, particularly those facing reelection, were also in opposition, and when the bill came from the Senate Finance Committee, the controversial disability provision was gone. Johnson pledged to have it restored when it reached the floor.

Concluding that only a few more votes would do the trick, LBJ and Bobby Baker quickly went to work. One of the people they needed was Robert Kerr, a member of the Senate Finance Committee with close ties in Oklahoma to the AMA. With Johnson's blessing, Kerr and Walter George worked out a compromise that called for reinstating the House disability provision to be financed by taxes paid into a new trust fund separate from Social Security. The other compromise provided for lowering the age of benefits for widows and retired working women and wives of retired workers to sixty-two.

With the revised bill in hand, the Johnson forces went into action rounding up votes. One target was George W. (Molly) Malone, the clumsy, red-faced senator from Nevada. A man of the far right whose propensity to deliver long, boring diatribes against free trade on the Senate floor made him few friends in Congress, his vote was as important as any other senator's. The pursuit of Malone was a classic of the Johnson method.

Johnson had gone out of his way on previous occasions to be cordial to Malone and had established goodwill with the senator. He knew that Malone was vulnerable at home on the issue of federal mineral subsidies, now sharply constricted by Eisenhower's parsimonious budget policy. At stake was a bill authorizing $69 million in federal tungsten purchases crucial to Nevada's economy. Malone needed this bill for his reelection bid two years ahead, and Johnson made a simple swap of favors: he would get the tungsten bill passed if Malone voted for the dis-

ability bill. Since few Republicans would defy the President on this issue, Johnson needed all the Democrats he could get and pressured unlikely Northeastern liberals such as Lehman of New York, Kennedy of
Massachusetts, and Green of Rhode Island to vote yes on the tungsten
subsidy. It passed. Malone was now in the majority leader's pocket.

When the Social Security bill came to the Senate floor, the vote
promised to be very close. Knowland had been doing some arm-twisting
of his own, reconverting some of the Republicans, including Joe Mc-
Carthy, whom Johnson had brought around. Baker's head count showed
a tie. Johnson had one ace-in-the-hole: party whip Clements, who until
this point had opposed the bill. Clements was fighting a very tough reelection campaign with the well-liked, attractive Republican Thruston
B. Morton, and the AMA, with strong links to the Kentucky tobacco industry, would destroy him if he voted for the bill. But the desperate Johnson convinced his second-in-command in an urgent cloakroom strategy
session to change his vote to yes. The bill passed, forty-seven to forty-five.
Eisenhower signed both the tungsten and the Social Security bills into
law.*

While Johnson was waging his legislative battles in Congress, he was
also once again fighting for control of the Texas Democratic delegation
to the August national convention. He and Rayburn agreed that they did
not want to see a replay of 1952, when pro-Eisenhower governor Shivers
and his followers were seated as delegates in preference to the loyalist
Texas liberals and moderates. Shivers was moving even further to the
right, and according to Hank Brown, a Texas AFL leader, Johnson felt
that it was necessary to "take him on . . . in order to maintain credentials
with labor and the Mexican-American and the Negro."[45] Rayburn came
up with a plan to push Lyndon for head of the delegation and as the
state's favorite-son candidate for president.

Johnson agreed to Rayburn's scheme. In May, at the Texas state convention in Dallas, LBJ faced the "Shivercrats" on the right and a liberal
group to his left in a fight for the soul of the state party. The Johnson
centrists won in what Reedy would later call "a display of extremely high
political courage," and kept the crypto-Republican Shivers forces from
hijacking the party.[46] The party liberals were more successful, however,

---

*Unfortunately, Clements's "aye" probably cost him his Senate seat. In November he lost to Morton
by fewer than five thousand votes. Ironically, two years later, Malone, too, went down to defeat in
Nevada.

managing to defeat Johnson's choice for national committeewoman, Mrs. Lloyd Bentsen, and electing one of their own. Still, overall, the Johnson forces had prevailed.

Now largely in control of his Texas delegation, Johnson went to Chicago as a favorite-son candidate. In the interest of party unity he hoped for a moderate statement in the national party platform on civil rights. The plank would have to be weak enough to win the Southerners, but strong enough not to embarrass the northern candidates with their black and liberal constituents. A major issue was whether to include a specific endorsement of *Brown v. Board of Education* and a demand for implementation of that decision. Fortunately for unity, Eleanor Roosevelt, the liberals' patron saint, agreed with Johnson that the party should omit specific endorsement of the antisegregation decision. The final version, adopted by the convention, was the moderate one. It declared that the Democrats would continue their "efforts to eradicate discrimination based on race, religion or national origin" with the knowledge that "this task requires action, not just in one section of the nation, but in all sections." It recognized that "recent decisions of the Supreme Court . . . relating to segregation . . . have brought consequences of vast importance to our nation as a whole and especially to communities directly affected," and that these decisions were now "part of the law of the land." The convention, however, rejected by "howling voice vote" the liberals' proposals "for the use of force" to stop any interference "with the orderly determination of these matters by the courts."[47] It also voted down their demand that the court expand the decision to include interstate transportation.

Meanwhile, the fight for the nomination raged in the convention hotel suites. Stevenson again hoped to be his party's nominee. He had fought a hard primary battle with Estes Kefauver until July, when the Tennessean withdrew. Now only Averell Harriman, the liberal New York governor, remained a threat, though not a very serious one. The media dismissed Johnson himself as a serious candidate; *Life* magazine pointed out that he "smelled of magnolias."[48] But Johnson had some support among the party leaders. Truman, for one, though he announced publicly for Harriman, told LBJ privately that "I'm opening this thing up so anybody can win—including you." Rayburn saw his friend's growing interest and deplored it. "I hate to see Lyndon get bit so hard by the presidential bug at this stage of the game. Stevenson's got it sewed up."[49]

Rayburn was right. John Connally's nominating speech pointed to Johnson's courageous battle against the pseudo-Democrats in Texas. He called Johnson a man for all sections and "the solid foundation stone upon which the strength of the Democratic Party has been rebuilt."[50]

But Stevenson was nominated on the first ballot; the majority leader got only eighty votes, mostly from his home state.

The convention's only real drama came when Stevenson, rather than designating a vice-presidential nominee, threw open the choice to the delegates. This would be the first time in memory that the nominee for the second slot would be chosen this way. The move disappointed several hopefuls. Johnson, for one, had been under pressure from Rayburn, Russell, and other southern friends to ask Adlai for the nomination for himself. By the time Johnson decided to try for it, Stevenson had made his decision for an open ballot.

The leading vice-presidential aspirants were Kefauver and his Tennessee colleague Albert Gore, Hubert Humphrey, and the relative newcomer to the Senate from Massachusetts, young John F. Kennedy. Johnson initially favored Humphrey but then switched to Kennedy, whom he thought might be useful to him in the future. When Johnson announced Texas's fifty-six votes for Kennedy from the floor, it looked as if the young man might make it, but then Minnesota switched from Humphrey to Kefauver and Tennessee released the Gore votes to Kefauver as well, starting a stampede that put the Tennessean over the top.

There would be a sad footnote to a convention that did little to further Johnson's career. Rebekah Johnson, bursting with pride at her son's accomplishments, came to Chicago to be with Lyndon and Lady Bird and to share in the excitement of a national convention. Her son introduced her to political celebrities and she had her picture taken with Harry Truman, Adlai Stevenson, and Eleanor Roosevelt. But Lady Bird observed that her mother-in-law had peculiar nodules on her arms. Ominously, these were soon diagnosed as symptoms of lymph gland cancer.

Back in Texas in September, Johnson found himself in the middle of another liberal-conservative imbroglio. This time it was a fight for the governorship between conservative Price Daniel and Ralph Yarborough, a liberal lawyer from Austin. Daniel had beaten Yarborough in the first primary, but because Pappy O'Daniel was also in the race, he had not received the needed majority, and the two leading candidates were forced into a runoff in late August. Johnson supported Price Daniel, and Pappy O'Daniel, who hated both Daniel and Johnson, urged his followers to shift to Yarborough. The runoff returns on August 25 were close and, as was the habit in Texas, they became the focus of electoral hanky-panky involving delays in reporting and vote manufacture. The Daniel people proved more enterprising and ingenious than their opponents and won. Yarborough later called it a "stolen election."[51]

In a near reprise of the May convention, the "Red Hots," led by Yarboroughites Kathleen Voight and Ronnie Dugger, sought to take over the party and write its platform at the state convention on September 11. Still determined to maintain his centrist dominance of the Texas Democrats, Johnson kept several Red Hot county delegations from being seated. After "one of the bloodiest [conventions] in state history," LBJ and his friends prevailed and passed a platform supported by Price Daniel.[52]

Johnson's role at Fort Worth, needless to say, angered the Texas liberals. George Reedy admitted that it had "caused some damage." On the other hand, Reedy noted in a memo to his chief, no one could "claim now that you are 'dominated by labor and left wingers.'" And besides, the "so-called 'liberals'" would have to go along with the party.[53]

The liberals were further annoyed by what they considered Johnson's limited support of the Stevenson-Kefauver ticket in the fall. Johnson promised Stevenson he would give his all for the ticket in the South and did in fact work for him. But it was an uphill fight in Texas, where Ike's popularity cut across class, and even racial, lines. In the end Johnson devoted more time and energy to supporting Democrats in general for the sake of retaining a Congressional majority than to the Stevenson-Kefauver ticket. The results were predictable. Eisenhower won a landslide victory. Stevenson lost Texas. Congress remained narrowly Democratic: 232 to 199 in the House and 49 to 47 in the Senate.

The events of late 1956 epitomized Johnson's perennial problem in maintaining a viable middle position without alienating either side in state politics. As columnists Evans and Novak pointed out, the senator had no "solid *Johnson* position in Texas," as other politicians such as Humphrey or Kennedy had in their home states. Johnson had to constantly test the Texas political waters and "could not afford to take a single step in national politics without looking over his shoulder to catch the reaction back home. . . . The boiling stew of Texas politics constantly threatened to spill over on him."[54] In later months Johnson struggled to appease his left opponents. When Fred Schmidt and Jerry Holleman of the Texas State Federation of Labor visited Washington in March 1957, they had a long talk with LBJ. Afterward Bill Brammer and George Reedy of the senator's staff took them to lunch and discussed further the recent bruising political battles in Texas. Brammer reported back to his chief that the visitors would return home satisfied that the senator "and they generally agree[d] on legislation for the working man" and that it was "pointless and destructive to carry on petty, partisan feuds within the framework of the Party back home." They promised to return to Texas "and try and put a stop to this business."[55] But despite the fence-mending, the constant turmoil of Texas politics undoubtedly encouraged Johnson's damaging political insecurities.

No sooner was the election past than Johnson faced a renewed challenge by the liberals over civil rights and the related issue of limiting Senate filibusters.

The pressures for a major federal civil rights measure were growing stronger by the day. One striking feature of the recent presidential contest had been the shift of many black voters to the Republican column. Eisenhower, by most estimates, had gotten 20 percent more black votes than in 1952. Undoubtedly, like other Americans, black voters were attracted primarily by the general's bland but reassuring presence, but according to Humphrey and other liberal Democrats, black voters were deserting the party because it had failed to take a strong stand on civil rights. The Democrats, Humphrey warned, were "digging their own graves by inaction. . . ."[56] On November 22, a clutch of liberal senators led by Humphrey, Paul Douglas, Wayne Morse, and Richard Neuberger issued a manifesto outlining a liberal sixteen-point program for the Democrats to enact in the first session of the new Congress. A key item was another push to curb filibusters.

More liberal thunder came from Paul Butler, Democratic National Committee chairman. Disgusted with the election results, Butler blamed Johnson and Rayburn for the Democrats' loss. They had cooperated too closely with the Eisenhower administration for leaders of an *opposition* party and had not provided effective leadership. In late November, Butler and other disgruntled liberals formed the Democratic Advisory Council as mouthpiece for the party's left and as a device to blur the party's image as an extension of Texas. Announcing that the Council would formulate liberal positions to challenge the Eisenhower administration, the insurgents invited twenty top Democratic officeholders, including Johnson and Rayburn, to join. Johnson tactfully declined on the grounds that "an additional committee not created by Federal law . . . would only cause delays and confusion." In fact, he feared that the DAC, in Harry McPherson's words, would be a "terrifically divisive force" within the party and harden the informal alliance between southern Democrats and Republicans. Once when McPherson urged a liberal policy on the majority leader, LBJ responded that he "didn't want Dick Russell . . . to walk across the aisle and embrace Everett Dirksen."[57] Most of the other Senate Democrats, with the exception of Kefauver and Humphrey, followed suit, forcing Butler to scale down the DAC's agenda.

Though he rejected the DAC, Johnson avoided a head-on collision with the group. It might have only a few members in Congress, but with important Democrats such as Eleanor Roosevelt, Harry Truman, Dean Acheson, and Professor John Kenneth Galbraith of Harvard on its roster, it wielded influence, and Johnson kept his innate skepticism to himself. He would like to be kept informed of their views, he told DAC members. "Johnson tried to cultivate us," Galbraith later told Merle Miller. "He would have various people myself included, down to the Ranch. It's a wonderful place to go, I may say."[58]

Though friendly to them on the surface, Johnson continued to resent the advanced liberals. He made an exception of Humphrey, whom he considered a reasonable man capable of compromise. But generally he found it hard to forgive them the difficulties they caused him and never ceased to justify his own political balancing act. In the last years of his life, commenting on these 1956 events, he told Doris Kearns:

> Just look at the [1956] election results and you've got the perfect way to measure the success of my leadership against that of all those intellectual liberals who supported Paul Butler and Adlai Stevenson. . . . Their method of campaigning—with their search for big issues and big fights with the Republicans—was tried twice and it failed twice, producing the greatest defeat ever suffered by the Democratic Party. Now you put that dismal record beside my method of campaigning for a Democratic Congress on the basis of the positive achievement of the Democratic Party, striving all the time to work out solutions rather than merely creating electoral issues, and what do you see but an unbroken string of successes for me and an unbroken string of failures for them. I was winning Democratic seats in the Congress while they were losing the Presidency.[59]

Johnson's political experiences made him detest ideological partisanship. Only when he could forge a consensus did he feel comfortable. Like others in the midfifties, he sincerely believed, moreover, that the ideologies and class resentments of the New Deal era were outdated. As aide George Reedy noted in a memo to his chief of December 1956, only "Negroes" were "interested in political programs that make an abrupt change from the past." Most other Americans were "concerned with stability and with improving the gains that have already been made."[60] Understandably, the party liberals considered him a trimmer. But even when, as president, he moved sharply to the left, he could never please the advanced liberals. Their constant carping would make him anxious until the end of his political career. Indeed, his sensitivity to criticism on both sides, particularly during the Vietnam War, eventually undermined his ability to function effectively and drove him from the White House.

But meanwhile, a new Congress beckoned, one with festering old issues and new ones that would test the mettle of the Senate majority leader.

CHAPTER 12

The Civil Rights
Act of 1957

C IVIL RIGHTS WAS IN THE AIR when Congress convened in 1957. The Deep South still said "never" to desegregation, but the nation as a whole favored ending Jim Crow, and in the upper South blacks were beginning to enter previously all-white schools in large numbers. In December 1956, following the Montgomery bus boycott led by Martin Luther King Jr., the U.S. Supreme Court had declared Alabama's Jim Crow transportation laws unconstitutional. An attack in the courts on the rest of legal segregation now seemed imminent. By early 1957 the clamor for racial justice had become loud and insistent, and many senators were demanding a major civil rights bill. Among Democrats, the spirit of the times was reinforced, as we saw, by the sense that the party needed a strong showing on civil rights to bring disaffected black voters back into the fold.

The rising tide of civil rights was both a danger and an opportunity for Johnson. He could no longer ignore the issue; he would have to take a stand. If he stuck with the South he would please Texas voters and his southern colleagues who had helped him become majority leader. But refusing to move would end any chance to become a truly national leader and deny him the ultimate goal, the White House. This was the matter uppermost in his mind when on January 3, 1957, he was reelected leader of the Senate by a slim margin, with liberal Mike Mansfield of Montana as his whip. But first there were Middle Eastern policy and the domestic budget to attend to.

On New Year's Day 1957 the president held a four-hour meeting with Johnson, Rayburn, and congressional leaders of both parties to discuss the chaotic and ever-troublesome Middle East. In mid-1956 Egyptian strongman Gamal Abdel Nasser had seized the vital Suez Canal from its European owners and closed it to Israeli shipping. In response, that October, in collaboration with France and Great Britain, Israel had invaded the Egyptian-held Sinai Peninsula and had soon retaken control of the canal. Angry that the French-British-Israeli plans had been kept secret from him and afraid that the Soviet Union would intervene on Egypt's side, Eisenhower forced the three nations to withdraw. The immediate crisis was soon past, but Arab-Israeli tensions continued and, with France and Britain humiliated, a power vacuum had appeared in the region.

At the New Year's Day meeting Eisenhower noted that the Soviets might now step into the Middle East cauldron. To counter this, he intended, he said, to ask Congress to provide open-ended military and economic aid for any Middle Eastern country faced with Communist aggression. "The existing vacuum in the Middle East must be filled by the United States before it is filled by Russia," he told the congressional leaders.[1]

Eisenhower assumed that his proposal—soon labeled the Eisenhower Doctrine—would meet with little resistance. But Congress is never happy to give a president *carte blanche* in foreign policy, and this time was no exception. But beyond this, the Democrats considered the doctrine a virtual alliance with the Arab nations and unfriendly to Israel. The Democratic Advisory Council, under Butler and Stevenson, attacked the doctrine, and former secretary of state Dean Acheson pronounced it "vague, inadequate, and not very useful."[2]

Johnson and Rayburn did not like the new policy as initially worded but did not intend to reject it completely. If Congress said no, they feared, Eisenhower's authority in the Middle East and the world, and with it America's, would be seriously damaged. They also hoped to avoid stigmatizing the Democrats as neoisolationists. What they wanted was a differently worded, less ambitious, and less precise declaration that did not favor one side over the other. With some help from their advisers they came up with a simple substitute, which they presented to Dulles. "The United States," this statement read, "regards as vital to her interest the preservation of the independence and integrity of the states of the Middle East and, if necessary, will use her armed force to that end."[3]

While Congress squabbled over the wording of the doctrine, the Middle East came to a new boil. In September the United Nations began to consider imposing sanctions on Israel, which, concerned for her security, had refused to withdraw all her troops from the territory she had occupied in the Suez War. Anxious to appease the powerful anti-Israeli Arab bloc, Dulles supported sanctions, as did Eisenhower. On February 3 Ike sent Prime Minister David Ben-Gurion a sharply worded telegram insisting that he comply with the UN resolution. Johnson, speaking for many of his fellow senators, including minority leader Knowland, warned the president and the secretary of state against "coercing" Israel. Speaking out authoritatively on foreign policy for the first time, in a letter to Dulles Johnson declared, "the United Nations cannot apply one rule for the strong and another for the weak; it cannot organize its economic weight against the little state when it has not previously made even a pretense of doing so against the large states." He hoped, he wrote, that Dulles would "instruct" the American UN delegation "to oppose with all its skill such a proposal [for sanctions] if it is formally made."[4]

Dulles did not reply to Johnson's letter. The lack of response and the tough sanctions policy in general infuriated Johnson. He and the administration were soon rushing toward a head-on collision. The crash did not come. On March 1, Israel announced to the UN General Assembly that it would pull out its troops.

Johnson's willingness to confront the administration over Israel has been seen as a bid for the Jewish vote for 1960: many Jews had supported Eisenhower in 1952 and 1956, and this defiance would win them back to the Democrats. Clearly Johnson hoped to gain Jewish support for his actions. Bobby Baker urged LBJ to make his letter to Dulles "available to every Jewish friend. . . ."[5] But the argument leaves out Johnson's personal feelings. Johnson was spontaneously sympathetic to underdogs and saw little Israel as a David surrounded by Goliaths who wanted to destroy it. More than this, however, Johnson was a philo-Semite. As we saw, as a young congressman he had procured an American visa for refugee conductor Erich Leinsdorf and worked to rescue Jews from the Nazis' grasp. He had many Jewish friends and, for some reason, identified with Jews. Harry McPherson, an imaginative man, basing his conclusion on LBJ's expressiveness and physicality, said that LBJ reminded him "of a six-foot-three-inch Texas, slightly corny version of a rabbi or diamond merchant on 44th Street [in New York]." "Some place in Lyndon Johnson's blood," he was convinced, there were "a great many Jewish corpuscles."[6] For most of his career Johnson would be considered by American Jews a good friend, and it would be one of the ironies of his life that after 1965, when Vietnam became an overriding issue, a disproportionate number of Jews would be among his outspoken critics.

Budget issues also pitted Johnson and the administration against one another during this session. On January 16 Eisenhower sent his budget to Congress asking for $71.8 billion, a peacetime high, with most of the increases in defense and related national security programs. Unfortunately for the president, his secretary of the treasury, conservative steel magnate George M. Humphrey, publicly objected to the budget, warning that if the government did not reduce the tax burden on the country there would be "a depression that will curl your hair." Not enough new jobs could be created, he added, "because we are just taking too much money out of this economy. . . ." Johnson soon joined the fray, questioning the "wisdom of this budget."[7] Eisenhower made things worse for himself when at a January 23 press conference he remarked, "If Congress can cut the budget, it is their duty to do it."[8]

Though Democratic liberals such as Arthur Schlesinger Jr. believed budget cutting made "neither political, moral, nor economic sense,"[9] Johnson saw it as a way to make political capital for his party and change its reputation for fiscal extravagance. Appropriations Committee chairman Carl Hayden was prepared to help Johnson pursue his strategy. "The Democrats," he told reporters, "are the party of economy."[10] He then began to trim the budget item by item, chopping out funding for programs he had always supported, including military preparedness. The process angered the president. "Now an unexpected phenomenon [has] occurred," he said sarcastically. "The Democrats inexplicably [have become] economy minded."[11] The Battle of the Budget was joined.

In the end, the congressional budget provided for more than $4 billion less than the president wanted, with $2.4 billion slashed from defense and $1 billion from foreign aid. Ironically, in the first few months of 1958 Congress not only restored the cuts but also added another $4.5 billion in appropriations. The Battle of the Budget had been a waste of time and a fake issue. Neither Johnson nor the Democratic Party had gained acclaim in the whole business.

Meanwhile, civil rights had been simmering. Not even Johnson was sure what he would do when Eisenhower resubmitted his civil rights bill to Congress in 1957. On January 11, Arthur Krock reported that Johnson and Knowland were cosponsoring "a proposal designed to permit an emphatic Senate majority to end debate on all 'motions' to take up 'measures,' as well as on the 'measures' themselves." This move—cloture— would be "a definite blow to most of Johnson's fellow Southerners," because it would prohibit them from burying bills "in the graveyard in which for years they have repeatedly interred major items of Federal 'civil rights' legislation."[12]

On January 12 the *New York Times* speculated that "as a Senator from Texas," Johnson might "fight" the Eisenhower civil rights bill. But it also declared that he "will not attempt to use his position as Democratic leader to keep [the civil rights bill] from reaching the floor," and did not foresee his participating "in the prospective filibuster" or obstructing "efforts to break it."[13] Other rumors flying around Washington had Johnson telling his southern friends that a bill was going to be passed whether they liked it or not and they had better "address themselves to its merits." Johnson in fact told a reporter that "the bill that was going to emerge had to have meaning and substance."[14]

There were, according to observers, several reasons for Johnson's new, more cooperative position. One was his yearning for the Democratic presidential nomination in 1960. As the *Times* explained, this was an impossible dream if he did not modify his "Dixiecrat record on civil rights." Ever alert to timing, the majority leader understood that Congress had to take some action on civil rights and that "a modified change" in the filibuster rules, "now possible at this session, would be a first step."[15] Harry McPherson suggested another possibility. Johnson, he wrote, felt that the race question "obsessed the South and diverted it from attending to its economic and educational problems; that it produced an angry defensiveness and parochialism. . . ."[16] Get rid of the race question and the South might finally overcome its age-old problems of ignorance and poverty.

On March 15, at a benefit dinner address in Raleigh, Johnson beseeched six hundred of North Carolina's leading Democrats to work for party unity. It was necessary, he declared, "to give a little and take a little" to unite the Democratic Party. Without specifically mentioning civil rights, he noted that "all of us—North and South—must give up the idea of crushing the other fellow and ramming our own pet ideas—no matter how nobly motivated—down his throat." Sectional differences, he insisted, were "insignificant alongside our real problems," which included conserving the country's natural resources, conquering cancer and heart disease, educating America's young to keep pace with the Soviet Union, helping the beleaguered farmers, finding peacetime uses of atomic energy, adjusting monetary policy to ensure prosperity, and "working effectively to maintain the integrity of the free world. . . ." There were other problems and "many disputes—some of them angry—that must be settled," he noted, but he gave no clue as to what these were or how they could be resolved.[17]

At this point few liberals expected much of the majority leader. Speaking for committed liberalism was Americans for Democratic Action

(ADA), an organization founded in 1947 by Eleanor Roosevelt, Arthur Schlesinger Jr., John K. Galbraith, Hubert Humphrey, Joseph Rauh Jr., and Walter Reuther to uphold the principles of FDR and the New Deal. The ADA disapproved of Johnson and in early 1955 Joe Rauh, in his acceptance speech as ADA head, had attacked the majority leader specifically. Also critical was the Civil Rights Leadership Conference, composed of activists from the Urban League, the NAACP, the AFL-CIO, the American Jewish Committee, and other organizations committed to ending racial discrimination.

Bit by bit the civil rights issue, pushed by the sheer force of history, moved to the front of the legislative agenda. Soon after the new Congress convened in January, Senator Clinton Anderson of New Mexico introduced a resolution to make it easier to invoke cloture to stop southern filibusters. The motion was defeated, but the vote was closer than a similar one four years earlier. Meanwhile, the Republicans reintroduced the weak civil rights measure that had failed in the previous session. On June 18 it passed the House by a large bipartisan northern and western majority.

But the Senate was the nut to crack. Johnson wanted a civil rights bill but could not afford a strong measure. It was certain to be defeated, and the majority leader would come out looking ineffectual. He needed to forge a centrist majority that would get a bill through Congress without provoking a sectional donnybrook. Here Johnson played a canny game. Western Democrats were public power advocates and had long struggled for federal funding of a high dam at Hells Canyon close to the Oregon-Idaho border that would provide cheap electric power for the whole Northwest. In 1956 the Hells Canyon high dam bill seemed certain to pass the House when Senate conservatives, many of them Southerners, defeated it by a close fifty-one-to-forty-one vote. Johnson had done nothing to save the bill, but when it came up again in 1957 he saw his chance for a little horse trading. Calling in all his political markers, he inveigled his southern friends into supporting the bill. It passed the upper house this time by a vote of forty-five to thirty-eight. An important contingent of Westerners, mostly liberals, who might otherwise push too far, were now beholden to the South and would be ready to compromise on civil rights.

Like the 1956 Republican measure, the bill that arrived in the Senate from the House was divided into four parts. Part I called for a Civil Rights Commission with power to investigate cases of racial discrimination and subpoena witnesses. It did not provoke serious opposition. Nor would many legislators object to Part II, which established a special civil rights division within the Department of Justice. Parts III and IV, however, promised to ignite a firestorm. Part III conferred new powers on the attorney general, including the right to initiate suits in school desegregation cases and to issue injunctions to prevent violations of voting rights and other civil rights. Part IV made illegal any attempt to prevent eligible voters from casting ballots in federal elections and gave the Justice Department power to initiate suits to provide relief. Federal judges would try violations of the law, and defendants would be denied the right of trial by jury.

Part III, conferring special powers on the attorney general, was not a new idea. President Truman had explicitly recommended it in 1946 as an element of his civil rights program. But it actually harked back to the late 1860s, when Congress controlled the defeated former Confederate states and could impose anything it wanted. Senator John Stennis of Mississippi angrily declared that the 1957 bill would have the effect of reviving a law enacted in "the inflamed Reconstruction era,"[18] and Southerners did not welcome the advent of a second period of "barbarism." They also feared that Part III would become a powerful weapon to enforce school desegregation. As for Part IV, many from Dixie professed outrage at denial of a basic constitutional right. But more important, certainly, they understood that local juries in the South were certain to be far more friendly to defendants who violated the act than federal judges.

Southern leaders shouted defiance. On July 2, even before the House measure arrived in the Senate, Richard Russell announced that passage of the bill would "cause unspeakable confusion, bitterness, and bloodshed" throughout the South. "You may as well prepare your concentration camps now," he warned his colleagues, "for there are not enough jails to hold the people of the South who will today oppose the use of raw federal power to forcibly commingle white and Negro children in the same schools and in places of public entertainment."[19] The bill, declaimed Senate Judiciary Committee chairman James O. Eastland of Mississippi, would "deny the southern states the fundamental base of the American system—and that is the right of self-government."[20]

It fell to Russell to get the bill buried, and he gamely tried to muster votes without Johnson's cooperation. On a key forty-five-to-thirty-nine vote upholding a resolution by Senators Knowland and Douglas to speed the measure through the upper house, Johnson, to smooth relations with Russell temporarily, voted with his fellow Southerners. The Senate would now proceed to the momentous debate on whether it should take up the first new civil rights bill since Reconstruction.

Johnson believed that a civil rights bill could pass the Senate in 1957 without strenuous southern opposition if it were limited to voting rights.

He agreed with George Reedy, then staff director of the Democratic Policy Committee, that by this time "Southerners felt guilty about depriving the Negroes of voting." They might not feel ashamed about segregated schools, or poor housing, or "depriving them of jobs . . . but they were defensive about the vote thing. That they couldn't justify." Southerners, Reedy said, took the Constitution seriously, and when they had to take a stand that defied the Constitution, it made them uneasy.[21]

LBJ also understood that he would have to make the bill more acceptable to the South. To prevent what the *New York Times* predicted would be "the granddaddy of all filibusters,"[22] Richard Russell would have to intervene with the southern conservatives. Liberals did not believe the original bill strong enough, but many influential Democrats, besides Southerners, had doubts of Part III's wisdom or even constitutionality.

Johnson began lengthy discussions with Russell, seeking advice from the man who had helped him become Senate leader. What would the South tolerate in a civil rights bill, and what would it do with the current proposal? Russell told Johnson that there were two basic preconditions to passage of a civil rights bill without a filibuster. One was the excision of Part III, and the other was the addition of a jury trial amendment. Russell took great pains to emphasize the compelling need to get rid of Part III. Confirming Reedy's opinion, he told Johnson if he could assure Southerners that it was simply a voting rights bill, they would let it come to a vote. But if Part III, granting the attorney general greatly expanded power to attack southern racial policies, remained, and if Johnson voted for it, his "name would be mud from the Potomac to the Rio Grande."[23] Russell's admission that the South could tolerate a voting rights bill was more than generosity to his protégé. He was worried that the Southern Democrat-Republican coalition was falling apart and that the race issue would accelerate the collapse. He also believed that if the South deployed the filibuster now, when public opinion had shifted toward civil rights, the outcry would force the Senate to change its rules of debate and the South would lose its most useful political tool forever. The passage of an acceptable voting rights bill might quiet the liberals for a while and forestall other civil rights changes that the South would find more difficult to swallow.*

With these matters in mind, Johnson and Russell concluded that the majority leader would keep a low profile for a while and see how things

---

*For their part, Senate liberals almost welcomed a filibuster. If the South obstructed federal civil rights legislation it might so anger the voting public that they would punish conservatives in the upcoming congressional elections.

were developing while at the same time seeking to build support for a jury trial amendment. Russell would oppose the bill, as it stood, on the Senate floor. Russell and Johnson also conferred with Eisenhower, hoping to make him backtrack on his own bill. The president, at a news conference on July 3, acknowledged that there were "highly respected men" who believed that "this is a very extreme law, leading to disorder." He now hinted that he might be willing to drop Part III and admitted that he did not understand parts of the bill and would have to talk the matter over further with the attorney general.[24]

When debate opened on the Senate floor on July 8, Russell proclaimed the South's opposition to the bill. For this measure, Johnson had turned the control of the Senate over to minority leader Knowland. As he sat at his front-row desk with his arms folded on his chest, Johnson's demeanor was almost aggressively neutral. He did remark, however, that the rest of the administration's legislative program would have to be delayed since everything must wait for the Senate to take action on civil rights. He also warned, coyly, that legislation for the Niagara Power Project, considered a high-priority issue by two key civil rights supporters, Senators Irving Ives and Jacob K. Javits of New York, would also be held up. The battle was now under way.

Johnson continued to maintain a low profile in the first few days of Senate hearings. He limited his public utterances to short speeches, distributed to the press in advance, praising the Senate for its statesmanlike behavior in debating the most troubling issue in years, and reassured everyone that considering the "climate of reason" within which the Senate was working, it was bound to "reach a meaningful conclusion." On July 11 the *New York Times* reported that the small group of southern liberals, led by Albert Gore of Tennessee, was trying to work out a compromise that would fully protect voting rights but "would withhold federal power to force school integration."[25] The Gore plan seemed to fall halfway between the administration's scheme and the do-nothing-at-all plan of the traditional Southerners.

In reality, Johnson was feverishly working behind the scenes, consulting with lawyers, calling in political chips, and wielding his formidable powers of persuasion to secure a workable compromise along the lines of the Gore plan. Highly respected Democratic elder statesmen Dean Acheson and Clark Clifford encouraged the forces of compromise by advising that Part III gave too much power to the Justice Department and upset the traditional checks and balances of American government. Johnson also consulted with the irreproachably progressive Clinton Anderson of New Mexico, who also believed that Part III should be eliminated and agreed to sponsor, along with Vermont's liberal Republican senator George Aiken, an amendment to this effect. Meanwhile, Vice President Richard M. Nixon and minority leader Knowland, never known for their liberal views, were working hard with strange bedfellows Senator Douglas and the ADA to save Part III and also to deny jury trial rights to violators of the law. After a few days of discussion, Johnson asked to begin formal Senate debate. With the majority leader in the affirmative, the Senate voted to bring the civil rights bill to the floor, seventy-one to eighteen.

Before the vote, Johnson told the Senate that his action was not to be taken as outright support for the bill as it stood. "But," he declared, "some of us, to whom this bill is unacceptable in its present form, are ready to allow it to be debated out of a decent respect for the convictions of others. Is it too much to hope for a reciprocal generosity for our convictions?" With his usual eye toward achieving consensus, he repeated, as a mantra, "I trust the results of the reasoned debate of reasonable men."[26]

Meanwhile, Johnson was being barraged by constituents confused over what was going on in the Senate and what part their senator was playing in the proceedings. Hundreds of letters and telegrams from Texans urged him to resist the civil rights bill. One telegram, from the racist Texas Citizens Council in Houston, read: "WE ARE TOLD YOU ARE READY TO SELL OUT THE SOUTH. IS THIS TRUE?" Johnson's staff answered all mail on the subject with a cleverly worded form letter:

> I do not know where you could have gotten the idea that I am supporting the "so-called bill for civil rights legislation now before Congress." Certainly I have made no statement to that effect nor have I intimated to anyone that I plan such support.
>
> The bill that has been introduced is one to which I am very much opposed, as I do not believe it would advance any legitimate cause.[27]

And, of course, he *was* opposed to the "bill that [had] been introduced"—but not to the one he would try to enact.

Immediately after the procedural vote Anderson and Aiken offered their compromise amendment. Then Eisenhower backtracked again on the original bill by seeming to come out in support of the Anderson-Aiken position. After thanking the Senate for bringing the bill to the floor, the president said that the most important thing they could do was to ensure black voting rights. At a press conference on July 17 he was questioned by Rowland Evans of the *New York Herald Tribune* about permitting the attorney general to bring suits on his own motion to enforce school desegregation in the South. The president expressed opposition to any Justice Department action "without any request from local authorities." On the general issue of civil rights, he urged caution. "I personally believe," he said, "if you try to go too far too fast in laws in this delicate field that has involved the emotions of so many million Americans, you are making a mistake."[28] By weakening his stand Eisenhower had effectively killed Part III. "The president," moaned Senator Douglas, "has pulled the rug out from under us."[29] Though Knowland, after conferring with Eisenhower, reported back that the president really wanted Part III retained, the Senate voted to delete it, fifty-two to thirty-eight.

The next order of business was Part IV, the right of jury trial for those who obstructed the law. In righteous wrath, Southerners wrapped themselves in Article Six of the Bill of Rights. Part IV, they insisted, denied fundamental constitutional protection. Civil rights advocates shot back that white Southern juries would never convict racist white Southerners no matter how egregiously they violated the law. A southern filibuster seemed likely.

Johnson had to find some way to uphold jury trials while convincing liberals that they would not weaken the bill. He soon found his rationale in an article by law professor Carl Auerbach in the liberal journal *The New Leader* delineating a clear difference between criminal and civil contempt cases. Auerbach had concluded that a split in the civil rights ranks over the jury-trial issue was "as unjustified as it is unnecessary."[30] A plaintiff guilty of a civil crime such as refusing to permit a black person to vote could clear himself of civil contempt charges by agreeing to modify his behavior. A jury trial was unnecessary in these cases. If, however, he persisted in defying the order to permit blacks to vote, he would be guilty of *criminal* contempt and so could be brought to trial before a jury.

Johnson consulted with his legal advisers, the old New Dealer Benjamin Cohen; Johnson's friend Abe Fortas; and Dean Acheson, the former secretary of state and Democratic Wise Man. They agreed with Auerbach's interpretation and helped draft various versions of an amendment to add jury trials in criminal contempt cases to the bill. The winning formula was an amendment submitted by the old western progressive Joseph P. O'Mahoney. By incidentally making jury trials easier for labor leaders in violation of the Taft-Hartley Act and so pleasing liberals and trade unionists, it strengthened the bill's support.

Still, civil rights partisans continued to resist the jury trial clause. Nor, at first, were many labor leaders converted. "Labor will not barter away," said James Carey of the Electrical, Radio, and Machine Workers, "effective protection of the right of a Negro to register and vote in return for the very dubious advantage that Senators O'Mahoney, Kefauver, and Church now appear to offer labor."[31]

Johnson was undeterred by his opponents. He understood that there would be no civil rights law without a jury trial title and continued to fight hard for it. Even Adlai Stevenson was convinced that it would be better to have a bill with the jury trial provision than no bill at all. Finally, in an attempt to break the deadlock and test the sincerity of those who supported jury trials, Senator Neuberger announced that if the O'Mahoney amendment was adopted, he would further amend it to make sure that the jury trial provision did not apply in areas where juries were selected only from the registered voters list, invariably "lily-white" throughout the South.

On the same Sunday that Senator Humphrey told the *Face the Nation* audience that the jury trial advocates did not have the votes, Cy Anderson, lobbyist for the twelve railroad brotherhoods, ran into a Johnson staff member at the Glen Echo Amusement Park outside Washington, where both men had taken their children for a day of fun. Convinced that labor unions could better protect themselves against criminal contempt cases with a jury trial and anxious to extract legislative favors from southern Senate leaders, Anderson told the Johnson staffer: "Any labor skate [sic] who is against trial by jury, ought to have his head examined."[32] Shortly after the chance encounter at Glen Echo, all twelve railroad brotherhoods sent telegrams to Johnson supporting the amendment. The tide soon turned. George Meany, head of the American Federation of Labor, came out for the amendment, as did John L. Lewis of the United Mine Workers. Even though Walter Reuther of the Auto Workers continued to oppose it, Democratic liberals in the Senate now had their out. If organized labor supported the jury trial amendment, they could as well.

Knowland and Johnson decided to call for a roll call on August 2. As the time drew near, both sides scurried to round up votes for and against the jury trial amendment. Knowland consulted with Humphrey, who told him he had enough votes to defeat the O'Mahoney amendment. Johnson began to call in favors, and Nixon and Johnson exchanged angry words near the Senate floor, with the vice president accusing the majority leader of using "his bullwhip on [his] boys tonight."[33] After a fourteen-hour debate, thirty-nine Democrats and twelve Republicans voted to attach the jury trial amendment to the civil rights bill. Nine Democrats and thirty-three Republicans opposed it.

Johnson was still not off the hook. The bill, with its new amendments, now had to pass the hurdle of the full Senate. The Republicans were unhappy with the bill. Eisenhower called it "largely ineffective" and threatened to veto it. Nixon labeled it "a vote against the right to vote."[34] Speaker of the House Joseph Martin predicted that the measure would probably have to be carried over to the second session. But Johnson was determined to secure passage and applied pressure. Just before the roll call, Johnson told the Senate:

> I tell you . . . there is no political capital in this issue. Nothing lasting, nothing enduring, has ever been born from hatred and prejudice—except more hatred and prejudice. Political ambition which feeds off hatred of the North or hatred of the South is doomed to frustration. There is a compelling need for a solution that will enable all Americans to live in dignity and in unity. This bill is the greatest step toward that objective that has ever been made.[35]

After an interminable debate, the Senate passed the bill on August 7, seventy-two to eighteen. Every southern senator voted nay except Johnson, Yarborough, Gore, Kefauver, and Smathers. Church reported that after the bill passed Johnson was "warmly and massively grateful, so much so that I was almost stifled in his embrace.[36]

The bill now went back to the House, where additional compromises were made on the jury trial amendment. Both the House and the Senate finally passed the revised bill on August 29, the Senate after a twenty-four-hour filibuster against it by grandstanding South Carolina senator Strom Thurmond, who angered Russell for defying the no-filibuster promise. It was now sent to the White House for the president's signature and finally, though reluctantly, signed on September 9.

The Civil Rights Act of 1957 was the first genuine civil rights measure to be passed since Reconstruction. Primarily a voting rights law, it was weaker than the liberals wanted, and many would be angry at Johnson for a long time. But among his fellow senators it seemed a good start, and afterward even some of Johnson's most impassioned Senate foes admitted that it broke the ice for later bills. The newly established Federal Commission on Civil Rights became an important educational instrument for the burgeoning civil rights movement and played a part in the development of future measures. Bayard Rustin, civil rights leader and special assistant to Martin Luther King Jr., later said: "I felt that the 1957 civil rights bill was a weak, but a very important bill. And while we had considerable questions about it, we all supported it on the basis that this would establish a very important precedent."[37]

Johnson gave much of the credit for the session's success to Bobby Baker. His record would not have been so good "if it had not been for the strong right arm named Bobby Baker," he wrote his protégé. "I only wish there were some way to make the words stronger."[38] The next year he would try to get Baker chosen as one of the Junior Chamber of Commerce's "outstanding young men of the year." But, of course, the civil rights triumph was Johnson's, requiring all the political talent he possessed in pulling together radically divergent groups, keeping his party from an open and possibly permanent split, and convincing enough Republicans to vote against the administration. He calmed the South so it would not filibuster. He persuaded the moderates and the liberals that the bill was the best that could be gotten at the time. He restored a measure of respect to the Senate, which had suffered a decline in its reputation since the McCarthy era, by showing the "nation and the world that this legislative body really works even on the toughest issue of all time. . . ."[39] And he enhanced his reputation as a national leader by forsaking the traditional position of his section without abandoning it completely. Johnson, himself, summed up his achievement:

> Maybe I voted wrong on some civil rights bills in the past, but I'm learning all the time. I got all I could on civil rights in 1957. Next year I'll get a little more, and the year after that I'll get a little more. The difference between me and some of my northern friends is that I believe you can't force these things on the South overnight. You advance a little and consolidate; then you advance again. I think in the long run my way may prove to be faster than theirs.[40]

And he would, of course, eventually more than fulfill his promises.

The civil rights battle had been chancy for Johnson and he believed, as did most observers, that he would have jeopardized his political career if the outcome had been different. But less than a month later, he got a chance to enhance his reputation without risk. On October 4, 1957, the Soviets announced that they had launched a man-made satellite, called *Sputnik*, into space. As it orbited Earth, beep-beeping so Soviet scientists could track its path, its signal was heard most shrilly by Americans, stunned at having been surpassed by the Soviets. America, seemingly at the forefront of modern science and technology ever since the atomic bomb, had been toppled from its pedestal.

LBJ was at the Ranch when the news broke. He, Lady Bird, and some guests took a walk along the Pedernales after dinner, peering at the night sky to see whether they could glimpse the little ball that had produced a "technological Pearl Harbor." Johnson remembered "the profound shock of realizing that . . . another nation [had achieved] technological superiority over this great country of ours."[41] He sprang into action, phoning members of his Preparedness Subcommittee and staff to talk about what could be done. Johnson proposed a Senate investigation to consider how to restore our technological leadership but promised to avoid blaming anyone for America's tardiness. By the time the subcommittee was ready to meet, the Soviets had launched *Sputnik II*, this time carrying Laika, a live dog. When the U.S. Vanguard rocket, our own satellite launcher, exploded on its launching pad the following month, America's humiliation seemed complete.

Johnson had been interested in space exploration since his days on the Armed Services Committee during his first Senate term. He had failed to interest Defense Department officials in a satellite research program then, and had had no more success with the Eisenhower administration. Even now, in the wake of *Sputnik*, the White House did not seem inclined to bold action. Confronted by the Soviet coup, White House chief of staff Sherman Adams said the United States did not want to get involved in an "outer space basketball game." The American people were not so dismissive, however. Not only had their pride been hurt; they were also worried that U.S. military advantage had been compromised and the Cold War balance of power shifted to the Soviets. As Johnson himself noted, "The Roman empire controlled the world because it could build roads. Later—when men moved to the sea—the British Empire was dominant because it had ships. Now the Communists have established a foothold in outer space."[42]

For LBJ and the American public the implications seemed clear. Yet the majority leader realized the need to tread a narrow line between demoralizing the nation by ranting about Soviet accomplishments and arousing it for battle to overtake the Soviet Union technologically. He was careful to accentuate the positive. "There is no reason," he declared in a speech at Austin, "why we cannot catch up and outstrip anyone else—providing we unite and decide to so. . . ."[43]

By the time Johnson opened the subcommittee's hearings in Washington on November 25, 1957, he had marshaled his usual roster of impressive legal talent, including Cyrus Vance and Ed Weisl to act as counsels. The investigation, which lasted into the following year, heard testimony from more than two hundred witnesses of scientific, industrial, military, and technological renown. Not only did the subcommittee consider weaponry and defense; it also dealt with space flight. Some of the testimony was disturbing. The Soviet Union was ahead of the United States in the development of ballistic missiles, had an R&D system that equipped it to produce new weapons faster than the United States, and was training scientists and technicians at a quicker pace than America.

There were several ways to narrow the military gap rapidly, the subcommittee report declared: an accelerated timetable for rockets already in the works, an early-warning antimissile network, and a reconstituted fleet of bombers. It became obvious as the hearings went on that America had to enter the space age as quickly as possible.

On January 31, 1958, the United States successfully lofted *Explorer I*, and the nation was relieved. But this was only the beginning. *Sputnik* had set off a world rivalry between the superpowers that, whatever its motives, would propel mankind beyond Earth and set its feet on the road to the stars.

Lyndon Johnson would play a critical role in the early stages of the space race. On February 8, he introduced a resolution to organize a Senate Subcommittee on Aeronautical and Space Science. It was approved seventy-eight to one, and he became its chairman. The new committee, assigned the task of creating a new American space program, recommended establishment of the National Aeronautics and Space Administration. NASA, which later commemorated LBJ by calling its headquarters in Houston the Johnson Space Center, began operation in October 1958 with Project Mercury, whose goal was manned space flight. In November President Eisenhower chose Johnson to represent the United States at the UN discussion of outer space control. His impassioned speech called for peaceful cooperation and a ban on military weapons in outer space.

George Reedy has charged that for Johnson the space program was pure expediency. It gave him a hot issue and a way to publicize himself as a statesman. When it came to more than talk, however, Reedy has written, the majority leader had to be pushed. The measure creating NASA was the work of his staff, he says, a feat "accomplished only by shoving papers into his hand to be read on the floor of the Senate."[44] It is hard to fully credit this description; Lyndon Johnson was too energetic, too intrusive to be led like this. But however attained, Johnson won new renown as a space expert. He rejoiced in his new role for its own sake but did not hesitate to use it as a means of self-advertisement. And self-advertisement at this moment seemed understandable. A presidential election year was approaching, and although Johnson denied that he would run for president, few observers took his disavowal seriously.

The year 1958 was also one of economic recession. By February more than seven million Americans were out of work. Some Democrats favored tax cuts to meet the crisis, but Johnson preferred a ten-point spending program, including a $1.8 billion housing bill, a $1.5 billion flood control bill, a $1.8 billion highway construction bill, and an extension of unemployment insurance compensation for an additional fifteen weeks. Unlike a tax cut, most of these would leave behind a residue of improved infrastructure for the nation. Congress passed the Democratic antirecession program, but Eisenhower, opposed to getting the government into "the countercyclical business on a huge basis,"[45] vetoed the bills.

Congress, however, was mostly occupied with foreign events in the spring and summer of 1958. In May Syria encouraged a revolt against pro-American Lebanese president Camille Chamoun, and in July the panicky Chamoun requested American troops. Eisenhower sent 9,000 Marines and 420 fighter planes to Lebanon to help him out, explaining that American lives might be in jeopardy. Johnson gave a speech in favor of the president's action in the Senate on July 15.

In August the Chinese Communists were on the move again, this time renewing their artillery attacks on Quemoy and Matsu, two small islands off Taiwan controlled by the Chinese Nationalists under Chiang Kaishek. Johnson quickly steered emergency appropriations to aid Chiang through the Senate.

By the time Congress adjourned in late August, Rebekah Johnson was near death from cancer. Johnson flew back to Texas to be at her side, hoping to brighten her remaining days. She died on September 12 and was buried in Johnson City on the banks of the Pedernales next to her husband. Her death, he later said, made him very sad. She had been a lifelong source of inspiration.

In November the congressional elections produced remarkable victories for the Democrats. The new House would have 283 Democrats and 153 Republicans, the new Senate 65 Democrats and 35 Republicans. The Senate sweep was one of the most impressive in that body's history, a result that Humphrey and other liberals ascribed to the wise course of the majority leader.

Sam Rayburn was not happy with the almost two-to-one margin in both chambers. "I'd just as soon not have that many Democrats," he said. "They'll be hard to handle. It won't be easy."[46] Besides sheer numbers, there would be an ideological problem. Many of the Democratic newcomers were liberals who would resist his and Johnson's more moderate dictates.

In the wake of the election Johnson wondered what the future would bring. But it was not just the new congressional liberals he was concerned about. He had gone as far as he could in the Senate, and his restlessness was surfacing again. He was seriously thinking, no matter what he said publicly, of running for president in 1960.

CHAPTER 13

To Run or Not to Run

N INETEEN FIFTY-NINE PROMISED to be a troublesome year for Lyndon Johnson. The 1958 congressional elections had been a liberal landslide. The Senate acquired ten new liberal Democrats, including Eugene McCarthy of Minnesota, Vance Hartke of Indiana, Edmund Muskie of Maine, Philip Hart of Michigan, and Thomas Dodd of Connecticut. Although Johnson was handily reelected majority leader, he quickly learned, as Sam Rayburn predicted, that the new Democrats in the Eighty-sixth Congress would be difficult to manage. When their majority was wafer-thin, the Senate Democrats had banded together under Johnson's aegis against the Republican enemy, aware that unity was necessary for survival. Now, with a thirty-seat Democratic edge, the dissenters could afford to be more independent. But the problem went beyond statistics: it was a collision between a pragmatic centrism and liberalism. Inevitably the new Senate was far more issue-oriented than the old, and that raised problems. According to Harry McPherson, the elections had "extremized, polarized the two parties, and the Southerners, being unable to go along with the northern Democratic brothers, would go over and join the Republicans frequently."[1] The clash would vex Johnson, who could never assuage his own liberal conscience and leanings. And to top it all, the majority leader would face a more formidable opponent than Knowland on the other side of the Senate aisle. The California senator had chosen to run for governor and had been replaced as minority leader by Everett M. Dirksen of Illinois, a supple master, in his own way, of the arts of political maneuver. Dirksen, in the end, would form an alliance with Lyndon Johnson, but no one could predict that outcome as the Congress opened.

More than impending political squalls vexed the majority leader in the months following the midterm elections. Senatorial power was losing its savor for Johnson, and so was much else. As a way of adding spice to his political life, he moved out of his cramped majority leader's quarters into a much larger space, formerly occupied by the District of Columbia Committee. Dazzlingly done up in green and gold by an interior decorator whom Johnson hired from New York, it was impiously nicknamed the "Taj Mahal." Meant not only to cheer up Johnson but also to impress his visitors, the new offices only helped a little. According to George Reedy, Johnson was passing through a full-blown midlife crisis in 1959–1960. He was "expressing dissatisfaction with his family, with his friends, with almost everything."[2] He wondered if he was not missing out on life by staying in politics. Reedy later described how Johnson once confided in him that life consisted of three parts. The first part of your life you spent preparing; the second you spent doing; the third you spent enjoying it. During this session of Congress Reedy believed it "just possible that he had reached the third stage and [felt] he better hurry up and enjoy it."[3] Yet on the other hand, Reedy mused, perhaps LBJ realized that he really had no capacity for leisure, "that he was not the type of person just to drop out and enjoy life."[4]

Almost as soon as the new Congress convened, Johnson provoked the liberals' ire by squelching their plan to stop filibusters by a simple majority. Though he then pushed through a change making it easier to invoke cloture on debates, both he and the dissidents saw this as the first installment of the coming power struggle between them. Then, in February, William Proxmire attacked Johnson on the Senate floor. The senator from Wisconsin had said just a few months before that LBJ was "an excellent party leader . . . [and] fair to everybody."[5] Proxmire, however, was angry with Johnson for rejecting his request for an appointment to the Finance Committee, possibly in retaliation for his own attacks on the oil depletion allowances. But he was also furious that Johnson had decided not to call further Democratic caucuses for the rest of the year. Under Johnson's leadership, he now complained, power was too "sharply concentrated." "The typical Democratic senator" had "literally nothing to do with determining the legislative program and policies of this party."[6] Wayne Morse publicly applauded the attack, and Douglas, Gore, and Joseph Clark of Pennsylvania murmured their support.

Proxmire's attack infuriated Johnson. In private he referred to his critic as "Senator Pissmire."[7] He finally responded publicly in the Senate toward the end of May, saying the Wisconsin senator was spreading "fraud" about his leadership to cover up his own deficiencies. He accused Proxmire of wanting a "fairy godmother or a wet nurse" to get his pet projects passed and said he did not have the "power . . . to bring two strong men into agreement by waving a wand." Johnson added, glancing at the Wisconsin senator, that when a senator wants something done and does not get his way, "he puts the blame on the leadership. It does not take much courage, I may say, to make the leadership a punching bag."[8] Johnson, who found it hard to take any sort of criticism, particularly when it was so public, told a reporter, "I am the best thing that ever happened to the liberal cause in the Senate. If I should die tomorrow, none of those bleeding hearts would be able to get their pet projects out of committee."[9] Years later, he told biographer Doris Kearns that the liberals exaggerated his control of the Senate and that "the theory that one man is able to tell sixty-four other senators how they shall vote is nonsense." He believed the problem had less to do with his leadership and more to do with the liberals' need to criticize things in general and him in particular. As he complained to Kearns: "First they tell me they want a strong leader . . . so they can get results. So I give them leadership and I get results. Then they change their tune, and say that what they really want is democracy, and participation, and decentralized leadership. Then, in the same breath, they contradict themselves. . . . The only link is their endless need to cut me up."[10]

Difficulties with the liberals within his own party were not new, but Johnson also encountered a surprise problem as the new Congress began. Subject to the new Twenty-Second Amendment, Eisenhower was a lame-duck president, and even Republican leaders were concerned about his seeming lack of interest in party matters. The Democratic victories in November were fueled by public anger at Republican policies, by organized labor's antibusiness attitudes, and by farmer discontent in the Midwest, as well as by the continuing recession. Voters had also been repelled when the president's trusted chief of staff, Sherman Adams, resigned after a House investigation revealed he had received a vicuña coat and other gifts from a New England industrialist and had made phone calls to government regulatory agencies on the businessman's behalf.

Johnson believed that with the president's right-hand man gone, the indecisive Eisenhower would be crippled on domestic issues. The majority leader planned to take advantage of this weakness by pushing a package of legislation similar to that of Franklin Roosevelt's First Hundred Days of 1933. In his talk to the Democratic caucus, even before the session opened, he proposed area redevelopment programs, a comprehensive housing bill, and the Temporary National Economic Commission (TNEC), modeled after the New Deal TNEC of 1938, to investigate the problems of unemployment, inflation, and economic growth. Though ostensibly a neutral investigative body, it was clear that the new commission would end up nailing the Republicans for chronic unemployment, creeping inflation, and retarded growth. Obviously most of this new legislation would cost money. But since Eisenhower did not seem capable of fighting back, Johnson did not anticipate any serious trouble.

The president fooled everybody by a surge of interest in politics and party matters that focused on balancing the budget. He refused to accept legislation that required major expenditures. In early January 1959 he told Dirksen and House minority leader Charles Halleck that he had a simple plan to combat the Democrats' contemplated spending spree. He would let Johnson and Rayburn deplete their energies passing the bills and then kill them with his "veto pistol." "Every sort of foolish proposal," he informed the two congressional leaders, "will be advanced [by the Democrats] in the name of national security and the 'poor fellow.' We've got to convince Americans that 'thrift' is not a bad word."[11] The Republicans would not attack the Democrats' proposals on their merits but on the grounds that they were busting the budget and were inflationary, a prospect that would frighten the average voter.

At the beginning of the new Senate term, Johnson had two major items on the agenda. One was a bill for new civilian airport construction and a major updating of air safety control equipment. Both kinds of facilities had been little improved since World War II. The other was a massive housing construction bill that included billions for urban renewal. Johnson also proposed a temporary unemployment compensation bill and extension of benefits for those still suffering from the recent recession.

By the end of January Eisenhower was making it quite clear through news conferences and messages that he would go after "spendthrift Democrats." He insisted it was not necessary to spend more money on health, education, and welfare to ensure progress. Johnson was now worried, with good reason, that the president would indeed veto his airport and housing bills. The liberals wanted to add additional funding to the housing and urban renewal programs, but instead Johnson decided to cut back to make the bills vetoproof. He had started the term with a grand flourish; now he was cautious. "Some of us," he told the Senate, "want to put a few roofs over people's heads. . . . It does not mean I am a spender because I want . . . a housing bill."[12] In the middle of February he assailed Eisenhower's picture of a thrifty executive branch and a profligate Democratic Congress and observed that while Eisenhower was unwilling to spend more money on social programs, he was increasing funds for civil defense, for the U.S. Information Agency, for mutual security, and for State Department salaries.

In the end there was no Hundred Days for Johnson. To pass airport and housing bills that the president would not veto, Johnson had to slash the funding, at which point he ran full tilt into angry liberals who accused him of betraying the Democratic mandate of November 1958. The unemployment compensation bill also seemed too puny to liberals. Democratic Senator Pat McNamara of Michigan wrote a public letter to Johnson accusing the Senate and its leadership "or . . . lack of it" of bringing "forth a mouse . . . [and] sadly enough, even this mouse was quickly throttled."[13] The same thing was true of practically every piece of social legislation that Johnson tried to get through Congress in 1959: nothing he proposed was broad enough to satisfy the liberals. And yet Eisenhower vetoed practically everything that appeared on his desk. By the middle of May the Republicans were publicly chortling over Democratic squabbling. In June both the liberal Democratic Advisory Committee and Johnson were counterattacking the Republicans for sabotaging Congress.

But the liberals continued to condemn Johnson as well. In fact, Paul Butler turned the anti-Johnson impulse into a crusade. On June 13 the Democratic advisory council denounced the president for threatening vetoes of major legislation "in an attempt to thwart one constructive and necessary measure after another." But it also charged Rayburn and Johnson with "accommodation." "Republican obstructionism has made the Democratic task in Congress doubly hard," said the council. "However, the people expect and are entitled to have in this Congress more tangible results of the mandate they gave a Democratic majority last November than they have received to date." The council then urged the Democrats in Congress "to use . . . [their] power and give the nation a significant program of constructive legislation regardless of Republican opposition."[14] The ADA chimed in soon after. Johnson and Rayburn had cooperated with Eisenhower and surrendered "before a shot was fired." The Democratic congressional leadership "had imposed its own veto on the Congressional majority."[15]

As Senate leader Johnson had always achieved what he wanted by compromise; going out on a limb violated his political essence. He believed that partial victories in areas such as redevelopment, housing and airport construction, and urban renewal were better than total defeats. He told his liberal critics: "If we have a choice between political issues and achievement, we will choose achievement."[16] As for Butler, the

Johnson people saw him as a Kennedy partisan whose ideological attacks did not have to be taken seriously.

At this point more Democrats in Congress favored Johnson's "legislation of the possible" than opposed it. A *Congressional Quarterly* poll of half the congressional Democrats showed that 53 percent of them stood behind LBJ.[17] Many, including some of the hard liberals, were anxious about the effects of Butler's continued attacks. "We are paying Butler thirty five thousand dollars a year," said one liberal senator, "to try to destroy the Democratic Party while Thruston B. Morton [Republican national chairman] would . . . do it free."[18] The *New York Times* attempted to explain why the liberals were so resentful. The "real reasons for the liberals' frustration go deeper than Senator Johnson . . ." noted a *Times* editorial. The liberal majority was not solid enough to override presidential vetoes and the congressional leadership had "to act with this fact of life in mind."[19] All the sniping and criticizing, however, made Johnson very uneasy, undermined his power in Congress, and brought these conflicts to the attention of the voting public.

One triumph for Johnson during this gloomy year was winning statehood for Hawaii. Since the end of World War II Congress had been seriously considering whether Alaska and Hawaii should become states. One argument against statehood was that neither was contiguous with any of the other forty-eight. Other objections were primarily political. Most politicians conceded that Hawaii would vote Republican and Alaska Democratic, providing a party balance if both were admitted to the Union. But Southerners and conservatives were uneasy about the large proportion of Asians in Hawaii's population and worried about the power of organized labor among Hawaiian plantation workers and longshoremen. These two groups opposed the entrance of Alaska as well because if it came in, Hawaii was sure to follow. Still, by 1958, most of Congress favored statehood for Alaska, and it was finally admitted as the forty-ninth state on January 3, 1959.

In March the Hawaii statehood bill was brought before the Senate. Unlike many Southerners, Johnson was not offended by the territory's racial potpourri. The Pacific island chain seemed a wonderful example of racial harmony, and he believed, naively, that its example could help the South with its own racial problems. In addition, admitting it as the fiftieth state would show the world that the United States truly believed in multiracial equality. Johnson was so enthusiastic about the idea that he proposed to establish an East-West Center at the University of Hawaii in Honolulu, where faculty and students from all over the world would gather to discuss and embrace intercultural harmony.

Johnson threw himself into the Hawaii statehood enterprise with his usual manic energy. He told Republicans that the president favored it so they might as well vote for it and teased Democrats that the Republican territorial governor of Hawaii was slated to come to Washington soon and they wouldn't want to let him take the credit for getting the bill passed. On March 11, the date of Hawaii governor William E. Quinn's arrival, the Senate passed the Hawaii statehood bill, seventy-six to fifteen. Daniel K. Inouye, soon to be the first representative from the fiftieth state, called it a "pure and simple civil rights bill. . . ."[20]

Hawaii statehood was, perhaps, the high spot of this congressional session for Johnson. Meanwhile, as he struggled with presidential vetoes and the rebellious members of his own party, his colleague Senator John Fitzgerald Kennedy was busily looking for an issue that would make the public notice him and promote his chances for a presidential run in 1960. The senator soon hit on corrupt practices in labor unions.

The unions had been under investigation since 1957 by the Select Committee on Improper Activities in the Labor and Management Fields, popularly known as the Senate Rackets Committee. Under chairman John McClellan of Arkansas and chief counsel Robert Kennedy, a younger brother of the Senator, the committee had revealed how trade union leaders often diverted money from pension funds into their own pockets, rigged union elections, physically intimidated opponents, took bribes from employers, and engaged in other illegal activities. McClellan's and Kennedy's concerns were obviously legitimate, but the committee's work had also been used by Senator Barry Goldwater and other conservatives to pillory honest, but poltically left, labor leaders, including the powerful and respected Walter Reuther of the United Automobile Workers, as subversive crypto-Communists.

Senator Kennedy was willing to capitalize on rising public disgust with labor unions. A member of the Labor and Public Welfare Subommitte, he had proposed in 1958 an innocuous bill framed merely to protect employee welfare and pension funds against predatory union leaders without bolstering the antiunion provisions of the Taft-Hartley Act. Though the Senate, with Johnson's support, had passed it eighty-eight to one, the House killed it. Too weak for pro-business congressmen, it was too stringent for those who favored labor. In 1959, with presidential nominating conventions less than a year away, Kennedy reintroduced the same bill. A this point Senator McClellan added what he called a Bill of Rights allowing union members to bring union leaders to court over practically any area of disagreement.

The measure, if passed, promised to create chaos in every union, corruptly managed or not. Opposed to the harsher changes, Kennedy asked Johnson whether he could floor-manage the bill to defeat the Mc-Clellan amendment. We have it on George Reedy's word that LBJ did not understand the complexities of union practices and often could not follow the intricacies of the evolving legislation. But as senator he was more liberal on labor than he had been in the House and maintained close ties to George Meany of the AFL-CIO. He himself did not like the McClellan proviso, but he could see what Kennedy was up to and sat on his hands. The Bill of Rights clause passed, forty-seven to forty-six. Kennedy was horrified. He had created a Frankenstein monster.

Johnson now deployed some rather underhanded trickery to get the McClellan amendment defeated. An aide brought to his attention that the proposed bill contained an obscure point detrimental to the South's position on civil rights legislation, and if permitted to stand, would speed up the process of school, as well as union, desegregation. The majority leader immediately showed this to his southern colleagues, who demanded reconsideration. The next day Humphrey, Clark, and one of the Southerners rewrote Kennedy's original bill, scarcely changing it, and in this form it passed the Senate, only to be defeated in the House, which seemed to be more antilabor than it was in the previous year.

Once unleashed, antiunion feeling could not be easily checked. The House became the target of pressure from antiunion employers who demanded a strong antilabor bill. Congressman Phillip Landrum, a Democrat from Georgia, and Republican congressman Robert Griffin from Michigan wrote the new bill, which Eisenhower, and a public disgusted with the labor practices they saw exposed in the televised Senate rackets committee hearings, supported. The House passed it, 229 to 201. When this measure came back to the Senate, John Kennedy refused to add his name to it. After minor changes the bill passed the Senate as well.

Johnson's role in all of this is unclear, but the consensus is that while he did not publicly support the Landrum-Griffin bill, he was not willing to throw his weight behind a more moderate measure. Although George Meany, president of the AFL-CIO, believed that without Lyndon Johnson an even more drastic bill would have passed, many labor leaders were disappointed with Johnson. Commenting on the passage of Landrum-Griffin, Texas AFL leader Hank Brown noted that the "National AFL leadership felt that Johnson did considerable foot dragging as far as labor was concerned. . . . They felt that Rayburn and Johnson were saying the right things, but they just weren't pressing. This showed up, in my opinion, in 1960 as to why Johnson got very little help out of labor in his bid for the presidency."[21]

In the end, then, Kennedy did not further his reputation as a competent legislator, and Johnson, who thought that he could embarrass

Kennedy without doing himself harm, unwittingly further alienated the liberals.

Much of what Johnson did during this session of Congress was informed by the impending presidential race. The prospect of running in 1960 both intrigued and repelled him. He could conceive of no higher goal than the presidency, yet he was full of uncertainty and constantly rehearsed his misgivings. Did he, personally, have the skills and knowledge to be leader of the Free World? Could he face the prospect of defeat? Could a Southerner ever hope to become president? Years later he told biographer Doris Kearns that no matter how well he planned a presidential campaign, his southern background would have thwarted him. And others, at the time, agreed. As Proxmire, still on the attack, told a labor group in Madison, Wisconsin, Johnson had "overcome his regional limitations to a remarkable degree" but was "still a Southerner."[22] Clearly a Southerner could not be trusted to be a truly national leader. All told, the presidential race fed Johnson's instabilities, and they in turn shaped his campaign. George Reedy would describe the course of Johnson's "presidential leanings" in 1959 as "the track of a cat through a fish market."[23]

One other factor may help explain Johnson's volatility during these months. He apparently was entangled in an intense emotional attachment to one of his staff, a young Texas woman who had been part of his Senate entourage for some years. More than one Johnson intimate has said his affair with the slightly plump, sweet-faced young woman was far more serious than most of Johnson's other involvements. She was essential to his comfort, providing the mothering and personal care he needed, especially when the Senate went into all-night sessions and someone had to lay out his toiletries and provide clean shirts. Perhaps the relationship was platonic, but most Washington insiders considered it passionate and carnal. Indeed, JFK's biographer Herbert S. Parmet describes one of Johnson's associates as believing LBJ "was sufficiently enchanted to consider leaving Lady Bird."[24] He broke off the relationship, apparently in 1960, but she remained within his social orbit after he had moved to the White House.

However wobbly overall, Johnson's presidential ambitions intruded in the confirmation hearings of Lewis Strauss as secretary of commerce. A retired World War II rear admiral who had competently chaired the Atomic Energy Commission for five years, the conservative and arrogant Strauss had antagonized many congressmen on the Joint Atomic Energy Committee, particularly its chairman, Senator Clinton Anderson. From opposite sides of the political spectrum, the two men became bitter personal enemies when Anderson complained that Strauss was too secretive in his dealings with Congress, and Strauss countered that Anderson did not understand the complexities of the situation. Anderson, who had little formal education, took this as a personal insult and did not forgive the slight. Both Strauss and Eisenhower knew that the admiral's bid for reappointment as AEC chairman would fail, and to save his career the president nominated him as secretary of commerce.

Most people expected that after a small fuss from Anderson's contingent, Strauss would be confirmed. In the entire twentieth century, only one cabinet nominee—back in 1925—had been vetoed by the Senate. But Anderson and the liberals were determined to give Strauss more than just a little bit of trouble. Strauss himself created additional problems for himself by answering questions in a slippery manner and by rude and supercilious behavior during the three-month-long hearings.

Johnson found himself in a peculiar position on the Strauss appointment. He had nothing against Strauss, who was not tainted by scandal or impropriety, but he did not want to further antagonize the liberals if he could avoid it. For their part, Strauss's supporters attacked his opponents as either Communists, a charge that Johnson no longer took seriously, or as anti-Semites, a charge that he did. Both Kennedy and Johnson had to take into account Jewish voters if they wanted to run in 1960 and did not want to risk their ire by voting against Strauss. Johnson stayed out of the way until the final tally, when he let it be quietly known that he was against confirmation. Several Democratic senators who were leaning toward Strauss now shifted their votes, and the admiral was not confirmed.

As majority leader, Johnson did not have to deal with foreign affairs in depth. In his own presidential administration William Fulbright's Senate Foreign Relations Committee would become a major player in the nation's foreign policy court. But during Johnson's leadership of the Senate, the committee, led by Theodore F. Green of Rhode Island, ninety years plus and deaf, played a muted role. When foreign concerns engaged the majority leader it was often because they had domestic political or policy implications.

One matter that had long troubled Johnson was the supposed Soviet superiority over the United States in education. America had "a lot of catching up to do and we ought to do it,"[25] he believed. On September 14, the day that Nikita Khrushchev was scheduled to address the United Nations in New York, LBJ proposed a "work now, pay later" plan to provide loans for college students. The bill would authorize government guarantees of a hundred million dollars' worth of loans a year to students, repayable after graduation. Although it was too late for this session of Congress, the Senate majority leader said he hoped to take action on the measure the following year. He added that although the rationale for his bill did not depend solely on the need to surpass the Soviet

Union, "it would be foolish to ignore the fact that we are in bad need of educated brain power in the modern world."[26]

The Soviet premier planned to visit Washington after his UN speech. Johnson thought it inappropriate for Khrushchev to address Congress and made sure the Senate was adjourned before the Russian arrived, but he did not object to a meeting with the Senate Foreign Relations Committee. Recalling how Nixon's "kitchen debate" with the Soviet leader in July at the American National Exhibition in Moscow had made the vice president a minor hero, he decided to meet the Soviet leader himself when he came to the capital. Lightning did not strike twice, however, though Johnson later reported that Khrushchev told him: "I have read your speeches. And I don't like any of them."[27]

Meanwhile, the race for the Democratic nomination was heating up. Rayburn "was very anxious for Lyndon to run," recalled James Rowe. "He did not think any Roman Catholic could win the election."[28] On October 17, though his candidate had not yet declared himself, the speaker took the bull by the horns and opened a twelve-room "Johnson for President" headquarters in Austin. For his part the majority leader was hinting that he would like to run and pointedly refused to contradict a Dallas newspaper report that while he was "not a candidate now, he is definitely 'available.'"[29] The uncandidate also expressed his pleasure at the formation of Johnson for President clubs in various places.

Whatever Lyndon's doubts, Lady Bird had obviously thrown *her* hat into the ring. The majority leader's wife found speaking in public a trial, but, determined to help her husband, she registered for a course at the Capitol Speakers' Club in Washington. The teacher, Hester Provenson, taught her how to relax, how to modulate and regulate her voice, how to organize her material, and how to assume the proper posture and bearing at the rostrum. Lady Bird also asked the upscale Dallas department store Neiman-Marcus to make red, white, and blue "Ladies for Lyndon" uniforms.

As the weeks of the Eighty-sixth Congress rolled by, LBJ's hesitation became more awkward. In 1960 he would be up for reelection. Did he want to run again for the Senate? He had mastered the Senate and probably would have little trouble continuing as majority leader in spite of liberal sniping. At this stage of his life the always restless Texan was tempted to go for the presidency, but he was pessimistic about his chances, worried about his health, and conflicted about taking the gamble.

Johnson wanted to president as much as he wanted anything. James Rowe thought Johnson wanted it "so much his tongue was hanging out." But he was so scared, according to Rowe, that the "other part of him said, 'This is impossible. Why get my hopes up? I'm not going to try. If I don't try I won't fail.'"[30] He refused to enter presidential primaries, though Hoosier senator Vance Hartke believed he would have no trouble winning in Indiana, and Kennedy, his rival, thought he had a good chance in West Virginia. He was afraid that his down-home speechmaking, appreciated in his own section of the country, would be regarded as hickish elsewhere. Once more Johnson's insecurities hurt him. It was a mistake to assume that he could avoid the public exposure, that he could count on his national reputation as a legislative leader to win the nomination.

Another error was underestimating John F. Kennedy. Johnson had little respect for his future rival. He considered him a "playboy" who would not put in the time and effort necessary to be a good president. "It was the goddamnedest thing," Johnson told Doris Kearns:

> Here was a young whippersnapper, malaria-ridden and yellah, sickly, sickly. He never said a word of importance in the Senate and he never did a thing. But somehow with his books and his Pulitzer Prizes he managed to create the image of himself as a shining intellectual, a youthful leader who would change the face of the country. Now, I will admit that he had a good sense of humor and that he looked awfully good on the goddam television screen and through it all he was a pretty decent fellow, but his growing hold on the American people was simply a mystery to me.[31]

Johnson unwittingly had put his finger on two very important factors that were in the process of transforming American elections. One was the ability to project charm on television; the other was "style." Johnson was perceived of as a "politician's politician," not as a "people's politician," according to a 1960 poll by Louis Harris for Kennedy.[32] Now that the media were more visual than verbal, the candidates had to "look like a president." The handsome, preppy Kennedy, speaking with his educated, New England accent, and accompanied by his beautiful, fashionable wife, was both charismatic and stylish. The awkward, lumbering Johnson, still not fitting his massive frame, with his provincial southwestern speech and mannerisms, and his craggy face, ever-changing with the emotions of the moment, unfortunately was neither. Nor was Lady Bird, for all her intelligence and dignity, a glamor girl.

Kennedy's one big liability was his religion. A practicing Catholic, he belonged to a religious minority still considered faintly alien. The one Catholic major party presidential nominee, Al Smith of New York, had been badly beaten in 1928, establishing in the minds of many Americans the conviction that a Catholic could not be president. But none of the Democratic hopefuls could use religion as a public issue, no matter how they might be tempted. The voters' hidden prejudices were one thing; blatant exploitation by a rival was quite another.

The best way to run for president, Johnson came to believe at the beginning of 1960, was to display his talents as a strong Senate leader and hope that the right people and the voters would appreciate it in the end. Perhaps the convention would be deadlocked, in which case he was sure he would be the logical choice. After all, he was the great consensus-builder, the master of conciliation. Wouldn't his fellow Democratic delegates realize that he was the perfect man to hold the party together when all others had failed? He soon began to emphasize his role as a responsible statesman, anchored on the Senate floor, carrying out congressional business while all the other candidates scurried around canvassing for delegates. Somebody had to be there, he kept saying, to "tend the store."[33]

The strategy was another mistake. As a Kennedy aide later noted, LBJ's "decision to stick to his Senate duties and enter no primaries at all was a fatal flaw in the Johnson campaign."[34] Johnson's liberal detractors did not intend to oblige the majority leader by making his Senate leadership in the Eighty-sixth Congress any easier. As soon as Congress convened for its second session, the Democratic liberals started to push him again for regular party caucuses, which he had resisted. Johnson temporarily defused the issue by assurances that any senator could invoke a meeting at any time by a simple request. Less than a week later, however, Senator Gore headed a short-lived drive to reduce Johnson's power by asking for the expansion of the nine-man Democratic Policy Committee and for choice of the policy committee's members by majority vote, a selection that was now made by Johnson as vacancies occurred. Gore then completely confused the issue by praising Johnson as "the ablest Democratic leader that has served this Senate in my lifetime."[35] In a Democratic caucus on January 13 the Democratic senators voted fifty-one to twelve to uphold the majority leader's authority as it stood.

Having crushed this revolt, Johnson could get on with more important Senate business. With a view to melting down his liberal opposition, he proposed a sweeping plan of social legislation calling for medical care for the aged, an increased minimum wage, federal aid to education, a depressed-areas bill, water conservation, and income equity for farmers based on the distribution of their surplus produce to the poor. All of these required government funding and were unlikely to pass.

Also on LBJ's agenda was a new civil rights bill, which would supplement the one passed in 1957. He preferred to delay additional civil rights legislation for several years but realized he could not and decided to take the initiative himself before a coalition of liberal Democrats and moderate Republicans took charge. According to George Reedy, Johnson was uncharacteristically careless about legislative strategy in this case. He had never acted "with less forethought, with less planning, with less consideration."[36] On January 20 the majority leader submitted a measure extending the life of the Civil Rights Commission, creating the Federal Community Relations Service to mediate local disagreements over segregation, conferring new subpoena powers on the attorney general to investigate voting rights violations, and banning transportation of explosives interstate to prevent bombings directed against civil rights workers. The bill was dismissed by Roy Wilkins of the NAACP as "an effort to block consideration of effective legislation," as a "liniment to cure a tumor. . . ."[37] Soon after, the White House outbid Johnson with its own measure, adding a provision making it a crime to seek to hamper a federal court order on school desegregation. Finally, a group of Democratic Senate liberals introduced their own bill granting the Justice Department power to initiate suits to compel school desegration, essentially restoring Part III of the 1957 civil rights law.

Senate action could not come too quickly, for the civil rights movement was once again heating up. On February 1 a group of well-dressed black students from North Carolina Agricultural and Technical College entered a Woolworth store in Greensboro, sat down at the lunch counter, and asked to be served. Blacks could buy food at the store but had to eat standing up. The students remained unserved at the counter for more than two hours, and when they left, they gathered on the street in a tight circle chanting the Lord's Prayer. The next day, and for many days afterward, they returned with a growing flock of fellow students and again requested counter service, behaving with decorum and dignity. Later that week, other black students duplicated their nonviolent protests at lunch counters in cities in North and South Carolina, Virginia, Florida, and Tennessee. By February 15, Johnson's deadline for beginning Senate work on a new civil rights measure, the sit-ins had spread to fifteen cities in five states. White students in the North, thrilled by the bravery of their fellow black students, soon began their own protest, picketing local outlets of retail chains where the protesters had been denied service. The new student activism was a electric shock to Martin Luther King Jr., whose Gandhian civil disobedience had, until now, been more a theory than a practice. The media were soon proclaiming that the civil rights movement had entered a new, more militant phase.

To keep his bill from being bottled up in the Judiciary Committee, on February 15 Johnson got the Senate to approve a minor House bill. This measure would become the pin board for civil rights amendments. "The Senate," Johnson declared, "is going to do what is right in this matter even though we do not satisfy the extremists on either side." At this point Richard Russell rose and, pounding on his desk, accused LBJ of a "lynching of orderly procedure in the Senate of the United States."

Civil rights advocates, he charged, were trying to "harass and hell-hack the southern people" in an election year.[38] To confuse matters, Wayne Morse, who supported civil rights legislation, objected to Johnson's strategy. The next day, the Senate voted down a southern attempt to delay further action on the bill for a week.

Conservative Southerners used every delaying tactic they could muster to stop the new civil rights bill, stretching the debate to fifty-three days. In response, Johnson instigated round-the-clock sessions. He also had forty army cots with bedding moved into Senate offices to ensure that fifty-one senators could be rounded up at any moment for an emergency quorum call. By refusing to yield and refusing to adjourn he hoped to wear the Southerners out. Ten days into these arduous sessions, Paul Douglas asked Johnson and minority leader Dirksen to help invoke cloture. Both leaders turned him down. Johnson knew if he supported cloture he had no chance of getting Russell to compromise on any civil rights bill. He had also more seriously offended the South this time by his pro-civil rights actions than he had in 1957 and he did not want to lose their backing completely, especially this year, when he was contemplating a presidential run.

Russell, of course, fought every amendment and used every obstructionist tactic he could muster. He divided the segregationists into teams, with each crew holding the floor for about four hours. At the end of their stint they would call for a quorum, forcing the sleepy and disheveled civil rights advocates to be available at all times while Russell's group could catch up on sleep and refreshment. Majority whip Mike Mansfield was very resentful, believing that the compromise measure that was eventually passed was due to fatigue. "We debated civil rights . . . unshaven . . . without ties, with hair awry, and even in bedroom slippers," he complained. It was not the "well rested" opponents of civil rights who had to compromise. "It was," he said, "the exhausted, sleep-starved, quorum-confounded proponents" who had to give in.[39]

It eventually became clear to Johnson that he had to break the impasse. The Republicans, with an eye on the election, also wanted some kind of civil rights bill passed that spring. LBJ got together with Eisenhower's attorney general, William P. Rogers, to come up with a compromise bill, keeping the provisions on voting rights and ridding it of the toughest sections on school desegregation and job discrimination. By now Russell himself had acknowledged that a new voting rights bill could not be avoided. This prompted liberals to accuse Johnson of conspiring with Russell to push through something innocuous that would not disturb the South. And, indeed, the bill could not have been passed without an agreement with Russell.

In any case, the measure that eventually got Congress's approval established a system of federal referees to register black voters in federal elections, extended the life of the Civil Rights Commission, and imposed criminal penalties for bombing and bomb threats against civil rights officials and civil rights workers. If not a breakthrough measure, it did reinforce the right to vote, the prerogative Johnson considered fundamental to all the others in achieving racial justice.

Signed by Eisenhower on May 6, the bill was weaker than most civil rights supporters would have liked. Yet the northern press generally praised it and commended Johnson's efforts in seeing it through. Editorial writers acknowledged its shortcomings but emphasized that "any measure that ensures an extension of the franchise is a forward step."[40] The southern press, however, perceived it as a defeat for Dixie, and many southern papers called Johnson a traitor to the region. He was "the southern Benedict Arnold," declared the *Florida Times-Union*. A headline in the *Augusta Herald* read: "South Is Betrayed Again by Johnson for the Sake of His Own Ambitions."[41] To make matters worse, Johnson knew that most liberals were disappointed with the new law. He tried to explain that he got the best bill he could with the votes he had. If he could have gotten a better bill, he certainly would have done so. Liberals felt, he said, "that they ought to have the whole loaf. And a lot of us would like to have a whole loaf, but you don't always get what you want."[42]

Just before the president approved the 1960 civil rights bill, foreign policy caught the nation's headlines. Eisenhower had planned a summit meeting in Paris with Soviet premier Khrushchev on May 15 and intended to visit the Soviet Union during the summer. But the Cold War thaw reversed abruptly when the Russians announced that they had shot down an American U-2 spy plane, equipped with high-tech cameras and radiation detectors, inside Soviet territory. At first the American government claimed that the U-2 was a weather research plane that had run into mechanical difficulties and wandered off course. On May 7, Khrushchev reported that the pilot, Francis Gary Powers, was alive and had confessed to spying. Then Ike admitted that he had authorized the flight and furthermore knew the United States had been conducting "extensive aerial surveillance" over the Soviet Union. Khrushchev upbraided Eisenhower and threatened to call off the summit meeting.

Kennedy used the occasion to criticize the president for jeopardizing the summit conference. Johnson took a different tack, if only to distance himself from his rival. In a speech to the Senate he noted that espionage did not cause the Cold War but was simply a necessary "by-product" and he hoped that the Soviet premier would not use this incident as an excuse for "sabotaging" the summit conference. He also promised an investigation to see "if blunders have been made" but emphasized that Khrushchev should not be permitted to use "this incident in such a way as to divide the American people and to weaken our national strength."[43]

Johnson also met with Sam Rayburn, Adlai Stevenson, and William Fulbright in an attempt to save the Paris conference, and under Johnson's aegis they sent a cablegram asking Khrushchev not to "torpedo the conference." By the time it was delivered to the Soviet embassy in Paris, the Soviet leader had in fact canceled the meeting and Eisenhower's visit to the Soviet Union. Later that month Johnson warned against allowing Soviet leaders to set "the standard of conduct upon which we must negotiate for peace with other nations." At a graduation ceremony in Oklahoma City, on the other hand, he declared that "We don't want a cloak-and-dagger America."[44]

Once more political observers assumed that Johnson's actions had been governed by his presidential ambitions. And they were right. He desperately wanted to show his expertise in world affairs to strengthen his position at the upcoming convention. And he may have made his point with a few of the foreign policy establishment. Soon after the Oklahoma speech, former ambassador to the Soviet Union Averell Harriman told Johnson he was just the man the country needed.

With the civil rights bill under their belt, members of the Eighty-sixth Congress lost interest in further legislation. Johnson simply could not get his fellow senators to concentrate on the rest of his social program. Three Democratic senators—Symington, Humphrey, and Kennedy—were actively running for office, as was the Senate's presiding officer, Vice President Richard Nixon. And the majority leader himself was more than a little distracted by all the election year political maneuvering.

During the months leading up to the convention Johnson continued to gyrate over his candidacy like a top. He made a few exploratory political speaking trips and covertly encouraged friends to gather delegates in various state caucuses but refused to enter state primaries. He did not understand—and he was not alone at this point in the evolution of American party politics—that the rules were changing and that the primaries were becoming the most important road to nomination. Major wins in early primaries produced "momentum" that often could not be stopped. Brokered conventions in smoke-filled rooms were fast becoming things of the past.

Besides the ever-loyal Sam Rayburn, Johnson actually had solid grassroots support. Moderate Southerners hoped a Texas president might finally end the Civil War; pragmatic Westerners liked Johnson's practical bent. He also had friends among midwestern moderates, old New Dealers, and Jewish voters. But was this enough? His indecisiveness over running drove away important political supporters. These people could have provided him with vital help and advice. Yet a small group of friends, such as John Connally and Senators Robert Kerr and Clinton Anderson, never gave up. His major weakness was among liberals who refused to see him as an acceptable candidate.

Yet he was not entirely without liberal support. In New York City, the bastion of liberal leadership and sentiment, Mary Lasker, an influential philanthropist and social leader, was a Johnson enthusiast. But Lasker had difficulty persuading New York liberals to endorse the Texan. Eleanor Roosevelt, the beloved *grande dame* of the Democratic Party's left, turned her down. According to Lasker, Mrs. Roosevelt queried her about LBJ's support for civil rights, and she had answered: "He's for civil rights." FDR's widow replied: "He's from the South, and it's impossible." Lasker also tried to persuade Dorothy Schiff, publisher of the liberal *New York Post*, and the paper's editor, James Wechsler, to support LBJ. They, too, were suspicious of his southern origins and could not be convinced. On the other hand, Phil Graham, publisher of the *Washington Post*, though not his wife, Katharine, who owned the *Post*, liked Johnson and had urged him to seek higher national office.

Indecisive, insecure, ambivalent, Johnson continued to hope he could ride to victory at the convention through his Senate connections; senators, after all, were powerful figures who often controlled their state's convention delegations. Yet to avoid disappointment, he tried to discourage his aide John Connally from advertising his run too openly. When Connally opened a Johnson headquarters in downtown Washington with a big "Johnson for President" sign, LBJ "raised hell" and forced him to take the sign down.[45] Journalist Jack Bell assessed LBJ's campaign bluntly. "Johnson fooled with it back and forth. He never got organized." Bell also criticized Johnson's Texas supporters for "fouling up things around the country."[46] But there was a psychological reason for the slow and tentative start. Johnson's failure to commit himself completely provided a fallback position, a rationalization he could use to assuage his disappointment if he lost. If he didn't enter the presidential contest full tilt, then his defeat could be blamed on his late announcement and his responsibilities in the Senate. And he still hoped, until a few weeks before the convention, that no candidate would arrive at Los Angeles with the necessary number of delegates. In the give-and-take of a brokered convention he could emerge victorious.

On May 7 Johnson won renomination to the Senate in the Texas senatorial primary, overcoming whatever doubts he had been harboring about his strength in his home state. Meanwhile, Kennedy was winning presidential primaries all across the nation. He took New Hampshire on March 8. On April 5 he won a surprise victory over Hubert Humphrey in Wisconsin. The Minnesotan had said he would withdraw if he lost in his neighboring state but changed his mind and decided to proceed on the primary trail. Humphrey managed to win in the District of Columbia and felt he would have an even better chance in strongly prolabor West Virginia, where the population was more than 95 percent Protestant.

The West Virginia primary now became the stage for a dramatic showdown. The Kennedy men were angry at Humphrey as a "spoiler." Even if he won, he would only preserve the field for a third candidate, such as Stevenson, Symington, or Johnson. Humphrey was still smarting over his loss in Wisconsin and was furious over the amount of money that the Kennedy forces were throwing around in a place where he felt he should by right have every advantage. The three other candidates were following the events closely, covertly and not so covertly helping Humphrey in his all-out war against JFK. Johnson, now wearing contact lenses probably more to help his image than his eyesight, made a two-day, three-state tour of West Virginia, Ohio, and western Pennsylvania. He was well received in Clarksburg, West Virginia, where he reiterated his line about the importance of "tending the Senate store."

On a chilly, rainy day West Virginians went to the polls and gave Kennedy a three-to-two victory. He now seemed unstoppable. The triumphant Kennedy could not refrain from sniping at his rivals when he came to New York City fresh from the primary. At a press conference, without mentioning the names of Symington or Johnson, he said: "No convention has ever nominated a man who avoided the primaries and elected that man president. And the 1960 Democratic Convention in Los Angeles is going to be no exception."[47]

Johnson and Symington kept insisting publicly that the nomination was still up for grabs. On May 31 Johnson's Texas backers took out full-page ads in eighteen newspapers, including the *Washington Post* and the *New York Times*, appealing to Johnson to declare his candidacy. Headed "Who Shall Lead Us?," the ads praised the qualifications and experience of the Senate majority leader and obliquely attacked Kennedy for his youth and inexperience. On June 1 the Scripps-Howard newspapers, backers of Eisenhower in 1952 and 1956, announced their support of LBJ for president. He was, they said, "the ablest and strongest Democrat available."[48]

Although he still had not announced by the middle of June, Johnson tried to convince the voters that it would be an open convention. In heavily Catholic New Jersey he scolded those who thought the convention was all "sewed up." He had not been an "active" candidate because of his duties as majority leader, he told his audience, but he knew he had lots of support in "many areas" of the country. Clearly referring to the West Virginia primary, he declared, "We Protestants have proved we'll vote for a Catholic. Now we want you Catholics to prove you can vote for a Protestant."[49]

For a time LBJ picked up further support. On June 30 a *Congressional Quarterly* poll of 407 journalists showed that 43 percent considered Johnson the strongest candidate, with Stevenson second at 30 percent and Kennedy third with 21 percent. On July 1, former president Truman held a press conference to announce that he had resigned as a delegate to the Democratic convention because he did not want to take part in what he considered a "prearranged affair" and implied that the proceedings in Los Angeles were being "controlled in advance" by Kennedy's "overzealous" supporters. He also said that Lyndon Johnson "deserves serious consideration at the convention."[50]

Johnson, in collaboration with Speaker Rayburn, decided to recess rather than adjourn Congress on July 3 and reconvene it in August after the nominating conventions. This "rump session" would give him additional leverage at Los Angeles by reminding the country and the delegates that the majority leader was a very important man.

Johnson could not know when he recessed the Senate in July that except for the upcoming "rump session," his twenty-four-year career in Congress was over. It had been a distinguished career. His Senate leadership, particularly, had stood out in an extraordinary way. Johnson, it could be argued, had been the greatest Senate leader since Stephen Douglas, a century before. Even Barry Goldwater, an intense political rival and his opponent in the 1964 presidential election, admired Johnson's Senate leadership. "He was a very good majority leader," Goldwater told Merle Miller. "If he had a job to do, we didn't go home at five or six o'clock. We went home when we got the job done, and it might be two or three days later, having been there all night, several nights. . . . When Lyndon Johnson said, 'This is going to be legislation,' you knew you weren't going to leave until it *was* legislation, until it was finished."[51] A finer, if more partisan, accolade came from Clark Clifford, Truman's close adviser and LBJ's future secretary of defense. Sometime toward the end of Johnson's Senate reign Clifford told an audience that the previous years would "not be known really as the Eisenhower years. They would likely be known as the Lyndon Baines Johnson years because he was supplying the leadership that the country needed."[52]

CHAPTER 14

Campaign Year 1960

D ESPITE THE HAMLET-LIKE IRRESOLUTION and preposterous backing and filling, it surprised no one when, on July 5, two days after Congress adjourned, Johnson finally announced formally his run for president. When asked by reporters about his chances at the convention, he claimed he might win on the third ballot. Significantly, he did not rule himself out of the vice-presidential nomination. Would he call himself a "conservative?" asked a reporter from the *Washington Post*. No, he said, he saw himself as a "man in the middle, progressive and prudent without being radical." With an obvious swipe at Kennedy's 1952 defense of McCarthy as a great patriot, and his absence when the senate voted to censure McCarthy in 1954, he noted that *he* was a "voting liberal when McCarthyism was at stake in the United States Senate."[1]

Johnson was forced to spend more time checking Kennedy at Los Angeles than collecting delegates for himself. According to political columnists Evans and Novak, the Johnson strategy had four parts. First, persuade Hubert Humphrey not to give up his forty or so delegates. Second, encourage the Stevenson candidacy, since the Stevenson delegates at some later time could be switched to Johnson. Third, induce favorite sons, such as Governor Robert Meyner of New Jersey, not to release their delegates. And last and most important, discredit Kennedy. Unfortunately, though negative campaigning was a common campaign device even then, it created enmity between the two men, who previously had cooperated on many senate issues.

Johnson thought that JFK was assailable on two points: his health and his father. The health issue was whether he had Addison's disease, a serious, sometimes fatal disorder of the adrenal glands. Recently doctors had found that injected cortisone could bring the disease under control, but it was still a dreaded ailment.

Even before Johnson entered the race, his backers were making health an issue. Proposing a medical test for all Democratic candidates, Mrs. India Edwards, a former Democratic national committeewoman, cochair of Citizens for Johnson, asserted that Kennedy definitely had Addison's disease. Doctors had told her, she declared, "that he would not be alive if it were not for cortisone."[2] The Kennedys admitted only to an "adrenal insufficiency," probably brought on by malaria contracted during the war. Jack himself acknowledged he now took cortisone, but only when he was working hard. His supporters tried to turn the health issue back on LBJ. Ted Kennedy, the youngest son of Joe, countered that Johnson still had not recovered completely from his heart attack.

Publicly LBJ avoided discussing the medical issue. Both he and Kennedy were in good health, he declared. But privately he told Peter Lisagor of the *Chicago Daily News* that he thought his Senate colleague was "a little scrawny fellow with rickets," making a small circle with his thumb and forefinger to describe the circumference of Kennedy's ankles.[3]

Then there was Joe Kennedy. When Harry Truman said it was "Pop, not the pope"[4] that disturbed him about JFK's candidacy, he was reflecting a common political opinion. Joseph P. Kennedy had worked his way out of Boston's Irish ghetto via Boston Latin School and Harvard College. Banking, distilling, stock market manipulation, and Hollywood filmmaking, all charged with ruthless energy, had made him an immensely wealthy man. He burned to make one of his four sons president of the United States and was willing to expend any amount of effort and money to do so. Unfortunately, he was a heavy cross for his sons to carry. During World War II he had, as ambassador to Great Britain, supported Neville Chamberlain's appeasement policies and skirted the edge of pro-Nazi views. Many political observers feared that such a brutally domineering, conniving, wrongheaded man could not fail to influence his son's views.

Johnson was not shy about raising the Joe Kennedy issue. He suggested that without the ambassador's wealth Jack would never be a candidate. Just before the official balloting at Los Angeles Johnson noted: "I wasn't any Chamberlain-umbrella policy man. I never thought Hitler was right."[5] Johnson also swiped at Kennedy's relatively youthful age of forty-three, saying that "Neither party has ever elected a man under forty-five to be president. . . . The vice presidency is a good place for a young man who needs experience."[6]

The Johnsonites' attacks helped trigger the war that would engulf LBJ and Robert Kennedy for the rest of their lives. His brother's campaign manager, Bobby had a history of vendettas against men he disliked. He had pursued Jimmy Hoffa, the corrupt Teamsters boss, like Inspector Javert pursued Jean Valjean in *Les Misérables*. If, in addition, the scoundrel attacked his family, he was remorseless. When Roy Cohn, chief counsel of Senator Joe McCarthy's Permanent Subcommitee on Government Operations, and for a time his boss, had smeared baby brother Edward Kennedy, Bobby had retaliated with a ferocious campaign to humiliate Cohn. Now, enraged at the innuendos about his older brother's health and his father's defeatism, he vowed revenge against LBJ. One morning, at the convention, he encountered at breakfast Johnson loyalist Bobby Baker. Baker complained that Ted Kennedy had been unfair about Johnson's heart condition. Livid, RFK shot back: "You've got your nerve. Lyndon Johnson has compared my father with the Nazis, and John Connally and India Edwards lied that my brother is dying of Addison's disease. You Johnson people are running a stinking damned campaign and you're gonna get yours when the time comes!"[7]

In any case, Johnson's four-point plan to get the nomination did not work, and the candidates and delegates streamed into Los Angeles for the July national convention with the young Massachusetts senator in a commanding lead. In a final desperate move, just before the nomination, John Connally arranged a televised LBJ-Kennedy debate before the Texas and Massachusetts delegations. This was a blunder. Kennedy disarmed everyone at the beginning by denying there was anything to debate since "I don't think Senator Johnson and I disagree on the great issues that face us."[8] Johnson pictured himself as a responsible, experienced leader and dismissed Kennedy as a youthful dilettante who missed quorum calls and roll calls. His criticism was clumsy and deftly outclassed by his opponent, who said he supported Johnson heartily for majority leader, implying of course that he meanwhile would be president. LBJ's old friend Jake Jacobsen later said this meeting was Johnson's "last gasp." Kennedy did such a good job, in his opinion, that he got "Johnson to where, when he got up, there wasn't much to say. You couldn't argue with a man who was treating you so good, and really it didn't come off as we had expected it to."[9]

Now there was nothing to do but wait for the balloting, with Kennedy supremely confident and Johnson mostly glum. On Wednesday the convention adopted, over southern dissent, a "big-budget" platform that included the most forceful civil rights plank in Democratic Party history, and then moved on to the balloting. Rayburn nominated Johnson, calling him "a man for all Americans, a leader matured by long experience, a soldier seasoned in many battles, a tall, sun-crowned man who stands ready now to lead America. . . ."[10] It was nice oratory, but a waste. The first ballot gave Kennedy the victory, with 806 votes to Johnson's 409, mostly from the South. The results were a bitter disappointment. One report has Johnson in a drunken rage that evening in the corridor outside his Biltmore suite, calling the Kennedys foul names.

What about second spot? It is clear that many Democratic pols believed that a Kennedy-Johnson ticket would be their best chance of winning. Southern party leaders, especially, feared that a Yankee Catholic would crash in flames without a Southerner by his side. Yet the party liberals and the labor barons were equally clear that Johnson was not acceptable. Kenneth O'Donnell, a Kennedy retainer and liaison with organized labor for his boss, later wrote: "The labor people had warned me repeatedly that they did not want Johnson on the Kennedy ticket," and he had given them and the liberals assurances on that subject.[11]

Enter Phil Graham of the *Washington Post*, an old friend of both Kennedy and Johnson. As we saw, Graham had long tried to transform the Texas senator from a regional and Beltway figure into a national leader. On Monday, with the Kennedy nomination on Wednesday all but certain, Graham and Washington journalist Joe Alsop had gone to the Massachusetts senator's hotel room and pleaded eloquently for Johnson as vice-presidential candidate. To the visitors' surprise, Kennedy responded enthusiastically. Johnson could help the ticket not only in the South but elsewhere in the country, he said, and he intended to make the offer. Kennedy had said the same thing to Congressman Tip O'Neill of Massachusetts. On Wednesday morning Graham and Kennedy rode together to the convention. Graham urged him to announce his choice of Johnson the following day.

Whatever he had told Alsop, Graham, and O'Neill, however, Kennedy in fact had already asked Clark Clifford to sound out Senator Stuart Symington of Missouri for the vice-presidential spot, and Clifford had taken this as a firm offer. But then, Thursday morning at about eleven, Kennedy dropped down to Johnson's Biltmore suite two floors below his own, and made *him* the offer. The proposal, brother Bobby later insisted, was pro forma; the freshly minted nominee wanted primarily to cement party unity and did not expect his offer to be accepted. We will never know. It is hard to believe that Kennedy and his staff did not understand that Jack, a New England Roman Catholic, was a hard sell in the South and that without a man like Lyndon on the ticket victory was remote. Jim Rowe claims he specifically told Bobby that since Jack was not "too popular in great areas of this country," Johnson was the only man to help "in the South and part of the West."[12] And yet, as Bobby's story goes, startled at the response, the candidate returned to his suite nonplussed. "Now what do we do?"[13]

Johnson and his advisers had been engaged in a debate over a possible offer that reached a crescendo with the nominee's visit. Johnson knew he could not expect to function as effectively in the future as majority leader as in the past. If Nixon won he would be facing a more vigorous Republican president than Eisenhower, while at the same time the liberals in his own party would demand more progressive social legislation. If Kennedy won, the focus of power in the Democratic Party would shift to the White House, and Johnson would be one man among many doing the president's bidding. If he remained majority leader, his job would be to push the Kennedy, not the Johnson, program through Congress. If he succeeded, the president would get the credit. If he failed, he would be blamed, and his enemies, including some of Kennedy's advisers, would be happy to emphasize the point to the media. Staying on in the Senate seemed a somber prospect. In a sense the choice to run for vice president was the choice to stay in politics.

The vice presidency, by giving him national visibility, was also a way to escape his reputation as a sectional politician. Though he would be running as a Southerner to balance the ticket, once vice president he would no longer be totally identified with one section. Moreover, he felt that he was the only man who could help bring the South back into the mainstream of American politics. According to Arthur Schlesinger Jr., a Kennedy loyalist, Johnson was saddened by the "fact that so much southern political energy was diverted from constructive channels to the defense of the past . . .fighting for lost causes. . . ." He would show them that it was possible to move ahead.[14]

And there was always the potential of inheriting the presidency, one way or another. As of 1960 no vice president in the twentieth century had ever been nominated for president after serving his term, but three presidents had died in office since 1901. As he told Clare Boothe Luce, Henry Luce's wife and former congresswoman from Connecticut: "Clare, I looked it up: One out of every four presidents has died in office. I'm a gamblin' man darlin', and this is the only chance I got."[15]

Yet Johnson did not want to seem eager. His supporters and financial backers in Texas had been assured that he was a serious candidate for the top spot. They would be offended if he accepted second place too avidly. Reluctance was also a bargaining ploy. Perhaps he could extract promises for expanded responsibilities and visibility for the vice president from Kennedy in exchange for accepting second place.

The weight of advice from friends and associates was favorable. Senate friends Robert Kerr and Clinton Anderson warned against accepting. Rayburn was initially skeptical. Campaign manager Connally was vehemently opposed. The idea that Johnson would join forces with a man whom he, Connally, had fought so hard to defeat rankled. But most others said yes. After talking to Louisiana congressman Hale Boggs, Rayburn concluded that without Johnson on the national ticket the Democrats would certainly lose. Rayburn hated Nixon, the likely Republican nominee, and did not want to see him get the White House. Senator Kerr also switched. "Lyndon," he told his friend, "if Jack Kennedy asked you to be his running mate, and if you don't take it, I'll shoot you right between the eyes."[16] Lady Bird, too, believing the vice presidency less stressful than the majority leadership, came down on the side of acceptance. Together these pushes and considerations had induced the majority leader to accept the offer.

What happened next is hard to untangle, and even historians who interviewed many of the participants do not agree. The true story, however, seems to go like this. Key Democratic liberals were outraged when they heard that Kennedy was planning to tap Johnson as the vice-presidential candidate. It was a horrible mistake, labor leaders Walter Reuther, Jack Conway, and Alex Rose told the nominee. When Bobby and O'Donnell, dispatched by the candidate to tell the union leaders of his decision, arrived in Reuther's suite, they came under furious attack. Bobby, O'Donnell reported, was "ashen."[17] Governor G. Mennen ("Soapy") Williams of Michigan remarked that he had been "so happy over the platform" but was now "ready to trade the platform for any other Vice Presidential nominee."[18]

But it was not only Johnson's ideology that put some Democrats off. People in the Kennedy camp were disturbed by the difference in personal style: the suave, cool, cosmopolitan, Harvard-educated man of the world versus the awkward, overbearing, unsophisticated graduate of a southern teacher's college. How could the two mesh?

The fury of the opposition dismayed the candidate, and hoping to extricate himself from his promise, he sent Bobby to see Johnson, in all, three times during the day. As Connally later told it, Bobby insisted that "Lyndon has got to get off this ticket. This convention is going to go crazy," he had announced. "He's got to withdraw."[19] To induce him to turn down the offer, Bobby proposed that Johnson take the Democratic National Committee chairmanship. Bobby later recalled of the last visit that he told LBJ, as they sat on the couch together, that there would be a lot of opposition to his nomination and that it would be an unpleasant experience. As he spoke his discouraging words, Bobby later insisted, the

Texan began to grow tearful. "I want to be vice president," he recalled the majority leader saying, "and if the President [sic] will have me, I'll join him in making a fight for it."[20] Nonplussed, Kennedy said that if he really wanted the spot, then his brother would confirm the offer. Meanwhile, apparently, having learned of Bobby's mission, Phil Graham got John Kennedy on the phone. Any liberal defections would most certainly be offset by southern gains, he told the nominee, and scolded him for acting in the Hamlet-like way of Adlai Stevenson. JFK responded that his brother had lost touch with the latest decision and asked Graham to tell the majority leader that the offer was firm. With Bobby still in the room laying out the difficulties of a Johnson nomination, Graham called JFK back and informed him what his brother was doing. The nominee then asked to speak to his brother and told him that the offer was a *fait accompli*. In Graham's contemporary report, Bobby listened stone-faced to Jack and angrily exclaimed, "Well, it's too late now," and slammed down the receiver.[21] When Bobby left the room, Johnson called him a succession of foul names. LBJ now went out and told the press that Jack Kennedy wanted him to be the vice-presidential candidate and that he had accepted the offer.

The maneuvering over the nomination was the ultimate source of the deep rift between Robert Kennedy and Johnson. As we saw, Bobby was a champion hater long before he met Johnson. He already despised the Texan for his campaign methods against his brother. But LBJ himself was a conciliator who had learned to work with men of differing temperaments and ideologies. He might have forgiven Bobby for opposing some piece of legislation, for example, but he could not forgive a man who had threatened his very future. In all likelihood Bobby was only transmitting his brother's actual hesitancy over the vice-presidential nomination, but LBJ believed that he had tried to annul Jack Kennedy's decision. The repercussions would be felt well past 1960 and ultimately damage both men.

The next day Governor David Lawrence of Pennsylvania, calling LBJ the "strongest Democratic leader in the history of the United States Senate," formally nominated him for vice president. This was the only name placed in nomination. With a few stray "nays" among the roar of "ayes," the convention confirmed the choice by voice vote. When the two Democratic leaders met with black delegates after the convention, Johnson told them the LBJ on his lapel button now stood for "Let's Back Jack."

Though some liberals remained bitter, Southerners, as Kennedy had hoped—diehard segregationists excepted—were pleased with the slate. Governor Buford Ellington of Tennessee had worried that his state would turn Republican in November. Now, he said, "I think this ticket will carry the state." Luther Hodges of North Carolina pronounced the Kennedy-Johnson team "perfect."[22]

Soon after the convention the Johnsons flew off to Acapulco to recuperate. They stayed at the estate of Mexican political leader Miguel Alemán and had the use of Alemán's yacht. They shopped for clothes and gifts in the shops of the luxurious resort town. In late July Johnson visited the Kennedy family summer compound at Cape Cod to discuss the campaign ahead. At the candidates' joint press conference on July 30, Johnson did most of the talking and joking with the reporters. He and Kennedy were compatible, he made clear, and any residual bitterness from the convention had evaporated. Johnson surprised the press by stating that neither he nor Kennedy intended to wage a regional campaign and, as a matter of fact, Kennedy was planning to go to Texas. "Between the two of us," he said, "we are going to cover everything."[23]

Actually, this was a compromise engineered by Jim Rowe; Kennedy had originally wanted Johnson to confine himself to the South, and it was still understood that LBJ's most important job was to deliver that section to the Democrats. Kennedy planned to concentrate on the northern cities. Rowe, whose experience in national politics dated from the midthirties, felt that both men should show themselves in areas where they were not known. A Montana Catholic who knew what it was like to be member of a small and suspect religious minority, Rowe told Kennedy: "You've got to let these people see you. You've got to show them that Catholics don't have horns."[24] It was equally important, Rowe felt, that Johnson should get exposure in places other than the South for any future quest for the presidency itself. LBJ balked at going to Chicago, California, and New York City, where the "liberals [would] cut me up and embarrass Jack Kennedy," but Rowe decided it was all the more reason he should campaign there. He could show them that he was indeed a national politician. As James Blundell, an old Johnson friend, later noted, "he went to all three places and was very successful."[25]

But first there was the "rump session" of Congress that Rayburn and LBJ had arranged in July to help Johnson with his anticipated presidential run. Johnson had intended to focus on four areas, including a rise in the minimum wage, medical care for the aged, a federal housing program, and federal aid to education. Unfortunately, when Congress reconvened on August 8, all of these initiatives failed. The minimum-wage bill floundered on two competing versions in the Senate and House, the health insurance bill was actually defeated in the Senate, the housing bill never made it to the floor, and conservatives saw to it that final action on federal aid to education was checked. The session was politically damaging. Instead of increasing his prestige as he had hoped, Johnson had only annoyed his colleagues, who found the sweltering three extra weeks in Washington galling when they wanted to go home to campaign. No one was as chagrined as the man at the top of the ticket. JFK's trusted secretary Evelyn Lincoln recalled her boss pacing up and down his office during that frustrating do-nothing period muttering, "I can't understand what Lyndon was thinking about."[26] Fortunately, the public soon forgot the Democratic fiasco.

As usual, campaigning began in earnest after Labor Day. In August a Texas court had given Johnson a cushion by ruling that it was legal for him to run both for senator and vice president at the same time. Texas politics being what they were, Johnson was now assured of returning to the Senate no matter what happened.

The vice-presidential nominee by now had committed himself to the liberal Democratic social and economic agenda, strong civil rights plank and all, and intended to fight for it as hard as he ever fought for anything. (On only one issue did he retain his sectional ties—tax depletion allowances for the oil industry.) And whatever he may have thought privately, he never publicly said anything negative about his running mate. As a matter of fact, he praised Kennedy effusively, enshrining him among heroes such as FDR, Woodrow Wilson, Thomas Jefferson, and Mr. Sam. Johnson talked repeatedly during the campaign about linking Boston, Massachusetts, with Austin, Texas, and declared that the Boston-Austin axis would combine the best of all possible worlds. He expressed his hope that Kennedy's religion would not be an issue. The South would transcend intolerance and prejudice and vote for the Kennedy-Johnson ticket. But he refused to pander to anyone. "Wherever I may go, I will never speak as a Southerner to Southerners, or as a Protestant to Protestants, or as a white to whites. I will speak only as an American to Americans—whatever their region, their religion, or their race."[27]

On September 7 a group of 150 leading Protestant clerics and laypeople, under the aegis of the Rev. Dr. Norman Vincent Peale of New York City's Marble Collegiate Church, expressed concern over Kennedy's Catholicism. A "Roman Catholic President," they announced, "would be under extreme pressure from the hierarchy of his Church to align United States foreign policy with that of the Vatican."[28] The religious issue, they declared, was the most important of the campaign.

Kennedy intended to answer this charge when he and Johnson went to Texas a few days later to campaign for the state's critical twenty-four electoral votes. They learned what awaited them when, at a meeting of the Dallas County Democratic Executive Committee, a speaker referred to them contemptuously as "Mister Boston Beans" and "Lyndon Benedict Johnson."[29] At the Alamo in San Antonio, on September 12, a large group of hostile picketers greeted the candidates. Two of the signs they carried read: "We want the Bible and the Constitution" and "We don't want the Kremlin or the Vatican."[30]

Johnson gave the hecklers what he called his "little ole war hero" speech, praising Kennedy for his brave rescue of the crew of the torpedoed PT-109 in World War II. "And when he was savin' those American boys," Johnson dramatically declaimed, "they didn't ask what church he belonged to."[31] Later that night, in Houston, Kennedy told the Protestant Greater Houston Ministerial Association that he did not speak for his church on public matters and that the church did not speak for him either. "Whatever issue may come before me as president—on birth control, divorce, censorship, gambling, or any other subject," Kennedy declared, "I will make my decision in accordance with what my conscience tells me to be the national interest and without regard to outside religious pressures or dictates."[32] Johnson, as well as most political observers, thought the performance outstanding, doing wonders to dispel religious antagonism. The next day, the candidates, now joined by Sam Rayburn, campaigned through Texas, feeling much more confident about the possibility that the state would vote Democratic in November.

Johnson continued to hammer away at the religious bigotry theme for the rest of the campaign. In Washington he criticized Nixon for failing to repudiate support from anti-Catholics and bigots who raised the religious question. In Owensboro, Kentucky, he charged that Nixon was campaigning for president as he had campaigned for other offices in the past. "They are always campaigns of fear," of "hate, that try to divide our country when it should be united."[33] This religious issue, he charged, would "backfire" against the Republicans. At the end of September, Johnson toured the Midwest, sometimes accompanied by former president Truman. In Columbus, Ohio, Johnson again chastised "those who would divide this country" on religious, racial, or regional grounds. Those people were "doing Nikita Khrushchev's work."[34]

Just before embarking on an October swing through the South, Johnson detoured to the Northeast. In New Jersey he ridiculed Richard Nixon as the "great misjudger of the decade." In New York he kissed babies and went to a kosher delicatessen, where he chomped on pickles while shaking hands. Lady Bird Johnson, also campaigning in New York, told a press conference that she was "extremely hopeful" about Democratic chances but did not want to sound too optimistic lest campaign workers slacken off. "My husband has always run scared," she said, and then translated this ambiguous phrase as a "Texas expression for 'Don't stop working,' and don't get too overconfident." Johnson also spoke before the Liberal Party, a small New York group financed largely by the Jewish-run garment unions. Many Jews were skeptical of Kennedy; his father's supposedly pro-Hitler views aroused suspicions toward the son. Johnson, however, had many Jewish friends, and his appearance before the Liberal Party helped shore up the ticket in vital New York. Johnson denounced Republicans for favoring the "privileged few" and stressed his own belief that "all people should be equal before the law."[35]

On October 6 the vice-presidential candidate set off on a thirty-five-hundred-mile whistle-stop tour of the South, traveling in an eleven-car train he called the *LBJ Victory Special* but that reporters nicknamed the *Cornpone Special*. He attracted governors, congressmen, and other state and local officials and provided lots of good copy. Meanwhile, Lindy Boggs, wife of Congressman Hale Boggs, took five other women, all dressed up in red, white, and blue outfits, and flew from city to city in advance of Lyndon's train to help stir crowd enthusiasm and dispel any overt acts of hostility. "Everything worked out beautifully," recalled Mrs. Boggs. "What southern gentleman is not going to receive southern ladies when they are coming to his state and his city?"[36]

One of Johnson's favorite campaign ploys was warning voters that Nixon, as president, would not be able to function with a Democratic Congress. In Chicago he referred to Nixon as a "dangerous candidate" because he ignored Americans' troubles by "claiming that they did not exist." In Los Angeles he informed students that Nixon was desperate and trading his gloves for a pair of "brass knuckles." In Missouri he said that the vice president was "jumping around like a cat on a hot tin roof."[37] And after the first Kennedy-Nixon debate on television, he joked about the vice-president's pale stage makeup. "Of course," LBJ told his audiences, "all of us Democrats who have been around him for eight years have known all along he's made up."[38]

Wherever Lyndon went, he effectively developed the campaign themes: He attacked religious prejudice, defended the party's strong civil rights stand, criticized Nixon, acclaimed the Boston-Austin axis, and cheered the union of North, South, and West. He undoubtedly persuaded many southern voters to support the ticket. He even got some of the doubting liberals to change their mind about him personally. The *New York Times* praised Johnson for being the "hardest-working speaker of the four stars now on the political circuit."[39] Johnson could not resist letting Kennedy know what a successful campaigner he was turning out to be. "I see you are losing Ohio," he told him during a telephone call on election night. "I am carrying Texas and we are doing pretty well in Pennsylvania."[40]

Johnson was undoubtedly effective at times, yet the campaign drained his stamina and disturbed his emotional balance. According to George Reedy, LBJ had begun to drink to excess during the months of indecision and self-doubt leading up to the convention. After it, he was haunted by his fear that Texas would go Republican and that he, on the ticket primarily to ensure his state's twenty-four electoral votes, would be blamed. During the campaign tours his temper was on a hair trigger and he would berate advance men and staffers unmercifully if anything went wrong. Jim Rowe later told Hubert Humphrey that he did not know "why his staff did not kill him. . . . They almost did several times."[41] He continued to drink too much. The vice-presidential candidate, Reedy wrote, was often occupied in "drunken prowls up and down hotel corridors," with his aides engaged in "frantic efforts to sober him up in the mornings so that he could make speaking engagements." At one point in El Paso, during the Texas circuit in September, Johnson "could barely see" when Kennedy joined the party for a joint appearance.[42] Fortunately, LBJ's recovery rate was rapid, and on that occasion, as on others, he proved effective before the voters. Fortunately, Lady Bird could usually stabilize him. "If it hadn't been for Lady Bird," recalled a friend, "Lyndon would have gone off the deep end many times."[43]

One of the most significant events of the campaign, and the one that many observers believe turned the tide in Texas, occurred in Dallas just days before the election. Up to that point Johnson had reason to worry about delivering the state's vote. Some of the Texas liberals were refusing to work for the ticket, and some of the conservative Democrats, under the leadership of former governor Allen Shivers, had joined Democrats for Nixon. On November 4, shrieking "We Want Nixon!," hundreds of hostile, angry people mobbed LBJ and his wife in the lobby of the Adolphus Hotel when he came to address a Democratic rally. Bruce Alger, the only Texas Republican congressman, had organized the crowd, which included John Tower, Johnson's Republican rival for the Senate. Alger himself was carrying a placard reading "LBJ Sold Out to Yankee Socialists." Other signs read: "Let's Beat Judas," "Let's Ground Lady Bird," and "LBJ—Counterfeit Confederate."[44] Some of the crowd were Junior Leaguers attending a Nixon rally across the street.

Before the Johnsons entered the hotel, one of the hostile women snatched Lady Bird's gloves and threw them in the gutter. Everybody was screaming insults at the Johnsons; some spat at them; one demonstrator hit Lady Bird on the head with a sign. Trying to push through the lobby, Lyndon and Lady Bird spent half an hour moving seventy-five feet. Mrs.

Johnson was quite frightened. "I just had to keep walking," she said later, "and suppress all emotions and be just like Marie Antoinette in the tumbrel."[45] But her husband was quite cool, instinctively understanding that if he behaved with dignity, he could turn the fracas to his own advantage. He asked the police to leave, telling them: "If the time has come when I can't walk through the lobby of a hotel in Dallas with my lady without a police escort, I want to know it."[46] The TV cameras recorded the whole scene.

In the end the incident worked resoundingly to Johnson's advantage. Many viewers were shocked by the sight of a rampaging mob attacking the Democratic vice-presidential candidate and his wife. Abruptly, Northerners who thought of LBJ as a racist Southerner and a rich, swaggering Texan saw him being attacked, cursed, and spat on by the very people he was supposed to be one of. The incident changed liberals' perceptions. It also gave Johnson and the Democratic ticket a boost in the South. Many fair-minded Southerners were mortified by the viciousness of the mob scene and its violations of the civility and cordiality that they prized. They did not want to be associated with Southerners who had participated in this outrageous affair. A Nixon backer lamented that it might have "set the Republican party in Texas back twenty years."[47]

When the Johnsons got to Houston they were warmly welcomed by people carrying signs that said: "We Apologize; We Love You." Senator Richard Russell, who had sat out all Democratic national campaigns since 1944, called Johnson and offered to help in the few days remaining before the election. Russell then campaigned in Texas and South Carolina. Johnson also managed to persuade other reluctant southern Democrats to join the campaign.

The night before the election, Johnson in Texas and Kennedy in Massachusetts appeared on national television. Johnson again stressed the Boston-Austin connection and talked about the grandson of two Confederates teaming up with the grandson of two Irish immigrants. The unity theme was uppermost in his mind. "Americans," he said, "are ready to lay aside the division of the Eighteen Sixties to meet the challenge of the Nineteen Sixties."[48]

The Kennedy-Johnson ticket won by a sliver, garnering 49.7 percent of the vote to Nixon's 49.6 percent. The Democrats received only 112,881 more popular votes than the Republicans out of more than 68.5 million cast. In the electoral college the Democratic vote of 303 to 219 seemed more impressive. But most political observers believed that JFK could not have been elected without the South. There, the Republicans carried only three states of the Old Confederacy: Virginia, Florida, and

Tennessee, with thirty-three electoral votes. And even in those states the Democrats made a strong showing. In Florida the vote was close, with a margin for Nixon of fewer than 50,000 out of 1.5 million. According to political analysts, only the fact that Tennessee had a large contingent of Protestant fundamentalists helped put Nixon in front. The Democrats took all the other southern states except Mississippi, winning eighty-one southern electoral votes. But above all, Texas, which had not supported a Democratic presidential candidate in twelve years, contributed twenty-four electoral votes to Kennedy and Johnson.

At the moment of victory, even members of the Kennedy camp most passionately opposed to Johnson acknowledged that his presence on the ticket had carried the election. "Old Lyndon put his prestige on the line," said a happy Texas Democratic official on the morning after. "He had to buck the religious issue, the platform, and the oil depletion allowance, and he wound up stronger than ever." Johnson himself declared: "This is one of America's finest hours." Soon after, he told political associates that he intended to be "the most influential Vice President" in American history.[49]

CHAPTER 15

Vice President

O N THE MORNING OF JANUARY 20, 1961, with seven inches of snow on the ground and eighteen-mile-an-hour gusts howling across Washington, Lyndon Johnson arose and put on a black cutaway morning coat, striped trousers, and a light gray double-breasted vest. Lady Bird chose an olive green suit and donned a mink coat to ward off the chill. A black limousine drove up to the house carrying the president pro tem of the Senate, Carl Hayden, and the House majority leader, John W. McCormack, the Johnsons' official escorts to the inauguration. The party drove to the east front of the Capitol, across from the Library of Congress, where the ceremony would take place.

A bright sun peeped through the clouds, but it was not enough to raise the temperature, and the electric heaters were unable to warm things up. On the small inaugural stand, the guests and dignitaries had their coats buttoned up to their necks except for LBJ, who seemed not to notice the cold.

The ceremonies began at noon. The famous black contralto Marian Anderson sang *The Star-Spangled Banner*. The poet Robert Frost, who could not see in the brilliant sun, recited his poetry from memory. Boston's Cardinal Cushing led a long prayer. At twelve-forty Sam Rayburn stepped forward to administer the oath to Lyndon Johnson. This was the first time that a Speaker had ever sworn in a vice president, but no one would disagree with the appropriateness of the choice. Holding a Bible given to him by his mother, and used nine times before as a member of Congress, Lyndon Baines Johnson officially became the thirty-seventh vice president of the United States. Later, at one of the inaugural balls, Mrs. Hugh Auchincloss, Jacqueline Kennedy's mother, danced with Johnson and, she told her daughter he was "very gallant and courtly." She "liked him very much."[1]

In many ways this day was the high point of Lyndon Johnson's vice presidency. The office was a dismal trap. In the past, when Johnson found himself in a subordinate position, he was able to use his talents to advantage. Either he became a favorite son, learning his seniors' techniques and sharing their confidences while basking in the attention and the favors they bestowed, or made the post into something more powerful and prestigious than it had been before.

But the vice presidency carried fundamental, irremediable limitations. The authors of the Constitution intended the holder of the office to be merely a stand-in for the president, ready if necessary to take over in the event of incapacity or death. Like an understudy waiting in the wings whose only chance to get on stage is when misfortune strikes, the vice president could only benefit from catastrophe. Otherwise, according to the Constitution, "The vice president of the United States shall be president of the Senate, but shall have no Vote, unless they be equally divided." This was the Founders' description of a relatively meaningless, mostly ceremonial role. Hubert Humphrey, who would also be a vice president with larger ambitions, told a story about a mother and her two sons. "One went to sea, and the other became vice president, and neither was ever heard of again."[2]

Lady Bird, on the other hand, was delighted to be wife of a vice president and was exhilarated by her new role. "I had a ball," she told Merle Miller. "I loved it. . . . We bought a beautiful home. We took a sizable share of entertaining the visitors; we did a lot of traveling—all things I enjoy and had done very little of before. But I would not say Lyndon shared my feeling. It was a life that was not nearly as pleasant for him as it was for me."[3]

Johnson sorely missed the power and prestige of majority leader. A month after the inauguration, Harry McPherson recounts, the vice president walked into the Senate cloakroom jammed with lounging, gossiping senators. In the past, when the majority leader had come by, a hush had fallen over the solons, as if the school principal had intruded into a group of raucous, mischievous schoolboys. Now, nothing happened. "He was no longer a member of the club. It was a very subtle thing, but you could feel it."[4]

Johnson's relations with his chief and his close advisers were touchy and unstable. There was a discrepancy in age, political talent, and experience between himself and the president. Kennedy was nine years younger than Johnson and had not yet earned his spurs. He had been in Congress eight years fewer than his vice president, had not been a particularly effective senator, and had no actual experience as a leader. JFK himself was aware of the differences between the two of them. "I spent years of my life when I could not get consideration for a bill," he told Arthur Schlesinger Jr., "until I went around and begged Lyndon Johnson to let it go ahead."[5] To Kennedy's credit, he also understood how touchy Johnson could be and tried to be as tactful as possible. He threatened to fire anyone on his staff who did not treat Johnson the way they would want JFK to be treated if their positions were reversed. He assigned him a posh six-room suite in the Executive Office Building. He expected to keep his vice president fully informed and to consult him frequently on legislation and public attitudes, sincerely esteeming his advice.

The president sought to accommodate LBJ on matters of appointments and patronage. It was at Johnson's urging, for example, that he selected John Connally as secretary of the navy, and Cyrus Vance, junior partner of his New York friend Ed Weisl, as general counsel for the Defense Department. He even acceded to Johnson's demand that he, not the senators from the state, as custom dictated, be given all patronage control beyond postmasters' appointments, in Texas. This effectively neutralized liberal Democrat Ralph Yarborough, Johnson's opponent back home.

Yet there was an underlying tension between the president and LBJ. Much of it had to do with style and personality. JFK did not relish the close company of the vice president. He complained to Evelyn Lincoln that Johnson wanted to travel with him on *Air Force One* whenever the two men were to appear together at a political conclave. Not only was it imprudent for the president and his stand-in to travel by plane together; JFK did not look forward to being confined to close quarters with his vice president. Kennedy also thought LBJ talked too much at meetings. After one, the president remarked, "We never got a thing done today. Lyndon never stopped talking."[6]

For his part, Johnson seldom felt at ease with the Camelot crew surrounding JFK. Predominantly Easterners, often Ivy Leaguers, they were remote from his own cultural circle. He lacked the cultivation of the Harvard intellectuals who advised the president. He could not converse about recent literature or the arts. He did not go to concerts, or movies, or plays. He was ill at ease at the various gatherings that the Kennedys held for outstanding scholars and cultural luminaries. For their part, the Kennedy entourage, despite the president's instructions, scorned him. They called him "Uncle Cornpone" and considered him a crude exhibitionist, a loud, clownish Texan.[7] Within Attorney General Robert Kennedy's social circle, the "Hickory Hill gang,"* the vice president was a favorite butt. At one point in late 1963 a gift to Bobby by his friends of an LBJ voodoo doll produced a great collective laugh. Hugh Sidey of *Time*, who disapproved of the disrespect for Johnson, later noted, "the merriment was overwhelming."[8] The provocations of Bobby and some of them," recalled Jim Rowe, "were really pretty outrageous."[9]

Johnson knew what the Kennedy people were saying in private, but tried to ignore it. He was determined to be, according to columnist William White, "first of all a *loyal* vice president,"[10] and publicly did everything in his power to live up to this principle as long as Kennedy was president. He never openly disagreed with anything that Jack did and went out of his way to make sure that he never uttered a critical word about the president even to his old political friends in the Senate. Johnson enjoyed poking fun at people and had a gift for making his rivals and enemies look ridiculous. His self-restraint toward Kennedy had to exact a considerable emotional price. But he was restrained not only by loyalty and piety. He also realized that he could not be a "breakaway" vice president, like John Nance Garner, who ended up antagonizing Franklin Roosevelt and being dropped from the 1940 ticket. If he could keep his discontents and resentments bottled up for eight years, he would stay on in 1964 and four years later get Kennedy's support for his own bid for the presidency.

Though he kept his tongue about the president to himself, Johnson sneered at the "Harvards" who surrounded him. His whole adult life had been dedicated to action and getting things done; the Kennedy crowd often preferred, he believed, to talk endlessly about theoretical issues rather than act. But he also felt insecure and resentful in their presence and, however much he chewed the president's own ears, seldom spoke up at cabinet meetings or even get-togethers with congressional leaders. Kennedy later complained to his friend George Smathers, "I cannot stand Johnson's long, damn face. He just comes in, sits at the cabinet meetings with his face all screwed up, never says anything. He looks so sad."[11]

Johnson's supposed reticence as a member of ExComm, the emergency steering committee during the 1962 Cuban Missile Crisis, aroused the contempt of the Attorney General, already prejudiced against LBJ.

---

*Named after the Robert Kennedy estate in the Virginia suburbs.

Bobby later gibed that during the tense meetings in late October, when the world seemed to totter on the edge of nuclear cataclysm, "Lyndon Johnson never made any suggestions or recommendations as to what we should do. . . ." After each meeting, moreover, he "would circulate and whine and complain about our being weak."[12] In fact, as the record shows, the vice president did speak up once or twice during the meetings, but he clearly felt out of his depth with such foreign policy whizzes as Secretary of State Dean Rusk, Secretary of Defense Robert McNamara, and national security adviser McGeorge Bundy, and for Bobby, who already viewed Johnson through grossly distorted lenses, his role on ExComm confirmed that the Texan was an ignorant lightweight unsuited to world leadership.

The gap between the nation's two top officials extended to their wives. Jacqueline Kennedy, a graduate of Miss Porter's in Farmington, Connecticut, had attended Vassar and the Sorbonne in Paris. She was clever, fashionable, and beautiful, spoke French like a native, and loved the arts. But she was snobbish and extravagant. She was clearly an adornment to her handsome husband, but she could not be counted on to undertake mundane political responsibilities, although when she did, she impressed everyone with her talent and style. She was jealous of her husband's other women and was often resentful and withdrawn. She poked fun at Mrs. Johnson's devotion to her husband, remarking at one point that "Lady Bird would crawl down Pennsylvania Avenue on broken glass for Lyndon."[13]

Lady Bird, in fact, was smart, plain, and practical, an excellent businesswoman, and, as Jackie observed, fiercely loyal to her husband. If Lyndon romanced other women, she did not let it affect their relationship, believing that no matter what else happened, she was the most important woman in his life. His first heart attack had drawn them closer than ever. She was a fundamental source of advice and kept well informed on all political matters. An article in the *Washington Evening Star* said that "the gentle manner of Mrs. Lyndon B. Johnson masks stamina, efficiency and a strong sense of purpose. She is feminine, friendly and folksy. . . ." When Johnson became vice president she formed a small class of four other Washington wives to learn Spanish because she felt "that this hemisphere is terribly important and [she] wanted to be able to speak the language of the people who live in it." Most people who met Mrs. Johnson liked her. As one Senate wife noted, she was "a warm person who always greets you with a gay smile and both hands outstretched."[14]

Kennedy left orders with his chief of protocol, Angier Biddle Duke, to "watch over [the Johnsons] and see that they're not ignored." They should be invited to all the parties. But often by the time Duke got the list of invitees, the vice president and his wife were not on it. "The real problems," Duke told Merle Miller, "were when the president would have some of the 'in-group' parties for Arthur Schlesinger, Mac Bundy, Kenneth Galbraith, and his friends that would come down from New York."[14] Duke would have to call the president on the afternoon of the day of the party to remind him to invite the Johnsons. But then, when they came, nobody paid much attention to them.

Numerous stories survive of the vice president's isolation at Kennedy functions. Hyman Bookbinder, a later War on Poverty official, recalled a 1963 occasion when Johnson was present at a White House ceremony presided over by Esther Peterson to unveil the president's Report on the Status of Women. At one point Peterson rushed over to Bookbinder with an anxious request: "Do me a favor. Lyndon's sitting out there in a corner and no one is talking to him. Please go and talk to him till four o'clock."[16] Harry McPherson recounted an evening he spent at the White House toward the end of the Johnson administration. He was sitting in the living room with the president and First Lady as Johnson was shuffling through some photographs. LBJ came across one of a lady he had met back in 1961 or 1962 when both he and JFK had been in New York to make speeches. After the oratory, the president's entourage had come back to the apartment of the president's brother-in-law Steven Smith for some late supper. Johnson described to McPherson the crowded living room where Kennedy sat in a large armchair surrounded by admirers, all craning to get the president's attention. The vice president found himself ignominiously in the outer circle. In his 1998 interview with the authors, McPherson could only imagine, from the distance of thirty years, "the level of self-pity and rage in him." Rather than remain, the vice president went to the empty library where, as a measure of his boredom, he actually picked up a book to divert himself. Soon after an attractive woman, the one in the picture, came in. She had left the living room, she said, because the "most interesting man in that room [had] left." She and the vice president spent until three or four in the morning alone, talking. Six years later, President Johnson remained grateful. As he remarked to McPherson in Lady Bird's presence: "Anytime she wants to come down here it's okay with me."[17]

Johnson's restraint in the face of contempt and rebuff was harder to achieve than he anticipated. He was a man of pride, passion, and energy who craved action and power and now had little outlet for the exercise of any of his abilities. His friend, lawyer Abe Fortas, was concerned about Johnson's state of mind. He told Justice William Douglas that "care should be taken that he is loaded with work—overloaded. This will serve his own peace of mind and it will also avoid the waste of his extraordinary talents."[18] Johnson knew his skills were being wasted. "Every time I came into John Kennedy's presence," he told Doris Kearns, "I felt like a goddamn raven hovering over his shoulder. Away from the Oval Office, it was even worse. The vice presidency is filled with trips around the world, chauffeurs, men saluting, people clapping, chairmanships of councils, but in the end, it is nothing. I detested every minute of it."[19]

He felt emasculated in this role and believed that other people now regarded him as insignificant. At a dinner party he pointed to his chauffeur and complained to a fellow guest: "He's been driving Senate majority leaders since Joe Robinson and when I got elected vice president, I asked him to come with me. At first he said 'No.' I said 'Why?' He said he liked to drive the majority leader because there was a man with real power. He said the vice president doesn't have any power at all." Then, recalling the site of the 1960 Democratic National Convention, Johnson added wistfully: "He's a pretty smart fellow, my driver. I wish I'd had him with me in Los Angeles."[20] Whether the chauffeur actually said this or not, it expressed Johnson's feelings of loss and demotion.

Johnson tried to escape the trap by enlarging his role. The effort would be stymied.

The attempt began even before the inauguration, when, on January 3, the sixty-four Democratic senators met for the party conference traditionally convened at the start of a new congressional session. The caucus unanimously chose an LBJ protégé, the professorial Montana senator Mike Mansfield, to succeed him as majority leader, and Mansfield, by Johnson's request, promptly asked the senators to allow the vice president-elect to attend the caucus and be permitted to preside over future caucuses of the Democratic senators.

Even Johnson's friends were appalled at the proposal. Recognizing that it would give the vice president control of caucus procedures and activities, five senators, including some of LBJ's strongest supporters, rose to protest. Others, who carefully praised Johnson for his past leadership, said that though the position of presiding officer of the Democratic caucus had no constitutional status, Johnson's demand was a threat to the separation of powers. "We might as well," growled Senator Gore, "ask Jack Kennedy to come back up to the Senate and take his turn at presiding."[21] As LBJ watched ashen-faced, many of his old cronies objected to the proposal. The vote was actually forty-six to seventeen to approve the Mansfield resolution, but the proud and emotional Johnson was irreparably hurt by the seventeen negative votes, mostly from liberals. "Those bastards sandbagged me," he fumed.[22]

Just after the meeting, as required by law, Johnson resigned as senator. He continued to anguish over the seventeen "nays" and what he perceived as his defeat, however. Seeking to distance himself from Johnson's influence, Mansfield soon after told the press that as majority leader he would not be "a circus ringmaster, the master of ceremonies of a Senate nightclub, a tamer of Senate lions, or a wheeler-dealer."[23] This, too, Johnson perceived as a slap in the face. Evans and Novak believe that "No other single event in those formative days of the New Frontier cut deeper, and none more influenced his conduct as vice-president after January 20. Indeed, he retired from the Senate—physically as well as legally."[24] LBJ attended one Democratic Senate caucus as vice president, but only to call it to order, immediately handing over the gavel to Mansfield.

When it came to Congress he felt like a powerless outsider among the people he had once so successfully dominated. And he could barely bring himself to help Kennedy in the legislative area, where his services would have been most appreciated. "Johnson pulled back . . . after that caucus," related a Kennedy aide. "He hadn't expected it, and it made him reluctant to approach senators."[25] At the weekly White House breakfast meetings for legislative leaders, Johnson was uncharacteristically silent. He looked tired and tense, giving his opinion only when specifically asked by Kennedy to offer one, usually mumbling his answers. In later months, as measure after measure introduced by the president came to naught in Congress, he was denounced by the liberal *New York Post* for not laboring hard enough to pass Kennedy's programs. Johnson took a perverse pleasure in remembering that the same newspaper had attacked him for trying to grab power at the Democratic conference on January 3.

A final bid for vice-presidential power was another defeat for Johnson. Shortly after the inauguration, an ambitious Johnson aide composed an executive order assigning to the vice president "general supervision" over many areas of government, including the National Aeronautics and Space Administration. After the president signed the executive order, it would officially direct all departments and agencies to send Johnson all reports, information, and policy plans that usually went to the president himself. Though dubious, Johnson sent it on to Kennedy. The president consigned the memorandum to oblivion. His refusal to sign it, coupled with the January 3 fiasco, convinced Johnson that he should confine himself to ceremonial duties. It was a course he would follow in the rest of his three years as vice president.

Though Kennedy refused to make Johnson de facto head of NASA, he recognized that his vice president, the author of the 1958 National

Aeronautics and Space Act, could be an invaluable help in the space program and asked Congress to replace the president with the vice president as chairman of the Space Council, an advisory group on space issues and a bridge between the civilian space exploration program and the military services. One of the chairman's jobs was the right to approve all major appointments.

Anxious to put a New Frontier stamp on the space program, Kennedy asked Johnson's help in finding a new civilian head of NASA. Johnson selected James E. Webb, a director of the Kerr-McGee oil company owned by his friend senator Bob Kerr of Oklahoma. Johnson also chose three high-level creative executives to study the space program and recommend ways that space exploration could be expedited.

In actuality, the Space Council had little power and afforded Johnson little scope for his energies. But the space program never ceased to excite his interest. Johnson urged Kennedy to speed up moon exploration, an idea that received a boost when, in April 1961, the Soviets sent cosmonaut Yuri Gagarin into orbit around Earth. After Gagarin landed safely, Kennedy sent a memo to Johnson, asking: "Can we beat the Russians to the moon?" LBJ's enthusiastic "Yes" encouraged Kennedy's famous request that Congress appropriate twenty billion dollars for a crash program to put a man on the moon and bring him back "before this decade is out."[26]

There is no question that Johnson considered the space program an exciting and worthy challenge. But like everything else, it was also an opportunity to attract attention and exercise power. As part of his official duties, he visited space installations across the country, making sure that the press was there to give him full coverage. At the end of each visit he shook everybody's hand and thanked them all profusely. Another opportunity for press coverage came when Alan Shepard made America's first manned space flight. A newspaper photo of this occasion showed the president and Jackie Kennedy watching a television set in the last seconds before blastoff while Johnson was pictured holding a telephone, looking as though he were directing the whole operation. In February 1962, when John Glenn became the first American to orbit Earth, Kennedy turned down Johnson's request to be in the Bahamas when the astronaut came ashore. But he could not entirely resist Johnson's importuning and permitted him to join the parades for Glenn in Washington and New York. Johnson ran true to form. In his eagerness to show how involved he was in the space enterprise, he upstaged Glenn and his wife by signing New York City's Guest Book before the Glenns. The *New York Herald Tribune* called Johnson a camera hog because he had managed to be in practically every photograph of the astronaut and his wife.

Johnson was involved in two other space and aeronautics projects. Kennedy asked him to head a special committee to research the possibility of building a supersonic transport that would fly at twice the speed of sound and compete with the parallel British-French project. This endeavor foundered on disagreements between Johnson and the administration's advisers over financing. Johnson wanted the federal government to subsidize a large part of it, but others thought that private industry should invest at least a quarter or more of the development costs. Eventually, on the advice of Defense Secretary McNamara, Johnson's recommendations were rejected, confirming that his power even in the field of aeronautics was limited.

A more important stage for the vice president than space was civil rights. Kennedy wanted him to be chairman of the Equal Employment Opportunity Committee (EEOC), established by Truman to encourage government contractors to hire minorities. At first Johnson was wary of the assignment. He supported the committee's purposes but was afraid that "any failure of the commission [sic] to put more Negroes into industrial jobs would bring the cynical reaction that he had . . . sabotaged the works."[27] He complained that the EEOC had no regular legislative budget and fretted about burning the last bridge to his southern constituency. Many of the biggest government contractors were located in the South and did not employ blacks except in menial positions. In some of these Dixie communities the companies were the main source of jobs, and if their contracts were canceled because of segregated employment policies, the local people would suffer economically. Johnson did not want to be blamed for their distress.[28] But he could not wiggle out of it. Kennedy insisted, and since Vice President Nixon had chaired the committee under Eisenhower, Johnson felt he had no choice but to accept.

Under Nixon's aegis the committee had only intervened when individuals themselves actually complained about discrimination in hiring. If the committee were to function more effectively, Johnson realized, it needed more power. He asked Abe Fortas to help him draft a more rigorous executive order to be presented to Kennedy for his signature. Fortas composed a statement that shifted the burden of proof from those experiencing employment discrimination to businesses seeking government contracts. It directed federal agencies to sign contracts only with companies that had pledged to comply with nondiscriminatory employment policies. Those companies also were responsible for getting labor unions, still largely segregated, to cooperate. Noncompliance would result in cancellation of government orders and possible inclusion on a blacklist for future contracts as well. Kennedy was pleased with Fortas's work and signed the order in March 1961.

To wield new powers Johnson needed new funds, but the committee had no money of its own. Recognizing that the South would veto any congressional appropriation, he wheedled over a million dollars from other government agencies. Senator Russell tried futilely to find the source of the agency's money. But Johnson would not tell him and "did not bend" in spite of the pressure.[29]

To exacerbate his southern difficulties, the first contractor to be charged with discrimination under the new order was the Lockheed Corporation, which had established one of its largest defense plants in Marietta, Georgia, Russell's home state. The Lockheed plant was totally segregated. Not only did Lockheed discriminate in hiring, it also would not allow blacks and whites to use the same cafeterias or washrooms. When Johnson took over the committee, Lockheed was negotiating a one-billion-dollar contract to build large transport planes for the air force. The company sent a report to the committee assuring it that there were no racial problems at Marietta. When Johnson's staff rejected Lockheed's claim, several southern committee members tried to get the agency to change its mind, and Russell himself "raised hell." Fortunately, Johnson inveigled Lockheed into promising to end discrimination in hiring, while the government, for its part, pledged to educate blacks for skilled jobs.[30]

The committee was not harmonious. Some members wanted to go slowly; some wanted immediate action. Some were for persuasion; others, for penalties. One of the staff directors, Robert Troutman, an Atlanta businessman who favored a moderate approach, came up with a "Plans for Progress" program that pledged business firms to renounce discrimination but that provided no enforcement mechanism. On the other side was liberal John Feild, who had previously served on the Michigan Fair Employment Practices Commission. Feild noted that there was a vast gulf between signing pledges and actually hiring minority employees. The government must flex its muscles to force compliance. "I have been impressed," Feild told a civil rights group, "with the educational value of a threat." Johnson himself endorsed exhortation rather than actual punishment. "Let's make it *fashionable*," Johnson would tell his staff, "to end discrimination."[31]

The antagonism between what *New York Times* reporter Peter Braestrup characterized as the "compulsory" and the "voluntary" factions attracted wide notice. Secretary of Labor Arthur Goldberg, trying to minimize the controversy, told Braestrup: "I like a little healthy diversity.

There is bound to be disagreement in a group as varied as this one."[32] He and the vice president were quite satisfied, they said, with the early two-thousand-person gain in jobs under the Plans for Progress agreements, and insisted that publicity was a valuable tool in getting big business to cooperate against racial discrimination. But United Auto Workers president Walter Reuther and Whitney Young Jr., head of the National Urban League, had doubts about the efficacy of the program. Herbert Hill of the NAACP said that the Plans for Progress agreements "resulted in more publicity than progress."[33]

Two days after the article appeared, Johnson wrote a letter to the *Times* defending himself and his committee. "Controversy, like beauty is frequently in the eye of the beholder," he wrote. "The facts are that people involved in different aspects of a program are quite likely to put heavier emphasis on that with which they are the most familiar." The committee's objectives were to ensure equal employment opportunities for all, a "goal . . . based upon considerations of both wisdom and morality." The committee operated a "compliance program, and . . . we mean business." The program was voluntary, but this did not mean that it relieved "employers of their obligation to comply with the executive order." "We must rid ourselves of the notion that there is one simple solution to this highly complex problem." Johnson concluded with a ringing civil rights endorsement. "Justice has been too long delayed by abstract procedural arguments. People are entitled to fair play and equal treatment now — while they can still enjoy its benefits — and it is my intention to sponsor any and every legitimate form of action that will produce results."[34]

The divisive Troutman-Feild fight was resolved by luck and adept maneuver. In the middle of the brouhaha, the executive vice chairman of the committee, Jerry R. Holleman, former head of the Texas state AFL-CIO, who had brought Feild into the committee in the first place, resigned from government service after admitting that he had taken a thousand dollars from fellow Texan Billy Sol Estes for political favors. To replace Holleman, Johnson appointed gradualist Hobart Taylor Jr., a black graduate of the University of Michigan Law School, who had long been a Johnson supporter. Then Johnson reorganized the committee, eliminating the jobs of both Feild and Troutman. With both men out of the way, Johnson appointed Taylor top staff director.

By the fall of 1962 Johnson and Taylor boasted that "Plans for Progress" had been signed by fifty companies holding billions of dollars of defense contracts. In January 1963 the committee held a much-publicized banquet at the White House for 250 representatives of companies participating in the plan.

Johnson was satisfied with slow but steady progress in the civil rights field and happy when his achievements came without stirring conflict. He really believed he could change employers' minds and improve compliance with nondiscriminatory hiring policies by persuasion and pressure rather than penalties. But Attorney General Kennedy, an official committee member, deplored his results. Bobby came to a couple of committee meetings, supposedly at the request of the president, asked a lot of pointed questions of the members, barked at their responses, and then brutally scolded the vice president in front of his colleagues, implying that he was an ineffective chairman. When Hobart Taylor tried to protest, Kennedy would not let him speak. After lecturing everyone that the president wanted more impressive results, he walked out. Johnson, thoroughly embarrassed, was silent and "slumped in his seat," according to an observer. He did not call another meeting for a long time. The vice president had been thoroughly and savagely undermined by the president's brother, fueling rumors that Johnson might be dropped from the ticket in 1964. Meanwhile, the attorney general had Taylor dismissed.

In reality the committee's achievements were substantial. According to William White, the number of blacks in top government jobs increased the first year of the committee's operations by 35 percent. On the middle level, black government employment rose 20 percent. Many jobs formerly held by whites in petrochemical plants in Louisiana and Texas, in shipyards in Mississippi and California, in food plants in Georgia, and in steel plants in Alabama, Texas, and West Virginia were now occupied by blacks. A total of 118 international and 338 affiliated local unions pledged to abolish segregation in their apprenticeship programs and lines of seniority. In Los Angeles, Johnson himself held meetings with the school board and local employers to discuss whether vocational training for minorities might be coordinated with the job needs of the community. Johnson and his committee, the forefather of the Equal Employment Opportunities Commission, set a precedent for government involvement in the area of creating and maintaining equal job opportunities.

Johnson's work on the committee forged a commitment to civil rights he had never felt before. The vice president made speeches all over the country, even in the South, on the need for equal rights and opportunities for minorities. His travels through the nation and meetings with black victims of discrimination personalized the civil rights issue for him. Here was another group of dependents whom Johnson, acting as a benevolent father, had a responsibility to take care of. Even if, in the early sixties, he still preferred a moderate approach, he determined that ultimately racial discrimination must go.

But John Kennedy failed to use the vice president's commitment and knowledge in pushing through what came to be the landmark Civil Rights Act of 1964. JFK was not a civil rights enthusiast. During his first two years, the Justice Department under Robert Kennedy sought to enforce existing laws and court decisions on voting rights and school desegregation. In the fall of 1961 the president sent federal marshals and troops to force desegregation of the University of Mississippi. He also issued an executive order, promised long before, to forbid discrimination in federal housing and in housing secured by federal loans. But neither he nor his brother understood, at this point, the depth of black people's feelings about second-class citizenship, nor did they have a strong moral commitment to changing the nation's racial orientation.

The administration's record in getting a major installment of federal support for civil rights was not impressive. In 1961 Congress refused to pass a measure to use a sixth-grade education as proof of literacy in states where a literacy test for voting existed, and the White House could do little to change its mind. More important, the administration seemed unable to rally its energies for a major new federal law that would plug the many loopholes left by the measures of 1957 and 1960. Majority leader Mike Mansfield was convinced that no Democratic president would ever get another civil rights bill through the Senate. He could "never persuade that many Republicans to vote for cloture," the Montana senator believed.[35]

In February 1963 Kennedy finally sent a civil rights bill to Congress. It was a weak measure that Martin Luther King Jr. and other civil rights activists considered "tokenism."[36] Republican leaders gleefully attacked the proposal as "thin" and belittled Kennedy's leadership on the issue.[36] Even the administration conceded the bill would have to be supplemented down the line.

Events forced the administration to take a bolder stand. In April and May King's Southern Christian Leadership Conference launched a campaign to desegregate Birmingham's downtown stores, federal buildings, and a suburban shopping mall. The city's segregationists, lead by the brutal public safety commissioner Eugene ("Bull") Conner, countered the marches and demonstrations with attack dogs and high-pressure fire hoses. The rage and violence—women recoiling from snarling dogs, adults and children knocked over by water jets—was brought vividly into American living rooms by network TV. The public, whether moved by common decency or frightened by violence, began to ask for a White

House response. Supported by his brother but opposed by most of the White House staff, Kennedy finally gave the order to draft a strong new civil rights bill.

Aside from the EEOC, Johnson had not been consulted on the administration's civil rights policy and was not shown the administration's new legislation during the early drafting. But he sought to make himself a player in the formation of the new initiative. On Memorial Day, speaking at Gettysburg, the vice president made an impassioned speech for immediate action to end discrimination. A hundred years before, he noted, the slaves were freed. But a century later "the Negro remains in bondage to the color of his skin." No longer could the nation ask its black citizens for "patience."

> The Negro says, "Now." Others say, "Never." The voice of responsible Americans—the voice of those who died here and the great man who spoke here—their voices say, "Together." There is no other way.
>
> Until justice is blind to color, until education is unaware of race, until opportunity is unconcerned with the color of men's skins, emancipation will be a proclamation but not a fact. . . .[38]

Johnson had his one and only chance to influence the pending civil rights bill when, in early June, the White House authorized JFK's close friend and aide Theodore Sorensen to solicit the vice president's views. Johnson told Sorensen what he thought—at length; the transcript of the phone call runs to twenty-seven pages.

The president, he said, must assume moral leadership of the civil rights issue. He must "make a moral commitment" to America's black citizens. He should go South and, while standing in Dixie, tell its citizens that the nation must adhere to the Golden Rule of do unto others. Kennedy was going to "have to ask the Congress to say that we'll all be treated without regard to race." Such a gesture would impress the South with his "courage," and even if white Southerners did not like what he said, they would respect him for it. Johnson could not resist complaining about being excluded from discussion with crucial senators and warned that as matters stood the administration would "be cut to pieces with this." The president would be "a sacrificial lamb."[39]

The exchange with Sorensen notwithstanding, Johnson had little direct input into the administration's major civil rights bill, and it predictably stalled in Congress.

But the question of the vice president's legislative role went beyond civil rights. Johnson believed, with good reason, that he had no real access to the seat of power in the Oval Office and that there was no sense fooling himself or others that he did. Everybody in Washington knew what was going on, and some senators were frustrated by the lack of leadership in Congress. "Here they've got the best legislative strategist," complained Senator Dennis Chavez of New Mexico, "a man who really knows how things are done on the Hill, how to push bills through the toughest committees . . . and they send him off on some stupid mission to Timbuctoo. . . . They must think Lyndon will steal their show."[40] Arthur Schlesinger Jr., a JFK partisan, explains the administration's policy:

> If Kennedy had allowed Johnson to conduct his congressional relations, he would in effect have made the vice president the judge of what was legislatively feasible and thereby have lost control over his own program. This was something no sensible president would do. Kennedy therefore relied on his own congressional liaison staff . . . calling on the vice president only on particular occasions.[41]

Perversely, while keeping the vice president at arm's length, the White House also resented his seeming indifference to the administration's legislative success. Presidential aide Ralph Dungan later recalled that Kennedy "thought that Lyndon ought to be up there [on Capitol Hill] beating their heads in."[42] Sorensen, too, later expressed disappointment with LBJ's apparent unwillingness to use his vaunted legislative clout to advance the New Frontier. In truth, Johnson could have helped more to get Kennedy's programs passed. But his wounded pride deterred him as much as anything else. In any case, he clearly felt some *schadenfreude* at the ineptness of the White House congressional liaison.

Johnson later remembered foreign travel as part of his vice-presidential ordeal, but it was in fact the one escape from the humiliations of the office. Kennedy had promised Sam Rayburn "to use Johnson's finesse at handling people on an international level."[43] Nixon, not especially talented in interpersonal relations, had performed a similar role for President Eisenhower.

Johnson went abroad eleven separate times, visiting 33 different countries and covering 120,000 miles in fewer than three years as vice president. Though he had not traveled extensively before, he was an enthusiastic goodwill ambassador for the United States. He represented his country when the new president of the Dominican Republic was inaugurated, went to Senegal for its Independence Day festivities, had an audience with Pope John XXIII, and then attended his funeral the following year.

Everywhere he went, Johnson handed out cigarette lighters and LBJ-engraved ballpoint pens. He serenaded a seventy-year-old woman selling vegetables in Finland when he learned it was her birthday. He often brought Lady Bird and Lynda with him and asked them to speak to the crowds. The Johnson women, well coached in a few choice phrases in the native language, would charm the audience. "He'd tell everyone he met, practically everyone he shook hands with," an observer told Merle Miller, "'Now you-all come to see me in Washington.'" John Kenneth Galbraith, then the ambassador to India, told a translator he hired to interpret for Johnson, "If Lyndon forgets and asks for votes, leave that out."[44]

Johnson often behaved like a caricature of the spoiled, provincial American abroad. He transported his seven-foot-long bed and his special pillows all over the world, insisting that a six-foot, three-inch man could not sleep in a shorter bed. He also took a shower attachment that sprayed out water in the hard, fine way he preferred, and brought along cases of his favorite scotch whiskey, Cutty Sark. He changed his plans precipitously, inconveniencing not only his own staff but also the personnel of the American embassies where he stayed. The reporters who accompanied him were not the familiar ones from Washington, and they were not inclined to be kind to him. They often related anecdotes, some merely funny, but others critical, building up a Johnson file that was usually uncomplimentary.

Johnson got along well with Third World people, though not necessarily their leaders. The peasants of India, Pakistan, Iran, and Vietnam liked his exuberance and Texas extravagance. He was less popular in places such as Scandinavia, where the citizens were prosperous, middle-class burghers. In his tour through Norway, Sweden, Denmark, and Finland in September 1963, he offended officials, the press, and the public generally by walking over some sacred graves, interrupting service at a state banquet, and snubbing local officials. George Reedy, who accompanied the vice president on his perambulations, later noted that "he was a boor throughout the Scandinavian trip."[45]

The State Department constantly worried that Johnson's gaffes would bring ridicule on the American government. For his part Lyndon complained that the State Department did not give him credit for knowing how to treat people. He considered his critics priggish and out of date. "We cannot demonstrate the essence and spirit of the American political system," he declared, "unless we get out of our limousines abroad as we would at home. After all, what dignity are we trying to prove—that of the office of vice president or that of the human race?"[46] Whatever his underlings felt, Secretary of State Dean Rusk had abundant confidence in the vice president. "There is no person in America," he said, "that can equal Johnson in knee-to-knee conversation with another man."[47]

One of his most important trips came in his first year as vice president, when he went to Southeast Asia on a fact-finding and morale-building mission. There had been a recent Communist insurrection in Laos and troubles in South Vietnam that threatened the downfall of pro-American president Ngo Dinh Diem. Kennedy wanted an evaluation of the Southeast Asia Treaty Organization and hoped to show our western Pacific allies that we were still interested in the region and would not desert them. Johnson went to Thailand, India, Pakistan, Taiwan, Hong Kong, the Philippines, and Vietnam. He met with the aged Generalissimo Chiang Kai-shek; with Prime Minister Jawaharlal Nehru of India; with the military dictator of Pakistan, Ayub Khan; and with Diem. Twenty-five reporters came along on a separate plane.

Johnson behaved with his usual ebullience, inviting Bashir Ahmad, an illiterate Pakistani camel driver who lived in a little mud hut, to visit the United States. It became a *cause célèbre* when the man took him up on his invitation, and the vice president, rather than look like a phony and disgrace the administration, had Bashir and his daughter come to the United States and visit his ranch. In this case Johnson was able to convert a potentially embarrassing situation into a public relations coup. "Still," said an observer with a sigh, "we thought it was just as well that of all those thousands of people, maybe tens of thousands that Mr. Johnson invited . . . only one ever showed up."[48]

But Johnson had been sent to Southeast Asia for a serious purpose, not just publicity. Diem was not an effective leader from the American point of view. He was corrupt, inefficient, and favored his own Catholic religious minority. He was despised by the peasants of South Vietnam. Could his regime be made more efficient and more popular? Could his backbone be stiffened in the fight against the Communists? LBJ was to promise American economic and additional military aid and report back to his chief.

Johnson, though initially reluctant to go, carried out the mission with bravura. He spent almost three hours with Diem and conveyed to him the president's views on improving the lot of the peasants and making his administration more efficient. He praised Diem as "the Winston Churchill of Asia."[49] After returning, he composed a long report for Kennedy, analyzing the economic and political conditions in the countries he visited. The report accurately foreshadowed future events in Southeast Asia. It also revealed the contrasting sides of his foreign policy ideology. On the one hand, he said, "the greatest danger . . . is not the momentary threat of communism itself." Rather, it stemmed "from hunger, ignorance, poverty, and disease."[50] On the other hand, he concluded, "the battle against communism must be joined in Southeast Asia with strength and determination to achieve success there—or the United States, inevitably, must surrender the Pacific and take up our defenses on our own shores."[51]

However confusing the message, it was clear that Johnson was not enamored of direct American intervention in the region. "Asian leaders, at this time," he noted, "do not want American troops involved in Southeast Asia other than on training missions. American combat troop involvement is not only not required, it is not desirable . . . because recently colonial peoples would not look with favor upon governments which invited or accepted the return this soon of Western troops."[52] He concluded with chilling clairvoyance:

> The fundamental decision required of the United States . . . is whether we are to attempt to meet the challenge of Communist expansion now in Southeast Asia by a major effort in support of the forces of freedom or throw in the towel. This decision must be made in a full realization of the very heavy and continuing costs involved in terms of money, of effort, and of United States prestige. It must be made with the knowledge that at some point we may be faced with the further decision of whether we commit major United States forces to the area or cut our losses and withdraw should our other efforts fail. We must remain master of this decision. . . . I recommend we proceed with a clear-cut and strong program of action.[53]

Tragically for himself and the country, Johnson himself would not remain master of it.

On August 13, 1961, the East German government, to check the hordes escaping from communism into the Western sectors of Berlin, tore down the barbed-wire fences that stood between East and West Berlin and replaced them with the notorious Berlin Wall. Unable to leave the country at the moment, Kennedy asked the vice president to go to Germany in his place to reassure our allies that we would not desert them. Johnson at first hesitated. Kennedy had ordered fifteen hundred additional American troops to West Berlin to reinforce the Western garrison. They would be sent by the autobahn, and no one could tell if the Soviets would try to stop them during this new crisis. War might break out at any time, and Johnson probably feared for his own safety. In addition, he was not convinced that Kennedy had anything substantial to offer our NATO allies and was putting him in a position in which he would look foolish. The president sent his brother Bobby to Johnson on yet another unpleasant mission: to order the vice president to Berlin, like it or not.

The trip turned out to be a triumph both for the United States and for Johnson. A large crowd met him at the Bonn airport when he landed, and wherever he went, thousands of Germans greeted him enthusiastically. As usual, he got out of his car to shake hands and kiss babies. When he arrived in Berlin he delivered a dramatic speech, choosing his words from the conclusion of the *Declaration of Independence*. He told the Germans:

> I have come to Berlin by the direction of President Kennedy. He wants you to know—and I want you to know—that the pledge he has given to the freedom of West Berlin and to the right of Western access to Berlin is firm. To the survival and to the creative future of this city we Americans have pledged . . . what our ancestors pledged in forming the United States: "Our lives, our fortunes, and our sacred honor."[54]

Johnson had not promised anything concrete, but his words stirred his listeners and helped restore morale.

For the next two years Johnson continued to travel widely, representing the United States at various official functions abroad. He frequently presided over the Senate as well, apparently, wrote Harry McPherson, "in the hope of breaking the record for attendance to that menial chore of the vice presidency."[55] He gave speeches throughout the nation on various occasions. But his heart was no longer in congressional politics, a situation made even worse by the death of Sam Rayburn in late November 1961. Everybody could see that he was unhappy and restless. He spent more time than ever in Austin looking after his television station and adding acreage to his ranch in the Hill Country. He also purchased a large home in Northwest Washington on top of a hill in the posh Spring Valley area of the District. *Les Ormes* was a French Provincial-style mansion, surrounded by pines and magnolia trees and furnished with French antique reproductions. Its former owner was his good friend famous party-giver and former ambassador to Luxembourg Perle Mesta. To make it more suitable for an elected American official, he Anglicized its name to The Elms.

The Johnsons spent three hundred thousand dollars remodeling the mansion, putting in a heated swimming pool, and piping Muzak into all the rooms. The new house did not help the vice president's state of mind. By 1963 he had become an invisible man. Comedians joked about his apparent disappearance from view and the *Texas Observer*, Ronnie Dugger's gadfly weekly, carried an article that asked cruelly: "What is an LBJ?" Harry McPherson remembered that during this period "He . . . drank a lot. He took up golf some . . . but not with enthusiasm."[56] Visiting The Elms one day with Abe Fortas for a swim in the pool, McPherson thought Johnson looked grossly overweight and sick.

His life as vice president, he concluded, was just an enormous frustration to him.

One penalty of his marginal role in the administration was anxiety over his future. Kennedy, he feared, would drop him from the ticket in 1964, killing his chance for a presidential run in 1968. "I'm going to be out of it for a second term," Lyndon moaned to a friend in the fall of 1963. "Jack has another man in mind for vice president."[57] Some of these fears were imaginary, a product of Johnson's bottomless need for approval, a need seriously unfulfilled in the Kennedy administration. Some of them fed on the endless rumors that floated around Washington, retailed by both the cognoscenti and the media. One of these involved an alleged meeting in Georgetown of Kennedy intimates who wanted Johnson off the ticket. Kennedy's personal secretary Evelyn Lincoln later claimed that the president had told her at the time that he was thinking of asking Terry Sanford, then governor of North Carolina, to be his running mate in 1964. "But it will not be Lyndon," he supposedly declared.[58] We cannot be sure of any of these stories, but it is clear that Johnson had some reason for his insecurities.

An additional worry surfaced in the fall of 1963 when Johnson was implicated in the shady business dealings of Bobby Baker, who had stayed on under Mansfield as secretary to the Senate Democrats. Baker was undoubtedly "very smart, very quick, indefatigable," and one of Senate leader Johnson's most valuable lieutenants.[59] But he was also greedy and ambitious, and he used his political connections to piece together lucrative business deals, including investments in an insurance company, a vending machine firm, and in a luxury motel-*cum*-nightclub in Ocean City, Maryland. Back in the fifties Baker had involved Johnson in an arrangement to buy life insurance from one Don B. Reynolds, who in turn bought advertising time on LBJ's Austin TV station and sent the senator an expensive Magnavox television set as a gift. Johnson had a mania for bargains. His later telephone conversations from the White House with hairdressers and haberdashers about cut-rate prices for services and garments for his family and staff are hilarious. Given this preoccupation and his passion for advancing the fortunes of KTBC, Johnson was probably guilty of this petty payola. Besides the dubious transactions that directly involved LBJ, Baker was accused, while working for Senator Johnson, of accepting payoffs for legislative favors to various business firms and using his influence to line his own pockets.

Baker's bubble burst in September 1963 when the *Washington Post* revealed that he had wangled a contract to install food vending machines in aerospace contractors' plants by trading on his connection with Johnson, a power in the American space program. Baker hired Abe Fortas to defend him, and on his advice refused to speak to his boss, Mike Mansfield, and other senators about his activities. In early October he resigned his Senate post. Shortly before Johnson and Kennedy made their ill-fated trip to Texas, Republican senator John Williams of Delaware, a man proud of his role in exposing influence peddling in the Truman administration, induced Reynolds to appear before a closed executive session of the Senate Rules Committee, where he testified about the gifts to the Johnsons in exchange for the life insurance purchase and reported Baker's claims that LBJ had accepted large bribes from General Dynamics for expediting a lucrative plane contract. Could this damaging testimony be kept from leaking? It seemed unlikely.

Johnson had remained Baker's friend even after he left the Senate. In early 1962 the vice president wrote his former right-hand man: "I do not know what I would do without Bobby Baker and I do not want to find out."[60] Though he had severed business connections with Baker, he worried that the investigation was part of a grand scheme by Robert Kennedy to nail him and have him dropped from the ticket in 1964. In fact, the Baker scandal may have helped LBJ. At one point, according to Kennedy's right-hand man Ken O'Donnell, the president told Florida senator George Smathers: "If I drop Lyndon, it will make it look as if we have a really bad and serious scandal on our hands in the Bobby Baker case, which we haven't, and that will reflect on me. It will look as though I made a mistake picking Lyndon in 1960. . . . Lyndon stays on the ticket next year."[61] At a press conference in the fall of 1963, when asked about Johnson's presence on the ticket in the next election, Kennedy answered affirmatively.

This was the way Kennedy felt in November 1963 when he and Johnson made arrangements for a trip to Texas together. Kennedy's standing in the polls had dropped to a 38 percent approval rating in Texas, an important state in his reelection strategy. He wanted to make sure Texas would remain in the Democratic column in '64. In addition, the two factions of the Texas Democratic Party—the conservatives, led by John Connally, LBJ's former aide, now governor; and the liberals, headed by Senator Ralph Yarborough—were bitterly feuding. The vice president was in the middle of the mess. The conservative forces seemed to be in the ascendancy and the extreme right wing, increasingly unhappy with Kennedy's civil rights and social programs, was becoming a major malign force in the state. The trip would be a joint effort to conciliate the two factions. The president would confirm his support for both Connally and Yarborough and express his confidence in Johnson. At the same time,

Johnson would solicit funds for the upcoming election and round up support for the president's programs.

There were premonitions that the visit would be a mistake. A month before, UN ambassador Adlai Stevenson had gone to Dallas for a meeting on United Nations Day. Right-wing extremists had distributed handbills with photographs of Kennedy and this message: "WANTED FOR TREASON. THIS MAN IS WANTED FOR TREASONOUS ACTIVITIES AGAINST THE UNITED STATES."[62] The militants heckled and booed Stevenson when he spoke and jostled and bumped him when he attempted to leave the hall. A lady picketer hit him over the head with a sign, and a man spat in his face.

Stevenson warned the president not to go to Texas. Louisiana congressman Hale Boggs agreed with the ambassador. "What I said to President Kennedy," Boggs told Merle Miller, "was that politics in Texas are so disturbed . . . that he was apt to get into trouble. I didn't mean that somebody was going to try to shoot him. I meant politically. And I remember he sort of laughed about that and said, 'Well, that makes it more interesting.'"[63] Johnson himself did not want to go to Texas, at least not at this time. He believed that the administration's popularity was simply "too low." It was Kennedy, Johnson later claimed, who insisted that the trip be made.[64]

The presidential party arrived in San Antonio on Thursday, November 21, to be greeted unexpectedly by friendly crowds. The reception was equally warm in Houston. Unfortunately, Connally and Yarborough continued to feud, and the senator refused to ride in the same car as Johnson. Johnson and Kennedy argued about the situation in the president's hotel room in Houston, and LBJ apparently had not calmed down when he left the room. The next morning, in Fort Worth, Kennedy asked Ken O'Donnell to inform Yarborough that if he didn't want to ride with Johnson, he could walk.[65] But at breakfast, whatever cross words had been spoken the night before, the president and Johnson seemed to have smoothed things over. "You can be sure of one thing," Kennedy told Johnson, "we're going to carry two states next year: Massachusetts and Texas." Smiling, Johnson replied: "Oh, we are going to do better than that, Mr. President."[66]

Despite a nasty, black-bordered advertisement in the *Dallas Morning News* accusing him of being soft on Communists, Kennedy was in high spirits when *Air Force One* landed in the brilliant sunshine at Love Field in Dallas. The president knew he was heading into what he called "nut country," but was philosophical, remarking that "if somebody wants to shoot me from a window with a rifle, nobody can stop it, so why worry about it?"[67]

On the way from the airport, the Connallys and the Kennedys were in the front limousine, behind the Secret Service cars, with the Johnsons and Yarborough silently and uncomfortably riding in the car behind. Although the crowds at the airport had not been especially enthusiastic, by the time the procession reached downtown Dallas, everybody was cheering, waving, and shouting. Nellie Connally turned to the Kennedys, delightedly exclaiming, "Well, Mr. President, you can't say that Dallas doesn't love you!" "No, you certainly can't," Kennedy responded, smiling.[68]

At about twelve-thirty Central Standard Time the car carrying the Kennedys and the Connallys made a left turn onto Elm Street in the shadow of the Texas School Book Depository. Three shots rang out. The president fell to the left, with a quizzical look on his face. Jacqueline Kennedy, her beautiful rose-pink suit splattered with blood, screamed, "Oh, no, no. . . . Oh, my God, they have shot my husband."[69] In a pause between the first and the second shot, Rufus Youngblood, the Secret Service agent in the limousine with Johnson, turned around quickly and pushed the vice president to the floor, sitting on his right shoulder to keep him down. Nobody knew what was going on, but the car radio indicated that the president had been hit by the shots, and the whole entourage was headed for Parkland Hospital.

When Johnson finally could leave the car at Parkland, he flexed his arms and ran his hands over his chest to ease the cramps from cowering on the car floor with a two-hundred-pound Secret Service agent perched on top of him. Rumors immediately surfaced that he, too, had been shot or had suffered another heart attack.

Just before 1:00 P.M., a priest went into the room where Kennedy was lying on a portable bed. A few minutes later, doctors announced that John Fitzgerald Kennedy was dead. At one-twenty Ken O'Donnell told Johnson, "He's gone." Assistant Press Secretary Malcolm Kilduff then addressed LBJ as "Mr. President," asking him whether he should make a formal announcement about Kennedy's death.[70]

The events of the next few hours would later create a media storm. Johnson's decisions would be attacked as insensitive to the Kennedys, especially the beautiful young widow. Yet they were understandable. Not knowing whether a conspiracy to murder the nation's leaders was afoot, Johnson decided to return immediately to Washington by *Air Force One*, the presidential plane, with Lady Bird and some of his own staff, along with the new widow, the casket carrying JFK's body, and the former president's aides. Seeking to confirm his legitimacy, he called the stricken brother, the attorney general, in Virginia, to ask whether he would object to an immediate swearing-in as president. To Bobby the concern seemed trivial and inappropriate considering the tragedy. Over the protest of Kennedy aide O'Donnell, Johnson then asked Jackie, still wearing her blood-stained pink suit, to be at his side aboard the plane while Judge Sarah Hughes administered the presidential oath of office. The judge's voice quivered and her hands shook as she administered the oath, the text of which had to be determined by a hurried call to Washington.

The flight back, as described in William Manchester's *Death of a President*, was undoubtedly a torture for the Kennedy loyalists. How could they not despair at the death of their shining hero and the wretched end to their own career hopes and not consider the very sight of his successor an offense? But we have the word of Jack Valenti that there was no actual "friction" between the two camps. "If there was, I was not aware of it," he later declared.[71] The two hours plus were difficult for Lyndon Johnson, too. Fate had suddenly made him the world's most powerful man, with no chance to adjust, to plan, to consider. Other presidents had succeeded through their predecessor's death, but none, since Theodore Roosevelt sixty-two years before, after his assassination. But one thing could not be gainsaid: plagued with doubts until the end that he would even retain second place for four more years, Lyndon Baines Johnson was now president of the United States.

Lyndon Baines Johnson was never as adorable again. LBJ at eighteen months.

Rebekah Johnson, Lyndon's refined, intellectual mother, about 1917.

Lyndon's first class at Welhausen Grade School in Cotulla about 1929.

Lyndon and Lady Bird on their honeymoon in Mexico City in 1934.

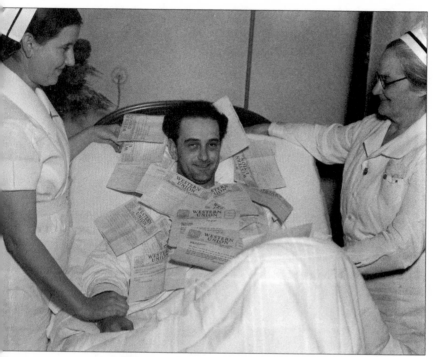

The young congressman-elect plastered with congratulations and telegrams, still looking wan from his appendectomy—but happy.

FDR greets newly elected congressman Johnson in Galveston in 1937. Governor Jimmy Allred is in the middle.

Lieutenant-Commander Lyndon Johnson being greeted by General Martin Scanlon in 1942 in the Pacific theater.

Congressman Johnson and Lady Bird with their two daughters in 1948.

Senator Johnson shows his affection for Sam Rayburn, one of his "daddies," on the speaker's seventy-sixth birthday in 1952.

Majority Leader Johnson speaking to a CIO group in his office. George Reedy and Lady Bird are present.

The famous photo showing the swearing-in aboard *Air Force One*, just hours after JFK's assassination. Jackie's clothing is still bloodstained.

LBJ staged the 1965 signing ceremony for the landmark Medicare bill at the home of Harry Truman, whose own health insurance bill had failed in Congress many years before. Behind LBJ and Truman are Vice President Humphrey, Bess Truman, and Lady Bird, her face hidden by the president.

The "treatment" took many forms. This was a mild version but, after all, the victim was the powerful senator from Georgia, Richard Russell.

Though from a former Confederate state, LBJ showed rare rapport with black Americans and did more for civil rights than any other president.

The Ranch—where LBJ relaxed (in his fashion) and renewed himself. This picture dates from the presidential years.

A thoughtful LBJ in April 1967 receiving a report on Vietnam from equally pensive General Westmoreland.

Despite his "eye for the ladies," LBJ loved his wife. Here, he and Lady Bird share a humorous moment.

In 1969 LBJ retired to the Ranch, let his hair grow long, gained weight, and came to look like a grizzled cowboy.

The Johnsons and the Nixons at the May 1971 dedication of the LBJ Library in Austin.

CHAPTER 16

"Let Us Continue"

A IR FORCE ONE TOUCHED DOWN at Andrews Air Force Base at 5:05 that evening. Before anyone could deplane, Bobby Kennedy climbed aboard and rushed back to where Jackie and the Kennedy aides were gathered close to the casket, ignoring Johnson as he brushed past. LBJ and his party were forced to wait until the casket was removed and Jackie and the Kennedy staff had left before reaching the tarmac. The new president somberly shook hands with the waiting crowd of friends and dignitaries and then, in the glare of floodlights, read a brief statement prepared by Jack Valenti and Bill Moyers:

This is a sad time for all people. We have suffered a loss that cannot be weighed. For me it is a deep personal tragedy. I know that the world shares the sorrow that Mrs. Kennedy and her family bear. I will do my best. This is all I can do. I ask for your help—and God's.[1]

Immediately after, Johnson, Lady Bird, and three of Kennedy's closest foreign affairs advisers—McNamara, McGeorge Bundy, and George Ball—left by helicopter for the White House grounds. During the short ride the president said that it was essential that they stay with him and give him "moral support."[2] At the vice president's office in the Executive Office Building, he met briefly with congressional leaders, wrote two touching letters to the Kennedy children, John-John and Caroline, and phoned key Americans to reassure them and ask for help. One phone call that anguished evening went to Richard Maguire, Democratic National Committee treasurer. Already looking ahead to November 1964,

Johnson asked Maguire to come see him to discuss "what we need to do and how we need to do it."[3]

Back at the Elms finally, Johnson found he could not sleep and joined aides Valenti, Moyers, and Horace Busby to watch TV. A painting of Sam Rayburn hung over the set and, raising a glass of orange juice to the portrait, Johnson said simply: "I wish you were here."[4] At midnight he went up to his bedroom, changed into his pajamas, and resumed watching TV with his aides. From time to time he leaned over to mention whom he wanted to see the following day. He finally went to bed at 3:00 A.M.

Johnson's first full day on the job was Saturday, November 23. It was a rainy day in Washington, and the dark clouds added to the sorrow that suffused the capital. The new president met with former presidents Truman and Eisenhower. Johnson spoke with legislative leaders of both parties, consulted with foreign policy officials, and held a twenty-five-minute cabinet meeting. After visiting with Jacqueline Kennedy, he walked with Lady Bird to view JFK's coffin lying in state in the Capitol Rotunda, and together they went to a prayer service.

The next day the Johnsons attended a special memorial service at St. Mark's Episcopal Church on Capitol Hill. Harry McPherson, a member of the St. Mark's congregation, observed the president wiping his eyes with his handkerchief as he listened to the minister's eulogy. Afterward the Johnsons went back to the parish house for coffee and, to the dismay of the Secret Service, shook hands with parishioners. "A lot of people were crying and holding his arm. It was immensely strengthening" to them, McPherson noted.[5]

On Monday the Johnsons, including Luci and Lynda, walked behind the Kennedy family in the funeral procession that wound through the streets of Washington. The FBI and the Secret Service were uncomfortable with the First Family's decision to join the cortege, since no one yet knew what had prompted Lee Harvey Oswald, by now the presumed assassin, to kill the president, and a wider conspiracy seemed possible. Jacqueline Kennedy later sent Johnson a long and effusive handwritten note thanking him for taking the risk and also for the simple and touching letters of condolence he had written Caroline and John. He had been "Jack's right arm," she said, and she appreciated his willingness to be vice president "to a man who had served under you and had been taught by you." "But more than that," she added, "we were friends, all four of us."[6] Whatever Jackie Kennedy's feelings in the future, at this painful moment she was clearly grateful to Johnson for his thoughtful actions after her husband's death, describing them as "extraordinary" and "magnanimous."[7]

From the outset Johnson labored under the shadow of the martyred president. For the rest of his political days he would be compared with the radiant young hero cut down in the prime of his career. And he was president by accident, by death, by murder! This horrified him as much as if not more than it did the rest of the nation. "I took the oath," he told Doris Kearns, "I became President."

> But for millions of Americans I was still illegitimate, a naked man with no presidential covering, a pretender to the throne, an illegal usurper. And then there was Texas, my home, the home of both the murder and the murder of the murderer. And then there were the bigots and the dividers and the Eastern intellectuals, who were waiting to knock me down before I could even begin to stand up. The whole thing was almost unbearable.[8]

For five years the Johnsons would also battle against the myth of "Camelot"—a time, it was said, when beauty, grace, wit, and charm had reigned in the White House—and they would be found wanting. For Lady Bird, relief from the struggle finally came in October 1968. As the LBJ administration was about to end, the First Lady noted in her diary that her predecessor's imminent marriage to the Greek shipping tycoon Aristotle Onassis, a coarse Caliban, had made her "strangely freer." "No shadow" now walked beside her "down the halls of the White House or here at Camp David."[9]

Despite the difficulties, Johnson carried off the transition with great flair. No one except his most carping critics could fault him for the considerate way he behaved toward the Kennedys in his early days in office. He treated the entire family with kid gloves, being especially careful of Bobby Kennedy's feelings, postponing his own move into the White House until December 7 out of respect for Jacqueline, and permitting the Kennedy children to attend the White House kindergarten until Christmas vacation. The relations with Jackie in these early days had more than a little guile in it. Johnson apparently feared that Jackie, the nation's reigning heroine, might support her brother-in-law for president the next year and stampede the delegates at the Democratic convention into a RFK nomination.

But his respect for his predecessor showed on a deeper level in his policy of "continuity." As he later wrote in his memoirs:

> Rightly or wrongly, I felt from the very first day in office that I had to carry on for President Kennedy. I considered myself the caretaker of both his people and his policies. . . . I did what I believed he would have wanted me to do. I never wavered from that sense of responsibility, even after I was elected in my own right, up to my last day in office. . . . I eventually developed my own programs and policies, but I never lost sight of the fact that I was the trustee and custodian of the Kennedy administration. . . .[10]

But continuity was more than a matter of personal loyalty; it was also a shrewd transition strategy. The nation needed reassurance that a new president did not mean a drastic shift of direction. On the day of the funeral Johnson told a group of state governors in Washington to attend the obsequies that "continuity without confusion has got to be our password and has to be the key to our system. . . . I am going to tell Congress that we intend to honor the commitments we have made at home, and abroad."[11] The next day, the stock market gained a record $15 billion, and the experts attributed the rally to "confidence in President Johnson."[12]

Continuity dictated the decision to keep Kennedy's advisers, from congressional liaison aides to the secretary of state. But their retention also reflected the new president's respect for his predecessor's judgment and his contacts with the nation's talent pool. Johnson here was revealing his sense that John Kennedy's cosmopolitanism gave him an edge over himself. Some of the legacies clearly did not work out. Several intense Kennedy partisans—Ken O'Donnell, Ted Sorensen, and Arthur Schlesinger Jr., for example—found working for LBJ distasteful and quickly left. But other Kennedy advisers, such as the director of White House congressional liaison, Lawrence O'Brien, Secretary of State Dean Rusk, Pentagon head Robert McNamara, and national security adviser McGeorge Bundy, stayed on to the end, or close to it, and became some of Johnson's most trusted counselors. As we shall see, the case of Attorney General Robert Kennedy, the ex-president's right hand, forms one of the great human dramas of Johnson's presidency, but he, too, would continue in office for almost a year. The quest for continuity would work in the short run. It would help reassure the public in an uncertain time and would ease the legislative path of the new president. But it would also saddle Lyndon Johnson with his predecessor's risky policy in Southeast Asia, which would damage his administration irrevocably.

One of the new president's goals was to win over the liberals who had long scorned him. Now that he was president, boss of the whole nation, he could finally come to terms with his own liberal doppelgänger. The day after the assassination, Joe Rauh was in Walter Reuther's suite at the Statler Hotel in Washington when the White House operator called to ask the UAW president for the phone numbers of David Dubinsky, I. W. Abel, David McDonald, and other prominent labor leaders. It was clear to Rauh that LBJ was determined to mend fences with the Democratic left. Soon after, LBJ asked Rauh himself to come to the White House for a visit. In the Oval Office, the president told Rauh "over and over again: If I've done anything wrong in the past, I want you to know that's nothing now—we're going to work together."[13]

Johnson moved into the White House the day after the funeral, bringing his own rocking chair to replace Kennedy's, and a larger, simpler desk than his predecessor's. On top of the desk he placed a silver scroll with a quill pen and pictures of Luci and Lynda. That day he met with Kennedy aides to discuss pending plans and ongoing business.

One of his visitors was Walter Heller, head of the Council of Economic Advisers, who told the president of Kennedy's plan for a major initiative in the new congressional session to combat the persistent poverty recently revealed in Michael Harrington's best-selling new book *The Other America*. Kennedy had read the book or, more likely, Dwight Macdonald's review of it in the *New Yorker*, and like other literate Americans, had been dismayed to learn that poverty survived in affluent America. In late 1962 Kennedy had asked Heller for facts and figures on poverty across the nation and in October 1963 gave him "the green light to pull together a set of proposals for a 1964 attack on poverty."[14] When Heller finished his account to the new president, Johnson exclaimed: "I'm sympathetic. Go ahead. Give it the highest priority. Push ahead full tilt."[15]

Johnson delivered his first major address as president the evening of November 27, less than a week after the tragic events in Dallas. Its importance clearly could not be exaggerated. Millions of Americans would be watching it on TV and get their first impression of him as president. It would influence the way his administration was regarded. The setting would have to show him off to best advantage. After much dickering, everyone finally agreed that Johnson would do best in the familiar environment of Congress.

Many in the auditorium were moved to tears as he spoke. His soft but solemn voice gave his delivery a dramatic power and underscored the mood of the nation. "All I have," he began, "I would have given gladly not to be standing here today." Paraphrasing the words "let us begin" in Kennedy's inaugural speech of 1961, Johnson intoned "let us continue," and used the word "continue" five times. As a memorial to the dead president, he asked Congress to act quickly to pass Kennedy's legislative program, his own program now as well: medical care for the elderly, federal aid to education, an all-out attack on mental illness, the conquest of space, and, "above all, the dream of equal rights for all Americans whatever their race or color." He wanted to "carry on the fight against poverty, and misery and disease and ignorance in other lands and in our own." His words on civil rights were loudly applauded by most of the legislators and dignitaries, but the Southerners in the audience, including Richard Russell, sat stony-faced, their hands at their sides.

If Johnson sought continuity with Kennedy's domestic policies, his attitudes toward other nations seemed less bellicose than his predecessor's. "In this age," Johnson said, "when there can be no losers in peace and no victors in war, we must recognize the obligation to match national strength with national restraint. We must be prepared at one and the same time for both the confrontation of power and the limitation of power. We must be ready to defend the national interest and to negotiate the common interest."

Johnson concluded with an affecting appeal for unity. He instructed the nation to resolve:

> that John Fitzgerald Kennedy did not live—or die—in vain. On this Thanksgiving Eve, as we gather to ask the Lord's blessing, and give him our thanks, let us unite in those familiar and cherished words:
> America, America,
> God shed his grace on thee,
> And crown they good with brotherhood
> From sea to shining sea.[16]

At the end, Congress greeted the speech with a thunderous standing ovation. All the Southerners now joined in as well. The media also applauded. The *Washington Post* said that the speech could not have been improved "by the alteration of one single sentence or a single sentiment." The *Cleveland Plain Dealer* noted that Johnson's words had inspired "the confidence of the world. . . ."[17] Thanks to speechwriter Sorensen and his own sense of the occasion, Johnson had sounded like a statesman and a leader, and, most important, like a president.

The address should have dispelled any doubts liberals might have felt about Johnson's commitment to civil rights and programs of social amelioration. In fact, they would get more than they would have under his predecessor. If Kennedy had had the vision, he lacked the skill. Johnson insisted that he had the same vision as his predecessor. "If you looked at my record . . . ," he told Walter Heller, "you would know I am a Roosevelt New Dealer. As a matter of fact . . . John F. Kennedy was a little too conservative to suit my taste."[18] And, Johnson felt, he also had the talent, well proven in his years as majority leader, to persuade Congress to act. "I loved Jack Kennedy, just like you," he told Richard Goodwin, a White House speechwriter, "but he never really understood the Congress. I do. And I'm going to pass all those bills you cared about. It's a once-in-a-lifetime opportunity, for you, for me, for the country."[19] Those of his friends who had insisted all along that he was a liberal, only more pragmatic than some, were delighted. His detractors, somewhat more skeptical, adopted a wait-and-see attitude.

And Johnson *would* be more liberal. His constituency was now two hundred million Americans, few of whom shared his fellow Texans' history and values. New York, Boston, San Francisco, Chicago, and Detroit were now more relevant than Dallas, Houston, and Lubbock. Organized labor, the Ivy League professoriat, the liberal foundations, the metropolitan press, and blacks counted for far more than in the past. And then there was the special vista of the American presidency. This was the pinnacle; one could not go higher. The only thing left to achieve was the applause of posterity. Now, finally, was the time to round off the triumphs of his liberal forefathers, to complete the program of his greatest predecessor and his own mentor, Franklin Roosevelt.

The day after Thanksgiving, Johnson appointed a commission to investigate the circumstances of the assassination. Rumors were already flying of left-wing and right-wing conspiracies, of the role of the Soviet Union, of the part played by Castro, and whether there had been other participants besides Oswald. With Congress pressing for its own investigation and the Texas authorities determined to get into the act as well, Johnson feared fouling the air with further overheated hearsay, though he was suspicious of the CIA, the Secret Service, the Cubans, and the South Vietnamese. Working shamelessly on a reluctant man's patriotism and his military service in World War I, Johnson induced Chief Justice Earl Warren, a liberal Republican from California, to head the group. The commission would be given all necessary powers, including subpoena powers, and would evaluate all "available information" concerning the assassination.

On the same day, Lady Bird filed an application with the Federal Communications Commission to transfer her controlling interest of 52.8 percent in the LBJ Company, which owned KTBC-AM and KTBC-FM and the KTBC television station, to two trustees. The company's name, moreover, would be changed back to the more impersonal Texas Broadcasting Company, and the stock would be held in a "blind trust" for her two daughters. Lady Bird would also no longer manage the station. The First Lady called this setting "her house in order," since her husband as president appointed members of the FCC, the agency that regulated broadcasting and television stations.

Johnson hoped to enact several measures in the time left before Congress adjourned for its Christmas break. He generally agreed that tax reduction and civil rights would have to wait until the new year. But he wanted to take care of the education and foreign aid bills in December.

He got some of what he wanted. In mid-December Congress passed the Higher Education Facilities Act, providing more than a billion dollars to build college libraries, classrooms, and laboratories for both undergraduate and graduate studies. Johnson had hoped to include a federal student scholarship program in the bill, but Congress balked at this demand. On December 16, calling it a monument to Kennedy, he signed the bill into law, using up almost a record number of pens. Three days later he signed a second education bill, which expanded assistance to vocational schools, continued aid to "impacted" public schools near military reservations or other federal installations, and increased loan funds for college students.

Congress was not as accommodating on foreign aid. Giving money to foreigners has not been wildly popular to Americans, particularly in the heartland, where the nation's connections with the rest of the world seem remote. On December 14 the House Appropriations Committee, chaired by Louisiana representative Otto Passman, a fierce xenophobe, reported out a $2.8 billion foreign aid appropriations bill, reducing the figure Kennedy had requested and Johnson expected by $1.7 billion. LBJ sharply criticized the House committee, charging that it would put American foreign policy "in a straitjacket."[20]

Meanwhile, there was the issue of selling wheat to the Soviet Union, currently in the midst of an agricultural crisis. Kennedy had favored such a sale as much to help the American farmer as to improve U.S.-Soviet relations. The Soviets needed loans to swing the deal, however, and the fiercely anti-Communist senator from South Dakota Karl Mundt induced the Senate to bar any federal agency from making such a loan.

Johnson considered the Mundt amendment a test of his power. Its passage would undermine his ability to pass his programs. Coming up in the new session were crucial bills that had stalled during the Kennedy administration and that were now part of his own 1964 legislative program. "If the legislators had tasted blood then [on the question of Soviet wheat credits]," Johnson later recalled, "they would have run over us like a steamroller when they returned in January."[21] Though Christmas was around the corner, he ordered the Senate-House conference committee to stay in session until they produced an acceptable bill and voted on it. This also meant calling back to Washington congressmen who had already left for the holidays. Members were understandably furious at the interruption in their vacation, but to cushion the blow LBJ ordered a "congressional airlift," a flotilla of military planes and helicopters, to pick up the absentees at their homes and bring them back. To further sweeten the pill, Johnson threw a party at the White House for them. Coffee, bourbon-laced eggnog, fruitcake, and Johnson's high spirits soon drained away resentment. At the end of the festivities, standing on a upholstered cut-velvet chair in the State Dining Room, the president thanked the members for attending and praised them as men and women who "labored through the vineyard and plowed through the snow."[22] The next morning, in an unprecedented dawn session, the House upheld the president's authority to use federal credit guarantees to sell wheat to the Soviets at his discretion. The out-of-town Democrats brought back by Johnson's "airlift" had made the difference.

With the wheat deal out of the way, Congress and the president could go home to celebrate Christmas. On the way to the Ranch, the Johnsons stopped in Austin to visit Governor John Connally, whose right arm was still in a sling from Oswald's bullet in Dallas. On this 1963 holiday stay LBJ was in an ebullient mood and delayed the Christmas turkey dinner to give fifty reporters and cameramen a tour of the house, showing off his collection of paintings and historical mementos, including a framed copy of a letter from Sam Houston to his great-grandfather and a desk supposedly used by Thomas Jefferson. The day after Christmas, Johnson held a press conference barbecue at the ranch attended by reporters, speechwriters, and cabinet officials carrying briefcases in one hand and plates of spareribs, sliced onions, pickles, and pretzels in the other. Standing on a hay bale set up as a speaker's stand, with microphone in hand, he announced that his new budget would propose increases in only two areas: the space program and a massive attack on poverty in the United States.

Walter Heller and Budget Director Kermit Gordon arrived at the Ranch on the twenty-seventh to discuss the antipoverty program that Johnson had signed on to just after Dallas. By this time the Bureau of the Budget and the Council of Economic Advisers together had drawn up a blueprint for a few "demonstration projects" to try out antipoverty approaches based on the Ford Foundation's "gray areas" experiments in community restoration. Johnson didn't like their scheme and sent Gordon and Heller, along with Bill Moyers and Jack Valenti, to the Ranch guesthouse where, at the kitchen table, they drafted an improved poverty bill based on the recent plan. The president considered this proposal too limited as well. He wanted something more ambitious and more politically resonant, he told his aides, something "big and bold" that would "hit the nation with real impact."[23] Why only a handful of demonstration projects? he asked Gordon and Heller. Have a program in every community that wanted one. The next day he told reporters at the Ranch that he intended to introduce a bill to reduce poverty when Congress assembled in January.

LBJ's vacation concluded with a two-day business visit with Chancellor Ludwig Erhard of West Germany. The two leaders agreed on the ultimate goal of a reunified Germany and the continued presence of American troops in the Federal Republic. After the business talks were over, Johnson and Erhard went to the nearby town of Fredericksburg, settled in the 1860s by German immigrants, to hear the choir at St. Mary's Parochial School sing a German version of "Deep in the Heart of Texas" to honor the chancellor:

> *Die Sterne bei Nacht sind gross und klar*
> *(Klatsch, Klatsch, Klatsch, Klatsch)*
> *Tief in das Herz von Texas.*[24]

With the successful visit of the German chancellor and the passage of the foreign aid and Soviet grain bills, Johnson seemed on his way to an effective foreign policy. The year 1963 ended on an up note.

In these early presidential months Johnson impressed everyone with his energy. A reporter, writing shortly after he came to the Oval Office, described him as "utterly cyclonic." Another wrote: "The man is all over the place. He's on the phone night and day. Visitors go in and out of his new office as if he were still on Capitol Hill. . . ."[25] This near-manic exuberance marked much of his first year as president. Elevation to Free World leader, the fulfillment of all his life's ambitions, walled off all the self-doubts and anxieties that had oppressed him so often in the past. It was also consistent with the ingrained emotional volatility of his personality.

"Compassionate" was the term Johnson used at the end of his first hundred days to describe the presidency he envisioned. Would his program have a label like New Deal or Fair Deal? asked a reporter during a television interview. He had not thought of any, he said, but he supposed that "all of us want a better deal, don't we?" During this interview, he also portrayed himself as a "progressive" who intended to be "prudent without having my mind closed to anything that is new or different."[26]

But LBJ needed to deflect the charge, invariably leveled at "progressives," that he was a spendthrift. The annual budget report was imminent and was rumored to propose federal outlays of $107 billion or $108 billion for the fiscal year, higher than any peacetime budget of the past. An ambitious program of social legislation made rapid economic growth essential, and that, in turn, Johnson believed, meant enactment of the $11 billion Kennedy tax cut bill, passed in the House but stalled in the Senate. But conservatives would accept the tax cut only if he could show that it would not produce massive deficits, and with outlays so high, that did not seem possible. The key to success was converting mossback Harry Byrd, chair of the Senate Finance Committee, an unyielding fiscal conservative who had bottled up the House bill for most of the year. At lunch at the White House in early December, Johnson told Byrd that the tax cut was "vital" to his programs. "I've got to have it." "Well, Mr. President," Byrd retorted, "I don't see how we can get a tax cut as long as this budget is so big." What if he could bring the budget in at under $100 billion? "Well," Byrd responded, then "we might be able to do business."[27]

During the next weeks Johnson, Heller, and Gordon hacked away at every item in the budget. Working night after night at the White House, often with department heads present, they chopped and pruned and pared. Johnson kept most of the budget work secret, but on January 20 he went public with his frugal intentions. With reporters present, he told a flock of Budget Bureau bigwigs assembled in his office that he intended to cut the federal electric bill drastically, beginning with the White House. The lighting bill at the Executive Mansion ran to several thousand dollars a month, he noted. "You don't accumulate unless you save in small amounts."[28]

In fact, Johnson had other goals for the headline-grabbing meeting besides proof of his frugality. Don Reynolds's testimony to the Senate Rules Committee about the Baker-Johnson connection was about to hit the papers, and the president hoped to deflect the public's attention. The maneuver worked, though he had to suffer with the tag "Lightbulb Johnson" for his trouble. The committee, controlled by the Democrats, issued a weak report, and the document made little public impression. This did not satisfy LBJ, however. There is some evidence that the White House contrived a smear campaign against Reynolds and Senator John Williams to undermine their credibility.

Meanwhile, the tax bill made progress. Continuing to stroke Senator Byrd's ego, Johnson sent Kermit Gordon with a copy of the fiscal 1965 budget to the senator's apartment at the Sheraton Park Hotel days before it was made public. Byrd received Gordon in his bathrobe and slippers and listened to him explain the details for half an hour. He was pleased; the budget came in at under $98 billion. On January 23 the Finance Committee approved the bill and sent it to the full Senate, which passed it by seventy-seven to twenty-one. On February 26 the president signed the measure, calling it "the single most important step we have taken to strengthen our economy since World War II."[29] LBJ gave credit to his predecessor and set aside four of the signing pens as souvenirs for the Kennedy family.

The key social program of the second session of the Eighty-eighth Congress was the unprecedented war on poverty. In all the years since

America's founding, the federal government had never bluntly announced its intention to terminate civilization's greatest social scourge. In many ways the new program was rooted in Johnson's own personal history. It harkened back to his own insecure childhood, to his teaching days in Cotulla, to his admiration of Franklin Delano Roosevelt and the New Deal, and to his experiences in the National Youth Administration. Now that he had power, this desire to rescue the poor took on an evangelical fervor. The antipoverty campaign would not only help the disadvantaged but fulfill as well America's moral obligation to all its people. And there were racial gains to be made, too. Johnson believed that racism fed on poverty. If blacks were able to make a living wage, whites would respect them more and prejudice would diminish. Finally, a campaign against poverty was good politics for 1964. He was "absolutely convinced," Irving Bernstein has written, "that poverty was a powerful campaign issue. . . ."[30]

Significantly, Johnson's January 8 State of the Union message did not link the war on poverty to Kennedy's unfulfilled agenda, though it was. This would be Johnson's own issue, one he hoped would help bring him out of Kennedy's shadow. In his enthusiasm for the new program Johnson got carried away. Gripped by his usual verbal extravagance and determined to rivet the public's attention, he pledged to conquer poverty for eternity and during his own administration to boot, promises far beyond anything that could possibly be fulfilled, given the fallibility of human beings and the imperfect nature of human endeavors. "The whole idea of declaring a big war on poverty," said his old friend Elizabeth Goldschmidt, "and ending it for all time, all the rhetoric of it appealed to him very much. In fact, I think he built the rhetoric far beyond that which had been planned by his advisers."[31]

Johnson knew that the nation could well afford a program to benefit the poor. It was growing richer every year, and if his proposed tax cut did what his Keynesian advisers said it would, it would grow even faster in the next few years. The growth of the GNP would automatically increase total tax revenues* and spare businessmen and the voters from the pain of surrendering larger shares of their own incomes. In effect, then, the costs of this program—and other programs—would come out of an ever bigger pie. And that is exactly what happened. As Leonard Hall, chairman of the Republican National Committee, ruefully noted, Johnson was "the only president to have prosperity and poverty going for him at the same time."[32]

---

*A later generation would call this "voodoo economics," but in the 1960s it seemed to work.

Johnson did not want to put the poor on a dole. He opposed massive "income maintenance" programs, to use the modern phrase, that would end poverty through straight gifts. In fact, like many conservatives, he feared the poor would squander straight cash. Speaking privately to Deputy Budget Director Elmer Staats about welfare payments to poor District of Columbia families, he complained, "They want to just stay up there and breed and won't work and we have to feed them. . . . I don't want to be taking any taxpayers' money and paying it to people just to breed."[33] Under his program people would get a "hand up," not a "hand-out." They would be taught new technical skills, better work habits, how to read and write. They would get better health care. These benefits would make them self-sufficient. Johnson always opposed subsidizing idleness. When, late in his administration, advanced liberals proposed a guaranteed annual wage, he refused to support it, though his successor Richard Nixon would endorse the scheme.

Johnson wanted the antipoverty program run out of the White House. He did not want the Departments of Labor; Health, Education, and Welfare; or Agriculture to have pieces of it. "The best way to kill a new idea is to put it in an old-line agency," he said.[34] Keeping it autonomous would also give the program greater visibility and prevent fragmentation. Heller and Gordon supported the president. Both believed that an independent agency would be more apt to experiment and innovate.

Johnson gave the task of working out the details of the new agency and its mission to Sargent Shriver, head of the Peace Corps. From a socially prominent Maryland family, Shriver had married Eunice Kennedy, a daughter of Joe Kennedy, and joined the powerful Kennedy clan. "Sarge" and his wife possessed a strong sense of noblesse oblige and were active in Catholic charities and a variety of social causes. In 1961 John Kennedy had picked his brother-in-law to head the Peace Corps, and Shriver had made it a success. LBJ's choice of Shriver undoubtedly exploited the Kennedy mystique. Shriver was a Kennedy, at least by marriage, but not one who resented Johnson's "usurpation" of the White House. He also had fine connections on the Hill. Shriver himself later declared: "I honestly believe that the principal reason why President Johnson wanted me to do it was that a large proportion of the congressmen and senators trusted me."[35]

Shriver embarked on the job of preparing an antipoverty bill with the same enthusiasm he had brought to the Peace Corps. He assembled a task force of former Kennedy associates, midlevel bureaucrats, and eastern liberal intellectuals to consider how to turn the Heller-Gordon plan into an effective piece of legislation. De facto head of this group was Adam Yarmolinsky, special assistant to Secretary of Defense McNamara, who had worked with Paul Ylvisaker, a social activist, on the pioneer Ford Foundation "gray areas" poverty programs. The task force in turn consulted nearly 150 labor, business, and agriculture leaders as well as educators.

From the outset the most innovative proposal was "community action." Borrowed from academic social theorists, it sought to raise income levels through "maximum feasible participation" of the poor in the planning and delivery of antipoverty services. Community Action would in fact create abuses and offend powerful politicians, but its idealistic proponents saw it as a powerful instrument for developing "community competence." Give the poor a role in deciding their own fate and you had solved half the problem of poverty. It is not clear that Johnson ever understood these goals. To him, community action was the up-to-date counterpart of his beloved National Youth Administration and seemed like a useful way to channel funds and services into city neighborhoods—neighborhoods, incidentally, where most of the voters voted Democratic.

Community action competed with other strategies during the task force deliberations. Meeting in a succession of makeshift headquarters scattered around Washington, some of the task force bureaucrats and experts favored direct federal job creation, like the WPA in the thirties. Shriver himself liked the idea of a Job Corps, a scheme to bring youths, mainly high school dropouts, to urban training and remedial education centers where, in a fresh environment, they could acquire skills and become productive members of society. Although the first "long, hot summer" of racial violence was still a year away, and crime statistics had not yet begun to soar, the public was acutely conscious of gangs and juvenile delinquency, so young people in their late teens seemed an obvious group to focus on. Perhaps poverty could be stopped with them before it was transmitted to future generations. The president was kept informed of the task force's work through aide Bill Moyers but seemed uninterested in the details.

Six weeks after it began its work, the task force presented Johnson with its proposal. On March 16, using this as a basis, Johnson sent a special message to Congress calling for a "nationwide war on the sources of poverty." He proposed a "total commitment by this president and this Congress and this nation to pursue victory over the most ancient of mankind's enemies. . . ." The war would not be "a struggle simply to support people, to make them dependent on the generosity of others," he noted. He wanted to give "people a chance." He saw his war as "an effort to allow them to develop and use their capacities . . . so they can share, as others share, in the promise of this nation." The president expected all these programs to be funded at under $1 billion and not jeopardize his $97.6 billion "economy budget."[36]

The Economic Opportunity Act (EOA) covered six titles. Title I created a Job Corps for young males (soon broadened to include young women), to be taught skills at training centers and camps, and a Neighborhood Youth Corps, to provide work-study programs to help underprivileged young men and women through high school and college. Title II authorized local communities to create plans to fight poverty and pledged federal government support for up to 90 percent of the costs of these community action programs in the first two years and 75 percent after that.

The remaining parts of the bill were less important. They sought to combat rural poverty through grants and loans to poor, marginal farmers; authorized employment and investment incentives to expand employment opportunities for the hard-core jobless; and proposed job-creating loans to small businesses. Title V sought to encourage states to provide basic literacy education and vocational training for both fathers and mothers on welfare so that they would eventually "secure employment or otherwise attain capability for self-support." Title VI, finally, established the Office of Economic Opportunity (OEO) and authorized it to "recruit, select, and train" volunteers" for a domestic Peace Corps, which would be assigned to Indian reservations, migrant labor camps, mental hospitals, and in some cases community action programs and the Job Corps. This program would eventually be called Volunteers in Service for America, or VISTA.[37]

This ambitious package was budgeted at a modest $962.5 million, but in fact only about half of it would be new money, funds not previously appropriated by Congress for social programs.

Mainstream liberals were quick to praise the bill. George Meany, head of the AFL-CIO, endorsed the program but reminded Congress not to forget housing programs, extension of the wage-hour law, and medical care for the aged. The general public, too, favored the programs. The pollster Oliver Quayle, asking about the antipoverty program in general without mentioning its specifics, found more than 60 percent support in New York, 67 percent in Pennsylvania, and 74 percent in Kentucky.[38] More critical was Americans for Democratic Action. Commenting on what it perceived as a too-limited budget, the ADA said: "We regret that this first battle is not to be fought in greater strength."[39]

Predictably, the chief opposition came from old-line conservatives. Republican leaders called the poverty war just a "packaging job" by

LBJ and an attempt to "give his own stamp" to a variety of programs that had been kicking around Congress for a long time. Far-right senator Barry Goldwater of Arizona attacked Johnson's "*Wizard of Oz* philosophy" and called the program a "Madison Avenue" trick by LBJ to win the 1964 election.[40] The conservative *Washington Star* sneered, "The poor will always be with us. And Lyndon B. Johnson will always be with the poor."[41] Most people agreed, however, that the poverty issue was too dramatic, "too emotion-laden and politically potent" for even Republicans in the end to oppose it too strenuously, particularly in an election year.[42]

Johnson was sure he had the votes for passage in the Senate but worried that the bill would be crippled by hostile amendments. Taking to the telephones, he told fellow Democrats that his prestige was on the line. Reverting to schoolteacherish ploys, he promised to put a "star in his book" for those who not only supported the bill but also convinced others to do so.[43] The two senators who deserved the most stars for their efforts were majority leader Mansfield and whip Hubert Humphrey, who dedicated many hours in the spring of 1964 to fending off amendments that promised to hamstring the measure.

The strategy in the more problematical House required Johnson to bypass the flashy and controversial representative from Harlem, Adam Clayton Powell, chairman of the Education and Labor Committee, and assign management of the bill to Phil Landrum, a Georgia conservative. Landrum was hated by organized labor for the 1960 antiunion Landrum-Griffin Act but, Johnson assured worried liberals, as a conservative white Southerner he would have a much better chance than Powell to get the antipoverty bill passed. Even so, the most hidebound Southerners remained opposed. Though the administration emphasized that more poor whites would benefit from the bill than blacks, the Dixie conservatives remained skeptical. In the South itself, certainly, blacks would benefit disproportionately, and besides, the programs would be racially integrated. Howard Smith of Virginia held up the bill in the House Rules Committee for as long as he could, reiterating all the old segregationist arguments against it. Johnson and his aides continued to apply pressure on the House in a campaign that one representative called "unprecedented."

Meanwhile, the president worked tirelessly that winter and early spring to raise the national consciousness on poverty. In January he sent Lady Bird to the bituminous coal district of Pennsylvania, where the mines had played out and where thousands were without work. There she posed with properly grim-looking miners to underscore the ubiquity of poverty. With or without LBJ, Lady Bird went on other publicity trips for the War on Poverty. The president himself spoke often on the subject to such diverse groups as the Business Council, the AFL-CIO, the Daughters of the American Revolution, and even the Socialist Party. At a meeting of the U.S. Chamber of Commerce, Johnson told businessmen that they lived on the side of the tracks where they had never really witnessed poverty. But the poor, he reminded them, were also human beings. "They get hungry, like you and me," he said, "and they have feelings like you and me. They deserve something better of our country."[44]

Johnson was not as interested as Kennedy in regional development, but he signed aboard when he realized that he could not ignore Appalachia in his War on Poverty. In April he submitted a revised version of the Kennedy Area Redevelopment bill, appropriating more than a billion dollars to revive Appalachia, and in May the Johnsons toured the region to push the measure and at the same time publicize the larger antipoverty campaign. On May 22 the *Washington Post* showed a picture of Lady Bird walking on a log to enter the home of Arthur Robertson in the Kentucky backwoods. Robertson, his wife, and their seven children lived in a three-room home "winterized" earlier in the year with a grant from the Farmers Home Administration.

In the end, to guarantee success, Johnson had to sacrifice Adam Yarmolinsky. No one on the antipoverty task force had done as much as Yarmolinsky to write the bill. He was close to Shriver and had been promised the position of deputy chief of the new Office of Economic Opportunity (OEO). But southern conservatives were suspicious of the New York City-born, Harvard-educated, combatively liberal and Jewish Yarmolinsky, who had pushed racial integration in the armed forces while at the Department of Defense. In early August, just before final debate and vote in the House, a group of North Carolina congressmen gave Johnson an ultimatum: Yarmolinsky would have to go or they would vote no. Days before, Larry O'Brien, head of White House liaison with the Hill, had given Johnson his House head count: The bill had only 203 of the 218 votes needed for passage. It would be close. On August 6 Shriver met with Landrum and the North Carolinians in Speaker McCormack's office and was told that the administration would lose eight North Carolina votes if Yarmolinsky were appointed to the OEO. When Shriver told them that the choice was not his to make, they suggested he call the president then and there. It took two calls from McCormack's office, but eventually Johnson agreed that Shriver could tell the holdouts that as director he would not choose Yarmolinsky as his deputy. Shriver would later say that it had been "the most unpleasant experience" he "ever had in the government of the United States."[45]

On August 8, 1964, the House passed the Economic Opportunity Act by 226 to 184, a majority large enough so that dumping Yarmolinsky was superfluous. That day, at a press conference, the president was asked about Yarmolinsky. Johnson was obviously not happy about his deed, no matter how necessary he believed it to be. He shut the reporter up with a sharp remark that Yarmolinsky was still at the Defense Department, ignoring the young bureaucrat's role in writing the War on Poverty bill and the shoddy truth that he had been sacrificed.

On the beautiful summer morning of August 24, in a Rose Garden ceremony, Johnson signed his antipoverty bill into law. "On this occasion," he declared, his voice brimming with emotion, "the American people and our American system are making history. For so long as man has lived on this earth, poverty has been his curse. . . . Today for the first time in all the history of the human race, a great nation is able to make and is willing to make a commitment to eradicate poverty among its people."[46] The remarks, broadcast on radio and TV, were clearly a contribution to the presidential campaign just about to begin.

LBJ sincerely yearned to end poverty in affluent America. But his political agenda made for a flawed outcome. The Economic Opportunity Act (EOA) would have benefited from more study and debate in Congress. Many of the individual titles were half-baked and would not stand up in practice. In his haste to create a record of accomplishment that would ensure victory in the fall election, he had also awakened desires and expectations among the poor that even the wisest and most benevolent Congress could not have satisfied. And yet Johnson had placed before the broad American public a problem that had previously concerned only an elite of leaders and intellectuals and for a time created a national consensus to try to solve it.

But there were other pressing matters to attend to in these transition months. By early 1964 the civil rights struggle was reaching a crescendo. Many fair-minded whites could no longer abide the abuses being visited on black Southerners: The humiliating "WHITES ONLY" signs at restaurants, movie theaters, and rest rooms; the clubbings, the fire hoses deployed like cannons, the snarling dogs when blacks sought to exercise their civil rights. The year 1963 had been one of accelerating racial turmoil, beginning with violently confrontational demonstrations in Birmingham, Alabama, in the spring and culminating in the August 28 "Jobs and Freedom" March on Washington that had attracted 250,000 people, black and white. When Martin Luther King Jr. told the crowd at the Lincoln Memorial that he had a dream that "the sons of former slaves and the sons of former slaveowners will be able to sit down together at the table of brotherhood,"[47] it plucked a chord that resounded through the country's heart. The march was the high point of the civil rights movement that year and perhaps the zenith of the whole "Second Reconstruction" that finally made blacks full members of American civil society. The time had arrived, activists concluded, for massive and decisive federal intervention to guarantee voting rights and end all remnants of segregation. And the public agreed. Between the fall of 1963 and the early spring of 1964 polls recorded surging public interest in moving on the civil rights front.

But it was not merely the accelerating civil rights trajectory that moved the president. Johnson's own yearnings had been stirred. He had long believed that segregation and racism hurt the South and relegated it to outsider status in the nation. It was now time to bring Dixie into the Union. But we must not discount Johnson's moral convictions. Lyndon Johnson wanted fervently to end segregation, discrimination, and disfranchisement, and now, as president, he was able to do it though he knew that *even* now he would have to expend political capital to achieve it. In later years Ramsey Clark, Johnson's third attorney general, wrote of LBJ's civil rights views: "There was a purity about it . . . in terms of commitment to principle, the ideal of equality, less fettered by political consideration than any other activity of government or out of government that I have been involved in. His period in the White House in civil rights was a period of stunning change. . . . I believe that there was a clarity of vision and a purity of purpose that was real and profound."[48] And Johnson's commitments would make a crucial difference. Without strong presidential leadership the momentum of the day could have been lost. It is hard to imagine an Eisenhower or a Nixon, whatever the *Zeitgeist*, achieving a giant installment of racial progress.

By the time he became president, LBJ was ready to "shove in" his whole "stack" on civil rights. Johnson knew that a strong civil rights bill would exact a price. It was "destined to set me apart forever from the South, where I had been born and reared," he later noted.[49] But he refused to be deterred. In the early weeks after Dallas he met with all the major black leaders to hear their thoughts and their ideas, and from the outset it was clear that he would be bolder than any of his immediate predecessor for the cause of racial equality.

The bill JFK had sent to Congress in June 1963, despite the president's initial qualms and reservations, was the most extensive civil rights measure ever proposed by the White House. Its major provisions established a sixth-grade education as proof of literacy for voting in federal elections; outlawed local laws excluding from public facilities any person on the grounds of race, color, religion, or national origin; gave the commissioner of education the right to establish school desegregation programs and the attorney general the power to sue noncompliant school boards; denied federal funds to state and local programs that discriminated; and established by statute the Commission on Equal Employment Opportunity to supersede the one created previously by presidential executive order.

The bill was stuck in the House when Kennedy died, held captive by Howard Smith's obstructionist Rules Committee. LBJ embraced the Kennedy measure and started the ball rolling by deploying the rarely used Rule 11, allowing rank-and-file members of a House committee to overrule the chairman. Professing to dislike the strategy "in the marrow of his bones"[50] as a denial of House tradition, Johnson pushed hard to take the bill away from the Rules Committee. The administration managers failed to get the required number of signatures, but there were enough dissenters to make Smith uncomfortable, and to save face, he began hearings on the bill in January. On the thirtieth House Resolution 7152 moved to the House floor for debate and for possible amendment.

During House consideration the president and Larry O'Brien kept close tabs on the bill's progress. White House aide Jack Valenti later remarked of reluctant congressmen, "We let them know that for every negative vote there was a price to pay."[51] The president also used the carrot. When Jake Pickle, LBJ's friend and successor as Representative from the Tenth District, voted for the bill, Johnson phoned to tell him how proud he was of him for defying Texas mores.

It proved impossible to fend off amendments. But not all were retrograde. "Judge" Smith, according to House majority whip Carl Albert, "was an unreconstructed nineteenth-century Virginian" who "spent his entire legislative life trying to ward off federal encroachments into the world in which he was born."[52] But he inadvertently expedited a social revolution in the United States. In the course of the H.R. 7152 debate he offered an amendment to the section on equal employment opportunity that added "sex" discrimination to the list of practices forbidden employers in hiring. Smith considered the amendment a poison pill that would help defeat the bill. No one, he was certain, would vote seriously for a measure containing such a feature. To his amazement, the proviso passed and then failed to scuttle the bill itself. On February 10 the House passed the civil rights measure, including the sex discrimination proviso, by 290 to 130, in a thoroughly bipartisan and sectional vote.

The House bill was an abomination to old-line southern senators, and no one expected it to escape a lethal Senate filibuster without substantial change. Kennedy could not have gotten a bill enacted without major compromise. But Johnson, a Southerner, made it clear that he would not tolerate concessions and would sacrifice other congressional business to get the measure through. Once more Johnson was forced to grapple with his liberal demons. "I knew," he told Doris Kearns, "that if I didn't get out in front on this issue, they [the liberals] would get me. They'd throw up my background against me, they'd use it to prove that I was incapable of bringing unity to the land I loved so much. . . . I had to produce a civil rights bill that was even stronger than the one they'd have gotten if Kennedy had lived. Without this, I'd be dead before I could even begin."[53] Johnson publicly stayed in the background during the fight over the Civil Rights Act, but he was everywhere behind the scenes cajoling and threatening southern senators. He even appealed shamelessly to sectional pride in himself. Did Southerners want to embarrass the only southern president since Zachary Taylor? If they did, they would never see another one again.

Even before the bill passed the House, Richard Russell gave notice that he would fight to the finish, as he had against each civil rights measure since 1957. In early March Russell told reporters he saw "no room for compromise" and would resist to the "last ditch."[54] But Dick Russell was now an old man in failing health and in the end would be no match for Johnson and the younger, stronger liberal senators who were resolved to get the bill enacted.

As the measure moved through the upper chamber, a reluctant or irresolute senator would hear from Johnson over the phone. The president pleaded and lectured in an effort to lock up the vote. If the man was not home when the White House called, Johnson would butter up his wife: "Now, honey, I know you won't let your husband let his president down." Occasionally he would reach one of the senator's children. "Now you tell your daddy," Johnson would coax, "that the president called, and he'd be very proud to have your daddy on his side."[55] He was shameless.

The White House tapped majority whip Humphrey as floor manager for the bill in the Senate, and the Minnesotan threw himself into the battle with his usual gusto. Each morning pro-civil rights senators and Justice Department lawyers from Robert Kennedy's staff gathered in Humphrey's office to plot strategy, stressing the importance of a bipartisan alliance against the intransigent South. The administration could count on continuing pressure from civil rights organizations, unions, and religious groups to influence the undecided senators. On April 28 Georgetown University hosted a meeting of the National Interreligious

Convocation of Civil Rights. During the sessions its members fanned through Capitol Hill offices, beseeching senators to pass the bill.

There was no way that invoking cloture could be avoided this time. It would be a near thing. Since the beginning of the century, twenty-seven cloture votes had been called and only five had received the needed two-thirds majority, none pertaining to civil rights. Here minority leader Everett Dirksen, a sonorous and platitudinous solon from Illinois, was a key person. A mild conservative, the "Wizard of Ooze" had always been able in the past to change course on national issues when he believed it necessary. Johnson and Dirksen had a close, though sub-rosa, relationship. The senator often visited the White House but came through the Diplomatic Reception Room so as not to be seen. On the second floor of the Mansion, recounted Jack Valenti, Lyndon and Ev would have a drink together and "chew the fat, reminisce, tell stories, laugh, and really enjoy themselves."[56] They would also horse-trade: a presidential favor for a Senate vote.

Now, in the spring of 1964, Johnson told his pal that he counted on his "deep-rooted patriotism"[57] to help get the civil rights bill through. But the president also understood that the Illinois senator could use some "pork" and promised him a Corps of Engineers project for Illinois. The White House strategists simultaneously told Humphrey to sweet-talk Dirksen and emphasize what a hero he would be if he assisted in invoking cloture. Humphrey later said he had "courted Dirksen almost as persistently as I did Muriel [Mrs. Humphrey]."[58] The Civil Rights Act would "go down in history," he told the gray-haired senator, and that, Humphrey noted, "meant, of course, that *he* [Dirksen] would go down in history, which interested him a great deal."[59]

But Dirksen was influenced as much by fear as by Johnson's and Humphrey's flattery. The senator dreaded inner-city violence during the hot summer if the Civil Rights Bill was not passed; by June there were already signs of trouble brewing in New York City. In the late spring, after much hemming and hawing, Dirksen came to his decision. Misquoting Victor Hugo, he declared, "No army can withstand the strength of an idea whose time has come."[60] With the minority leader aboard, after almost two months of debate and the longest filibuster in Senate history, on June 10 cloture passed, 71 to 29. Every senator was present and voting, including Clair Engle of California, dying of a brain tumor and brought to the proceedings in a wheelchair. Unable to speak, he indicated his "yes" vote by pointing to his eye.

There were still pestiferous amendments to get out of the way, 115 in all. All told there were 106 Senate roll-call votes on the bill. It was clear that the real battle was over, however, when at one point, Richard Russell was speaking and Massachusetts senator Edward Kennedy cut him off, telling him his time was up. Dick Russell had never been treated so rudely before. As Russell took his seat, he had tears in his eyes. Finally, Dirksen came up with a "revised" bill, one that was almost a duplicate of the strong measure the House had passed in February. The one proviso that diluted the bill somewhat was the "Mrs. Murphy's clause," exempting from nondiscrimination provisions boardinghouses with no more than five rooms to rent. Nine days after cloture was invoked, the Dirksen bill passed the Senate, 73 to 27. On July 2 Johnson signed into law the most comprehensive civil rights act in the nation's history.

Suddenly he was a liberal hero. Anthony Lewis, a columnist for the *New York Times*, noted that "this country's first Southern President since Reconstruction" had "made it all possible by his outspoken commitment to Negro Rights. . . . Nearly everyone has . . . forgotten the chaos and bitterness into which civil rights legislation had fallen last autumn. It seemed then that only a miracle could save it. . . ."[61] In 1968 the prominent black novelist Ralph Ellison contributed an essay to a book about the programs of President Johnson. Ellison wrote:

[P]erhaps I am motivated here by an old slave-born myth of the Negroes— not the myth of the "good white man," nor that of the "great white father," but the myth, secret and questioning, of the flawed white Southerner who while true to his Southern roots has confronted the injustices of the past and been redeemed. Such a man, the myth holds, will do the right thing however great the cost, whether he likes Negroes or not, and will move with tragic vulnerability toward the broader ideals of American democracy. . . . When all of the returns are in, perhaps President Johnson will have to settle for being recognized as the greatest American President for the poor and for the Negroes, but that, as I see it, is a very great honor indeed.[62]

Was Johnson happy? Not really. Bill Moyers recalled seeing him the evening the Civil Rights Act passed. The media were ringing with pronouncements about the "historic" event: How unprecedented! What an achievement! Yet LBJ, the author of this triumph, had managed to snatch defeat from the jaws of victory. He was "depressed" that evening, Moyers reported. When he asked him why, Johnson replied: "I think we've just delivered the South to the Republican Party for the rest of my life and yours."[63] LBJ was right, of course: The white South is now almost solidly Republican, in part because the Democrats broke the back of Jim Crow. But only an emotionally impaired man would have made the point at such an exalted moment.

Poverty and civil rights were not the only matters on Johnson's mind in the spring of 1964. The country faced a massive railroad strike that threatened the movement of mail, food, and manufactured goods and promised to shut down commuter train lines. Economic chaos loomed. The issues were featherbedding—excessive staffing—as well as job security and paid vacation time. In March 1963 the U.S. Supreme Court had allowed the railroads to institute new work rules but also agreed that the unions had an equal right to strike, confirming the impasse. That August, confronted with a midnight strike deadline, Congress prohibited a railroad walkout until the end of February the following year. Meanwhile, an arbitration board concluded that the railroads had the right to end featherbedding, and in the wake of this decision, management began firing superfluous workers.

At 4:30 A.M. on April 8, the Railroad Brotherhoods, preferring to take on one railroad at a time, struck the Illinois Central, stranding four thousand Chicago commuters in unlit passenger cars. The angry owners announced that they would retaliate with strict new work rules to go into effect after midnight on April 10. The local strike now seemed likely to mushroom into a nationwide work stoppage. Fearing mass layoffs in railroad-dependent industries and the possibility of food shortages in the big cities, LBJ moved quickly to head off the strike.

Acting by the president's direction, Secretary of Labor Willard Wirtz called an emergency meeting with labor and management in Washington. After wrangling through the night, both sides refused to budge. A national shutdown now seemed certain unless Johnson himself intervened. Wirtz told the president to stay out of it and let the strike take place. The opposing positions were so entrenched that if the president asked for a strike delay he would be refused and humiliated. A short strike, moreover, might actually lead to a settlement. But Johnson was being pushed from the other side as well. A prolonged strike, some of his close advisers told him, could be a national disaster, and the public would blame him for inaction. He must intervene.

The struggle between the railroads and the Brotherhoods was of long standing. Neither Eisenhower nor Kennedy had been able to resolve it, and Johnson was intrigued by the idea that he might finally broker a permanent agreement. Hours from the strike deadline he summoned to the White House Roy E. Davidson, grand chief engineer of the International Brotherhood of Locomotive Engineers, representing labor, and management's James E. (Doc) Wolfe, chairman of the Railway Labor Conference. They should accept a twenty-day delay during which both the strike and the rules changes would be suspended while negotiators tried to work out a compromise. Both sides went to dinner, and when they came back, management had agreed to the delay; labor refused. The president now asked the labor leaders to meet with him separately in the Oval Office and presented new proposals already cleared with management: The postponement would be cut to fifteen days and there would be two new negotiators. When the labor leaders refused to agree, the president promised that the issues that most concerned the union would be dealt with. "Please give me time," he implored. "I am your president. I'm new on this job. I'm coming to you for the first time." He promised to "personally ride herd over the negotiations and see to it that there is good-faith bargaining." He appealed to their patriotism and then, switching on his southern folksiness, turned to fellow Texan Charles Luna, head of the Brotherhood of Railway Trainmen. "Charley, it's not one of those damn Yankees asking you."[64]

Less than two hours before the deadline, the union leaders agreed to cancel the Illinois Central walkout and put off the national strike for the fifteen days of negotiations that Johnson requested. The next morning, labor and management, joined by two new negotiators, New York City labor expert Theodore W. Kheel and Professor George W. Taylor of the Wharton School, met in a comfortable room at the Executive Office Building. The president dropped in from time to time. "Hi ya, fellows, how ya doing?" he kibitzed. Through the negotiations he gave the participants pep talks or read them dire figures from Walter Heller's office about the harm a railroad strike would do to the country. He walked around the room, looking over their shoulders, reading what they wrote on their pads. At one point he decided they needed some coffee to keep going and rummaged around the EOB until he found an old coffeepot. He then sent a messenger to an all-night convenience store to bring back several cans of coffee.

On April 21 the negotiators reached a tentative agreement with representatives from labor. Management was still not appeased and was additionally concerned that a bill giving the industry greater latitude in setting freight rates was stuck in the House Rules Committee. Johnson knew a good trade when he saw one. The president vowed to get the freight-rate bill to the floor. He also promised that the Treasury would review the question with the IRS of allowing depreciation for bridge and tunnel construction. Half an hour later, Doc Wolfe came in to tell the president the owners would settle.

With victory in hand, the exuberant Johnson shoved Davidson, Wolfe, Wirtz, and Reynolds into the presidential limousine. Accompanied by a police escort, the car raced through Washington rush-hour traffic to television station WTOP for the announcement that the negotiations had been successful. In the end, neither the IRS nor the House Rules Committee paid any attention to the president's requests, but the new contracts were already signed, and everyone was relieved that the problem had been solved. For Johnson, the railroad dispute was a personal triumph. It was his first major achievement not linked in some way to the martyred Kennedy.

By the spring Johnson had earned the confidence and gratitude of the American public. He had every reason to be pleased and optimistic. In April a Gallup poll announced that 77 percent of the American people approved of the new president. Yet once more his moods seemed disconnected from reality. His volatility emerged vividly that same month at an informal meeting with some prominent editors in Georgetown at the home of newspaper columnist Max Freedman. The president arrived at the late-evening gathering unexpectedly, full of bounce and enthusiasm. He regaled the editors with stories and mimicry and teased fellow guest Senator Humphrey about a possible vice-presidential candidacy in November. When Eugene Patterson of the *Atlanta Constitution* introduced himself, Johnson said he knew who he was and promised then and there to appoint him to the Civil Rights Commission, demanding an immediate response. One of the journalists present later said: "He was so exuberant, so high, that some of us wondered about his mental stability."[65]

But then came the crash. The meeting broke up at 2:00 A.M., and LBJ offered to drop Patterson off at his hotel. In the presidential limousine, bending forward with his head in his hands, he told the editor of all his fears. The Kennedys and the "eastern crowd" had nothing but contempt for him. They considered him a rube. As for his fellow Southerners, they distrusted him on civil rights while, at the same time, blacks distrusted him because he came from the South. He could see serious trouble ahead. "You just wait and see what happens when I put one foot wrong."[66]

These emotional swings might have crippled Johnson. At times they did mar his relations with colleagues and associates and impair his judgment. Yet they did not keep him from functioning on the broad presidential stage. In hopes of making his individual mark before the fall election, this spring Johnson resolved to leapfrog the New Deal–New Frontier programs to a new agenda to improve the "quality" of life for all Americans, not just the poor and the deprived.

Back in the midfifties, after a decade of postwar prosperity, Arthur Schlesinger Jr. had called for a new "'qualitative liberalism' dedicated to the bettering of people's lives and opportunities."[67] By the opening years of the 1960s the sense that national happiness required more than material abundance had seized the minds of many liberal thinkers. Now that most Americans were comfortable materially, something had to be done to enhance people's spiritual, moral, and aesthetic existences. When Eric Goldman, a Princeton history professor, now Johnson's cultural adviser, wrote to assorted intellectuals around the country asking them what should be the "general thrust" of the administration, all agreed that "it was important, even urgent, for President Johnson to use his office in a conscious effort to alter American values." The best-selling historian Barbara Tuchman noted that "the time [had] come to shift the emphasis from the material to the moral." Norman Podhoretz, editor of *Commentary*, an influential magazine of intellectual and political comment, called attention to the problem of living "in a society in which goods are abundant and work loses its force as the organizing principle of the individual's existence. . . ."[68]

These ideas were in the air, then, when in April 1964 Johnson called Bill Moyers and Richard Goodwin, a former Kennedy aide, now administration speechwriter, to go for a swim in the White House pool. Johnson had more than exercise on his mind as the three naked men paddled around. The president told his aides he had two concerns. He wanted to get elected in his own right, and he wanted to pass some exciting new legislation. He had pulled the stalled Kennedy programs "out of the ditch." Now it was time to move on. "We've got to use the Kennedy program," he said, "as a springboard to take on the Congress, summon the states to new heights, create a Johnson program, different in tone, fighting and aggressive." As the president swam toward the end of the pool, he suddenly turned. "Now, boys . . ." he told the two young aides, "you start to put together a Johnson program, and don't worry about whether it's too radical or if Congress is ready for it. That's my job."[69] The two men quickly got to work.

A good time to spell out new ideas would be at the University of Michigan commencement exercises later in May. In 1947 Secretary of State George Marshall had used the Harvard graduation to announce the Marshall Plan. Johnson would use the occasion at Ann Arbor to lay out a new domestic agenda. He would also take the opportunity to provide some unifying phrase for the Johnson programs, some lively label to distinguish it from Kennedy's "New Frontier" and also serve in the coming election campaign. The "better deal" tag that Johnson had used in a television interview earlier in the year had, fortunately, not caught on. Goodwin preferred "Great Society," which he may have borrowed from others, and Johnson had tried it out in a few minor speeches he gave that spring and found that it suited him. When Goodwin sat down to write the May address, "Great Society" was the term that stuck. A Harvard-trained lawyer, Goodwin was an intellectual in touch with the cutting-edge thinking of the Cambridge–New York circle, and the speech reflected his contacts. Much of the Great Society agenda laid out that spring day represented the fancies and speculations of academic thinkers, but by their announcement on this special occasion they shaped the Johnson record.

Ninety thousand people had gathered at Michigan Stadium on May 22 to celebrate the university's 120th commencement and to see the president of the United States receive the honorary degree of doctor of civil laws. It was a sunny day, and the parents, faculty, administrators, and dignitaries were in the cheerful and receptive mood appropriate to graduations. On a platform draped with the university's blue and gold bunting, Johnson promised to "assemble the best thought and broadest knowledge from all over the world" to find ways to make American society the best in the world. "The challenge of the next half century," he declared, "is whether we have the wisdom to use [our] wealth to enrich and elevate our national life, and to advance the quality of our American civilization. . . ." Americans had "the opportunity to move not only toward the rich society and the powerful society, but upward to the Great Society."

That Great Society would be something new in the world. It would be "a place where every child can find knowledge to enrich his mind and to enlarge his talents," where "leisure is a welcome chance to build and reflect, not a feared cause of boredom and restlessness," a place where "the city of man serves not only the needs of the body and the demands of commerce but the desire for beauty and the hunger for community." The Great Society would allow men and women to "renew contact with nature. . . ." It would "honor creation for its own sake and for what it adds to the understanding of the race. . . ." In the Great Society people would be "more concerned with the quality of their goals than the quantity of their goods."

Johnson asked the audience whether they would "join in the battle to build the Great Society, to prove that our material progress is only the foundation on which we will build a richer life of mind and spirit."[70] His listeners roared out their affirmation. The crowd in fact had applauded enthusiastically twenty-nine times during the speech, and the president was euphoric on the plane ride back to Washington.

The national public was almost as enthusiastic as the audience at Michigan Stadium. The times were ripe for change. The country was rich and getting richer and could afford to be generous. For many mid-level Americans in 1964, moreover, Johnson's Great Society promised to complement and enhance their own plans and aspirations. But other discontents would soon come to the fore. As the sixties advanced, segments of America hitherto mute or amorphous—black nationalists, radical students, feminists, militant Hispanics, and social nonconformists—would grow restless and aggrieved and grope for expression and recognition. Many would see the Great Society as a mockery or an evasion. And even in 1964, support for the president's vision, if wide, was shallow. Before long many middle-class voters would conclude that the Great Society had raised hopes and expectations unrealistically, had reinforced the very discontents it had sought to abate, and had created other discontents never foreseen.

But much of the peril to the Great Society would derive from events abroad, for even during this interregnum year there loomed the shadow of Vietnam.

The division of Vietnam at the seventeenth parallel by the Geneva Accords of 1954 had not been considered a permanent solution by the Communist government of Ho Chi Minh in Hanoi. Determined to create a united Communist state under its sole rule, the Hanoi regime deployed trained guerrilla forces, the Vietcong, and, later, North Vietnamese regulars inserted through the Demilitarized Zone, to attack the Saigon government and its supporters. To avoid a disastrous "domino" effect in Southeast Asia, after the French abandoned Vietnam at the time of Geneva, Eisenhower had made the United States the major financial backer of the anti-Communist regime in Saigon. Between 1955 and 1961 the U.S. Treasury spent a billion dollars on South Vietnam to prop up the South Vietnam government and provide training and equipment for the poorly organized and led South Vietnamese army.

Kennedy was a determined "cold warrior" who accepted the inexorable struggle between communism and the "free world." On taking office he had launched a major buildup of both nuclear and conventional weapons. His foreign policy outside of Europe emphasized aggressive, nonnuclear responses to the "liberation wars and popular uprisings" against the "imperialists" that, in January 1961, Premier Khrushchev had pledged the Soviet Union to support all over the world. Kennedy had been uncertain how far to go in defending American interests in Vietnam. No more than Eisenhower did he want to be sucked into a land war in Asia. He rejected advice to send troops to Laos, one of the successor states of French Indo-China, to protect a pro-American government, and accepted neutralization there as a solution. But he worried that if the more strategically important South Vietnam went Communist, the rest of the world would consider America weak and doubt our commitment to containment. Even historian Arthur Schlesinger Jr., a strong Kennedy partisan, agrees that JFK was overcommitted to "action diplomacy, an approach that was a tripwire for trouble."[71]

Kennedy increased the American presence in South Vietnam substantially and bet on Ngo Dinh Diem to stave off the Communist threat. As we saw, Diem had not been an effective defender of his ill-formed country against the Communists, and in mid-1961 Vice President Johnson had gone to Vietnam at his chief's behest to help change his policies. In the months following Johnson's visit, Diem, a Catholic convert, harassed the Buddhists, triggering a wave of hunger strikes and fiery self-immolations by protesting priests that aroused world dismay. In the fall of 1963 Kennedy, once Diem's strong supporter, abandoned him. Without American protection, Diem was assassinated by his enemies in early November, and a motley succession of generals took over in Saigon. By expediting the overthrow of Diem, the administration had implicitly made an additional commitment to the South's continued autonomy. By this time there were sixteen thousand American advisers, military and political, in South Vietnam helping to defend the pro-Western Saigon government, and the first Americans had died as the result of enemy action. Though the young president could not settle his mind on Vietnam, at the time of his death he was apparently being dragged, willy-nilly, into the morass of a land war in Southeast Asia.

Johnson at the outset simply followed in what he perceived as his predecessor's footsteps. As we saw, in these early months after the assassination he sought to establish continuity between the Kennedy administration and his own. He was especially emulative in foreign relations, where he felt least sure of his footing. The new president kept in place almost all of Kennedy's top foreign policy advisers—Secretary of State Dean Rusk; Secretary of Defense Robert McNamara; national security adviser McGeorge Bundy; his brother, Assistant Secretary of State William Bundy; McGeorge Bundy's NSC deputy Walt Rostow; and George Ball, under secretary of state for economic affairs. With the exception of Ball, all were protohawks. According to Clark Clifford, on the issue of Vietnam, Johnson "encountered a practically unanimous sentiment among his senior advisers. . . . [T]hey all said . . . the domino theory is unquestionably so." The "president proceeded at that time on the basis of a solid phalanx of advice from the main advisers in the field that this is what we had to do."[72]

But the policy transmission process may have been more confused—and absurd—than direct. White House press secretary George Reedy thinks that on Vietnam Johnson was the victim of a "simple misunderstanding." In the first meeting in the White House after Kennedy's assassination, staffers from both the Kennedy and Johnson camps were present, he notes. The Kennedy people were "looking to him [Johnson] for a cue to their future conduct." *He, on the other hand, was looking to them for a cue as to what Kennedy would have done.*" During the months that the Kennedy advisers stayed on, Reedy thinks it very likely that Johnson believed Kennedy would have pushed forward with the war, while the Kennedy advisers considered this Johnson's own choice. As Reedy points out, Kennedy staffers later claimed that their man had intended to leave Vietnam after the 1964 election, but he doubts that they really knew. "They did not make this remarkable discovery," he wrote, "until *after* Vietnam became unpopular."[73]

In truth, his advisers' views did not entirely conflict with Johnson's own inclinations. The president's understanding of twentieth-century history, especially the abysmal appeasement chapter of Munich, would not allow him to surrender part of the Free World to Communist subversion without a fight. Shortly after the triumphant Ann Arbor speech, Johnson discussed American policy in Southeast Asia at a news conference. In Vietnam, he said, he would be guided by four principles: One, "America keeps her word." Two, "The issue is the future of Southeast Asia as a whole." Three, "Our purpose is peace." Four, "This is not a jungle war, but a struggle for freedom on every front of human activity."[74] The formula was implicitly a commitment to a major Cold War responsibility, though it is not clear whether the president intended it that way.

And yet Johnson resisted escalation of the American investment. One historian has claimed that he considered success in Vietnam and at home as part of the same progressive package. In both cases, says Lloyd Gardner, he saw a benevolent American government as uplifting, improving, reforming the lives of ordinary people. His scheme to develop the Mekong Delta in Vietnam in his mind paralleled the Tennessee Valley Authority of the New Deal and appealed to him in its own right; it was not merely a means to forestall a Communist takeover in South Vietnam.[75]

But in fact, Johnson understood the Vietnam struggle as the mortal enemy of his domestic programs. History, he believed, proved this. Woodrow Wilson's New Freedom had been terminated by World War I. World War II had aborted the New Deal. Truman's involvement in Korea had weakened his administration and damaged his legislative effectiveness. "Once the war began," Johnson told Doris Kearns in 1970, "then all those conservatives in Congress would use it as a weapon against the Great Society." He could see it coming as he brooded over the mess in Vietnam. In a pungent metaphor, he noted: "If I left the woman I really loved—the Great Society—in order to get involved in that bitch of a war on the other side of the world, then I would lose everything at home."[76]

In recorded private telephone conversations of late May 1964 with McGeorge Bundy, Richard Russell, and UN ambassador Adlai Stevenson, we hear the president's deep personal anguish and doubts. He fears, he says, getting into another Korea and being forced, as there, to fight the Chinese. On the other hand, he worries about the Republican reaction in the coming presidential campaign if the administration does not act aggressively. Nixon, Rockefeller, Goldwater, and Lodge all will try to crucify him if they can. He also knows that men suffer and die in wars undertaken for reasons of grand world strategy, however valid, and it gives him pause. He tells both Russell and Bundy that one of the White House marine guards is the father of six children. He would hate to send that man to Southeast Asia to risk his life. In the conversation with Bundy the president asks for alternative options and seems intrigued by Bundy's description of pundit Walter Lippmann's proposal to negotiate a face-saving arrangement with Hanoi to "neutralize" South Vietnam and then leave, accepting the inevitable takeover of the South by the Communists. As he tells Stevenson, in what could serve as a summary of his views: "I shudder to get too deeply involved there."[77]

Yet Johnson prepared for that very contingency. Rejecting Truman's disregard of Congress when he decided to intervene in Korea, he asked his advisers in the spring of 1964 to prepare a standby resolution for Congress authorizing the chief executive's use of force in Southeast Asia if needed. At this point Americans were not thinking very much about Vietnam. Polls taken in the spring revealed that two-thirds of the nation was scarcely aware of events in Southeast Asia.† By contrast, most Americans knew about the proposed Great Society and liked it. In June the plan for a congressional resolution on Vietnam was shelved. Yet during the summer, as the Saigon government threatened to crumble under the blows of the Vietcong, the president worried that Vietnam would be converted by the Republicans in the fall into an effective antiadministration weapon.

Johnson hoped to soft-pedal Vietnam during the presidential campaign. But he could not avoid reacting that summer to what seemed a blatant provocation by the Hanoi regime.

---

†Though, among those who knew of the problem, a majority wanted to stay out of it.

The challenge occurred in early August. On the second, as the USS *Maddox* steamed through the Gulf of Tonkin between the island of Hainan and the North Vietnamese coast, it was attacked by three Communist torpedo boats. The *Maddox* had been collecting data on North Vietnamese radar and ship movements and helping the South Vietnamese navy in attacks on enemy coastal bases. The North Vietnamese were monitoring the American ship's activities. The *Maddox* exchanged fire with the North Vietnamese ships and, aided by American carrier jets, seriously damaged them. Two days later the captains of the *Maddox* and another American destroyer in the gulf, the *Turner Joy*, reported that Communist vessels had launched torpedoes at them.‡ Johnson had responded mildly to the August 2 attack, but after the apparent second round, concluded he must act with force. Hours after receiving the message about the *Turner Joy* he ordered planes from U.S. carriers cruising off the Vietnam coast to bomb North Vietnamese torpedo boat bases and oil storage facilities. That evening the president appeared on TV after the eleven-o'clock news and told the nation that "aggression by terror against peaceful villages of South Vietnam" had now "been joined by open aggression on the high seas against the United States of America." Though he was ordering a retaliatory American air strike, he noted, this was a "firm but limited response." "We seek no wider war," the president intoned.[78]

The North Vietnam attacks, real or imagined, created both a danger and an opportunity for Johnson. Soon after the Tonkin Gulf attacks, Senator Barry Goldwater, the air force reserve general whom the Republicans had nominated for president in mid-July, issued a statement that "we cannot allow the American flag to be shot at anywhere on earth if we are to retain our respect and prestige."[79] Johnson knew he was "being tested."[80] As Robert Anderson, Eisenhower's secretary of the treasury and a moderate Republican, told the president in a telephone conversation, "You're going to be running against a man who's a wild man on this subject. Any lack of firmness he'll make up. . . ."[81] The Tonkin Gulf incident gave Johnson the opportunity to assert the administration's resolve and at the same time to confer on his Vietnam policies the constitutional legitimacy he had wanted for some time.

---

‡There may not have been a second attack on August 4. The American radar had possibly been registering turbulent weather conditions or even a school of fish rather than torpedoes. McNamara later admitted that he was uncertain that the second attack ever took place.

Meeting with congressional leaders the day after his TV appearance, the president described the incident and asked their support for a joint resolution drafted by McGeorge Bundy. This statement authorized the "President as Commander in Chief, to take all necessary measures to repel any armed attack against forces of the United States and to prevent further aggression."[82] On August 7 the House of Representatives unanimously passed the Gulf of Tonkin Resolution; the Senate followed up with only two dissenting votes. The public, like Congress, largely approved of Johnson's action. Whatever Congress's intentions—and however limited the initial purposes of the president himself—his critics would claim that he and McNamara considered the resolution a "blank-check authorization for further action,"[83] a virtual declaration of war.

No one doubted that Johnson's nomination at the Democratic National Convention in Atlantic City was a sure thing. Yet the president was too anxious to enjoy the ride. Besides Vietnam, he worried about the fallout from Bobby Baker's dealings. In January, at a press conference, Johnson brushed off the free stereo set as a simple gift from "an employee" with whom he had at times exchanged small presents.[84] Three weeks later, on a TV program interview, he repudiated his old friend in a shameless way. Asked about his "protégé" and "friend," he shot back that Baker was a Senate employee and "no protégé of mine."[85] But the issue did not go away. In February Baker had been called before the Senate Rules and Administration Committee to testify about his dealings and, in "a hippodrome atmosphere," had repeatedly invoked the Fifth Amendment against self-incrimination. Johnson was also concerned about charges of influence and corruption regarding his radio and television empire that were appearing in the *Wall Street Journal* and the *Washington Star*. To top it all, he had managed to offend the nation's dog lovers when, on the White House lawn, he had pulled his pet beagles' ears, and when they yelped, said that it hadn't hurt them at all.

Potentially the most politically damaging event of the summer was the growing restlessness in the black ghettos. In mid-July, following the killing of a fifteen-year-old black boy by an off-duty New York City policeman, Harlem erupted in an orgy of looting, arson, vandalism, and brick-throwing that soon spread to Brooklyn and to Rochester, New York.

Johnson deplored the rioting on its own terms, of course, but he also feared its effect on what would soon be called "backlash." Already the archsegregationist governor of Alabama, George Wallace, was harvesting votes, and Democratic votes at that, for reversing the civil rights clock and limiting federal social programs perceived as too problack. In the recent Maryland, Wisconsin, and Indiana Democratic primaries, playing on white resentment of supposed favoritism toward blacks, Wallace had won a third or more of the ballots. The rage in black ghettos could only make the backlash worse. The president invited civil rights leaders to the White House and asked them to restore peace. The black leaders themselves believed that defeating Goldwater was critical at this point. Pleading for calm, they requested of the black community a "broad curtailment if not total moratorium of all mass marches, picketing and demonstrations until after Election Day . . ."[86] Fortunately, ghetto grievances and disappointments and the sense of wrong were still at modest levels, and the riots soon petered out.

Another pothole on the nomination road was the "Bobby" problem. The president did not trust or like Robert Kennedy. Ever since the vice-presidential foul-up in 1960 he considered JFK's brother an adversary. For his part, though circumspect in his public acts and utterances, the attorney general considered Johnson an intruder. Johnson had used the nation's sorrows and guilts over John Kennedy's assassination to prod Congress into enacting his programs during the remaining months of the Eighty-eighth Congress, but he now wanted to get out from under the Kennedy mystique. "I don't want to get elected because of the Kennedys," he told a Kennedy friend in the spring of 1964. "I want to get elected on my own. That's a perfectly normal feeling, isn't it?"[87] Unfortunately, the attorney general considered himself JFK's rightful heir and wanted the vice-presidential nomination as the next step to the White House. Bobby acted, LBJ believed, "like *he* was the custodian of the Kennedy dream, some kind of rightful heir to the throne."[88] Johnson did not intend to allow his administration to go down in history as a way station between two Kennedy presidencies.

There was a strong element of obsession in Johnson's response to Robert Kennedy. Bobby aroused all LBJ's atavistic insecurities and sense of inferiority. The Kennedys represented for Johnson—as for his successor Nixon—a standard of glamor and sophistication unattainable to a poor boy from the provinces, no matter how successful. But the reaction was not entirely irrational. The assassination still evoked powerful responses from liberal voters toward the Kennedy name, and these subtracted from Johnson's own strength. And there were practical reasons as well for disregarding Bobby's vice-presidential ambitions. Goldwater's nomination had made Bobby dispensable. The liberal Northeast, formerly Johnson's weakest region and the one area in which having RFK on the ticket might help, now became Johnson's strongest bulwark. A symbol of civil rights enforcement, however qualified, Bobby was a political liability in the South and West, where the Republican candidate was strongest. Polls showed that one-third of the South's Democrats would desert the party ticket if Bobby were on it; only one in twenty-five would be unhappy with Hubert Humphrey.[89]

In late July Johnson decided to end the Bobby problem decisively. He summoned the attorney general to his office and told him that his weakness in the South and West made it inadvisable for him to be the vice-presidential candidate. He praised Kennedy's talents, assuring him that he had "a unique and promising future in the Democratic Party."[90] LBJ asked the attorney general to help in the coming campaign. When Kennedy refused to issue a public statement withdrawing from the race, Johnson was forced to take action. At a televised press conference on July 30, the president, using the formula suggested by elder statesman Clark Clifford, announced that he did not intend to consider as vice-presidential possibilities any of his present cabinet members or any of those who met regularly with the cabinet. Kennedy later joked that he was "sorry [he] took so many nice fellows over the side with me."[91]

Johnson was not generous toward his adversary. He later gloated to reporters that when Kennedy received the bad news, he gulped, "his Adam's apple going up and down like a Yo-Yo." Johnson gulped himself to illustrate the point.[92] To avoid igniting pro-Kennedy sentiment at the convention, moreover, he induced the arrangements committee to postpone a memorial film about JFK, to be introduced by Bobby, until after the vice-presidential nomination, when it could do no harm.

With the Kennedy matter solved, Johnson hoped for a convention that would be completely under his control, from the program arrangements to the content of the party platform. He looked forward to a love feast and a grand party consensus. Yet the Johnson melancholia once more asserted itself. With a nomination and then electoral victory as certain as anything can be in politics, he told Lady Bird that he was considering withdrawing from the race. In fact, in John Connally's words, "there was about as much chance of him withdrawing in 1964 as there was for a snow storm in Panama."[93] But even if, in his heart of hearts, he did not feel these doubts, he *did* want to win big, bigger than Roosevelt. Only that would appease his ego.

Johnson would not get the harmonious convention he craved. That spring, Operation Freedom Summer had drawn hundreds of young civil rights workers to Mississippi, the heart of Dixie darkness, to register black voters for the fall campaign. Three of them, two whites—Andrew Goodman and Michael Schwerner—and one black—James Cheney—disappeared in June and were feared murdered by Klansmen. Johnson asked his friend FBI director J. Edgar Hoover to saturate the state with agents to find the missing young activists and arrest the perpetrators. On

August 4 the FBI found the bullet-ridden bodies of the three missing civil rights workers buried in an earthen dam in Philadelphia, Mississippi. Meanwhile, other activists in the state had established the Mississippi Freedom Democratic Party (MFDP) and, in extralegal "freedom primaries," had elected state delegates to the forthcoming national convention.

Although they had no legal case, the Mississippi insurgents asked the Democratic credentials committee in Atlantic City to seat them rather than the "Jim Crow regulars." At preconvention hearings, middle-aged sharecropper Fanny Lou Hamer, beaten mercilessly by whites for trying to vote, argued eloquently that the MFDP was the group that most closely supported Johnson's beliefs and programs and therefore, official or not, deserved to be recognized. Johnson faced a dilemma. Most of the Mississippi regulars would probably cross party lines and vote for Goldwater in November, but Johnson could not support their expulsion without antagonizing the rest of the South. Liberal Democrats, however, demanded that at least half of the MFDP delegates be seated. If the credentials committee rejected this formula, the liberals had sufficient strength to bring a minority report to the convention floor.

Knowing as we do the outcome of the election, we cannot see it as a close call. But Johnson professed to be worried. On August 9 he called Walter Reuther to chastise him and Hubert Humphrey for allowing the MFDP and its counsel, Joe Rauh, to disrupt the convention. "The only thing that can screw us good is to seat that group of challengers from Mississippi," he told the UAW president. "There's not a damn vote that we get by seating those folks."[94] Five days later, with the issue still unresolved, he warned Humphrey of the strength of the John Birch Society and Goldwater in the South and of how seating the MFDP could be a disaster. "So this is an extremely dangerous election. Now the thing that makes it more dangerous than anything else—I am telling you, if I know anything I know this—if we mess with a group of Negroes that were elected to nothing, that met in hotel room . . . and throw out the Governor and elected officials of the state [of Mississippi]—if we mess with them, we will lose fifteen states without even campaigning." "Why in the living hell," he asked Humphrey, "do they [the black leaders] want to hand . . . Goldwater fifteen states?"[95]

Though he had stamped his ticket for civil rights, Johnson had no use for militants, and certainly not those who threatened his own goals. In the interest of a peaceful convention the president ordered the FBI to keep close watch on the doings of the MFDP and the contingents of SNCC and CORE activists in Atlantic City. Under Hoover's lieutenant, Cartha DeLoach, black FBI agents infiltrated the MFDP's strategy meetings in the basement of the Union Baptist Temple, and tapped the phones at CORE and SNCC headquarters. DeLoach later confessed that it was a mistake for the FBI to have "accepted the assignment in the first place. . . . At best it was demeaning; at worst it was a serious breach of the law."[96] Johnson's response was obviously excessive but it accurately expressed his fears and self-doubts.

The Democratic National Convention officially opened on Monday, August 24, in Atlantic City, New Jersey, a gaudy seaside resort with once-elegant, now seedy, grand hotels, and a honky-tonk, fast-food, souvenir-shop-lined six-mile boardwalk. Though determined to reject the activists' demands, Johnson secretly helped negotiate the compromise scheme that Humphrey, Reuther, and black leaders Martin Luther King Jr., Bayard Rustin, and James Farmer finally thrashed out. Two MFDP leaders would be chosen as delegates at large with full voting rights; the rest of the Freedom Party delegates would sit on the convention floor as "honored guests." The regular Mississippi delegates, meanwhile, would be seated only if they pledged allegiance to the national ticket. In addition, in 1968, four years hence, and at each national convention thereafter, the party would reject delegations from states that based voting on race or color.

Militant black leaders considered the scheme a sellout and demanded its rejection. Joe Rauh opposed the compromise, too, but could not withstand the pressure to make a deal. Reuther, whose UAW Rauh represented in Washington, told Rauh that if the arrangement failed, Johnson might lose the election. Rauh was amazed. "Are you serious?" he responded. "Goldwater has been nominated! How can you lose it?"[97] The president himself kept threatening to reject the nomination if the squabble was not settled through a compromise. "I'm just about ready to sign off," he told press secretary George Reedy.[98] Though skeptical, Rauh yielded, and eventually concluded it was not a bad arrangement. In the end, the convention accepted the compromise plan and seated two Freedom Party delegates. The battle left a residue of resentment, however. Most of the regulars from Alabama and Mississippi refused to sign the pledge and walked out. For their part, many civil rights workers were offended by the administration's half a loaf. Their disappointment and sense of betrayal by Johnson and the Democrats would accelerate the growing militancy of younger civil rights workers that marked the rest of the decade.

Meanwhile, the final vice-presidential choice hung fire. Johnson had tried to create suspense by not revealing his running mate until the last possible moment. In fact he had probably settled on Humphrey long before. The president considered Humphrey unstable and a blabbermouth and was not certain he could be relied on not to hurt the administration. To reassure himself, in late July he asked aide James Rowe, a Humphrey partisan, to extract from the senator an ironclad loyalty oath. Humphrey would have "to go all the way" with LBJ on his platform, views, and policies. Johnson promised to listen to his vice president's opinions. But he didn't "want to have to kiss the ass of a vice president." An hour later, after Rowe had reported back to Humphrey, the senator himself called the White House to give the required pledge. "I can assure you—unqualifiedly, personally, and with all the sincerity in my heart," he told Johnson, that he had his "complete loyalty." "And that goes for everything," he added. "All the way . . . right to the end of the line."[99]

But as the convention approached, Johnson played games, leaking other names besides Humphrey's, some plausible, some preposterous, for the sake of sustaining suspense. In the end the public front-runners were the two senators from Minnesota, Humphrey and Eugene McCarthy, and Senator Thomas Dodd of Connecticut. McCarthy and Dodd, both Catholics, could presumably provide religious balance for the ticket. Concluding that Johnson had Humphrey in mind all along and was merely using him, McCarthy withdrew his name from consideration. Dodd was never a serious contender; he was on the list merely to heighten the drama. On August 26 the president had Humphrey and Dodd fly down to Washington from the convention. He spoke to both men in the Oval Office and finally told Humphrey that he was "it." The grateful senator reiterated his loyalty. The two men then strolled out to the White House grounds and announced the decision to waiting reporters.

That Wednesday evening, as Johnson winged his way to Atlantic City, a roaring crowd of delegates nominated him by acclamation. Upon landing, the nominee announced his choice of Humphrey as his running mate. On Thursday the president and the TV public watched the outpouring of love for the Kennedys at the convention that he had anticipated and feared. Bobby was cheered for an astounding twenty-two minutes as he stepped to the podium to introduce a film, *The Thousand Days*, poignantly recounting his martyred brother's three years in the White House. Johnson himself could not excite equal enthusiasm. After Humphrey's rousing acceptance speech, the president's own seemed lackluster—flat and too long. The gala to celebrate his fifty-sixth birthday, however, lifted his mood. At a Texas-style celebration atop the convention hall, guests, paying a thousand dollars apiece, could nibble hors d'oeuvres, gawk at a giant red, white, and blue map of the United States cake, watch ethnic singers and dancers perform, and sing "Happy Birthday" to the birthday boy. The proceedings were televised and a national audience viewed the president cutting his cake, taking a big slice for himself, and swallowing every crumb. Meanwhile, on the beach outside the hall, pyrotechnists fired off three tons of rockets and Roman candles. The spectacular birthday party seemed a fitting climax to Johnson's time of glory. "I've been going to conventions since 1928," Johnson pronounced, "and this one is the best of all."[100]

Johnson started with the advantage of incumbency, and every presidential deed or remark reported in the media was campaign fodder. At first he stayed off the campaign trail, but by the end of September he was itching to do battle.

Johnson launched his active campaign on September 28 as a whistle-stop tour through New England. Deep in Kennedy country, he got as enthusiastic a response as he could have wished. The crowds were "so thick and friendly," Jack Valenti reported, that it was like "trying to pull your way through a big mass of molasses. . . ."[101] It was the delirious New England reception, Valenti claims, that provided the first inkling that a landslide victory was in the making. From then on, the travels were nonstop. All told, Johnson spent forty-two days on the stump, covered more than sixty thousand miles, and made almost two hundred speeches. He shook so many hands that his own right hand was soon swollen and bleeding. He gave many awkward "Mr. President" speeches to stuffy audiences. But when he let down his hair, he hit his stride. His cornpone style was well suited to the 1964 campaign. As his motorcade wound through the streets of a town, he stopped the car. "Come on, folks," he would call from his limousine through a bullhorn. "Come on down to the speakin'. You don't have to dress. Just bring your children and dogs, anything you have with you. It won't take long. You'll be back in time to put the kids in bed." A few blocks farther, he would stop again and repeat the routine. When the crowd had assembled at the designated place, the president regaled them with his Great Society programs, reminisced about his colorful ancestors and his boyhood in Texas, and related amusing political stories.[102] His frenetic campaign pace did not derive from fear of losing to Goldwater; he just wanted the biggest margin of victory in American presidential history.

From the outset Johnson enjoyed a huge lead over his opponent. The president had won the public's heart with his dignified and calming behavior after the assassination. His decisive action during the Eighty-eighth Congress on the stalled domestic legislation of his predecessor further enhanced his image. The public agreed with the conclusion reached by Harry McPherson, reminiscing after Johnson left the White House: "However history gets redone, nothing can redo the fantastically competent job . . . the superb job he did in those early months."[103] The times were with him, moreover. His Great Society, still rudimentary, suited the generous, compassionate mood of middle-class voters. The civil rights issue was still working for him, though attitudes toward race were beginning to change and would not remain an asset for long. And then there was prosperity. The economy was booming, never a bad circumstance for an incumbent seeking reelection.

Goldwater's political extremism contributed to Johnson's decisive lead from the outset. The Republican National Convention at San Francisco had left the Grand Old Party seething with resentments. When Governor Nelson Rockefeller of New York denounced extremists at the Cow Palace as "kooks," he had been booed and hissed by Goldwater supporters. Then, in his acceptance speech, Goldwater had refused to reach out to his opponents. "Extremism in the defense of liberty," he had declared, was "no vice! [And] . . . moderation in the pursuit of justice" was "no virtue!"[104]

The Republican candidate, however amiable a man, went into the campaign weighed down by a huge load of negatives. Just before the Republican convention, he had voted against the civil rights bill, and later, while the newly minted nominee, would vote against the Economic Opportunity Act. Over the years Goldwater had offended organized labor, Social Security pensioners, and friends of public power. Most damaging was his apparent willingness to use nuclear weapons to achieve his foreign policy objectives. "When you say 'nuclear,'" Goldwater had explained, "all the American people see is a mushroom cloud. But for military purposes, it's just enough firepower to get the job done."[105]

Outside a few pockets where the John Birch Society and the White Citizens' Councils flourished, even the Republican press favored Johnson in 1964. Only three big-city newspapers supported Goldwater, and the usually Republican popular magazines *Life* and the *Saturday Evening Post* came out for Johnson. The *Post* castigated Goldwater as a "grotesque burlesque of the conservative he pretends to be. He is a wild man. . . ."[106] Even big business supported Johnson. A committee of business leaders, including auto magnate Henry Ford II, Joseph Block of Inland Steel, and Edgar Kaiser of Kaiser Aluminum, worked for Johnson's election and collected millions from some of the country's major corporations for his campaign. Every sector in America except the hard-core right would be going "all the way with LBJ." Johnson, it appeared, would get something close to his precious consensus.

On the campaign trail Goldwater continued to be his own worst enemy. "Every time Barry opened his mouth," bemoaned a liberal Republican, "he was campaigning for Lyndon."[107] As damaging as the pronunciamentos themselves were the places where he delivered them. The Republican candidate attacked Social Security in the retirement haven of St. Petersburg, Florida; he condemned the poverty campaign in impoverished West Virginia; he denounced cotton subsidies in Memphis, home of the Cotton Exchange. As the campaign advanced, the Republican candidate began to back off from some of his more extreme remarks. But it was too late to reverse his image, especially the public's perception of him as a trigger-happy warmonger. The gleeful Democrats used his more outrageous utterances for their own benefit. One Democratic campaign sticker read "Goldwater for Halloween." Another proclaimed "Vote for Goldwater and Go to War." A notorious Johnson-Humphrey TV commercial, aired once and then withdrawn, showed a little girl picking petals from a daisy while in the background a nuclear countdown is heard. After the bomb detonates and the mushroom cloud emerges, Johnson's voice is heard intoning: "These are the stakes. To make a world in which all of God's children can live, or go into the dark. We must either love each other or we must die."[108]

Yet Goldwater had a few cards of his own to play. The public still perceived LBJ as a wheeler-dealer who had derived great wealth from the government-regulated communications industry and had associated with shady political operators. To stave off a Goldwater charge that Lyndon had used his public office to build his fortune, Abe Fortas hired the well-regarded accounting firm of Haskins and Sells to do an audit. This placed Johnson's holdings at a relatively modest $3.3 million. The Republican national chairman called the Haskins and Sells figure "incredibly low," like "New York listing the value of Manhattan Island at $24."[109] But since no evidence of malfeasance was found, Goldwater dropped the matter in his campaign.

But the Republican candidate may have gotten more mileage out of the corrupt associates charge. The Arizonan lashed out again and again on the ethics issue, accusing Johnson of disreputable friends and shady morals. "To Lyndon Johnson, running a country means . . . buying and bludgeoning votes."[110] Goldwater raked up charges that his opponent had used Bobby Baker's connections for personal gain. He also charged that Johnson had invested in a number of business deals with Billy Sol Estes, a freewheeling Texas entrepreneur who had illegally parlayed the federal agricultural price support programs into a fortune. In fact, Johnson had accepted minor financial support from Estes during his 1954 reelection bid and had welcomed his help during the 1960 vice-presidential campaign, but their relationship had been tenuous, and a House subcommittee had found no evidence that Johnson or his associates had helped Billy Sol's West Texas agricultural empire. As for Bobby Baker, Johnson had already repudiated his old friend, but it helped that the Senate deferred hearings on the case until after the election. Though the Republicans undoubtedly scored some points on the ethics issue, Johnson's poll ratings remained high.

Johnson feared repudiation in the South, his own section, because of the Civil Rights Act. To assuage regional feelings he dispatched Lady Bird and a contingent of southern ladies, wives of Democratic officials, on a whistle-stop tour through Dixie to remind Southerners that the Democratic presidential candidate was one of their own. In early October the *Lady Bird Special*, consisting of two communications cars, six Pullman sleepers, and two dining cars, left Alexandria, Virginia, for New Orleans, sixteen hundred miles away. The president himself joined the ladies at Raleigh and then got off, only to meet them once more at their New Orleans terminus.

The one truly jarring event of the campaign occurred on October 7, when the Washington, D.C., police arrested Walter Jenkins, one of the president's most trusted aides, in a YMCA bathroom on a charge of disorderly conduct, a euphemism for homosexual activities. The forty-six-year-old Jenkins, father of six children, one named Lyndon, was a friend and confidant of the entire Johnson family and privy to all of the most private twists and turns of Johnson's life. Abe Fortas and Clark Clifford tried to get each of the three Washington dailies to bury the incident on compassionate grounds. Jenkins had suffered a "nervous breakdown," would be going to the hospital for a rest, and would resign his position, they said. The Washington editors agreed to sit on the item, but after reporters learned of a similar arrest incident in 1959, the less merciful United Press sent the story out over its wires. In the middle of a presidential campaign, the news that an aide who knew all the White House secrets might be open to blackmail became an instant campaign threat.

Johnson was flabbergasted when he heard of Jenkins's mishap. "I just swear I can't believe this," he exclaimed to Abe Fortas. In a phone call to her husband campaigning in New York, Lady Bird, a kind woman who put human relations before expediency, urged the president to find a job for Jenkins at KTCB. She, meanwhile, would make a public statement of sympathy to the Jenkins family. Johnson, who often reversed her priorities, tried to warn her off, but Lady Bird persisted. "If we don't express some support to him . . . we will lose the entire love and devotion of all the people who have been with us," she told him.[111] Lady Bird made her sympathy statement, and it was politically wiser than silence or harsh repudiation of the president's old friend. Johnson told Jenkins to resign but refused to condemn him publicly. A week later the FBI cleared Jenkins of posing any threat to "the security or interests of the United States in any manner."[112] Fortunately, the ouster the next day of Nikita Khrushchev as leader of the Soviet Union grabbed the nation's headlines and buried the Jenkins affair in the back pages.

Johnson's finest campaign moment came soon after the Jenkins incident. On October 9, at the Jung Hotel in New Orleans, he boldly faced the racist lion in its own den. In a rambling speech to a Democratic fund-raiser, he appealed to the South's regional pride and latent populism. For decades Dixie had been distracted and weakened by division over race, he said. The recent Civil Rights Act had won two-thirds of the Democrats in Congress and three-quarters of the Republicans. The South must accept that decision. "I am not going to let them build up the hate and try to buy people by appealing to their prejudice." In a flashback to the populism of his youth, he then recounted what an old southern senator had told Sam Rayburn years before. The veteran politician remarked how race in effect had kept the South from acknowledging its real enemies, the corporate exploiters, and how he "would like to go back down there and make one more Democratic speech. . . . Poor old state, they haven't heard a real Democratic speech in thirty years. All they ever hear at election time is nigra, nigra, nigra!"[113] The president got a five-minute standing ovation.

As Johnson anticipated, Goldwater tried to make an issue of foreign policy, especially Vietnam, where he claimed the United States was not being aggressive enough against the Communist enemy. The Kennedy-Johnson record in foreign policy, he charged, was one of "drift, deceptions, and defeat."[114] Johnson better understood the public mood. He portrayed Goldwater as a man of war and himself as a man of peace. He made extravagant statements about his intentions that would plague him later. At Manchester, New Hampshire, he told his audience that while "others are eager to enlarge the conflict by supplying American boys to do the job that Asian boys should do," that "action would offer no solution at all to the real problem of Vietnam."[115] He repeated versions of this promise at other places on the campaign trail. In the heat of the 1940 election campaign, Franklin Roosevelt had denied he would send American "boys . . . into any foreign wars." FDR had suffered no ill effects when America went to war in 1941. But that was World War II, a "good war." Vietnam was a "bad war," and Johnson's remarks would haunt him in the months ahead.

But the torments were still in the future. On November 2 LBJ and Lady Bird flew back home to Texas. Anticipating victory, he confided in an old friend: "It seems to me tonight that I have spent my whole life getting ready for this moment."[116] The next day, the Johnsons voted in Johnson City shortly after the polls opened. For the remainder of the day the president was fidgety and preoccupied. There was nothing else he could do to affect the results; waiting was his only option. The Johnsons went back to Austin for dinner at the Driskill Hotel, the site of so many important events in the president's political life. They watched some early returns and then attended the reception of old friend John Connally at the Governor's Mansion. By now, the outcome was clear, and the Johnsons and their daughters went to Austin's Municipal Auditorium, where the band was playing "The Eyes of Texas Are Upon You." Thousands of cheering people awaited his victory statement.

Lyndon Baines Johnson achieved one of the greatest electoral sweeps in American history. He received more than 61 percent of the popular vote and the largest electoral vote ever, except for FDR's in 1936. Best of all, the Eighty-ninth Congress would have the biggest Democratic majority in both houses since the New Deal era. Many of the freshman congressmen had traveled to victory on Lyndon Johnson's coattails, and they would surely remember their debt to the president. For Johnson it was extraordinary ego balm. "It was," he told biographer Doris Kearns, "a night I shall never forget. Millions upon millions of people, each one marking my name on their ballot, each one wanting me as their president. . . . For the first time in all my life I truly felt loved by the American people."[117]

It now remained to be seen whether this landslide could be translated into a legislative program equal to its extraordinary dimensions.

CHAPTER 17

High Water

BASKING IN HIS SPECTACULAR NOVEMBER TRIUMPH, Johnson spent the rest of 1964 relaxing on the Ranch with Lady Bird while taking short trips to Washington. On November 17 the Johnsons were back in Washington, where they celebrated their thirtieth wedding anniversary. The president surprised his wife with a twelve-pound sponge cake, adorned with entwined wedding rings, yellow sugar roses, white sugar doves, and nine photographs. The main picture had been taken on their honeymoon and showed the smiling young Johnsons standing on a Mexican-type gondola in the floating gardens at Lake Xochimilco with Lady Bird carrying a bouquet of flowers. On December 18 the Johnsons were back at the White House where, with a flick of a switch, the president lit the nation's Christmas tree, bedecked with five thousand red and white bulbs, and predicted that a new star was rising in the sky, "the star of peace." Standing coatless in the twenty-five-degree temperature, he said that the brightness of the lights expressed "the hopefulness of these times."[1]

This should have been an exhilarating period for Johnson. He had fulfilled his highest political ambition, and the only constituencies left were posterity and the historians. Yet even now Johnson could not be happy. He was beginning his new term with advantages that few presidents had enjoyed before, but he feared that his edge could quickly dull. He was determined not to waste his mandate, as FDR had done after the stunning victory in 1936 when he tried to pack the Supreme Court. LBJ knew that both the public and Congress would not hesitate to attack as soon as he made a misstep. As he told a meeting of congressional liaison officers gathered in the Fish Room of the White House in January, he had to move fast. "Now, look," HEW's Wilbur Cohen would report his words, "I've just been reelected [sic] by the overwhelming majority and I just want to tell you that every day while I'm in office, I'm going to lose votes. I'm going to alienate somebody."[2] He predicted, with tragic accuracy in this case, that something would come up, "either something like the Vietnam War or something else where I will begin to lose all that I have now. . . . So, I want you guys," he exhorted, "to get off your asses and do everything possible to get everything in my program passed as soon as possible, before the aura and the halo that surround me disappear. Don't waste a second. Get going *right now*. . . ."[3] Johnson would make similar cautionary statements to a dozen other groups.

And he was not only uncertain of his power and his reputation; he was unsure of his very existence. Would he survive a full term, given his medical history? There would be a quality of urgency about the Johnson legislative program during the Eighty-ninth Congress that can only be explained by a subconscious fear of early death. Johnson would be accused with reason of pushing new laws out the congressional door in half-digested form without due regard for their administration and proper enforcement. The process would undermine his political support and diminish his historical reputation. It is easy to believe that his judgment was impaired by something more elemental than a calculation of political ebbs and flows.

Johnson could count on one of the most efficient legislative machines of any president. His chief of liaison with Congress was Larry O'Brien, a Massachusetts publicist who had worked the Hill for Kennedy and been induced to stay on after the assassination. O'Brien and his chief aides—Mike Manatos for the Senate and Henry Hall Wilson for the House—were extraordinary salesmen for the Great Society. They spent hours in congressmen's offices, on the phone, in bars and restaurants, sweet-talking holdouts. They counted votes to see where the weak spots were on vital roll calls. O'Brien often reported the status of legislation to the cabinet and scolded department heads when they seemed not to "be moving that bill."[4] The president himself, of course, was a legislative phenomenon. Few congressmen could withstand the famous treatment of cajolery, moral blackmail, physical intimidation, and bulldog persistence. In his persuasive role Johnson was often described as a force of nature, irresistible in its power to move even the most firmly planted objects. Lee White, special counsel to the president from 1965 to 1966, described him as a "pit-bull terrier" when it came to legislation. "It didn't make a darn bit of difference what else came along on his radar screen. If he had a piece of legislation that was important in front of him, that's what he focused on."[5] Johnson also understood the constituent pressures on members of Congress and the need to recompense them for helping him, especially when that help entailed taking an unpopular stand in their districts.

And the president drove his subordinates ruthlessly to keep the bills rolling. Wilbur Cohen recalled an occasion in April 1965 when he and O'Brien were in majority leader Mike Mansfield's office just off the Senate floor, pushing hard to get some more bills through the congressional mill before the Easter recess. "Larry and I sat in Mansfield's office and we alternately kind of laughed and commiserated with one another on the business of getting more bills passed that afternoon." Johnson called and spoke to O'Brien. The President plaintively asked: "Well, can't you get another one or two yet this afternoon?" And Larry said: "No, I think we've done as much, Mr. President, as we can."[6]

No one worked nine to five at the White House; they had to be ready to serve the president at any time. As in the days when he had been Congressman Kleberg's legislative aide, Johnson demanded utter dedication from the people who worked for him.

Some presidential aides would recall working with LBJ as an ordeal. Harry McPherson said Johnson had a talent for malicious mimicry that he wielded against selected people. His outspoken press secretary, George Reedy, was one of his chief targets. It was also hard to deal with LBJ's ego and energy. As McPherson remembered, "He sucked all the air out of the room" when he entered. His insensitivity often backfired. As the end of his administration approached, Johnson tried to talk McPherson into returning to Austin to run simultaneously the LBJ Presidential Library, the Johnson School of Public Affairs, and the Johnson TV station. Knowing the president's "relentlessness," McPherson declined.[7] Yet others would downplay Johnson's tyrannical behavior. Douglass Cater, who became a Johnson "idea man" in 1964 and stayed on as the White House expert on education and health issues, admitted that LBJ "burst out sometimes." But "Big Daddy could beat you one moment and hug you and invite you in to eat. I read about other presidents whose aides never had a meal with them. Hell, it was hard to avoid a meal with Lyndon Johnson."[8] He could also be incredibly generous. Reedy, who acknowledged that LBJ had a cheap streak, also noted in wonder, "Why, the guy gave me a brand-new Lincoln car!"[9]

Nothing, however, helped Johnson get his legislative program through Congress as much as the electoral triumph of November 1964. According to O'Brien, who had keenly felt the frustration and failure under Kennedy, "it was Johnson's landslide . . . that turned the tide. . . . The President had a mandate."[10]

As was true of the War on Poverty bill, much of the Great Society legislation of the Eighty-ninth Congress originated in task forces, men and women with expert knowledge in relevant fields who closely studied the issue at hand—health care, education, environment, recreation, urban blight—and proposed remedial legislation. Johnson created fifteen task forces in 1964 and another twenty-seven from 1965 to 1968. Their deliberations were private to avoid the intrusion of partisan politics, an approach that opponents would later criticize.

Johnson wasted no time outlining his legislative agenda. On January 4 he gave his second State of the Union address before a joint session of the House and the Senate. No one present could fail to remember the previous year, when he had spoken to Congress in the shadow of his slain predecessor. This time, the speech, interrupted by waves of applause, did not mention Kennedy once in its four thousand words. It emphasized, as had the May 1964 Ann Arbor address, how the daily lives of America's people could be enhanced. "We seek," he declared, "to establish a harmony between man and society which will allow each of us to enlarge the meaning of his life and all of us to elevate the quality of our civilization."[11] He described the task as threefold: keeping the economy growing, opening opportunities for all Americans, and improving the texture of life for all.

Consistent with his profound faith in education, he proposed to spend $1.5 billion to help every student at "every stage along the road to learning," from preschool through college. Since "greatness require[d] not only an educated people but [also] a healthy people," he endorsed new medical research, improved health care for poor children, regional medical centers providing advanced diagnosis and treatment, new support for medical and dental education, and community centers for the mentally ill. To elevate city life he asked for a cabinet department of housing and urban development. Crime could be controlled through the training of local enforcement officers and by putting the latest scientific techniques at their disposal.

A more beautiful America was also part of his dream, a goal that Mrs. Johnson soon made her First Lady's project. He envisioned preserving a "green legacy" for America's children. Along with conservation and the reduction of air and water pollution, he wanted "more large and small parks, more seashores and open spaces than have been created during any period in our history." To encourage creative achievements he proposed a national foundation for the arts, which would include federal grants to promote music, theater, and dance, and funds for museums. He promised to stimulate basic science by strengthening university programs. And for government to be able to "serve these goals" it would need to be "modern in structure, efficient in action, and ready for any emergency." To appease the cheeseparers, Johnson promised: "Wherever waste is found I will eliminate it."

In the speech's foreign affairs section he suggested that Soviet leaders visit the United States to learn about it firsthand and proposed that they and their American counterparts appear on television in their respective countries. He professed "special ties of interest and affection" for the free republics of Latin America and promised to strengthen these ties as well as to increase U.S. commitment to the Alliance for Progress. In regard to Vietnam, he noted that there "Communism wears a more aggressive face." He justified the American presence in Southeast Asia on the grounds that "a friendly nation" had asked for our help, that we had pledged our help, and that three presidents had supported that pledge. With no hint of just how much it would cost him, he vowed, "We will not break it now."[12]

According to the *Washington Post*, Congress was amazed by the speech. LBJ had asked for more than any president in the past. Liberals were pleased; even Pennsylvania senator Joseph Clark, usually skeptical of Johnson's actions, praised it highly. Conservatives inevitably thought it promised too much and worried about the costs. Senator Dirksen described it as "a glowing blueprint for paradise." Its weakness, he said, "was that it undertakes to redress every need both foreign and domestic. . . ." But a moderate Democrat, Senator Vance Hartke of Indiana, summed up the feelings of much of the congressional majority. The "President's hand is on the pulse of America," he declared. "He knows our past intimately and sees our future clearly."[13]

The 1965 State of the Union message was not just rousing words. Johnson meant business. Three days later he sent Congress a message called "Advancing the Nation's Health," which proposed hospital care for the aged under Social Security as a top priority, along with a plan for regional health centers to provide everyone with access to modern medicine. On January 13 he submitted his education message, asking for $1.5 billion in federal aid to education, with children in low-income families the first priority. His program, which also included expanded college scholarships and money for supplemental educational services, including remedial reading clinics and psychologists, would furnish aid at every level, from preschool to graduate school.

The next day he asked Congress to enact a new immigration bill designed to eliminate the bigoted national origins quota system devised under the Johnson-Reed Act of 1924. Admission to the United States would now be based on skills and family ties rather than race, nationality, and ethnicity.

Johnson's focus in these opening days of his full term was decidedly domestic. On January 18, a columnist for the *Washington Post* called LBJ's foreign policy agenda a "holding operation." LBJ backpedaled on a multilateral nuclear force. He did not recommend solving the troubles of the Atlantic Alliance, he planned to curtail foreign aid, and he expected to carry on the struggle in Vietnam at its existing levels. "The presidential tone," wrote Chalmers M. Roberts, the *Washington Post's* chief diplomatic correspondent, ". . . sounds like a pullback from the activist period of American world interest during the Kennedy years. . . . [T]here is a sense of withdrawal in the air."[14]

Two days before the inauguration, Johnson's approval rating rose to 69 percent. A Harris survey reported people's favorable impressions derived from what they saw as LBJ's "friendly, warm personality," his ability to work hard, and his intelligence. Many regarded him as "straightforward and vigorous" and "a good family man." Only a small percentage considered him a "wheeler-dealer" or thought he was "too corny."[15]

By this time visitors were streaming into Washington to become part of the biggest inaugural jamboree in the nation's history. Two hundred thousand people were invited to join in the various inaugural festivities, including all the Johnson relatives and Lynda and Luci's teenage friends from Texas. The Pennsylvania Railroad planned to run thirteen special trains to the capital from Philadelphia alone. Twenty-two information booths were set up at Washington area hotels, motels, and transportation centers. And a record-breaking crowd of 1.2 million lined up, forty deep at some spots, on the partly sunny, cold day along Pennsylvania Avenue and at the Capitol to watch the inaugural parade. At the swearing-in ceremony itself Lady Bird, at the suggestion of her husband, held Rebekah Johnson's Bible, on which LBJ placed his hand for the oath of office.

The president later said he enjoyed every minute of the inaugural round and danced his way through all the balls, singling out for partners the wives of representatives and senators whose votes he wanted for his Great Society programs. His last stop was the ball at the Sheraton-Hilton, where he danced exclusively with ladies from Texas. When he left the hotel he admonished the celebrants: "Don't stay up late. We're on our way to the Great Society."[16]

By the beginning of February, the Eighty-ninth Congress was in furious motion. The Senate had already passed bills to help Appalachia, fight water pollution, and implement the international coffee agreement. The House at the same time was working on Medicare and aid to education.

Meanwhile, the very disaster that Johnson feared was in the making. In the previous months, as fall gave way to winter, Vietnam was entering a crisis phase that the administration could not ignore. South Vietnam had not stabilized after Diem's assassination. Rather, the country had experienced a violent succession of military juntas and strongmen, each fecklessly seeking to consolidate his power and unify the country. By the early fall of 1964 mobs were rampaging through the streets of Saigon, Buddhists and Catholics were once more at each other's throats, and criminal gangs were attacking innocent citizens.

At this moment of decision Johnson had three choices in Southeast Asia. One was a Munich-like withdrawal. The second was a limited war of restrained military action confined primarily to the South. The third was an all-out war, including bombing every North Vietnamese target available and, if needed, a ground troop invasion of the North. An appeasement policy was not conceivable to a man who had been an ardent interventionist during the late 1930s. All-out war promised to generate massive domestic opposition, cost too much, and risk drawing the Chinese and the Soviets into the conflict and possibly escalate into World War III. Faced with these alternatives, Johnson chose the middle-of-the-road policy, "graduated pressure" that would match the level of American response to the reaction of the enemy, though with a lid on the whole. The danger here was stalemate, and, of course, this is the very outcome that ensued.

Experience as well as expediency may have inspired the limited-war policy. During the October 1962 Cuban missile crisis, Johnson had attended the Ex Comm meetings where Kennedy had decided to defer a military attack on Cuba in favor of a naval blockade. Only if the "quarantine" failed, the president had concluded, would the United States launch air and ground attacks against the Communist installations. And, of course, the strategy had worked: Khrushchev had withdrawn the missiles without American air attacks or invasion. The success of gradual escalation in Cuba had impressed Johnson and, more significantly, perhaps, had persuaded his closest advisers on Vietnam, Secretaries McNamara and Rusk and national security adviser MacGeorge Bundy, all three active members of Ex Comm.

But if Johnson rejected the "victory" option, he did so over the opposition of most of his military advisers. As military historian R. H. McMaster has recently claimed, Johnson "brought with him to the presidency a low opinion of the nation's top military men."[17] He thought most of them were little better than air force general Curtis LeMay, who would suggest bombing Vietnam "back to the stone age." He believed he understood better than any of them, including the Joint Chiefs of Staff, that achieving American ends in Vietnam did not require invading North Vietnam or deploying nuclear weapons.

It has been said that limited war was the sure formula for failure. It is the hardest to fight, especially by a democracy, for it requires a degree of patience that the voters, and especially American voters, do not have. It was also unsuited to Johnson's own temperament. George C. Herring has written that Johnson was "a restless and impatient man waging war against an enemy who thought in terms of years, not days, centuries, not decades."[18] And yet it is hard to believe that a "victory" strategy would not have been a still worse disaster, one that would indeed have precipitated a major war between the two Cold War blocs. What we are left with is choice one, then: withdrawal from Vietnam. That would have been for the best, after all, as most of us now believe. But no one in the White House in early 1965 foresaw the road to hell that stretched ahead.

The Vietnam entrapment accelerated in the months following the presidential election. On November 30 General Maxwell Taylor, Henry Cabot Lodge's replacement as U.S. ambassador in South Vietnam, took off for Washington after declaring, "I'm going to recommend to the president that we put American troops in this country."[19] Taylor's views still seemed extreme at this point, but the administration did agree to step up intelligence patrols along the North Vietnamese coast, to be followed by escalating air strikes first against guerrilla infiltration routes and then direct bombing raids against North Vietnam. Fear of encouraging further disruption delayed this scheme. But the political situation in South Vietnam soon grew worse. By late January a group of younger South Vietnamese military men, led by Air Marshal Nguyen Cao Ky and General Nguyen Chanh Thi, had staged another coup, which destabilized the country further. Soon after the takeover, five thousand rampaging students trashed the United States Information Service library in Hue. Growing anti-American sentiment raised fears that the Saigon government might begin to negotiate with the Communists and, in effect, surrender. In a memo of January 27, McGeorge Bundy and McNamara told the president that current American policy of waiting for "a stable government" in South Vietnam could "lead only to disastrous defeat." The United States could either use its "military power in the Far East . . . to force a change in Communist policy" or it could "deploy all . . . [its] resources along the track of negotiation, aiming at salvaging what little can be preserved with no major addition to our present military risks."[20] Both men noted that they personally favored the first option—using military power.

Before taking action, Johnson sent Mac Bundy to Vietnam for further reconnaissance. On February 7, three days into the national security adviser's visit, the Vietcong attacked the South Vietnamese army headquarters and the U.S. Air Force base and barracks at Pleiku, 240 miles north of Saigon. Eight Americans were killed and more than a hundred wounded. Bundy phoned his boss to urge retaliation against the Communists, and Johnson immediately ordered American planes to attack North Vietnamese military installations across the seventeenth parallel. The Flaming Dart reprisal attacks were soon repeated in response to a Vietcong assault on a U.S. barracks at Qui Nhon.

Back in Washington, Bundy recommended transforming the retaliatory strike into a program of "graduated and sustained" bombing of North Vietnam. At a National Security Council meeting, with key congressional leaders present, Johnson approved the strategy as likely to defeat aggression "without escalating the war." But still doubtful, he invited former president Eisenhower to meet with him and his advisers at the White House to consider what to do. Meanwhile, Vice President Humphrey weighed in on February 15 with a memo to the president that foreshadowed much later criticism of the administration's Vietnam policy. Humphrey warned that the American public was "worried and confused" and would not support a massive intervention in Vietnam. Given the spectacular November election victory, it should be possible for the administration to risk attack from the right on Vietnam, the vice president declared. On the other hand, if the United States "embroiled deeper in fighting in the next six months," political opposition would "steadily mount" and cause serious damage to the rest of the administration's policies, including "socially humane and constructive policies generally."[21] George Ball also dissented, but Ike's conclusion that a bombing campaign could weaken Hanoi's resolve confirmed Johnson's decision. Bundy urged the president to announce the bombing decision publicly. He refused. With his Great Society programs moving steadily through the legislative mill, he did not want to distract Congress. And despite Humphrey's conclusion, he feared that calling attention to the bombing campaign would ignite the political right, which would then demand a far more aggressive approach.

On March 2, without fanfare, Johnson launched Operation Rolling Thunder. Targeted initially against Communist infiltration routes for men and supplies into the South, it spared Hanoi, Haiphong—the major North Vietnam port of entry—and other important targets in the North. Its chief purpose was to "send a message to Ho Chi Minh," not seriously damage North Vietnam and its offensive capacity. The military leaders considered it feeble and futile. As Admiral Thomas Moorer, commander of the Pacific Fleet, later remarked, "Ho Chi Minh never got the message."[22] Yet Johnson recognized the gravity of his decision, remarking lugubriously that "We've got a bear by the tail."[23]

Meanwhile, the president pressed ahead with the Great Society. In a special message to Congress on February 8 he called for measures to "rescue our cities and countryside from blight." We should landscape our highways, plant more trees, provide for more urban open spaces, better control air and water pollution, and remove unsightly auto junkyards close to major highways. Commenting that motor vehicles should not be permitted to "tyrannize the more leisurely human traffic," he asked for walking, hiking, horseback, and bicycle trails. He promised to include in his budget sufficient funds to start up the various beautification programs and to call a White House Conference on Natural Beauty for mid-May.[24]

On March 2 the president asked Congress for a new cabinet-level Department of Housing and Urban Development. Noting that "throughout man's history, the city has been at the center of civilization," Johnson said that the "modern city can be the most ruthless enemy of the good life, or it can be its servant. . . ." He identified the major problems of city life as those of "housing and education . . . increasing employment . . . ending poverty . . . and racial discrimination." These were of such "scope and magnitude" that only "representation at the highest level of government" would be able to solve them.[25]

In his recommendations for highway beautification, area redevelopment, and attention to the cities, the president, as we saw, was following an agenda created by the thinkers and social scientists of the new age of affluence. Education, however, was an old issue and a personal issue for Johnson. From the time he taught school in Cotulla, he considered education a magic engine to lift people out of poverty and improve their lives. Vice President Humphrey thought LBJ "was a nut on education . . . he . . . believed in it, just like some people believe in miracle cures."[26] But most Americans agreed with the president's view. It is a defining piece of American mythology that poverty, social inequality, racism, and crime can be expunged if everyone has access to good schooling. By the 1960s most Americans also agreed that the public schools were in crisis, beset by overcrowded classrooms, underpaid teachers, bad teaching, and a soaring pupil dropout rate. In 1964 the news that the armed services had to reject more than a quarter of all draftees because they were unable to read or write at the eighth-grade level seemed to confirm the terrible state of American schools.

The worst problems clearly occurred in poor neighborhoods, and it was widely assumed that inferior education was closely tied to lower expenditures per student. Since American public elementary and secondary schools were administered through thousands of local school districts and financed by a combination of state and local taxes, schools in wealthier districts and states were better funded than poor ones. Federal aid seemed the only way to smooth out the inequalities. "I knew," Johnson said, "that unless the federal government could step in and render necessary assistance, many American children would be doomed to inferior education, which presaged an empty future. Not only would those children suffer but so would their country."[27]

From Andrew Jackson on, American presidents had favored diverting federal money to local schools, but each attempt had foundered on one or more of three issues: racial segregation, local control of neighborhood schools, and the separation of church and state. By the opening of the Eighty-ninth Congress the segregation issue had been settled by Title VI of the Civil Rights Act of 1964, prohibiting racial discrimination in federally funded programs. But the other two remained.

The "religion of localism" in the finance and governance of the common schools was devoutly embraced by Americans. The twenty thousand or so local school districts appealed to American individualism and suspicion of big government, provided jobs for thousands of administrators, and suited rich suburbanites who could concentrate their tax money on the education of their own. Local control had the strong backing of the state boards of education, which feared federal intrusion into their bailiwicks.

An even tougher problem was religion. Catholics opposed federal aid to education if parochial schools were not cut in. But including the parochial school system stirred the ire of an ill-sorted alliance of secular liberals and conservative Protestants. Some Southern Protestant fundamentalists objected to aid to Catholic schools simply because they disliked Catholicism. Liberal Protestants and Jews, staunch defenders of the church-state separation principle, opposed aid to *any* parochial schools, including their own. President Kennedy, a Catholic, had, in 1961, tried to bypass the difficulty by proposing to confine aid to building classrooms and paying teachers' salaries. Many Catholics protested bitterly that the measure still discriminated against them. When this, and two subsequent measures, came to a vote in Congress, many northern Catholic Democrats joined with Republicans and Southerners, traditional enemies of federal aid to education, to shoot them down. It was necessary to find a formula that would circumvent the religious problem as well as reduce fears of federal intrusion and control.

In 1964 Johnson appointed a task force of businessmen and academics under the leadership of liberal Republican John Gardner, president of the Carnegie Foundation, to study the nation's educational needs and to recommend a way to break the impasse. At the same time, Francis Keppel, chosen head of the federal Office of Education by Kennedy and retained by Johnson; Secretary of Health, Education, and Welfare Anthony Celebrezze; Assistant Secretary Wilbur Cohen; and others were also working on possible solutions. The drafters held many meetings with educators, professional organizations, and religious groups to maximize support for federal aid and minimize their particular objections. The two chief antagonists to be reconciled were the National Education Association, the public school teachers' union, adamantly opposed to dividing the pot with the Catholic schools; and the National Catholic Welfare Conference, representing the Catholic hierarchy.

What finally worked was a scheme to provide benefits to poor *students*, without regard to religion, rather than to the schools themselves. This was not without precedent, since in 1947 the Supreme Court had decided that New Jersey could provide state funds for busing parochial school children because the money helped the students primarily. Kennedy refused to use this loophole because he thought a Catholic president would not be able to get away with it. Johnson, a Protestant, could afford to be more flexible. The breakthrough was, in Keppel's words, a plan where "money would go to the public schools but the services it purchased would be available to all pupils, no matter where they went to school, whether in public institutions or nonpublic. . . ."[28]

Introduced immediately following Johnson's January 12 special message, "Toward Full Educational Opportunity," the Elementary and Secondary Education Act (ESEA) had five titles. Title I, backed by the bulk of the funds, targeted "educationally deprived children" and authorized money for school districts on the basis of the number of children from families earning two thousand dollars or less or who were on public assistance. It was up to the districts themselves to choose the appropriate schools, and to the schools to choose the appropriate students. This local control would pacify people who worried about federal intervention. Title II provided money for library resources, textbooks, and instructional materials and would be made available to both public and parochial school children. This section contained the all-important compromise worked out between public and religious school educators that allowed the rest of the bill to proceed. Title III made provision for supplementary education centers to supply educational services and programs such as physical education and recreational facilities, remedial instruction, adult education, and educational counseling that were unavailable at local schools. Title IV funded regional education laboratories in universities. The last title appropriated funds to make state departments of education more efficient and sensitive to students' needs.

Hearings on the bill began in the House on January 22, with Secretary Celebrezze and Commissioner Keppel testifying that the legislation was designed to bring poor people into the economic mainstream by snapping the cycle of poverty. After them came a stream of friendly witnesses, mostly educators, school principals, and school superintendents. One member of the opposition charged that it seemed to be just a gravy train for school administrators. Some conservative witnesses were still opposed to federal aid to education on principle; some liberals felt the bill was not financially generous enough. Johnson plunged into the legislative process in February and March, coaxing and wheedling members of the powerful National Education Association and making his usual phone calls to legislators still on the fence. At one point, when a leading education subcommittee member, Democrat Edith Green of Oregon, a fierce champion of church-state separation, threatened to "jump the reservation," the president invited her to the White House for a chat and gave her a signed portrait of himself.[29] The House finally approved the bill on March 26.

Johnson hoped ESEA could be voted on by the Senate without amendment to avoid delay. It would be difficult, he knew, since, as Congress often joked, "if the House passed the Ten Commandments the Senate would amend this to provide either nine or eleven."[30] But the president got what he wanted. In the Senate, floor manager Wayne Morse, who would prove to be an implacable Johnson enemy over Vietnam, this time helped the administration by getting his colleagues to reject eleven amendments. "The stakes are too high for the children of America," Morse declared on the Senate floor, "for us to run the risk of jeopardizing this legislation in conference."[31] On April 19 the Senate passed it seventy-three to eighteen.

Johnson called ESEA "the most significant education bill" in congressional history. At a victory celebration he told his guests, "I worked harder and longer on this measure than on any . . . since I came to Washington in 1931 — and I am proud of it."[32] He arranged to have the signing ceremony at his old one-room, tin-roofed school, one and a half miles from the Ranch. Standing beside him was his first teacher, Kate Deadrick Loney, "Miss Katie," now seventy-two. Some of his former students from the Cotulla school were also there, and a few of the Sam Houston High School debaters he had coached in 1930. The Eighty-ninth Congress, he said at the ceremony, would be "remembered in history as men and women who began a new day of greatness in American society." The act would "bridge the gap between helplessness and hope for more than five million educationally deprived children." He had chosen his old school for the signing ceremony because, he wistfully remarked, he wanted to go back to "the beginnings of my own education—to be reminded and to remind others of that magic time when the world of learning began to open before our eyes."[33]

But the president had little time to savor his legislative triumph; Vietnam kept demanding his attention like some unruly child. The bombing campaign, designed to cow the Communists by demonstrating the power of America if defied, only stiffened the resolve of Ho Chi Minh and his lieutenants. Despite Rolling Thunder, with each passing month more supplies and arms, largely donated by the Chinese and the Soviets, reached the Vietcong in the South, brought painfully down the Ho Chi Minh Trail. By now well-trained Vietnamese regulars were beginning to arrive in numbers in the South to reinforce the guerrillas. Meanwhile, continued political instability in Saigon weakened the already feeble capacity of the Army of Vietnam (ARVN) to counter the Communist campaign.

For some time General William Westmoreland, the square-jawed, ramrod-straight West Pointer who took command of the American Vietnam military mission in 1964, had been warning that stopping the Communists would require American combat troops "in division strength."[34] Soon after, LBJ approved the first dispatch of U.S. fighting men. On March 8, thirty-five hundred marines in full battle dress waded ashore near Danang to be greeted on the beach by smiling young women who, treating them like tourists just off a Hawaiian cruise ship, placed flowered leis around their necks. The marines at first were assigned the defense of the Danang perimeter. Their mission was soon expanded to include help for ARVN units under attack.

It was at this point that the nation's campuses became staging areas for opponents of the emerging war in Vietnam. By now a cohort of students and younger faculty had evolved beyond the prudent conformism of the 1950s. Immersed in the same postscarcity cultural environment that inspired the Great Society, they had soaked up a new sensibility defiant of authority, committed to personal authenticity, and passionately dedicated to equality and social justice. Johnson and the Great Society might have enlisted these young men and women, and, in fact, federal programs such as VISTA, Head Start, and the Peace Corps did draw on their idealism. But Vietnam would disillusion them and taint the president and his policies. It would ultimately dissolve their faith in their nation's leaders and its institutions.

It was more than ironic that the first organized protests against the Vietnam War erupted at Ann Arbor, where Johnson had delivered his Great Society speech in May 1964. On March 24, in response to Rolling Thunder, students and faculty at the University of Michigan conducted a "teach-in," a twelve-hour marathon of discussions, speeches, and lectures on the subject of Vietnam that drew three thousand students and several hundred faculty. Few defended American policy. The teach-in movement soon spread in successive waves to campuses all across the country. For a time the State Department sent spokesmen to present the administration's position. But before long, the hostile receptions convinced administration officials that their "truth teams" were a waste of time.

Johnson said he welcomed constructive criticism and was glad he lived in a "nation where, in the midst of conflict . . ." its citizens could exercise free speech."[35] But the protests upset him, and on April 7, at Johns Hopkins, he replied to his critics. His speech, "Peace Without Conquest," delivered before a thousand faculty and students and a television audience of sixty million, sought to satisfy both the emerging "doves" and "hawks."

Johnson pleaded eloquently for strong American resolve. We were in Vietnam because since 1954 "every American president" had "offered support to the people of South Vietnam." He intended to keep the promise. Beyond that, Americans must "strengthen world order." If we abandoned Vietnam, people all over the world would lose confidence in "the value of American commitment, the value of America's word." If we backed down, the result would be an "even wider war." His objective was the total independence of South Vietnam, and America would do whatever was necessary to reach that objective. "We will not be defeated. We will not grow tired. We will not withdraw, either openly or under the cloak of a meaningless agreement." He hoped that peace would come soon but noted that it rested in the hands of others.

Now, to appease his dovish critics, he shifted gears. He was ready to begin "unconditional discussions" to end the Vietnamese War, he declared, although any settlement would have to include an independent South Vietnam. Johnson, who naively believed that people all over the world had the same goals as Americans, also proposed a billion-dollar American investment in an economic development plan for Southeast Asia that in the future could include North Vietnam. Harking back to his beloved Hill Country, where lives had been improved by the building of dams and expanding the electric grid, he foresaw development of the Mekong River, which could eventually provide "food and water and power on a scale to dwarf even our own TVA." He concluded on a pacific note. "We will choose life," he declared. "And so doing we will prevail over the enemies within man, and over the natural enemies of all mankind."[36]

The response to the speech was generally favorable. Letters and telegrams on Vietnam, noted a White House memo, "shifted from five to one against the president to better than four to one in his favor."[37] Many European and nonaligned nations also responded approvingly. Yet the president had failed to please the skeptics. Pundit Walter Lippmann, whom the president had hoped to win over, pointed out that "unconditional discussions" were far less conciliatory than "unconditional negotiations." Lippmann would soon claim that "the president is in grave trouble."[38] Nor were the Communist countries moved. The day after the speech, a headline in the *Washington Post* screamed: "Peking Scorns President's Peace Offer."[39] North Vietnam then announced its terms for ending the war: withdrawal of all American troops, the end of foreign bases in Vietnam, the recognition of the National Liberation Front (the Vietcong), and the reunification of Vietnam without foreign interference. In other words, total victory. The Communist countries and North Vietnam were not going to be bought off so easily.

And neither was the antiwar movement in the United States. On April 17, Students for a Democratic Society, which the war would soon transform into the New Left flagship, held the first major anti-Vietnam protest rally in Washington. With the temperature in the eighties, twenty thousand people showed up at the Washington Monument to denounce the war. One of the organizers, Paul Booth, a Swarthmore undergraduate, told the *New York Times* what the president himself believed: "We feel passionately and angrily about things in America, and we feel that a war in Asia will destroy what we're trying to do here."[40]

Johnson had been exhilarated by the deployment of the marine battalions at Danang. "Now I have Ho Chi Minh's pecker in my pocket," he chortled.[41] He obviously did not. In the spring of 1965 it was impossible for an American to venture a few miles out of Saigon without an armed escort, so effective were the Vietcong irregulars in the countryside. On March 30, three hundred pounds of *plastique* in the trunk of a gray Renault exploded in front of the American embassy in Saigon, wounding fifty-two Americans. The South Vietnamese government continued to disappoint the Americans despite another coup in early 1965 that brought to power the team of Nguyen Cao Ky, the swaggering young air force general who made himself prime minister, and Nguyen Van Thieu, the new chief of state, an infantry general. The two men brought a measure of stability to the South Vietnamese government, but they proved generally no more honest or democratic than their predecessors. Worst of all, they did not succeed in making the ARVN a truly effective fighting force.

Meanwhile, the president faced turmoil much closer to home than Southeast Asia. In late April civil war broke out in the Dominican Republic. Johnson ordered four hundred marines to land, ostensibly to protect American lives and property. Actually, he and his advisers feared that the opponents of the existing regime, led by Juan Bosch, were infiltrated with Castro-inspired Communists, and the administration soon dispatched more troops. Eventually more than twenty-two thousand American soldiers and eight thousand American sailors took part in the operation. Though aware that his actions would again evoke the phrase "Yankee imperialism," Johnson said he "could not risk the slaughter of American citizens."[42] He also justified his actions on the grounds that he had to stop the spread of Castroism. "The American nations cannot, must not, and will not," he announced, "permit the establishment of another Communist government in the Western Hemisphere." He invoked Kennedy's memory, recalling that less than a week before his death, JFK had warned against "the establishment of another Cuba in this hemisphere."[43] In the end, an OAS peacekeeping team arranged a cease-fire among the squabbling Dominican factions. On June 3 LBJ announced he had ordered the withdrawal of all American marines. The intervention had cost the United States $150 million.

Though a minor affair, the Dominican intervention marked a turning point for Johnson in foreign affairs. Liberals, uncomfortable with his Vietnam policies, now began to criticize him openly, aggressively, and often. Americans for Democratic Action roundly denounced Johnson over the Dominican intervention, and academics wrote angry letters to the newspapers. The liberal press was quick to climb on the anti-Johnson bandwagon. "Mr. Johnson's tough action," complained *The New Republic*, "is cheered loudest by those who want only strongman right-wing governments in Latin America."[44] James Reston of the *New York Times* described Johnson as "all over the place." He summed up what many political observers were feeling: "Nobody is very worried about the Dominican Republic, but the feeling persists that disorderly policymaking or capricious personal judgments could one day cause much more serious trouble elsewhere."[45]

While still entangled in the Caribbean, Johnson had to give further attention to Vietnam. During the spring Westmoreland and American generals in Vietnam on fact-finding missions brought new pressure on the president to increase the American commitment. The United States, they believed, must move beyond a defensive posture, creating enclaves free of Vietcong and carrying the fight directly to the enemy. As General Earle C. Wheeler, chairman of the Joint Chiefs of Staff, bluntly remarked, "No one ever won a battle sitting on his ass."[46] This meant more troops, American troops, who would go on the offensive and finally bring the war to a successful close. The administration complied in small, barely noticed increments, so that by early May there were more than forty-six thousand American fighting men in South Vietnam. In June Westmoreland cabled the Pentagon that North Vietnamese regular army units had crossed the border into the South and that Soviet bombers and jet fighters had arrived in Hanoi and would soon enter the fray. Meanwhile, the ARVN was suffering from both serious battle losses and a high desertion rate. Westmoreland said he needed another 41,000 troops now and 52,000 later, a total in Vietnam of 175,000, to defeat the Communist takeover. These would not merely protect American installations; wherever they were needed, they would also actively engage the enemy.

Johnson consulted everyone in sight before making a decision on this momentous demand. The administration's house dove, George Ball, advised caution. The United States, he feared, was repeating the Indo-China experience of France. If we must send combat troops, we should treat it as an experiment to be limited in duration and magnitude. Secretary of Defense McNamara's response took the form of a long paper composed in late June. McNamara had been a professor of business at Harvard and then a brilliantly successful executive at Ford Motor Company before being tapped by JFK to head the Department of Defense. Johnson considered McNamara "the smartest man" he had "ever met," and took his advice seriously. Now, at this turning point, the secretary outlined three possible options in Vietnam: Withdraw as soon as possible; fight an enclave war and prepare the South Vietnamese to take over; follow the generals' advice and present the enemy with the options of real negotiation or destruction. McNamara told the president that he favored the third choice. He would give Westmoreland his troops, and go beyond that by stepping up the bombing campaign and mining Haiphong Harbor to stop resupply of the enemy. He also advised calling to active duty 225,000 military reservists in civilian life, a move that, by massively disrupting the lives of many civilians, would commit the American people to the war as no other action could. In response, Mac Bundy called the McNamara proposal "rash to the point of folly."[47] By this time the president had approved further combat contingents for Vietnam, bringing the total to about 75,000 men.

Still, Johnson continued to vacillate, conferring constantly with his advisers and members of Congress. To tap the collective wisdom of the foreign-policy establishment, Johnson sought out the views of prominent elder statesmen who had molded United States internationalist foreign policy since World War II. The "Wise Men" had been first assembled as a group by Johnson during the 1964 presidential campaign to provide the foreign-policy expertise he felt he needed to make himself a credible candidate. Their membership would vary, but on this occasion they included former secretary of state Dean Acheson; World War II general Omar Bradley; former head of the Marshall Plan Paul Hoffman; Robert Lovett, an influential subcabinet officer in the Truman administration; Roswell Gilpatric, Kennedy's under secretary of defense; John McCloy, former American proconsul in post-1945 Germany; and others. Meeting on July 8 and 9 and briefed on Vietnam, they advised the president to be tough. The men who had constructed the postwar anti-Soviet containment policy saw Vietnam inevitably through the prism of the larger Cold War. To turn tail in Southeast Asia was as inconceivable as yielding to the Soviets on Berlin or Greece or Turkey. Yet we must avoid bringing the Soviets into the war, they said. Concluding that an enhanced bombing campaign would incite the Soviets more than a ground campaign, they approved of sending combat troops. Speaking for the group, Gilpatric proposed applying "whatever amounts of military power may be needed, perhaps as much as brought to bear in Korea fifteen years ago."[48] McCloy told Rusk and McNamara: "You've got to do it. You've got to go in."[49] Later that evening Acheson and several colleagues visited the president at the White House. Johnson complained to them that he had no support on Vietnam from anyone and predicted that entanglement in Asia would kill his domestic programs. As Acheson later wrote his former chief Harry Truman: "I blew my top & told him . . . that he had no choice exept to press on. . . ."[50] However much he demurred, the Wise Men's hawkish advice deeply impressed the president.

Still, Johnson remained tortured by uncertainty. Senator John Sparkman of Alabama recalled that during that 1965 summer he was "literally torn to pieces" by the situation. Press secretary George Reedy believed "that period was the most anguished I ever saw. He wanted to do anything, anything rather than send more troops."[51] The torment of those weeks activated Johnson's mood-swing disorder. Bill Moyers, now press secretary, later recalled that his depression was "never more pronounced than in 1965 when he was leading up to the decision about the buildup in Vietnam." He spent a lot of time in bed with the covers over his head. The situation in Vietnam would have been hard for any sensitive leader to handle emotionally, but Johnson was particularly agonized. He regarded American soldiers as his "boys," as if they were part of his family. Lady Bird told historian Robert Dallek that "the worst time was the boxes coming back on the train" with the fallen heroes "heading for their final resting place back home. . . ." Moyers said that LBJ was not depressed all the time. There were many things that would brighten his mood, like the passage of one of his Great Society bills. "But always," Moyers maintained, "when he returned to the subject of Vietnam this cloud in his eyes and this predictably unpredictable behavior" would return.[52]

The time for decision came in late July. From the twenty-first on, the president huddled with his civilian and military advisers and congressional leaders at a half dozen meetings to consider the next big step in Vietnam. All except Ball agreed that now was the time to make a major ground troop commitment. Johnson had probably made up his mind already, but he remained torn by doubts. At a meeting with military and Pentagon civilians on the twenty-second he raised the question of public reaction to a quantum leap of intervention. Would "the Congress and the people . . . go along with 600,000 people and billions of dollars 10,000 miles away?" he asked. Secretary of the Army Stanley Resor reassured him: The "Gallup poll shows people are behind our commitment."[53]

Determined to avoid "dramatics," on July 28 Johnson held a news conference where, tucked into the middle of other subjects, he announced that he planned to send 50,000 more fighting men to Vietnam, raising the total to 125,000. To keep up American strength elsewhere, he would order accelerated draft calls, but he would not ask for a reserve call-up, a move he understood from past experience would set off alarm bells among the general public.* He restated his willingness to go to the conference table with the Communist leaders in Hanoi to discuss a negotiated settlement. In defending the American presence in Vietnam, he once more cited the promises of three presidents, insisted that a Communist-dominated Asia was a threat to America's national security, and reiterated his fear of another Munich if the United States withdrew. On a "personal note," he confessed that he did not find "it easy to send the flower of our youth, our finest young men, into battle." It was, he declared, "the most agonizing and most painful duty of your president."[54] As Johnson later noted in his memoirs, "Now we were committed to major combat in Vietnam."[55]

---

*The option had been discussed at the July meetings but rejected. Johnson remembered how controversial had been Kennedy's call-up of the reserves in 1961, after Khrushchev's challenge over Germany at the Vienna summit. He did not want to repeat the experience.

Could Johnson have taken a different tack? Critics have asked why he did not duplicate Kennedy's Laos ploy: Patch up an agreement to "neutralize" the region and then allow the Communists to quietly take over. Kennedy "lost" Laos but suffered no political ill effects from the decision. Walter Lippmann and others, as we saw, had suggested this approach. In many ways it was the policy by which Nixon finally extricated the United States from the Vietnam swamp. But these examples do not reckon with LBJ's insecurities and vulnerabilities. Kennedy was a cosmopolite, the son of a diplomat. As a young man he had written a best-selling book on European power politics during the 1930s. Once past his shaky early Bay of Pigs start, and particularly after the 1962 Cuban Missile Crisis, JFK moved comfortably in international affairs and seemed a masterful player on the world scene. The public, presumably, would have trusted a Kennedy decision to give up on Vietnam. Johnson did not have the experience or the confidence to back down. Nor would the press and the public, which later denounced him for the Vietnam morass, have spared him had he decided to back out. Neither would the political right. The "Democratic right and the Republicans . . . would have torn him to pieces," Jack Valenti later insisted.[56] And we must always avoid the temptations of hindsight. Despite the French experience, few could foresee that the mighty United States, the best-armed nation in the world, would find the Vietnam Communists such formidable foes. No one, in William Bundy's later words, realized how "extremely tenacious" the North Vietnamese would be.[57]

There was also a misperception in Washington of the South Vietnamese's will to survive as an independent people. In truth South Vietnam was not a nation. The administration hoped it was, and sought to ensure that it would become one. "Nation-building" was a refrain much used by administration officials to describe American Vietnam goals. The policy was backed by economic aid and technical advice to the Saigon government and by excruciating efforts to force the Saigon juntas to legitimize their regimes through open, honest elections. But South Vietnam, though many of its inhabitants did prefer the Saigon government to the Communists, never did become a country and never could rally its people to sacrifice for the good of the whole.

But more to the point, no one anticipated that more Americans would die in the Vietnam War than in Korea.

Public opinion backed the escalation of July and continued to support the war for many more months. Even the liberal press by and large endorsed the president on Vietnam for the rest of 1965. Not so the intellectuals. The hostility of the nation's cultural elite to the president's foreign policy exploded in Johnson's face at the White House Festival of the Arts. The event, conceived by Princeton historian Eric Goldman, the Johnson White House intellectual-in-residence, was intended to honor luminaries from the fields of music, film, dance, photography, literature, painting, and sculpture, and give the administration improved cultural grades. Scheduled for June, it turned into an opportunity for the artists and literati to express their outrage at Vietnam. Poet Robert Lowell first accepted the invitation and then had loud, public second thoughts. In a letter prominently featured on the front page of the *New York Times*, Lowell spurned the invitation, thereby turning an innocuous cultural event into a foreign-policy protest. "Although I am very enthusiastic about most of your domestic legislation and intentions," Lowell wrote, "I nevertheless can only follow our present foreign policy with the greatest dismay and distrust. . . ."[58] Most of the invitees accepted and participated, but Lowell articulated what many in the creative and intellectual communities actually felt about Johnson at this point. The president, initially excited about the festival, was mortified by the rejections and almost did not show up himself.

Johnson's advisers warned him that 1965 was not the time to submit any additional civil rights bills. In a meeting with Martin Luther King Jr. in December, after his return from Oslo to accept the Nobel Peace Prize, the president told the black leader that the poverty program should be a sufficient installment of benefits for blacks for now. King demurred: There was a serious voting rights issue that must be addressed. King later quoted the president: "Martin, you're right about that. I'm going to do it eventually, but I can't get a voting rights bill through this session of Congress."[59] King did not intend to wait until Johnson was ready. Just after the new year he was in Selma, Alabama, to announce that blacks would push the federal government to action by "marching by the thousands to the place of registration."[60]

Selma was just what the civil rights doctor ordered. Seat of Dallas County, it was an old Black Belt town where the relations between the races had barely altered since slavery days. Only 156, or 1 percent, of the county's black voting-age population were registered to vote. King's marches succeeded in goading Dallas County sheriff Jim Clark, a man who fit the Hollywood stereotype of a bigoted southern lawman, into mass arrests, of children as well as adults.

King appealed to the federal government for support. Through his young lieutenant Andrew Young, he contacted Lee White, the president's adviser on civil rights, and asked Johnson to go on record in support of voting rights. After meeting with King briefly on February 9, the president responded at his February 12 press conference:

All Americans should be indignant when one American is denied the right to vote [he said]. The loss of that right to a single citizen undermines the freedom of every citizen. This is why all of us should be concerned with the efforts of our fellow Americans to register to vote in Alabama.[61]

On March 3 the Selma leaders, defying an order from Governor Wallace, announced that they intended to march to the state capital at Montgomery to submit a petition of grievances. Four days later, as the demonstrators approached the Pettus Bridge across the Alabama River, state troopers attacked them with tear gas, nightsticks, chains, and electric cattle prods. As many as a hundred people were injured. Television cameras caught the violence, with ABC breaking into its movie *Judgment at Nuremberg*, a dramatization of the 1946 Nazi war crimes trial, with footage of the violence in Alabama. The parallel was stark. "Bloody Sunday" touched a nerve among millions of fair-minded Americans. In the next few days thousands of blacks and whites showed their concern by sympathy marches in cities all over the country.

Meanwhile, back in Atlanta, King decided that he would personally lead a second march across the Pettus Bridge and then on to Montgomery, the state capital, fifty-four miles away. When a federal judge issued an order to delay the march, the administration urged King to obey it. King refused but, unwilling to offend the legislators whom he hoped would enact federal voting rights legislation, he accepted a face-saving device. He and the marchers would cross the bridge but would stop when they reached a line of state troopers on the other side. There would be no violence this time by either side. On March 9 King led almost two thousand marchers, singing "Ain't Gonna Let Nobody Turn Me 'Round," onto the bridge and halted when he saw the state troopers. After offering a prayer, he turned the marchers back. King avoided violence, but that night a white Unitarian minister from Boston, James Reeb, was clubbed to death by four white men in Selma to the cries of "Hey, nigger-lover."[62]

Johnson was appalled by Reeb's murder and immediately phoned the minister's wife to offer his condolences and the government's help. Meanwhile, the judge who had issued the restraining order withdrew it, clearing the way for the aborted march to Montgomery to proceed. A violent clash between civil rights demonstrators and Alabama state police and racists now seemed imminent.

Though prodded by Harry McPherson and Abe Fortas and personally outraged at the Pettus Bridge violence, Johnson refused to send federal agents to protect the marchers. He did not want to make a martyr of George Wallace or weaken the moderate voice in the South by a massive federal intrusion. At this point Wallace asked to see the president at the

White House. LBJ would now have a chance to use reason rather than brute force to deal with the crisis.

The meeting between Wallace and the president on March 13 was a quintessential LBJ performance. Johnson seated Wallace across from his rocking chair on a squishy sofa into which the governor sank. Looming over his compact guest, the president accused Wallace of condoning brutality and demanded that he order Alabama voting officials to register blacks. When the governor protested that he could not persuade those officials, LBJ retorted: "Don't shit me about your persuasive powers, George. Why, just this morning I was watching you on television . . . and you was attacking me. . . . And you know what? You were so damn persuasive that I had to turn off the set before you had me changing my mind." Johnson invoked the judgment of history to change the governor's mind. Did "George" want "a Great . . . Big . . . Marble monument" that read " 'He Built'?" Or did he prefer "a little piece of scrawny pine board laying across that harsh, caliche soil" that read " 'George Wallace—He Hated'?"[63] Johnson left the Oval Office briefly to let the governor properly absorb the browbeating, and when he returned he apparently told him that he must support black voter registration and stop the violence. If the disorders continued, the governor would have to find a face-saving way to request federal intervention. Walking to the White House Rose Garden with Wallace, Johnson told reporters that the governor had agreed that blacks must be registered and accepted the need to protect demonstrators against attack. He also announced that he would be sending Congress a voting rights bill the following week. Several days later, after Wallace informed the president that the state of Alabama could not afford the costs of protecting the civil rights marchers, LBJ federalized the Alabama National Guard to do the job and added U.S. marshals and regular army military police. King's march to Montgomery would be protected.

On March 15 Johnson addressed a joint session of Congress on prime-time television. Speaking with unaccustomed passion, he outlined what he wanted in a voting rights bill and asked Congress to pass it quickly. "Should we defeat every enemy," he said, "should we double our wealth and conquer the stars, and still be unequal to this issue [of equal rights for black Americans], then we have failed as a people and as a nation." This was not a Negro problem, nor a southern problem, nor a northern problem, he asserted. "There is only an American problem. And we are met here tonight as Americans to solve the problem." The cause of American Negroes "must be our cause, too. Because it is not just Negroes, but really it is all of us who must overcome the crippling legacy of bigotry and injustice." At this point Johnson paused dramatically and, raising his arms, uttered words with such resonance that they brought Congress and all the justices of the U.S. Supreme Court to their feet with cheers and applause: "And we . . . shall . . . overcome!"[64] The phrase from the civil rights freedom anthem had stirred Johnson's listeners to the bone and established his solidarity with the civil rights movement. Viewing the speech in Selma on TV, Martin Luther King Jr. cried. Even SNCC militant John Lewis praised the speech, calling it "historic, eloquent, and more than inspiring."[65] When Johnson left the rostrum he encountered House Judiciary Committee chairman Emmanuel Celler. "Manny," the president said, "I want you to start hearings tonight."[66]

The voting rights bill Johnson sent to Congress on March 17 was a relatively simple document for a law intended to reverse a hundred years of political injustice. One of the prime weapons southern states had used in disfranchising voters was the literacy test, but it was hard to tell how many voters were actually turned away from the polls on these grounds. Attorney General Nicholas Katzenbach had come up with a formula to ferret out voter discrimination. If a state used literacy tests or comparable exams to establish voter eligibility and if fewer than 50 percent of *all* its voting-age citizens voted or were registered to vote in 1964, it would be presumed that racial discrimination existed. If discrimination was discovered, literacy tests would be automatically prohibited in that jurisdiction. If local officials continued to discriminate, the U.S. attorney general, upon petition of twenty or more local residents, could send examiners to inspect applications and enroll eligible voters directly. Under this formula, literacy tests would be automatically suspended in Mississippi, Virginia, Louisiana, Alabama, Georgia, and South Carolina. The law invalidated payment of a poll tax as a prerequisite for voting and made violations of its provisions criminal acts.

On March 21 King and thirty-four hundred followers set out for Montgomery. Four days later, now twenty-five thousand strong, the marchers reached their destination and heard King deliver a stirring address from the steps of the Capitol building. That night a white woman from Detroit, Viola Liuzzo, mother of five children, and a member of the march's transportation committee, was driving from Selma to Montgomery on Highway 80. She was shot to death. LBJ acted quickly, appearing on television with FBI director J. Edgar Hoover at his side to denounce "the horrible crime" and announce that four members of the Ku Klux Klan had been arrested. Since murder is not a federal crime unless committed on federal property, the Klansmen would be tried instead for violating Mrs. Liuzzo's civil rights. She was murdered, he said, by the "enemies of justice who for decades have used the rope and the gun and the tar and feathers to terrorize their neighbors," and he reiterated his request that Congress act speedily on the voting legislation.[67]

By now southern resistance in Congress to ending black disfranchisement was largely broken. Events in Alabama helped. But Johnson also applied "the treatment," so successful in the past. The president was constantly on the phone, lining up votes. According to James Farmer, head of the Congress of Racial Equality, he was "cracking the whip. He was cajoling, he was threatening . . . whatever tactic was required with that certain individual, he was using."[68] On May 9 one of the staunch southern senators said, "We know we're licked."[69] On May 25 the Senate voted cloture, ending southern filibuster attempts in the upper house.

In Congress the liberals prevailed broadly. They strengthened the bill to include federal inspection of counties where voting discrimination existed whatever the cause and, at the behest of the New York delegation, added a bilingual literacy provision for areas in which at least 5 percent of the population did not speak English. The Senate passed the bill 77 to 19, on May 26. The House passed it on July 9 by 333 to 85. On August 3 and 4 the House and Senate, respectively, adopted the conference committee report.

To dramatize the importance of the new law, Johnson went to the Capitol on August 6 to sign it on Congress's own turf, something no president had done in twenty-five years. The Voting Rights Act, he noted, would "strike away the last major shackle" of the Negro's "ancient bonds." Blacks must now register to vote because their future and their children's future depended on it. If they did this, he noted, they would find "that the vote is the most powerful instrument ever devised by man for breaking down injustice and destroying the terrible walls which imprison men because they are different from other men."[70]

The law accomplished what it intended. Four days after its passage Johnson sent federal examiners to Mississippi, where, in Dallas County, black voter enrollment increased almost instantly from 320 to 6,789. In four years the number of southern black voters rose from 1 million to more than 3 million. The number of elected black officials soon followed. In the six states predominantly affected by the law, the figure for blacks in elected office soared from seventy to almost four hundred in four years. Johnson feared that the new law would destroy the Democratic Party in the South. He was not wrong. The Republican surge in Dixie since the 1960s represents in part the defection of southern white voters from the party that gave them the Voting Rights Act of 1965. Yet the law also made black Americans full citizens and set limits to the petty abuse and discrimination they had long suffered at the hands of local and state governments.

During these triumphant spring days of 1965 Johnson proposed one further step toward his shining goal of a free and equal society. In May a report researched and written by Assistant Secretary of Labor Daniel Moynihan came into the hands of the president and his aides. *The Negro Family: The Case for National Action* described how more and more black children were being raised by unmarried mothers. Even in two-parent black families fathers did not earn enough, and the mother was the major provider, leading to the development of a matriarchal family structure that failed to socialize children, especially male children, well. It was important then that jobs be available for black males.

Johnson decided to speak to the issue of blacks' persistent economic disadvantage at the Howard University commencement in June. It was in this speech, written by Richard Goodwin and Moynihan, that Johnson—surely without realizing its implications—announced what would be called affirmative action, the source of so much controversy in later years as his successors and the federal courts clothed the principle in ever more elaborate garments. At Howard, Johnson described the growing economic chasm between the races and blamed it on "centuries of oppression and persecution." The nation must compensate for these injustices. "You do not take a person who, for years, has been hobbled by chains and . . . bring him up to the starting line . . . and still believe that you have been completely fair." It was "not enough to open the gates of opportunity. All our citizens must have the ability to walk through those gates." The nation must seek "equality" "not just . . . as a right and a theory, but equality as a fact and equality as a result." Johnson promised to call a fall conference whose object would be "to help the American Negro fulfill the rights which—after the long time of injustice—he is finally about to secure."[71] Johnson was inadvertently sowing the seeds of racial resentment.

Alas for further racial progress, on August 11, only five days after the voting rights signing ceremony, Watts, a black neighborhood in Los Angeles, erupted in violence.

Like other racial upheavals of the decade, Watts was triggered by rage at the police, who in Los Angeles were particularly detested by black citizens. The six days of mayhem triggered thirty-four deaths, three thousand arrests, and property losses from arson and looting of more than two hundred million dollars. It required fourteen thousand National Guardsmen to restore order. Though there had been trouble and violence in Harlem the year before, it was Watts that marked the onset of the "long, hot summers" that would afflict the decade.

The president was at the Ranch for a long weekend when he heard the news. Joseph Califano Jr., his new assistant, borrowed from the

Pentagon, phoned from Washington to tell him about Watts, but Johnson wanted desperately to distance the administration from the troubles and did not return the calls. He finally contacted Califano on Saturday and ordered that not a single federal official set foot in Los Angeles without his permission. The next day, after learning that his subordinates had authorized an army airlift of supplies to the California National Guard, he phoned again. Califano should issue a statement praising the local and state officials for bringing the violence under control.

Watts trapped the president in an uncomfortable dilemma. He could not condone the violence, but he did not want to pander to white backlash sentiment. He must salve the wounds of the ghetto but not reward rioters. On August 15 Johnson denounced the rioters but acknowledged the remaining legitimate grievances of the black community. It was not enough "simply to decry disorder," he noted. It was also necessary to remedy the lack of hope, skills, and education, and other shameful deficiencies of the slums and "strike at the unjust conditions from which disorder largely flows. . . ." "We must not," he warned, "let anger drown understanding if domestic peace is ever to rest on its only sure foundation—the faith of all our people that they share, in opportunity and in obligation, the promise of American life."[72] Johnson also came through with some useful racial Band-Aids. In early September he authorized a flock of new or expanded minor federal programs for Watts in the areas of adult education, legal aid, manpower training, health services, and business development. As we know, these did not transform the Los Angeles black ghetto into a paradise, and there were still the upheavals in Cleveland, Detroit, and Newark to come.

In some ways Watts marked a reversal in the administration's response to the civil rights movement. The White House reaction to the riots was "one of despair," Harry McPherson recalled. The president and his aides believed it "would almost certainly jeopardize a lot of what [the administration was] trying to do." "It seemed to justify the worst feelings of the racists in Congress and in the press" and imperiled further civil rights legislation. More ominous, "it worked a very severe and immediate strain on the coalition of liberals."[73] The president himself expressed these pessimistic views more colorfully. "Negroes will end up pissing in the aisles of the Senate, and making fools of themselves, the way . . . they had after the Civil War and during Reconstruction. . . . Just as the government was moving to help them, the Negroes will once again take unwise actions out of frustration, impatience, and anger."[74] There was more than expedient considerations behind this annoyance, however. Johnson always expected gratitude from the beneficiaries of his largesse. That was essential for the give-and-take of politics. But blacks had instead betrayed him; they had proven disloyal.

But the worst effects of racial turmoil still lay ahead. During the summer of 1965, the president was busy signing bills he had championed, and his approval rating among all voters stood at 69 percent. On June 21 he approved a $4.7 billion reduction in excise taxes. On July 14 he signed the Older Americans Act, establishing an administration on aging under the Department of Health, Education, and Welfare. On July 26 he created a national crime commission, calling it the beginning of "a war against crime."[75] On August 9 he approved the Health Research Facilities Construction Program, which authorized construction of new hospitals and medical schools, expanded the National Institutes of Health, and doubled medical research funding for the next three years. He also announced the upcoming development of a task force to set up goals for the Great Society in "education, health and happiness."[76] On August 10 he put his name on a housing act that included a rent subsidy of $30 million for low-income families.

But the most consequential piece of legislation in the summer of 1965 was Medicare. Federally sponsored health insurance had been discussed since before World War I, when Teddy Roosevelt's Bull Moose Party, borrowing from European and Australian examples, made it part of their 1912 platform. Franklin Roosevelt had considered adding federal health insurance to his Social Security legislation in 1935, but capitulated to the organized medical profession's opposition rather than sacrifice the other important features of the landmark Social Security bill.

After World War II, when the spectacular breakthroughs of medical science escalated the demand for doctors and hospitals, private insurance became an increasingly popular way to insure good health care and prevent financial catastrophe for individuals and families afflicted by costly illness. During these years labor unions extracted health insurance coverage from employers as part of their members' benefits under union-management contracts. Meanwhile, the American Medical Association (AMA), realizing that private health insurance helped guarantee compensation for doctors' expensive services, announced its support for voluntary, private health insurance. By 1960 more than a hundred million Americans were covered by private health reimbursement plans.

But millions remained uncovered. Some of the uninsured used free clinics or charity wards in emergencies, but others went without medical services for years on end. The elderly suffered disproportionately, since as a group they had more health problems than younger people, had lower incomes than average, and, now past their working years, lacked job-related health insurance. With Americans living longer and medical and hospital costs mounting, the problem of medical care for the elderly began to loom larger in the public consciousness.

In 1949 Harry Truman, a passionate partisan of a universal federal health care system, had submitted to Congress the Murray-Wagner-Dingell bill, providing federal money for medical needs to be financed through payroll deductions. The AMA denounced it as "socialized medicine" and spent more than three million dollars to defeat it. The bill never made it out of the House Ways and Means Committee. In the upper chamber, the new junior senator from Texas had been sufficiently concerned with alienating conservative constituents to vote against the Truman plan.

By 1960 so many Americans agreed that something had to be done to help the elderly and the poor pay their medical bills that the organized medical profession gave begrudging support to the federal Kerr-Mills bill. A state-administered health scheme, this covered the costs of X rays, drugs, and private nursing as well as fees to doctors, dentists, and surgeons, and paid for up to six months of hospitalization. But the bill required a large "deductible" and was "means tested" to eliminate all but the "medically indigent" from its provisions. The measure became law in 1960.

Reformers found Kerr-Mills unsatisfactory. Many states refused to join the system because it imposed heavy costs. Means-tested medical benefits, moreover, stigmatized their recipients. Liberals had long advocated health insurance covering all retired persons as a natural extension of the Social Security system. This would deal with the particularly acute problem of the aged, but had the additional advantage of targeting a group—"old folks"—then still considered especially deserving of society's solicitude. The King-Anderson Medicare bill, submitted by Kennedy to Congress in 1962, covered all Social Security recipients for hospital and nursing home costs but omitted a surgical benefits provision and said nothing about doctors' fees. Although this was a limited measure, union groups and older Americans rallied to its support, writing thousands of letters urging its passage. The AMA helped defeat Kennedy's version of Medicare by a massive campaign against it and against two other Kennedy attempts to get a medical insurance bill enacted.

Johnson was determined to rescue Medicare. He could justify his vote on the Truman national health insurance bill as refusal to accept an extreme measure. In 1956, however, as majority leader, he had maneuvered the Senate into accepting a disability clause in the updated Social Security measure by a single vote. Johnson had a special empathy for the old and ill. According to Wilbur Cohen, assistant secretary of Health, Education, and Welfare who would guide Medicare over the political hurdles, the president worried about "people who became old and indigent and sick and disabled and he wanted to do something for them."[77] Johnson also knew a popular position when he saw it. Countrywide support had been building during the previous decade, and requests had been streaming into the White House from older Americans asking the president to push Medicare. Finally, LBJ considered medical reform part of the Kennedy legacy he had specifically promised to translate into action.

In August 1964, before the presidential election, Johnson induced the Senate to attach a hospital care provision to a House bill increasing Social Security payments. Though the bill became deadlocked in the House-Senate conference committee and failed to pass the Eighty-eighth Congress, this was the first time that at least one house of Congress had approved the health insurance principle. During the presidential campaign, enacting medical care for the aged was a major Johnson selling point.

One of the biggest stumbling blocks to Medicare besides the AMA was Congressman Wilbur Mills, chairman of the House Ways and Means Committee, which had jurisdiction over Social Security programs. A prissy-looking, bespectacled Harvard Law School graduate from Kensett, Arkansas, Mills was admired for his ability to sort through the intricacies of complex financial legislation. He was also known as one of the most cautious members of Congress. Though a conservative Democrat, sympathetic to the AMA's position, he was exquisitely sensitive to changes in public opinion, particularly those from the voters in his district and state. The electoral landslide of 1964 had changed the composition of the Ways and Means Committee. Two new Democratic members, both Medicare supporters, could help vote the bill out of committee no matter what the chairman did. Add the growing clamor from voters in favor of Medicare, and Mills could see the handwriting on the wall.

Johnson sent his special health care message, "Advancing the Nation's Health," to Congress on January 10. Incorporating a comprehensive measure including augmented community health services, scholarships for medical and dental students, and regional medical centers, its first section was hospital insurance for seniors. The administration proposal was the top priority for the new Eighty-ninth Congress, and the bills were given the legislative numbers H.R. 1 and S. 1 in the two houses. Refusing to be left behind, the Republicans introduced their own medical insurance scheme for the elderly. "Bettercare" was a voluntary plan through private insurance companies subsidized by the federal government; the elderly could join or not, as they wished. Though over-all a more conservative measure than the administration's bill, unlike H.R. 1 and S. 1 it covered doctors' fees, drugs, mental hospital stays, and other medical costs, as well as hospital stays.

Many elderly Americans believed that the government intended to pay their doctors' costs as well as hospitalization, and rather than let the Republicans steal the Democrats' thunder, Mills proposed revising the administration proposal to incorporate physicians' services costs. Johnson was delighted with the changes. "Just tell them to snip off that name 'Republican' and slip those little old changes into the bill," he exclaimed.[78] Mills also added one more ingredient, a Kerr-Mills-type "means-tested" component to help the indigent with their health care expenses whatever their age: For all those unable to pay their medical bills there would be a joint federal-state program (Medicaid) that the experts estimated would cost an additional five hundred million dollars.

The Mills bill now had three layers: the original Democratic plan for compulsory hospital insurance under Social Security; a government-sub-sidized voluntary insurance program to cover doctors' bills; and the Med-icaid section, providing matching federal grants to states to pay medical bills for welfare recipients and for the disabled, the blind, the aged, and children in single-parent families. On March 23 the House Ways and Means Committee approved the bill. The whole House passed the mea-sure soon after, 313 to 115.

The bill then went to the Senate Finance Committee, where its chairman, conservative Harry Byrd of Virginia, a friend of Johnson's but an opponent of Medicare, seemed likely to hold up the hearings. In very Johnsonian fashion, the president forestalled a delay by appearing to-gether on national television with nine influential congressional Demo-crats, including Byrd, by his side. Eight of the congressmen praised the scheme fulsomely, but the nonplussed Byrd, who had not been told why he had been summoned to the TV station from his Virginia farm, sat mute. Finally the president turned to his old pal and asked him to "make an observation." When Byrd declined, Johnson then asked him whether he knew of anything that "would prevent . . . [hearings] coming about in reasonable time—there is not anything ahead of it in the committee?" Byrd was trapped. He knew of nothing that would delay hearings in the Senate Finance Committee, he said. "So when . . . it is referred to the Senate Finance Committee, you will arrange for prompt hearings . . . ?" the president coaxed. Byrd softly said yes. With an immense smile, John-son faced the television cameras. "Good!" he exclaimed. "Thank you very much, gentlemen."[79] This was the first time the "treatment" had ever appeared on national TV!

With the formidable Byrd obstacle removed, the Senate began consideration of the bill. Senator Russell Long of Louisiana, who had been mistakenly assigned floor leadership of the measure, loaded up the administration measure with his own proposals. On July 9 the Senate passed this clunky bill by sixty-eight to twenty-one. It was now up to Mills to clean up the law to conform to the House measure. As Long watched in dismay, in the joint House-Senate conference meetings Mills lopped off almost all the Senate's additions to the House bill, and on June 27 and 28 the House and Senate passed the Medicare law.

But there was still one more scene to play. Many AMA members were threatening to boycott the law; the doctors had to cooperate or Medicare would be an empty gesture. Cohen advised the president to reassure them that they would not "be kicked around by the government. . . ."[80] Johnson agreed and on June 29 summoned to the White House representatives of the AMA, then meeting in New York. The president snowed the doctors. Feeding their own inflated self-image, he talked of how wonderful doctors were, how when his daddy was sick the doctor would come and sit with him all night. He talked about how great America was and how the country owed so much to those who had made it great but were now old and sick. He asked the AMA bigwigs for help in implementing the law. Several times the seated president rose to his feet, forcing the doctors to rise in unison, a physical act that acknowledged that he was president of the United States and the boss. But he also noted from a memo on his desk that "reasonable charges" for the doctors' services would be determined by the insurance companies, which the medical profession pretty much had in its pocket. Commenting on the performance, an aide present noted that he had "never seen anything like it."[81]

With an unerring flair for what a later time would call photo ops, Johnson flew to the Harry S. Truman Library in Independence, Missouri, for the signing ceremony. In his accompanying remarks, he praised his predecessor's role and told the crowd of 250 that Americans loved Harry Truman "not because he gave them hell—but because he gave them hope." He then signed the bill on a table that Truman had used to authorize the Truman Doctrine and sign the treaty of peace with West Germany, giving the first pen to Truman and the second to his wife, Bess. He also presented them with the first two applications for Medicare cards. "I am glad," said Mr. Truman, "to have lived this long."[82]

Without question the new law would confer enormous benefits on many Americans. It vastly improved the health and well-being of millions of poor and aged Americans. But, joined with other well-meaning Johnson medical programs, it also unleashed the demon of medical inflation for a generation. The feature of the new law allowing doctors to charge "reasonable" and "customary" fees based on those "prevailing" in their communities was virtually a blank check for medical practitioners to line their pockets. But it was probably the unavoidable price of getting the bill past the hurdle of organized medicine. Ultimately Congressman Phil Landrum would prove to be right. "The day will come," he declared, "when the medical profession will hail this bill as saving their profession from the socialized medicine they so rightly fear."[83]

Enactment of Medicare was the consummation of a thirty-one-year battle, and President Lyndon Johnson and his commitment to a "Great Society" had gotten it done. The "education president and the health president" had accomplished much by the summer of 1965. On August 10, 1965, Tom Wicker wrote in the *New York Times*, "The list of achievements is so long that it reads better than the legislative achievements of most two-term presidents, and some of the bills—on medical care, education, voting rights . . . to pick a handful—are of such weight as to cause one to go all the way back to Woodrow Wilson's first year to find a congressional session of equal importance."[84]

Johnson later insisted that the turning point in his presidency came just past midsummer in 1965, smack in the middle of his greatest domestic triumphs. By September 1965 he "began to sense a shift in the winds," he wrote in his memoirs. "I knew intuitively that there would be growing resistance to further legislative action." Throughout the fall, he said, congressional leaders from both parties advised him that the country "needed time to catch its breath . . . to consolidate and digest the laws we had already passed." Looking back to late 1965 from just after Nixon's victory in 1968, Wilbur Cohen believed that not only was Congress beginning to balk; the American people "thought that he [Johnson] was . . . going too fast. They couldn't understand all this rush of legislation. . . ."[85] And Vietnam was also looming larger as a hurdle to domestic legislation. LBJ marked as the actual turnaround date the moment when Congress failed to pass home rule for the District of Columbia. "This defeat," he believed, "was a clear sign that the winds of reform would not blow again as hard as they had through the remarkable first session of the Eighty-ninth Congress."[86]

He exaggerated, of course. Johnson was always so sensitive to disagreement or disapproval that any loss jolted him. There were only two other administration measures of consequence that failed to pass in the fall of 1965: the appropriation for rent supplements, and the repeal of Section 14(b), the right-to-work section of the Taft-Hartley Act, which nobody expected to get through Congress anyway. A few setbacks did not signify the end of his program. Other Great Society legislation remained in the pipeline, to be passed during the rest of 1965 and in the second session the following year. But he was correct in his assessment that the impetus for reform was declining. And it was certainly true that his spectacular success in getting Congress to do *everything* he wanted reached its climax in August 1965.

One source of letdown was the unraveling of the War on Poverty. The most extravagant expression of Great Society idealism, by mid-1965 the measure was creating more problems than answers in the age-old battle against one of humanity's chief calamities.

Created in August 1964, the Office of Economic Opportunity did not make its first War on Poverty grants until January, after the presidential election. During those early start-up months the OEO pulsated with enthusiasm and a sense of mission, reflecting the young band of idealists collected by agency head Sargent Shriver. Shriver himself was an idealist, though one who had proven his management skills as chief of the Peace Corps, a job he continued to hold for months after he took on OEO. Shriver's relations with the president were initially good. In LBJ's eyes he was a Kennedy, but the best of the lot and, after all, only a brother-in-law. By choosing him to lead the War on Poverty the president was confirming a bond with the glamorous Kennedy clan without creating a serious rival.

Shriver's job was nearly impossible. The agency itself was divided between those who, in the emerging New Left spirit of the day, wanted to use the OEO, and especially the community action programs (CAPS), as a tool to empower the poor, and those who saw the CAPS primarily as useful ways to distribute social benefits. The same division could be found among participants in the War on Poverty in the field as it unfolded. The mayors of the big cities—New York, Chicago, Philadelphia, San Francisco, Los Angeles, for example—resented and feared the loss of control over millions in federal funds. Mostly Democrats, their complaints that neighborhood people, activists, and hustlers, not they, were handing out money and creating jobs rang a loud bell in Congress and the White House. Among some of the local people, meanwhile, the new fountain of federal money seemed an opportunity to upend local power structures and enhance grassroots democracy.

The community action programs quickly became storm centers of controversy. In every poor community there were opportunists who considered the War on Poverty a gravy train offering good jobs, at astounding pay, for themselves personally, and opportunities for power-enhancing patronage. But even the community idealists were often a trial to people in power. By mid-decade the new radicalism and black separatism had spread among the ghetto young, creating a cohort of militants who saw community action as a chance to revolutionize the masses. It is no accident that the Newark Community Union Project, founded by Students for a Democratic Society (SDS) leaders Carl Whitman and Tom Hayden, clashed with Newark mayor Hugh Addonizio over sponsorship of VISTA groups in the city. During the summer of 1965, HARYOU-ACT in New York, the local Harlem CAP, besides bowing to blackmail by hoodlums who threatened to riot if not paid off, sponsored the Black Arts Repertory Theater School run by militant playwright Imamu Baraka, still calling himself LeRoi Jones. Jones put on antiwhite plays, including *Jell-O*, in which Rochester, the comic black valet on Jack Benny's popular TV show, turns on his white exploiters, including Benny, and kills them all. The press gave wide publicity to these excesses, and they soon came to the president's notice.

The Jobs Corps, too, got a lot of negative media attention. The Job Corps camps brought hundreds of inner-city youths and young men and women from Appalachia to special training camps outside metropolitan centers to learn marketable skills. These were often the hard-core unemployed, and unemployables, and they were not always upright citizens. Before long the newspapers were featuring stories of violence, drunkenness, drug abuse, and thievery, as well as complaints from neighboring householders, that confirmed many of the prejudices of white, middle-class Americans about the nation's underclass.

The mainstream response to these excesses was predictable outrage. When the Associated Press in November wrote up the summer doings of HARYOU in New York, the White House received a barrage of angry letters. An Illinois lady called the LeRoi Jones enterprise "a training school for radical strife" and asked how long the country was "going to tolerate the complete lack of common sense in a program as this. . . ." A man in California wrote to protest "*my* tax money being spent to produce plays of hate." Another lady, from Oregon, wrote that she had never "heard of such a horrible example" of "foolish . . . expenditures" as described in the AP article.[87] A small sample, apparently, of the total received by the White House, these letters were passed along to the OEO for reply.

More telling to the president, probably, were the complaints of big-city mayors. By May many of them were angry and, at the National Conference of Mayors in St. Louis, were prepared to endorse the resolution of John Shelley of Francisco and Sam Yorty of Los Angeles attacking the OEO for failing "to recognize the legal and moral responsibility of local officials who are accountable to the taxpayers for expenditures of local funds."[88] In the end the resolution failed to pass; most of the mayors were

Democrats and did not want to embarrass the administration. But to appease them the White House ordered Vice President Humphrey, in St. Louis to address the conference, to reassure the city leaders that the president would not ignore their voices.

During the summer, Shriver had one shining success—or what at first seemed like one. This was Head Start, an early education program designed to give poor preschoolers a leg up in developing the intellectual and social skills that middle-class children acquired from their parents. Johnson was very taken with the idea and wanted at first to call it "Kiddy Corps." It not only promised to soak up leftover poverty funds; it also seemed a sure winner. Shriver would later say that while middle-class white folks might not be happy distributing largesse to belligerent ghetto youths who seemed bent on riot and looting, few could resist children. "There's always been a prejudice in favor of little black children," he told an interviewer in 1977.[89]

Head Start was launched in mid-February at a White House tea party presided over by the First Lady. It was rushed into operation in June to take advantage of the summer vacation, when unused school buildings and schoolteachers would be available. By the fall it had scored a public-relations home run, and on August 31 Johnson announced at a White House meeting of educators and psychologists that Head Start would become a permanent one-year program for 350,000 poor children. What had started as a trial run had now "been battle-tested" and "proved worthy."[90]

Head Start's success notwithstanding, the War on Poverty weighed Johnson down. At first he defended it and the way Shriver and his agency administered it. But Johnson soon came to regard it, and especially the community action programs, as an incubus. James Gaither, an assistant to Califano, remembered that community action gave the president more "political heat" than anything but Vietnam.[91] In a display of self-pity that grew increasingly frequent as troubles multiplied, Johnson concluded that OEO officials as a whole were not to be trusted. Wilbur Cohen remembered that the president told him often that he would never appoint people from the OEO to other government jobs. "Well, I don't want to appoint that fellow," Cohen quoted the president as remarking, typically. "He's from OEO. He's disloyal to me. He's a troublemaker."[92]

Johnson's assessment of his administration's turning point was a retrospective conclusion from his memoirs published in 1971. In fact, when the first session of the Eighty-ninth Congress adjourned in late October, he seemed delighted with its work, calling it "the greatest in American history." And, as the polls showed, the general public strongly applauded the results as well. Yet, as usual, Johnson could not enjoy his success. Under the surface, he was discontented. A *Washington Post* columnist in late August described his mood as "withdrawn and somber."[93] LBJ believed that the people who counted—the "Harvards," the liberals, the press—after a brief honeymoon—were again skeptical of him, if not outright hostile and contemptuous. The *New Republic* confirmed LBJ's feelings of insecurity: "How nice it is to have a man who gives what liberals have asked for generations, plus the fun of kicking him around, too."[94] Even if *The New Republic* was being ironic, it certainly described the views of a substantial number of liberals. No matter what he accomplished, they would always make fun of him at best and hate him at worst.

Without question Johnson's personal habits contributed to his bad image with liberals, especially the elite contingent from the Northeast. He had none of the tokens of high culture: an Ivy League degree, an interest in the arts, a capacity for abstract thought, and a taste for the latest intellectual fashions. But beyond this, he had a coarse personal streak that offended the more fastidious of his advisers. In many ways he resembled that other southern populist Huey Long, who received important visitors in his pajamas and displayed execrable table manners. Johnson delighted in forcing his staff to share the calls of nature with him. The habit, probably intended to show who was boss, dated at least from his days with Kleberg, when he offended office secretary Luther Jones by giving him dictation while on the toilet. He continued this crude behavior into the presidency. The liberal Texas journalist Ronnie Dugger recalled a visit to the White House late in Johnson's term. After talking to Dugger for some time the president went off to the bathroom to relieve his bowels, leaving the door open. Dugger could hear "loud expulsive sounds mixed with his continuous talking." Meanwhile, "one of his young men squatted down just outside the open door and made notes."[95] The "young men" had to take it, but one author has claimed that the president's publicly displayed toilet habits helped drive from Washington the Secretary of the Treasury C. Douglas Dillon, a charter member of the eastern elite.[†]

The public only occasionally saw the president's uncouth side. The time he pulled his beagle by his ears, and the later incident at the hospital, where he showed his gallbladder operation scars to the reporters, are

---

[†]Actually, Dillon denied the charge made in David Halberstam's book *The Best and the Brightest*. LBJ, he later wrote, never subjected him to the ordeal described. Dillon did not refute, however, that Johnson subjected others to it. See letter of Dillon to Thomas Johnson of February 5, 1973, attached to the Dillon *Oral History*, LBJ Library.

instances. He tried for dignity in his presidential appearances and usually erred on the side of a charmless, stiff formality. Everyone who knew him agreed that he was far more effective in small groups, where his earthy humor and grasp of facts invariably impressed his audiences.

More damaging was his emerging "credibility gap." Kermit Gordon believed that it probably dated from Johnson's coy behavior over his first budget back in 1964. But as a phrase it was probably first used in print— as the headline for his column of December 5, 1965—by Murrey Marder, the *Washington Post*'s diplomatic correspondent. Marder described the growing belief of political observers, the media, the intellectual community, and well-informed citizens—the "sub-Establishment of national life"—that the White House was not being honest with the public. The skeptics were "not beatniks, draft card burners or dyed-in-the-wool critics of Government policy." Although the suspicions began with official pronouncements about various events in Vietnam, they became even more conspicuous with what seemed like exaggerated rationalizations for the military intervention in the Dominican Republic. Since the Vietnam problem was ongoing, once distrust was established, it was almost impossible to restore confidence that administration explanations were true. "The public search for detailed fact," wrote Marder, "collides not only with the standard diplomatic desire for secrecy. It also encounters President Johnson's obsession with secrecy in Government operations as a whole."[96]

Johnson claimed that Vietnam had made him secretive. This was not true. He was never a fan of full disclosure. He invented and distorted some of his past and the history of his family. He never escaped the talltale heritage of the frontier. As a politician, he jealously guarded important information until it suited his purposes to reveal it. His legislative task forces, for example, were enjoined to strict secrecy. But Johnson might have preserved his reputation if he had only refused to discuss matters he wished to hide. Instead, he dissembled and was then caught in a lie. Hugh Sidey of *Time* magazine was certain that Johnson actually believed many of his misleading statements. Whatever the shape of the problem, however, it is clear that Vietnam amplified his instinctive close-to-the-vest responses and undermined his public credibility.

There were many reasons why Johnson and the press did not get along. A man notoriously sensitive to the public and private needs of fellow politicians, he had little empathy for reporters. He assumed they had no personal lives and was indifferent to inconveniencing them with abruptly altered travel plans. He would, for example, refuse to release information about whether he was going to visit the Ranch for the weekend and then have Reedy or Moyers announce on Friday afternoon: "Get your bags out, we're leaving at seven o'clock tonight for Texas." The news-men, according to Jack Valenti, "would just climb the wall with fury."[97]

Johnson's bad relations with the media would damage his adminis-tration after 1965. Notoriously avid of attention and sensitive to criticism, he kept a battery of TV sets at the White House and the Ranch con-stantly tuned to each of the networks to learn what they were saying about him and his doings. He was what a later generation would call a "control freak." This served him well in getting laws on the books. But the press was resistant to his pokes and pulls, his rewards and retaliations. While majority leader he could easily control the small circle of re-porters assigned to him. As president he became the hot focus of national media attention and simply could not apply his micromanagement skills to so large and so diverse an entity. He tried to oversee the news flow by limiting what subordinates could tell the press, and he engaged in an early version of spin control. But, with the exception of close friend William S. White, the White House press corps, bound by professional principles, proved more independent than he liked.

Johnson did not understand the newspeople. As we know, reporters and columnists are not robots. They have opinions and agendas and in-terests. But Johnson could not conceive that they might also have profes-sional standards. According to Reedy, he "could not believe that any story about a political personality had been written just because it hap-pened. In his mind, it was something that had been inspired by either the friends or the foes of that personality."[98] The president could not fathom why the press did not respond to his requests and favors like the politicians. He considered the press ingrates. He would invite a colum-nist or a reporter to the Ranch or to the White House, and that reporter would then knife him in the back in a story. One early instance was at Eastertime 1964, when the president crammed four reporters, three of them women, into his Lincoln and set off on one of his ninety-mile-an-hour tours of his Ranch property. Johnson considered this a treat, but the media folk were terrified. As if in revenge, they reported that while hurtling along the narrow back roads the president was tippling from a cup of beer and graphically describing the generative organs of his prize bulls. The account, widely disseminated, made Johnson seem simultane-ously reckless and coarse. The *Time* magazine story the following Mon-day called the president "a cross between a teen-age Grand Prix driver and a back-to-nature Thoreau in cowboy boots."[99]

Yet the poor relations were not entirely the president's fault. The me-dia folk were indeed moved by prejudice as well as principle. Mostly gut liberals, at least at the reporter level, when they saw him in 1964 as the bulwark against the right-wing demon Goldwater, they gave him the benefit of every doubt. Generally the Great Society and civil rights legislation got a good press, too. But Vietnam, once past the early phases, enraged them. Thereafter, Johnson was irreversibly flawed—in his character, his manners, his tastes.

By mid-1966 the White House had become painfully aware of the president's "image" problem. The chief informant was Robert Kintner, a journalist and former TV executive whom Johnson had known since the 1930s. In April 1966 Kintner joined the White House staff to serve as a two-way conduit between the administration and the press, and his memos to the president were soon major sources of information and advice, drawing on his many media contacts.

In late June Kintner briefed LBJ on the views of Walter Ridder, of the Ridder chain of midsize newspapers in the Midwest and on the Pacific Coast. Ridder had told Kintner that LBJ's reputation was "one of 'maneuverer' rather than what he and I both know to be the facts—that of a sincere, well-informed leader."[100] The president seemed to be trying too hard to get public support. He should be more relaxed; his public appearances should be more informal. He should also pay less attention to what the Washington press corps said about him.

But the serious damage from the media skepticism and the credibility gap was still in the future. In these fall and winter months of 1965 Johnson still had many defenders. "In my judgment," wrote Roscoe Drummond in a syndicated column a month after Marder's December article appeared, "Mr. Johnson has done nothing to justify lack of trust between himself and the American people. . . ."[101] At the beginning of 1966 a Gallup poll found the president the "Most Admired Man" in the world for the third straight year.[102]

Well into 1966, LBJ would continue to get most of his bills passed. In early September he signed a measure creating the Department of Housing and Urban Development, ending a five-year fight. He later named as its head Robert Weaver, the first black ever appointed to a cabinet-level position. Two weeks later he approved a bill establishing the National Endowments for the Arts and the Humanities, modeled after the National Science Foundation established fifteen years previously.

No element of the Great Society fits so well its quality-of-life attribute as this law. In Europe public patronage had for many years funded orchestras and theatrical and opera companies as well as individual artists and performers. But in the United States, the federal government had done little for the arts aside from the New Deal's short-lived Federal Arts and Federal Writers projects, which had provided incomes for unemployed creative artists. Prodded by his wife, John Kennedy had tried to augment the federal government's role in the arts but had gotten little besides a National Council on the Arts and Cultural Development, an advisory agency with few powers and little money. LBJ, as we have seen, did not have sophisticated cultural tastes. When he could pry himself away from his first love, politics, his preferences ran to popular music and middle-brow art. He seldom read a book. As vice president he could barely tolerate the Kennedy White House cultural soirees. Aide Harry McPherson believes that his cultural indifference diminished his administration by cutting him off from artists and intellectuals. On the other hand, Lady Bird liked theater and art and often arranged trips of her own to New York to see plays that interested her, and she paid visits to Washington museums with Lynda. The First Lady had an ally in Abe Fortas, Johnson's close friend ever since his House days, a man who played the violin almost at a professional level and who took high culture seriously. Playing to the theme of cultural and spiritual enrichment as a core piece of the Great Society, together wife and old friend helped turn LBJ into a patron of the arts. The humanities became linked to the arts through Johnson's need to appease the academics and literary intellectuals.

In his January 1965 State of the Union address LBJ asked Congress to "recognize and encourage those who can be pathfinders for the nation's imagination and understanding."[103] Two months later he sent a bill to establish a National Foundation on the Arts and Humanities to Congress. The bill that passed the House and Senate in mid-September was little more than a foot-in-the-door sort of measure. It established a National Endowment for the Arts and a parallel National Endowment for the Humanities, with a meager 5 million dollars apiece to dispense as grants to individuals and organizations. More would come later, ironically much of it under Richard Nixon. Still, it was a breakthrough that Johnson sought to make the most of among the people who rejected him as a rube and a philistine.

In the September 29 Rose Garden signing ceremony for the new law, Johnson said the new foundation would have an "unprecedented effect on the arts and humanities of our great nation."[104] He was not entirely wrong. The amount of money initially appropriated was a mere token, and even when the sums rose after Johnson's term, America was not transformed into Periclean Athens. But under the National Endowment for the Arts, many communities experienced for the first time the pleasures of high culture in live performances. Existing cultural institutions expanded; new ones were created. Dance companies, especially, would spread and blossom under the gentle rain of federal money. The humanities endowment, for its part, would sponsor ambitious projects of historical and literary editorship and subsidize individual scholars, authors, and social scientists. Today the national endowments are under siege by conservatives, philistines, free marketeers, and assorted skeptics, but all things considered, the money was well spent.

Johnson proved as much of an innovator in the natural as in the cultural environment, helping to launch what his secretary of the interior, Stewart Udall, called the "Third Wave" of the conservation movement. LBJ's presidency coincided with a new public consciousness of both the dangers and the possibilities in the nation's natural endowment. By the midsixties a sense of environmental fragility, spurred by Rachel Carson's 1962 best-seller *Silent Spring*, had appeared. So, too, had a new understanding of ecological relationships and a new reverence for nature inspired by the writings of ecovisionaries such as Aldo Leopold and James Gilligan, who believed in the deep spiritual quality of unspoiled, undeveloped nature. Stewart Udall had read Carson, and he and his assistants had been impressed by the concepts of the new ecological movement. Udall was a Kennedy holdover but was close to the Johnsons. Lady Bird, who had a special love for flowers and the landscape, relied on Udall, a former congressman, to get her highway beautification bill through Congress. The president himself had a natural affection for the land and accepted Udall's guidance. If the secretary declared "'This is good for the land and good for the people,' he bought it," Udall later said.[105]

Johnson signed on to much pending Kennedy environmental legislation and during the summer of 1964 helped get it through Congress. The new laws included a trust fund for federal land acquisition and a Wilderness Act setting aside federal land that would be kept permanently pristine, without development. Simultaneously, Congress passed a cluster of bills creating federal parks, preserves, historic sites, and seashores.

After the 1964 election the pace of preservation and protection accelerated. In a special message to Congress on the physical environment in early February, Johnson announced a "new conservation" infused with the spirit of ecologically informed environmentalism. The new view, he proclaimed, insisted that "beauty must not just be a holiday treat, but part of our daily life." It was concerned not "with nature alone" but "with the total relation between man and the world around him." Its goal would be "not just man's welfare but the dignity of man's spirit." It sought not only to "protect the countryside" but also to "salvage the beauty and charm of our cities." The message also talked much of water pollution, which had severely befouled the nation's lakes and rivers.[106]

Johnson's concern for water and air pollution had been anticipated by Democratic senator Edmund Muskie of Maine, a man whose environmental concerns gave him the nickname "Mr. Clean." During previous Congresses Muskie had introduced bills to control and reduce water and air pollution, but they had been blocked in committee by conservatives. Back in 1959, when he was Senate majority leader, Johnson had punished the liberal Muskie for his bumptious, disrespectful attitude by giving him second-class committee assignments. Now, in the Eighty-ninth Congress, he turned to the Maine senator for help in getting the antipollution measures he wanted.

Two water quality measures were already wending their way through Congress when Johnson transmitted his February environmental message. Muskie's strong Senate bill passed in late January. The House bill was a weaker law that gave the states too much authority to set standards. In the conference committee to reconcile the two versions, Muskie and the administration prevailed, however, and the law as enacted allowed the federal government to augment state standards if these did not prove adequate.

Clean air was another concern of the administration. As of 1963 American cars were inefficient gas-guzzlers and pollution-spewers. Industry, too, especially oil refining, was a major poisoner of the atmosphere. Johnson had signed the Clean Air Act of 1963, a weak measure that authorized Washington to establish air quality standards but gave it little authority to enforce them. Deeply dissatisfied with the law, Muskie introduced S. 306, a stronger measure, during the Eighty-ninth Congress, but without consulting Johnson. LBJ was close to the auto industry. Henry Ford II had supported him against Goldwater the year before and was one of his favorite business tycoons. Besides, a Texan could understand the danger of contaminating the rivers but had, as his birthright, a natural rapport with big cars. The administration initially sought to delay the Muskie bill and then gave it begrudging support. What finally passed was a weak measure that even the president could only call "a hopeful beginning" at the October 20 signing ceremony.[107] In that ceremony, Johnson quoted Rachel Carson: "In biological history, no organism has survived long if its environment became in some way unfit for it; but no organism before man has deliberately polluted its own environment." With his usual grandiosity the president promised to "rewrite that chapter of history."[108]

On October 3, as the momentous first session wound down, Johnson signed a major immigration reform bill. In the shadow of the Statue of Liberty, with Ellis Island nearby, he ended with the stroke of his pen the xenophobic, national origins quota system in place since the 1920s. The National Origins Act of 1924 discriminated harshly against eastern and southern Europeans in favor of northern Europeans and denied naturalization rights to Japanese-born residents. Besides contracting the whole stream of newcomers to the United States, it imposed a stigma of inferiority on those American citizens whose families had come from places such as Italy, Poland, Russia, and Greece. Over the years the system came under attack from liberals and ethnic defense groups as racist and as cruel to those foreigners who most needed and deserved refuge in America.

The Kennedys remembered keenly the discrimination the Irish had encountered in mid-nineteenth-century Boston. John Kennedy, who had authored a book on the immigrant origins of Americans, deplored the existing quota laws, and in mid-1963, after months of bickering with the conservative committee chairmen of the House and Senate, submitted a bill to Congress ending the nationality quota system and providing for reuniting families separated by immigration regardless of nationality. Hearings on the bill were held up by the immigration subcommittee of the House, and nothing had been done by the time he went to Dallas.

Johnson favored liberalization of the nation's immigration laws. He had few if any ethnic prejudices. He was familiar with the German Americans who had settled in the Hill Country. He had good rapport with Mexican Americans. During the 1930s he had witnessed, and opposed, the cruel exclusion from the United States of Jewish refugees desperately fleeing Nazi persecution, a shameful page in American history. When briefed on the immigration issue by Myer Feldman, a Kennedy aide, he immediately signed aboard the movement to revise the nation's immigration laws. In his first State of the Union message, in January 1964, Johnson noted:

> In establishing preferences, a nation that was built by immigrants of all lands can ask those who now seek admission: "What can you do for our country?" But we should not be asking: "In what country were you born?"[109]

Thereafter Johnson pushed hard for immigration reform against the resistance of conservative Michael Feighan of Ohio, head of the Immigration and Nationality Subcommittee of the House Judiciary Committee.

The administration's bill got nowhere until after the 1964 presidential landslide. Now, with more urban northern Democrats on the immigration subcommittee, the bill slipped easily through the legislative process, passing the House in August 1965 and the Senate in late September. The new law ended the national origins quota and gave preference as immigrants to relatives of those already in the United States as well as to skilled workers and to members of the artistic, scientific and professional communities, all on a first-come, first-served basis. It restricted total Eastern Hemisphere annual immigration to 170,000 and set a ceiling of 120,000 on arrivals from Latin America. Excluded from these limits were relatives of American citizens.

Johnson was proud of his accomplishment. And well he might be. Like many Great Society laws, the 1965 immigration law had some unforeseen negative consequences,‡ but it did finally make amends for a standing insult to millions of Americans whose ancestors had been judged inferior.

Less than a week after the signing ceremony on Liberty Island, LBJ was in Bethesda Naval Hospital for surgery. He had been feeling good since his major heart attack, but the day after Labor Day he suffered severe abdominal pains. The doctors told him was it was a diseased gallbladder and advised him to have it removed. The operation, on October 8, was successful. Doctors removed his gallbladder and a urethral stone in the same abdominal incision. The next day he signed thirteen pieces of minor legislation, read some briefings on world affairs, dictated some letters, and received visits from family and staff. The official press releases stressed how well he was doing, but the fifty-seven-year-old Johnson was actually in a great deal of pain. During his recuperation he showed reporters his scar to prove that he had not had another heart attack, as rumored. The photograph of the president pointing to his bare belly was widely published in newspapers and magazines. It made Johnson a laughingstock. One Washingtonian snidely suggested calling him "The Abdominal Showman."[110] The ridicule was unfair. Considering the wild rumors that circulate when a president is in the hospital and given Johnson's history of heart problems, his wish to confirm the medical reports is understandable. It is a measure of the president's vulnerability that the action backfired, causing him embarrassment and pain.

Johnson also had reasons for satisfaction during this period. A report from the Office of Business Economics said that the nation's economy was outperforming the most hopeful predictions made earlier in the year and that the gains were across the board, covering every major part of the economy except homebuilding. The Gross National Product was growing at 5 percent annually, as fast as in the extraordinary previous year. It was among the best of all the industrialized nations.

And public opinion still seemed to be with him on Vietnam. True, the October 17 weekend was marked by antiwar protests all over the

---

‡Most notably, the exaggerated definition of family members would allow many immigrants not otherwise qualified to get legal admission to the United States. Some critics have also been unhappy with an end to the preference for Europeans.

country, but Johnson had reason to believe that the general public was getting fed up with the naysayers. Opinion polls indicated that there was widespread support for Johnson's Vietnam policies. A *New York Times* front-page story reported the parades, blood donations, information programs, and rallies being planned by those who supported the military commitment in Southeast Asia. Voluntary enlistments in the armed forces were up since the summer. Even at the colleges where antiwar support was strongest, most students still supported the president. At Yale, where Vice President Humphrey was due to speak on October 21, a leaflet prepared by student leaders declared, "We feel that there is little support at Yale for groups which have attempted to impede troops movements and encourage students to obstruct the draft."[111]

Still fatigued from his operation, the president left the hospital on October 21, planning to spend the rest of the year after Congress adjourned recovering at the Ranch. For the twenty-two months since Kennedy's assassination, his pace had been so hectic that the doctors advised him to take an extended period to convalesce. But there were still a few bills waiting for him to sign before he could relax in Texas.

The first gave him enormous pleasure and pride. The highway beautification bill really belonged to Lady Bird, who had made "The Beauty of America" her special project. She had suggested the bill to her husband and had traveled through the countryside planting trees and making speeches for upgrading the appearance of America's highways. In May she had taken a well-publicized scenic tour through Virginia in a chartered bus full of cabinet wives, Public Roads and Parks Service officials, and forty members of the press.

The measure faced immense hurdles. The Outdoor Advertising Association, the billboard lobby, conducted a robust campaign against it, buttressing their drive with the usual obstructionist states' rights argument. State and county highway officials, fighting to prevent money being deflected from construction and repair of the immense interstate system, also opposed the bill, as did proprietors of junkyards and scrap yards, often located along the shoulders of major highways. Though backed by a diffuse public dislike of the commercialization and defacement of the highway system, the organized forces for "beautification" were far weaker, consisting primarily of female-dominated road councils and garden clubs.

Johnson knew how formidable the measure's opponents would be, but he considered the bill a gift to his wife. As he told his staff, "You know, I love that woman and she wants that highway bill. By God, we're going to get it for her."[112] But this time the vaunted Johnson juggernaut failed. In the end, the president got far less than he and the reformers wanted. The Highway Beautification Act forbade billboards and junk-yards within a thousand feet of an interstate but allowed them in commercial and industrial zones. In determining exempted zones the states, rather than against the more aggressive federal authorities, would decide. All costs for administration and for removal of unsightly features would be assessed against the Treasury, rather than the sacred Interstate Highway Trust Fund, and the president's request that the states be required to use a third of the money they received from the federal government for secondary roads for easier access to recreation and scenic areas was eliminated.

Johnson himself deserved some of the blame for the bill's weaknesses. His strong personal feelings impaired his judgment. "I must inform you," Larry O'Brien wrote the president on September 18, "that our performance on the Highway Beauty Bill has fallen far below the standards of our usual work." Administration managers had created confusion and annoyed friendly members of Congress.[113] "Much of the fault," Joseph Califano later wrote, "lay with the president for the one inept legislative experience I witnessed and participated in as a member of his staff."[114] But the president was also undermined by White House staffers who considered the bill frivolous. It was Lady Bird's bill, not a true administration measure. In fact, the highway beautification movement expressed the fragile outer edges of the quality-of-life sensibility, and it is not surprising that it could not prevail against the entrenched interests opposed to its goals.

But however imperfect, the president made the most of the measure. The bill signing took place in the East Room of the White House, where a blue velvet backdrop featured blow-up photographs of roadsides defaced by junkyards side by side with scenic, tree-lined highways. As the Marine Band played "America the Beautiful," LBJ noted that the law would "enrich our spirits and restore a small measure of our national greatness."[115] It was only a "first step" in beautifying the landscape, however; there would be others. Johnson gave the first pen and a big kiss on the cheek to his wife.

LBJ still had some fifteen bills left to approve before the 1965 legislative year was over. The most important was the higher education bill, proposed on January 12 at the same time as ESEA.

As we saw, LBJ had boundless faith that education would cure all that ailed individuals and society. Rooted in his own experience and training, it was reinforced by the era's conventional wisdom that nurture counted far more than nature. In the case of higher education, the relevant lesson was the "human capital" concept that the engine of modern economic growth was the knowledge in people's skulls, not merely the brute machines of the factories. LBJ did not have to fight for the bill the way he did for ESEA. The church-state issue did not apply, and there were no powerful institutions opposed. The bill was ably handled by his supporters in Congress, and the president's strong support clearly counted.

The new measure, an expansion of a Kennedy bill, provided for federal support of college tuition scholarships, low-interest student loans, and work-study programs for low- and middle-income students. It authorized funds for libraries and for small and newly developing colleges. It extended the life of the National Defense Education Act, a post-*Sputnik* measure to strengthen science, mathematics, and language education, and also set up a National Teacher Corps to pay the education costs of those who agreed to teach for up to two years in elementary and secondary schools in poor areas. The cost of all this? Roughly $785 million—far more than the original administration bill, yet a small part of the total cost of higher education in the United States.

The president signed the bill on November 8 at his alma mater, now called Southwest Texas State College, before a crowd of more than three thousand, who had packed the gym to hear the college's most famous alumnus speak. Johnson referred proudly to the two dozen education bills that had been passed by the Eighty-ninth Congress. That Congress had done "more for the wonderful cause of education in America than all the previous 176 regular sessions of Congress put together."[116]

Now the president could go back to the Ranch to rest and recuperate. He had reason to be pleased with his accomplishments. Even for a man not recovering from surgery, the year had been a prodigiously full one. He had sent 115 legislative recommendations to the Hill and had signed 89 into law.

The highly productive year ended on an up note. On Christmas Eve the Johnsons made a happy announcement. Their younger daughter, Luci, age eighteen, had become engaged to be married to Airman Patrick John Nugent. The wedding would take place the following summer. In addition, a "head to toe" physical examination on December 29 had revealed that the president was in "fine condition."[117] The last day of 1965 found LBJ working at his desk, looking forward to a New Year's Eve party given by the Driskill Hotel for the White House press corps. The second session of the marvelous Eighty-ninth was just ahead. Would it be as productive as the first? Was there more room for breakthroughs and triumphs?

CHAPTER 18

Guns vs. Butter

J OHNSON'S LONG STATE OF THE UNION MESSAGE on January 12 stressed his continued dedication to the Great Society. He had criticized President Truman in 1950 for pursuing both guns and butter during the Korean War, but guns and butter were exactly what he asked for now.

"This nation is mighty enough . . ." he told Congress, "its society healthy enough—its people strong enough—to pursue our goals in the rest of the world while building a Great Society at home." The War on Poverty must continue with "vigor and determination." Congress must pass a new civil rights bill, the third in three years, which would ban discrimination in federal and state jury selection and prohibit discrimination in both the sale and the rental of housing. He recommended a further massive drive against water and air pollution and an urban slum rebuilding program "on a scale never before attempted." He proposed a crime prevention program accomplished "by building up law enforcement and by revitalizing the entire federal system from prevention to probation." He came out for consumer laws against false labeling on packages, harmful drugs and cosmetics, and deceitful interest and credit charges, as well as a highway safety act and an increase in the minimum wage.

And there was more. A new cabinet-level Department of Transportation was essential to "meet the needs of industry" and "the right of the taxpayer to full efficiency and frugality." The Treasury should subsidize a new supersonic transport plane and finance export of the Great Society to other nations through an International Education Act and an

International Health Act. Referring to unfinished business of the first session, he asked Congress to repeal Section 14(b) of the Taft-Hartley Act, enact home rule for the District of Columbia, and appropriate money for rent supplements and for the Teacher Corps, which had not yet been funded. He promised a number of special messages in the near future to explain his proposals in detail.[1]

Johnson could not ignore Vietnam in this prolix message. In the media, news about Southeast Asia seemed to be eclipsing everything else. Only a year and a half earlier, during the 1964 campaign, the polls showed that the voters were indifferent to foreign-policy issues. The most recent polls revealed the public's confusion about what exactly should be done in Vietnam, but the indifference was gone; American voters were obviously deeply concerned about the issue. And well they might be. By the end of 1965 there were more than 185,000 American combat troops in Vietnam, and 1,350 had already been carried home in body bags.

By now the failings of overall strategy in Vietnam were becoming apparent to McNamara and other policymakers. Westmoreland, with his newly beefed-up command, envisioned a four-phase war to be activated concurrently. He would deploy troops to protect American bases along the coast and around Saigon. Additional forces would be sent to the Central Highlands to block any Communist attempt to cut the country in two. These were holding actions and would not themselves stop the enemy. For this purpose he planned large-scale "search and destroy" missions to pursue the enemy wherever he could be found and if possible entice him into battle where American firepower would decimate his forces. The fourth phase would be a mop-up operation. Meanwhile, American bombing would choke off the flow of supplies and troop reinforcements available south of the demilitarized zone, while a "pacification" program would seek to check the guerrillas by winning the "hearts and minds" of South Vietnamese villagers.

The strategy did not work. The Communists refused to face the ARVN and American forces in direct battle. They hid when pursued, and they attacked by stealth. American forays often produced air balls: The enemy was somewhere else when the blow landed, and the only results were some burning thatch and bone-weary marines. Nor did the bombing interdict reinforcements. The enemy was able to nullify the air raids by an amazing system of infiltration over the jungle-shrouded Ho Chi Minh Trail. Each increment of American troops brought additional Communist forces. Escalation begat counterescalation in what came to seem, by early 1966, an endless sequence. As for the "hearts and minds" of the villagers, they were either indifferent to the blandishments of the

Americans or remained positively hostile to the corrupt government in Saigon.

The military blamed the president for the stalemate. In early November they asked for another 113,000 troops. They also proposed more rigorous interdiction of supplies and a major increment in the bombing campaign. The United States should mine Haiphong Harbor and heavily bomb Hanoi itself. When they presented their plan at an Oval Office meeting, Johnson exploded. According to marine general Charles Cooper, "he screamed obscenities, he cursed [the Joint Chiefs] personally. . . . He . . . accused them of trying to pass the buck for World War III to him."[2]

That fall the antiwar movement touched a new level of passion and drama when a Quaker pacifist, Norman Morrison, doused himself with kerosene just outside McNamara's window at the Pentagon and lit a match. In late November SANE, a group of respectable middle-class and middle-aged doves formed in the fifties to stop nuclear testing, brought thirty thousand marchers to Washington to demand a negotiated peace. It was during this demonstration that for the first time protesters were heard chanting: "Hey, hey, LBJ, how many kids did you kill today?"

Johnson always insisted that he paid no attention to the protesters. But he did. A man for whom admiration was like manna, he suffered deeply from the activists' taunts and slurs. He also began to fear weakening resolve among his closest advisers. In late November Westmoreland had cabled Washington asking for two hundred thousand more troops in 1966. The request, opening the prospect of war without reasonable end, was disturbing. McNamara flew to Saigon to consult the general and learned that, despite the bombing, the Communists were moving two hundred tons of supplies a day down the Ho Chi Minh Trail. The news, McNamara later wrote, "shook me and altered my attitude perceptibly."[3] The secretary returned home to suggest changing course. At a meeting on December 17 in the Cabinet Room he told the president, "We have been too optimistic." The United States had to "explore other means."[4] Encouraged by a Soviet promise to use its influence with Hanoi to negotiate if the Americans stopped the bombing, on December 27, following an early thirty-hour Christmas truce, Johnson agreed to a pause in the bombing campaign against the North. This could be extended day by day to test Hanoi's response. Simultaneously he dispatched envoys by special presidential jets to major cities around the world to ask foreign leaders for help in turning the bombing pause into wide-ranging negotiations to end the war. In hours, Humphrey was off to Japan, India, and the Philippines; Arthur Goldberg, American UN ambassador, to Paris and London.

The pause remained in effect when Johnson delivered the January State of the Union speech, and he was still hopeful that his peace initiative would bear fruit. The United States, he said, would "meet at any conference table, we will discuss any proposals . . . and we will consider the views of any group." But he did not dwell on Vietnam excessively. He reiterated more than once that Vietnam should not be allowed to distract from the Great Society. He was certain that "we can continue the Great Society while we fight in Vietnam." Do not take the war out on the poor, he warned. His conclusion expressed Johnson's idealism at its purest: "Scarred by the weaknesses of man, with whatever guidance God may offer us, we must nevertheless stand alone with our mortality, strive to ennoble the life of man on earth."[5]

Even Johnson's loyal supporters were skeptical that he could get his full domestic agenda. Just before the speech, an administration stalwart, Representative George Grider of Tennessee, warned there was little chance that the nation would "be able to afford expansion of social programs in the next term and there may even be some cutting back."[6] To pay for both guns and butter, the budget that Johnson submitted to Congress two weeks later was a record $112 billion, including a supplemental request for the Vietnam War of $12.7 billion and a hint of new taxes.

By late January it became clear that the bombing pause was getting nowhere. The Communists called the pause a trick and insisted that the United States must cease for good all hostile acts against the Democratic Republic of Vietnam before they could consider negotiations. Johnson concluded that Ho was merely using the halt as an opportunity to increase traffic in men and matériel over the Ho Chi Minh Trail and for repairing damaged roads and bridges. Johnson would later say that the pause was one of the great mistakes of the war. He "had been suckered into and nothing had come from [it] and that he'd gotten bad advice on it."[7] On January 31, after thirty-seven days, he ordered the bombing resumed.

The Vietnam problem for Johnson was exacerbated by his own volatile feelings. He had, as we have seen, always ridden an emotional roller coaster, though with steeper downs than ups. Now, whenever the news from Vietnam was bad, his depression intensified. An expert in political maneuver, he began to stumble. In formulating his 1966 policies, Johnson expected his greatest opposition to come from conservatives and "hawks," who wanted to escalate the war in Vietnam. But he misjudged the mood of a Congress weary of the enormous bulk of legislation passed in 1964 and 1965. Even without the crisis in Southeast Asia, probably some time was needed to digest the Great Society programs that had already been passed. The president, however, chose to push an ambitious agenda and had ample reason to expect a balky Congress. But Johnson was totally surprised when much of the antagonism began coming from congressional friends more interested in criticizing his foreign policy than passing Great Society measures.

The senator from Arkansas J. William Fulbright was not your usual southern courthouse politician. A Rhodes scholar and a former law professor at the University of Arkansas, he was a cosmopolitan gentleman who after he came to the Senate moved up quickly to chair the prestigious Foreign Relations Committee. A personal friend of Johnson's, Fulbright had supported the Gulf of Tonkin Resolution in 1964. He had disagreed with the president over the Dominican intervention but had remained a Johnson supporter generally. As the months passed, however, Fulbright concluded that the United States did not belong in Vietnam. As a predominantly white country, we represented an alien culture, and our intrusion aroused natural antagonism among Asians. Besides, Vietnam was damaging our all-important relations with the Soviet Union. In the past, Fulbright had always held hearings of his committee in private, without publicity. But now, beginning on January 27, he proposed to put the president's policy on trial in full view of the TV cameras.

Another disillusioned Johnson supporter was Senator Vance Hartke. As a freshman Democratic senator from Indiana in 1958, Hartke had quickly become a protégé of the powerful majority leader. Now, as a member of the Senate Finance Committee, he was concerned that the escalating cost of the war would in fact smother Great Society programs. Just before Johnson had to decide whether to end the Christmas bombing pause, Hartke wrote a forceful letter asking him not to resume the attack and persuaded fourteen Democratic colleagues to sign it. He released it to the media on January 27.

Johnson's public response was brusque but polite. He thanked the writers for telling him how they felt, but noted that he alone had the power to make the decisions. Inwardly Johnson could scarcely contain his anger. When he took a group of Indiana party workers on a tour of the White House he snubbed Hartke and soon began referring to the Indiana senator in public as "obstreperous." In private he called him by a slang name for the male sexual organ. In addition, Johnson induced the Department of Agriculture to refuse to reappoint Hartke's people to the agricultural stabilization committees in Indiana. In effect, he turned Hartke into a major enemy.

This retaliatory response marked the president's progressive loss of control when faced with "that bitch of a war." The harsh vindictiveness was not effective. His problem with the Indiana senator was seen by many observers as an "ironic symbol" of a "revolt against Johnson." In

March a *Washington Post* writer asked: "Is President Johnson's legislative honeymoon finally headed for the rocks?" The reporter did not commit himself to a definite answer, but he noted that the "durability of the remarkable marriage is being seriously questioned at the Capitol for the first time."[8] Johnson was able to make new friends among the younger senators. Fred Harris of Oklahoma and Gale McGee of Wyoming were among the new faces who supported him on Vietnam. He even reconciled with an former liberal foe, Senator Paul Douglas, a stalwart anti-Communist who backed him on Southeast Asia, and promised to help him with his reelection campaign. But the loss of his old friends was particularly distressing and contributed to his growing suspicion of others.

On the same day the Hartke antiwar letter appeared, LBJ submitted his annual economic message. Johnson described the economy in glowing terms. "Our nation's industries, shops, and farms—our workers, owners of businesses, professional men and women—prosper today far beyond the dreams of any people, anytime, anywhere," he declared.[9] But for the first time he raised the specter of inflation. By the end of 1965, despite an interest rate hike by the Federal Reserve Board of Governors, the upward pressure on prices was becoming apparent and could not be disguised. Until now, whenever he referred to dampening the economy, he had used the term "appropriate fiscal action." He hoped that voluntary efforts by business and labor would be sufficient to check price rises, he now said, but if not, he was prepared to take more stringent steps, an actual hike in personal and business income taxes.

This was a sour note indeed. LBJ had tried from the outset to make the war as palatable as possible. Never frank about his spending proclivities, he sought to hide the financial costs of Vietnam because he distrusted the American people's stamina in the face of sacrifice. One method was to shift Social Security tax revenues, hitherto sequestered in a separate fund, to the general revenue column, thereby reducing the Treasury deficit—on paper. McNamara was a willing abettor of Johnson's fiscal deception, though he may also have misled the president. The defense secretary hid costs from Congress, the Treasury, and the Council of Economic Advisers. He told the Defense Department controller to falsely assume the war's end at the end of the 1966–1967 fiscal year to keep outlay estimates low. He evaded questioners who asked him bluntly what the American taxpayer was paying for the war. And apparently he fudged the figures to the president himself. As Irving Bernstein notes, not until late November 1966, at the Ranch, did McNamara admit that the war was draining as much as $20 billion a year from the economy.[10]

Johnson's fiscal evasions would prove to be a double mistake. Most important, they allowed inflationary pressures to build past the point of effective restraint. But hiding the fiscal pain may also have had a paradoxical effect on public morale. A good case could be made for not inflicting pain on a public unconvinced of the danger from Communists half a world away. But another argument could be made. Louis Heren, a British biographer of LBJ, has noted that most people associate war with some sort of sacrifice and austerity and that pain actually can build civilian morale by convincing people that they "are doing their bit for the war effort."[11] In effect, then, Johnson was inadvertently undermining public resolve in the face of a dogged enemy who would not give up.

To steal the spotlight from Fulbright's scheduled Vietnam hearings and to demonstrate his constructive "nation-building" interests, in early February Johnson arranged a three-day meeting in Hawaii with Vietnam's chief of state, Nguyen Van Thieu, Prime Minister Nguyen Cao Ky, and General Westmoreland. In Honolulu the general told him that the summer troop reinforcements had prevented defeat but could not produce victory. He asked for more troops, and Johnson, "intense, perturbed, and uncertain how to proceed," according to the general, reluctantly agreed to increase the current 184,000 to a whopping 430,000 by the end of the year.[12] The president was less accommodating to the South Vietnamese leaders. Johnson was not happy with the performance of America's ally, either on the battle front or behind it. American observers believed that the Saigon government was failing to rally the South Vietnamese people, in part because it ruled arbitrarily, without consent. Thieu and Ky would be expected, the president said, to push a new, democratic constitution and free elections. These would legitimize the Saigon government and, incidentally, appease some domestic protesters against U.S. policy in Southeast Asia. Meanwhile, Johnson would dispatch a team under Secretary of Health, Education, and Welfare John Gardner to Saigon to look into the performance of South Vietnam leaders and American civilian and military officials, and to investigate progress in the fight for "the hearts and minds" of the Vietnamese people. In the final meeting with the Saigon leaders and the general, Johnson noted, not for the first time, that it was time to "nail the coonskin to the wall."[13] Westmoreland was amused by the perplexed looks on the faces of Ky and Thieu at this remark.

The Declaration of Honolulu, issued after the meeting, pledged to continue the struggle until victory was achieved, but also stressed social and economic reforms in South Vietnam. The Saigon government would work for "the eradication of social injustice," and for building a "modern society in which every man . . . has respect and dignity."[14] The United States would, while aiding the military effort, "wage other efforts in the South to make the dream of a better life a reality."[15] If carried out, it would basically have amounted to a neocolonial "Americanization" of Vietnam. But, of course, it was not implemented. Like every American effort to the very end to bolster the South Vietnamese, it was an exercise in futility, with much of the blame assignable to Saigon's incompetence and indifference. And in the end the Honolulu conference failed to overshadow the Fulbright hearings a few days later.

These televised sessions featured Maxwell Taylor and Dean Rusk as well as a wide array of experts on Southeast Asia and foreign policy generally. Fulbright grilled Taylor and Rusk hard but could not budge them. Rusk, particularly, fought back, insisting that America had a "vital stake" in the Vietnam outcome. The chairman called retired general James Gavin to testify for an "enclave" policy to hold off defeat until a negotiated peace could be arranged. Revered foreign policy expert George Kennan testified that the United States had no vital interest in Vietnam. Millions of Americans watched the hearings, and many wrote Fulbright to vent their anger at Johnson. In their wake Wayne Morse proposed a bill to repeal the Gulf of Tonkin Resolution. It failed, and in the end the hearings proved less damaging than the administration feared.

Meanwhile, Johnson was itching to get back to the Great Society. On February 15 he wrote to Speaker John W. McCormack to remind him of two issues left over from the previous congressional session. He wanted Congress to appropriate funds for the Teacher Corps and for rent subsidies. The corps was part of the Higher Education Act of 1965 and, though Congress had approved it, it had failed to fund it. The rent supplement had passed the previous session as part of a federal housing bill but had been openly attacked as "socialistic" and covertly attacked as likely to bring black families into white neighborhoods. It had been dropped in the joint conference committee on appropriations. In the letter to McCormack, Johnson said that strict income limits for rent supplement recipients would be imposed and that the housing to be subsidized would be modest. It would not include more than one bathroom per apartment, for example. The Teacher Corps had been targeted by groups opposed to further federal intrusion into local schools and by schoolteachers' unions, fearful of competition for jobs from uncredentialed young people. Both bills, as well as other administration spending proposals, had drawn the fire of anti-inflationists. "Call it walking inflation, call it creeping inflation," intoned Senate Republican minority leader Everett Dirksen. "I don't care what you call it. Somewhere, somehow, there has to be a halt in programs of the Great Society." If the choice was between a tax increase or a cut in spending, he certainly preferred the latter.[16]

In April, Congress cut Johnson's requested $13.2 million for the Teacher Corps to a paltry $9.5 million. It was barely enough for the corps to survive.* The rent subsidy fared no better. The House approved a miserly $22 million allocation by an eight-vote margin. Then the Senate Appropriations Committee took it out of the 1966–1967 budget bill. The White House applied pressure, and the Senate restored the cut. When the rent supplement was finally passed, in September, Congress funded it with a meager $22 million. The final bill, moreover, gave local authorities the right to exclude from their jurisdiction any project they did not approve of. It was, in the end, a minimal bill, producing, after five years, only forty-six thousand new housing units for the poor. Still, the passage of even a pale shadow of the original bill saved the administration from humiliating defeat in an area that the president considered important.

The tightening budget constraints forced Johnson to shift from costly capital projects to consumer and environmental protection measures, programs with low price tabs. In a special "Consumer Interests" message to Congress on March 21, he asked for passage of legislation long hanging fire to protect buyers from deceptive packaging and from bewildering credit arrangements. Though not costly, these proposals were controversial. Food producers had been trying to fend off a "truth in packaging" law for years; banks and personal finance companies had been lobbying to defeat "truth in lending" proposals for as long. In 1966 the opposition managed to strip the packaging bill of its provision mandating uniform standards of size and weight. Truth-in-lending legislation had to wait until 1968 for enactment.

Immediately after the consumer message, Johnson sent a child safety bill to Congress. As on other occasions, Johnson was in part responding to a personal experience. This time it was his distress when the son of his closest domestic adviser, Joseph Califano, ended up in the hospital after swallowing a bottleful of aspirin. "There ought to be a law," he told Califano, "that makes druggists use safe containers. There ought to be safety caps on those bottle so kids like little Joe can't open them."[17] The proposed bill targeted commonplace childhood hazards such as aspirin of the fruit-flavored children's kind and toys that contained "hazardous substances." The administration also wanted controls over toy Easter ducklings containing pesticides, arsenic, or disease-causing bacteria.

---

*At the end of September Congress finally appropriated an additional $7.5 million, which allowed the corps' teachers to begin serving in poverty area schools. The Teacher Corps survived, but it was always on short rations.

Automobile safety was another item on Johnson's wish list of consumer measures. In 1965 a young Harvard Law School graduate, Ralph Nader, wrote a sensational exposé of the automobile industry, *Unsafe at Any Speed*, that quickly became a best-seller. Nader called the automobile manufacturers legal killers for putting comfort, style, and horsepower before drivers' safety. The industry had failed to produce a "safe, nonpolluting and efficient automobile."[18]

In March 1966 the administration introduced a weak auto safety bill that called for voluntary industry standards before any federal mandate was imposed. Nader, a witness before the House subcommittee considering the bill, called it a "no-law law."[19] A few days later the *New York Times* revealed that GM had hired private investigators to ferret out "lurid details" about Nader's life. The article made the young lawyer a folk hero and gave his cause enormous publicity. Johnson now put his shoulder behind a stronger bill. In an April message he lambasted the industry for raising "picayunish" objections to federal standards. "We can no longer tolerate unsafe automobiles," he declared. "The alternative to federal standards is unthinkable. . . ."[20]

Stirred to action by the Nader affair, Congress passed two important transportation safety measures during 1966. One was the National Traffic and Motor Vehicle Safety Act, which required federal safety standards on all new automobiles after 1968 and established federal quality standards for tires. Passed the same day was a bill requiring each state to abide by federally approved highway safety programs by December 31, 1968. Failing to do so would cost the state 10 percent of federal construction funds. At the White House ceremony for the bills' signing, LBJ said that safety was "no luxury item, no optional extra," and warned the automobile makers to "build in more safety without building on more costs."[21]

However pleased with the progress of domestic programs, from 1966 on, there was never a time when the president could forget the Vietnam War. On March 26 a total of 450 pickets marched in front of the White House. Fifty thousand paraded in New York, and other mass rallies were held in other American cities as part of the Second International Days of Protest. At New York's Central Park, eighty-one-year-old Rev. Abraham Johannes ("A.J.") Muste, a tireless and devoted worker for peace and social justice all his life, called for Johnson to discard his "mistaken policies" and "end the war now."[22] A nonscheduled speaker, novelist Norman Mailer, was given the microphone for a few minutes. "Lyndon Johnson knows," he said, "that when 60,000 people . . . will go out and march down Fifth Avenue being heckled, there is an incredible potential resistance to the war. . . ."[23] According to the newsletter of the National

Coordinating Committee to End the War in Vietnam, antiwar activities all over the world during the three days between March 25 and 27 amounted to the largest and most far-reaching peace demonstrations in history.[24]

Johnson got a sorely needed emotional boost when, in April, he went to Mexico to dedicate a statue of Abraham Lincoln. At the Mexico City airport, festooned with red, white, and blue flowers and the flags of both countries, he was warmly greeted by President Gustavo Díaz Ordaz and a crowd of about 25,000. "If I could have my one wish granted," Johnson said after reminding his listeners that he had spent his honeymoon in Mexico, "it would be that we could live in a world where we had the same peaceful relations with other nations that we have with the people of Mexico."[25] The president was ebullient when he returned to the Ranch after his Mexican visit.

But his mood soured when he read the *Washington Post* the following day. The lead on a *Post* front-page story was: "Vietnam is expected to upstage domestic issues as Congressmen return to work on Capitol Hill this week after an Easter recess." And a column on the editorial page was headlined "Shadows of War Darken the Polls." The piece, by Marquis Childs, noted "the striking contrast between the President of a year ago and the President today. . . ." The year before, "buoyed by the record landslide of 1964 Johnson was at the floodtide of his capacity as a persuader and organizer." That had changed. "Today the President concentrates almost entirely on Vietnam. His closest advisors say he rarely thinks or talks about anything else. And as the pressure of the dilemma bears down, he is increasingly irritable and impatient. He finds the war in all its aspects a hair shirt. . . ."[26]

Meanwhile, Fulbright continued to attack the president over Vietnam. In April Fulbright linked the war to Johnson's domestic policies. "In concrete terms, the president simply cannot think about implementing the Great Society at home while he is supervising bombing missions over North Vietnam," he declared. "There is a kind of madness in the facile assumption that we can raise the many billions of dollars necessary to rebuild our schools and cities and public transport and eliminate the pollution of air and water while also spending tens of billions to finance an 'open-ended' war in Asia."[27] The United States was "succumbing to the arrogance of power" by equating "its power with virtue and its major responsibilities."[28]

As we have seen, one way that Johnson rationalized staying in Vietnam both to himself and to the public was by analogy to Munich in 1938, when the European democracies had appeased Hitler and reaped the whirlwind of World War II. Most of the country's intellectuals had supported Franklin Roosevelt when he brought the United States into that war. Now this same group of people agreed with Fulbright when he rejected the parallel. "The treatment of slight and superficial resemblances as if they were full-blooded analogies—as instances of history 'repeating itself'—is a substitute for thinking and a misuse of history," Fulbright pronounced. Rubbing salt in Johnson's wounds, he quoted Winston Churchill, the European leader most identified with opposition to appeasement at Munich. "Appeasement from strength is magnanimous and noble and might be the surest and perhaps the only path to world peace."[29]

On May 11 Johnson answered Fulbright's "arrogance of power" charge in a speech at Princeton University. The "exercise of power in this century has meant for all of us in the United States not arrogance but agony," he asserted. "We have used our power not willingly and recklessly ever, but always reluctantly and with restraint." He declared that the United States, unlike powerful nations in the past, "has not sought to crush the autonomy of her neighbors." Nor had it been motivated by "blind militarism. . . ." We had only sought to check "devastating aggression." In the end, our nation had not "followed the ancient and conceited philosophy of the 'noble lie' that some men are by nature meant to be slaves to others."[30] In the next few days he abandoned his judicious defense and turned harshly on his critics. Speaking to congressional Democrats, he sarcastically referred to his audience as some of his "very old friends as well as some members of the [Senate] Foreign Relations Committee." Soon after, in an address in Chicago, he called his Vietnam opponents "nervous Nellies" who in the face of war losses would "turn on their leaders and on their country, and on their own fighting men."[31]

Johnson continued to press forward on his domestic agenda, however. On April 29 he sent a new civil rights package to Congress, providing for a national Fair Housing Act, augmented protection of civil rights workers, an end to discrimination in jury selection, and a broadening of the attorney general's authority to bring desegregation suits. The fair housing provision touched especially sensitive nerves. The two previous administration civil rights measures conformed to the public's sense of fair play over discrimination in voting, jobs, and access to public accommodations. The new law got many Americans where they lived—literally. It banned racial and religious discrimination in the sale, rental, and financing of housing. It covered all types of housing, including the upstairs back room rented to a boarder by the fictional Mrs. Murphy—the *cause célèbre* during the fight for the 1964 civil rights bill. It applied to private homes in the suburbs as well as apartment houses in the cities. The bill awakened some of the worst nightmares of whites: violent neighborhood crime and plummeting property values. For blacks, relegated to decrepit slum housing at exorbitant prices, it represented a long-overdue opportunity to break out of the physical ghettos. A modified version of the bill made it through the House this session but was blocked in the Senate by the opponents of the housing provisions.†

By the time LBJ introduced his new civil rights program the civil rights movement itself was escaping the bounds of integrationism and nonviolence and transmogrifying into a militant separatist movement that frightened and offended the broad center of the white public. In May the staff of the Student Nonviolent Coordinating Committee (SNCC), meeting in Tennessee, elected as their new chairman the militant and charismatic Stokely Carmichael. Carmichael was an advocate of "black power," which repudiated integration and glorified separation. "Integration," in Carmichael's view, was "a subterfuge for the maintenance of white supremacy." It reinforced, among both black and white, "the idea that 'white' is automatically better and 'black' is by definition inferior."[32] As a by-product of the black power doctrine, SNCC, and the equally militant CORE, expelled white civil rights activists from membership.

Black power became news just before twenty-four hundred delegates, representing a "cross section of American life," arrived to attend the June 1–2 White House Conference on Civil Rights. Most of the delegates had been carefully selected for moderation. But clearly a new combativeness had invaded the civil rights movement. Militants among the delegates insisted that there be sessions on the controversial Moynihan Report, a document that seemed to blame the black family for African American failure. Others demanded impractical further massive infusions of tax money into new programs for the poor. There were also rumblings of opposition among blacks to the administration's Vietnam policies. Still, the moderates remained in control. When the president appeared at an evening session to introduce Solicitor General Thurgood Marshall, leader of the NAACP legal team in the landmark *Brown* school-desegregation decision, Johnson was cheered with gusto. "I came here today at the end of a long day to tell you that we shall not turn back," he told participants.[33] But in truth he did not want to move forward too fast, either. Though Johnson had unwittingly opened the affirmative action Pandora's box in his Howard University speech, he hoped

---

†The administration introduced it again in the next Congress and it eventually passed as the Fair Housing Act in April 1968. It proved, in the end, largely ineffective in ending segregated housing.

the civil rights movement would continue along a moderate path, one where he could comfortably be the drum major. "It was an unexpected and flawless triumph," McPherson would later write of the conference. But "it was about the last one he would have."[34] Whether he knew it or not, LBJ was becoming increasingly irrelevant to the movement he had done so much to bolster.

As the summer approached, college and university graduation ceremonies became focal points for antiwar protests. At Amherst, students walked out of the commencement to denounce giving Secretary of Defense Robert McNamara an honorary LL.D. A week later, McNamara was the butt of almost two thousand student and faculty antiwar demonstrators at New York University's graduation ceremonies. On June 4 the *New York Times* published a three-page advertisement signed by more than sixty-four hundred professional men and women, mostly academics, urging the administration "to cease all bombing, North and South, and all other offensive military operations immediately." It should also "evaluate seriously whether self-determination for the Vietnamese as well as our own national interest would not be best served by termination of our military presence in Vietnam."[35]

Johnson waited until 1967 to mount a major counteroffensive against his Vietnam critics, but at a news conference on June 18 he answered his opponents:

Here in the United States, I believe that our people are really determined to see this thing through. In recent primary elections not one single candidate was able to make opposition to the resistance of aggression in South Vietnam a successful position that led him to victory. A minority of our people, it is true, are willing now to pull out. Another minority are prepared to see us use our total power. The rest of us . . . are determined that this nation honor its responsibility and its commitment to help Vietnam turn back aggression from the North. . . . [36]

At the end of June Johnson authorized American bombers to attack fuel storage depots adjacent to Hanoi and Haiphong, North Vietnam's major port city. For the first time the air raids would hit targets near major population centers. The administration defended this escalation of Rolling Thunder on the grounds that North Vietnam had itself expanded the war in the South. In fact, Johnson was being pushed by his military advisers to step up the air attacks. But the president insisted on micromanaging the bombing, choosing the targets himself from a list submitted by the generals. Jack Valenti remembered observing McNamara and the president in the Situation Room examining potential attack sites. "The president would say, 'I don't want to hit SAM site six because that's [blank] miles from Hanoi and I'm afraid we'll overshoot it. So let's leave that alone and hit SAM site five instead.'"[37] Johnson on this occasion actually told one reporter that he had approved the raids because he "had to do something to help the morale of the Joint Chiefs. We weren't winning and they were frustrated."[38] But in a speech in Omaha, he professed to believe that the military actions he approved "have already begun to turn the tide."[39] On July 5 he told a Texas news conference that more than half of the total fuel storage capacity of North Vietnam had been destroyed.

Meanwhile, doubts of the war's winnability began to seep through the very walls of the White House and the Pentagon. In the summer of 1965 Richard Goodwin, the writer and idea man who had authored the Great Society speech, left the administration, convinced that Lyndon Johnson had developed frightening paranoid tendencies. In 1966 Goodwin would become an important antiwar leader and later help found the dump-Johnson movement. In November the Ford Foundation invited national security adviser McGeorge Bundy to take over its presidency. Dismayed at the continuing escalation and afraid Johnson no longer trusted him, in February Bundy would resign to go to New York. The most consequential doubter of all was Robert McNamara. His trip to Vietnam in late November, as we saw, had shaken his confidence and prompted the Christmas bombing pause. Not until mid-1967 did he tell the president the depths of his doubt, but he would never again believe that the war could be won.

By mid-1966 Vietnam had forced an open confrontation between the president and Bobby Kennedy and turned them into snarling enemies. When Bobby ran for the U.S. Senate from New York in 1964, Johnson, a loyal Democrat, had helped him. On a two-day tour from Buffalo to Brooklyn the two appeared together on the same platform several times. The president would put his arm around the scrawny senatorial candidate and announce: "This is ma boy, I want you to elect ma boy."[40] In November Bobby had won by a 700,000-vote majority, far less than the 2.7 million by which the president carried New York.

Despite the campaign, enmity between LBJ and RFK continued, undoubtedly fanned by the journalists' sure instincts that a feud made good copy. Kennedy supported the president's Great Society; no Democrat from New York could do otherwise. But Kennedy resented the kudos Johnson received and the contrast often drawn between Lyndon's legislative successes and the supposed failure of his brother Jack. One observer noted that when Johnson addressed joint sessions of the Ninetieth

Congress, the newly seated Bobby "seldom clapped; he just seemed to smolder."[41]

Overt policy disagreements with the administration began over the invasion of the Dominican Republic, which the senator considered a repudiation of his brother's generous and democratic policies toward Latin America. Then, when Kennedy went on a fact-finding trip to South America in November 1965, the president and his advisers assumed Bobby was gearing up for a presidential run against Johnson in 1968.

But it was Vietnam that snapped the last connective tissue between the two men. Bobby had not started as a dove. In the spring of 1964 he had explained to a friend that he believed that his brother felt that "we should win the war,"[42] though it was not clear, he said, whether that meant sending combat troops. Vietnam as an issue had not ruffled the 1964 senatorial campaign, but in May 1965 the new junior senator from New York gave a speech criticizing the administration's bombing campaign as likely to drive more South Vietnamese into the arms of the Vietcong. "Victory in a revolutionary war," Bobby noted, was "not won by escalation, but by deescalation."[43] In February 1966 the senator further provoked the president and his advisers by his support for including the Vietcong in any peace negotiations that might be arranged. By midsummer Kennedy followers and loyalists were beginning to talk seriously of organizing a national anti-Vietnam campaign, and some were pondering the possibility that the senator might openly challenge Johnson on 1968.

Johnson's troubles at home competed with troubles abroad. On July 12, three nights of rioting began on Chicago's West Side when police shut off an illegally opened fire hydrant in a black neighborhood. When the disturbances were over, 2 blacks were dead, many police and civilians were injured, and almost 400 people had been arrested for looting, throwing stones at police cars, or damaging property. Later that month, there was a serious riot in Hough, a black section on Cleveland's East Side. During the tumult, more than 250 fires were started by angry blacks, who shot at firemen trying to extinguish the blazes. There were also racial disturbances in Brooklyn, and scattered racial flare-ups continued in Chicago during the rest of the summer.

Johnson inevitably appealed for calm and deplored the riots. On July 23 he told a luncheon of businessmen and labor leaders in Indianapolis that "riots in the streets do not bring about lasting reforms . . ." but actually made "reform more difficult by turning away the very people who can and must support reform." The uprisings must be stopped "not only to protect the society at large" but also "to serve the real interests of those for whose cause we struggle."[44]

LBJ received a small respite from domestic and foreign problems on August 6 when his younger daughter, Luci, married Patrick Nugent at Washington's Roman Catholic Shrine of the Immaculate Conception. A ninety-minute nuptial Mass was followed by a seven-hundred-guest White House reception with champagne punch and an eight-foot high wedding cake. Though the beaming president seemed to enjoy the ritual, and, said Lady Bird, did not look at his watch "one single time during the service,"[45] even at the wedding he could not escape the mounting opposition. Billing the occasion as a family affair rather than a state function, the First Family had barred TV cameras from both the church and the reception, giving permission only for pictures of arriving guests. Yet it could not prevent antiwar demonstrators from picketing both the shrine and the White House, to protest scheduling the event on the anniversary of the Hiroshima atomic bomb attack in 1945.

Johnson responded to antiwar activity and declining popularity by a series of new peace offensives. On August 24 he approved the proposal of the Association of Southeast Asia for an all-Asian parley to end the Vietnam War. He also announced his support for reconvening the peace conference at Geneva and repeated his desire to attend "a conference anywhere I think it would be helpful."[46] Later that month he told the Soviet leaders that in spite of the war in Vietnam he and they could still try to work toward world peace together. It should "not stop us from finding new ways of dealing with one another." Since American goals in Vietnam were limited, merely those of "trying to protect the independence of South Vietnam . . . ," the USSR should not feel threatened. "We seek in Southeast Asia," he said, "an order and security that would contribute to the peace of the world—and in that, the Soviet Union has a very large stake."[47]

Johnson continued his peace offensive in late October by a Pacific trip, accompanied by Lady Bird and a team of advisers, to consult with leaders from Australia, New Zealand, South Korea, South Vietnam, Thailand, and the Philippines. The junket was primarily a maneuver to sell the American public on the war and was a modest success. At stop one, in New Zealand, the first thing Johnson saw when he left his plane were signs reading "Bobby Kennedy for President." Yet generally the crowds were cordial and, acting as though campaigning for office at home, Johnson got out of his car to shake hands and dispense his friendly, corny greetings. In Australia he ignored antiwar protesters and bags of green and red oil paint thrown at his limousine. He was determined to be upbeat, repeating that "Australians are the kind of people I can go to the well with."[48] When he reached Manila, thousands of cheering people greeted him along the eight-mile route from the airport to the city. But there was an antiwar demonstration in front of his hotel, and some placards called him a "modern Hitler."

The meeting in the Philippine capital included interviews with Westmoreland and Ky on the military situation. Ky told him that the Vietcong were on the verge of collapse; Westmoreland assured the president that "by every index, things were improving. . . ." "[W]hile there was light at the end of the tunnel, we had to be geared for the long pull." The enemy was at a disadvantage but was "relying on his greater staying power."[49]

The conference itself reiterated the now standard tactics of dealing with Vietnam by both carrot and stick. Johnson promised to withdraw American troops within six months if North Vietnam "withdraws its forces to the North" and "ceases infiltration" of South Vietnam. But the conference communiqué also declared that military efforts would continue "as long as may be necessary, in close consultation among ourselves, until the aggression is ended." The document included a four-point "Declaration of Peace" that stated: (1) "aggression must not succeed"; (2) "the bonds of poverty, illiteracy, and disease" must be shattered; (3) "economic, social, and cultural cooperation with the Asian and Pacific region" must be shored up; and (4) the Allies "must seek reconciliation and peace through Asia." In a speech concluding the meeting, Johnson noted that "all of those who have an appetite for the territory of someone else" should be warned "that when they do attack their neighbors, the friends of their neighbors will be there to resist it."[50]

On impulse, before returning home, Johnson flew to Cam Ranh Bay, a giant American military base in South Vietnam. Leaving the plane, he waded into a crowd of friendly troops, shaking hands, as he always did, as if soliciting votes for a Texas election. Later, at the officers' club, before a group of field commanders, he repeated a favorite phrase: "May the good Lord look over you and keep you until you come home with the coonskin on the wall."[51]

Thousands came to greet the president when he arrived at Dulles International Airport on November 2, and Johnson addressed the crowd of well-wishers. The Manila meeting, he said, had "rejected the voice of the appeaser and the heel of the aggressor." It had also "agreed that our goal is an honorable peace. . . ." He was "much more confident and much more hopeful" than he had been before the trip to Asia, he told his audience.[52] In fact the meeting had done little to further American goals in Vietnam, but it did temporarily revive public confidence. A poll taken just after Johnson returned showed that 65 percent of American adults still approved of the president's handling of Vietnam. In the summer of 1966 the economy, buoyant since the tax cut, began to falter. On July 25 the stock market suffered its largest one-day decline since the Kennedy assassination. More serious was the looming budget deficit for 1967, triple the $1.8 billion Johnson had calculated in January, when his figures did not even include the additional outlays on Vietnam. Extra money would have to come from somewhere, and most of his economic advisers favored a tax hike to check the growing threat of inflation. In August Johnson met with congressional leaders of both parties to test the waters on an income-tax increase, but in fact there was little likelihood of a tax jump in an election year. "You'd have trouble getting more than fifteen votes," predicted House minority leader Gerald Ford. "You wouldn't even get that many," chimed in Carl Albert, Democratic House leader.[53] One practical suggestion to raise revenue was the repeal of the investment tax credit that business had gotten in the Kennedy administration, a tack that both Wilbur Mills and Senate Finance Committee chairman Russell Long said they would accept. This would increase federal tax revenue and at the same time dampen inflation-producing business investment. After the stock market dropped even more sharply in late August, Gardner Ackley, Heller's successor as chairman of the President's Council of Economic Advisers, pushed hard for repealing the investment tax credit. Congress went along, and LBJ signed the bill into law just after Labor Day. This was really a stopgap measure that did not provide nearly enough to cover the escalating costs of guns and butter.

The fall of 1966 was a relatively good time for the president on the legislative front. On September 23 Johnson signed the bill raising the minimum wage for the thirty million workers already covered from $1.25 to $1.60 and extending coverage to more than ten million workers in restaurants, hotels, and retail stores. "Another coonskin on the wall" was the way Johnson excitedly described the creation of a second new cabinet post on October 15 as he signed the bill establishing the Department of Transportation. The new department would include the railroad, highway, and aviation administrations, a partially independent National Transportation Safety Board, and, in peacetime, the coast guard. At the signing ceremony in the White House the president talked about the "mammoth task" of unsnarling, organizing, and building a national transportation system.[54]

On the same day, Johnson signed five bills establishing national recreational areas, including Point Reyes National Seashore near San Francisco; Guadalupe Mountains National Park in western Texas; Pictured Rocks National Lakeshore on the southern shore of Lake Superior in Michigan; Bighorn Canyon National Recreation Area in Montana and Wyoming; and Wolf Trap Farm Park in Virginia, designated as a performing arts center. Johnson signed a bill creating the Indiana Dunes National Lakeshore a few weeks later. The President called these new areas collectively "a milestone in the history of conservation" and said they would restore more land for parks and playgrounds "than we lose to housing, highways, airports, and shopping centers." Then turning to his wife, who was standing behind him, he joked, "And if we don't stop Mrs. Johnson from going out there, we'll be increasing it some more."[55]

In another round of legislation Johnson extended the federal government's power over the environment. The Clean Waters Restoration Act set water quality standards for intrastate waters, and authorized money for construction of sewage treatment plants and for research on water purification, industrial water pollution, and waste treatment. Johnson also approved a bill protecting species of wildlife threatened with extinction, and a rivers, harbors, and flood control bill that authorized construction by the Army Corps of Engineers of forty federal water projects in twenty-five states.

Before Congress adjourned it gave Johnson another significant piece of his Great Society agenda, the Demonstration [Model] Cities Act.

To thoughtful sixties Americans, the cities seemed to be battlefields where social health and social decay struggled to prevail. All the nation's pathologies—poverty, racism, crime, disease—found havens there. So did America's healthy parts—the arts, education, wealth creation, new ideas. The fate of the cities would be a test of American civilization itself.

Urban renewal in the fifties and early sixties meant rebuilding city business districts and constructing high-rise apartment buildings to entice the white middle class back to the city centers. In the process, site residents, mostly poor and black, were often evicted from their homes. The new Demonstration Cities program would keep the poor in place, where they would benefit from a liberal transfusion of federal money and expertise. It envisioned cooperation by government, business, labor, whites, and blacks in upgrading housing, schools, transportation, health care, recreation, and police services in inner cities to make them more livable and humane places. The scheme originated with Walter Reuther,[‡] head of the United Automobile Workers' Union, whose membership included thousands of black workers. In a letter to the president in May 1965, Reuther had proposed "an urban TVA to stop erosion of cities and

---

[‡]Its roots, however, can be traced to Johnson's 1964 Task Force on Metropolitan and Urban Problems, headed by Robert Wood of MIT.

people." The government should create "research laboratories for the war against poverty and ugliness in the urban environment." He suggested six large cities—Los Angeles, Washington, D.C., Philadelphia, Chicago, Houston, and Detroit—where the government would build "full and complete and organic neighborhoods for fifty thousand people to give meaning to our *ability* to create architecturally beautiful and socially meaningful communities of the twentieth century. . . ."[56]

The scheme appealed to the president, but he delayed submitting a bill to Congress until after it created the new Department of Housing and Urban Development and he had appointed the black economist Robert Weaver, head of the Housing and Home Finance Agency, to head it. Then, after the Watts riots in August, he selected a new task force headed by Robert Wood to put together a detailed proposal for "Demonstration Cities," as the scheme was first called. Under pressure from the president, the task force multiplied Reuther's six cities to sixty-six—six large, ten medium and fifty small—so that as many states and cities as possible would benefit and, presumably, remember the Democrats gratefully at election time.

By January 1966, when the administration's bill reached the House and the Senate, Congress was more reluctant than it had been the year before to commit itself to sweeping social experimentation. Liberals thought the funding too stingy. Conservatives thought the idea pandered to blacks and objected to its price tag. The bill languished, and in May the *New York Times* thought the measure doomed. "All signs on Capitol Hill suggest that the 'demonstration cities' program is dead," a *Times* piece said.[57] The president would not give up, however, and at a Democratic leadership breakfast on May 31, 1966, he called the bill "the most important domestic measure before the Eighty-ninth Congress and to the future of the American cities." He was determined to get the bill passed before the Eighty-ninth Congress adjourned.[58]

Lackluster leadership on the House Banking and Currency Committee led administration strategists to focus on the Senate. Passage in the upper house would force the hand of the other chamber. The bill was turned over to a Democrat from a rural state, Edmund Muskie of Maine, to shepherd through. This was a shrewd move to impress other senators from rural states. If the senator from Maine, whose state was without a single large city, thought the bill sufficiently important to fight for its passage, it might be worthy of support. For a time it looked as if the bill would fall victim to the Johnson-Kennedy feud. At hearings before the Executive Reorganization Subcommittee, administration spokesman Robert Weaver came under ferocious attack from Bobby Kennedy and Senator Abraham Ribicoff of Connecticut, John Kennedy's first secretary of health, education, and welfare, for supporting a timid, inadequately funded bill. It seemed to many observers as if the two senators belonged to the opposition party, and in a sense they did: They had become rallying points for the emerging anti-Johnson forces within the Democratic Party. With some modifications and a reduction from $2.3 billion to $900 million in funds for two years, the Senate passed the bill on August 19.

Now, with the bill in the House, Johnson himself got into the act, touring the Northeast to promote it. "Give us action . . . and American cities will be great again," he asserted in Syracuse during a three-day swing.[59] Though many were turned off by the urban violence during the summer, the administration prevailed on religious, civic, business, and labor leaders to support it. A group of "big business progressives," as James Reston called them, including David Rockefeller, Henry Ford II, and Edgar Kaiser, announced that "America needs the demonstration cities bill" to deal with "disease and despair, joblessness and hopelessness, excessive dependence on welfare and the . . . threats of crime, disorder, and delinquency." In addition, they stated, it was fiscally sound and "in our business judgment it deserves to be ranked as high on any list of national priorities as any program we know."[60]

As finally passed in the House on October 14, the bill provided for funds to rebuild urban slums, for development of entire "new towns," and for "incentive grants" to stimulate extensive, area-wide planning. Those cities using the grants would have to upgrade health, education, welfare, and other social services so that the "total environment" of the area's residents would be improved. To avoid a touchy issue, the bill's final version did not include a provision for further desegregation in housing, which had been in the president's original plan.

Johnson signed the bill in the White House East Room on November 3. In his remarks he called the measure "Model Cities" rather than "Demonstration Cities." As target of so many rallies, his feelings were understandable. "Don't ever give such a stupid goddamn name to a bill again," he admonished Califano as they walked back from the signing ceremony.[61]

Many contemporaries considered Model Cities a path-breaking measure, on a par with the civil rights bills and Medicare. They were mistaken. Underfunded, spread too thin, sabotaged by his successor, the bill accomplished little. The slums, the ghettos, the crime, and the squalor of American cities remained.

The midterm congressional elections on November 8 posed a dilemma for Johnson. He hoped to retain a cooperative Democratic

Congress for 1967 and 1968 against the historical odds. But how could he help? His own poll ratings were sagging as the public became more impatient with Vietnam and racial change. Johnson also remembered FDR's disastrous effort in 1938 to purge conservative Democrats who had opposed his New Deal programs. Would campaigning for Democrats end up being self-defeating? The president dithered for some weeks and then decided to dispatch a flock of administration officials, including the vice president, on the campaign trail. The week before he left on his Asian trip, Johnson decided to campaign himself. The centerpiece of the swing would be signing ceremonies at appropriate sites for the remaining 1966 Great Society bills. America's biggest shopping center would be the best place for the truth-in-packaging signing. Minnesota, "the land of ten thousand lakes," would obviously be the best place to approve the Clean Water Restoration Act, and so on. But then he had second thoughts. Many Democrats were certain to be defeated in the traditional off-year backlash, and his own prestige and his Great Society would be tarnished by their losses. Johnson abruptly canceled the trip. Democrats who had counted on his presence resented his change in plans. The anger was intensified by Johnson's denial that any such trip had been planned. In an irascible attack on the media, he claimed that "all those canceled plans primarily involve the imagination of people who phrase sentences and write columns and have to report what they hope or what they imagine."[62] His denial did not help the credibility gap; it was too patently untrue.

The president tried to make the best of the midterm election results. It was difficult. The Republicans gained forty-seven House and three Senate seats, leaving the administration with *party* majorities in both houses but virtually eliminating the *liberal* majorities. A major loss for Johnson was steadfast liberal and recent ally Paul Douglas, running for a fourth term in Illinois, who fell victim to white backlash. After the election, new press secretary George Christian told reporters that Johnson "obviously wishes every man that he wanted elected were elected" but that the Senate elections still left the Democrats with a "pretty good majority."[63] It was obvious, however, that the losses would affect Johnson's ability to get additional legislation through Congress, and Democrats were worried that House Republicans would hamper continued financing of Great Society programs already enacted. Another unhappy omen was that of forty-four House Democrats elected in the Johnson landslide in 1964, many credited with saving Great Society bills in the House, more than half were defeated in the new election. Former vice president Richard Nixon, who had campaigned tirelessly for Republican candidates, was quick to gloat. Calling the election results "the sharpest rebuff of a president in a generation," he said it spoke to Johnson's "lack of credibility and lack of direction abroad."[64]

Johnson kept his aplomb. At a news conference after the election, he admitted that "the other party strengthened its position," but "as a good American," he lied, "I think we are all glad to see a healthy and competent existence of the two-party system."[65] Later that month he announced that he intended to charge ahead, proposing new measures to Congress and getting renewed funding for the Great Society programs already in place. He admitted that it would be a grueling fight. "I think it will be more difficult for any new legislation we might propose."[66] Meanwhile, a Louis Harris poll on December 5 revealed that public approval of the president was down to 43 percent, an all-time low.

Clearly the months ahead would be difficult for a president whose energies were flagging, whose foreign policy seemed so problematical, whose emotional security relied so heavily on approbation, and whose formerly adroit political footing was failing. "The very qualities that had led to Johnson's political and legislative success," Doris Kearns would write, "were precisely those that now operated to destroy him: his inward insistence that the world adapt itself to his goals; his faith in the nation's limitless capacity; his tendency to evaluate all human activity in terms of its political significance; his insistence on translating every disruptive situation into one where bargaining was possible; his reliance on personal touch; his ability to speak to each of his constituent groups on its own terms. All these gifts, instead of sustaining him, now conspired to destroy him."[67]

CHAPTER 19

Retreat

T HE YEAR FOLLOWING THE 1966 MIDTERM ELECTION was the nadir of Johnson's presidency. From the start it did not go well. Democratic governors, meeting in December in White Sulphur Springs, West Virginia, questioned his effectiveness as both national and party leader. According to Governor Warren E. Hearns of Missouri, frustration over Vietnam, excessive federal spending, declining support for the Great Society, and "public disenchantment with the civil rights programs" had eroded the president's support. Johnson would have lost Missouri by a hundred thousand votes if he had run in 1966. The Democrats, he said, might be better off with some other candidate than Johnson in 1968.[1]

That same month Bill Moyers, the owlish young Texas minister who, as White House aide, had helped design the Great Society and whom LBJ had treated virtually as a son, resigned as press secretary. Moyers's brother had recently committed suicide, and he now had to support both his parents and his brother's family. He needed desperately to improve his finances. But there was more than these private reasons for his departure. Moyers feared that his boss had lost his emotional balance and resented being blamed by the president for the credibility gap. Johnson, for his part, was convinced "Billy Don" leaked inside White House information to reporters and doubted his loyalty. Moyers's lunch with Bobby Kennedy at Washington's Sans Souci Restaurant on the very day he resigned clinched Johnson's conclusion that he had long been a Kennedy spy in the White House.

Another bad sign was an article by James Reston in the *New York Times* accusing the administration of poor management. By late 1966, problems with the War on Poverty and other programs had damaged the president's reputation as an executive. The "fact is not only clear but undisputed," Reston wrote, that the White House was "poorly organized to administer the domestic programs" it had enacted. Reston blamed LBJ himself. The president was "reluctant to delegate power over those homefront activities to the vice president, or anyone else, and suspicious of political institutions of any kind." And Reston acknowledged the legislative gluttony problem. "The administration has put through more social and economic programs in the last two years than it can absorb."[2]

Nor were the Johnsons allowed to enjoy the year-end holidays in peace. On Christmas Day, antiwar demonstrators defied cold winds to picket near the Ranch, passing out anti-Vietnam leaflets and carrying signs reading "LBJ, LBJ, How Many Kids Were Napalmed for Christmas Day?" Meanwhile, the media predicted trouble with the less liberal Ninetieth Congress, their prophecies fueled by polls showing Capitol Hill backing for the president slipping badly and Democrats just as likely to oppose him as Republicans. Just before the New Year began, the dean of Washington columnists, Walter Lippmann, expressed doubts that Johnson could "achieve any of the goals he proclaimed a year ago."[3]

Despite the protesters, a long stay at the Ranch improved the president's health, still fragile from another operation in December for a benign throat polyp and repair of his gallbladder scar. But it did little to bolster his emotional state. He complained about feeling "trapped by events" and "boxed in" by his lack of control over national and world happenings.[4] Yet he put on an optimistic face at a year-end press conference. The Great Society must proceed, he told reporters, "the nation can afford to continue . . . to fight wars on both fronts." The American people had "much to be thankful for" and the country would "have a good year."[5] Few shared his public confidence.

Johnson scheduled the 1967 State of the Union address for January 10 so he would not detract from minority leader Everett Dirksen's birthday party or preempt *Gomer Pyle*, *Green Acres*, and *Petticoat Junction*, Tuesday night's popular television shows. As he told aide Joe Califano, "I don't want millions of people looking at me for an hour and thinking 'This is the big-eared son of a bitch that knocked my favorite program off the air.'"[6] In fact, Johnson managed to get 59.6 percent of all TV watchers, according to the Nielsen ratings.

He began by citing the accomplishments of the previous three years, reiterating the progress in education, medical care for the elderly, and job training. The nation had "succeeded in creating a better life for the many as well as the few." But the important question was "whether our gains shall be the foundations of further progress, or whether they shall be . . . abandoned by a people who lacked the will to see their great work through." He did not believe the country wanted to "quit" at this point.

On Vietnam it was impossible to be upbeat. Having been rebuked for credibility, he sought for candor. "I wish I could report to you that the conflict is almost over," he said. "This I cannot do. We face more cost, more loss, and more agony. For the end is not yet." Though he welcomed peace initiatives and diplomatic discussions, "we must firmly pursue our present course. We will stand firm in Vietnam." He also endorsed the end to wiretapping and bugging except in national security cases, and then only with the "strictest safeguards."

Here Johnson was not being candid. His own record on covert surveillance was a curious one. Harry McPherson has insisted that his chief despised wiretapping. Yet in practice Johnson was not fastidious about official snooping. During 1965 and 1966 the FBI, convinced that Martin Luther King Jr. was a Communist dupe, had been listening in on King's activities. Buggings of the civil rights leader's hotel rooms showed that King was a lusty man who enjoyed the attentions of young women. Hoover had sent the tapes on to Johnson who, by all reports, relished the raunchy words and earthy noises. McPherson has denied that the president had asked for this information, "and yet, like all of us, [he] was impressed by what they revealed."[7] Beyond this, Johnson had a Dictabelt taping system on all his phones and recorded important conversations, outgoing and incoming. As for the "bugging ban" recommendation of the State of the Union address, most observers considered it a backhand slap at Robert Kennedy, during whose tenure as attorney general the FBI had stepped up electronic surveillance.

The least pleasing part of the speech undoubtedly was the request for a tax increase. Prices had risen about 3 percent since December 1965, twice the pace of the previous six years, and could no longer be ignored. Now, in the State of the Union message, Johnson proposed a surcharge of 6 percent on both corporate and individual income taxes "to last for two years or for so long as the unusual expenditures associated with our efforts in Vietnam continue." They would be terminated as soon as possible, he promised.

Implicitly recognizing shifting public opinion, Johnson used the phrase "Great Society" only once, but that did not stop him from calling for new domestic programs. His wish list included a Social Security benefits increase and an expansion of Medicare; Head Start for three-year-olds, with a new Follow Through program for early education; the end to age discrimination in the workplace; full funding for the Model Cities program; a truth-in-lending law; an air quality act; anticrime legislation; and aid to American Indians and migrant farm workers. He also proposed a Corporation for Public Broadcasting, which would channel both public and private funds into noncommercial television and radio facilities. After piling high the plate, he said he wished the nation could do even more, but realized that other commitments were making "heavy demands on our total resources." Notwithstanding, he resolved to "do all that we can with what we have—knowing that it is far, far more than we have ever done before, and far less than our problems will ultimately require."[8]

The message received mixed reviews. Columnist Joseph Kraft felt Johnson had begun to close the "credibility gap." Joseph Alsop called it "the most candid and least phony-pious [speech] he has ever delivered. . . . "[9] There were plenty of complaints, however. Martin Luther King Jr. said that the president had been neglectful of civil rights. Johnson was backtracking in his commitment. James Reston scornfully referred to the speech as "guns and margarine."[10]

Within days, Vietnam eclipsed other news when American planes attacked targets near Hanoi, the first such raid in nearly a month. The White House declared that only military targets had been attacked and civilian populations spared. But after the Viet Cong published a detailed report, the administration acknowledged the likelihood of civilian casualties, though suggesting that Communist surface-to-air missiles (SAMs), aimed at attacking planes, had caused the casualties. Vietnam once again seized the headlines when the president submitted his budget message on January 25 asking for $169.2 billion, with defense spending at a record-breaking $74.1 billion.

It was now impossible to deny that the war was beginning to crowd out the Great Society fiscally. Many of the domestic social programs had been enacted with modest appropriations on the understanding that there would be increased funding each year out of growing federal revenues. This growth no longer seemed likely. In this budget, Great Society programs were slated for a nominal $1.9 billion increase. Liberals immediately took Johnson to task, decrying the downsizing of domestic programs. But LBJ was not fully responsible. Besides the president's own caution in asking funds for domestic programs, control of the two subcommittees of the House Appropriations Committee that would shape the Great Society budget for the next two years had, with the recent election, fallen into the hands of conservatives.

The portion of the 1967 State of the Union speech that had drawn the most applause was the "safe streets" anticrime proposal. Americans now believed the nation was in the grip of a potent crime wave. And they were right; the midsixties saw a sharp rise in crimes against persons and property. In the cities particularly, violent crimes were soaring, and more and more honest citizens worried that criminals had taken over "the streets." Johnson did not intend to let the Republicans make capital of the issue at his expense, and in February he delivered a message on crime and drugs, incorporating a Safe Streets and Crime Control Act proposal. Aware that local and state governments had to shoulder most of the responsibility for curbing crime, the president endorsed federal grants to upgrade their criminal justice systems. Federal money would help build modern crime labs, community correction centers, and police academies. The grants, he said, "would encourage innovative efforts against street crime, juvenile delinquency, and organized crime."[11] Johnson urged Congress to enact tough gun control laws and devote its attention to the growing problem of narcotics addiction.

The day of the crime message also marked a new low in the president's relations with Bobby Kennedy. For weeks a controversy had swirled around William Manchester's family-authorized account of the assassination of JFK in Dallas. As originally written, the work had depicted Johnson as a boor, insensitive to the feelings of the bereaved family, and a man whose macho Texas culture in some way explained the tragic events in Dallas. Though softened after Jacqueline Kennedy threatened to sue Manchester for using personal material about herself, when published it still portrayed LBJ harshly. LBJ was hurt by the depiction and resented the Kennedys' apparent unwillingness to delete the slurs on him while fighting to protect their own reputation. He complained to Abe Fortas and assorted aides that the book was intended to drive him from the White House in favor of Bobby. "I believe," he told Fortas, "that Bobby is having his governors jump on me, and he's having his mayors, and he's having his nigras, and he's having his Catholics."[12] Many of the president's friends agreed with his conclusion.

Worse was to come. In early February *Newsweek* reported that the North Vietnamese had proposed new peace terms to RFK while he was in Paris on a European tour: If the Americans ceased for good their bombing campaign, Hanoi would talk about ending the war. The president and Secretary Rusk had little faith in freelance Vietnam negotiators who promised breakthroughs. But aside from chagrin that his nemesis was meddling in the peace negotiations, for the moment Johnson was in an optimistic mood about Vietnam and had no intention of calling off Rolling Thunder without assurances that the Communists would not use it to reinforce and resupply their forces in the South. Johnson believed that the New York senator had leaked the story to the press to force his hand, and he was furious.

Previously, at most private encounters, the two men had been polite. Now, at a meeting in the White House on February 6, with national security adviser Walt Rostow and Under Secretary of State Nicholas Katzenbach both present, Johnson ferociously attacked the senator. It was, Katzenbach remembered, "Johnson at his absolute worst."[13] According to *Newsweek*, the president told Kennedy that he and his friends, if they persisted, would have "the blood of American boys . . . on your hands."[14] One Kennedy associate claimed the president threatened "to destroy" Bobby and "every one" of his "dove friends." "You'll be politically dead in six months."[15] The senator allegedly called the president a son of a bitch and told him, "I don't have to sit here and take that. . . ." After forty-five heated minutes, Kennedy left and, at Johnson's insistence, denied the peace overture story to the press. "I never felt," Kennedy told reporters, "that I was the recipient of any peace feelers." But whether the peace feelers had been real or imaginary, the meeting between Johnson and Kennedy, Rostow confirmed, had been "very rough."[16]

It was at this point that Kennedy made the final break with Johnson over Vietnam. He had sniped at the administration before but had never denounced its Vietnam policies publicly at length. Now, on March 2, on the Senate floor, in a speech written by Richard Goodwin and Arthur Schlesinger Jr., Kennedy turned his guns on the war as conducted by the White House. He admitted that previous administrations, including his brother's, had had a hand in the debacle. But that was not important. In passionate terms he called the war a human "horror" that must be stopped. Why not, he asked, test the North Vietnamese's professions by ending the bombing at once and agree to negotiate within the week?

The speech enraged the president. He had tried to dissuade Kennedy from making it. After it was delivered, administration officials denounced it. When Johnson himself responded to Kennedy's speech a week later, however, he sounded reasonable and conciliatory. After noting that the United States had ceased its bombing five times previously without result, he insisted that he did not "want to quarrel with anyone." He must grant critics, he said, "the same sincerity" he claimed for himself.[17] Yet Johnson could not resist questioning Bobby's motives. Soon after, in a dinner speech to the Democratic National Committee, he asserted that the public would reject "a dishonorable peace . . . bought at the price of a temporary lust for popularity."[18]

By 1967 Vietnam had become the dominant administration concern, crowding out most domestic issues. Back in the happier days of 1965 Johnson had begun to meet on Tuesdays for lunch at the White House with McNamara, Rusk, McGeorge Bundy, Joint Chiefs chairman Earle Wheeler, and special invited guests to discuss Vietnam. These meetings became more frequent in the months that followed and in 1967 were supplemented by additional Vietnam discussion lunches in the presidential dining room, its walls appropriately decorated with Revolutionary War scenes. The diners often focused on bombing targets, with the military asking authorization for more of them while the civilians typically demurred. At first the discussions were free-ranging—all opinions were welcome. By 1967 the president began to exclude the doubters. He had also begun spending long hours after 3:00 A.M. in his bathrobe and slippers in the White House basement Situation Room, reading the latest reports from Saigon. At a televised news conference in early 1967, Johnson admitted, "I go to bed every night feeling that I failed that day because I could not end the conflict in Vietnam."[19] Johnson later insisted to his biographer Doris Kearns that he never slighted his domestic policy for the war, and showed her a chart, listing a breakdown of the time he spent on domestic issues and Vietnam, to prove it. But as Kearns explained, the domestic hours were often purely ceremonial occasions, including award presentations, Rose Garden chats, and meetings with representatives of various civic groups.

On February 8, in celebration of Tet, the Vietnamese lunar New Year, Johnson announced a four-day cease-fire. That same day he wrote to Ho Chi Minh asking for direct peace discussions, hoping he would get an answer during the truce. He said he was "prepared to order a cessation of bombing against your country . . . as soon as I am assured that infiltration into South Vietnam by land and by sea has stopped." He spoke of both sides avoiding provocations so that it would be "possible . . . to conduct serious and private discussions leading toward an early peace."[20]

No more than at other times did these peace feelers stir a favorable response. And why should they? Ho and his colleagues had an entirely different agenda from that of the United States. They did not intend to allow part of their country to remain outside their control. The South must be wrested from the imperialists and all Vietnam unified under a "people's" regime. The American goal of an independent, Western-oriented government in Saigon was not acceptable. For the sake of reducing the pain, the Communists might consider something less than an immediate takeover, but they did not intend to accept terms that hindered their ultimate goal of one Vietnam under their rule. If the war cost thousands of Vietnamese lives and wrecked the country's infrastructure, it was also proving costly for the Americans. The Communists could not expect to defeat the American military in the field, but in the long run they hoped that domestic dissent would undermine American resolve.

Under the circumstances, Ho's reply was predictable. After the usual denunciation of America's destructive and inhumane acts in Vietnam, the Communist leader repeated the standard "four points" of official Communist policy as preconditions for a Vietnam settlement: The American government "must stop the bombing definitely and unconditionally, and all other acts of war against the Democratic Republic of Vietnam"; it must "withdraw . . . all its troops and those of its satellites"; it must "recognize the National Liberation Front [Vietcong]"; it must "allow the people of Vietnam to settle their problems by themselves." As for talks concerning a settlement, there would be no serious discussions until the United States "unconditionally halt[ed] the bombing as well as all other acts of war against the Democratic Republic of Vietnam."[21] Soon after, Ho made a similar reply to a request by Pope Paul VI that both sides make greater effort to find a peaceful solution.

Clearly Johnson had no intention of accepting the four points. They were a formula for surrender. As for an unconditional bombing halt to trigger negotiations, during the four days the truce lasted, American reconnaissance revealed that the Hanoi government had undertaken large-scale resupply of its troops in the South. LBJ soon ordered the bombing raids to resume.

The following month LBJ asked for an increase in monthly draft quotas. At the same time, a presidential advisory commission proposed reorganizing the Selective Service system, ending student and occupational deferments. It also recommended calling the youngest men first and picking draftees "at random," using a fishbowl or a computer. Johnson backed the lottery plan for nineteen-year-olds, expecting it to become fully operational by 1969, but delayed announcing his opinion on undergraduate deferments. But he ended all postgraduate deferments except for those in medical and dental schools. He also insisted that the failure to negotiate was the fault of the Vietnamese. "I do not think," he said at a March news conference, "that we can stop half the war while the other side continues to kill our men, to lob their mortars into our air bases, to seize South Vietnam by force."[22]

After Ho rejected Johnson's "peace bid," Vance Hartke wrote the president urging him to ask U Thant, secretary-general of the United Nations, to arrange a limited cease-fire. Johnson answered him in a two-page letter:

> Hanoi has never acknowledged that it is involved in South Vietnam or that it has carried out "acts of war" against South Vietnam or against us. Each time we ask Hanoi, whether openly or in secret, to give us some indication of what they are willing to do in return for a lessening of the level of our actions, we get only the same well-grooved propaganda record: "Stop the bombing."

Besides, he noted, the consideration was not "who stops what first. We have said we are prepared to act first—provided the other sides give us assurance of what it will do in response."[23]

During 1967 militant peace protests kept pace with the escalating war. On February 15 a total of twenty-five hundred women, under the aegis of Women Strike for Peace, gathered in front of the Pentagon, shouting antiwar slogans and waving banners and placards reading, "Don't draft our sons to burn and destroy" and "Drop Rusk and McNamara, not the bomb." When marching and chanting under Secretary of Defense McNamara's window did not bring him out, they charged up the Pentagon steps. After the Pentagon demonstration some of the women went to Capitol Hill to see their congressmen or joined the gathering at the Metropolitan AME Church to hold their own "hearing" on the war.

Determined not to let the grim Vietnam situation deter him domestically, the day after the bombings resumed, Johnson sent a special message to Congress on the need for further civil rights legislation. The proposed Civil Rights Act of 1967 called for a fair housing law, a ban on discrimination in both federal and state jury selection, an extension of the Civil Rights Commission for another five years, and strengthening the Equal Employment Opportunity Commission by granting it "cease and desist" powers it did not then possess. A few days later he asked Congress to protect consumers to assure the safety of household products, meats, medical devices, and diagnostic tests. Congress, however, moved slowly on all these issues; everyone and everything seemed more mired than ever in Southeast Asia.

In mid-March LBJ addressed a joint session of the Tennessee legislature on the occasion of the bicentennial of Andrew Jackson's birth. He announced the retirement of Henry Cabot Lodge as ambassador to Vietnam and the appointment of Ellsworth Bunker, former ambassador to India, in his place. Mostly on the defensive these days, the president emphatically justified his Vietnam policy. He understood why Americans were confused by the "barrage of information about military engagements," but, he insisted, the "strengthening of allied forces in 1966 was instrumental in reversing the whole course of the war." Although American representatives were ready to discuss peace at any time, "reciprocity must be the fundamental principle of any reduction in hostilities." He also complained that his actions were constantly criticized while those of "the Vietcong go largely unnoted in the public debate." He was tired of "this moral double bookkeeping."[24]

On March 20 Johnson set out for Guam on *Air Force One* for a two-day conference with South Vietnam leaders, ostensibly to introduce

President Nguyen Van Thieu and Prime Minister Nguyen Cao Ky to a new team of American civilian advisers for Vietnam. Actually Johnson was desperately seeking some way to lessen the American commitment. If the South Vietnam leaders could be compelled to bear the brunt of the fighting, the burden on the United States would be eased. And if they could be forced to accept into the Saigon government elements of the National Liberation Front, the Vietcong, negotiations might be opened. Collateral issues to be addressed were the progress of his other war—rural pacification and the rebuilding of South Vietnam. Johnson at times, as we saw, identified the peasants in Southeast Asia with the farmers of the Texas Hill Country and believed that economic progress and political freedom were the keys to making their lives better. Pacification would be the Great Society brought to Vietnam. To give credibility to this "nation-building" agenda Johnson induced David Lilienthal, former director of the New Deal's Tennessee Valley Authority, to come along to the conference.

The meeting itself was inconclusive. To demonstrate progress in democraticizing South Vietnam, Thieu and Ky presented Johnson with a copy of the new Vietnamese constitution, approved only a short time before. The Americans and the Saigon leaders discussed land reform, food supplies, inflation control, black-marketeering, and corruption, as well as long-range economic planning. But as for reducing the American military investment, reality intruded. Westmoreland had flown in from Saigon to brief the conferees on the military situation. The general had no illusions about the ability of South Vietnam to win the war by itself. More, not less, Americanization was necessary, he stated. For the Communists to be stopped he would need at least 80,000 more troops, bringing the total to 550,000. When asked to provide a duration estimate for winning the war, the general stated: "As things now stand it may take ten years."[25] Lilienthal, who was seated to the president's right, saw him blanch.

The Guam meeting did not brief well. Back in Washington, McNamara, who was fast losing confidence in winning the war, could not avoid telling reporters that the military authorities, both American and South Vietnamese, thought the war could go on indefinitely unless the American investment was augmented. Johnson himself admitted when he returned that "We did not adopt any spectacular new programs. . . . The nature of this war is not amenable to spectacular programs or easy solutions."[26]

Inter-American affairs took much of the president's time during the spring of 1967. In mid-April he went to Uruguay to meet with Latin

American leaders in hopes of reviving the Kennedy-inspired Alliance for Progress, now showing serious signs of fatigue. Johnson himself had less confidence than his predecessor in America's capacity to bring democracy's blessings to the Latin American masses and had converted the Alliance primarily into an anti-Castro, anti-Communist device combined with a trade expansion feature. One item of his agenda now was a Latin American common market, with American seed money to help it become a reality. Even here, however, Vietnam intruded. The President of Ecuador denounced the United States for spending so much time, energy, and money in Vietnam while "at their very door nations are trembling with guerrillas, and misery corrodes not only the body but the very soul and minds of the people."[27] Although Congress had already refused to give the president the increased amount of money for Latin America he had requested, he promised to try again.

Johnson returned to Washington to face an intensifying and deepening peace movement. At the ADA's spring convention its national board supported Joseph Rauh's resolution condemning LBJ's Vietnam policy and pledging to support any candidate in 1968 who would work for the war's "peaceful resolution on honorable terms."[28] An ominous new development was the growing defection of black Americans. After months of debate, Martin Luther King Jr. decided to join the April 1967 demonstration sponsored by the National Mobilization Committee to End the War in Vietnam (the Mobe). King had not wanted to share the platform with representatives of the Old and the New Left, and many of his advisers believed that he should not allow the peace movement to eclipse his civil rights activities. But King also did not want to miss the boat. As Dave Dellinger, a pacifist antiwar activist, boasted, the Mobe was "going to have the biggest antiwar march that ever took place . . . with or without Martin Luther King," and King "was going to be left behind in history if he didn't come."[29] And it was in fact the largest protest march since the Vietnam War began—and King joined it, breaking with Lyndon Johnson, the man who had done so much to advance the civil rights movement and the cause of the poor. On April 15, at New York's United Nations Plaza, 125,000 people heard King deliver the keynote address. "Let us save our national honor—stop the bombing," he entreated.[30]

Two weeks later, Westmoreland, brought home for a visit to help reassure the politicians and the general public, told Congress that "backed at home by resolve, confidence, patience, determination, and continued support," the United States would "prevail in Vietnam over the Communist aggressor." To hearty cheers, he informed the legislators that America could successfully prosecute the war if it could overcome "our

Achilles heel . . . our resolve."[31] Westmoreland repeated the theme of "resolve" soon after in a speech in New York. Dissent at home, he noted, gave the Communist enemy "hope that he can win politically that which he cannot accomplish militarily."[32] The general may have inspired the converted, but he offended the doves in Congress. Fulbright considered his remarks an implied threat. "This criticism of dissent will lead to a charge of disloyalty," he complained, "and from that . . . probably to treason."[33] Senator George McGovern denounced the idea "that it is American dissent which is causing the Vietnamese to continue the war." By using this argument, the administration was "only confessing the weakness of its own case. . . ."[34]

But, of course, the North Vietnamese did count on the frailty of American resolve. Johnson was dead right that the peace movement was undermining the American war effort. Ho Chi Minh's high card was patience, not military power. The Communists would outlast the Americans. When North Vietnamese troops went South to fight the American "invaders," Father Ho told them, "Your mission is to fight for five years or even ten or twenty years."[35] But outlasting the Americans meant more than just accepting losses; it also meant surviving until the growing disenchantment with the war on the American home front undermined the invaders' morale. On many occasions during the painful, endless months of battle the Communist leaders would be encouraged by the turmoil in American cities and on American campuses. And, of course, they were ultimately correct. It was loss of will on the home front that led ultimately to the final cease-fire and American withdrawal soon after.

Johnson tried to seem philosophical about the antiwar protests. "We deplore and disagree with folks who burn our flag and who take rather extreme measures," he told a press conference in May 1967. But "so far as they express an honest difference of opinion, we expect it. We rather think that we will always have it in our form of government."[36]

This was Johnson's public stance on dissent. Behind the scenes he was far less tolerant. The president found the heckling, the picketing, the denunciations excruciating personally. By 1967 he was followed everywhere by hostile peace demonstrators and forced to confine his public appearances to military bases and other tightly controlled environments. The antiwar movement activated the paranoid streak in the president, a response that even Lady Bird acknowledged. He had always believed he could get any reasonable person to see his point of view, and when people, individually and in the mass, refused to see the light, he was quick to detect devious and self-serving motives. No aspect of his presidency so frustrated his yearning for consensus as the war, and the president allowed his frustration to overwhelm his faith in freedom to dissent.

LBJ was a good friend of FBI director J. Edgar Hoover and his lieutenant Cartha DeLoach.* This friendship at times served the nation well on the race front. Hoover never escaped his upbringing in that segregated southern city, pre-1960 Washington, D.C., but, pushed hard by the president, he turned the FBI into an effective agent against the Ku Klux Klan and other white racist groups resisting the civil rights revolution of the decade. But Johnson also tried to enlist the FBI in his hunt for Communist influence in the antiwar movement. As early as April 1965 he summoned Hoover to the White House and told him that he had no doubt "in his mind" that "communists" were "behind the disturbances" against the Vietnam War.[37] He ordered Hoover to dig into the matter.

Hoover could never demonstrate a clear connection between the antiwar movement and Communist foreign governments, but to please his boss and friend, he served up SDS and the New Left as substitutes. Dissatisfied with the FBI's results, the president enlisted Director Richard Helms of the CIA. The agency's mid-November report was no better. "We could find no evidence of any contact between the most prominent peace movement leaders and foreign embassies, either in the United States or abroad," it concluded.[38]

But Johnson persisted to the end of his administration to encourage surveillance as well as action against dissenters he considered outside the pale. In 1956 Hoover had created the COINTELPRO program to infiltrate left-wing groups and, through "dirty tricks" of the kind later blamed on Nixon, to discredit, confuse, and undermine them. In the later sixties Hoover extended these operations, not sanctioned by law, to embrace SDS student activists, black militants such as the Black Panthers, and the antiwar movement. It is difficult to say how much Johnson knew about Hoover's extralegal activities, but he obviously approved the administration's legal challenges to the antiwar movement. Under attorneys general Nicholas Katzenbach and Ramsey Clark the Justice Department brought indictments against draft card burners and military personnel who refused combat on the grounds of conscience. In early 1968 a federal grand jury in Boston would indict a clutch of antiwar leaders, including baby doctor Benjamin Spock, Yale Protestant chaplain William Sloane Coffin, and Marcus Raskin of the Institute of Policy Studies for conspiring to discourage compliance with the Selective Service Act. Johnson's counterattack did not derail the antiwar movement, but it did exact a heavy toll of money and energy.

---

*Robert Dallek believes that Johnson's good relations with Hoover derived in part from his fear that the FBI files included information about his sexual peccadilloes. See Dallek, *Flawed Giant*, p. 408.

Nor was the news on the domestic front any better that spring of 1967. Every day the press reported new setbacks for Johnson's social programs. On May 18 the Republicans helped kill new funds for rent subsidies, the worst defeat the Great Society had suffered in three years. The school aid bill and the Model Cities program were also getting battered in Congress. In addition, now that King had joined the antiwar forces, he felt free to criticize the president on other grounds. King charged that butter was losing out to guns; funds that could have gone into the poverty programs were going into the Vietnam War, and the war had "broken" the civil rights movement. Johnson denied these charges. He was not retreating from his commitments; he was in for "the long pull." He also warned his critics that "bitterness and strife and separation will not and cannot build anything; they can only destroy."[39]

That spring another nationwide rail strike threatened to tie up the country. And in addition to Vietnam, the burgeoning peace movement, and the recalcitrant Congress, Johnson faced a predicament in the Middle East.

In early 1967 tensions in that complicated portion of the world were fast coming to a head. Egypt, under President Gamal Abdel Nasser, had turned to the Soviet Union for friendship and armaments after unsuccessfully courting the United States and its allies. On May 16 Nasser asked UN secretary general U Thant to remove UN troops from the Egyptian-Israeli border, where skirmishes had been occurring for many months. A weak man, U Thant complied, though he knew that he was removing a major barrier to an Egyptian attack on Israel. Johnson cabled the Israelis and the Soviets to "remain cool." He also wrote to Nasser expressing sympathy for "the pride and aspirations of your people," but urged him to "avoid war as his first duty." If Egypt exercised restraint, Johnson promised, he would make another attempt "to find a solution to the old problems there."[40] Nasser ignored him, blocking access to the Israeli port of Eilat and depriving his enemy of its outlet to the Red Sea. He also spoke ominously about a "holy war" against Israel. On May 23 Johnson declared the blockade "illegal and potentially disastrous to the cause of peace." But, hoping to forestall a preemptive strike by either side, he added that "the United States strongly opposes aggression by anyone in the area, in any form, overt or clandestine."[41] He also advocated swift UN intervention.

The crisis in the Middle East posed a tricky problem for Johnson. He had opposed the Eisenhower Doctrine, promising American military aid to any Middle Eastern nation resisting Communist armed aggression. Designed to appease the Arabs, it placed Israel and her hostile neighbors on an equal footing. As majority leader he had also opposed Republican-approved UN sanctions against Israel. Shortly after Kennedy's assassination, LBJ told an Israeli diplomat, "You have lost a very great friend, but you have found a better one."[42] Though it was not always politically expedient, he "had a deep feeling of sympathy for Israel and its people, gallantly building and defending a modern nation against great odds and against the tragic background of Jewish experience."[43] He had, as we saw, defied the country's aversion to Jewish immigration before World War II and helped rescue hundreds from the horrendous fate of the Holocaust. Enhancing his natural predilection were the facts that he had many Jewish friends and that Jews were substantial contributors to the Democratic Party and to Johnson in particular. His friendship with Ed Weisl Sr. and Leonard Marks went back many years. Weisl and Marks had helped Johnson acquire his TV stations. Arthur Krim, an entertainment tycoon, was a major Johnson fund-raiser in 1964 and later. Yet complicating his feelings was the fact that many Jews, especially younger ones, opposed his policies in Vietnam and were conspicuously active in the antiwar movement. Johnson resented the pressure on him to take a strong pro-Israel position, though in the end his sympathies prevailed.

Diplomacy quickly reached an impasse. Fearing a joint Soviet-Egyptian campaign to wipe out their nation and drive the Jews into the sea, on June 5 the Israelis launched a preemptive land, air, and sea strike against Egypt. Within hours Jordan, Syria, Lebanon, and other Arab states attacked Israel. When a State Department spokesman, echoing Woodrow Wilson in 1914, declared that the United States was "neutral in thought, word, and deed," American Jews bridled. Johnson responded that his attachment to Israel was as firm as ever and instructed Secretary of State Dean Rusk to revise the word "neutral" to "nonbelligerent."[44]

By the third day of the war, though they had all their enemies on the run, the Israelis expressed their willingness to accept a cease-fire. The Arabs did not respond, and Israeli troops continued to advance, chasing the Egyptians out of the Sinai Desert, seizing the West Bank of the Jordan River, reopening the Gulf of Aqaba, and capturing the Old City of Jerusalem, long part of Jordan. A new crisis seemed to be in the making when, through error, so they claimed, the Israelis attacked the USS *Liberty*, a U.S. Navy communications vessel, with planes and torpedo boats, killing thirty-four Americans. Ambassador Abba Eban immediately offered an apology and promised compensation. Johnson decided to accept the apology without reprimand, though some of his advisers were furious and urged him to punish Israel.

On June 9 Israel took the Golan Heights in Syria and seemed poised to capture the Syrian capital, Damascus, itself. By now the UN negotiator was working out a cease-fire agreement between the belligerents.

Meanwhile, Soviet prime minister Aleksei Kosygin, anxious to rescue his Arab clients, called Johnson on the hot line, never used before, to declare that the situation in the Middle East had reached catastrophic proportions. Unless Israel halted its military operations, Kosygin declared, the Soviet Union would take "necessary actions, including military." Johnson immediately ordered the Sixth Fleet, cruising a hundred miles off the Syrian coast, to move closer to shore, serving notice to the Soviets that the United States would brook no Soviet interference. But at the same time, LBJ called Kosygin to tell him that the United States was "pressing Israel to make the ceasefire completely effective and had received assurances that this would be done." The Israelis, for their part, concluding that they had taught their enemies enough of a lesson and taken enough territory, were finally ready to cease hostilities. On June 11, the fighting stopped. Israel had won a stunning, one-sided victory.

One sidelight of the Six-Day War was the meeting at Glassboro, New Jersey, between Johnson and Kosygin. Shortly after the Mideast fighting ceased, the Kremlin announced that the Soviet premier would come to New York to speak before the UN General Assembly. Johnson's advisers believed it would be useful for the two men to meet on American soil. How could he ignore a tailor-made opportunity on his own shores? Rusk thought it would mean "an enormous political loss" if he passed up the chance. Walt Rostow thought it would yield major gains, helping LBJ to protect his "flank to the left and among the columnists."[45] Johnson himself had often declared that he would travel anywhere in search of peace, and he needed little persuading. He wanted to convince the Soviet leaders that the United States, through its support of Israel, was not seeking to humiliate the USSR. Beyond this LBJ hoped to push his plans to limit nuclear arms and reduce the threat of a nuclear holocaust. LBJ in fact was a pioneer in arms control efforts. Paul Warnke, at the time a member of McNamara's Pentagon and later chief U.S. arms reduction negotiator, would credit him with triggering the processes that concluded with SALT I, antiballistic missiles and nuclear nonproliferation agreements.[46]

The first problem was finding a mutually acceptable meeting place. Johnson did not want to go to New York, a hotbed of antiwar activism; protesters of every stripe would drown out the meeting, perhaps literally, with distracting noise. Kosygin did not like Washington because he feared criticism from other Communist nations that he was consorting with the enemy in its own capital. The two sides finally settled upon the quiet southern New Jersey college town of Glassboro, close to Philadelphia and midway between New York and Washington. On June 23 the two leaders met in the Georgian-style home of the president of Glassboro State

College. The questions discussed were the Middle East and Vietnam, with antiballistic missiles and nuclear nonproliferation as secondary topics.

The Glassboro summit accomplished little. Neither side yielded on any matter, though both expressed their ardent desire for world peace and agreed they would keep in "direct" contact with each other. Johnson, putting the best face he could on it, thought the meeting had done some good. "It does help a lot to sit down and look at a man right in the eye," he said, "and try to reason with him, particularly if he is trying to reason with you. We may have differences and difficulties ahead but I think they will be lessened, and not increased, by our new knowledge of each other."[47] If Glassboro accomplished little of substance, it made people feel better to see the two superpower leaders talk. It could only reduce international tensions. Johnson's ratings in the polls went up in the afterglow of the meetings.

June was a good month for Johnson all in all. On June 14 he nominated Thurgood Marshall to the U.S. Supreme Court, the first black ever chosen for the highest court. Remembering FDR's problems with the "nine old men," Johnson had elevated his good friend Abe Fortas to the Court two years before. Fortas would not only vote the right way, he would also keep him informed about the Court's intentions. Marshall's nomination would now clinch the majority for Great Society programs and also help knock down challenges to the administration's civil rights legislation.

On June 17 leaders of the six railroad unions postponed the threatened railroad strike indefinitely, taking the pressure off both the president and Congress. At the end of June, the long fight to save the Teacher Corps was successful when the Senate passed the bill and sent it to the White House. Though the program was modified, the administration considered its core preserved, and that was a victory.

But the president had little time to savor his gains. American casualties were rising in Vietnam, and the peace movement was becoming bolder and ever more militant. *Newsweek* called the United States "A Nation at Odds" in its cover story for July 10 and commented that "not since the 1930s has an American president been subjected to such scurrilous attack as has Lyndon Johnson."[48]

By the summer Johnson was losing confidence in Westmoreland's strategy of attrition. McNamara was having even deeper doubts. The bombings had produced little; Communist men and supplies still arrived in South Vietnam, matching every increase by the United States. "Ho Chi Minh is a tough old SOB," McNamara privately complained to his staff. "And he won't quit no matter how much bombing we do."[49] In a memorandum sent to President Johnson in May, he had observed that

Hanoi had no intention of negotiating until after the 1968 presidential election. "Continuation of our present moderate policy, while avoiding a larger war, will not change Hanoi's mind. . . . Increased force levels and actions against the North are likewise unlikely to change Hanoi's mind, and are likely to get us in even deeper in Southeast Asia. . . ."[50]

Yet despite misgivings, in early July Johnson decided tentatively to give Westmoreland the extra troops he had requested at Guam, but dispatched McNamara to Vietnam to negotiate the exact figure with the general. In Saigon the defense secretary listened to the optimistic reports of Westmoreland and Ellsworth Bunker, the new U.S. ambassador, and found his growing doubts for the moment assuaged. He returned claiming that the war was winnable if Westmoreland got his reinforcements. "There is not a stalemate," he told the president.[51] At the same time, however, he refused to buy the generals' faith in the endless bombing campaign. In mid-August the administration made public its decision to send an additional forty-seven thousand troops to South Vietnam.

McNamara had scarcely finished briefing Johnson on his trip when riots broke out in Newark, New Jersey, igniting the worst summer of racial violence in the nation's history. When the National Guard and state troopers were called in to quell the Newark disturbances, gun battles erupted between rioters and the law enforcers. New Jersey's governor Richard J. Hughes, calling it a "criminal rebellion,"[52] phoned the president for help. Johnson promised Hughes whatever he needed, but in the end was relieved that the governor was able to handle it without federal troops.

Detroit exploded in the early morning hours the following week. In 1967 the Motor City had a progressive mayor sensitive to ghetto problems, a city administration with many black officeholders, and a booming economy. Millions of dollars in antipoverty and urban-renewal funds had flowed into the city, but relations between blacks and the police were tense, mirroring those in Newark and other cities. When police raided an after-hours club on the city's West Side, they detonated the worst race riot in decades.

Acting on a request from Republican governor George Romney, this time the president sent in federal troops. Six battle-scarred days later, forty-three people were dead, more than a thousand were wounded, five thousand were homeless and jobless, and four thousand fires had destroyed thirteen hundred buildings.

Republicans blamed Johnson for the riots and demanded a congressional investigation. He had indulged the rioters, they charged, failing to protect law-abiding citizens, and looking the other way when "hatemon-

gers" traveled "from community to community inciting insurrection."[53]
The left attacked him for insufficient attention to the ills of the ghettos
and called for a "Marshall Plan" for the cities. Black leaders were critical. Martin Luther King Jr. insisted on a federal jobs creation program
for every poor person in the cities. Meanwhile, H. "Rap" Brown, the
militant head of SNCC, called Johnson "a white honky character" and
a "mad wild dog . . . outlaw from Texas. . . ."[54] Within the administration itself, Robert Kintner advised the president to find some poultice
to quickly slap on the ghettos' wounds. "Large sections of the country,"
he wrote the president in a confidential memo, were "unenthusiastic"
about the Model Cities program and the War on Poverty as ways of mut-
ing urban insurrection. The programs were simply "too long run." Instead Johnson should consider a "jobs for all" program like Roosevelt's
WPA.[55]

Johnson found himself on a high wire forced to perform a difficult
balancing act. He was not, of course, indifferent to the ghetto grievances,
but he could not seem to condone the riots without deeply offending
many moderate white voters and undermining whatever social generosity
remained in the nation. He also could not afford to antagonize the civil
rights leaders and the left-liberals by harshly condemning the militants
and feeding the bigots. Johnson quietly sent seven of his staff members
into fourteen of the nation's ghettos to assess the situation. On July 27,
speaking live on television, the president set aside the following Sunday
as a day for prayers of reconciliation. He ordered special riot-training
standards for National Guardsmen. "We have endured a week such as
no nation should live through . . ." he said sorrowfully, "a time of violence and tragedy. . . . This is not a time for angry reaction," Johnson
advised the nation, "it is a time for action starting with legislative action
to improve life in our cities." He said the "violent few" should be "condemned." "But let us remember," he pleaded, "that it is law-abiding Negro families who have suffered most at the hands of the rioters."[56]

Under congressional pressure, the president appointed a National
Advisory Commission on Civil Disorders to investigate the causes of the
riots and recommend measures to avert such social spasms in the future.
As chairman he selected the Democratic governor of Illinois, Otto
Kerner, with John V. Lindsay, the liberal Republican mayor of New
York, as his deputy. Johnson asked the commission to avoid politics and
work quickly but without making hasty judgments. "Let your search be
free," he said encouragingly, "untrammeled by what has been called the
'conventional wisdom.'"[57] As we shall see, when the report finally appeared, he would feel betrayed.

August brought two unpopular moves: authorization for the forty-five thousand additional solders for Westmoreland, and a request that Congress enact a 10 percent surcharge on individual and corporate income taxes to raise $4.7 billion in additional revenue.

The tax hike, of course, had been pending for at least a year. Johnson had already advised Congress in July to start working on an income-tax increase after they came back from their summer vacation. At a press conference in the Fish Room of the White House, he promised to do his part by cutting programs, though he hoped the damage would be minimal. He knew that he could not pay for both guns and butter without a tax increase. But once again he feared for the health of the Great Society. "All hell will break loose on our domestic program," he predicted more than once when he contemplated the tax hike option.[58] And he was right. The halls of Congress were soon resounding with schemes to cut funds for elementary and secondary education and the War on Poverty. And before long the proposal to fund a public broadcasting corporation was fighting for its life.

The biggest impediment to action on the tax front was Wilbur Mills. The chairman of the House Ways and Means Committee did not like the surcharge. The president had to choose between the war and his social programs, Mills believed. He personally preferred funding the war.

After months of negotiating, it was clear that the administration did not want to make the deep domestic cuts that Mills felt were necessary to get Congress to pass the tax increase. Mills later told the Johnson Library's Oral History Project that he was merely trying "to describe the circumstances that would have to be brought to bear in order to get the 10 percent increase passed. The President knew what I was doing. He couldn't buy it."[59] Before very long it was clear that the tax increase was dead until the following year.

Congress was stewing in general that summer. Instead of vacationing at home, members were stuck in steamy Washington dealing with seemingly insuperable problems. "It's not just the war and the riots," said one grumpy legislator. "It's all this and taxes, too."[60] Their fretfulness had already defeated the $20 million Rat Extermination Act that Johnson had proposed in a special message on urban and rural poverty. The act would have provided the funds for the eradication and control of rodents in slum neighborhoods. Johnson was particularly moved by the thousands of ghetto children who, social workers said, were bitten by rats every year. But the House was heartless, refusing by a vote of 207 to 176 to even debate the bill. Conservatives made fun of it, calling it a "civil rats bill." A Republican representative from Virginia said: "I think the 'rat smart thing' for us to do is to vote down this rat bill rat now."[61]

But the president would not be laughed off, considering it a "personal challenge" to see the bill passed. In the end, Congress reconsidered and included a rat control provision in the Partnership for Health Act, which Johnson signed in December. The legislation authorized $589 million for grants to the states for health services and planning, $40 million of which was earmarked to check rodent infestation.

As August wore on, Johnson's Vietnam critics would not let up. On the "dove" side, Senator Fulbright told the American Bar Association that "the Great Society has become a sick society." Referring to the War on Poverty and Vietnam, he noted that "each war feeds on the other, and although the president assures us that we have the resources to win both wars, in fact we are not winning either. . . . Together the two wars have set in motion a process of deterioration in American society. . . ."[62] Meanwhile, Senate majority leader Mike Mansfield scolded the president for asking for more troops and recommissioning the battleship *New Jersey* for use in Vietnam. Republicans, whose support for the Tonkin Gulf Resolution enabled Johnson to claim that he had received a mandate to pursue the Vietnam War, now asked him to reconsider. Did that resolution need "modification in light of changing political and military conditions" and is "alternative legislative action . . . necessary?"[63] Johnson answered them in a televised press conference, challenging them to revoke the Tonkin Gulf Resolution if they did not approve of his leadership. Though he denied the war was stalemated, he warned that it would "get tougher as it gets along."[64] This statement did not silence his dovish congressional critics. In September, fifty-two House members, Republicans as well as Democrats, asked for a formal review of Vietnam policy. Their aim, they said, was not to criticize the president but merely to give Congress some responsibility in the area of foreign policy.

Hawks, too, assailed the president's policies, though their argument was that he was too timid. A report by the Preparedness Subcommittee of the Senate Armed Services Committee bitterly assailed McNamara for "shackling the true potential of airpower," permitting North Vietnam to build up "the world's most formidable anti-aircraft defenses." McNamara should pay more attention to the Joint Chiefs, it warned. It was "high time . . . to allow the military voice to be heard in connection with the tactical details of military operations."[65] Neither Johnson nor McNamara would comment on the report, but administration loyalist Mike Mansfield angrily replied that the subcommittee was really attacking the president, since McNamara acted under Johnson's orders.

In the middle of August, influential senators from both parties had insisted that unless the South Vietnamese government agreed to impartial national elections, they would demand the withdrawal of U.S. troops.

On September 3 the South Vietnamese went to the polls, electing General Thieu as president. Truong Dinh Dzu, a lawyer, running as a peace candidate who favored negotiations with the Viet Cong, did surprisingly well, however, bolstering the sense that the elections were fair. Though there was plenty of evidence of corruption, the fact that there had been a large turnout while war was raging seemed impressive to those Americans not inclined to question too closely their country's policies in Southeast Asia.

At the end of September the administration announced a new policy intended to bring Hanoi to the bargaining table. Until now the North Vietnamese had insisted that the price of negotiations was a permanent cessation of all bombing of the North, in addition to withdrawal of all American troops from the South and recognition of the Vietcong. But in June, contacts with Hanoi through two French scientists and Henry Kissinger, then a Harvard professor of government, suggested that less stringent limits might be acceptable. Johnson did not intend, of course, to remove American troops unilaterally. Nor did he intend to recognize the guerrillas' legitimacy. But he was willing to stop the bombing campaign under less demanding terms than the United States had previously imposed. Instead of reducing their military activities in the South in exchange for a bombing halt, all Hanoi need do was not increase its infiltration of men and supplies. On September 29, in a speech to the National Legislative Conference in San Antonio, Johnson announced that the United States would be "willing to stop all aerial and naval bombardment of North Vietnam" if this would "lead promptly to productive discussions." While discussions proceeded, however, "North Vietnam would not take advantage of the bombing cessation or limitation."[66]

LBJ was surprised when the North Vietnamese rejected this "San Antonio formula" on October 17 as "only trickery."[67] The answer must be, Johnson believed, that "they still hope that the people of the United States will not see this struggle through to the very end." The North Vietnamese were wrong, in Johnson's opinion:

I think it is the common failing of totalitarian regimes that they cannot really understand the nature of our democracy:

- They mistake dissent for disloyalty.
- They mistake restlessness for a rejection of policy.
- They mistake a few committees for a country.
- They misjudge individual speeches for public policy.[68]

But Johnson was whistling in the dark by now. The North Vietnamese had more accurately judged the mood of Americans than their president. October 1967 saw the most widespread and militant antiwar protests to date, a culmination of the accelerating feeling of dissent sweeping through the country. The *New York Review of Books*, expressing the growing apocalyptic mood of the nation's left intelligentsia, had described earlier in the year how to make a Molotov cocktail to aid in overthrowing the "system." Now, on October 12, it published a statement signed by 121 intellectuals, "A Call to Resist Illegitimate Authority." The manifesto condemned the war on moral as well as legal grounds. The signers promised "to organize draft resistance unions, to supply legal defense and bail, to support families, and otherwise aid resistance to the war in whatever ways may seem appropriate."[69] In the language of the antiwar movement, "protest" had now hardened into "resistance."

Stop the Draft Week would follow a few days later. On Saturday, October 21, a sunny, mild fall day in Washington, fifty thousand to a hundred thousand protesters gathered to demonstrate against the war. The peaceful rally at the Lincoln Memorial, replete with speeches, songs, and bitter denunciations of LBJ, was followed by a slow procession to an officially designated Pentagon parking lot across the Potomac. There the demonstration turned angry as activists, some carrying Viet Cong flags, shouted obscenities and hurled eggs and bottles.

Determined not to let the protest get him down, the president put in a busy day at the White House. He worked in his office, conferred with Vice President Humphrey and others in the White House garden, met visitors from Laos, and only occasionally asked for news about the demonstration. He also signed a few bills, including one that increased police security in Capitol Hill buildings and grounds. After the weekend was over and the protests had receded, he warned both North Vietnam and the American peace movement that the United States will "stay the course in Vietnam."[70]

One administration official with a closer view of the demonstration was Robert McNamara, who was at his Pentagon office that day and who went to the roof to observe the action. The secretary of defense no longer believed in the war. Just before a November 2 meeting of the Wise Men, called by Johnson ostensibly to consider new ideas but actually to confirm the old, McNamara submitted a brutally frank memo to the president. "Continuation of our present course of action in Southeast Asia," the secretary wrote, "would be dangerous, costly in lives, and unsatisfactory to the American people." The memo estimated that the year ahead would bring an additional eleven thousand to fifteen thousand American dead and another thirty thousand to forty-five thousand serious casualties without bringing the country "enough closer to success, in the eyes of the American public, to prevent the continued erosion of popular support for our involvement in Vietnam." The secretary then proposed a halt in the bombing to spur negotiations, announcement of a policy of stabilization, and a transfer of greater responsibility to the South Vietnamese.[71]

Johnson did not show this memorandum to the Wise Men, nor did he let them see other written materials that cast doubt on the possibility of a military victory and suggested that the damage to American foreign policy of a withdrawal from Vietnam would be limited and manageable. LBJ was tortured by doubts, but he refused to consider the war stalemated. The Wise Men meeting was intended more to reassure the president and confirm his policy than to challenge him. And reassure him it did. The elder statesmen—including Clark Clifford, McGeorge Bundy, Dean Acheson, Omar Bradley, Averell Harriman, Abe Fortas, and others—unanimously rejected withdrawing "without a satisfactory settlement with the North."[72] Though conscious of weakening public resolve, they suggested a stepped-up public relations campaign. In effect, their report was a "validation" of existing policy, in Walt Rostow's later words, "the last validation of the strategy of the president, by . . . the establishment that had emerged at the time of Henry Stimson and Franklin Roosevelt."[73]

As for McNamara's memo, Johnson never acknowledged it. But it obviously hurt him. McNamara later said that it "raised the tension between two men who loved and respected each other . . . to the breaking point."[74] For some time the defense secretary had wanted to leave the cabinet to take the vacancy as head of the World Bank but did not want to desert the president. Now, with mixed feelings, the president took up the suggestion and on November 30, announced that McNamara would be leaving for the World Bank. Thirty years later McNamara still did not know "whether I quit or was fired."[75]

Actually, there had been some forward motion on the domestic front during this turbulent fall. One area of progress was in women's rights, where Johnson was prepared to use the federal government to overcome discrimination. Johnson was a child of a patriarchal society, not a "sensitive" man of our own feminist era. He clearly respected women who resembled his mother—cultivated, strong, aspiring. Lady Bird epitomized the type. He had many women friends who worked in politics and who had helped him in various ways during his career. Elizabeth Wickenden and Alice Glass were good examples. But he also consigned many women to a different category: creatures to provide solace and physical pleasure.

Johnson, as we saw, was not a faithful husband even in his congressional days. Not the satyr that Jack Kennedy was, he apparently used his power—the "ultimate aphrodisiac," as Henry Kissinger has famously said—to draw attractive young women into his bed. Booth Mooney, a Johnson aide and speechwriter, later wrote that LBJ "at times" gave "the impression of being . . . as horny as a billy goat in the spring of the year."[76] As vice president, Johnson reputedly had used his Senate office suite for assignations. The reporters came to call it "the nooky room."[77] George Reedy, in his scathing book on LBJ, refuses to name names, but claims convincingly that Johnson appointed a number of his bed partners to White House jobs, primarily as secretaries. Some of these mistresses, according to Reedy, were competent women, but others had the rest of the White House staff shaking their heads in disbelief. In a 1998 telephone interview with the authors, Reedy described what delight Johnson took in acting as Pygmalion to pretty young women whose makeup and dress he would supervise and to whom he often gave expensive gifts. Finally, there is the claim of Carl Rowan, who served Johnson as ambassador to Finland and as director of the U.S. Information Agency. In the wake of the charges against Bill Clinton of presidential sexual misdeeds, Rowan reported that a White House employee had told him how LBJ had forced his attentions on her while she was visiting the Ranch in 1965.[78] Another story that merits attention concerns an encounter at the 1960 Democratic National Convention. Johnson, it was reported, was standing in a reception line greeting admirers when a pretty woman slipped a key to her hotel room into his hand. Johnson pocketed the key and later that day came to her room for a romp. When he left he offered his hand with a sprightly: "Ah want to thank you for yore help to my campaign."[79]

We cannot prove any of these allegations. Reporter Nancy Dickerson thinks Johnson flirted with lots of women, but it did not necessarily mean that he wanted to "jump in bed." She admitted that Johnson had propositioned her in a motel, but it came to naught. "I loved being with LBJ," she wrote, "but sex had nothing to do with it. I enjoyed him because power is fascinating."[80] But only a naïf can doubt that Lyndon Johnson had sexual trysts not only while in Congress, but also as vice president and president.

What did Lady Bird think of her husband's wanderings? Booth Mooney quotes her admission to Barbara Walters after Johnson's death that "Lyndon was a people lover and that did not exclude half the people in the world—women. Oh, I think perhaps there was a time or two . . ." And then she stopped, unwilling to continue the thought further.[81] In a recent TV interview, obviously alluding to her husband's peccadilloes, she admitted that Lyndon had hurt her. But, she continued, he also made her believe in herself and, as she said, "I loved my share of my life with him."[82]

But beyond such personal considerations, Johnson appreciated women's potential as a voting block. Though Kennedy had set up the President's Commission on the Status of Women in 1961, he had been reluctant to move on their recommendation that the federal government appoint more women to important federal jobs and thus serve as an example to private industry. Here Johnson could outclass Kennedy by acting quickly. Hoping to garner favorable publicity for his plans, back in early 1964 he gave an interview to the *Washington Evening Star* explaining his intentions for women's advancement. In a front-page story, he told Isabelle Shelton that he would appoint at least fifty women to important government jobs and end the custom of reserving the top jobs for men. He intended to "make the upgrading of women in American life one of the major goals of his administration." He hoped that private industry and the professions would be influenced by his actions. "Women," he told Shelton, "have the stickability, courage and never-say-die attitude that you don't find in a man. They never give up when they believe something deeply. And they have the imagination, initiative and ingenuity that I like."[83]

There were not 50 immediate vacancies to fill, but by October 1965 he had appointed 120 women to key positions, including spots on the Atomic Energy Commission, the Equal Employment Opportunity Commission, the Department of Agriculture, and to many federal judgeships. One of his most publicized female appointees was Betty Furness, a former movie actress best known for demonstrating Westinghouse refrigerators in the commercial breaks during television coverage of the 1952 presidential conventions. Furness became special assistant to the president for consumer affairs. Though the ultraliberal *Nation* scorned this appointment as "another case of image-making,"[84] Furness's flair for public relations stood her in good stead as an able and energetic consumer advocate.

The administration took other actions to advance women in the federal government. It abolished the practice of "men only" civil service examinations and of specifying sex in classified advertising for jobs. On October 13, 1967, the president issued Executive Order 11375, forbidding gender discrimination in federal jobs and by private employers with government contracts. The order became the legal foundation for most of the sex discrimination suits that have marked employee relations in our own day. Mary Keyserling, head of the Women's Bureau at the Department of Labor from 1964 to 1969, believes that the Johnson years were "a time of unprecedented progress" for female wage earners. As she told Merle Miller: "I think women realized more gains in many ways during this period than at any comparable period in our history."[85] Even while his overall poll ratings plunged in the later months of his presidency, his support among women remained high.

Though legislation had stalled during most of 1967, there was some movement by the fall. On October 3 Johnson signed a bill expanding the vocational rehabilitation program and authorizing two new programs for deaf-blind youths and adults and for migrant workers. A few weeks later he approved an extension of the Appalachian Regional Development Act of 1965. On November 3 he signed into law the appropriations bills for the Housing and Urban Development Department, including funds for rent supplements and the Model Cities program. Both bills provided less money than the administration asked for, but Johnson considered passage "a legislative miracle—the opposition was that strong." Still, he added, "it was no victory for 200 American cities which have already submitted model-city applications" and "no victory for the 30,000 poor families who will be denied . . . decent housing . . . because the rent supplement program was cut."[86] On the same day he established an advisory panel on urban disorder under the chairmanship of Richard J. Hughes.

On November 7 Johnson approved the Public Broadcasting Act of 1967, a "quality of life" bill that expressed the cultural elitism of the Democratic Party's reform wing, heavily weighted with intellectuals and academics.

It was a Kennedy appointee, Federal Communications Commissioner Newton Minow, who, with his famous remark that commercial broadcasting and television was a "vast wasteland," had fired the opening shot in the sixties war to elevate the intellectual level of broadcasting. In 1962 Congress voted more than thirty-two million dollars in funds for the construction of educational television stations. By 1966 more than a hundred such stations had gone on the air. The act did not provide funds for programming, however, and so did little to fulfill the dream of making high culture and science knowledge available to a broad national audience. Many in the Johnson administration, notably Secretary of Health, Education, and Welfare John Gardner, hoped to enhance this unsubstantial setup by generous federal aid. The result was a breakthrough in the history of noncommercial broadcasting.

In February Johnson submitted a measure to create the Corporation for Public Broadcasting, with modest funds for the production of educational radio and television programs, free of advertising or political control. This aid would be allocated to noncommercial stations and individuals, and the corporation itself would not be permitted to own or operate a TV or radio station. The stations receiving federal funds were prohibited from editorializing or taking sides for or against any candidate for political office. Though some representatives regarded the proposed corporation as a "Frankenstein," it passed the House by 265 to 91. The Senate passed it by voice vote.[87†] Johnson signed the bill into law in early November.

Johnson interrupted his bill-signing activities for a few days to tour military bases in honor of Veterans Day. At Fort Benning, Georgia, he attacked those who made the war a topic "for cocktail parties, office arguments or debate from the comfort of distant sidelines."[88] Spending the night on the USS *Enterprise*, the first American nuclear-powered carrier, the president proposed to meet with North Vietnamese leaders aboard a neutral ship in neutral waters if it would lead to a settlement of the war.

Johnson returned to Washington to face harsh new challenges. A new Harris poll revealed that only 23 percent of the American people thought he was doing a good job, an all-time low. Nor was Vietnam's popularity moving in the right direction. Those who wanted the nation to get out of Vietnam "as quickly as possible" nearly doubled, from 24 percent in July to 44 percent in late October. In a television address a few days later, Johnson again defended his war policy, asking his critics to be more cautious before making "irresponsible" and "untrue" statements. There was a difference, he asserted, between responsible dissent and "storm trooper bullying, throwing yourself down in the road, smashing windows, rowdyism, and every time a person attempts to speak to try to drown him out."[89]

By this time there had appeared a formidable "dump Johnson" movement organized by Allard Lowenstein, a young liberal activist with ties to the civil rights movement. Lowenstein and other younger Democrats, many attracted to politics by the idolized Adlai Stevenson, had for months been agonizing over how to give political expression to their anti-Vietnam views. Some, such as Joe Rauh, were willing to settle for a peace plank in the 1968 party platform. But others were determined to deny Johnson renomination. In August 1967, at a chance meeting on a plane trip to California, Lowenstein asked Bobby Kennedy to challenge the president in the upcoming Democratic primaries. When Kennedy demurred, the Conference of Concerned Democrats, organized soon after, turned to Senator Eugene McCarthy of Minnesota. After dithering

---

†By 1979 there were more than four hundred public broadcasting stations receiving federal grants and providing listeners and viewers with a varied menu of classical music, hard news, documentaries, popular science, and other programs of educational interest not available on commercial broadcasting.

for weeks, in late October McCarthy agreed to run. He announced his candidacy on November 30.

Still waiting in the wings was Bobby, whose initial rejection seemed tentative and whose advisers were involved in a passionate debate over the pros and cons, practical and moral, of challenging the incumbent Democratic president. Publicly, the New York junior senator proclaimed his intention to support LBJ in '68, but his disgust with the war and his contempt for the president remained unshakable. Johnson himself had no doubt that Bobby would run. Senator George McGovern later quoted the president during these weeks: "That little runt will get in. The runt's going to run. I don't care what he says now."[90] We do not know what Johnson thought of the challenge at this point. Probably, like most savvy politicians, he considered it quixotic. But given his insecurities, he could not have been happy at the prospect of facing his nemesis Bobby in the court of public opinion. When Dan Rather asked Johnson whether he would run in 1968, he answered he would "cross that bridge when the time comes."

Congress did not adjourn until December 15, making the session the fifth longest since World War II. On November 20 Johnson signed the bill establishing a National Commission on Product Safety and urged Congress to pass the rest of the consumer protection acts still in the hopper. The next day he signed the Air Quality Act, giving HEW responsibility for designating air quality control regions in polluted areas. The states would have the job of setting and enforcing the standards. The bill was a compromise, and at the signing ceremony LBJ warned that "either we stop poisoning our air, or we become a nation in gas masks, groping our way through the dying cities and a wilderness of ghost towns."[92]

There was no longer quite the same air of exhilaration at bill-signing ceremonies as there had been at the beginning of the Great Society. In fact, sometimes Johnson seemed downright vexed. Remarking with some annoyance at the signing ceremony for the Product Safety Act that this was the "first major consumer law that I have signed this year," he said it should have been the twelfth. He was most concerned that Congress pass the meat inspection and the flammable fabrics legislation. "Nobody in this country," he declared, "ought to ever take a chance on eating filthy meat from filthy packing houses . . ." no matter "how powerful the meat lobby is." He also wanted to "protect our families against fabrics that flame . . . without any warning."[93] In the end he got what he wanted on these two issues. Johnson signed the bill strengthening the 1953 Flammable Fabrics Act on December 14. It extended its prohibition to all clothing and household and office interior furnishings made of fabric, put the Commerce Department in charge of mandatory flammability standards, and established a national advisory committee. The following day he signed the Wholesome Meat Act of 1967, updating the basic meat inspection act passed in 1906 and plugging many of its loopholes. Present at the signing, sitting in a wheelchair, was eighty-nine-year-old Upton Sinclair, whose sensational muckraking novel *The Jungle* had exposed the unsanitary conditions in the meat industry and directly inspired the 1906 law.

Before Congress adjourned, Johnson signed a bill barring discrimination by employers against workers between forty and sixty-five years of age. This measure would became the primary shield of older workers in a society steadily aging. Other important legislation squeezed in at the end of the session were refunding of aid to elementary and secondary education and for the War on Poverty and foreign aid. The president had called for an increase in Social Security payments in his 1967 State of the Union speech. He wanted them raised 15 percent. Congress finally passed a bill in December giving twenty-four million people increases of at least 13 percent beginning in February. The measure also increased the base salary subject to Social Security taxes and the Social Security tax rate in 1969.

What made this bill particularly controversial was the amendment tacked on by Wilbur Mills freezing federal funds to Aid to Families with Dependent Children (AFDC). Mills was responding to the growing dismay of many Americans at the "welfare mess" and their sense that, though children should not be made to suffer for the sins of their parents, something had to be done to prevent the abuse, extravagance, and fraud under the existing system. Still unformed and tentative, these views were beginning to challenge the conventional liberal wisdom and would, of course, in the 1990s, carry the day. Under the Mills formula there would be no additional federal matching funds to the states beyond those as of February 1968, and mothers on welfare would have to register for jobs. However weak, this was the first attempt to tie welfare payments to a work commitment from recipients.

The bill caused a furor. Liberals were horrified at the welfare revisions. Leon Shull of Americans for Democratic Action declared the freeze on AFDC "cruel" and the work training requirement "callously wrong."[94] Welfare rights activists testifying before the Senate Finance Committee denounced the pending legislation. One welfare mother from New York said she did not believe "we should be forced to work," threatening that although "we, the welfare recipients, have tried to keep down the disturbances among our people . . . the unrest is steadily growing."[95] Liberals in the Senate promised to filibuster the bill but were out-foxed by Senate whip Russell B. Long, who brought the conference report to the floor when the liberals were not there and made sure it was immediately adopted. Johnson himself was opposed to the welfare provisions, meeting with Mills to persuade him to withdraw the harsh amendments. Mills could not be talked out of it, despite Johnson's plea that the freeze was unfair and would hurt the poor and their children. In the end Johnson was advised to sign the bill but make his opposition to the freeze and work incentive understood by Congress before it came to his desk.

Although 1967 was a bad year for Johnson, he could take comfort and pleasure in his family. He enjoyed his grandson Patrick Lyndon Nugent and allowed him to crawl around the floor of the Oval Office while Grandpa conducted business. He had joked with reporters after the baby was born: "Patrick Lyndon," he said, "doesn't seem to be nearly as concerned with the problems of the world as I am."[96] On December 9 his older daughter, Lynda, married marine captain Charles Robb in a lavish White House ceremony. Lady Bird wrote in her diary that her daughter looked beautiful in her "long-sleeved, high-collared, white silk-satin gown," but she herself was watching her husband, whose gaze at the bride was "such a mixture of tenderness and farewell." She noticed that "His hair was whiter than I have ever seen it," and she felt "full of tenderness for him."[97]

And all things considered, the legislative record in Congress could have been worse. Forty-eight percent of the administration's bills had passed. Some of these were refunding of earlier programs; some did not attract much public notice at the time of their passage but became more important in later years. One of these was the food stamp program, first enacted in 1964 as a nonmandatory program with an authorization of two years. In 1967 Johnson asked for a permanent extension of food stamps with no authorization ceiling. Congress granted him only a two-year extension but extended it again for one more year in 1968.‡

Yet clearly there had been a drastic decline in the legislative success rate. Congress had refused to pass the administration's civil rights bills. The truth-in-lending bill passed the Senate but not the House. Wilbur Mills blocked the income-tax surcharge. The right-to-privacy bill that Johnson had made a special part of his crime and drugs message in

---

‡By 1969 a total of 3.2 million people were getting food stamps, but allotments were skimpy and federal participation represented a small proportion. The Nixon administration, in 1970, responding to what was perceived as a widespread national hunger problem, federalized the program and made the benefits more generous. So the extension of food stamps that Johnson requested in 1967 turned out to be a permanent legacy of the Great Society.

February was approved by a Senate subcommittee but did not reach the Senate floor. And a highway beautification request was first drastically slashed and then kept from reaching the House floor.

The administration claimed to be satisfied with the first session of the Ninetieth Congress. "The Ninetieth Congress is a Democratic Congress," declared Larry O'Brien, now the postmaster general, "and it is passing Democratic proposals sought by a Democratic president." It had not demolished Great Society programs, as the pessimists had predicted. In fact, said O'Brien, "the president's programs had been retained and expanded." "The Great Society programs," added Joseph Califano, "are here to stay."[98]

But administration partisans were being too upbeat. In fact, the first session of the Ninetieth Congress had been a holding action. As Congress adjourned for Christmas recess, further movement in 1968 on the social agenda seemed problematical. As for Vietnam, Joseph Califano later wrote: "As 1967 ended, Johnson couldn't seem to deliver victory on the battlefield or negotiations for peace, no matter how many troops and bombs he committed to the effort or how many diplomatic feelers he extended to North Vietnam, and the American people were beginning to have second thoughts about him."[99]

CHAPTER 20

Renunciation

J OHNSON TOOK TO THE ROAD after Congress adjourned, going first to
California to cheer up GIs wounded in Vietnam and then to Honolulu where, in a driving rain, he was confronted by angry antiwar
demonstrators. After a stop in Pago Pago he flew to Australia to attend the
funeral of his friend and supporter Prime Minister Harold Holt, who had
drowned in a swimming accident. In Canberra he conferred with President Thieu about settling Saigon's differences with the Vietcong and, by
making them into friends, perhaps detaching them from their North
Vietnamese patrons. He then flew to Cam Ranh Bay in South Vietnam,
the second time in fourteen months. At the giant American supply base
he talked to General Westmoreland and Ambassador Ellsworth Bunker
and visited with the troops and assured them, "We're not going to yield
and we're not going to shimmy."[1] The next stop was Pakistan, to see President Ayub Kahn, and after that Rome, to meet the pope. Johnson told
Paul VI that he was pleased that his daughter Luci was a convert to
Catholicism, but the Holy Father was more interested in Vietnam and
why America was continuing the war. Johnson, for his part, asked Paul to
press the Catholic Thieu to open talks with the Viet Cong. After a meeting with the president of Italy, Johnson flew home on Christmas Eve.

As 1968 began, most Americans took it for granted that Johnson
would run for reelection. The man simply would not be able to walk off
the stage where he had performed his bravura act for so many years.
Within the White House itself, midlevel staff were feeding the president
polling data as late as March 30 to show that he would defeat his two

chief rivals for the nomination and win the election in November against any likely Republican. Though Washington was rife with rumors that the president would not run again, few pundits doubted he would. As late as February 17, columnist Carl Rowan wrote that the chances of his not running "can't be better than a million to one."[2]

In fact LBJ was carefully weighing the pros and cons. Though *Time* had named him "Man of the Year" for the second time in four years, Vietnam and Democratic dissension were draining the physical and psychic energy he would need to spend another grueling term in the White House.

The Johnson family was divided over his running again. Lady Bird was opposed to another term. She had wished from the start, she later explained, "that he would leave after his first full term, when he would have accomplished as much as he could, and there would still be time . . . for a quiet life together."[3] But she admitted in her diary that she was "so uncertain of the future that I would not dare to try to persuade him one way or the other."[4] Luci was against it on medical grounds. She wanted a living father, she said. Lynda was more ambivalent. As a daughter, she preferred that he not run, but as a citizen she hoped he did. As she told her mother, her husband, marine officer Charles Robb, was going to Vietnam, and "there will be a better chance of getting him back alive and the war settled" if Lyndon Johnson remained president.[5]

Johnson had been flirting for some time with the idea of not running. Without telling anyone, in 1967 he had commissioned an actuarial study of his life expectancy, providing the experts with medical histories of all the men in the Johnson family, including himself. The results were chilling. He would die at age sixty-four, they said. It was as close as any prediction can be: He died at sixty-four and a half. Johnson would later link his mortality to the public good. In 1971 he told a member of his retirement staff, Leo Janos, that he felt the American people had suffered by having too many presidents die in office.[6] But this concern for the voters seems an after-the-fact rationalization. In fact, LBJ had always been terrified of dying young and clearly thought giving up the presidency would buy some extra years.

But health concerns were not the only inducements to leaving. Johnson felt he had completed his mission, or as much as was possible. He talked of further installments of social legislation, but he had virtually exhausted the pool of ideas that he had inherited from his predecessors or that his own advisers had formulated in his first four years. And the few new ones being proposed did not appeal to him. When Sargent Shriver and other antipoverty warriors suggested some form of guaranteed annual income for the chronically poor, whether in the form of a negative income tax or through some other device, Johnson shot the proposals down as too extreme.

And then there was Vietnam. It was like some horrible skin disease that had spread over his presidency and would not yield to treatment. He and his advisers seemed incapable of effecting a cure. Perhaps someone else could. And Bobby? Could he face the humiliation of having the nomination stolen from him by the man he considered his personal nemesis?

Those closest to Johnson were aware that he was seriously considering retirement. According to Lady Bird and press secretary George Christian, he was actually thinking of making a withdrawal statement at the end of his 1968 State of the Union speech. But he feared becoming an impotent lame duck for the rest of his term and refrained. Later he told Christian, "I thought about it, but when I got over there I got to thinking about laying out this big program before Congress and telling Congress, 'This is the program I want done and, by the way, I'm not running for reelection.' So I just decided it was kind of strange and didn't do it."[7] He was obviously still leaving the door open. Meanwhile, there would be a lot of work to do before the elections and many surprises along the way.

The new year had just begun when Johnson, speaking to reporters at the Ranch, sounded the alarm at the burgeoning deficit in the United States balance of payments and the depletion of the Treasury's gold supply. The condition had been long in the making. In the Bretton Woods agreement of 1944, the world's trading nations had created a mechanism for stabilizing international currencies by pegging them to gold valued at thirty-five American dollars per ounce. The system relied on the willingness and the ability of the United States to buy and to sell gold at the stipulated price. For almost twenty years following Bretton Woods, it worked. Interchangeable with gold, the American dollar served as a reserve for international currencies. During this period the world-dominant American economy easily carried the burden of stabilizing the Free World monetary system.

By the late sixties severe strains had appeared. As Europe and Japan recovered from World War II they began to compete for America's international customers while at the same time giving American industrial producers a hard run for their money at home. Simultaneously the American economy became increasingly dependent on foreign raw materials, especially petroleum. Further burdening the balance-of-payments situation were Americans' tourist expenditures, investments abroad, and foreign military commitments.

All these, taken together, had begun to erode Bretton Woods by the early sixties. Then came Vietnam. As Arthur Okun, last head of the Council of Economic Advisers under Johnson, noted in 1969, there was "no dimension of the American economy in the last three and a half years which hasn't been touched by Viet Nam."[8] The war exacerbated the balance-of-payments problem by increasing Treasury spending abroad, especially in Southeast Asia. More important, it unleashed domestic inflation.

By 1968 Johnson's "guns and butter" policy had broken down. As we saw, he had come in with a balanced budget in 1965. Then, in fiscal year 1966, the Treasury's income fell behind outgo by $3.8 billion. In fiscal '67 the deficit went to $8.7 billion. Now, at the opening of 1968, the expected deficit for the year was $28 billion. This was almost the same sum as, in the Defense Department estimate, the cost of American obligations in Vietnam for that year.

Deficits plus full employment equal inflation. During the years 1961–1965 consumer prices had risen on average 1.3 percent annually. By the second half of 1967 they were rising at the rate of 3.8 percent; for the first third of 1968 at 4.4 percent. Inevitably America's balance of payments went berserk. Higher domestic prices made foreign goods even more attractive to American consumers, and the trade deficit went to more than $3 billion in 1967, threatening to soar far beyond this the following year.

With the Free World awash with American dollars, the bankers began to worry that the United States could not continue to pay out gold on demand at thirty-five dollars an ounce. Dollars began arriving at the Federal Reserve to exchange for gold while it was still possible. America's gold reserve began to drain away. And then there was Charles de Gaulle. The "Grand Charles," regretting France's loss of "grandeur," resenting Anglo-Saxon "arrogance," and disapproving of America's course in Southeast Asia, did what he could to undermine the dollar. Air France planes arrived in New York carrying French surplus greenbacks to exchange for gold. In late November the governors of seven central European banks, meeting at Frankfurt, pledged continued support to the dollar gold reserve at thirty-five dollars an ounce. But the drain continued.

It was this threat that the president was seeking to counter on New Year's Day at his ranch press conference. Johnson called for extensive changes in the way the country did business with other nations and announced strict government controls on private investments overseas. He would ask Congress to give the Federal Reserve Board new power to tighten controls over foreign lending, he told reporters. He would also take steps to reduce federal spending overseas by reducing the number of American civilians employed abroad. The president pleaded with Americans to limit "nonessential" travel outside the Western Hemisphere. He intended to encourage the flow of funds "back to our shores" by attracting more foreign investments and more international tourists and would work to develop a long-range program to stimulate U.S. export sales. He would not "tolerate," he said, a deficit that might threaten international monetary stability. Nor could he stand for a deficit that "could endanger the strength of the entire free-world economy, and thereby threaten our unprecedented prosperity at home."[9]

Johnson's remarks had an almost immediate effect. The dollar rose sharply overseas and, in the first three months of 1968, the gold drain diminished. In March, however, there was an abrupt run on the gold markets in Europe that once more jeopardized the integrity of the dollar and tripped off what historian Robert Collins has called "the most serious economic crisis since the Great Depression."[10] On the fourteenth, gold sales hit a historic single-day record at four hundred million dollars, and American tourists found it impossible to use their traveler's checks or exchange their dollars for European currency. To bolster the dollar Great Britain complied with an American request to shut down the London gold market. The Senate soon rushed through a bill removing the 25 percent gold cover against American currency, thereby freeing the entire American gold supply to meet monetary commitments and preserve the thirty-five-dollar-an-ounce price of gold. The crisis subsided.

On January 15 the Ninetieth Congress reconvened. Members were waiting for Johnson's State of the Union address before considering any important business, and there was barely a quorum present in either chamber. The president, now back in Washington, was still working on the speech, insisting to his speechwriters that it be kept as short as possible.

As aide Joseph Califano would later write, the preparation of the 1968 State of the Union message "became a battleground for the President's mind."[11] On one side was Secretary of the Treasury Henry Fowler, a conservative who pushed for sharp cuts in Great Society programs to reduce inflationary pressures. At the other end was Califano himself, an unreconstructed liberal who urged the president to stick to his Great Society guns. In a memo of early December Califano took note of Johnson's fears that Ways and Means Committee chairman Wilbur Mills would demand cutbacks in domestic programs to give the administration the tax surcharge it wanted. The president, Califano wrote, should confront Mills without yielding. Califano also addressed the signs of growing public concern over faltering presidential leadership. The president should respond to Americans' concern by a strong statement that "can give them a sense of hope. . . ."[12]

The president's speech, as prescribed, was brief, a mere four thousand words. Johnson got to the bad news first. "[O]ur country is challenged at home and abroad," he intoned. In Vietnam "the enemy had been defeated in battle after battle" during the past year, yet, hoping to break the American will to fight, they persisted in sending "men and matériel across borders and into battle, despite his very heavy losses." Johnson qualified the call for resolve by affirming his commitment to peace "at the earliest possible moment" and reiterated that he was "exploring the meaning of Hanoi's recent [peace] statement." Any talks, however, had to be established on the basis of his San Antonio formula of September 1967.[13]

On domestic matters the president's words betrayed no sense of lessened possibilities. As Califano would later note, Johnson may have been uncertain about what he would seek from Congress in December 1967, but one month later he was "willing to spend whatever capital he had left—and it was dwindling fast—to get his work done without waiting for the war to be over."[14] Without mentioning the Great Society once by name, Johnson reiterated its informing vision. The fundamental question was not how to achieve abundance when there was plenty for all, but "How can we all share in our abundance?" He asked Congress to pass those social measures still pending, and he proposed several new ones.

Johnson expressed his concern about the growing crime and violence in the cities, the rapidly rising medical costs, the low wages paid to farm workers, the lack of decent shelter for all families, and the still badly polluted urban rivers and air. "We have lived with conditions like these for many years," he admitted. But what we used to find "inevitable, we now find intolerable." He appealed to Congress to pass the new versions of the Higher Education Act, the Juvenile Delinquency Act, the Highway Beautification Act, and the measures to conserve the California redwoods left over from the first session. The Senate had passed the truth-in-lending, fire safety, and pipeline safety laws; it was time for the House to act on them. He wanted to see enactment of leftover civil rights legislation, including laws providing for fair jury trials, equal employment, and fair housing. He also called for new job and consumer bills, child health programs, medical cost control laws, and a ten-year campaign to build six million new housing units for low- and middle-income families. In addition, he proposed farm support programs, additional antipollution legislation, and stricter drug control laws. And he hoped Congress would pass the income-tax surcharge to help pay for his programs and "continue our economic expansion, which has already broken all past records."

Though his tone was somber, Johnson refused to be pessimistic. He was confident that America could master its difficulties. "If ever there was a Nation capable of solving its problems," he declared, "it is this nation. If ever there were a time to know the pride and excitement and hope of being an American—it is this time." He concluded on a hopeful note to polite applause. "This, my friends, is the State of our Union, seeking, building, tested many times this past year—and always equal to the test."[15]

LBJ's largely upbeat words did not deceive the knowledgeable. Observers were quick to note the differences between the 1968 speech and previous ones. Vietnam, this time, got far more attention than domestic programs. And there was also a major difference in audience response. The assembled representatives, senators, and other dignitaries lacked the enthusiasm that accompanied his words in 1965. In the view of one columnist, the speech "reflected the weariness and anxiety of a nation plunged into a seemingly endless war abroad and growing division and disorder at home."[16]

Whatever Johnson really believed about his chances with Congress, he pushed ahead. The week after the State of the Union speech, he asked the legislators to pass a five-point civil rights program. In his message accompanying submission, he denounced the "voices of the extremists on both sides" and noted that "the more we grapple with the civil rights problem . . . the more we realize that the position of minorities in American society is defined not merely by law, but by social, educational and economic conditions."[17] In February, in a speech in Dallas, he more forcibly reaffirmed his support of the Great Society than he had in months. "The Great Society that is designed to help people," he declared to much applause, "is here to stay."[18]

But when Johnson submitted his budget for fiscal 1969, it was clear that something had to give. He asked Congress for $186.1 billion, conceding that it might not be enough to cover the expenses of the war. This was the first budget since he took office in which he removed some of the butter on the nation's table to pay for the guns. The budget allocation for Great Society spending had gone from $6.9 billion in 1965 to $20.8 billion in 1969; Vietnam, which added virtually nothing to the nation's bill in 1965, would cost $26.3 billion in 1969. Just a year before, in the 1967 budget message, he was able to say that funding for "new and vital" Great Society programs would not be curtailed to pay for Vietnam.

But Wilbur Mills had been pushing Johnson to reorder his priorities, urging him to "pause in this headlong rush toward ever bigger government,"[19] and the president, hoping to persuade Mills to cooperate on the 10 percent surcharge, was now paying attention.

Echoing the words of his State of the Union speech, LBJ would be tested many times in the year ahead, with an especially heavy load dumped on him in the weeks immediately following the speech. This was a time, the president later remembered, when he "felt that [he] was living in a continuous nightmare."[20] Soon after the State of the Union message HEW Secretary John Gardner resigned, explaining that he believed Johnson should not run for reelection. When asked why he felt this way, Gardner replied: "I . . . think we're in a terrible passage in our history and that you cannot do what needs to be done." To his surprise, Johnson said he agreed.[21]

And a terrible passage the next few months would prove to be. On January 23 a flotilla of North Korean patrol boats captured the USS *Pueblo*, a lightly armed American intelligence vessel with highly sophisticated data-gathering electronic equipment, forcing it into a North Korean port and imprisoning its eighty-three-man crew. The North Koreans claimed the *Pueblo* had violated their territorial waters. The United States asserted that the ship had actually been in international waters, twenty-five miles off the coast, and demanded the release of the vessel and its men. To meet the emergency, Johnson called back to active duty almost fifteen thousand air force and navy reservists and requested that the UN Security Council consider sanctions against North Korea. Although the acute phase of the *Pueblo* crisis was over quickly, negotiations dragged on for months, finally culminating in the release of the men, but not the ship, in December, after almost a year. Combined with an uncovered plot to assassinate an American ally, South Korean president Chung Hee Park, only a few days before, and Hanoi's intransigence over coming to the bargaining table, the *Pueblo* incident seemed part of a grand Communist design to thwart the United States in East Asia.

Then came the Tet offensive, the turning point in the war. North and South Vietnam's biggest holiday, Tet marks the lunar New Year and is commemorated by a week of festivities. Both sides in the war had observed a truce at Tet in the past, and the United States had honored them. This time, however, the Communists had prepared for the occasion their most powerful strike against the enemy, one that would "decide the fate of the country" and "end the war."[22] The blow, they hoped, would repeat Dien Bien Phu, which had destroyed the morale of the French colonialists and led to the Geneva agreements liberating North Vietnam. Tet was an ideal time for such an attack. The enemy would be observing the holiday; South Vietnamese government offices would be closed, and ARVN soldiers would be on leave to visit their families. In fact, the Americans were no more alert than their allies. In Saigon, Ambassador Ellsworth Bunker threw a party in Tet's honor, inviting everybody to come "see the light at the end of the tunnel,"[23] a phrase that was then circulating among the American military. General Westmoreland confessed years later that though he knew the enemy was planning a large campaign, "I frankly did not think they would assume the psychological disadvantage of hitting at Tet itself, so I thought it would be long before or after Tet."[24]

The Tet holiday began after midnight on Tuesday, January 30. Less than a hour later, seventy thousand Vietcong and North Vietnamese regulars struck at five of South Vietnam's six largest cities, thirty-six of forty-four provincial capitals, sixty-four district capitals, and fifty assorted hamlets. At 3:00 A.M. a huge explosion shattered the U.S. Army's Tactical Operations Center fifteen miles from Saigon. Vietcong troops in the capital also attacked the airport, the presidential palace, and the headquarters of South Vietnam's General Staff. Some of the most violent fighting occurred in the beautiful northern city of Hue. A former capital, Hue had handsome boulevards, a park-lined River of Pefumes, and temples, palaces, towers, and moats modeled on the Chinese imperial city of Peking. After capturing the Citadel, the ancient fortress in the city's center, North Vietnamese troops proceeded to destroy buildings and massacre residents. One observer described what was left of the city as a "shattered, stinking hulk, its streets choked with rubble and rotting bodies."[25]

For Americans the most alarming part of the offensive was the attack on the U.S. embassy in Saigon by a nineteen-person Vietcong suicide squad dressed in civilian clothes. Blasting a hole through the front wall, the commandos entered the embassy compound. Marine guards kept them from invading the embassy building itself, but they retreated to the courtyard, where they crawled behind large flower tubs and continued to launch rockets at the building. After six hours of fighting all nineteen were either dead or badly wounded. Seven Americans were killed in the fighting. Though the attack had failed, Americans were shocked that the Vietcong could actually penetrate the center of American power in Vietnam.

It is difficult to overestimate the impact of Tet. The Communists did not achieve their goals. The South Vietnamese people did not repudiate their rulers, nor did they welcome the National Liberation Front as their saviors. Vietcong losses, moreover, were much greater than those of the Americans or the South Vietnamese. Thousands of hidden Communist sympathizers and agents had come to the surface and were slaughtered, devastating the guerrilla forces. But Tet was a catastrophic setback for the Americans and the South Vietnamese, too. The ARVN lost more than three thousand troops, the pacification program was dealt another blow, and almost one million new refugees were unleashed on an already strained South Vietnamese economy. But far more important, the attack was a psychological disaster for the United States and the Johnson administration. The Communists proclaimed Tet an astounding victory, and many Americans agreed. Vietnam had long since become a "living room" war where American TV viewers saw brutal images of fire, death, destruction, and agony on the nightly news. In no previous American conflict had the public been exposed so directly to the truth that war was hell. The flickering images of the Tet fighting made it difficult to deny that the American cause had not suffered a devastating blow.

By now many of the nation's reporters, anchors, editors, columnists, and publishers believed the war in Vietnam was "unwinnable," and it molded their perceptions of Tet. The first accounts, emphasizing the assault on the embassy, gave the impression that the Vietcong had actually occupied the embassy building, the very seat of American power in Vietnam. The symbolism was potent. Although the stories were later corrected, the initial feeling of dismay left a deep impression. The president's aide Harry McPherson, who spent his workday in the White House, confirmed the psychological power of the negative media barrage. He was "more persuaded" by what he "saw on the tube and the newspapers," he later told a historian, than by his "own interior access to confidential information. . . ."[26]

No news report was as damaging to the administration as Walter Cronkite's February 27 "Special" on Vietnam. The admired avuncular anchor of CBS's *Evening News*, Cronkite was a hawk who since 1965 had accepted the benevolent "nation-building" administration line on Vietnam. His faith in the war was beginning to erode when, in mid-February, while Tet offensive bullets were still being exchanged, he had flown to Vietnam. What he saw pushed him over the line, and his half-hour televised report, seen by millions, ended with an unprecedented editorial comment: "It is increasingly clear to this reporter that the only rational way out . . . will be to negotiate, not as victors, but as an honorable people who lived up to their pledge to defend democracy, and did the best they could." Johnson did not respond publicly to the Cronkite program, but Bill Moyers later reported that the president watched it and as he turned off the set had remarked: "If I've lost Cronkite, I've lost middle America."[27]

Notwithstanding the president's pessimism, the administration fought back. At a press conference on February 2 Johnson told reporters that

Westmoreland had assured him that the North Vietnamese attack was "not . . . a military success." Striking at the media, he remarked that "we do not believe that we should help them in making it a psychological success either."[28] He plugged the same line with congressional leaders. At a February 6 breakfast meeting with top Democrats, Johnson claimed "there was no military victory for the Communists. . . . Just look at the [Vietcong] casualties and the killed in action."[29] But the press refused to be convinced. When journalists at a State Department "backgrounder" persisted in depicting Tet as a Vietcong victory, the exasperated Secretary Rusk barked out: "There gets to be a point when the question is whose side are you on?"[30]

Privately, Tet shook Johnson's own confidence. When national security adviser Walt Rostow, Mac Bundy's successor, burst into a White House foreign policy meeting with the news that the Vietcong were shelling Saigon and the American embassy, the president had reacted spontaneously: "This could be very bad. . . . This looks like where we came in."[31] In the next few days he sought solace in religion, gliding off to St. Dominic's Church, with his Secret Service guards, to pray and sing hymns. Johnson would never publicly concede that Tet was a major American reverse. "The Tet offensive was, by any standard," he wrote in his 1971 memoirs, "a military defeat of massive proportions for the North Vietnamese and the Viet Cong." He was sure that "historians and military analysts" would come to consider it "the most disastrous Communist defeat of the war in Vietnam."[32] But, of course, he was wrong: Whether right or wrong, they would consider it the beginning of the end.

For weeks after Tet, the war in Vietnam continued without change. Johnson feared that one Communist target, Khe Sanh, in the northwestern corner of South Vietnam, would turn into another Dien Bien Phu. The Communist attack on the marine base had actually only been a diversion to deflect attention from the pre-Tet buildup, but Johnson considered it a major test of strength and will and authorized 10,500 more marines and army airborne troops to Vietnam and a step-up in the air attacks against the enemy as well. Hanoi, he opined, had never really wanted peace negotiations. Tet was "an answer any schoolboy should understand."[33]

But the defense of Khe Sanh, ultimately successful, was virtually the last installment of escalation. Tet marked the Vietnam watershed for LBJ as well as the war itself. It damaged his public standing irreparably. In the six weeks that followed Tet, his overall approval rating plummeted from 48 to 36 percent; his war leadership approval dropped from 40 to 26 percent. It was in the wake of Tet that he concluded that further commitment was a bottomless hole that could never be filled in.

Johnson came to this conclusion reluctantly and only by allowing himself to be led by the foreign policy elite who had helped steer the nation into the Vietnam imbroglio in the first place. These men wielded enormous moral influence over the president, and their conclusions in March 1968 that more troops, more money, more weapons, and more sacrifice would not break the stalemate finally halted the open American commitment to win and began the process of withdrawal.

The reevaluation was triggered by the military's overreach. In the wake of Tet, Westmoreland and the Joint Chiefs saw an opportunity to push the country to a final commitment to win at any cost. More troops, they concluded, now that the Communists were on the ropes, and a call-up of the military reserves, would mark the end to the limited war they had been forced to fight and give them a chance for complete victory. On February 23 General Earle Wheeler, chairman of the Joint Chiefs of Staff, came to Saigon to evaluate the military situation and report to Johnson on what further reinforcements were necessary. Wheeler and Westmoreland agreed that substantial troop increases were imperative— in fact, 206,000 more. These would be used to regain the military initiative, stop the enemy attack, and restore security in the cities, towns, and other heavily populated sections of the countryside. If the requests were refused, Wheeler claimed, the United States must be "prepared to accept . . . reverses."[34]

Wheeler's request backfired. Read at a State Department luncheon meeting on February 27, the report caused consternation. McNamara, no longer at the Pentagon but still advising the president, protested that it would force a reserve call-up of 150,000 men, an additional $10 billion for fiscal 1969, and an accelerated draft. "I've repeatedly honored requests from the Wheelers of the world, but we have no assurance that an additional 205,000 [sic] will make a difference in the conduct of the war."[35] Stunned by McNamara's vehemence were Clark Clifford, McNamara's designated successor; Joe Califano, the president's domestic affairs adviser; and Harry McPherson, Johnson's trusted counselor and chief speechwriter. Each saw it as a sign that the ground had shifted. On the drive back to the White House Califano remarked to McPherson: "It really is all over." The Texan concurred: "You bet it is."[36]

LBJ returned to Washington the next day from a morale-boosting visit with troops about to leave for Vietnam, followed by a stay at the Ranch. One of his first acts was to create the Clifford task force, to consider the troop increase request in all its aspects and ramifications. "Give me the lesser of evils," he instructed Clifford.[37] That evening Johnson called in elder statesman Dean Acheson, Truman's secretary of state and chief author of the Cold War containment policy that had guided the United States in the postwar period. Acheson, as we saw, had supported LBJ on Vietnam but now was dubious. When confronted by the anxious president with the demands of Wheeler and his colleagues, he bluntly stated: "With all due respect, Mr. President, the Joint Chiefs of Staff don't know what they're talking about." When Johnson remarked that it "was a shocking thing to say," Acheson replied: "Then maybe you ought to be shocked."[38] To get his informed thinking on choices in Vietnam, Johnson agreed to provide Acheson with the raw data as he received it instead of "canned briefings."

The Clifford group got to work immediately. Johnson trusted the handsome, debonair Clifford, a prominent Washington lawyer who had been Truman's naval aide and a perennial adviser to Democratic presidents. Although Clifford had been a hawk, he had been disturbed when he discovered on a summer visit to the Far East in 1967 that America's allies in the western Pacific area were not especially worried about the Vietnamese Communists and were reluctant to aid the American effort to stop Hanoi. The trip had left him "puzzled, troubled, concerned" and feeling perhaps that "our assessment of the danger to the stability of Southeast Asia and the western Pacific was exaggerated."[39] Nevertheless, as a member of the November 1967 wise men conclave, he had concurred that the president should stay the course. Clifford's fellow advisers on the new task force included Dean Rusk; CIA director Richard Helms; General Maxwell Taylor, Kennedy's Joint Chiefs chairman; Walt Rostow; Treasury Secretary Fowler, and top Pentagon civilians Paul Warnke and Paul Nitze. Warnke headed the Bureau of International Security Affairs, a division of the Defense Department swarming with Pentagon doves. He and many of his colleagues had long nurtured serious doubts about Vietnam and were prepared to provide Clifford with a turnaround strategy when he came in as McNamara's successor. On March 1 Clifford was still a hawk, though a shaky one. By March 4, after three days of intense discussion, he emerged a dove. Clifford would profoundly disappoint LBJ, though in the end the president would find it impossible to resist his firm moral pressure.

The Clifford task force considered a variety of issues. Would the extra men requested do the job, or would the enemy merely match any American buildup? Would bombing end the war, or could the Communists absorb the punishment? The answers when the questions were put to the military men were all pessimistic. One of the most critical issues was the financial cost of escalation. Unless the nation was prepared to accept still higher inflation or further danger to the international monetary system, stated Secretary Fowler, there could be no escape from either raising taxes or cutting back drastically on domestic programs—if the administration insisted on the additional 206,000 troops.

In the end, the task force recommended a strategy of "population security along a demographic frontier" proposed by Warnke. This meant abandoning the costly search-and-destroy attrition approach of Westmoreland and his colleagues and concentrating on protecting the cities, which would effectively limit the American commitment and American casualties. Specifically, the Clifford group endorsed an immediate increase of 22,000 soldiers, a strengthening of the strategic reserve, and heightened pressure on the South Vietnamese government to shoulder more responsibility for the war. It advised against a new peace initiative and, for the moment, reserved judgment on the full Wheeler-Westmoreland request pending subsequent study of new tactics in resolving the situation in Vietnam. The proposal, if accepted, would slow escalation, not reverse it.[40]

Clifford handed Johnson his report at a White House meeting on the early evening of March 4. He told the president that the Wheeler-Westmoreland request was "a watershed." "Do you continue down the same road of more troops, more guns, more planes, more ships?" The answer was no. "We are not sure that a conventional military victory, as commonly defined, can be achieved," he continued. The task force was split on whether to actually send those 206,000 or so extra men. "But all of us wonder if we are really making progress toward our goal."[41] National security adviser Walt Rostow noted that it was a pessimistic appraisal, and the next day, at one of the Tuesday lunches, urged the president to reject it in favor of a full reserve call-up. The public would support him if he made a "rally-around-the-flag" patriotic appeal. Johnson was not moved by his hawkish adviser. The Clifford report had gotten through to him and tipped him over the line. He would not send the troops requested.

Meanwhile, Rusk advised Johnson that a limited halt in the bombing might jump-start peace negotiations. Since the rainy season made flying dangerous and would restrict air force raids over North Vietnam, there was no military advantage to be gained by not stopping them for a while. Until now the president had opposed any reduction of the bombing, but he believed that the United States was actually in a position of strength because North Vietnam had suffered heavy losses since Tet and might be more willing to negotiate. Also, Johnson could not ignore polls revealing rapidly decreasing popular support for the war. He was beginning to change his mind and told Rusk to prepare a statement favoring a bombing pause.

Though the *Washington Post* had some inkling of changes in the wind when it revealed on March 3 that the administration was conducting a "major reassessment" of the war,[42] the public paid little attention to the process until the following week, when a *New York Times* three-column headline blared: "WESTMORELAND REQUESTS 206,000 MORE MEN, STIRRING DEBATE IN ADMINISTRATION." The information in the article was reasonably accurate, if somewhat dated. The *Times* correctly observed that Tet had deeply changed official attitudes and created the "sense that a watershed has been reached. . . ."[43] The piece angered the president, who was certain it came from one of the dovish Pentagon civilians. Johnson detested leaks; they represented disloyalty. He also resented being nailed down. He was still wavering.

On the following two days, Secretary of State Rusk was grilled for eleven hours by the Senate Foreign Relations Committee. Before the harsh glare of television cameras, he told the committee that Vietnam strategy was "being reexamined from A to Z" but that the president had still not come to any hard conclusions. Chairman Fulbright had no patience with Rusk. Our Vietnam policy, he said, has had "effects both abroad and at home that are nothing short of disastrous."[44] The committee agreed with Fulbright, as did 139 members of the House, who sponsored a resolution asking for a total reevaluation of American policy in Vietnam.

Congress now contained as many doves as hawks. And the shift went beyond Capitol Hill. Even influential diplomats, some military leaders, foreign policy specialists, and some staunch conservatives were publicly changing their minds toward the war. General Maxwell Taylor was "amazed" at the roster of people who were defecting. "The same mouths," he recalled, "that said a few months before to the president, 'You're on the right course, but do more,' were now saying that the policy was a failure."[45] All this disharmony was tearing down Johnson's confidence, pushing him bit by bit toward modifying his own stand.

While the fallout from Tet was still rocking the administration, Johnson experienced another rebuff. On March 1 the National Commission on Civil Disorders, established following the 1967 Newark and Detroit ghetto riots, issued its report, commonly called the Kerner Report, after its chairman, Otto Kerner, the governor of Illinois. The commission was dominated by the liberal mayor of New York, John Lindsay, a Republican who felt no loyalty to the president. Giving only minor credit to the administration for improving the circumstances of American blacks, the commission concluded that the nation was "moving toward two societies, one black, one white—separate and unequal." Further, white racism was the sole cause of black poverty, rage, and disorder: "Discrimination and segregation have long permeated much of American life; they now threaten the future of every American."[46]

Johnson loathed the report. He disagreed that the United States was as deeply split along racial lines as Kerner and his colleagues maintained. He deplored placing the blame for the riots on white racism; the charge would only offend white members of the Democratic coalition: the urban bosses, the labor barons, the white ethnic voters. He was also angry that the report failed to acknowledge his own decade-long efforts in behalf of African Americans. And finally, he bridled at the report's recommendations: a vast array of new programs that would cost some thirty billion dollars to implement. Didn't the commission members know that Congress would refuse to pass such legislation?

Johnson was slow to comment publicly on the report. Then, to quash talk that he was ignoring it, he told a news conference that while it was "thorough" and "comprehensive" and contained "many good recommendations," he did not agree with all of it. He would have it carefully studied to see which proposals could be carried out. "From time to time," he added, "I am sure that we will not only be acting upon other things in the report but some things not covered by it." He also noted that "you cannot correct the errors of centuries in four years or forty years."[47]

March 12, the date of the New Hampshire presidential primary, was for Johnson another telling day. Johnson's name was not on the ballot; any vote for him had to be a write-in. Nor did he campaign in the state. Under the circumstances the numbers were not that bad: The president actually edged out Eugene McCarthy in the popular vote by 49.4 to 42.2 percent. But once more, he had suffered a shattering psychological blow. The results were everywhere taken as a defeat. The vote had turned on Vietnam, and the conservative voters of New Hampshire, for conflicting reasons,* had repudiated the president's policies.

McCarthy's showing brought Bobby Kennedy into the race. His policy disagreement with Johnson had been predominantly over the president's Vietnam policy. With Johnson's cool response to the Kerner Report, he now believed that the president had given up on the cities and their festering racial and economic problems. Now New Hampshire made it seem that LBJ could be beaten. Convincing himself that the cerebral and dithering Minnesota senator could not win in November, he prepared to throw his own hat in the ring.

---

*It appears that almost as many voters opposed Johnson's policies on Vietnam because they were too timid as because they were too aggressive. The president had suffered the fate of the middle-of-the-roader.

But first he felt he must give the president one more chance to find his way out of the Vietnam morass. Taking up a suggestion of Chicago mayor Richard Daley, Kennedy proposed to Clark Clifford that Johnson make a public acknowledgment that his policy was a failure and appoint a commission to decide how to extricate the United States from its plight. The members of the commission would be named by Kennedy. If the president complied, he would not run against him.

It is inconceivable that a savvy politician such as Robert Kennedy, one who knew LBJ well, could expect such a scheme to be acceptable. Johnson would sooner acknowledge that he was a child-molester than swallow such a proposal. And he did not. At a meeting on March 13 with Kennedy and Ted Sorensen, now a Robert Kennedy aide, Clifford agreed to speak with the president, but first pointed out that Bobby's chances of getting the nomination and then winning were not very good. That afternoon, Clifford told the president about Bobby's plan. Johnson turned it down unequivocally: It would seem like a political deal; it would encourage Hanoi; it would usurp presidential authority over foreign policy. Given the dovish membership Bobby had proposed, the commission's report was a foregone conclusion. Clifford phoned Sorensen and Kennedy and, with the president on the line, rejected the proposal. On March 16 Bobby announced that he, too, would seek the Democratic presidential nomination and would contest the remaining primaries with McCarthy. "I do not run for the Presidency merely to oppose any man," Kennedy declared, "but to propose new policies . . . to end the bloodshed in Vietnam and in our cities."[48] For the rest of the month he continued to attack LBJ, at one point denouncing him for dividing the United States as "never before in our history."[49]

The Vietnam reappraisal process continued on March 25 when, at Clifford's suggestion, Johnson again convened the Senior Advisory Group, "the wise men," at the State Department to discuss Vietnam. For two days its members—McGeorge Bundy, Acheson, Henry Cabot Lodge, Douglas Dillon, George Ball, Cyrus Vance, and others—listened to briefings by the generals and civilian experts, pondered what they had heard, and met with the president. Their deliberations completed the task of reevaluating Vietnam begun by the Clifford task force three weeks before.

Johnson had told the military men not to give the wise men "an inspirational or a gloom talk." "Just give them the factual, cold, honest picture as you see it."[50] In response, the generals were mostly upbeat. Wheeler reported a "sharp turnaround" both in the military position and in morale in Vietnam since February. It was the "doom and gloom" in the United States that might undermine things. General Creighton

Abrams, who would soon be chosen as Westmoreland's successor in Vietnam, stated unequivocally that the enemy could never launch another offensive like Tet. He also said the South Vietnamese would be able to undertake more of the fighting once the current military buildup was completed.

On the afternoon of March 26 Johnson, along with Generals Wheeler and Abrams, met with the participants to hear their conclusions. Mac Bundy, speaking first, told the president that the wise men had significantly shifted their attitudes since their meeting in November. "[A] great many people—even very determined and loyal people—have begun to think that Vietnam really is a bottomless pit," declared the former national security adviser, the man who had prompted the president to send the first combat troops to Vietnam. "I must tell you," he added, "what I thought I would never say, that I now agree with George Ball."[51] In various ways Bundy's views were echoed by Lodge, Dillon, Acheson, and, not surprisingly, Ball himself. A few of the wise men—Abe Fortas, Maxwell Taylor, and elder military statesman Omar Bradley—demurred, defending the old line, but as Clifford later noted, "you could feel it, you could just sense it, it was just a great big swing around from almost unanimous belief in the rightness of our cause in the first group and a substantial shift in the second group the thrust of which was that we should not continue to pour blood and treasure into Vietnam but that we should give the most careful consideration to seeing if we couldn't find some way to negotiate ourselves out of Vietnam."[52]

Johnson listened to the pundits with his small grandson Lyn Nugent squirming on his lap. He had heard most of what the majority had said before, but he was dismayed by their preference for "disengagement." As the grayheads filed out, the president cornered Ball and complained: "Your whole group must have been brainwashed and I'm going to find out what [Philip] Habib[†] and the others told you." The next day the president had the briefers repeat to him what they had said to the senior advisers. Johnson apparently decided that they had not been the source of the change of heart. Like almost everyone else, he later concluded, they had been misled by the media reports on Tet.

Johnson would defend his Vietnam policies till his dying day. In his memoirs he blamed the defection of his advisers on their concerns over dissent at home and the social problems of the cities. "They seemed to

---

†Philip Habib was deputy assistant secretary of state. He was one of the group's civilian briefers and he had, in fact, been skeptical of the existing course.

be saying," he wrote, "that anything that happened in Asia or the rest of the world was less important than the strains we were suffering at home." The retired president rejected their argument that Vietnam precluded domestic social peace. Rather, he believed "in 1965 and in 1968 (and today)" that "abandoning our commitment in Vietnam would generate more and worse controversy at home, not less." To the end Johnson remained firmly committed to the domino defense. Abandoning the South Vietnamese "would bring vastly greater dangers—in Laos, Cambodia, Thailand, and elsewhere, including India and Pakistan—than would a policy of seeing our commitment through in Southeast Asia. . . . There was no question in my mind that the vacuum created by our abdication would be filled inevitably by the Communist powers."[53]

These remarks were part of LBJ's postpresidential defense. But in March 1968 he came to a fork in the road and chose the one he had not previously traveled. He would not only refuse the generals' troop request; he would also take the advice of Rusk to halt the bombing above the twentieth parallel, without asking the Communists to stop their resupply effort. This was not exactly the categorical "Out now!" approach of the passionate peaceniks. It was, rather, a decision to stop escalation and shift the defense burden gradually to Saigon, but it was a major turning point nonetheless.

By late winter Johnson had also reached a pivot point in his political life. Should he continue in office? Or should he leave public life? In early February the president and his advisers had begun to discuss a major TV address that would, in the wake of Tet, stiffen the nation's resolve to go the distance in Vietnam. Its focus shifted with the drift of Johnson's advisers from confidence to doubt. It was at the first speechwriting session, on February 27, that the Westmoreland troop request so outraged Clifford, McPherson, and Califano. Yet as late as March 22, a week before the scheduled delivery, the speech was still a hard-line document.

It was during the last three days that Clifford and McPherson, an anguished and unacknowledged dove, turned things around. At a State Department meeting on March 27, William Bundy, Rusk, Rostow, and McPherson listened to Clifford pour out his feelings against further escalation. He knew the business community and the legal establishment, he said, and they were "no longer behind this war."[54] The speech as written was just more of the same and should be changed. McPherson volunteered that the president had too much invested emotionally in the war to change, but Rusk and Rostow, surprisingly, did not speak out strongly against Clifford's position. After lunch Clifford told the group: "I think Harry ought to go back and write a new draft based on what we have agreed to here, a new kind of speech."[55]

On March 28 Clifford and McPherson gave the president two speech drafts, the first "about war," the second "about peace."[56] The president himself would choose which one he wanted. To McPherson's delight when he came to the Oval Office at ten the next morning, he found Johnson making small changes on the dovish speech. Bursting with excitement, he phoned Clifford after he left the room. "We've won!" he shouted. "The president is working from our draft!"[57]

The speech would be the occasion for more than announcing a new Vietnam policy. Here was the chance for Johnson to make his political swan song as well. He would tell the American people he did not intend to run for reelection.

Fears of mortality played their part in the renunciation. As we saw, neither the president nor his family believed he would survive another term. Johnson also feared humiliation. On Tuesday Wisconsin would hold its Democratic primary and McCarthy would certainly win in a landslide. And then would follow, probably, a dreary succession of primary defeats to Bobby! The likely course of events would be more than he could bear. And in truth, Johnson had little physical or emotional energy left to continue performing the duties of the presidency, let alone reserves for another presidential campaign. On March 26 Theodore White, the best-selling chronicler of recent American presidential elections, visited Johnson for the first time in the four years since his last campaign opus. He was "shocked" by what he saw.

> When I had last spoken to him, during the exuberant campaign of 1964, Lyndon Johnson had bestrode the nation's politics like a bronco-buster. Now he seemed exhausted. His eyes, behind the gold-rimmed eyeglasses, were not only nested in lines and wrinkles, but pouched in sockets blue with a permanent weariness. His forehead was creased. . . . He spoke in an undertone, with a softness, a tiredness. . . . The contour of his large body reflected his exhaustion as he slouched in a large rocking chair, his feet lifting to a carpet-covered footstool, his slate-blue suit rumpled, his hand jingling something in the left pocket; nor did he ever stir to those famous gestures that accompany a classic Johnson performance.[58]

Joe Califano, too, observed the president's fatigue in late March when he sat in the Oval Office listening to Johnson muse about the political future. "The President was slumped in his chair and he looked very tired," Califano later wrote. Johnson remarked that he knew he was tired because his eyes hurt. "They . . . always hurt when I'm very tired."[59]

But LBJ remained hesitant until the very last moment. On Sunday, with the speech scheduled at 9:00 P.M., Johnson had joined a group of senior Democrats to consider reelection strategy. The polls were optimistic about his chances overall despite the likelihood that he would lose badly to McCarthy in the Wisconsin primary. The president said nothing to the party leaders to deter them from their plans. Nor did he stop former North Carolina governor Terry Sanford, head of the Johnson-Humphrey reelection committee, from leaving Washington later that day to observe the Wisconsin contest.

Johnson invited the Cliffords to join the First Family and the Rostows at the White House before the speech and stay afterward for dinner. While dressing, the president asked the defense secretary to come to his bedroom. There, as he put on his tie, he handed Clifford a sheet of paper. He intended, he said, to append it to the speech later that evening. It said:

> I have concluded that I should not permit the Presidency to become involved in the partisan divisions that are developing in this political year. . . . Accordingly, I shall not seek, and I will not accept, the nomination of my Party for another term as your President.

The Johnson family and a few of the president's closest friends and associates knew about his decision by this time, but Clifford was astounded. "You've made up your mind?" he asked. "Yes. . . . Totally," Johnson replied."[60]

At nine that evening, seated behind his Oval Office desk, Johnson spoke calmly to the national television audience, betraying none of the inner turmoil that had tormented him for months. He wanted to speak "of peace in Vietnam and Southeast Asia," he said. Hanoi, he noted, had "failed to achieve its principal objective" during the Tet offensive. It was possible that they might try such an attack again, but it still would not work. However, many men on both sides would die. "And the war will go on. There is no need for this to be so."

The president promised to take "the first step to deescalate the conflict" by immediately and unilaterally "reducing—substantially reducing—the present level of hostilities." He had ordered the cessation of bombing in an area including "almost 90 percent of North Vietnam's population, and most of its territory." Only in the "area north of the demilitarized zone where the continuing enemy buildup directly threatens allied forward positions and where the movements of their troops and supplies are clearly related to that threat"‡ would the attacks continue. "Whether a complete bombing halt becomes possible in the future will be determined by events."

---

‡The provision in an earlier draft that bombing would cease only north of the twentieth parallel had been modified to include the whole region above the DMZ.

Now came the speech "about peace." The United States, he announced, was prepared to "send its representatives to any forum, at any time, to discuss the means of bringing this ugly war to an end . . . ," and he called on Ho Chi Minh "to respond positively and favorably to this new step toward peace." He expected South Vietnam to make a greater effort in its own defense, but more American "support troops" would still be needed in the next five months, totaling 13,500 men. He also defended his past policies by reiterating his belief that "a peaceful Asia" was "far nearer to reality because of what America has done in Vietnam," and reminding the nation of Munich by restating that the American presence in Vietnam was "helping the entire world avoid far greater conflicts than this one."

He repeated his warning about the economy, insisting that the deficit be reduced. The war's expenditures had taken a heavy toll, and Congress had not acted on the need for a tax surcharge. If it failed to act "promptly and decisively," the president said, it would raise "very strong doubts . . . about America's willingness to keep its financial house in order."

At nine thirty-five Johnson was finally ready. As he glanced at Lady Bird sitting out of camera range, he raised his right arm, signaling that he would go through with it. The tone of his voice softened as he began this last part of the speech. "For thirty-seven years in the service of our Nation . . . I have put the unity of the people first . . . ahead of any divisive partisanship." Unfortunately, the United States was now profoundly divided, and the divisions threatened to undo all the gains made since he took office. Those gains "must not now be lost in suspicion and distrust and selfishness and politics. . . ." He therefore could not permit "the presidency to become involved in the partisan divisions that are developing in this political year." Viewers had no time to wonder what he meant. His next words repeated the phrase Clifford had seen. "Accordingly, I shall not seek," he declared, "and I will not accept, the nomination of my party for another term as your president."[61] When he finished and the cameras were turned off, Lady Bird walked over to her husband, threw her arms around him, and said, "Nobly done, darling."[62]

The public reaction was electric. The White House got forty-nine thousand telegrams and thirty thousand letters in the next few days, most of them favorable. Many of the writers praised the president for sacrificing his own career to unify the nation. Antiwar activists were thrilled; McCarthy and Kennedy supporters were reported to be jubilant. European leaders were also supportive, even the skeptical Charles de Gaulle of France, praising LBJ for his "act of reason and political courage."[63] The *Washington Post* summed up the favorable response the day after the speech: LBJ "has made a personal sacrifice in the name of national unity that entitles him to a very special place in the annals of American history. . . . The President last night put unity ahead of his own advancement and his own pride."[64] Johnson's popularity skyrocketed from a 57 percent disapproval rating before his speech to 57 percent approval after it. It was not all kudos, however. Many of Johnson's friends were appalled, and some of his opponents were unforgiving. Senator Fulbright attacked the peace proposal as "a very limited change in existing policy . . . not calculated to bring a response from North Vietnam."[65] The leadership in Saigon seemed disturbed by Johnson's decision not to run, fearing that it would be, in the words of a Vietnamese diplomat "a turning point in the war—in favor of North Vietnam."[66] Yet the response to both the peace initiative and the renunciation was overwhelmingly positive.

The renunciation energized Johnson's legislative programs. Prospects for passage of the fair housing bill, the truth-in-lending bill, funding for OEO—all lagging badly—immediately improved. "The president could [now] come up stronger in Congress on all his programs," said the chairman of the liberal Democratic Study Group, James O'Hara of Michigan. "Members can support him explaining that he knows more about the problems than they and that he has no political ax to grind."[67] On April 2 the Senate voted to pass a 10 percent surtax.

A few days after Johnson's dramatic announcement, Hanoi said it was ready to open peace talks. LBJ immediately agreed to "establish contact." But it soon became clear that peace was still far away. Such large differences remained between the two sides, particularly over the extent of the bombing halt, that months would pass without fruitful negotiations.

The nation had little time to consider the difficult road to peace. On April 4 Martin Luther King Jr. was assassinated by an escaped white convict while King was in Memphis to help sanitation workers in their strike for higher wages. Johnson, as we saw, had at times been skeptical of King and had listened with relish to the FBI's clandestine tapes of his sexual peccadilloes. By early 1968 King's attacks on the administration's Vietnam policies gave the president further grounds for anger. Yet Johnson understood the explosive potential of the foul deed. He canceled an imminent trip to Honolulu for talks with Westmoreland and Ellsworth Bunker and appeared on national TV to condemn the murder and implore "every citizen to reject . . . blind violence. . . ."[68] He also called Coretta King and the ailing father of the civil rights leader to express his condolences. Still, the president feared the worst. Referring to the boost from the renunciation, he told Califano: "Everything we've gained in the last few days we're going to lose tonight."[69]

Acting quickly, Johnson convened a meeting of black leaders and congressional bigwigs for the morning after the assassination. He refused to invite the black power firebrand Stokely Carmichael as beyond the pale. The meeting was tense. Many of the distraught civil rights leaders and black politicians vented their rage at the way their people had been treated for so long. The president pleaded for calm and asked the congressmen to accelerate pending civil rights bills, including a fair housing law.

Later that day Johnson proclaimed a national day of mourning for Sunday, April 7, and asked Congress to meet in a joint session "at the earliest possible moment" to hear his proposals "for action — constructive action instead of destructive action — in this hour of national need." He believed "deeply" that "the dream of Dr. Martin Luther King Jr. had not died with him." Whites and blacks, he continued, "must and will now join together as never in the past to let all the forces of divisiveness know that America shall not be ruled by the bullet but only by the ballot of free and of just men."[70]

But no amount of oil would calm the waters of racial rage that now welled up. Within hours riots exploded in 168 cities all over the country. In Washington, Chicago, Baltimore, and Kansas City, the rioting and looting were particularly severe, but New York, Boston, Pittsburgh, San Francisco, Philadelphia, and Detroit, as well as many other large and small cities across the United States, also cowered under threat of fire and destruction. The rioting in Washington was, of course, especially dismaying to Johnson. Smoke from arsonists' fires could be seen from both the White House and the Capitol. In the District of Columbia black militants helped to fan the flames, and Carmichael was in the thick of the action. Despite his dismay, the president kept his sense of humor. When Califano showed him a report that Carmichael intended to burn down Georgetown, the gentrified D.C. neighborhood where many of the city's liberal pundits and antiwar journalists lived, Johnson grinned and exclaimed: "Goddamn! I've waited thirty-five years for this day!"[71] In the end the president had to order the mobilization of federal troops to restore calm in the nation's capital.

Johnson did not go to King's funeral. Both the FBI and the Secret Service told the president that it was likely that an attempt would be made on his life if he went to Atlanta. In his place, he sent the vice president. The memorial service was not only an occasion of sorrow but also of politicking, with presidential candidates Bobby Kennedy, Eugene McCarthy, Richard Nixon, and Nelson Rockefeller in conspicuous attendance, along with all the prominent black leaders.

In what seemed to be a fitting memorial to Dr. King, on April 10 Congress passed and sent the fair housing bill to Johnson for signing. This was the third important civil rights act of his presidency, and it had seemed unlikely that such a bill would pass this session, since a similar one had failed to get through the more liberal Eighty-ninth Congress. On its face the bill promised major social change. It made it a federal crime to threaten or harm civil rights workers and, in response as much to ghetto disorders as to Ku Klux Klan mayhem, to cross state lines to provoke a riot or to demonstrate, transport, or manufacture explosive or incendiary devices for use in civil disorders. But its heart was the fair housing provision. As of January 1, 1970, it would be illegal to discriminate in the rental or sale of about 80 percent of the nation's housing. This seemed to promise an end to residential segregation, a condition that penalized blacks severely and bolstered race discrimination in America. But in truth, unlike the 1964 Civil Rights Act and the 1965 Voting Rights Act, the measure accomplished little. White homeowners, real estate agents, builders, and insurers managed to undermine the law's intent by subterfuge. Housing remained one of the last redoubts of separation by race. Still, at passage, the bill seemed like another triumph for racial integration.

Meanwhile, the promised peace talks with North Vietnam lagged. The initial sticking point was where the conference should be held. Fifteen cities were considered before agreement. On May 3 Johnson finally announced that the United States and North Vietnam had agreed on Paris, the obvious choice from the outset, as the site for peace discussions on May 10. Johnson warned against too much optimism at this stage. "This is only the very first step," he informed the audience in a nationally televised news conference. "There are many, many hazards and difficulties ahead."[72]

And there were. Administration advisers disagreed over the strategy to be deployed in Paris. Rusk remained deeply suspicious of the Communists and insisted that Hanoi be told that the bombing would cease only if the North Vietnamese stopped infiltration in advance. Clifford preferred a softer approach, closer to the San Antonio formula of no increase in the resupply during negotiations in exchange for a bombing halt. The discord, Clifford believed, measured the difference between a real move toward disengagement and essentially more of the same — the continued pursuit of victory, even if with a smaller commitment of American manpower. The conflict was fought out in drafting instructions for W. Averell Harriman, whom Johnson appointed chief U.S. negotiator in Paris. In the end the instructions were sufficiently ambiguous so that

Harriman, a dove, had considerable maneuvering leeway. The military feared Harriman's dovish stance, and on the plane to Paris, General Andrew Goodpaster, representing the Joint Chiefs, argued that nothing be done to "endanger American lives." The president, he insisted, had not instructed the delegation "to end the war on 'the best terms we can,'" as Harriman claimed. "Those are *not* our instructions."[73]

The talks began as scheduled but became deadlocked over the role of the Saigon government in the discussions and the preconditions to an American bombing halt. The Communists wanted the South Vietnamese excluded from the talks as American puppets while, simultaneously, they demanded that the National Liberation Front, the Vietcong, be included in any discussions of the future of South Vietnam. They also insisted on total evacuation of American forces from Vietnam and refused to promise anything in exchange for a complete, "unconditional" bombing halt. Neither side was willing to budge. Johnson soon became convinced that the Communists were using the discussions almost entirely for propaganda advantages, a view reinforced in June when the Vietcong, in the president's words, "mounted a savage, indiscriminate attack on Saigon—on the government of South Vietnam and on ordinary citizens alike."[74]

The quadrennial presidential campaign proceeded as the turmoil in the nation over the war, on the streets and the college campuses, built to a crescendo. The campaign would be deeply infused with its effects. On April 27 Humphrey declared that he would be a candidate for the Democratic nomination. Even before his announcement, Secretary of Agriculture Orville Freeman endorsed his fellow Minnesotan. Johnson was furious and ordered the other cabinet members and other White House appointees to stay out of the nomination struggles in the Democratic Party or "get out of the government." "I can't have the government," he ranted on the phone to aide Joseph Califano, "torn apart by cabinet officers and presidential appointees fighting among themselves about Kennedy, McCarthy, and Humphrey."[75] This is what he meant, he claimed, by his pledge of March 31 that he would "not permit the Presidency to become involved in the partisan divisions that are developing this political year."[76] With an extraordinary level of churlishness, he even instructed his cabinet not to attend the luncheon for Humphrey marking his announcement.

Johnson's attitude toward his vice president revealed LBJ at his worst. He despised disloyalty, but Humphrey had been loyal, almost to a fault. Johnson told Doris Kearns that he himself had been a loyal vice president but he gave himself only a B grade. "Humphrey," he said, "was an A or A plus."[77] And should the shared ignominy and obscurity of that trivial job not have evoked some sympathy for his own vice president? Joseph Califano believes that Johnson's hostile response derived from his infatuation with Nelson Rockefeller, the liberal Republican governor of New York who was a major contender for his party's nomination in Miami. Califano was a perceptive man close to LBJ, but this seems puzzling in a lifelong partisan Democrat.

In all likelihood HHH's candidacy brought to the surface the president's painful ambivalence toward his renunciation. He could not face the risks, personal and political, that running again raised, but he resented the man who benefited from his withdrawal. Perhaps a Republican successor seemed the less humiliating alternative to himself. In a convoluted way Johnson seems to have played the classic part of a dog in the manger.

In May Johnson signed a domestic bill that he had been pushing for some time and had mentioned in his 1967 State of the Union speech. This was the Truth-in-Lending Act that, as its major provision, required that consumers be advised of the cost of credit. This would be done by disclosure of interest rates and all charges on revolving credit accounts and disclosure of the "true" annual interest rates of first mortgages on houses. The bill also provided that workers could protect 75 percent of their take-home pay after taxes from garnishment. In the past their entire salary could be garnished, and the mere fact of garnishment was often used by employers as an excuse for firing them.

Also in May, the tax surcharge issue was finally resolved. The Senate bill, passed on April 2, imposed a ten-billion-dollar surcharge but required the administration to reduce spending by six billion dollars, a move that was aimed primarily at domestic social programs. The House bill did not even contain a tax hike, and the fate of the surcharge depended on the joint conference committee resolution. Johnson tried to get Wilbur Mills to induce the committee to compromise, but the Arkansas Democrat refused to change the Senate's collective mind. The president had consented to make the original cuts reluctantly in order to get the tax hike out of committee. Procrastination, he believed, was "courting danger," and Congress should "bite the bullet" and "pass a tax bill without any ands, buts, or ors."[78] But he resented being blackmailed, and six billion dollars seemed more than he could bear. "We have very serious problems in the cities that should be met," he said, "very serious problems with the poor that need more attention."[79]

Johnson's advisers were split over the tax hike. Those more concerned with the war than social problems pushed hard for the tax increase. "The international consequences will be very grave if there is no tax bill," declared Rusk. "It is just absolutely essential."[80] Liberals, on the other hand, wanted to make sure the money was there for domestic programs and thought six billion dollars too steep. At a May cabinet meeting, HUD Secretary Robert Weaver expressed dismay that cities' programs would be cut. His conscience would not permit him to accept the higher figure. The secretary of labor agreed with him. "I wouldn't pay one single penny," insisted Willard Wirtz, "not one single penny. . . . Don't go below your budget, Mr. President. Don't surrender. . . ."[81] The battle spilled over into the public forums. The American Bankers' Association, the Chamber of Commerce, and other conservative business lobbying groups rushed to support major spending cuts to accompany the tax hike. Labor, education groups, city officials, and churches weighed in on the other side. The AFL-CIO executive council attacked "the meat-ax approach to cutting the budget."[82]

Johnson still hoped to save the Great Society and made one more push for less drastic cuts. He told a group of businessmen that six billion dollars would "sow more seeds of despair and frustration by cutting off the very programs that are so vital to human well-being"[83] and urged them to speak out to this effect. But the president was unable to light an effective backfire, and the House-Senate conference committee refused to budge. On June 21, despite a flurry of last-minute wire-pulling and lobbying on the Hill, the House accepted the conference report.

On June 28, without ceremony, Johnson signed the bill, which included the 10 percent income tax surcharge and the six-billion-dollar federal spending cut package. Yet he got his way in the end. Congress was incapable of cutting even four billion dollars in spending, and Johnson certainly would not make any more reductions than he had to. Whatever may have happened to its spirit, the body of the Great Society survived. Its programs would continue, and even grow, for the next twenty-five years.

The civil rights leaders might have influenced the course of the tax debate, but by this time the civil rights movement was tearing itself to pieces over black power. Among the younger leaders, "instrumental" politics with practical goals had given way to "expressive" politics more concerned with establishing identity and defying "whitey" than with concrete benefits. Valuable, perhaps, as therapy for the spiritual and psychological wounds of black Americans, the new militancy neglected the realities of a nation where blacks were only one-tenth the population and could only accomplish their goals with the support of millions of white liberals.

But there would be one last integrationist campaign. Martin Luther King Jr. and his Southern Christian Leadership Conference had fought the separatism and militancy of CORE and SNCC. The SCLC had been pushed left by the radicals, but they retained their faith in the political road to progress. Before his death, King had conceived of a massive campaign to force Congress to enact bold new antipoverty laws. Poor people of all backgrounds and ethnicities would converge on Washington, D.C., and camp out on the Mall. They would stay there, bearing witness, until Congress funded massive programs of jobs and aid for the nation's poor. Led by King's successor, the Rev. Ralph W. Abernathy, in May and June, caravans of the poor—blacks, Native Americans, Mexican Americans, and Puerto Rican Americans—arrived in the nation's capital. In West Potomac Park, a mile from the White House, they built shacks out of plywood and canvas, named the settlement Resurrection City, and announced that they intended to stay until Congress fulfilled their demands. Unfortunately, the weather did not cooperate. Rain began the third week of May and continued for a month with little relief, turning Resurrection City into a squishy mess, creating health problems, and appalling Washington's citizens and tourists. In addition, leadership was incompetent, money was scarce, and ethnic differences weakened any semblance of unity. Although about fifty thousand people came to celebrate Solidarity Day on June 19—Juneteenth, the anniversary of slave emancipation in Texas in 1865—the Poor People's Campaign quickly petered out. People began to drift away, and Resurrection City closed down on June 26, shortly after the Interior Department declined to renew its permit.

The president had serious doubts about the goals and the methods of the Poor People's Campaign. Given the political realities, its demands were preposterously grand. Besides, it might provoke further violence and disorder. Johnson was also horrified by the squalor of Resurrection City. Attorney General Ramsey Clark remembered how upset the president was at the aesthetic desecration of the nation's capital, the city he loved and that represented the qualities he held most dear. "To see these pitiful poor people with their ugliness and misery sprawled on the monument grounds," Clark said, "really hurt him, deeply hurt him. . . ."[84] When McPherson suggested that the president invite Abernathy and Coretta King to the White House for Sunday breakfast, he refused. Yet at the same time Johnson told his cabinet members to give time to delegations from the campaigners and to be courteous to them. He also told them to avoid promising generous federal aid; he did not want to reward disrupters of the nation's capital.

While the Poor People's Campaign was converging on Washington, the president tried to put an optimistic face on the social tensions and divisions that had begun to appear insoluble to many concerned citizens. Aside from his concern for appearances, he was defending his own record of achievement on the racial front. If the critics and naysayers were right about the state of the nation's race relations, what had his five years in office accomplished? In New York on May 20, he said he refused to accept the "diagnosis of fatal sickness in our society," and he rejected the "diagnosis of deep racism because . . . people [are] struggling as never before to overcome injustice." He denounced those who were "bad-mouthing our country all day long, all week long." Although admitting that "poverty, racism, ignorance, and illness still plague us," he contended that the country was moving toward the eradication of these "age-old ills."[85] At a speech in Fort Worth on May 29 Johnson repeated his conviction that the United States was making progress, but he expressed his bafflement at why few seemed to realize it. "Why do we take so little comfort," he asked, "in the undeniable triumphs of the past few years? Why do we scarcely seem to notice how far we have come—and in how short a time—toward solving problems that have plagued our democracy for generations?" In every way, he declared, "we have moved closer—much closer—to solving our problems."[86]

Johnson's optimism would prove hollow. A few days later, on June 5, after narrowly defeating McCarthy in the California primary, Bobby Kennedy was assassinated by a young Palestinian who resented his pro-Israel positions. Johnson had been incensed by Bobby's attacks on his programs and policies during the twelve weeks of the senator's transcontinental campaign against McCarthy for the Democratic nomination. Johnson felt that he had done far more than his predecessor in improving the lot of blacks and the poor. He believed, moreover, that his Vietnam policy was merely an extension of JFK's. And yet Bobby was running off with the minority voters and the antiwar people. Still, he was authentically appalled when he heard of the fatal shots at the Los Angeles hotel. "Too horrible for words," he exclaimed when Walt Rostow phoned him with the news.[87] Immediately ordering Secret Service protection for all the candidates and their families, Johnson spoke on nationwide television to express his revulsion at the shooting. There were "no words equal to the horror of this tragedy," he said. Americans must stop the violence "that tears at the fabric of our national life." He exhorted people against overreacting and making far-reaching generalizations about the sickness of our society. But the murders of Martin Luther King Jr. and of John and Robert Kennedy were "ample warning that in a climate of extremism, of disrespect for law, of contempt for the rights of others, violence may bring down the very best among us."[88]

The president established a commission to examine the causes of violence in America and appointed Milton Eisenhower, brother of the thirty-fourth president, to head it. One question he wanted the commission to consider is still being pondered today: "Are the seeds of violence nurtured through the public's airwaves, the screens of neighborhood theaters, the news media and other forms of communication that reach the family and our young?"[89] He also proclaimed June 9 a day of national mourning, with U.S. flags to fly at half staff on all federal property.

Lady Bird and the president came to the Requiem Mass for Kennedy at St. Patrick's Cathedral in New York City. As he entered the gothic edifice on Fifth Avenue, Johnson knew he was intruding into a hostile camp, where many of the mourners despised him and even blamed him in some indirect way for the tragedy. But all went well, thanks to the calming words of Archbishop Terence Cooke. At the end of the service, the Johnsons were instructed to leave first. On the way out they passed Ethel Kennedy, who said to Lyndon, "You have been so kind."[90] The Johnsons flew back to Washington to meet the funeral train and attend the burial services at Arlington National Cemetery. The president was visibly moved by the assassination and the ensuing memorial ceremonies, but his aide Harry McPherson later wrote that "Robert Kennedy's murder stirred such a hurricane of emotions that it was difficult for him to speak about it."[91] Whatever LBJ's personal ambivalence about King and Kennedy, he was truly appalled at the epidemic of violence in the land he loved.

He almost seemed to be trying to convince himself that the two recent murders were not symptomatic of more serious failings in American society when he spoke at the graduation exercises of the Capitol pages on June 11. It was essential, he declared, to "distinguish between the twisted logic of a political assassin and the inherent decency of the vast majority of the people."[92]

At this point the rule of reason seemed particularly important to LBJ, and he was especially pleased at UN approval of the Nuclear Nonproliferation Treaty, which, when it went into effect, would prohibit nuclear powers from distributing nuclear weapons or information about them to other nations and forbid nonnuclear nations from constructing nuclear weapons or explosives. He thought it was possibly "the most important step toward peace" in UN history. The president was so anxious to announce his pleasure at this step in ending the arms race that on June 12 he flew to New York in stormy weather to address the General Assembly before it adjourned. "I believe this treaty can lead to further measures that will inhibit the senseless continuation of the arms race," he told the

UN delegates. "I believe it can give the world time—precious time—to protect itself against Armageddon."[93] The following day LBJ was present at a White House ceremony celebrating the United States-USSR Consular Treaty—the first bilateral treaty ever signed between the two countries—which set up conditions under which each nation could establish consulates within the other's boundaries. Before the month was up, he approved the long-delayed award of a Moscow-to-New York route for the Soviet airline Aeroflot. At the White House ceremony on July 1 marking the signing of the Nuclear Nonproliferation Treaty, he announced that the United States and the Soviet Union were planning to start talks on restricting offensive nuclear weapons and defensive antimissile systems in the near future. According to White House officials, Johnson had taken the first step in this direction by writing to then Soviet premier Nikita Khrushchev in January 1964. At the signing ceremony Johnson said he believed that "man can still shape his destiny in the nuclear age—and learn to live as brothers."[94] In addition to being remembered for the Great Society, aides said Johnson hoped to be recognized as the president who initiated the process of Soviet-American cooperation.

Johnson also wanted to address the problem of urban crime before he left office. Murders, armed robbery, rapes, and other violent felonies had been proliferating as the sixties approached their end. In many ways the surge was linked to the spirit that infused the entire decade: a sense of grievance, of entitlement, of the illegitimacy of hierarchies and established institutions, of personal fulfillment, of instinctual indulgence. The Great Society had benefited from the new spirit; it had also, arguably, encouraged it. Yet Johnson, of course, abhorred mindless violence and sought to check it. Twelve hours after Kennedy's death Congress passed a crime bill barring the interstate shipment and out-of-state purchase of handguns. Johnson called the bill a "halfway measure" that did not regulate "the deadly commerce in lethal shotguns and rifles," and he asked the legislators to give him a much tougher gun control law. Yet the president signed the scarcely changed final version of the Omnibus Crime Control and Safe Streets Act on June 19, commenting that it did "more good than bad." Again, he asked Congress to pass stricter controls on rifles, shotguns, and ammunition in the near future. The bill that was signed also established the Law Enforcement Assistance Administration in the Justice Department to administer grants to the states to upgrade their criminal justice and law-enforcement operations. It permitted wiretapping by federal, state, and local officials while prohibiting this conduct by private parties and forbidding the sale or distribution of eavesdropping devices by private parties in interstate commerce. Johnson thought permitting all levels of government to snoop "in an almost unlimited variety of situations" was "unwise." He asked Congress to repeal this provision and said he would insist that the federal government eavesdrop only in national security cases and then only if the attorney general so authorized.[95]

His lame-duck status after March 1968 seemed to give Johnson more, rather than less, emotional drive to push domestic social legislation. It was an opportunity, wrote Joseph Kraft, syndicated columnist for the *Washington Post*, for him to do things and "advance programs that previously had to be muted or even withheld for political reasons." Kraft warned that the president, in both his domestic and Vietnam agendas, was going "far beyond what his popularity in the country or his majority in Congress would sustain. To push much further as a president on the way out . . . at this juncture . . . carries a real risk of confirming the country in what is an almost pathological suspicion of politics and government."[96] But Johnson craved further legislative achievements before he left politics forever. Before his term ended he would sign a full complement of bills furthering his social agenda.

Conscious of time quickly passing, Johnson thought he could guarantee the existence of the Great Society long after his term was over by ensuring a liberal Supreme Court. He hoped to preserve the progressive racial settlement he had brokered and the delicate church-state balancing act for funneling federal funds to parochial schools. When Chief Justice Earl Warren, father of the activist liberal Court, informed the president that he intended to retire, Johnson turned immediately to his good friend Supreme Court associate justice Abe Fortas, "the most experienced, articulate, and intelligent lawyer" he knew, a man who would "carry on the Court's liberal tradition."[97] To fill Fortas's slot as associate justice he nominated another friend, judicial moderate Homer Thornberry of the Fifth Circuit Court of Appeals, a fellow Texan.

The nominations were in trouble right from the start. The president and Fortas had been friends since 1937, the year they both came to Washington, Johnson as a freshman member of the House, and Fortas as assistant director of the Public Utilities Division of the Securities and Exchange Commission. Johnson had elevated Fortas to the Court in 1965 when Justice Arthur Goldberg, painfully arm-twisted by the president, quit to become American chief delegate to the UN. Thornberry was an even older friend, first meeting Johnson as a page in the Texas legislature when Johnson's father was a member and young Lyndon hung around the state Capitol. Thornberry took over LBJ's House seat in 1948 when Johnson went to the Senate.

Johnson expected charges of "cronyism" to be leveled against the appointments. And in the case of Fortas, there would be other difficulties as well. Though a member of the third branch of government, Fortas continued to advise the president, a practice that seemed to violate the federal Constitution's separation-of-powers doctrine. The president had come to rely on Fortas for advice and even emotional support. The justice, in turn, came close to idolizing LBJ. In his memoirs Johnson would defend the continuing relationship of justice and president as grounded in precedent. "Our history," he wrote, "is filled with examples of Supreme Court Justices who not only advised Presidents but carried out political chores for them, and those examples go back to Chief Justice John Jay of George Washington's administration."[98] But practices were now stricter, and the close relationship gave the conservatives a handle to defeat the nomination.

But Republicans were not only annoyed at what they perceived as blatant cronyism. They also sought to deny LBJ the opportunity to fill a slot on the Supreme Court, particularly that of chief justice, at the end of his term. Such a move, if successful, would deprive a Republican president, if elected in November, of the opportunity to nominate a conservative. Senate majority leader Mike Mansfield asked the Republicans not to make a political issue out of Fortas's nomination. "President Johnson is not a lame-duck President," he told the Senate. "If one were to carry that shallow reasoning to its conclusion, any time a President was elected to a second term he would become a lame duck on the very first day of that term."[99] Clark Clifford, however, had no illusions about the damaging effect on the nomination of LBJ's renunciation. In Clifford's opinion, if LBJ had done it before March 31, he would have gotten his nominations through. He also believed that the president should have chosen a moderate Republican, rather than Thornberry, for the associate justice's spot to placate the Republicans.

But opposition to Fortas crossed party lines. Many moderate Democrats were skeptical of the associate justice. Southerners disliked his pro-civil liberties record, especially his crucial fifth vote in favor of the *Miranda* decision, which sought to guarantee legal counsel to an accused person even if indigent. Conservatives and police believed that *Miranda* pampered criminals and encouraged crime. They, and other social conservatives, also perceived Justice Fortas as soft on pornography, though in fact he was not as committed a civil libertarian as some of his colleagues on the Court.

To add to the list of opponents, Johnson had inadvertently offended Richard Russell by stalling on a nomination to a federal district court of a man the Georgian had recommended. Russell was so angry he ended their twenty-year friendship, writing to LBJ that he did not want to be regarded "as a child or a patronage-seeking ward-heeler. . . ."[100] Feeling he was no longer bound to support the president's Supreme Court nominees, Russell told the Republicans he would help them defeat Fortas.

There were, finally, anti-Semitic undertones to the mounting antagonism to Fortas's appointment. "One southern senator . . . said to another," Harry McPherson later told Merle Miller, "'You're not going to vote for that Jew to be chief justice, are you?'"[101] Senator James Eastland was overheard at a cocktail party admitting that "after [Thurgood] Marshall," he "could not go back to Mississippi if a Jewish chief justice swore in the next president."[102] If anti-Semitism hurt Fortas, it also had its uses. The president had Califano contact automaker Henry Ford to point out, "it wouldn't be a good thing for the country for the first Jewish Chief Justice to be turned down." He also told a Jewish White House aide from Chicago to get "every Jew out there in Illinois to go up to Dirksen and thank him for his support."[103]

But nothing helped. By an eleven-to-six vote, the Judiciary Committee recommended the nomination in September. But then the opposition really went to work. Led by conservative Republican senator Robert P. Griffith of Michigan, Fortas's adversaries launched a filibuster. While the senators were talking round-the-clock, it came out that Fortas had taken fifteen thousand dollars to teach a nine-week course at American University Law School. His law partner Paul Porter had raised thirty thousand dollars from five businessmen and given the money to the university, which then gave half to Fortas for the course. This appeared to many to be tainted money. When the administration asked for a vote to end the filibuster, it failed by fourteen votes. At this point Fortas withdrew his name from consideration for chief justice but remained on the Court as an associate justice.

LBJ was crushed by this defeat. A year later, Lady Bird told an interviewer she believed the hostility to the Fortas nomination represented "the rising anger against Lyndon and mostly the rising anger against liberalism."[104]

When, the following year, Fortas resigned from the Court for taking a twenty-thousand-dollar fee from a shady financier, Louis Wolfson, the president remained loyal. In his memoirs, published two years after Fortas left the Court, Johnson wrote: "The truth is that Abe Fortas was too progressive for the Republicans and the southern conservatives in the Senate, all of whom were horrified at the thought of a continuation of the philosophy of the Warren Court."[105] Interviewed at the Ranch after he left Washington, he remarked sadly about Fortas: "I made him take the justiceship. In that way, I ruined his life."[106]

As the summer wore on, the presidential candidates often got more front-page headlines than the president. Despite the peace talks in Paris, not much progress was being made in winding down the war. In a meeting between Johnson and South Vietnamese President Thieu in Honolulu in mid-July, the two leaders discouraged hopes for deescalation of the war unless the Communists drastically changed their policies. Before seeing Thieu, LBJ had a jarring discussion with Clark Clifford, who had just returned from a trip to Saigon. Clifford told his chief that he did not believe the South Vietnamese leaders wanted the war to end. They were the beneficiaries of five hundred thousand American protectors and "a golden flow of money."[107] Nor did they understand that now, with Johnson president, they had their best chance of a favorable peace. All the other major candidates were less committed to continuing the war than he. Johnson conveyed some of Clifford's ideas to Thieu, but to little effect.

Things were now going somewhat better for Johnson on the domestic side. On July 10 he reminded Congress that there was still a lot more work to be done and that if they did not act quickly he might even issue an executive order to bring them back after the conventions to finish their business. He mentioned the bills he considered vital, in order: higher education, poverty appropriations, gun control, housing, health manpower, and assorted environmental and consumer laws.

Johnson had high hopes for the Housing and Urban Development Act, passed in the summer of 1968, the most sweeping housing bill passed by Congress in almost twenty years. Passed in the summer, the law provided $5.3 billion for a three-year program to construct or refurbish 1.7 million housing units for low-income families. It sought to encourage low-income families to buy homes by providing an interest rate subsidy. It made Federal Housing Authority insurance available to families whose previous credit rating had been poor. It established federal subsidies to make rental housing more available to low-income families by helping in the construction or rehabilitation of rental and cooperative housing. The bill expanded existing rent supplement and Model Cities programs and authorized the establishment of joint private-sector and government-subsidized personal and property flood insurance for homes and small businesses in areas susceptible to floods. It sought to involve business as well as nonprofit groups in slum clearance and required that, wherever feasible, construction projects should employ local people and construction contracts should be awarded to locally owned companies.

The president signed the bill in front of the new Housing and Urban Development Building, receiving much applause as he remarked: "Today we are going to put on the books of American law . . . the most far-sighted, the most comprehensive, the most massive housing program in all American history."[108] In fact, the measure proved disappointing. Congress provided little of the needed money, and even before Johnson's death, he admitted that it had achieved little.

Johnson signed a few other bills before the Democratic nominating convention. The Wholesome Poultry Products Act made poultry sold within a state subject to federal poultry inspection standards and provided financial and technical aid to the states for establishing inspection systems on a par with those of the federal government. On August 17, in Austin, Johnson signed laws to create an Eye Institute within the National Institutes of Health and to create new schools of nursing, dentistry, and medicine and expand many existing ones. Johnson was especially pleased with the provision creating improved scholarship support for students of nursing.

A more controversial law was the highway bill. During the Ninetieth Congress, the original 1965 highway beautification bill had come under strong attack, particularly by the billboard lobby. Women's clubs and conservation groups had counterattacked, but their voices were drowned out by conservative congressmen and business interests. The original law survived in a weakened state, and by 1968 the conservationists were disgusted, calling the law a "fraud on the public expectations."[109] In March Johnson asked Congress to revitalize the Highway Beautification Act, but members ignored him and in the end gave the administration only 10 percent of the funds requested for billboard removal and weakened federal power to determine standards for billboards. It also reduced the protection afforded roadside parklands by the original bill. Pennsylvania's Joseph Clark called it "a significant victory for the uglifiers."[110] LBJ toyed with the idea of vetoing the weak measure. But afraid that his veto would not be sustained and the Democrats embarrassed in an election year, he signed the bill at the last possible moment.

In the week preceding the Democratic National Convention, there were some foreign policy developments that caught the public's attention. There had been speculation that Johnson intended to unilaterally stop the bombing in Vietnam. He would do it either to aid the talks in Paris or to give the Democratic Party a boost at home. He effectively ended the rumors with a speech to the convention of the Veterans of Foreign Wars on August 19. The United States would take no further actions to deescalate the Vietnam War unless North Vietnam indicated its serious intention to make peace, he told the veterans. Since March 31 the Communists had continued to push southward and make preparations for future attacks. "The next move must be theirs," declared LBJ. "We are willing to take chances for peace but cannot make foolhardy gestures for which our fighting men must pay the price."[111]

If Johnson could not bring the war in Vietnam to an end, he had hoped to score major diplomatic gains in his negotiations with the Soviet Union. There were plans in the works for another summit conference and a visit by Johnson to the Soviet Union in October, which his press office was just getting ready to announce publicly. If he could get new agreements advancing world peace, it might help the Democrats in the November elections. But the Soviets shattered all such hopes when they invaded Czechoslovakia with two hundred thousand troops on August 20 to topple reformer Alexander Dubcek, who had replaced the hard-line Stalinism of the previous Czech government with a more liberal regime.

Johnson had received a message from Soviet ambassador Anatoly Dobrynin informing him of the invasion before Radio Prague reported it to the Czech people. This communication, after justifying Soviet actions, expressed the hope that "current events . . . not harm Soviet-American relations," to which the Soviet government "attache[d] great importance."[112] LBJ immediately called the National Security Council together into emergency session to determine how to proceed. Meanwhile, he instructed the American UN ambassador to "join with others in the Security Council" to uphold the "charter rights of Czechoslovakia and its people" and condemned the action in a short television speech the following day. Johnson told reporters that he was shocked by the "tragic news." "The Soviet Union and its allies," he declared, "have invaded a defenseless country to stamp out a resurgence of ordinary human freedom. It is a sad commentary on the Communist mind that a sign of liberty is deemed a fundamental threat to the security of the Soviet system."[113] The United States had no intention of intervening, but Secretary of State Rusk nevertheless wanted to express its deep concern for the plight of a UN member "so desperately periled as they are at the present time."[114] Johnson's handling of the Czech crisis was almost uniformly supported by congressional leaders.

The Czech invasion was a blow to Johnson's hopes that he would go down in history as the president who ended the Cold War. In the wake of the incident, the U.S.-Soviet summit meeting was postponed, and although the Nuclear Nonproliferation Treaty had gone to the Senate, after conferring with some of its members, Johnson realized he had no chance of having it ratified at this point. Besides their revulsion at the

Soviets' brutal invasion, some Republicans sought to delay the treaty until after the election. Then if a Republican became president, they would share the credit for a major breakthrough in the Free World–Communist struggle.

Meanwhile, the Democratic Convention in Chicago fast approached in an atmosphere pulsing with tension. No year since the end of World War II was as full of turmoil and foreboding as 1968. The assassinations of Martin Luther King Jr. and Bobby Kennedy, the riots in a hundred city ghettos, the escalation of campus violence, and the grim news from Vietnam all contributed to an apocalyptic mood. Now, as the delegates assembled in the Windy City, another chapter of a clamorous year was about to begin, and Lyndon Johnson, despite his renunciation, would be in the thick of it.

CHAPTER 21

Winding Down

L BJ DID NOT INTEND TO GET INVOLVED in the 1968 election after his withdrawal in March, but as the Democratic Convention approached, his political juices began to flow. He simply could not let go, not after twenty years at the vortex of momentous events. If nothing else, he needed confirmation that he had made a difference to the nation and the American people, had achieved as much as his great predecessor Franklin Delano Roosevelt. Johnson could not believe that at the final moment of decision the party would turn its back on him. John Connally later told how aide Marvin Watson was sent to Chicago to solicit a "draft" from the delegates. He himself, meanwhile, was dispatched to confer with southern governors who headed their state delegations.

A draft was not realistic. The governors, Connally noted, were emphatic: "No way," they said.[1] Johnson's March withdrawal had been a relief to many Democrats: He would no longer be a dead weight on the party. He still had friends and supporters among the party regulars. Chicago mayor Richard Daley, extending an enthusiastic invitation to the president and Lady Bird to attend the Chicago convention, was effusive in his praise. "The majority of Chicagoans," telegraphed Daley, "know you have been one of the greatest presidents of all time and have carried out the awesome responsibilities of president in a manner that is a credit to your country, your family and the Democratic party."[2] But not many thought LBJ could head a winning ticket. The best chance the Democrats had for success was distancing themselves from Johnson and his disastrous policy in Vietnam. Most of the party leaders, even the loy-

478

alists, knew this. When the president asked Louis Harris whether he should attend the convention, the pollster advised him that he might very well be booed there. And Harris was right. His name was not booed, at least on the convention floor, but few pictures of Johnson would be in evidence at Chicago and almost none of the speakers would refer to him by name.

Johnson always claimed to be a loyal Democrat. Back in 1953 he had described himself as "a Democrat of conviction—not out of habit," and called the Democrats "the party that is best for America."[3] Yet during 1968 his party loyalty took second place to his ego. Of all the alternatives to himself, he preferred his successor to be the Republican governor of New York, Nelson Rockefeller, a pragmatic liberal in his own mold and a long-term friend. Unfortunately, meeting in Miami at the beginning of August, the Republicans nominated Nixon for president and chose the obscure Maryland governor, Spiro T. Agnew, as his running mate. During the summer George Wallace, the Alabama backlash leader, entered the race as a third-party candidate through a ballot petition drive. His running mate would be the bellicose ex-air force chief of staff, General Curtis E. LeMay, who had urged using nuclear weapons to win the war. It could not be clearer that a victory for either Nixon or Wallace meant repudiation of all that Lyndon Johnson held dear. What was uncertain in the president's mind was whether a Democratic victory would be markedly different.

Though a draft evaded him, Johnson simply could not remain aloof from the Chicago convention. He hoped to make it do his bidding and had reason to believe he could. Many of the delegates, especially from the South, were in his debt. Mayor Daley was his good friend. His partisans ran the convention security system and doled out tickets to the hall to their favorites. He dominated the Platform Committee.

The convention had been timed to coincide with Johnson's sixtieth birthday and would have served as a triumphal renomination showcase had he stayed in the race. Now, at least, he expected to address the delegates and bask in their applause. Johnson set his speechwriters to work while editing their drafts at the Ranch. Determined that his presidency receive the appreciation it deserved, he dispatched aides Harry McPherson and Larry Levine to Los Angeles to prepare a film about his five White House years to be shown to the delegates.

Well before the convention's opening day the signs pointed to bedlam both inside the amphitheater and on the streets near the delegates' hotels. For weeks student radicals, peace activists, and counterculture militants had been girding to raise hell in Chicago against the

administration's continued support of the war. The Yippies, counterculture zanies led by Abbie Hoffman and Jerry Rubin, planned a tumul-
tuous Festival of Life to show up the Democrats' "festival of death." Yip-
pie fliers promised to unleash chaos and hold the convention up to
ridicule. Rubin later admitted, "We were not just innocent people who
were victimized by the police. We came to plan a confrontation. . . ."[4]
The Mobe and the more sober peace groups and the McCarthy and
Kennedy troops prepared their own demonstrations.

Richard Daley was determined to prevent disaster. The first party
convention held in Chicago since 1956, the year he became mayor,
would not be turned into a circus. He intended to show his city to best
advantage. Hizzoner was an old-fashioned urban politician who identified with the white working class, believed in respect for authority,
and despised troublemaking students and radicals. During the racial disturbances of the year before he had ordered the Chicago cops to shoot
looters and arsonists. Daley assigned all 11,900 of Chicago's police to
twelve-hour shifts during convention week and released hundreds of
plainclothes detectives for exclusive convention duty. In reserve there
would be 15,000 Illinois National Guardsmen and regular army troops
equipped with rifles and flamethrowers. Daley's antagonism and his well-
publicized advance planning thinned the ranks of the demonstrators.
But those who came were more than enough to rock the city, the party,
and the nation. As the delegates debated, bargained, and canvassed in
the hotels and in the amphitheater, demonstrators and police in riot gear
clashed on the streets. The TV crews and news photographers caught the
swinging clubs, breaking glass, shrilling sirens, and billowing tear gas in
their lenses. Like millions of other Americans, Johnson would be a horrified observer of the violence on the streets of Chicago. It would dissuade
him from leaving the Ranch.

Pandemonium on the streets was matched by turmoil in the conventional hall itself. From day one the delegates fought over the plank on
Vietnam, with the main issue when to stop the bombing. The Mc-
Carthy-McGovern-Kennedy people called for an "unconditional" cessation of all bombing in North Vietnam and "mutual withdrawal of all
United States forces and all North Vietnamese troops from South Vietnam . . . over a relatively short period of time." They also urged the
Saigon government to reconcile with the Vietcong and include them in
a coalition South Vietnamese government. The president shot the plank
down. "This . . . just undercuts our whole policy," he told Humphrey.
"[B]y God, the Democratic Party ought not to be doing that to me."[5] The
administration's plank rejected "a unilateral withdrawal" and promised to
halt the bombing only when it was certain that it did not threaten the

lives of American troops on the battlefield.[6] The administration loyalists also pushed a plank praising "the initiative of President Johnson which brought North Vietnam to the peace table" and calling for Hanoi to "respond positively to this act of statesmanship."[7]

The administration plank won by a vote of 1,567 to 1,041, provoking a major dove demonstration in the amphitheater. As the results were announced, peacenik delegates, wearing black armbands, took up the chant "Stop the war!" "Stop the war!" while actor-folk singer Theodore Bikel, a New York delegate, led the doves in singing "We Shall Overcome," the civil rights anthem.[8] The losing Vietnam plank became the minority report of the platform committee. Democrats had applauded Johnson's renunciation in March as a noble, selfless act. His reputation had soared. Now his refusal to see further than his own needs made him once more a villain. His willfulness would damage Humphrey and contribute to the party's defeat in November.

For the nomination itself, Humphrey was the front-runner from the outset. But his candidacy raised problems. Many delegates worried that he was too closely associated with Johnson. Early polls, moreover, showed him behind Nixon in the actual fall race. Even some hawk delegates agreed it might be wise to "dump the Hump." Johnson himself was less than encouraging to his vice president. LBJ distrusted Humphrey, and when he announced his candidacy in April, new tensions developed between the two men. The Minnesotan naturally hoped for Johnson's support, but the president balked and in fact seemed to go out of his way to belittle and demean his vice president. Looking at an evening newspaper with pictures of Humphrey and Senator Eugene McCarthy, each holding crying babies, Johnson joked: "That's the way I feel when I look at the two candidates, like crying."[9] On another occasion he told a friend that Humphrey was out of step with the times. "Hubert's just too old-fashioned, he looks like, he talks like he belongs to the past."[10]

But if not Humphrey, who? Some Robert Kennedy supporters sought to rally his orphaned delegates behind McCarthy. But when the resentments between the two camps foiled this move, a group of Kennedy people turned to dovish senator George McGovern of South Dakota. Five days before the convention, Ted Kennedy, the only surviving Kennedy brother, raised hopes of another alternative to Humphrey. Making his first public appearance since Bobby's assassination, the Massachusetts senator promised to "pick up a fallen standard."[11] Many Democrats, including Mayor Daley, fearing a Humphrey defeat would drag down local candidates, begged Ted to run. Johnson himself was certain that the Kennedys were plotting to take the nomination away from Hubert. Though skeptical of the vice president, he recoiled at another Kennedy and finally rallied his supporters for Humphrey. By the time the convention opened, the young Massachusetts senator had withdrawn.

On August 28 Johnson finally buried all hopes for a draft. In a message, read to the convention by Chairman Carl Albert, Johnson declared that his decision not to run was "irrevocable. . . . I ask therefore that my name not be considered by the convention. I wish to express my deep appreciation to all those who might have wished me to continue. . . . During the remaining months of my term as president, and then for the rest of my life, I shall continue my efforts to reach and secure those enduring goals that have made America great—peace abroad and justice and opportunity at home."[12] Johnson was renouncing the presidency forever.

Serenaded by an uncharacteristically sentimental White House press corps singing "Happy Birthday," the president celebrated his sixtieth birthday at the Ranch. Meanwhile, at the old Chicago Coliseum, three thousand people attended an "unbirthday party" for LBJ held by the Mobe, the major national peace organization. The celebrators listened to speeches by Dave Dellinger and novelists William Burroughs and Terry Southern, and watched performances by comedian Dick Gregory and folk singer Phil Ochs. Everyone laughed when Gregory cracked, "I've just heard that Premier Kosygin has sent a telegram to Mayor Daley asking for two thousand Chicago cops to report for duties in Prague immediately."[13]

Johnson could not understand why the protests persisted. Wasn't he trying to make peace in Vietnam? "After withdrawing from the race and getting the Paris peace talks with the North Vietnamese under way," recalled Larry Temple, a Johnson aide, "he thought those people would find the situation more satisfying."[14] When asked for his comment on the Chicago disorders, LBJ, through his press secretary, Christian, said he deplored violence. When asked further which violence he was deploring, that of the demonstrators or of the police, Christian replied, "All kinds of violence."[15]

With mayhem raging in the streets, on Wednesday, August 28, the delegates in the amphitheater chose a presidential candidate. McCarthy and McGovern received nominations, and they and their partisans enjoyed their brief moment on national TV. But Humphrey, with the support of southerners, big-city mayors, and trade union leaders, took the nomination on the first ballot, with Maine senator Edmund Muskie as his running mate.

Humphrey smiled for the cameras, of course, but was privately depressed by the prospects ahead. McCarthy announced that he would campaign for the Democratic doves but refused to stand with Humphrey on the platform when the nominee gave his acceptance speech. "I was a victim of that convention," the vice president said after the election, "as much as a man getting the Hong Kong flu. I felt when we left that convention we were in an impossible situation. I could've beaten the Republicans anytime—but it's difficult to take on the Republicans and fight a guerrilla war in your own party at the same time. Chicago was a catastrophe."[16] A *Newsweek* columnist was convinced "had Nixon written the script himself, he could scarcely have improved upon it."[17]

Not only did the nominee have to confront the Republicans and the party dissidents; he was forced to take on the president as well. Humphrey's advisers were certain he must detach himself from Johnson to win. But he could not make the break. In his acceptance speech at the convention, the vice president hewed closely to the administration's line on Vietnam. He also lavishly praised Johnson's accomplishments.

> [W]hat we are doing is in the tradition of Lyndon B. Johnson, who rallied a grief-stricken nation when our leader was stricken by the assassin's bullet and said to you and said to me, and said to all the world: "Let us continue." . . .
>
> And in the space of five years since that tragic moment, President Johnson has accomplished more of the unfinished business of America than any of his modern predecessors.
>
> And I truly believe that history will surely record the greatness of his contribution to the people of this land.

At the end, he stepped over the edge into fulsome excess. "And tonight to you, Mr. President, I say thank you. Thank you, Mr. President." Glad to have Johnson off their backs, the delegates broke into loud applause; only a few scattered boos ruined the effect.[18]

Johnson was naturally pleased with Humphrey's praise. But it did not reconcile him to the vice president's candidacy. Even in the best of times he was ambivalent about HHH; at worst he could be cruel and contemptuous toward him. Now, feeling sorry for himself, he acted petulant, ungenerous, and unhelpful. He was soon expressing qualms about his vice president's ability to "pull the party together during the campaign." And even if he were able to unite the Democrats and win, he asked, "What kind of a president [would] he make?"[19] Johnson's assessment of Humphrey was that he was "all heart and no balls."[20] In mid-September columnist Jack Anderson reported that Johnson was telling intimates that he expected Nixon to win. The president, Anderson explained, found it intolerable to "play second fiddle" to Hubert and "he is more concerned about his own place in history than about electing Humphrey."[21]

Dreading that President Humphrey would end the war by surrender on January 20, 1969, Johnson initially may have preferred Nixon. In

September Averell Harriman, back in Washington briefly from the stalled Paris peace negotiations, asked Clark Clifford if the president really wanted his vice president to lose the election, as had been rumored among the American delegation. "If you agree it is just between you and me," the defense secretary replied, "I believe you're right: The President wants to see him defeated."[22] Humphrey's physician and close friend Edgar Berman, in a posthumous biography of the Minnesotan, recounts that late in the campaign two Democratic leaders asked Johnson to do a whistle-stop tour for Humphrey through the border states into Texas. Looking directly into their eyes, Johnson said, "Why? Nixon is supporting my Vietnam policy stronger than Hubert."[23] The tour was never made. And Nixon did what he could to keep Johnson in a neutral corner by professions of respect for his opinions and reassurances that he would do nothing to give comfort to Hanoi.

From the beginning, Humphrey was behind his Republican opponent and barely ahead of George Wallace. The vice president had little money to improve his standing. Many of the usual party donors, offended by the violence in Chicago and discouraged by Humphrey's poor early polls, refused to open their pocketbooks. This established a vicious circle: Low funds restricted print and TV ads, thereby reducing Humphrey's standings in the polls. Poor prospects, in turn, discouraged contributors from pulling out their checkbooks.

Almost all of Humphrey's troubles stemmed from his inability to separate himself from the administration's Vietnam policies and convince the voters that he could bring peace. Doves pleaded with the vice president to break with the administration, preferably by endorsing an unconditional bombing halt. He could not bring himself to do it. Johnson did not help matters. Insisting that, until January 20, he alone was the commander in chief, he kept Humphrey in ignorance about the latest twists and turns at the Paris peace talks. He even chided the candidate publicly for his painful efforts to sound upbeat on Vietnam. After Humphrey predicted in a speech in Houston that American soldiers might soon be coming home, LBJ said with a snarl, "When is he going to learn that I'm still the president?" He then made it a point to state at an American Legion convention in New Orleans that "nobody can predict" when American boys would leave Southeast Asia "because we are there to bring an honorable, stable peace to Southeast Asia and nothing less will justify the sacrifices that we and our allies have made."[24] The White House pooh-poohed rumors that the candidate and the president were at odds and justified Johnson's statements at New Orleans by explaining that the president has "to state and restate government policy, whether or not there is a campaign going on."[25]

The president's New Orleans statement infuriated Humphrey. Johnson had "pull[ed] the rug out from under me," he griped. It was "not an act of friendship."[26] Humphrey soon came to see his chief as his enemy. "With the trouble I've had in this campaign all because of him, you'd think he'd at least respect my loyalty. . . . I think I've had Lyndon Johnson around my neck just long enough. . . . I'm fed up to here with him and his tantrums."[27] Yet Humphrey remained publicly loyal to the administration and blamed the media for the seeming troubles between him and Johnson. "The press wants to divide us—me and the president," he protested. "That makes their stories."[28] Johnson was a father figure to Humphrey and his good opinion remained important to him.

At the end of September Humphrey was fifteen points behind Nixon in the Gallup poll, and disaster loomed. Then a stop in Seattle on the twenty-eighth finally shocked Humphrey into action. Antiwar protesters in the Seattle Arena gallery taunted him unmercifully with cries of "Fascist! Fascist!" and "Dump the Hump!"[29] The Secret Service and Seattle police were forced to drag the demonstrators out of the hall, resisting all the way. The press played up the event as symptomatic of a collapsing campaign. Clearly he had to do something drastic to keep himself in the race. Humphrey's advisers had been insisting for weeks that he must outbid the president on peace terms with the Communists, and Johnson was aware of the temptation. The president asked Humphrey to postpone any new stand until the North Vietnamese actually began serious negotiating in Paris. He pressed the candidate's loyalty buttons hard. "I've given up the presidency, given up politics, to search for peace," he told his vice president. "It's broken my heart—in a way, broken my back. But I think I can get these people at the conference table if you will help."[30]

But this time Humphrey put his own fate first. In a nationally televised speech at Salt Lake City on September 30, he finally issued his declaration of independence. The words were prudent:

> As President, I would stop the bombing of the North as an acceptable risk for peace because I believe it could lead to success in the negotiations and thereby shorten the war. . . . In weighing that risk—and before taking action—I would place key importance on evidence—direct or indirect—by deed or word—of Communist willingness to restore the demilitarized zone between North and South Vietnam.

He qualified his statement further by saying that if the North Vietnamese showed "bad faith" he "would reserve the right to resume the war." He also proposed "an immediate cease-fire, with United Nations or other international supervision, and supervised withdrawal of all foreign forces from South Vietnam."[31]

The Salt Lake City declaration was at most a small step beyond the administration's position. The North Vietnamese were not impressed, and one of their leading diplomats sneered at its terms. The public and the media, however, hearing that he "would stop the bombing" and ignoring his qualifications, *perceived* it as a significant break. So did Johnson. George Ball, now a Humphrey adviser, had called Johnson before the speech to read him the Vietnam passages. After listening, Johnson prodded Ball to tell the press "that this doesn't mark any change from the line we've all been following." Ball would not comply. "I'm sorry, Mr. President," he replied, "but that's not quite the name of the game."[32] Joseph Califano later claimed that the president never forgave Humphrey for the speech.

But Humphrey himself felt liberated. On the plane back East from Salt Lake City the candidate was in a good mood for the first time in weeks, singing the words of an old black spiritual: "Ain't gwine study war no more."[33] The speech had other fortunate consequences. In early October, Americans for Democratic Action, which had been dragging its heels, finally endorsed Humphrey, although it maintained it was still "far from satisfied" with his stand on Vietnam and urged him to divorce himself from "errors of the past."[34] Most important, the declaration of independence saved the campaign from bankruptcy. Financial contributions, mostly in small amounts, started pouring in.

During the fall Johnson was not just watching the three candidates duke it out; he was also attending to his place in history. There was legislation to approve, much of it dealing with conservation and the environment. On September 30 he signed into law the $1.3 billion Colorado River Basin Act, authorizing construction of a four-hundred-mile system of dams and aqueducts to supply drinking and irrigation water and hydroelectric power for the rapidly growing cities of Phoenix and Tucson and other areas of central and southern Arizona. On the same day he approved a bill expanding the National Wilderness Preservation System and a few days later one to create the fifty-eight-thousand-acre Redwood National Park in northern California. In these fall weeks Johnson also signed legislation banning the mail-order purchase of handguns, shotguns, and rifles; extending federal aid programs for regional medical projects; providing health care for migratory workers; augmenting the food stamp program; and funding construction subsidies for U.S. shipbuilders. Another bill increased the penalties for possessing stimulants, hallucinogenic drugs, and "pep pills" and barbiturates without a prescription. "It is measures like this, and not talk about crime," Johnson said at this signing, "that strengthen the hand of our police and give our families protection."[35]

No congressional session surpassed the record of the first session of the Eighty-ninth Congress for productivity. But the Ninetieth Congress's second session achieved a respectable record for a nation squabbling about so many issues. And in an election year! Although LBJ did not get all that he wanted and was disappointed by some of the bills actually passed, he had managed to get his anti-inflation tax increase, an open housing bill, and much in the way of consumer and conservation legislation. The biggest congressional defeats for Johnson were the fiasco over Fortas and the failure to pass the Nuclear Nonproliferation Treaty. It seems clear that the president's decision in March not to run freed Congress, bickering about the war, the economy, and social trends, to put aside its differences and stop spinning its wheels.

Though he never regained his regard for Humphrey, as election day neared, Johnson finally rallied to his side. The ice may have been broken by Lady Bird, who never lost her affection for Hubert. In early October the First Lady, in an address to the Democratic Women's Club convention in Louisville, Kentucky, declared that Nixon and Wallace would reverse the clock on social progress. "Will America," she asked, "having forged so far ahead under President Kennedy and President Johnson toward a more just and compassionate society, now turn back?"[36] Speaking in a state that had voted for Nixon in 1960, Johnson in 1964, and now was leaning toward Wallace, she emphasized the successes of her husband's administration but pointedly gave Humphrey credit for helping to make such achievements as Head Start, Medicare, the Job Corps, the nuclear test ban treaty, and progress in civil rights possible. Mrs. Johnson pledged to work hard for Humphrey and promised to initiate a letter-writing and telephone campaign to get others to support him. She generously praised Hubert. "He is without vindictiveness and bitter hatred and God knows our country needs that today. He is a builder, a unifier, who does not try to set American against American. He does not pander to the fears in the souls of our people—he calls on the best that is in us— the affirming spirit of hope."[37]

It is unclear whether the First Lady's speech reflected a change of mind on her husband's part or an independent decision. Yet soon after, the president followed Lady Bird's lead. On October 10 he made his first full-scale political speech of the campaign. In a nationally broadcast radio talk sponsored by the International Ladies' Garment Workers' Union, he enthusiastically endorsed the Democratic ticket and strongly denounced the candidacies of Nixon and Wallace. Appealing to voters to support "progressive Democratic leadership," he attacked George Wallace as a man who would "seek to divide our country and our people, to set them against each other in mutual fear and suspicion." Then, spoofing the Republican campaign slogan, Johnson said that "Nixon is the one" who "cast the tie-breaking vote that killed aid to education" when he was the vice president; "Nixon is the one who said that Medicare 'would do more harm than good.'" And, he added, "they know that Nixon is the one who speaks for the Republican Party—that always opposes so much vital and progressive legislation." After retailing the negatives of the GOP candidate, Johnson finally brought himself to praise the vice president. He had asked Humphrey to run with him in 1964 "for one simple reason": He was "the best-qualified man to serve as President, in the event that I did not serve out my term." He lauded Humphrey's patriotism and his "great capacity to do good" and said he "looked forward to the day when Humphrey will assume the splendid misery—the burdens and the magnificent opportunities of the President of the United States."[38]

During these waning days of the presidential campaign, Johnson began to inch toward a full bombing halt in Vietnam. In September Harriman had told the president that he thought Hanoi might finally be serious about "making progress." On October 9 the North Vietnamese themselves indicated that if the United States ceased the bombing totally they would admit the South Vietnamese to the bargaining table. Before proceeding, Johnson wanted assurances from Ambassador Bunker and General Abrams. "Tell them," Johnson instructed, "we are thinking of going ahead [with a complete bombing halt] if we do not take an unwarranted gamble with the safety of our men, and I want their completely frank reactions—with the bark off."[39] Bunker and Abrams both gave their approval. On October 14 Johnson discussed the situation with his senior advisers, all of whom agreed it was time to "go ahead." The president seemed genuinely worried that he would be accused of trying to influence the election. "Some people will call it a cheap political trick," he fretted. Clark Clifford responded that he should not be bothered by this consideration. "There comes a time in the tide of men's affairs," he told Johnson, "that is a time to move."[40] Later that day the president met with the Joint Chiefs, who unanimously approved a bombing halt with certain conditions. The United States would maintain aerial surveillance of North Vietnam, and in the event that Hanoi violated its promises, bombing would be resumed. After meeting again with the senior advisers, LBJ was prepared to act. "I don't want to have it said of me," he revealed to them, "that one man died tomorrow who could have been saved by this plan. I don't think it [peace] will happen, but there is a chance. We'll try it."[41]

LBJ wanted the new peace talks to be conducted in strict secrecy. There were too many pressures and crosscurrents swirling about that might play havoc with the negotiations. But signs of a breakthrough soon began to emerge in public view: successive visits by Ambassador Bunker with Thieu; "tantalizing comments" by the North Vietnamese in Paris; and leaks by the Australian prime minister. Reporters soon were calling the White House, demanding to know what was up. Press secretary George Christian attempted to "cool" the speculation until real progress was made and issued a statement, approved by the president, saying, "There has been no basic change in the situation: no breakthrough."[42] But the press refused to be fobbed off, and speculation continued.

On October 16 Johnson made a conference call to all three presidential candidates to inform them of progress on the bombing halt. He was careful to tell Nixon that the discussions were not politically inspired. He was not trying to elect a Democrat in November by producing a peace rabbit from the hat at the last moment. The progress derived, he insisted, from a new flexibility in Hanoi. Humphrey was insulted that he was not informed privately and first, but Nixon's response was more significant. Despite Johnson's assurances, the Republican candidate was certain that the Democrats were planning an "October surprise" that would elect his opponent. Nixon believed that Johnson had promised him to remain neutral in the campaign and was angered by this apparent betrayal. The call soon became public knowledge. Republicans in general were suspicious of the purported breakthrough. Republican senator George Murphy of California announced that a peace move at this time was "suspect." Why was this not done "six months ago or a year ago?"[43] The next day the press reported that Humphrey had gained in the polls, moving up to within 5 percentage points of Nixon.

Meanwhile, in Paris, Harriman was trying to prevent slippage. The United States would stop the bombing: period. But North Vietnam would cease infiltration of men and supplies across the demilitarized zone and stop attacking South Vietnamese cities. North Vietnam still considered Saigon a "puppet" government, and Saigon, for its part, did not want to meet with the National Liberation Front. Harriman came up with an "our side, your side" formula to circumvent both adversaries' reluctance to negotiate with representatives they considered illegitimate or unacceptable. The two negotiating parties could decide whom to include on their side, and the other side could tacitly ignore who they were. This way, both antagonists could take part in the peace talks without having to acknowledge the other as an "independent entity." Without completely committing themselves, the North Vietnamese privately implied they would "know what to do" when the United States stopped the bombing. They also informally agreed, after some resistance, that serious peace talks would begin four days after the bombing stopped, a condition that Johnson thought was crucial, since the opportunities for new conditions might increase with each day's delay in getting to the conference table. He was also worried that this time, if the enemy used delayed peace talks to gain a military advantage, world public opinion would make it impossible to resume bombing.

In the end the definitive talks did not take place. South Vietnam president Nguyen Van Thieu could not bring himself to tolerate facing the Vietcong at the conference table. Their participation, he claimed, would undermine the morale of the South Vietnamese people and the army. But more important was a hidden consideration. Thieu knew that a peace breakthrough would help the Democrats, and now that Humphrey was sounding like a dove, that would hurt South Vietnam. The hawkish Nixon would probably get Saigon more favorable terms at the bargaining table. As Johnson later wrote, he had "reason to believe [the South Vietnamese] had been urged to delay going to the Paris meetings and promised they would get a better deal from a Nixon administration than from Humphrey."[44]

The words hid the details of a Byzantine intrigue to sabotage the talks of the kind usually found only in Hollywood thrillers. At its center was Madame Anna Chennault, the widow of an American military hero, General Claire Chennault, commander of the China-based Flying Tiger Air Corps detachment during World War II. Chinese-born, Madame Chennault was a leading member of the China Lobby, a pro-Chiang Kai-shek group fiercely opposed to any concessions to Red China. An ardent Republican, renowned hostess, enthusiastic fund-raiser for the GOP, and vice chair of the Republican National Finance Committee, she was in close contact with the Saigon government. Madame Chennault advised her friends in Saigon, according to Clark Clifford, that "no more progress should be made in conducting the peace conferences because the South Vietnamese could get a better deal from the new Nixon administration than they could get from the Johnson administration." Clifford also confirmed that the president was fully informed, through wiretaps and surveillance by U.S. intelligence agencies, about her activities. "She even had a code name," Clifford recalled. "She was called 'Little Flower.'"[45] Behind these maneuvers, Johnson was certain, was the Republican candidate himself. To an angry Johnson this smacked of "treason," and he made sure, through Everett Dirksen, that the Republican candidate knew that he was aware of what he was doing. Through Senator George Smathers, Nixon denied the charges and then, days before the voting, called the president directly to disavow the Chennault intrigues. In fact, there is historical evidence that he and his close advisers knew of, and approved of, her activities.

Certain of Republican perfidy, as Election Day neared, Johnson stepped up his campaigning for Humphrey. In late October, in a speech dedicating a flood-control project in Kentucky, LBJ accused the Republican candidates of being "wooden soldiers of the status quo." They would "scrap" all the progress the Democrats had made and, reiterating his programs for health, civil rights, and education, he pleaded with his audience to vote for Hubert Humphrey.[46] In New York City the following day, Johnson again attacked the Republicans. They "defer problems," while the Democrats "face problems." He then promised to "do everything I can to see that Hubert Humphrey and Edmund Muskie are elected on November 5." In addition, he praised Humphrey as "beyond question" the American "best prepared by intelligence, experience, compassion, and character" to be president.[47]

On October 31, after renewed assurances from the Joint Chiefs of Staff that a bombing halt would be "a perfectly acceptable military risk,"[48] LBJ took to nationwide television with another electrifying speech. With fatigue apparent on his face he announced that he had ordered a complete halt of all air, artillery, and naval bombardment of North Vietnam "in the belief that this action can lead to progress toward a peaceful settlement of the Vietnamese war." Now the United States had every justification in expecting "prompt, productive, serious, and intensive negotiations in an atmosphere that is conducive to progress." He warned, though, that there might be additional fighting ahead because "arrangements of this kind are never foolproof" and that there would be "some hard negotiating because many difficult and critically important issues are still facing these negotiators." He did not know who would be the next president, but he would try mightily to "lighten his burden as the contributions of the Presidents who preceded me have greatly lightened mine." And most of all, he would do everything he could to "move us toward the peace that the new President—as well as this President and, I believe, every other American—so deeply and urgently desires."[49]

On November 1 the bombing runs stopped, but to no political avail. Thieu remained unrelenting. Speaking to the South Vietnam National Assembly on November 2, he declared that he would never join the talks in Paris if he had to share the conference table with the NLF. Leaders in Saigon noisily condemned Johnson for selling out to Hanoi. Thieu would delay his acceptance of peace talks until three weeks after the election, too late to affect the results.

Johnson might have tipped the election to Humphrey by leaking Nixon's role in derailing the peace negotiations. But LBJ evidently feared that Nixon could be crippled as president by charges that as a private citizen he had interfered in high-stakes foreign policy negotiations.

Ironically, Johnson only postponed the fate that befell Nixon five years later for a similar disregard of constitutional processes. Inconsistently, Johnson sent William Bundy to inform Humphrey of the Republican maneuvers, hoping *he* would blow the whistle on his opponent. Humphrey balked. The evidence implicating Nixon personally seemed too oblique. Besides, the evidence the president had collected came from illegal wiretaps and other dubious sources. When Bundy filled Humphrey in on the details of Madame Chennault's intrigues, the vice president said, "It would have been difficult to explain how we knew about what she had done."[50] In the end Humphrey could not bring himself to implicate Nixon. Johnson was furious with the vice president, believing it was "the dumbest thing in the world not to do it."[51] It probably confirmed his doubts of Hubert's ability to lead the country.

By this time Johnson was exhausted from the tensions of negotiating the bombing halt, and he flew to the Ranch to recuperate. It was in Texas that he would cast his vote for Hubert Humphrey, who now trailed Nixon in the polls by only 2 percentage points, well within the statistical margin of error. On the Sunday before the election, Humphrey came to Houston for a huge rally. At the Astrodome that night, after a musical program starring Trini Lopez and Frank and Nancy Sinatra, Johnson and Humphrey stood together on a platform for the first time in the campaign. The president, not yet over a cold, called the vice president a "healer and a builder" who strove "not to generate suspicion and fear among our people, but to inspire them with confidence in their ability to live together." Alluding, perhaps, to Nixon's role in Thieu's recalcitrance, Johnson assailed the Republican as a "man of narrow partisanship" who had indulged in "clever campaign tactics of concealment and evasion." With unintentional prescience, he questioned Nixon's integrity. "No man can come to the presidency compromised in honor and lacking public trust," he noted. Such a man "will fail, and the people with him."[52]

On Election Day, President and Mrs. Johnson voted for Humphrey and Muskie in Johnson City at the headquarters building of the Pedernales Electric Cooperative, organized with the federal assistance Johnson had procured as a young congressman. Four years before, Johnson had felt on top of the world. Now he was in no mood to talk to reporters. Lady Bird was more cheerful, telling the press, "I hope you-all voted absentee."[53] Driving home in their white Lincoln Continental, they stopped the car for a few moments to watch a hay baler working in a field. Four years previously, they had driven flush with victory through Austin, whose streets were so jammed with crowds that the car could barely move in the direction of the state Capitol where LBJ was planning to address the crowd from the steps.

On November 5, 1968, Richard Nixon was elected president by fewer than half a million votes out of more than seventy-two million cast. In the postelection commentary, few observers fingered Johnson for Humphrey's loss. But, in fact, LBJ was partly responsible. In a race this close every bit of aid could have made a difference. Paying more attention to his personal frustrations, jealousies, and hurts, and indulging his patriarchal inability to cede responsibility and power, he failed Hubert Humphrey, the Democratic Party, and the cause of political liberalism.

Johnson made no immediate statement to the press about Humphrey's defeat, but it is clear that the president was unhappy. In addition, two important old Democratic Senate veterans had lost their bids for reelection. Wayne Morse, a former thorn in his side for whom he now felt affection, was defeated in Oregon. One of his closest friends in the Senate, Mike Monroney, was tossed out in Oklahoma. Johnson's press secretary said he was depressed, that the day after the election was one of those several "low days" he had been experiencing since his decision not to run. The President sent telegrams to both the winner and the loser. To Nixon he said:

> The responsibilities of leadership today are probably heavier than they have ever been before. They are certainly too heavy and too important to be also encumbered by narrow partisanship. . . . You can be certain that I shall do everything in my power to make your burdens lighter on that day when you assume the responsibilities of the president.[54]

Johnson telephoned Humphrey in Minneapolis on election night when his defeat became clear. Humphrey remained the loyal follower to the end. "Well, Mr. President," he replied, "it looks like I didn't make it. I'm sorry I couldn't do it for you. I just want to thank you for all the help."[55] Johnson later sent him a telegram:

> You fought well and hard. You have carried your convictions and the standard of our party with eloquence and magnificent courage. In twenty years of national service, you have had no finer hours than those of the past few weeks—in which you awakened the support and interest of millions of our people.[56]

On the bright side for Johnson in the fall of 1968 was the birth on October 25 of his first granddaughter, seven-pound, eight-ounce Lucinda Desha, born to daughter Lynda Robb. After handing out cigars and candy to reporters, he announced that the baby was healthy and vocal and "is already expressing herself." Lady Bird noted that "it was the only press conference I remember in recent months where everybody was content with the news!"[57] The First Lady, winding up her beautification program in Washington, D.C., had a park named for her on an island, newly planted with dogwood trees and daffodils, in the middle of the Potomac. On November 18 the Johnsons attended a reception at the Smithsonian Museum of History and Technology to celebrate their thirty-fourth wedding anniversary. More than a thousand Texans, in town for the Cowboys-Redskins football game, came to greet their state's most prominent couple. Lyndon gave his wife a sentimental letter as his present, and Lady Bird gave her husband a copy of a diary entry written on February 13, 1941, recording a White House dinner given by FDR that Mrs. Johnson had attended wearing an evening gown.

Johnson had two months to go as president, and there was still legislative and diplomatic work to do. There were also the problems of the transition. LBJ was determined to provide a smooth changeover to the new administration and to make sure that Nixon would not be hobbled by decisions rushed through by the Democrats at the last minute. "We have had five wonderful and productive years," he told his cabinet. "Let's all take care that . . . we do not diminish our contribution by rash, eleventh-hour actions carrying consequences, which have not been carefully considered at all levels of government . . . and by the president."[58] But there were some rough spots nevertheless.

On Veterans Day Nixon and his wife were guests of the Johnsons at an all-afternoon visit to the White House that included briefings for the president-elect and his aides by Secretary of State Rusk, CIA director Richard Helms, Clark Clifford, and others. Nixon called the briefings "completely candid and most helpful." He described Vietnam as "at the top of the list" in diplomatic importance and, noting that the country could not "afford a gap of two months in which no action occurs," declared that as long as Johnson was still president and Rusk secretary of state, "they could speak not just for this administration but for the . . . next administration as well."[59]

Relations between the two men soon hit bumps. A few days following the meeting, Nixon claimed that LBJ had agreed to consult him before making any important changes in diplomatic policy. This amounted to what the New York Times called a veto in fact if not in name over foreign policy during the transition period. Johnson believed that Nixon was attempting to be copresident and was miffed. In an unscheduled news conference the following day, he denied that he would be sharing his power. The "decisions that will be made between now and January 20th will be made by this President," he emphatically announced. After

January 20 it was a different story and he would "try to do anything" he could "to make Mr. Nixon's burdens easier."[60]

Johnson honestly tried to cooperate with the president-elect, but it proved hard to convince the media of his goodwill. On November 19, at the Annual Equal Opportunity Awards Dinner of the National Urban League, he spoke of the progress his administration had made in civil rights and called for continuing commitment to the struggle. "We have come a long way . . ." the president told his audience. "For as long as I live, I shall remain joined with you in fighting for that right to opportunity."[61] Johnson was annoyed when the *Times* and other observers said he had "indirectly challenged" Nixon to equal his record in civil rights and had obliquely criticized Nixon's economic policies. Johnson protested that this was not his purpose; the speech was meant to encourage blacks to keep up the effort.

The following month, when he spoke to the Business Advisory Council, he asked—unnecessarily, surely—for big business to back Nixon. He drew an analogy of the nation to an airliner in a storm with Nixon as the pilot. If the pilot and the plane went down, so would all the passengers. "If you ask me what you can do as a passenger in the plane," declared Johnson, "I say this: Sit there and try to find ways to help that pilot get that plane through those storms . . . and on the ground with a minimum of division."[62] He asked fellow Democrats not to act like dogs in the manger and not to "spend the next four years in partisan sniping." He suggested, in the official publication of the Democratic National Committee, that they act like the congressional Democrats did during his reign as majority leader when Eisenhower was president. When the new administration submitted acceptable programs, the opposition party should support them. On the other hand, "when we feel that the Administration is moving too slowly in certain areas—or not moving at all," Johnson added, "the Democrats must take the initiative just as we did in the 1950s. We cannot wait four years to continue our work on the national agenda." Remarking that the Democrats still controlled Congress, he exhorted them to remember that "in a very real sense the future of progressive legislation will rest with Democrats, as it always has."[63]

Clearly LBJ was trying to rise above his personal chagrins and disappointments. At least one columnist knew what that resolve cost. "The grace with which Lyndon Johnson is handing over the reins is admirable in every respect," wrote Charles Bartlett, "but particularly in terms of the gargantuan anguish which it nobly conceals."[64]

On December 12 Johnson met with the president-elect in the Oval Office for two hours. While the two leaders conferred, Lady Bird and

Luci entertained Mrs. Nixon and the Nixons' daughter Tricia, showing them around the living quarters in the White House. Meanwhile, press secretary George Christian chatted with his designated future counterpart, Ron Ziegler. Johnson and Nixon discussed Vietnam, the Middle East, and other world problems, and LBJ's last State of the Union message, to be delivered before Nixon's inauguration. They also talked about LBJ's plans for the Lyndon B. Johnson School of Public Affairs and some of the things he would need back home in Texas as an ex-president. The president reiterated that he would help in every way possible and direct his cabinet and White House staff to cooperate with newly named officials. But the media were still fomenting trouble. On this same day columnists Evans and Novak revealed that Nixon was disturbed by LBJ's plans for a last-minute meeting with Soviet premier Alexei Kosygin.

Making what was his last official trip abroad as president, on December 13 Johnson strolled a few feet across the Mexican border from El Paso, Texas, to meet with Mexican president Gustavo Díaz Ordaz. In a chilly winter sun on the new Pasa del Norte Bridge that linked the two countries, the two presidents set off a small explosion that rerouted the Rio Grande River under a 1963 agreement worked out by former presidents Kennedy and Adolfo López Mateos to solve an old boundary dispute. "Together," Johnson proudly declared, "we have shown that borders between nations are not just lines across which men shake their fists in anger. They are also lines across which men may cross hands in common purpose and friendship. And we have done so."[65]

Johnson spent the last few weeks of his presidency primarily in ceremonial activities. The crowds were generally sparser than in the glory days, and his words were often wistful. At the dedication of a low-cost housing demonstration project in Austin, the band failed to appear, and the press was asked to fill up the rows of empty seats in sight of the television cameras. "When I became president," LBJ said pensively, "there were a lot of things that I wanted to do. Some of them have been done. Far too many remain to be done. . . . My goals were simple. I wanted a house for every family, and I wanted food for every family. I wanted schools for every family. I wanted health for every family."[66] Back in the capital for the Christmas tree lighting ceremony on the south end of the Ellipse, Johnson remarked that it was the sixth and last time he would be pushing the button to turn on the national Christmas tree.

On a happier note, in the last few weeks new funding for his cherished Great Society helped create, so the president hoped, enough "momentum" to catapult the programs past possible budget cuts by the Nixon administration. During these final days the Model Cities program received a shot in the arm when Seattle, Washington, received nineteen million dollars' worth of federal grants. The Model Cities program had been delayed by the law's complicated provisions, by red tape, and by interagency feuding, It would never accomplish LBJ's optimistic goals. But the slow beginnings did not spoil the president's pleasure. As Secretary of Housing and Urban Development Robert Wood promised, "Other cities with plans under review can expect a decision shortly."[67] The president was also pleased when on December 22 North Korea released the eighty-two-person crew of the *Pueblo* in time for Christmas, although he called their eleven-month detention totally unjustified. He also ordered an investigation of the crew's charges that they had been beaten and abused.

Johnson was proud of his role as a prime mover in the space program and was elated when the *Apollo 8* mission astronauts orbited the moon ten times at the end of December and returned safely home. Before the final splashdown in the Pacific he had been figuratively biting his nails. "Well done," he exclaimed when they were reported safe. "We know," he added, "that all the engineering marvels in the world could not take away one whit of our commitment and admiration for the three of you who were out there in the vastness of space."[68] Johnson awarded gold medals to the astronauts—Frank Borman, James Lovell Jr., and William Anders—at a White House ceremony in January 1969, with members of all three branches of government, the diplomatic corps, and hundreds of citizens and dignitaries attending. The astronauts in turn presented Johnson with a photograph of the earth taken from space, which they described as "a picture of the Ranch."[69]

Even on his last Christmas in the White House, Johnson remained concerned with his failure in Vietnam. The *Washington Post* reported that peace in Vietnam was "the president's abiding preoccupation as his days in office slip away." In his last Christmas message to the troops he called them "patriots who manned the watchtowers in a time of peril so that we might live as free men." But he spoke wistfully of a "world brightened with the hope of peace."[70]

Johnson's mood in his last few weeks of office was often somber and even withdrawn. With retirement so near, he was dismayed at the emptiness that lay ahead. To give up an active public life and the enormous power he had held for so many years would have daunted someone with deeper internal resources than Johnson's. Besides, he felt unappreciated for all the things he had accomplished in the domestic realm. Rather than kudos, he was leaving under a cloud. The eastern intellectuals still did not understand him; the media despised him; and millions of ordinary Americans blamed him for his botch of Vietnam. At the church near the Ranch on the Sunday before the New Year, instead of turning around frequently to look at the congregation, as was his custom, he sat quietly and listened to the sermon. With the familiar members of the press corps tracking Richard Nixon around the country and unknowns now assigned to him, aides were not sure whether he would attend the White House correspondents' New Year's Eve party in San Antonio. And, in fact, he remained at the Ranch surrounded by family, friends, and neighbors. At midnight the Johnsons helicoptered to Lake LBJ to attend a party arranged by the chairman of United Artists, Arthur Krim, the man who was handling the sale of LBJ's memoirs and Lady Bird's diary.

The days preceding departure from the White House were full of sentimental farewell occasions. On January 6 the president and Lady Bird attended a nostalgia-filled farewell reception in the cafeteria of the Longworth Office Building. Johnson admitted to having had misgivings at times about Congress while he was president. But it had been his "home for so long and I love it so deeply," he added.[71] He joked that he might have made the wrong decision not to run in March, since Congress had just voted that day to raise the salary of the next president by a hundred thousand dollars. The four hundred guests showered the president with affection and praise. Both Republicans and Democrats cheered when the Johnsons entered the room, and members of both political parties stood on the reception line to greet the president. He even shook hands with Allard Lowenstein, now a New York congressman, the activist who had engineered the dump-Johnson drive before the 1968 election. As a gift, the Johnsons were given a history of the Capitol in six different languages.[72]

Farewell parties are invariably awash with ephemeral sentiment and nostalgia. Yet so many festive send-offs were held for the Johnsons in January that it was hard to believe he had been so reviled. A society writer described a party in New York given by Brooke Astor, Mary Lasker, the Krims, the Laurance Rockefellers, and other prominent businessmen and philanthropists as "really a love-in for Lyndon and Lady Bird."[73] Speaking in the Grand Ballroom of the Plaza Hotel on this occasion, the president, wearing a gray dinner suit with charcoal satin lapels and a gray shirt, said he had made a difference in people's lives. It did not really matter to him what "ultimate judgment" historians would make about his administration, he declared, "but whether there was a change for the better in the way our people live."[74]

Determined to go out with his "chin up" and his "chest out," Johnson decided to give his last State of the Union speech to Congress in person—a practice largely discontinued after John Adams—rather than sending a final message to be read by a clerk. Lady Bird cried at his official good-bye to Congress, though she claimed later that it was part sobbing and part laughing over the antics of her grandson, eighteen-month-old Lyn Nugent, who was allowed to stay up past his bedtime to attend. It was an emotion-filled event for all the members of the Johnson family. Three full minutes of standing applause, whistling, and cheering greeted the president when he entered the chamber of the House of Representatives to deliver his farewell speech. It was sober and subdued. He talked about the problems that had been plaguing the country through "several decades and administrations"—urban unrest, poverty, crime, unequal educational opportunity, the dangers of nuclear war, the crises in the Middle East and Vietnam. But he believed progress had been made in the previous five years, that a watershed had, in fact, been reached. "We finished a major part of the old agenda," he announced, listing voting rights for blacks, federal support for schools, conservation measures, and Medicare. Some of the achievements were fully launched, but other commitments still needed "additional funding to become a tangible reality." And if these promises were broken, "it would be a tragedy for our country." Therefore Congress should do the following: increase support for the Model Cities program; appropriate funds to construct more than half a million housing units for needy families; and charter an Urban Development Bank to lend money to communities at reduced rates to build schools, hospitals, parks, and other public facilities.

Dismayed that the United States was behind fourteen other nations in infant mortality, Johnson asked Congress to provide "decent medical care for all expectant mothers and for their children during the first year of life." Children and their families should also be protected from the costs of catastrophic illness. He instructed Congress to approve an overall rise in Social Security benefits of at least 13 percent. The fight against poverty required an ongoing commitment and a resolve not to grow impatient with its failures. To win it, Congress should reorganize the entire antipoverty program and approve a request of $3.5 billion for job training programs in the coming fiscal year.

He hoped Congress would "vigorously" enforce the "prohibition against racial discrimination" in the Fair Housing Act of 1968 and "extend the vital provisions of the Voting Rights Act for another five years." He also urged Congress to provide the full three hundred million dollars it authorized for the Safe Streets Act. He mentioned his disappointment at the failure to license and register firearms and hoped the legislators would do something about it in the next session.

His remarks about Vietnam were platitudinous. He assured Congress that "the prospects for peace are better today than at any time since North Vietnam began its invasion . . . more than four years ago." He then paid a "personal tribute" to American soldiers, exhorting his fellow countrymen to give them their "unstinting support while the battle continues" and their "enduring gratitude when their service is done." He himself felt "honored to be their commander in chief." He also hoped the Senate would confirm the Nuclear Nonproliferation Treaty and that arms talks with the Soviet Union would be recommenced shortly.

He concluded with some personal words to Congress. He had decided to deliver the address in person for two reasons, he noted. One was philosophical: He still felt he had something to say about the issues before the nation. The other was sentimental: Here he briefly recounted his thirty-eight years in Washington. He thanked former presidents Truman and Eisenhower and invoked the memory of Sam Rayburn and John Kennedy. He acknowledged the help of Hubert Humphrey, John McCormack, Carl Albert, Everett Dirksen, and Gerald Ford. He asked Congress to be understanding of President-elect Nixon. "The burdens he will bear will be borne for all of us. Each of us should try not to increase them for the sake of narrow personal or partisan advantage." In conclusion, he hoped:

> it may be said, a hundred years from now, that together we helped to make our country more just for all its people—as well as to ensure the blessings of liberty for our posterity. I believe it will be said that we tried.[75]

As he left the dais and walked up the aisle, stopping to shake hands, members of Congress, many with observable tears in their eyes, sang "Auld Lang Syne."

Johnson continued to work in the few days left before departing office. The day after the farewell speech he presented Congress with a record budget of $195.3 billion. He predicted back-to-back surpluses rather than the anticipated deficit contingent on a year's extension of the 10 percent surtax. He had been resisting the idea of continuing the surtax, especially since the president-elect had said he opposed it. But some of his aides, including Califano, risking his wrath, continued to press for its inclusion, believing it the only way to fund the Great Society programs in the year ahead. In the end, not only did Johnson accept the inevitability of extending the tax surcharge but also managed to convince Nixon to support it publicly as well.

In the weeks following his farewell speech the bumpy diplomatic ride resumed. In late November Thieu finally agreed to send representatives to Paris to talk peace with the Communists, but when they arrived, they and their adversaries, in what Clark Clifford thought "one of the silliest discussions" he had ever participated in,[76] could not agree on seating arrangements at the conference table. South Vietnam wanted a conventional rectangular table with two long sides. The National Liberation Front and the North Vietnamese would be seated on one side, testifying to their identity, while the Americans and the South Vietnamese would sit opposite them. Hanoi demanded a four-sided table giving an independent status to the Vietcong. The negotiators looked at nine different configurations before agreeing on January 16 to a round table with no sides that would concede nothing about the NLF's status. In the end, the Saigon leaders willfully insisted that the talks not begin until the following Saturday, after Nixon was sworn in as president, to keep Johnson from getting the credit. "I regretted," Johnson wrote in his memoirs, "more than anyone could possibly know that I was leaving the White House without having achieved a just, an honorable, and a lasting peace in Vietnam."[77] In the end the negotiations bogged down, and it would take four more years for peace to arrive.

The last farewell before the inauguration took place at the National Press Club. Johnson was both upbeat and sad. He joked with the reporters, many of whom had been highly critical of him, telling them that "all is forgotten." He "never doubted" their "energy" or "courage" or "patriotism," he told them, and accordingly he had asked General Hershey, director of Selective Service, to "get in touch immediately with each of you." More seriously, he said his deepest regret on relinquishing the presidency on January 20 was that "peace has eluded me." Recognizing that reporters were already sharpening their pencils to write their summations of his career, he remarked that the measure that had pleased him the most was the 1965 Voting Rights Act. It was "almost like Lincoln's Emancipation Proclamation." After a few more jokes, the scheduled hour was up, and Johnson left for the last time. Several hundred people were waiting for him on the street, all in a friendly mood, waiting to say good-bye.[78]

On Johnson's last night in office, he and Lady Bird hosted a small buffet dinner in the living quarters of the White House for his staff. It was another nostalgiafest. A marine quartet played background music, and when they struck up "Hello, Dolly," rendered as "Hello, Lyndon" at the triumphant 1964 convention, many guests became misty-eyed. For most of the evening LBJ seemed to be in a good mood, teasing his staff, telling jokes, and remembering the good times. But he also reminisced about his mistakes, admitting, for instance, that he had not done enough to keep the friendship of William Fulbright, his outspoken critic on Vietnam. Johnson also announced that as his last action as president, he was going to add more than 7.5 million acres of federally owned public lands to the National Park system.

At this gathering he offered advice for the future to some of his closest staff members. Cornering aide Joseph Califano near the White House elevator, he remarked that now that he was leaving the government he would finally begin to make some money. Califano should

> First, invest it in land. This Nixon knows nothing about the economy and it's going to go to hell. Second, when you pay your income taxes, after you figure them out, pay an additional five hundred dollars. It's not enough for Nixon to win. He's going to have to put some people in jail. Third, the more you succeed, watch out for jealous people. Jealousy and sex drive people to do more damn mean and crazy things than anything else.[79]

At about 11:00 P.M., after singing "For He's a Jolly Good Fellow" and the inevitable "Auld Lang Syne," the party broke up. When the last guest was gone, Johnson went over to the West Wing to do some final work at his desk. In his memoirs he wrote: "I wandered lonely through the empty offices, silent now after so many months of activity, to make sure that everything was in order for the Nixon takeover the next day."[80] Then he went to bed.

Washington, D.C., was gloomy, cold, and wet on the morning of January 20, 1969. A northeast wind chilled spectators' bones the day Richard Nixon was inaugurated as thirty-seventh president of the United States. At 11:37 A.M. Johnson walked out of the Capitol rotunda as the Marine Band played his final "Hail to the Chief." While waiting on the platform for the ceremonies to begin, he found the television cameras trained on him and immediately began telling jokes to the people around him, making them break out in laughter. Most of the other principals, including the Nixon and Agnew families, were solemn and subdued, trying hard to keep warm in the freezing drizzle. Hubert Humphrey seemed very grave, and his wife, Muriel, was weeping. The only person who appeared unreservedly happy was Lady Bird, resplendent in a peach-colored coat. Vivacious and smiling through her husband's last official appearance as president, she was obviously looking forward to getting him back to private life.

But before returning to Texas and repose there was the very last good-bye. Clark Clifford and his wife, hoping to spare the Johnsons the Trumans' lonely experience of returning to Missouri without a proper departure ceremony, had arranged to give a postinaugural farewell luncheon in their honor. The party, Clifford later said, was "one of the most heartwarming experiences" either he or the president ever had.[81] It was limited to close friends, but hundreds of people had learned about it in advance and gathered on the Cliffords' front lawn in Bethesda, Maryland. Clifford was relieved to see that most of the crowd were well-wishers. Some were carrying signs reading *WELL DONE, LYNDON* and *WE STILL LOVE YOU, LYNDON*.[82] The sign that most amused Lady Bird proclaimed *LBJ IN '72*, which reversed to *LYN IN 2004*.[83] Johnson was so gratified to see the friendly swarm, he shook hands and kissed a few babies, just as in the old days. "They didn't come to see the *president*," he excitedly told Clifford, "they came to see Lyndon Johnson." He brought his little grandson out to the front porch, holding him up for everyone to look at, while he and Lyn thrilled to their cheers.[84] LBJ himself remembered the party as "carefree" but full of nostalgia:

> This was an assembly of old friends who had traveled roads both rough and smooth together for many years; and together we had helped to write a rather remarkable chapter in American history. These were people who had been with us in sunshine and sorrow.[85]

Before he left the luncheon, he awarded Medal of Freedom citations to Dean Rusk, Clark Clifford, Averell Harriman, Walt Rostow, and William S. White. Then it was time to go. The Johnsons drove to Andrews Air Force Base to board *Air Force One*, the same plane on which LBJ was sworn in as president just over five years before. They were sent off with a twenty-one-gun salute. On the flight back, Johnson was loquacious and cheerful, discussing his feelings about leaving the presidency. First, he said, he was concerned for Mr. Nixon and "what he'll be facing up to." But then he realized he didn't have to worry anymore about every single thing that was going on. Referring to the nuclear launching codes that had accompanied him everywhere for the previous five years, he confessed it was "a great relief just to know that I can ride by myself on the ranch—that there will not have to be the man with the bag there." He felt "wonderful," he said.[86]

The Johnson presidency was over.

CHAPTER 22

Last Days

I N HIS LAST WEEKS IN OFFICE, Johnson had insisted he would be happy without the turmoil of political life. He planned to relax, he said. "They had me building empires, sailing ships, flying airplanes, meeting astronauts and everything else. But I am just not going to do any of those things." He wanted to spend some time being lazy. He wanted to "enjoy being with Lady Bird for a while." "She will get tired of me before very long. But we are going to sleep late. . . . [and we] will just take things easy."[1]

But could he? Action, political action, was the core of his being, and he had never learned how to unwind. In retirement there would be many things besides politics to occupy his time, but it is hard to say whether he found them very satisfying. Observers disagreed on his state of mind during these final years. A few days after Nixon's inauguration Johnson sold the rights to his memoirs to Holt, Rinehart, & Winston for more than $1.5 million. The project would last many months, give him a focus, and drain off surplus energy. Some of his friends reported that ranch chores, managing the Texas Broadcasting Company, and supervising the building of the new presidential library kept him happy. But even his partisans admit he suffered from periods of depression, and his relapse into smoking, drinking, and overeating suggests a fatalism about his life. Younger daughter Luci much later told Robert Dallek that leaving politics had been for her father like "committing . . . suicide."[2]

Two days after leaving Washington, LBJ was sitting under an oak tree on the Ranch, holding a press conference. Wearing slacks and a suede-trimmed western-style jacket, he spoke with the reporters for more than an hour, then changed into a tie and a tweed sport coat for picture-taking. He admitted that he missed presidential power. "I'm sure that anyone who's been as active in public affairs as I have will notice it when they call the roll," he said. But he added that he wanted to "miss it—it hurts good."[3] Reporters thought his mood was not as brave as his words. At times, they said, he seemed wistful, ambivalent, and not particularly confident. But Lady Bird was clearly elated to be back at the Ranch. Attired in a bright red dress, she served lemonade and cookies to the newspeople and joked about all the clothes that were "coming home from Washington." How would she find room for them at the Ranch? "The closets looked big when we built them," she mused. Posing for pictures at the end of the conference, Johnson warned the photographers to be careful about ruining the grass. "I have only one lawn," he wisecracked, "and I don't want to give it to my country."[4] He was gracious at the press conference, but he obviously found it trying. The next day, when a photographer accosted him as he was driving off the ranch in a small pasture vehicle, LBJ asked him to go away. "Look," Johnson protested, "I let you take pictures yesterday. I'm just a citizen. Let me alone."[5] The intruder complied.

Johnson's return to civilian life was buffered by a government-provided financial position better than that of any other outgoing president. Some of his perks came from older laws—the Presidential Transition Act of 1933 and the Former Presidents Act of 1958. Some derived from measures proposed by Johnson himself. The Presidential Transition Act gave him a onetime allowance of $375,000 to ease the adjustment to civilian life. Part of this would pay for personnel to answer the hundreds of letters he continued to receive. After that he would receive $80,000 a year for office expenses. His pension amounted to $25,000 a year. It now seems small, but 1969 dollars bought about five times as much as today's. Added to this, however, was a separate congressional pension, based on his service in the House and Senate, of about $22,000 a year. In addition, he would have lifetime Secret Service protection for himself and Lady Bird, free medical care, and free postage. Assuming he would want to stay informed about political doings around the nation and the world, before he left office he wheedled complimentary subscriptions to leading newspapers and magazines, including the *New York Times*, the *Washington Post*, the *Baltimore Sun*, *Time*, *U.S. News & World Report*, *Life*, and *Newsweek* as well as daily papers from Dallas, Houston, and Austin. The two air force sergeants assigned him as White House valets accompanied him to the Ranch for an indefinite stay.

Beyond his pension income and personal retirement perks the Johnson family was in excellent financial shape. Neither Lyndon nor Lady Bird talked much about their personal finances. Their reticence was mandated by good breeding but reinforced by the attacks on them for the way they had acquired their media empire. LBJ had no qualms about identifying his personal property. He used a branding iron to literally stamp his initials on every piece of physical property and on the covers of every document dealing with his policies, programs, and accomplishments. But his personal finances were off-limits.

In fact, the Johnsons were rich. During the 1964 campaign an auditing firm estimated his net worth at about $3.5 million. To insulate himself from charges of using his political power to line his pockets, soon after he became president, Johnson had placed the family fortune in a blind trust headed by A. W. Moursund, a longtime friend and business partner who practiced law in Johnson City. By 1969 the trustees, who had the power to buy and sell assets, had increased the portfolio to an estimated $15 million to $20 million. Johnson's real-estate holdings were extensive, totaling about fifteen thousand acres. Besides the six-hundred-acre main Ranch, on the banks of the Pedernales, there were five more ranches, as well as lakeside parcels scattered through the Hill Country, and residential lots in Austin. One of his ranches bordered a lake, and there Johnson kept a powerboat, which he zoomed across the waves as recklessly as he drove his cars around his Pedernales spread. The Johnson communications empire included the Texas Broadcasting Company, with its radio and television stations in Austin; Capitol Cable Company; the Muzak franchise in Austin; and broadcast operations in Victoria and Bryan, Texas, Ardmore, Oklahoma, and Lafayette, Louisiana. Though LBJ and Lady Bird were not on record as owning any stock in banks, the "Johnson group," made up of individuals and corporations close to the Johnsons, as well as family trust funds, owned stock in every bank in Austin.

One of the retirement benefits that pleased Johnson most was the LBJ Library, established by the Presidential Libraries Act to encourage the preservation of presidential papers in institutions operated by the National Archives and financed by private funds. By the time he left the White House, the library was already under construction atop the highest hill in Austin, overlooking the University of Texas campus and the state Capitol. The structure, when finished, was monumental. The chief architect, Gordon Bunshaft, was determined not only to satisfy Johnson but also to come up with an edifice that would describe the man he was building it for. It would have to be "strong and virile—with no frills," said Bunshaft. "He's very strong, you know. . . . There's nothing 'chicken' about him."[6] In fact, the building was an immense, charmless, almost windowless white marble cube. Johnson's future quarters on the top floor of the building were designed to resemble the Oval Office, and when completed the roof would feature a helicopter landing pad. In drawing up the plans, the builders, to guard against any would-be assassin, carefully calculated the distance and angle from Johnson's office windows to the University Tower, a few blocks away on campus.*

The building would house millions of pages of manuscript, more than any previous president had amassed, along with vast collections of photographs, audiotapes, and hundreds of film canisters, including the home movies Lady Bird took of her husband's first congressional campaign in 1937. Even before LBJ left office, Dr. Joe B. Frantz, a University of Texas professor of history, began work on a massive oral history project for the collection, interviewing more than five hundred colleagues and friends of Johnson, from his earliest days through his presidency. LBJ, in his usual grandiose style, insisted it would be "the best presidential library in the world."[7]

And nearby would be another memorial to Johnson, the Lyndon Baines Johnson School of Public Affairs. Designed to train students for careers in government, the school excited him as much as the library. LBJ enthusiastically composed a list of people he would ask to speak at the school. Referring to two black power militants, he told Hubert Humphrey, "I'm going to invite Stokely Carmichael and Rap Brown and we're going to have a free-for-all debate. I'm going to show 'em what free speech really is." The construction of both institutions would be mostly financed by the regents of the University of Texas, who considered his effects a "vital part of our nation's historical heritage."[8] The school would need sizable endowments, however, to keep it running. Part of it would come from the Lyndon Baines Johnson Public Affairs Foundation.

Until the library was completed, LBJ ensconced himself in a teak-paneled office on the top floor of the ten-story Federal Office Building in Austin that he had occasionally used when he was still president. But to LBJ's chagrin, the telephone company soon began to remove the 330 telephone lines connecting the Ranch to his friends, neighbors, Washington, D.C., and the rest of the world. Used to maintaining contact with whomever he pleased, whenever he pleased, he sorely missed the complicated circuitry. A Nixon aide promised that lines would be left at

---

*Texans still remembered that in 1966 a deranged young man, Charles Whitman, had killed fourteen innocent people on campus firing his rifle from the University Tower.

the Ranch so he could keep in touch with his successor, but this scarcely replaced the incomparable communications network he had enjoyed as president.

LBJ hoped to become part of the University of Texas community but declined a regular course schedule, confessing that he "didn't want to make any eight-o'clock classes."9 Actually, the relationship that developed between him and the university was equivocal. Both the UT student radicals and the Austin hippies rallied their troops to make LBJ's life difficult, with SDS promising to demonstrate if Johnson taught any classes. Meanwhile, other, less politicized critics were muttering about the scale of the buildings being constructed for the library and the school. LBJ, they charged — not incorrectly — would not simply be housing his papers, but, like an Egyptian pharaoh, erecting a pyramid to himself. The UT faculty had mixed feelings about Johnson's presence in the university's environs. Some, who hated the man and his policies, were afraid that Johnson would manipulate a takeover of the university. Others simply did not want him around as a reminder of the hated war. But a few were delighted, and many others simply took his presence in stride. Housing Johnson's papers on campus seemed "proper, even logical" to Roger W. Shattuck, liberal professor of Romance languages. "The proportion has been violated, perhaps," he added, "but he is, after all, the president and a man of considerable ego."10 Shattuck did complain that his teaching assistants were being shortchanged office space, while Johnson was engrossing all the room he needed. In the end the former president was not offered a professorship and was said to be very angry.

Less than a week after Nixon's inauguration, Johnson was back on the front page of the New York Times with two columns devoted to his postpresidential life. The February issue of Reader's Digest, soon after, contained an article "In Quest of Peace" by LBJ, discussing his policy in Vietnam. In words that were both bitter and tormented, he admitted that the war had contributed to his renouncing a second term. But he defended his escalation policies. To refuse to intensify "our effort when the enemy mounted an all-out drive to take South Vietnam and unhinge all of Asia" would have been worse than what ensued. Labeling the "credibility gap" a myth, he said that the administration had "tried many ways to explain our foreign policy decisions." Critics faulted him for not rallying the people to sacrifice and resolution, as Winston Churchill had rallied Britain in World War II. But even Churchill's eloquence "was unable to get a hearing until his nation was in mortal danger." His profoundest hope, he wrote, was that "America's resistance in Vietnam will discourage future aggressors."11

Later, on his first trip outside Texas since Nixon's inauguration, Johnson expressed his disappointment with the way the Paris peace talks were progressing. Touring the Herbert Hoover Presidential Library in West Branch, Iowa, with Lady Bird, he told reporters, "We haven't made the progress I wish we had made." When asked whether he thought resigning the presidency had furthered peace, he admitted it was not as effective as he had hoped.[12]

Vietnam would haunt Johnson all through his retirement years. When asked by *Time* correspondent Richard Saltonstall, just after he left Washington, if there was anything he would have done differently, Johnson thought for a moment. Then he said, in an almost inaudible voice, that "although he would have to reread his diary, March 5, 1965, was a day he might. . . ." At this point his voice became so faint, said Saltonstall, that he could not hear him though he was sitting just inches away.[13] March 5, 1965, was the last day Johnson could have canceled the orders to land marines in Vietnam, the mission that launched America's direct combat role in Southeast Asia. Was Johnson admitting that U.S. military involvement in Vietnam was a mistake?

For the first months after leaving office, Johnson spent much of his time puttering around the ranch, going to cattle auctions, and taking short vacations in Florida and the Bahamas. The press had to be satisfied with speculation about his future—most of which assumed he would soon be up to something dramatic. The media were disappointed that the man who for so many years had provided such spectacular copy as both villain and hero was simply marking time while he pondered his next moves. In a June article titled "Johnson's Friends Assert He's Happy As Texas Rancher," Roy Reed wrote, almost peevishly, "there was a widely held belief, particularly among the less sympathetic, that [Johnson] would get the fidgets in a matter of days, that he would shortly thereafter begin pestering his friends, then would begin abusing his enemies and finally would simply burst upon the State of Texas in an explosion of wrath and restlessness and take over everything in sight that was worth having, from politics to commerce."[14]

But Johnson continued to hibernate and, while waiting for LBJ to do something newsworthy again, the media had to be content with reporting his unannounced attendance at a Van Cliburn concert, Lady Bird's appearance at a country club tea in Austin, or sightings of the couple visiting the family cemetery. During the spring the Johnsons dedicated a recreation center in Fredericksburg, Texas, the only one of its kind in the Hill Country, called the Lady Bird Johnson Municipal Park. A picture of the former First Couple appeared on the front page of the *New York*

Times with an accompanying article, but this was really small potatoes, and the press kept yearning for something more substantial.

Johnson broke into the news again in mid-July at the launching of *Apollo 11*, the culminating mission of the program that landed the first men on the moon. Invited by Nixon to Cape Canaveral to attend the event, LBJ claimed he had an unpleasant time at the launching. As he told biographer Doris Kearns, he was seated in the bleachers with thousands of other people, perspiring in the "glaring sun," while waiting for the real celebrities to arrive. He had not wanted to be there in the first place, he said, but felt he could not turn down the invitation.

Johnson's perception was a revealing trick of the mind. In reality, he was treated like an honored guest. More popular as ex-president than in his last months in office, he was greeted by a cheering crowd as his limousine drove up to the Cape Kennedy Hilton. Later, he attended a luncheon given by the president of Gannett Newspapers honoring James Webb, the former administrator of NASA whom Johnson had named in 1961 to lead the country's space program. Guests at the event were handed gag newspapers featuring a story about LBJ and Webb going to the moon. At the launching itself, photographs of the Johnsons watching the blastoff show a pleased Lady Bird and an applauding LBJ. As for seating, the ex-president was given a place of honor next to Vice President Agnew, and various dignitaries came by to shake hands and say hello. But apparently nothing could compensate Johnson for his loss of power. He had ceased to be, in his eyes, the most important man in the world, and it distorted his memory of the event. One cannot gainsay his psychological discomfort. "It was worse than I thought," he told Kearns. "I hated people taking pictures of me when I felt so miserable. . . . I hated their questions. . . . Each conversation was like a goddamn quiz. . . . All I kept thinking of was how much I wanted to be home, walking through my fields, and looking after my cattle."[15] But we must not take seriously his claim that he had been deliberately, or carelessly, humiliated.

Nixon, in fact, proved cordial on other occasions, too. He invited Johnson and his family to lunch at the Western White House in San Clemente, California, to celebrate Johnson's sixty-first birthday. Nixon put a great deal of thought and effort into the birthday lunch. A Mexican mariachi band playing "Happy Birthday" greeted Johnson. Nixon waved his arms and led his family and staff in the singing, followed by a chorus of "The Yellow Rose of Texas." The birthday cake was inscribed "Happy Birthday President Johnson" and was frosted with yellow roses and bluebonnets.

After the festivities the Johnsons flew eight hundred miles north to the dedication of the Lady Bird Johnson Grove in Redwood National Park near Eureka. The event honored both the ex-president and his wife for their contributions to conservation and beautification. At the dedication of the three-hundred-acre grove of coastal redwoods that day, both Republicans and Democrats praised Lady Bird for her tireless work for the environment. A plaque at the grove commemorated her "devoted service to the cause of preserving and enhancing America's natural beauty for the enjoyment of all the people." Displaying some sparks of the old warrior, LBJ then spoke for ten minutes about conservation, of the solitary ordeal of being president, of his pride in his grandchildren, of the love and loyalty of his "womenfolk," and of his desire to help Nixon achieve the most desirable objective of all, "peace among nations of the world."[16] After the festivities, the Johnsons boarded an air force plane for the flight back to Texas.

During his postpresidential years Johnson's spirits swung between despair and euphoria. Retirement is a time of mixed feelings: regrets about past omissions, mistakes, and defeats, and pleasure at new freedoms and new options. Johnson was a passionate man who had experienced powerful highs and devastating lows during his working life, and his retirement evoked similar reactions. Johnson sought to fill his retirement life by cultivating relations with his family and those friends who had survived the ups and downs of his presidential career. He had never been a pal to his children. No president perhaps can be. But as he lost political power, he was able to take some comfort from those closest to him. "I have got," he boasted, "the best family in the world."[17] He often expressed great pride in his two sons-in-law and genuinely doted on his two grandchildren. Johnson affectionately called little Lyn "Khrushchev" because his squat little-boy shape reminded him of the former Soviet premier. Though it might seem improbable in a man whose lifelong interest had been politics and little else, Johnson could amuse his grandchildren "for hours with the same repetitive game long after most other adults would have lost their patience," according to Doris Kearns. And he was very tender with Lady Bird. There were many demonstrations of his love for her on a "daily level—in the gentle touch of his hand on her knee as they road in the car . . . in the warm crinkly smile with which he greeted her after being separated for less than a day."[18]

Yet the family was not enough, and that first year, especially, he often felt blue. But no one who came to visit or to interview him at the Ranch could be sure which Johnson he would get. When old friends Tex Goldschmidt and his wife, Elizabeth, came in the spring of 1969, Johnson was in the dumps, and Lady Bird was almost frantic trying to cheer him up. He refused to be comforted by talk of his presidential achievements, the visitors later reported, and insisted on discussing only the remote past.

Johnson's protective friends vigorously denied the rumors of melancholy. One told a reporter that "he surprised a lot of people, including me. We kept waiting for the decompression. But there hasn't been any."[19] Robert Hardesty, an LBJ speechwriter and collaborator on *The Vantage Point*, his published memoirs, insisted that "Johnson was just having a hell of a good time. He had fits of depression of course, but he was enjoying himself and doing things he wanted to do, for the first time."[20] The ex-president seemed in better spirits when he visited Washington. In early 1970 Clark Clifford saw LBJ in the capital on three separate occasions and he "looked awfully well."[21]

During the summer and fall of 1969 Johnson was busy with two major intellectual projects: writing his memoirs and overseeing the work on the library and school. With the help of longtime foreman Dale Malechek he was also running the Ranch with the same attention to detail he had devoted to politics, touring the grounds, overseeing his workmen, and checking on his animals. In the mornings he would hold ranch meetings, resembling presidential briefings, where he instructed his hands on their daily chores. He wanted his spread to be the best and to produce the best beef and finest eggs in the country, he told them. "I want each of you to make a solemn pledge," he said in the same exhorting tone he used at the White House, "that you will not go to bed tonight until you are sure that every steer has everything he needs." And, he added, the hens should be treated "with loving care."[22]

During his political career he had read voraciously at night the memos, reports, and briefings submitted by his aides. Now his night reading matter included progress reports on the number of eggs laid that week by his two hundred chickens. He was always looking for ways to improve his prize Herefords and the coastal Bermuda grasses they consumed. He worried about the weather and fretted about machinery and equipment that needed to be fixed almost as passionately as if it were a matter of national security. Bernard Weisberger, a historian who interviewed LBJ for *American Heritage* in 1970, reported being driven around the Ranch in a light green Continental by Johnson himself after business was concluded. The ex-president had two speakers in the car and used them to call out questions to his workers. At one point he stopped the car and beckoned someone over. When the man arrived, "he launched into a long discourse on an . . . irrigation pipe that was leaking . . . and that he wanted fixed."[23] Dale Malechek told one visitor about the time he was milking the cows at 6:00 A.M. when Johnson appeared in pajamas and slippers and bombarded him with questions. The sorely tried foreman joked: "Gee, I hope he runs again for president."[24]

Johnson was also deeply interested in the activities at his birth house, down the road, dedicated as a historic site in June 1970. Situated alongside the Pedernales River and run by the National Park Service, it had quickly become a tourist attraction, drawing more than a hundred thousand visitors the first summer. Johnson checked the license plates of the cars in the parking lot to see what states they came from, kept count of the number of visitors, and worried about attendance figures. He kept count of the admission receipts, claiming that if they were good enough he could raise salaries of the staff by two dollars an hour. As Kearns noted, Johnson was still assessing his popularity and trying to predict how people would regard him in the future.

Besides presiding over the Ranch, attending University of Texas football games—a late-acquired passion—playing golf, and swimming in his pool, LBJ was reported to be engrossed on his memoirs. In fact, he found he could not write and tried to tell the story of his presidency to a tape recorder. But even this proved difficult for him, though he came to Austin from time to time to discuss chapters with Walt Rostow, now a professor of economics and history at UT; Harry Middleton, future director of the LBJ Library; and Robert Hardesty, one of his speechwriters. To everyone's surprise, Johnson took on a part-time collaborator on his memoirs, Doris Kearns.

The child of parents who had never finished high school, Kearns had fought her way through college and graduate school on scholarships and fellowships. She became an assistant professor of government at Harvard and assistant director of the Kennedy Institute of Politics, and in 1967 coauthored an anti-Johnson article in the *New Republic,* "How to Remove LBJ in 1968." Despite the article, shortly after she was picked as a White House fellow.

LBJ had danced with her several times at a reception for the White House fellows and ended up sending her to work for Secretary of Labor Willard Wirtz for her year's internship. After Johnson renounced reelection, he assigned her to his own staff and she stayed on after the fellowship expired. When he got back to the Ranch, he begged her to help him on his memoirs. She could not say no. For months, beginning in late 1969, while teaching in Cambridge and marching and organizing for peace in Washington, she commuted to Texas. At the Ranch she took notes on his rambling monologues about his past and his opinions about people and politics. He came to rely on her, not only for help in writing his book but also for understanding the eastern intellectuals, who had passionately opposed him and who he believed had brought him down. "If I had been a young teacher at the University of Texas," Kearns reflected, "our relationship could never have happened. The fact that I was from Harvard was very important."[25]

Because they spent so much time tête-à-tête, and swam, and took long walks and drives together, rumors began to fly that there was a romantic relationship between the two. A 1971 article in *Parade* magazine hinted at an affair, angering LBJ and outraging Lady Bird, who admitted she had let Kearns come to the Ranch too often. Johnson's closest friends firmly believed that it remained platonic. And they were surely right. She herself maintained that their connection never became romantic. His attachment to Kearns seems to belong in the realm of personal validation rather than libido. As we have seen, for his entire career LBJ's soul had been a battlefield between his expedient impulses and his idealistic, liberal nature. In his mind Kearns epitomized "the Harvards" who had spurned him, and her understanding and compassion, her willingness to listen, met his need to justify himself to his critics on the left. Talking to Kearns must have done wonders for his conscience. Whatever the truth, Johnson needed a friend to whom he could pour out his triumphs and disappointments, and she met that craving.

By the fall of 1969, as the LBJ Library neared completion, more than a dozen staff members from the National Archives were sorting through Johnson's massive collection of papers, and former aides were processing the more confidential material. LBJ had excluded three categories of papers from access to researchers: personal correspondence, documents that involved his family or private affairs, and papers relating to national security or foreign policy that could "injure, embarrass, or harass any person." These, however, would be subjected to periodic review. Like their owner, the papers were soon generating controversy. At the annual meeting of the Southern Historical Association, a number of leading scholars complained about restrictions governing their use. Dr. Chester A. Newland, first director of the library, defended the need for "judicious" restrictions in an article in the current *Library Chronicle*, and Lady Bird said in an interview that she was helping to process the material and hoped to "make it available to scholars as quickly as possible." Other critics of the project doubted its objectivity. Republican senator John Williams of Delaware dismissed it as a project that "emphasizes [the former president's] achievements and forgets his mistakes."[26] To allay such criticism, Johnson sought to hire a staff with acknowledged professional credentials.

LBJ came back to the White House for the first time since Nixon's inauguration shortly before Christmas in 1969 to confer with the president on foreign affairs. In a two-hour breakfast meeting on December 11, the two leaders discussed the Nuclear Nonproliferation Treaty, U.S. relations with Japan, the strategic arms limitation treaty with the Soviet Union, and, of course, the situation in Vietnam. When Johnson left, the *New York Times* described him as "uncharacteristically reticent."[27] As the two men walked onto the North Portico of the White House, a crowd of tourists and reporters were milling around. Though he used to relish personal contact with the public and the press, he now seemed disinclined to engage with either group. He smiled at the press corps, shook hands with a scattering of tourists, and swiftly stepped into the waiting limousine without uttering a word.

Johnson concluded his first year of retirement with a television interview seen on CBS on December 27. This was the first of three such programs, based on anchorman Walter Cronkite's visits to the Ranch in September and October. In Cronkite's memoirs the ex-president appears on this first occasion as a boorish figure, sitting at the table for lunch with the CBS production crew wearing nothing but shorts covered by a bathrobe. As he waves his arms to punctuate his stories, this garment keeps coming apart. Lady Bird, Cronkite reported, was acutely embarrassed, especially since there were women as well as men on the CBS crew. When she could catch her husband's attention she gestured to him to close his robe, only to have it fall apart again when he began another story. Because of his heart problems, LBJ was on a strict diet and complained about it all through lunch to a chorus of sympathetic murmurs from his guests. As each course appeared and particularly when dessert arrived, he looked at Lady Bird to see if she was watching, and when she was looking away, like a child defying his mother, sneaked food from the plates on either side of him, an old habit of his.[28]

The first tape aired on TV, "Why I Chose Not to Run," showed a tense Johnson. He seemed in quick succession self-doubting, self-critical, self-justifying, and perhaps self-deluded. In all three interviews he refused to acknowledge the fact that he had done anything under duress. He had been master of his own fate, making his own choices, he insisted. Some of his claims were simply unbelievable. He told Cronkite that he felt certain he could have been reelected if he had run in 1968. He had had "more doubts about what would happen in the '64 campaign than . . . what would happen in the '68 campaign." He also claimed that Humphrey lost the election because he made concessions to the peace faction in his September speech in Salt Lake City.

Other assertions were revealing, if not fully credible. As he told it, it was Lady Bird's advice that convinced him to run for president in 1964, though he had substantial doubts about doing so. He also promised her he would announce his retirement before the 1968 campaign. He explained that the reason he did not withdraw after his State of the Union message was that after making all his recommendations to Congress, he did not want to "conclude it by saying, 'but I'm quitting. I'm throwing in the towel, and you go on and do this by yourself.'" He repeated the standard postpresidential platitudes about being happy that he could "go to bed after the ten-o'clock news and to sleep until daylight the next morning." In a statement that seemed more self-pitying than authentic, he told Cronkite that he had never been an ambitious man who wanted power more than anything else and that it was not true that his "greatest desire was to occupy the top job in American political life." Then, in a rather extraordinary confession for a nationwide television program, he revealed how tortured he was at times since he left office. He wasn't sure he had ever been up to being the president, he confided. Not only did he feel he was disadvantaged by the place he was born, his relative poverty, and his narrow education, but also he had "a general inability to stimulate and inspire and unite all the people of the country, which I think is an essential function of the Presidency." "Now," he added, "I have never really believed that I was the man to do that particular job. I have always felt that every job that I had was really too big for me."[29]

In the next segment, shown on February 6, 1970, LBJ discussed his action and those of his advisers in Vietnam. Appearing no more relaxed than in the first, Johnson was critical of his opponents while defending his response to the Tonkin Gulf incident and explaining his actions in the wake of the Tet offensive. Once Congress passed the Tonkin Gulf Resolution, he felt he had unlimited authority to do what he thought necessary to protect American troops and prevent further aggression in Southeast Asia. He did not ask for a declaration of war at the time, he said, because he was afraid North Vietnam had secret treaties with the Soviet Union and Communist China that would have automatically led to a much larger conflagration. But he had not deceived the American people. Congress knew exactly what it was doing when it passed the resolution, and "when the going got hard, when the road got longer and dustier, when the casualties started coming in, why, there were certain folk started looking for the cellar." Even more scornful of his archcritic from Arkansas, one of four senators who had introduced the bill in the Senate, Johnson said, "It was a shame somebody didn't think of calling it the Fulbright Resolution. . . . Don't tell me a Rhodes scholar didn't understand everything in that resolution. . . ."

The one Vietnam mistake he acknowledged was failing to impress the American people with all the peace overtures he made to Ho Chi Minh. He had been "willing to go anywhere, anytime, talk about anything," he insisted again. He was chagrined that following each attempt to negotiate, he was attacked for not handling it right, while his critics said "not one word about Ho Chi Minh." Johnson expressed disgust with the defeatist attitude of the public after Tet. People should have seen it for the Communist disaster it was. Instead it became a "psychological victory for them in the United States that they could not win from our men on the battlefield." Johnson sought sole credit for deescalating the war in 1968. He was not coerced into refusing the Wheeler-Westmoreland request for an additional 206,000 troops by the wise men and other government advisers. The views of these men who were demanding a change of policy neither shocked nor surprised him. "Something you're already doing couldn't shock you a great deal," he declared. According to Johnson, it was Dean Rusk, generally considered more hawkish than some, who instigated the bombing halt. Clark Clifford, thought to be more of a dove, actually suggested a conditional halt. In answer to why he made both the announcement to retire and to reduce the bombing of North Vietnam on the same night, Johnson said he wanted to use both "as a basis for getting all the steam I could toward a possible peace move."[30]

In the last interview, shown on May 2, Johnson offered his account of Kennedy's assassination, adding nothing new except that his first thought after hearing JFK was dead was that it might be "an international conspiracy and they were out to destroy our form of government and the leaders in that government." Some of the things he said about the Warren Commission's findings that Lee Harvey Oswald acted alone were deleted on the "ground of national security."

Actually the press and the public found more interesting his complicated feelings about the Kennedys and the Kennedy aides he inherited. He described his relationship with his predecessor as not close but "friendly, cordial, but not personally intimate." He believed that had Kennedy lived, he intended to include him on the ticket in 1964. Johnson admitted that he felt he was living in Kennedy's shadow. Everything he said and did was unfavorably compared with the former president. He thought that the public approved of Kennedy's conduct of the office, his way of dealing with things, his accent, and his background more than they did of his own actions, accent, and background. Kennedy "was a great public hero," Johnson told Cronkite, "and anything I did that someone didn't approve of, they would always feel that President Kennedy wouldn't have done that . . . that he wouldn't have made that mistake."

And he had harsh words for some of the Kennedy aides he had retained to preserve continuity and carry to fruition his predecessor's policies. He blamed their actions on their differences in point of view as well as the "fact that some of the people who served did not share either the desire or the hopes that I had for the country and for the government." He accused them of undermining him and his administration. He claimed that they "bored from within to create problems for us and leaked information that was slanted and things of that nature. A good many of them resigned at certain periods and left the impression that the government was not in keeping with their views and so forth." In answer to Cronkite's question whether his enemies belonged to a cult led by Bobby Kennedy, Johnson said, "I can't answer that question honestly and directly; I don't know." Then he moderated his accusations, saying he believed that some of the Kennedy folk acted the way they did out of grief at their leader's death. He particularly praised Theodore Sorensen. In the end, Johnson said he did everything he could to enact Kennedy's program and that it was only after he "finished writing and completing and enacting and inaugurating and putting into action the dreams" that his predecessor had had that he moved to programs of his own. The interview concluded with a heartfelt statement by Johnson that "I don't want anyone to ever say that I ever let him down for a moment."[31]

At the beginning of March, less than a month after the second interview aired, Johnson was admitted to the Army's Brooke General Hospital in San Antonio with severe chest pains. The doctors were worried about another heart attack and kept him under observation with continuous electrocardiographic monitoring. Finding no evidence of a new heart attack, they released him, and fewer than two weeks later he was back at the Ranch with instructions to rest and restrict his activities for a while.

By the beginning of April 1970 he was back in Washington, to attend the wedding of the daughter of his old friend columnist William White. He and Lady Bird stayed at the home of Lynda Bird Robb in Virginia. He visited Nixon and the "West Terrace Press Center," brand-new facilities for reporters that had cost the government more than half a million dollars. Calling it "a wonderful improvement," Johnson asked Nixon: "Is there the same improvement in the stories?" Nixon said he only hoped there were.[32] On this visit to the capital, he had lunch with the Texas delegation and then appeared on the House floor, where proceedings stopped for half an hour so people could line up to shake his hand. Greeting the former president on the receiving line in the House was Allard Lowenstein of New York, founder of the dump-Johnson movement, who told him that he had been worried when he heard about his chest pains the previous month and now was relieved to see him looking well.

It was probably during this trip that the Johnsons attended a dinner party at publisher Katharine Graham's home. The next day the ex-president came to the *Washington Post* offices downtown and spent four hours with reporters and editors, defending both Vietnam and the Great Society and presenting a general *apologia pro vita sua.* Two of the reporters later described his performance "as overpowering." Johnson "thumped on the table, moved back and forth vigorously, grimaced, licked his lips, gestured with his arms, slumped back in his seat, switched from a sharp to a soft story, and kept the conversation going from the moment he sat down at the table until . . . Lady Bird . . . sent in a note reminding him that he should come home to rest."[33] As he left, the *Post* and *Newsweek* people burst into spontaneous applause.

The spring of 1970 was a busy time for Johnson. Ignoring his doctors' advice to rest and relax, he was more active publicly than at any time since Nixon's inauguration. On May 1 Johnson was a guest of honor in Chicago at a fund-raiser for the Cook County Democratic Party, headed by Mayor Daley. In this first public address since leaving office, Johnson called on all Americans to support Nixon's policies in Southeast Asia, remarking that it hurt the country to "present the image of a disunited land that is reeking with dissension with no one person in authority," and restating how hard it was to get "Hanoi to listen." He did not specifically endorse Nixon's controversial April 30 decision to send American troops into Cambodia, but he said he hoped the president would have "the prayers and support of all people who love freedom; he has mine."[34] At the end of the month he was in Washington again to pay tribute to the retiring Speaker of the House, seventy-eight-year-old John W. McCormack, and to star at a fund-raiser for the national Democratic Party, which was pleading poverty in the 1970 congressional campaigns.

During the summer LBJ was even busier, showing what seemed to be a revived interest in politics. On July 15 he attended and spoke at a dinner in honor of his old adversary in Texas Democratic politics Senator Ralph Yarborough, who was running against Lloyd Bentsen Jr. in the Democratic primary. Five days later Johnson invited the major Texas Democratic candidates to the Ranch to discuss how to stop fighting and form a united front against the Republicans. At a fund-raiser in August LBJ gave what the *Houston Post* described as "a keynote address for a revival campaign of the state and national Democratic parties."[35] In September he helped kick off the U.S. Senate campaign of Lloyd Bentsen, who had defeated Yarborough.

Johnson turned sixty-two on August 27 and celebrated his birthday quietly with his family. On August 28 he presided at a seminar on economic policy, "The Years Ahead," at the new Lyndon B. Johnson State Park, to be formally dedicated the following day. Two hundred students, economists, and businessmen were present at the invitation-only event, but the proceedings were piped outside the park through loudspeakers, and reporters heard the speeches while being served soft drinks and beer by Johnson's staff. Among the featured speakers were Johnson's Secretary of the Treasury, Henry Fowler, and former chairman of the Council of Economic Advisers Walter Heller, who criticized Nixon's economic policies. Appearing much heavier than when he was president, Johnson played peacemaker, telling the crowd, "I hope we will temporarily suspend pointing the finger of blame. We have one president and one economy, and we are all in this boat together." LBJ also told the group that he planned more seminars in the future on "such subjects as environment, population control, food, health, beautification, arms limitation, education and foreign affairs."[36]

In November Holt, Rinehart, & Winston published *A White House Diary*, the journal Lady Bird kept from November 22, 1963, to January 20, 1969. The 806-page book was based on the tape recordings Mrs. Johnson made almost daily during the five years her husband was president. It described the endless social obligations and perpetual fixed smiles demanded of a First Lady. It portrayed the struggle between the public and personal side of her life and particularly her difficult effort to bring up her two daughters without stinting on her attentions to them. It covered the public figures and issues that made up American life during that time.

It described Johnson's commitment to civil rights and to his concept of a Great Society, her devotion to conservation and beautification as well as their mutual shock and dismay at Kennedy's assassination, and her husband's ambivalence toward some of the aides he had acquired from the former president. It related her ambiguous relationship with Jacqueline Kennedy. It confirmed her husband's version of his decision to retire and her own reaction to the possibility of another term in office. "I do not know whether we can endure another four-year term in the Presidency," she had written. "I face the prospect of another campaign like an open-end stay in a concentration camp." It depicted the intense stress on Johnson of the Vietnam War. After dinner with the Clark Cliffords and columnist Joseph Alsop, the president had recounted how, in the spring of 1964, Alsop told him, "If you don't commit troops you're going to preside over the first real defeat of the United States in history. There's no other honorable way out of Southeast Asia." In another entry, written a year later, the president said, "I can't get out. I can't finish it with what I have got. So what the hell can I do?" The reviews were mostly positive, though some critics complained that the details about what she wore and what she ate were repetitive and overwhelming. "History and a great many people," reviewer Marya Mannes wrote in the *New*

York Times Book Review, "will remember her as a valuable woman, largely immune from the antagonisms her husband aroused, who gave the best of herself to her family and to her country."[37]

Refusing to stay in bed with a bad cold in the middle of January 1971, Johnson was admitted to Brooke General Hospital in San Antonio with possible pneumonia. There was no indication of cardiac trouble, and after a few days he was sent back to the Ranch to recover.

After a relatively quiet spring, LBJ eagerly awaited the official opening of the Johnson Library on May 22. On a muggy but breezy day in Austin, 3,000 people, Democrats and Republicans alike, from President Nixon to would-be president Hubert Humphrey, from future secretary of state Henry Kissinger to former secretary Dean Rusk, attended the ceremony, along with a flock of celebrities. Two thousand antiwar demonstrators also showed up, but were kept away from the ceremony by Texas Rangers and highway patrolmen. Later, after a celebratory barbecue dinner on the library grounds, 250 protesters tried to disrupt the proceedings by throwing bottles, cans, and rocks at the police, ripping the wiring from three official cars, and deflating their tires. Twenty-seven were arrested. On the other hand, General Westmoreland and Robert Binder, the University of Texas student president, who had just been participating in the peaceful part of the antiwar demonstration, ended up shaking hands.

The library, when finished, was a simultaneous monument to scholarship and to its chief subject. Visitors got their first view of the photographic record on the first floor, with a huge blowup of LBJ as a five-year-old in a cowboy hat. The five-story Great Hall displayed massive murals etched in magnesium and weighing close to a ton recording LBJ's career as a congressman with FDR, as a senator with Truman, as the Senate majority leader with Eisenhower, as vice president with John F. Kennedy, and then, alone, as president. The library also housed hundreds of mementos, including personal letters from the pope, Albert Schweitzer, Khrushchev, and Ho Chi Minh; the lace and satin wedding gowns of his daughters; a tape of the LBJ campaign song "Hello, Lyndon"; and the plumed hat Carol Channing wore in a White House performance of *Hello, Dolly!* The area that quickly became a favorite of tourists was the exact-detail, seven-eighths-scale replica of the Oval Office on the top floor, closed only when Johnson himself was using it as a workplace.

Wearing his favorite shirt, suit, and tan tie, Johnson opened the ceremonies with a short speech on the lawn outside the library. "Here are thirty-one million documents," he explained, "to be preserved for the nation—for all who care to review and evaluate—and they will reflect what man can do and cannot do in one life." The collection, he explained, recorded the negatives as well as the positives of his presidency. "It is all here: the story of our time—with the bark off," he declared. "There is no record of a mistake, nothing critical, ugly, or unpleasant that has not been included in the files here." The library will "show the facts, not just the joy and triumphs, but the sorrow and the failures, too," he said. After the barbecue, some guests went with LBJ to tour the School of Public Affairs; others went to a Mexican fiesta party given by Luci Johnson Nugent and her husband, Pat, at the student center, which Lyndon and Lady Byrd attended after the school tour. The day had, as one guest summed it all up, "all the ingredients of a golden wedding celebration, a twenty-fifth alumni reunion, and a Sunday school picnic."[38]

Spoiling LBJ's delight at the opening of his library was the publication a few weeks later by the *New York Times* of top-secret documents, which it dubbed the *Pentagon Papers*. Commissioned by then secretary of defense McNamara to assist future scholars in determining how the United States became involved in Vietnam, the seven thousand pages of analysis and official documents had been leaked to the press by Daniel Ellsberg, a protégé of McNamara who had become a dove as the war dragged on. The Nixon administration was livid at the theft and publication, though the data did not cover the Nixon years. After the first excerpt appeared, the Justice Department sought to block further publication but was overruled by the U.S. Supreme Court.

The incident offended Johnson. Read a certain way, the *Papers* seemed to implicate him in early sub-rosa plans for escalating the war. At a lunch at the LBJ Library shortly after the first installments came out, Johnson reflected on his Vietnam policies. As always on Vietnam, he was ambivalent. On the one hand, he said, Kennedy had made a mistake by not sending more than sixteen thousand military advisers to South Vietnam in the early 1960s and had aggravated the situation by waiting so long before sending in more men. He also thought he had made a mistake by not establishing some kind of censorship, not as a cover-up of mistakes but to prevent the enemy from learning the next round of American action. "My God," he exclaimed, "you can't fight a war by watching it every night on television."[39]

Then, according to Leo Janos, present at the meal, Johnson began to defend his policies against the assertions and implications in the newspapers. All through 1964, he maintained, he really did not want a major war in Vietnam and hoped it would be possible to negotiate his way out of it. As the situation worsened, he tried to proceed slowly with the troop

buildup to avoid igniting prowar sentiment and to keep Hanoi from asking China for direct military help. He also noted that he did not want to
repeat Truman's error in Korea by going in without the approval of Congress. Johnson was angry at the claim that he used the Tonkin Gulf incident as justification for an attack. "Hell," he said, "the Communists hit
us there twice." He did nothing following the first attack, "hoping it was
either a mistake or the action would not be repeated." But when they hit
us again the next day, he declared, he was compelled to take action.
"And just about every member of Congress," he huffed, "was marching
right along with me." One accusation that particularly got his goat was
that he had been covertly planning to start bombing North Vietnam during the 1964 campaign. Johnson claimed it was "absolutely untrue." He
had vetoed five requests by the military for retaliation bombing raids in
the North. He admitted he had contingency bombing plans, but he
wanted to hold off as long as he could. "Finally," he said, "they attacked
our base in Pleiku in February 1965, destroying many planes and killing
a lot of our men. I was forced to act. I felt I had no choice."[40]

To take his mind off the still-swirling criticism of Vietnam and recapture the euphoria of the library dedication, later that summer LBJ
and Lady Bird invited the public to attend a fund-raising ceremony to expand the library's information and guide services. The "you-all come" invitation increased the average two thousand visitors a day to more than
eighty-six hundred by Sunday, August 1. That evening Johnson and Lady
Bird, both wearing light-colored suits in the Texas heat, autographed
book, photographs, postcards, pamphlets, and other memorabilia. Since
LBJ's memoirs had not yet been published, they autographed copies of
Lady Bird's book *A White House Diary; To Heal and Build: The Programs
of President Lyndon B. Johnson*, edited by James MacGregor Burns; and
A Family Album, by Rebekah Johnson. Johnson kept urging the large
crowd to go into the library and buy some more books, promising to stay
and sign them all. The schedule called for an hour of autographing, but
by the time the crowds had thinned, the Johnsons had been signing for
four hours. When asked if the autograph parties would be a regular event
a library official said, "Gee, I hope not."[41]

The *New York Times* began excerpting Johnson's memoirs in October before they were published in book form. Controversy erupted almost immediately. Johnson had written that he had appointed Arthur
Goldberg as UN ambassador because John Kenneth Galbraith had told
him that Goldberg was "bored" and "restless" on the Supreme Court.
Goldberg scaldingly contested LBJ's version of the event. He had, rather,
been coerced by the president to leave a job he enjoyed. But beyond

this, he considered faulty Johnson's account of his own efforts as UN delegate to deescalate the war and hasten peace in Vietnam. "Americans should not have to derive their information about these events [in Vietnam]," he declared, "only from the president's self-serving and biased statements in a document which purports to be, but in fact is not, the history of the events which have so profoundly affected all of us." Goldberg called Johnson's book "Orwellian," referring to the "newspeak" propaganda of the novel 1984.[42]

Goldberg had a personal ax to grind, but in truth *The Vantage Point* was a disappointing book. Ghostwritten by Kearns, Hardesty, and Middleton, it was, at Johnson's insistence, a sanitized account of his presidency that lacked its putative author's bite and earthiness. It resembled many of Johnson's formal "presidential" speeches—rather dry and lifeless.

By the fall of 1971 Johnson conveyed the impression that he had come to terms with his life. "I want to keep fit, young, interested, and happy," he told a Texas political writer. As part of this goal, he had found pursuits far from politics. Blaming it on "the trials and tribulations of Christmas," Johnson started smoking again in December 1971, a habit he had given up more than fifteen years earlier after his first heart attack, though he had occasionally relapsed thereafter.[43] But his resumed smoking aside, it seemed that by this time Johnson had found a better balance in his everyday life. He enjoyed swimming and built a plastic bubble over his pool at the ranch so he could exercise every day, even during the winter. Lady Bird revealed that she and her husband often rode horses together. "We have," she said, "a deep sense of oneness with the land . . . and we love it. We can ride for hours—ride over that eroded hillside country of Texas—and be at utter peace."[44] Never before patient with spectator sports, he now developed a passion for watching football and baseball, showing up with Lady Bird, Luci, and Patrick at Super Bowl VI in New Orleans and cheering on the Dallas Cowboys to a 24–3 victory over Nixon's team, the Miami Dolphins.

LBJ seemed to be in good spirits as 1972 began. For some years the Johnsons, often accompanied by family members and the ex-president's aides, had been taking winter vacations in Acapulco. This February they stayed at an oceanfront villa owned by Miguel Alemán, former president of Mexico, who had collaborated with LBJ on several Mexican land deals. LBJ did not travel light. He brought his own air-conditioning units and his own liquor, food, bottled water, and his cook, supposedly to avoid the "Montezuma's Revenge" that attacked his guests in 1970 after they ate local produce. On this trip he visited Las Pampas, Alemán's ranch in the Mexican interior. Characteristically, while enjoying his luxurious life, he was worried about the poverty of the ranch workers and their large families. Johnson would lecture the Mexican workers' wives about birth control, using a translator to make sure he got his points across. Back in the States, he sent the ranch families vitamins, clothing, blankets, and birth-control pills. "If I became dictator of the world," he said, "I'd give all the poor on earth a cottage and birth-control pills—and I'd make damn sure they didn't get one if they didn't take the other."[45]

Just before the Johnsons' Acapulco vacation, LBJ attended an education symposium at the LBJ Library. After the closing session he released 250,000 documents involving education, including material on the task force reports and the behind-the-scenes decisions on the sixty education laws passed by his administration. The recommendations of one such task force, kept secret until now, proposed a $1.25 billion program to integrate black students in inner-city schools with whites in suburban schools.

Most of the speakers praised Johnson for his efforts on behalf of education, but there were some dissenters. John Marland, Nixon's commissioner of education, noted that the Johnson administration had not solved the learning problems of disadvantaged children, who amounted to 20 percent of the nation's schoolchildren. A speech by Johnson concluded the two-day symposium. He was proud of his accomplishments, he declared; indeed, he would not apologize either for his reputation as an "arm-twister" or for what was in the education documents. "Whatever is there, whether it's for the good or for the bad, and I hope it's for the good," Johnson said, "I believe the papers will prove helpful for putting into perspective our problems and giving us some answers and solutions."[46] Though just a few years since the Great Society, Johnson believed "another great social surge" would occur soon and that arguments that we could not afford it were simply not true. "The country," he declared, "has the money to do anything it's got the guts to do." It was important to "convince those who pay the bills" that renewed social action was necessary.[47]

Johnson also had some things to say about politics and the upcoming election in another television interview with Walter Cronkite, "Lyndon Johnson Talks Politics." He foresaw a "knock-down, drag-out" contest in 1972 but hoped it would not be too divisive. "[W]e don't have to get personal and . . . question men's motives and their patriotism. . . ." Without acknowledging his own reliance on rich supporters, he blamed the high cost of running for office for making candidates "beholden to groups and people with means." Even though office seekers felt they were not influenced by having to raise money, "they are one way or the other, consciously or subconsciously, sometimes both." He admitted that money had played a part in his campaigns but, ignoring his debts to the Browns and the Texas oilmen, illustrated his case with the more innocent example of his ten-thousand-dollar loan from Lady Bird for his first congressional race. He looked back on his years as Senate leader as a "very productive period—and a very enjoyable period" in his public life, implying that his presidency was less delightful. When he discussed his own administration, he was very kind to Congress. Members were "better to me than they were to any other presidents I've known." And he said the military never kept him in the dark or tried to influence him on Vietnam. He would not "pass the buck." He was willing to take the responsibility for his military decisions, even if they were bad ones. They must fall "on my broad shoulders."

He was not especially eager, he said, to go out on "the cold chicken circuit" again, but would help his fellow Democrats if it seemed necessary. And if it helped his party or his country by stating his views, he would do that, too. Though respectful toward his enemies through most of the interview, he concluded with a dig:

> Most of the time I think we can better serve our country by letting those who have the responsibility and have the information . . . [speak up], but if I think they're doing it wrong and it's bad, I will speak up, because there were plenty of them spoke up during my time.[48]

He was right: He would never travel the cold chicken circuit again. While visiting daughter Lynda and her family in suburban Charlottesville, Virginia, Johnson awakened on April 7 with racking chest pains. A rescue squad ambulance came speeding to the house at 4:00 A.M., and the Robbs' doctor soon arrived with a mobile coronary care unit from the local hospital, where Johnson was taken. Dr. Willis Hurst, the cardiologist who treated Johnson for his almost fatal heart attack when he was Senate majority leader, flew up from Atlanta. With a grim and tired Lady Bird by his side, Hurst told the press that Lyndon had suffered a second heart attack. Mrs. Johnson said she thought her husband's condition had been brought on by "three . . . very strenuous days" of emotional and physical strain, including attending funeral services for a political colleague in Tennessee.

Dr. Hurst had informed Lady Bird privately that her husband's arteries were so blocked he might "die suddenly, and it wouldn't "matter if the five best cardiologists in the United States are in the room."[49] Though Johnson was not told how serious his condition was, he sensed the end, and after a week in the Virginia hospital, he demanded to go home. If he was going to die, he wanted to die in Texas. When Lady Bird demurred, he told her he intended to go with or without her. The Johnsons departed soon after this ultimatum. So hasty was their exit that the staff at Charlottesville was not even notified, and after hearing the rumor that Johnson had left, discovered LBJ's empty wheelchair in the parking lot.

After flying to San Antonio, Johnson was taken by wheelchair to Brooke Army Hospital. A week later, while in the hospital, he suffered a flurry of irregular heartbeats, which Dr. Hurst said was ventricular tachycardia, a warning of possible further serious damage to his heart. Sent home to the Ranch at the end of April, he returned to the hospital for tests in May. It was then announced that he had developed permanent congestive heart failure as a complication of his recent attack and required digitalis. By June, he seemed to be better, however, and he made a public appearance at a folk music festival in Kerrville, Texas, where he clapped his hands and stomped his feet in time to the music. But in late July he was back at Brooke Army Hospital with nausea and chest pains. After a few days, when the doctors were sure that he had not had another heart attack, he was again released.

For the last six months of his life Johnson would be constantly afflicted with chest pains. According to his aide Leo Janos, a "series of sharp, jolting pains . . . left him scared and breathless." He had a portable oxygen tank next to his bed, and from time to time, particularly in the afternoon, when the pain seemed worse, lay down and turned on the tank to help him breathe. He no longer drove his trademark Lincoln; he was chauffeured where he wanted to go. He told his friends he was "hurting real bad."[50]

During these last months Johnson seemed indifferent to survival. Against his doctors' advice, he continued to smoke and only intermittently stayed on the low-cholesterol, low-calorie diet they prescribed. In fact, he and friends at times would drive to Austin and gorge on hamburgers. At one point his weight ballooned to 235 pounds. He also began to have severe stomach pains, diagnosed as diverticulosis, an outpouching of the intestinal walls that occurs with aging. The doctors recommended surgery to stop the worsening pains, but he refused. Johnson flew to Houston for a consultation with world-renowned cardiologist Dr. Michael DeBakey. DeBakey concluded that his patient's heart was too damaged to undergo any kind of surgery, including a coronary bypass. After his death, when people were second-guessing whether the operation would have saved his life, four of his doctors, including DeBakey, issued a statement reviewing his condition. "Coronary bypass surgery does not revitalize destroyed heart muscles," it stated. "The poorest results occur in patients with inadequate heart function. Unfortunately, President Johnson was in this category."[51]

In early July the Democrats had held their presidential nominating convention in Miami Beach. Apprehensive that there would be demonstrations and violence, Larry O'Brien and others warned Johnson not to attend. And, in fact, a group of 150 Yippies torched a ten-foot-tall portrait of Johnson in front of Convention Hall as a warning to whoever was the 1972 candidate not to "turn into another LBJ."[52] But in any case, LBJ's health problems in the spring and summer of 1972 prevented him from being there. He supported Edmund Muskie for the nomination, although he later remarked that Muskie could never become president because he lacked "the instinct to go for his opponent's jugular."[53] During the convention he conferred by phone with both Muskie and Mayor Daley on how to stop South Dakota senator George McGovern from getting the nomination. Johnson was certain that McGovern was much too liberal. But besides, the South Dakotan was one of the first senators to protest escalation of the war in Vietnam. Yet LBJ refused Daley's request that he speak out publicly against McGovern before the convention.

It took Johnson a month after McGovern's nomination—by the very forces that lost to Humphrey at Chicago four years before—to endorse him publicly. In mid-August, in an eight-paragraph statement to *The Standard*, a weekly newspaper in Fredericksburg, Johnson said he supported his party's present presidential ticket. He could not ignore the differences that existed between himself and the candidate. "It is no secret," his statement read, "that Senator McGovern and I have widely differing opinions on many matters, especially foreign policy. . . ." However, it continued, "the Democratic Party can accommodate disagreements." Although the endorsement was qualified, Texas McGovernites, clutching at straws, claimed it was "a major plus" and "the greatest boost" they had had "for the Democratic ticket since it was completed."[54]

A few days later, McGovern and vice-presidential candidate Sargent Shriver, Johnson's old War on Poverty war czar, came to the ranch to meet with LBJ. A photograph in the *Washington Post* amazed readers. Not only were the two former adversaries smiling and chatting amiably, but also the peace candidate, with his short hair, suit, and tie, looked as conventional as possible, while the former president, wearing a checked work shirt and sporting long white hair down to his shoulders, resembled an aged hippie. McGovern himself remembered that the former president at this meeting "looked like General Custer." He also recalled that LBJ smoked eight or ten cigarettes and that Lady Bird watched him with a faint smile. "If there is such a thing as a sad smile," McGovern said, "she had a sad smile."[55]

The candidates and the ex-president had lunch together, talking cordially for three hours and parting on amiable terms. McGovern described the meeting as "most friendly."[56] But Johnson admitted to reservations. "Now on the war. I think you're crazy as hell," he told McGovern, "and you think I'm crazy as hell; so let's just not talk about that. Let's talk about America and about this election." The master politician suggested that the candidate stress his "homespun, down-to-earth background" and let people know he was proud of his country."[57] McGovern later wrote that LBJ gave him "very good advice and I wish I'd done more of it."[58] In the end, however, except for this meeting at the Ranch and the letter to the *Standard*, Johnson stayed out of the 1972 campaign. Actually, LBJ surprised many people by giving McGovern even this limited support. His friends explained that he wanted it to be said that he died a Democrat.

Speechwriter Horace Busby came to the ranch in September to help Johnson write his first public speech since his most recent heart attack, a talk to be given at the Scott and White Clinic in Temple, Texas. Though he meant to be upbeat about his beloved America, LBJ began it on a note that reflected his own sad prospects:

> With the coming of September each year, we are reminded, as the song says, that the days are dwindling down to a precious few. By the calendar, we know that soon the green leaves of summer will begin to brown; the chill winds of winter will begin to blow; and—before we are ready for the end to come—the year will be gone.[59]

At the Lady Bird Johnson Awards ceremony in Stonewall the following month, LBJ talked directly about his health. He was feeling well, he said, but was following an old woman's advice: "When I walks, I walks slowly. When I sits, I sits loosely. And when I feel a worry coming on, I just go to sleep. That's what I'm doing now."[60] But Johnson was not following this formula, nor was he paying much attention to the doctors' admonitions. When chided about his chain smoking, he said, "I'm an old man, so what's the difference?" He loved smoking and missed it terribly all those years that he had stopped, he noted. "Anyway," he rationalized, "I don't want to linger the way Eisenhower did. When I go, I want to go fast."[61]

Yet he obviously hoped for a few more years. As late as December 1972 he was talking to Horace Busby about becoming active again in 1973. "After the inauguration," he said, "we'll have four years behind us and I think I can speak up a little more. I've got some programs up there that are kicking around and I'd like to go more places and see more people again." What he had in mind was trying to liberalize and strengthen the Texas Democratic Party, which fifteen years before he had fashioned into one of the most powerful state parties in the country. In the previous election both blacks and Mexican Americans had shown little enthusiasm for the party's conservative candidates, and Johnson found this very troubling. In addition, the Republicans were pulling away white voters. When Busby asked him about his health, he said he was "just fair," but confessed he was taking nitroglycerin pills, "swallowing . . . [them] like a goldfish gulping crackers." He hoped he could "rest up in the sun" on his annual vacation in Mexico and feel restored. "But it's not good," he admitted.[62]

In November the Johnsons celebrated their thirty-eighth wedding anniversary. LBJ told newsmen that he believed he was "going to be as good as new by the new year."[63] Though, of course, he hoped his health would improve, he was also methodically preparing for the end. During his retirement he had devoted a great deal of his prodigious energy to his business interests and managed to double his wealth. He now owned property in Texas, Alabama, Mexico, and the Caribbean as well as his television stations and a photographic supply company in Austin. Regrettably, in the last year of his life, all his business dealings were conducted without the help of his longtime partner and boyhood friend A. W. Moursund. They had quarreled about some business matter, possibly the purchase of a bank. All Johnson would say about the rupture was that "The judge and I have split the blanket."[64] The breach was never repaired, and Johnson died without a reconciliation with Moursund.

In December LBJ donated the Ranch to the public for use as a historical exhibit of the "entire life of a president." The gift included their home, which they would continue to live in as long as they wanted, the other buildings on the ranch, and more than two hundred acres of crops and grazing land. As long as the Johnsons were living there, tours would include only the exterior of the ranch buildings. The one exception was the interior of the airplane hangar, which would contain various exhibits, and tourists would be able to see a film on the workings of the Ranch. The new site would be in addition to those areas managed by the National Park Service containing his birthplace and boyhood home. Also acquired by the National Parks Foundation were a forty-seven-acre tract and a log cabin in nearby Johnson City that LBJ's grandfather Sam Ealy Johnson used as headquarters for his cattle drives, and the one-room Junction Schoolhouse, which Johnson attended when he was four years old.

Despite the cardiac pain, Johnson made two public speeches in the month before his death. One was a routine appearance at the Dallas Press Club awards dinner. The other, a fitting last act, summed up his matchless civil rights achievements and conveyed his fighting spirit at its best.

The occasion was a two-day civil rights symposium on December 11 and 12, 1973, attended by a thousand guests to mark the opening to the public of a large selection of his administration's civil rights documents. Black leaders Roy Wilkins, Vernon E. Jordan Jr., Barbara Jordan, and Patricia Roberts Harris were there as well as Hubert Humphrey and former chief justice Earl Warren. The weather was uncharacteristically cold for Austin, with the "worst ice storm in years" blanketing central Texas. Planes flying the guests to the symposium had to land at San Antonio, where buses picked them up for the drive to Austin, inspiring jokes about "forced busing." Despite the weather, the Johnsons drove in from the Ranch, sitting through the meetings on the first day and attending the reception that night. Speakers on that day included Hubert Humphrey and Vernon Jordan, executive director of the National Urban League. Both men called on President Nixon to revitalize the civil rights movement. Humphrey was particularly emotional, warning Nixon that there could be "no more harsh indictment than his having failed to lead the United States in this critical and urgent area of domestic concern."[65]

Johnson was exhausted by the time he got back to the Ranch that evening. He was in such pain that the doctor had to make a predawn visit. Both the doctor and Lady Bird strongly advised him not to return for his speech the second day. But Johnson would not listen; he could not absent himself from a meeting on one of the most significant aspects of his administration. When the passion of Vietnam had receded, he expected he would be primarily remembered for his achievements in civil rights and on behalf of the common people. Lady Bird had grave doubts, but she later said: "I now realize it was all right that he went, because he knew what he was spending and had a right to decide how he wanted to spend it."[66]

So he came with Lady Bird at his side, wearing his "dark blue presidential suit and those flawlessly polished oxfords," and spoke in spite of noisy quarreling between the liberal and radical black leaders. He delivered a rousing twenty-minute speech, interrupted only at one point by his swallowing a nitroglycerin pill. The opening of this latest collection of papers would provide, he hoped, the documentary evidence that would lead to positive judgments by future scholars. As he told the symposium audience, the cache of documents just released "holds most of myself and holds for me the most intimate meaning" of "anything in the library."[67] He said he didn't want to spend two days talking about what had already been done because not enough progress had been made and he himself was ashamed that in six years he had not been able to do more. The problem of black inequality was the "concern and responsibility" of the whole country. "The black problem," he declared, "remains what it has always been, the simple problem of being black in a white society. . . . To be black," he agreed, "is to be proud, is to be worthy, is to be honorable. But to be black in a white society is not to stand on level and equal ground. . . . Whites stand on history's mountain and blacks stand in history's hollow. . . ." It was important, he said, that "we get down to the business of trying to stand black and white on level ground. . . ." Once again he endorsed affirmative action, a policy he had first proposed in the Howard University speech of 1965. He called for programs that would help blacks gain equal footing, including scholarships, more minority trainees in labor unions, and stronger efforts by professional and business "to make sure that blacks qualify for advancement up the promotion ladder." He noted that some people would be shocked and dismayed at these proposals because they "ask that special considerations be given to black Americans rather than giving equal consideration to all Americans," but they were to be expected since he had spent a lifetime "listening to the language of evasion."

He concluded with the stirring words of Martin Luther King Jr., which he in turn had used to support the passage of the 1965 voting rights bill:

> We know there's injustice. We know there's intolerance. We know there's discrimination and hate and suspicion. And we know there's division among us. But there is a larger truth. We have proved that great progress is possible. We know how much still remains to be done. And if our efforts continue and if our will is strong and if our hearts are right and if courage remains our constant companion, then, my fellow Americans, I am confident we shall overcome.

Harry Middleton, now director of the LBJ Library, had wanted an unruffled conference and was dismayed when a group of civil right militants demanded a chance to denounce the racism of the Nixon administration. Middleton consulted Johnson, warning him that there might be a demonstration if the militants were not allowed time on the program. He was not afraid of a demonstration, Johnson responded. After all, he had seen lots of them. The dissenters should be given time to speak. "We're talking about equal rights," he said, "and I think that you and I would not really want people to leave here thinking that they were not going to get their chance to say something. So I think we ought to give them some time."[68]

When given the rostrum, the Rev. A. Kendall Smith of the New York Task Force on Racism and Roy Innis, national director of the Congress of Racial Equality attacked the conference for presenting only "establishment" viewpoints. They demanded an extension of the meeting or a follow-up session and asked that the participants make the symposium "more than an empty ritual honoring one man. . . ."[69] Smith added: "For the symposium not to expand and deal with a new definition of equality is to refuse the sun of a new day."[70] Then Clarence Mitchell of the NAACP scolded the radicals by pointing out that if Johnson had the bravery to "speak against white demagoguery," he, Mitchell, would, wherever he was, "speak against black demagoguery."[71]

At this point, adrenaline coursing through his tired, sick body, LBJ remounted the stage and gave a performance that belied his fatigue, his pain, his ill health. Using all his old political skills to bring the divided crowd together, he delivered a rousing exhortation for people to reason together. Like Ted Williams and his last at-bat home run, Johnson did what he had done so well at his best. Spicing his words with his favorite brand of folksy stories, he asked that everyone "counsel together," keeping cool and without anger and "finally come out with a program with objectives. . . ." He believed if they presented it to Nixon, "without starting off by saying he's terrible, because he doesn't think he's terrible . . ." they might be pleasantly surprised at his response. LBJ himself couldn't offer them "much go-go at this period" of his life, but he could "provide a lot of hope and dream and encouragement. . . ." He would even "sell a few wormy calves now and then and contribute. . . ." And "until every boy and girl born into this land, whatever state, whatever color, can stand on the same level ground, our job will not be done." He had hit the ball clear over the fence, and the crowd went wild. People rushed to the stage to congratulate him, to shake his hand and touch a piece of history. As Hugh Sidey said, "If any questions lingered about what Lyndon Johnson had tried to do for his country, they were answered right then."[72]

It took Johnson a while to recover from the symposium, but he was well enough to celebrate Lady Bird's sixtieth birthday on December 22. In observance of Christmas, their four grandchildren turned on the lights on a huge cedar tree across the river from the Ranch. Lady Bird would have fond memories of that last holiday season together. LBJ took his grandchildren for a ride in a lawn mower around the airplane terminal on the Ranch. They called him Boppa, and when he came out dressed like Santa Claus, one of them climbed up on his lap and exclaimed, "This isn't Santa Claus. It's Boppa!" Lady Bird would reminisce that they had "lived the last bit to the fullest."[73]

Three funerals marred Johnson's last weeks. One was for Hale Boggs, the prominent Democratic congressman from Louisiana, who had vanished on a plane flight to Alaska. Another was for a busload of Austin schoolchildren who had died in a crash on the way to a church affair. The third was for Harry Truman, who passed away the day after Christmas. Johnson, accompanied by Lady Bird, their two daughters, and two sons-in-law, flew to the funeral in Independence, Missouri. LBJ and President Nixon led the funeral procession at the Truman Library. Later, Johnson stood at Truman's casket with his head bowed. Lady Bird thought these occasions "very real, harrowing emotional experiences" that had added to the stress on his heart.[74]

In a last interview with Walter Cronkite, taped at the ranch ten days before his death, Johnson reviewed his entire civil rights record, including the period when he was not as active as he was later. Johnson explained that he had not always seen "the special plight of the black man as clearly . . ." as he had later in his political career. Cronkite asked him when he had had his "moment of revelation." In response, Johnson rehearsed his evolving recognition of the inequities suffered by people of color and included his experiences teaching in Cotulla when he got his "real deep first impressions of the prejudices that existed and the inequity of our school system between whites and browns." He learned more at the National Youth Administration when he dealt with young "blacks and browns" and "saw the inequalities of our system then." He talked about the necessity for compromise on civil rights, about the "half a loaf" 1957 civil rights bill, and about his difficulties with filibustering by southern senators. Cronkite recalled some of the criticism leveled against him for holding back when, for example, as vice president, he headed the president's Committee on Equal Employment Opportunity. Why had he not moved faster at these times? He did not have the votes or the power until he became president, he said. It was his realization that:

> I was the President of all the people and all the people were looking to me to correct the inequalities and inequities and injustices and there was something I could do about it, I concluded that now that I have the power I'm going to use it every way I could. . . .

In this last interview LBJ gave generous credit to Truman for much of the agenda of the Great Society, calling himself only the "catalyst" who happened to be there at the right time. The interview was a curious mixture of Johnsonian pride and self-abnegation.[75]

The Cronkite interview aside, the beginning of January was quiet for Johnson. He and former economic adviser Walter Heller visited Southwest Texas State University at San Marcos to take part in a seminar. Johnson also attended the inauguration in Austin of the new governor of Texas, Dolph Briscoe, on January 17. A staff photo in the *Austin American Statesman* shows Johnson at the event, head resting on his fist, looking tired and thoughtful. Citing health reasons, LBJ decided not to go to Washington for Nixon's second inaugural and chose instead to be with Lady Bird at a tree-planting ceremony on the road between the LBJ ranch and the state park.

On Wednesday the seventeenth, two Hill Country neighbors, Mr. and Mrs. J. O. Tanner, came for a visit. The Tanners feared that their church activities, which included public baptisms in the Pedernales River, would be adversely affected by the expansion of the LBJ historical park. Johnson reassured them that they need not worry and then told them he did not have much longer to live. Tanner, the church superintendent, said he didn't think Johnson was joking, and Mrs. Tanner remembered, "He said it three times."[76]

Johnson gave a different impression to Paul Bolton and his wife, who visited the ranch Friday night. For many years a news anchorman on KTBC, Bolton reported that LBJ was "just like his old self" during dinner.[77] Early on the morning of January 21, LBJ phoned Jack Valenti, who, like so many LBJ aides, had remained in Washington. Johnson talked about taking his annual vacation in Acapulco and invited Jack and his wife, Mary Margaret, to join him and Lady Bird. The two old associates spoke for about forty-five minutes, with Johnson complaining about his angina and hoping that he would feel better in Mexico. Joshing Valenti about golf, LBJ accused him of moving his ball in the rough. When Valenti denied it, Johnson kidded that he would get the Secret Service to put him "under heavy surveillance" so that when they next played he could "get the proof" on him.[78]

Dr. Hurst's prediction that no one would be able to save him when the next severe heart attack occurred proved correct. Lady Bird cooked breakfast for her husband on the morning of January 22. Finding him somewhat quiet but "in good spirits," she decided to drive to her office in the library in Austin. After Lady Bird left, Johnson spent some time on the phone with various aides and associates. Then Jewell Malechek, his foreman's wife, chauffeured him around the Ranch to inspect the fencing. Later, after lunch, Johnson went to his bedroom to take a nap.

At three-fifty he called the Ranch switchboard, specifically asking, without giving a reason, that Mike Howard, a Secret Service agent, come to his room "immediately." Howard was not there, but the operator called agents Ed Noland and Harry Harris, who rushed in with a portable oxygen machine. LBJ, his face "dark blue," was lying on the floor, next to his bed, on his back. He appeared to be dead, but Noland applied mouth-to-mouth resuscitation, while Harris called Dr. David Abbott in Johnson City to come at once. Four minutes after LBJ's call, Howard arrived and tried external heart massage. It did not help. Meanwhile, Lady Bird, who was in a car near the library, was informed by two-way radio that her husband had been stricken. Johnson was placed on a private plane with the three agents and Jewell Malechek and the doctor aboard and was flown to Brooke Army Hospital in San Antonio. The sad entourage touched down at 4:35 P.M., and Dr. Abbott pronounced him dead before they took the body off the plane. Lady Bird met the plane in San Antonio, flying in from Austin by helicopter.

Johnson's body was brought back to Austin to lie in state at the LBJ Library. There the Johnson family stood by the etched murals of Johnson and the four past presidents, where they greeted the people who came to pay their respects. Johnson's Texas friends and colleagues stood vigil by the coffin during the night. Thousands of ordinary Texans came to say good-bye. A Dallas woman said she had stood in line for about two hours. "I would have stood in it for another two hours," she added, "if necessary." Lady Bird was moved by all the tributes. "It is the hope of the Johnson family," she said, "that individuals will express their feelings by doing something in their own community to make life better . . . for those communities."[79]

On the afternoon of January 24, a cold but sunny day in Washington, the gray metal coffin was carried on a horse-drawn caisson from the White House to the Capitol. Black Jack, the same gelding who had pulled Jack Kennedy's coffin ten years before, followed behind, riderless with black boots placed backward in his stirrups. At the Capitol rotunda, Johnson lay in state for seventeen hours while President Nixon and the nation's leaders, as well as common folk whose lives Johnson tried so hard to improve, filed past the casket. His friend Jake Pickle, now congressman from Johnson's old district, gave a ten-minute eulogy, followed by Dean Rusk. The former secretary of state said that "a thousand years ago in more robust times he would have been called Lyndon the Liberator."[80] One of the most acute assessments was Hubert Humphrey's: "He could take a bite out of you bigger than a T-bone steak and the very next day he would put his arms around you like a long-lost brother."[81] Reporter Nancy Dickerson thought that "in death [his enemies] could not tarnish the moment which belonged to those loyalists who had stood by him through the years and knew how hard he had tried, especially on Vietnam. . . . No man could have tried harder."[82] Lady Bird was composed, but when she looked at the coffin, a reporter saw her face as "a special study in love and loss and acceptance. . . ."[83]

And then it was back to the Texas Hill Country for the last time. The motorcade carrying the body traveled from Austin to the banks of the Pedernales as relatives, neighbors, and friends looked on. Hundreds of people were present, including LBJ's eighty-nine-year-old aunt, Jessie Hermine Johnson Hatcher, the only surviving child of Grandfather Sam Ealy Johnson. A ninety-two-year-old black man was there, too. He told Luci that "a tree would have had to fall over me to keep me from being here today."[84]

LBJ was buried next to his grandparents and parents in the family plot to the singing of "The Battle Hymn of the Republic." His friend Father Wunibald Schneider, priest at the Stonewall Catholic church, gave a eulogy in his Hill Country German accent. Father Schneider called LBJ "an ordinary man" but one who "had an extraordinary love for each and every one of us."[85] Making it an ecumenical service, the Rev. Billy Graham gave a eulogy as well. Then it was the turn of Johnson's old friend and protégé John Connally: "Along this stream and under these trees he loved he will now rest. He first saw light here. He last felt life here. May he now find peace here."[86] Master Sergeant Patrick Mastroleo of the Third Infantry blew "Taps" on a bugle. Lyndon was laid to rest in the ground near an old oak tree.

The cease-fire agreement in Vietnam, concluded on January 13, was announced the day Johnson died.[†] Some in the media, preferring to see it as the final irony of his life, claimed that he had not known that the war that destroyed his presidency had ended. Lady Bird denied the story. The administration had kept the ex-president informed of the negotiations. "I think his friends should be told," she declared, "that fate was kind. Lyndon did know that peace had come."[87]

[†]It was not formally signed by the participants until January 27.

Notes

Chapter 1: Beginnings

1. Bill Porterfield, *LBJ Country* (Garden City, N.Y.: Doubleday, 1965), p. 1.
2. Ronnie Dugger, *The Politician: The Life and Times of Lyndon Johnson* (New York: W. W. Norton, 1982), p. 25.
3. Hugh Sidey, *A Very Personal Presidency: Lyndon Johnson in the White House* (New York: Atheneum, 1968), p. 14.
4. Dugger, op. cit., p. 61.
5. Robert A. Caro, *The Years of Lyndon Johnson: The Path to Power* (New York: Alfred A. Knopf, 1982), p .3. The story may be apocryphal. Another version has it that years later LBJ's grandfather wrote a friend: "My grandson is as smart as they come and I expect he'll be a Senator by the time he's forty." See Larry L. King, "Bringing Up Lyndon," *Texas Monthly* (January 1971), p. 85.
6. Dugger, op. cit., p. 55.
7. George Reedy, *Lyndon B. Johnson: A Memoir* (New York: Andrews & McMeel, 1982) p. 22.
8. Doris Kearns, *Lyndon Johnson and the American Dream* (New York: Harper & Row, 1976), p. 41.
9. Ibid., p. 42.
10. Rebekah Baines Johnson, *A Family Album* (New York: McGraw-Hill, 1965), p. 30.
11. Kearns, op. cit., p. 22.
12. Alfred Steinberg, *Sam Johnson's Boy: A Close-up of the President from Texas* (New York: Macmillan, 1968), p. 11.
13. Caro, op. cit., p. 53.
14. Johnson, op. cit., p. 30.
15. Paul Conkin, *Big Daddy from the Pedernales: Lyndon Baines Johnson* (Boston: Twayne, 1986), p. xi.
16. Johnson, op. cit., p. 18.
17. Kearns, op. cit., p. 27.
18. Caro, op. cit., p. 68.
19. Philip Rulon, ed., *Letters from the Hill Country: The Correspondence Between Rebekah and Lyndon Baines Johnson* (Austin, Tex.: Thorp Springs Press, 1982), p. 28.
20. Dugger, op. cit., pp. 60–61.
21. Rulon, op. cit., p.19.
22. Johnson, op. cit., photographic reproduction folio of pictures following p. 32.
23. Sigmund Freud, "On Narcissism: An Introduction," *The Standard Edition of the Complete Psychological Works of Sigmund Freud*, vol. 14 (London: Hogarth Press, 1957), p. 82.
24. Kearns, op. cit., pp. 24–25.
25. From a telephone interview with Isabelle Shelton, social reporter for the *Washington Star*, March 21, 1964. Transcribed in Michael Beschloss, ed., *Taking Charge: The Johnson White House Tapes, 1963–1964* (New York: Simon & Schuster, 1997), p. 295.
26. Ibid, p. 295.
27. Kearns, *op. cit.*, p. 25.
28. Ibid.

29. Beschloss, op. cit., pp. 295–296.

30. Larry King, "Bringing Up Lyndon," *Texas Monthly* (January 1971), p. 82.

31. Robert Dallek, *Lone Star Rising: Lyndon Johnson and His Times, 1908–1960* (New York: Oxford University Press, 1991), p. 49.

32. Dugger, op. cit., p. 84.

33. Clifford and Virginia Durr, *Oral History*, Tape 2, pp. 23–24, LBJ Library.

34. Kearns, op. cit., pp. 36–37.

35. Dugger, op. cit., p. 85.

36. Caro, op. cit., p. 84.

37. Steinberg, op. cit., pp. 3, 28.

38. Sam Houston Johnson, *My Brother Lyndon* (New York: Cowles, 1970), p. 10.

39. King, op. cit., p. 80.

40. Caro, op. cit., p. 131.

41. Ben Crider, *Oral History*, p. 9, LBJ Library.

42. Ibid., p. 2.

43. Dugger, op. cit., p. 79.

44. Quoted in Dugger, op. cit., p. 70

45. Kittie Clyde Leonard, *Oral History*, p. 8, LBJ Library.

46. Ibid., p. 13.

47. Dugger, op. cit., p. 89.

48. Kearns, op. cit., p. 24.

49. Dugger, op. cit., p. 87.

50. Rebekah Johnson, op. cit., p. 20.

51. Emmette Redford, *Oral History*, Interview 3, p. 15, LBJ Library.

52. Ibid., p. 21.

53. Kearns, op. cit., p. 40.

54. Sam Houston Johnson, op. cit., p. 22.

55. Kearns, op. cit., p. 43.

56. Sam Houston Johnson, op. cit., p. 23.

57. Caro, op. cit., p. 126

58. Kearns, op. cit., p. 44.

59. Steinberg, op. cit., p. 34

60. Rebekah Johnson, op. cit., p. 20.

61. Harry Provence, *Lyndon B. Johnson: A Biography* (New York: Fleet, 1964), p. 34.

62. Kearns, op. cit., p. 45.

Chapter 2: College

1. Doris Kearns, *Lyndon Johnson and the American Dream* (New York: Harper & Row, 1976), p. 46.

2. Ben Crider, *Oral History*, p. 7, LBJ Library.

3. Ella SoRelle Porter, *Oral History*, p. 23, LBJ Library.

4. Robert Caro, *The Years of Lyndon Johnson: The Path to Power* (New York: Alfred A. Knopf, 1982), p. 160. *College Star*, December 17, 1929. Willard Deason, another White Star member, much later, disputed this interpretation of Johnson during his college years. According to Deason, not many people caled Johnson "Bull," though he agreed that Johnson "bulled his way around campus all right." See Robert Hardesty, ed., *The Johnson Years: The Difference He Made* (Austin: Lyndon B. Johnson School of Public Affairs—University of Texas, 1993), p. 128.

5. Merle Miller, *Lyndon: An Oral Biography* (New York: G. P. Putnam's Sons, 1980), p. 28.

6. Ibid.

7. Harry Provence, *Lyndon B. Johnson: A Biography* (New York: Fleet, 1964), p. 35

8. William C. Pool, Emmie Craddock, and David Conrad, *Lyndon Baines Johnson: The Formative Years* (San Marcos, Tex.: Southwest Texas State College Press, 1965), p. 131. From the *College Star*, June 12, 1929, p. 2.

9. Caro, op. cit., p. 150.

10. Kearns, op. cit., p. 56.
11. Caro, op. cit., p. 163.
12. Sam Houston Johnson, *My Brother Lyndon* (New York: Cowles, 1970), p. 29.
13. Kearns, op. cit., p. 66.
14. Miller, op. cit., p. 33.
15. Ibid., p. 31.
16. Caro, op. cit., p. 173.
17. Pool et al., op. cit., p. 95. This was from an interview by Emmie Craddock of H. M. Greene, September 16, 1964.
18. Dugger, op. cit., p. 121.
19. Vernon Whiteside as quoted in Caro, op. cit., p. 176.
20. Ibid., p. 177.
21. Miller, op. cit., p. 30.
22. Caro, op. cit., p. 190.
23. Dugger, op. cit., p. 122.
24. Caro, op. cit., p. 195.
25. Merle Miller, op. cit., p. 37.
26. Alfred Steinberg, *Sam Johnson's Boy: A Close-up of the President from Texas* (New York: Macmillan, 1968), p. 52.
27. Caro, op. cit., p. 204.
28. Caro, op. cit., p. 198.
29. Ibid., p. 205.
30. Ella SoRelle Porter, *Oral History*, p. 27, LBJ Library.
31. Gene Latimer, *Oral History*, Interview 2, p. 1, LBJ Library.
32. Ibid., p. 25, LBJ Library.
33. Dugger, op. cit., p. 127.
34. Steinberg, op. cit., p. 66.

Chapter 3: Congressional Secretary

1. Doris Kearns, *Lyndon Johnson and the American Dream* (New York: Harper & Row, 1976), p. 70.
2. Ibid., p. 73.
3. Clarke Newlon, *LBJ: The Man from Johnson City* (New York: Dodd, Mead, 1964), p. 50.
4. Ronnie Dugger, *The Politician: The Life and Times of Lyndon Johnson: The Drive for Power, from the Frontier to Master of the Senate* (New York: W. W. Norton, 1982), p. 167.
5. Merle Miller, *Lyndon: An Oral Biography* (New York: G. P. Putnam's Sons, 1980), p. 40.
6. Dugger, op. cit., p. 172.
7. Alfred Steinberg, *Sam Johnson's Boy: A Close-up of the President from Texas* (New York: Macmillan, 1968), p. 69.
8. Miller, op. cit., p. 43.
9. Gene Latimer, *Oral History*, Interview 2, p. 51, LBJ Library.
10. Booth Mooney, *The Lyndon Johnson Story* (New York: Farrar, Straus, 1964), p. 18.
11. Miller, op. cit., p. 45.
12. Dugger, op. cit., p. 166.
13. Robert Caro, *The Years of Lyndon Johnson: The Path to Power* (New York: Alfred A. Knopf, 1982), p. 223.
14. Latimer, op. cit., p. 12.
15. Caro, op. cit., p. 233.
16. Miller, op. cit., p. 41.
17. Ibid., p. 43.
18. William S. White, *The Professional: Lyndon B. Johnson* (Boston: Houghton Mifflin, 1964), p. 109.
19. Philip Rulon, *The Compassionate Samaritan: The Life of Lyndon Baines Johnson* (Chicago: Nelson-Hall, 1981), p. 49.
20. Caro, op. cit., p. 286.

21. Ibid., p. 263.

22. Ibid., p. 276.

23. Steinberg, op. cit., pp. 91–92.

24. Miller, op. cit., p. 41.

25. Ibid., p. 50.

26. Letter, James C. Patillo to Mrs. Lyndon Johnson, October 28, 1955, Papers of James Cato Patillo, LBJ Library.

27. Miller, op. cit., p. 49.

28. Lewis Gould, *Lady Bird Johnson and the Environment* (Lawrence, Kans.: University Press of Kansas, 1988), p. 10.

29. Eric Goldman, *The Tragedy of Lyndon Johnson* (New York: Alfred A. Knopf, 1969), p. 343.

30. Dugger, op. cit., p. 176.

31. Ibid., p. 177.

32. Ibid., p. 177.

33. Kearns, op. cit., p. 80.

34. Caro, op cit., pp. 299–300.

35. Miller, op. cit., p. 44.

36. Dugger, op. cit., p. 179.

37. Miller, op. cit., p. 44.

38. Kearns, op. cit., p. 82.

39. Dugger, op. cit., p. 180.

40. Caro, op. cit., p. 301.

41. Goldman, op. cit., p. 346.

42. Dugger, op. cit., p. 181.

43. Ibid.

44. Gould, op. cit., p. 16.

45. Goldman, op. cit., p. 345.

46. Marie D. Smith, *The President's Lady: An Intimate Biography of Mrs. Lyndon B. Johnson* (New York: Random House, 1964), p. 57.

47. Goldman, op. cit., p. 243.

48. Paul Conkin, *Big Daddy from the Pedernales: Lyndon Baines Johnson* (Boston: Twayne, 1986), p. 72.

Chapter 4: Young Bureaucrat

1. Letter, [Mamie S. Kleberg] to Lyndon Johnson, [April 25?, 1932], Pre-Presidential Confidential File, Box 2, LBJ Library.

2. Merle Miller, *Lyndon: An Oral Biography* (New York: G. P. Putnam's Sons, 1980), p. 54.

3. Ronnie Dugger, *The Politician: The Life and Times of Lyndon Johnson: The Drive for Power, from the Frontier to Master of the Senate* (New York: W. W. Norton, 1982), p. 185.

4. Miller, op. cit., p. 54.

5. Jesse Kellam, *Oral History*, Interview 1, p. 6, LBJ Library.

6. Miller, op. cit., p. 56.

7. Alfred Steinberg, *Sam Johnson's Boy: A Close-up of the President from Texas* (New York: Macmillan, 1968), p. 96.

8. Robert Caro, *The Years of Lyndon Johnson: The Path to Power* (New York: Alfred A. Knopf, 1982), p. 368.

9. Philip Rulon, *The Compassionate Samaritan: The Life of Lyndon Baines Johnson* (Chicago: Nelson-Hall, 1981), p. 60.

10. Kellam, op. cit., p. 18.

11. Ibid., p. 19.

12. Dugger, op. cit., p. 189.

13. Caro, op. cit., p. 360.

14. Doris Kearns, *Lyndon Johnson and the American Dream* (New York: Harper & Row, 1976), p. 86.

15. Steinberg, op. cit., p. 107.

16. Kearns, op. cit., p. 86.

17. Sam Houston Johnson, *My Brother Lyndon* (New York: Cowles, 1970), p. 54.

18. Dugger, op. cit., footnote 3, p. 434.

19. Miller, op. cit., p. 60.

20. Steinberg, op. cit., p. 111.

21. Dugger, op. cit., p. 196.

22. Ibid., p. 199.

23. Kellam, op. cit., p. 22, LBJ Library.

24. *New York Times* (April 11, 1937).

25. Hugh Sidey, *A Very Personal President: Lyndon Johnson in the White House* (New York: Atheneum, 1968), p. 13.

26. Dugger, op. cit., p. 200.

27. Ibid., p. 202.

28. Ibid.

29. Kearns, op. cit., p. 89.

30. Clarke Newlon, *LBJ: The Man from Johnson City* (New York: Dodd, Mead, 1964), p. 72.

31. Miller, op. cit., p. 22.

Chapter 5: New Deal Congressman

1. Campaign memo, 1937, Box 1, Johnson House Papers, LBJ Library.

2. Robert Caro, *The Years of Lyndon Johnson: The Path to Power* (New York: Alfred A. Knopf, 1982), p. 494.

3. Alfred Steinberg, *Sam Johnson's Boy: A Close-up of the President from Texas* (New York: Macmillan, 1968), p. 128.

4. Merle Miller, *Lyndon: An Oral Biography* (New York: G. P. Putnam's Sons, 1980), p. 74.

5. Ibid., p. 72.

6. Caro, op. cit., p. 501.

7. Ibid., p. 460.

8. Ibid., p. 461.

9. Ronnie Dugger, *The Politician: The Life and Times of Lyndon Johnson* (New York: W. W. Norton, 1982), p. 209.

10. Caro, op. cit., p. 471.

11. Paul Conkin, *Big Daddy from the Pedernales: Lyndon Baines Johnson* (Boston: Twayne, 1986), p. 93.

12. Miller, op. cit., p. 71.

13. Steinberg, op. cit., p. 133.

14. Rebekah Baines Johnson, *Letters from the Hill Country: The Correspondence Between Rebekah and Lyndon Baines Johnson*, edited by Philip Rulon (Austin: Thorp Springs Press, 1982), p. 49.

15. Dugger, op. cit., p. 216.

16. Clifford and Virginia Durr, *Oral History*, Tape 1, p. 24, LBJ Library.

17. Dugger, op. cit., p. 207.

18. D. B. Hardeman and Donald C. Bacon, *Rayburn: A Biography* (Austin: Texas Monthly Press, 1987), p. 237.

19. Steinberg, op. cit., p. 135.

20. Ibid., p. 139.

21. Ibid., p. 129.

22. Joseph Rauh Jr., *Oral History*, Interview 1, p. 2, LBJ Library.

23. Robert Caro, "The Johnson Years: Johnson Goes to War," *New Yorker* (November 6, 1989), p. 72.

24. Ibid., p. 93.

25. Caro, *The Years of Lyndon Johnson*, p. 541.

26. Clifford and Virginia Durr, *Oral History*, Tape 1, p. 7, LBJ Library.

27. Caro, *The Years of Lyndon Johnson*, p. 453.

28. Ibid.

29. Caro, "The Johnson Years," p. 72.

30. Nancy Dickerson, *Among Those Present: A Reporter's View of Twenty-five Years in Washington* (New York: Random House, 1976), pp. 138–139.

31. Ingrid Winther Scobie, *Center Stage: Helen Gahagan Douglas, A Life* (New York: Oxford University Press, 1992), p. 172.

32. Walter Jenkins, *Oral History*, Interview 3, p. 9, LBJ Library.

33. Ibid., pp. 25, 27.

34. Caro, *The Years of Lyndon Johnson*, p. 482.

35. Ibid., pp. 476–492.

36. Conkin, op. cit., p. 293.

37. Robert Dallek reports the incident based on his 1988 interview with John Connally. See Dallek, *Lone Star Rising: Lyndon Johnson and His Times, 1908–1960* (New York: Oxford University Press, 1991), p. 190.

38. Dickerson, loc.. cit.

39. Clifford and Virginia Durr, *Oral History*, Tape 1, p. 25, LBJ Library.

40. Eric Goldman, *The Tragedy of Lyndon Johnson* (New York: Alfred A. Knopf, 1969), p. 351.

41. Ibid.

42. *Time* (March 20, 1939).

43. Miller, op. cit., p. 75.

44. Ibid.

Chapter 6: Rehearsal for the Senate

1. Robert Dallek, *Lone Star Rising: Lyndon Johnson and His Times, 1908–1960* (New York: Oxford University Press, 1991), p. 198.

2. Alfred Steinberg, *Sam Johnson's Boy: A Close-up of the President from Texas* (New York: Macmillan, 1968), p. 145.

3. *New York Times* (April 30 and May 1, 1940).

4. Robert Caro, *The Years of Lyndon Johnson: The Path to Power* (New York: Alfred A. Knopf, 1982), p. 598.

5. Jerry Sinise and Jackie Pruett, *Lyndon Baines Johnson Remembered* (Austin: Eakin Press, 1985), p. 44.

6. Ronnie Dugger, *The Politician: The Life and Times of Lyndon Johnson: The Drive for Power, from the Frontier to Master of the Senate* (New York: W. W. Norton, 1982), p. 224.

7. Caro, op. cit., p. 629.

8. Ibid., p. 630.

9. Ibid, p. 637.

10. Ibid., p. 632.

11. Merle Miller, *Lyndon: An Oral Biography* (New York: G. P. Putnam's Sons, 1980), p. 76.

12. Joe B. Frantz, *Thirty-seven Years of Public Service: The Honorable Lyndon B. Johnson* (Austin: Shoal Creek Publishing Company, 1974), p. 95.

13. Sinise and Pruett, op. cit., p. 46.

14. Miller, op. cit., p. 77.

15. Ibid., p. 81.

16. Booth Mooney, *The Lyndon Johnson Story* (New York: Farrar, Straus, 1964), pp. 39–40.

17. Philip Rulon, *The Compassionate Samaritan: The Life of Lyndon Baines Johnson* (Chicago: Nelson-Hall, 1981), p. 78.

18. Steinberg, op. cit., p. 162.

19. Dugger, op. cit. p. 226.

20. Miller, op. cit., p. 83.

21. Steinberg, op. cit., pp. 164–165.

22. Caro, op. cit., p. 678.

23. Dallek, op. cit., p. 214.

24. Steinberg, op. cit., pp. 165–166.

25. Rowland Evans and Robert Novak, *Lyndon B. Johnson: The Exercise of Power* (New York: New American Library, 1966), p. 14.

26. Dallek, op. cit., p. 215.

27. Mooney, op. cit., p. 43.

28. Caro, op. cit., p. 704.

29. Mary Rather, *Oral History*, Interview 2, p. 19, LBJ Library.

30. Caro, op. cit., p. 711.

31. Miller, op. cit., p. 84.

32. *New York Times* (July 6, 1970).

33. Dugger, op. cit., p. 229.

34. Ibid., p. 228.

35. Dallek, op. cit., p. 221.

36. Miller, op. cit., p. 87.

37. Walter Jenkins, *Oral History*, Interview 1, p. 15, LBJ Library.

38. James H. Rowe Jr., *Oral History*, Interview 1, p. 16, LBJ Library.

Chapter 7: Time Out for War

1. Marie Smith, *The President's Lady: An Intimate Biography of Mrs. Lyndon B. Johnson* (New York: Random House, 1964), p. 59.

2. Doris Kearns, *Lyndon Johnson and the American Dream* (New York: Harper & Row, 1976), p. 94.

3. Merle Miller, *Lyndon: An Oral Biography* (New York: G. P. Putnam's Sons, 1980), p. 89.

4. Alfred Steinberg, *Sam Johnson's Boy: A Close-up of the President from Texas* (New York: Macmillan, 1968), p. 187.

5. Miller, op. cit., p. 89.

6. *New York Times* (August 22, 1941).

7. Kearns, op. cit., p. 95.

8. Robert Dallek, *Lone Star Rising: Lyndon Johnson and His Times, 1908–1960* (New York: Oxford University Press, 1991), p. 230.

9. Kurt Singer and Jane Sherrod, *Lyndon Baines Johnson: Man of Reason* (Minneapolis: T. S. Denison, 1964), p. 156.

10. James Reston Jr., *The Lone Star: The Life of John Connally* (New York: Harper & Row, 1989), p. 75.

11. Ibid., p. 76.

12. Ronnie Dugger, *The Politician: The Life and Times of Lyndon Johnson* (New York: W. W. Norton, 1982), p. 242.

13. Martin Caidin and Edward Hymoff, *The Mission* (Philadelphia: J. B. Lippincott, 1964), p. 41.

14. Letter, Charles Marsh to Lyndon Johnson, May 20, 1942, Pre-Presidential Confidential, Box 3, LBJ Library.

15. Reston, op. cit., p. 81.

16. Caidin and Hymoff, loc. sit.

17. Ibid., p. 79.

18. Ibid., pp. 119, 125.

19. Ibid., pp. 167–168.

20. Booth Mooney, *The Lyndon Johnson Story* (New York: Farrar, Straus, 1964), p. 46.

21. Dallek, op. cit., p. 239.

22. Dugger, op. cit., p. 249.

23. James Rowe, *Oral History*, Tape 1, Interview 5, p. 19, LBJ Library.

24. Dugger, op. cit., p. 251.

25. Dugger, op. cit., p. 251.

26. Caidin and Hymoff, op. cit., pp. 195–196.

27. Clarke Newlon, *LBJ: The Man from Johnson City* (New York: Dodd, Mead, 1964), p. 104.

28. Steinberg, op. cit., p. 198.

29. Philip Reed Rulon, *The Compassionate Samaritan: The Life of Lyndon Baines Johnson* (Chicago: Nelson-Hall, 1981), p. 86.

30. Miller, op. cit., p. 102.

31. Dugger, op. cit., p. 266.

32. Ibid., p. 268.

33. Ibid., p. 269.
34. Robert Caro, *New Yorker* (December 18, 1989), p. 52f.
35. Ibid., p. 58.
36. Miller, op. cit., p. 108.
37. Walter Jenkins, *Oral History*, Interview 7, p. 8, LBJ Library.
38. Dugger, op. cit., p. 273.
39. Ibid., p. 255.
40. Dugger, op. cit., p. 255.
41. Steinberg, op. cit., p. 283.
42. "Lady Bird Johnson: The Texas Wildflower," *Biography*, ABC News Productions.

Chapter 8: "Landslide Lyndon"

1. Alfred Steinberg, *Sam Johnson's Boy: A Close-up of the President from Texas* (New York: Macmillan, 1968), p. 213.
2. Ibid., pp. 216–219.
3. William S. White, "Texan Tells Grief of 'Young Guard,'" *New York Times* (April 13, 1945).
4. Booth Mooney, *The Lyndon Johnson Story* (New York: Farrar, Straus, 1964), p. 53.
5. Robert Caro, *The Years of Lyndon Johnson: Means of Ascent* (New York: Alfred A. Knopf, 1990), p. 122.
6. Clark Clifford, *Counsel to the President: A Memoir* (New York: Random House, 1991), p. 387.
7. Merle Miller, *Lyndon: An Oral Biography* (New York: G. P. Putnam's Sons, 1980), p. 111.
8. Ibid., p. 114.
9. Ronnie Dugger, *The Politician: The Life and Times of Lyndon Johnson* (New York: W. W. Norton, 1982), p. 299.
10. Philip Rulon, *The Compassionate Samaritan: The Life of Lyndon Baines Johnson* (Chicago: Nelson-Hall, 1981), p. 101.
11. *Congressional Record*, 79th Cong., 2nd sess. (April 13, 1946), pp. 2154–2155.
12. Miller, op. cit., p. 113.
13. Caro, op. cit., p. 136.
14. Dugger, op. cit., p. 305.
15. *Congressional Record*, 80th Cong., 1st sess. (May 7, 1947), pp. 842–843.
16. *Congressional Record*, 80th Cong., 2nd sess. (March 5, 1948), p. 1056.
17. Dugger, op. cit., p. 106.
18. Caro, op. cit., p. 37.
19. Rebekah Baines Johnson, *A Family Album* (New York: McGraw-Hill, 1965), pp. 18–19.
20. *Dallas News* (June 1, 1946), quoted in Seth McKay, *Texas and the Fair Deal* (San Antonio: Naylor, 1954), p. 165.
21. Doris Kearns, *Lyndon Johnson and the American Dream* (New York: Harper & Row, 1976), p. 100.
22. Steinberg, op. cit., p. 238.
23. Miller, op. cit., p. 117; James Reston Jr., *Lone Star: The Life of John Connally* (New York: Harper & Row, 1989), p. 124.
24. McKay, op. cit., p. 167.
25. Steinberg, op. cit., p. 241.
26. Mooney, op. cit., p. 56.
27. Dugger, op. cit., p. 309.
28. Miller, op. cit., p. 118.
29. Reston, op. cit., p., 130.
30. Miller, op. cit., p. 120.
31. Ibid.
32. *Houston Post* (June 8, 1948).
33. Dugger, op. cit., p. 316.
34. Miller, op. cit., p. 122.
35. *Dallas News* (August 21, 1948).

36. *Austin American* (August 25, 1948).

37. Sam Houston Johnson, *My Brother Lyndon* (New York: Cowles, 1970), p. 77.

38. Caro, op. cit., p. 380.

39. Dugger, op. cit., p. 338.

40. Bruce Allen Murphy, *Fortas: The Rise and Ruin of a Supreme Court Justice* (New York: William Morrow, 1988), p. 91.

41. Reston, op. cit., p. 155.

Chapter 9: Freshman Senator

1. Booth Mooney, *The Lyndon Johnson Story* (New York: Farrar, Straus, 1964), p. 65.

2. Harry Provence, *Lyndon B. Johnson: A Biography* (New York: Fleet, 1964), pp. 87–88.

3. Ronnie Dugger, *The Politician: The Life and Times of Lyndon Johnson* (New York: W. W. Norton, 1982), p. 344.

4. Merle Miller, *Lyndon: An Oral Biography* (New York: G. P. Putnam's Sons, 1980), pp. 142–143.

5. Dugger, loc. cit.

6. Provence, op. cit., p. 86.

7. Doris Kearns, *Lyndon Johnson and the American Dream* (New York: Harper & Row, 1976), p. 103.

8. Ibid., p. 104.

9. Ibid., p. 105.

10. Miller, op. cit., p. 141.

11. *Congressional Record*, 81st Cong., 1st sess. (March 9, 1949), pp. 2012–2019.

12. Dugger, op. cit., p. 345.

13. Monroe Billington, "Lyndon Johnson and Blacks: The Early Years," *Journal of Negro History*, vol. LXII, no. 1 (January 1977), p. 38

14. Letter, Lyndon Johnson to David Botter, January 21, 1949, Pre-Presidential Confidential, Box 3, LBJ Library.

15. Dugger, op. cit., p. 346.

16. Paul Douglas, *Oral History*, pp.1–2, LBJ Library.

17. Walter Jenkins, *Oral History*, Interview 9, Tape 2, p. 27, LBJ Library.

18. James Rowe, *Oral History*, Interview 5, tape 1, pp. 36–37.

19. Miller, op. cit., p. 146.

20. Robert Engler, *The Politics of Oil: A Study of Private Power and Democratic Directions* (Chicago: University of Chicago Press, 1961), p. 319.

21. Dugger, op. cit., p. 352.

22. Steinberg, op. cit., pp. 296–297.

23. Dugger, op. cit., p. 354.

24. Harry McPherson, *Oral History*, Interview 1, Tape 1, p. 21, LBJ Library.

25. Michael Janeway, "Lyndon Johnson and the Rise of Conservatism in Texas," an honors thesis for B.A. at Harvard University (1962), p. 21.

26. Eric Goldman, *The Tragedy of Lyndon Johnson* (New York: Alfred A. Knopf, 1969), pp. 380–381.

27. *Congressional Record*, 81st Cong., 2nd sess. (July 12, 1950), p. 9988.

28. *Congressional Record*, 81st Cong., 2nd sess. (July 12, 1950), pp. 9988–9989.

29. Alfred Steinberg, *Sam Johnson's Boy: A Close-up of the President from Texas* (New York: Macmillan, 1968), p. 305.

30. *New York Times Magazine* (June 17, 1951).

31. *Congressional Record*, 82nd Cong., 2nd sess. (December 12, 1950), p. 16458.

32. *New York Times*, May 19, 1951.

33. *Congressional Record*, 82nd Cong., 1st sess. (January 5, 1951), p. A38

34. Jenkins, op. cit., Interview 10, Tape 1, p. 30, LBJ Library.

35. Marie Smith, *The President's Lady* (New York: Random House, 1964), p. 207.

36. Ibid., p. 206.

37. Jenkins, op. cit., Interview 11, p. 3, LBJ Library.

38. Steinberg, op. cit., p. 323.

39. Ibid., p. 324.

40. Ibid., p. 326.
41. Alfred Steinberg, *Sam Rayburn: A Biography* (New York: Hawthorn, 1975), p. 275.
42. Dugger, op. cit., footnote 11, p. 471.
43. Mooney, op. cit, p,. 85.
44. Miller, op. cit., p. 153.

Chapter 10: Minority Leader

1. Sam Houston Johnson, *My Brother Lyndon* (New York: Cowles, 1970), p. 82.
2. Booth Mooney, *The Politicians: 1945–1960* (Philadelphia: J. B. Lippincott, 1970), p. 172.
3. Bobby Baker and Larry King, *Wheeling and Dealing: Confessions of a Capitol Hill Operator* (New York: W. W. Norton, 1978), p. 37.
4. Letter, Lyndon Johnson to Baker, February 10, 1953, Pre-Presidential Confidential File, Box 1, LBJ Library.
5. Letter, Robert Baker to Stewart Alsop, May 23, 1955, Pre-Presidential Confidential File, Box 1, LBJ Library.
6. Ronnie Dugger, *The Politician: The Life and Times of Lyndon Johnson* (New York: W. W. Norton, 1982), p. 379.
7. Ibid., p. 380.
8. *New York Times* (January 3, 1953).
9. Doris Kearns, *Lyndon Johnson and the American Dream* (New York: Harper & Row, 1976), p. 132.
10. Merle Miller, *Lyndon: An Oral Biography* (New York: G. P. Putnam's Sons, 1980), p. 155.
11. Kearns, op. cit., pp. 132–133.
12. Joseph Rauh, *Oral History*, Interview 1, p. 14, LBJ Library.
13. Miller, op. cit., p. 156.
14. Mooney, op. cit., p. 90.
15. Kearns, op. cit., pp. 113–114.
16. Robert Mann, *The Walls of Jericho: Lyndon Johnson, Hubert Humphrey, Richard Russell, and the Struggle for Civil Rights* (New York: Harcourt, Brace, 1996), p. 155.
17. Baker and King, op. cit., p. 70.
18. *New York Times* (April 20, 1953).
19. Ibid (July 28, 1953).
20. Mooney, op. cit., p. 97.
21. Dwight D. Eisenhower, *Waging Peace, 1956–1961* (Garden City, N.Y.: Doubleday, 1965), p. 593, footnote.
22. Stephen Ambrose, *Eisenhower: The President* (New York: Simon & Schuster, 1984), p. 155.
23. Baker and King, op. cit., p. 90.
24. Alfred Steinberg, *Sam Johnson's Boy: A Close-up of the President from Texas* (New York: Macmillan, 1968), p. 360.
25. Booth Mooney memo to Lyndon Johnson, April 4, 1954, Pre-Presidential Memo File, Box 2, LBJ Library.
26. *New York Times* (May 7, 1954).
27. Sam Houston Johnson, op. cit., p. 90.
28. Baker and King, op. cit., p. 94.
29. Miller, op. cit., p. 162.
30. Miller, op. cit., p. 166.
31. Rowland Evans and Robert Novak, *Lyndon B. Johnson: The Exercise of Power* (New York: New American Library, 1966), p. 82.
32. David Oshinsky, *A Conspiracy So Immense: The World of Joe McCarthy* (New York: Free Press, 1983), p. 377.
33. Evans and Novak, op. cit., p. 85.
34. Robert Mann, op. cit., p. 137.
35. Robert Hardesty, ed., *The Johnson Years: The Difference He Made* (Austin: Lyndon Baines Johnson Library, 1993), p. 145.

36. Steinberg, op. cit., p. 380.

37. *Congressional Record*, 83rd Cong., 1st sess. (February 16, 1953), p. 1097.

38. Memo, Jake Pickle to Lyndon Johnson, April 5, 1954, Pre-Presidential Memo File, Box 2, LBJ Library.

39. Memo to Senator Johnson, Pre-Presidential Memo File, Box 2, LBJ Library.

40. *New Republic* (August 9, 1954), p. 7.

41. Ibid.

42. *New York Times* (October 29, 1954).

Chapter 11: Majority Leader

1. *Newsweek* (June 27, 1955), p.24.

2. Richard Neuberger, "Making a Scapegoat of Lyndon Johnson," *New Republic* (July 4, 1955), p. 9.

3. Robert Mann, *The Walls of Jericho: Lyndon Johnson, Hubert Humphrey, Richard Russell, and the Struggle for Civil Rights* (New York: Harcourt, Brace, 1996), p. 147.

4. Harry McPherson, *Oral History*, Tape 1, p. 4, LBJ Library.

5. Merle Miller, *Lyndon: An Oral Biography* (New York: G. P. Putnam's Sons, 1980), p. 175.

6. *New York Times* (March 13, 1955).

7. *Newsweek* (June 20, 1955).

8. Miller, op. cit., p. 178.

9. Ibid.

10. "The Texan Who Is Jolting Washington," *Newsweek* (June 27, 1955), pp. 24–26.

11. McPherson, op. cit., p. 17.

12. Miller, op. cit., p. 174.

13. Alfred Steinberg, *Sam Johnson's Boy: A Close-up of the President from Texas* (New York: Macmillan, 1968), p. 454

14. Miller, op. cit., p. 175.

15. *New York Times* (July 4, 1955).

16. *Congressional Record*, 84th Cong., 1st sess., (September 28, 1955), p. 555.

17. Roland Evans and Rober Novak, *Lyndon B. Johnson: The Experience of Power* (New York: New American Library, 1966), p. 91.

18. Ibid.

19. Walter Jenkins, *Oral History*, Interview 14, p. 6, LBJ Library.

20. *New York Times* (July 2, 1955).

21. Steinberg, op. cit., p. 418.

22. Booth Mooney, *The Lyndon Johnson Story* (New York: Farrar, Straus, 1964), p. 137.

23. James Cain, *Oral History*, p. 13, LBJ Library.

24. *Newsweek* (Novermber 7, 1955).

25. Jenkins, op. cit., p. 14.

26. Letter, Juanita [Roberts] to Senator [Lyndon Johnson], Washington, D.C., July 30, 1956, Pre-Presidential Memo File, Box 4, LBJ Library.

27. Letter, Lyndon B. Johnson to Dorothy Nichols, September 16, 1955, Pre-Presidential Memo File, Box 1, LBJ Library.

28. Memo, Booth Mooney to Johnson, August 11, 1955, Pre-Presidential Memo File, Box 3, LBJ Library.

29. Memo, George Reedy to Johnson, August 19, 1955, Pre-Presidential Memo File, Box 3, LBJ Library.

30. Letter, Robert Baker to Lyndon Johnson, November 22, 1955, Pre-Presidential Confidential File, Box 1, LBJ Library.

31. *New York Times* (November 23, 1955).

32. Evans and Novak, op. cit., p. 153.

33. Letter, Robert Baker to Lyndon Johnson, December 20, 1955, Pre-Presidential Confidential File, Box 1, LBJ Library.

34. *New York Times* (January 2, 1956).

35. James Rowe, *Oral History*, Interview 1, Tape 1, p. 27, LBJ Library.

36. William S. White, *New York Times* (March 11, 1956).

37. Document quoted in *New York Times* (March 12, 1956).

38. Bobby Baker and Larry King, *Wheeling and Dealing: Confessions of a Capitol Hill Operator* (New York: W. W. Norton, 1978), p. 71.

39. William S. White, *The Professional: Lyndon B. Johnson* (Boston: Houghton Mifflin, 1964), p. 211.

40. Merle Miller, op. cit., pp. 187–188.

41. *New York Times* (July 23, 1956).

42. Miller, op. cit., p. 190.

43. White, op. cit., p. 212.

44. *New York Times* (March 24, 1956).

45. Miller, op. cit., p. 194.

46. George Reedy, *Lyndon Johnson: A Memoir* (New York: Andrews & McMeel, 1982), p. xiv.

47. *New York Times* (August 16, 1956).

48. *Life* (May 21, 1956).

49. Booth Mooney, *The Polticians, 1945–1960* (Philadelphia: Lippincott, 1970), pp. 245–246.

50. Robert Dallek, *Lone Star Rising: Lyndon Johnson and His Times, 1906–1960* (New York: Oxford University Press, 1991), p. 503.

51. Steinberg, op. cit., p. 442.

52. Dallek, op. cit., p. 505.

53. Memo, George Reedy to LBJ, 1956, Pre-Presidential Memo File, Box 4, LBJ Library.

54. Evans and Novak, op. cit., p. 242.

55. Memo, Bill Brammer to Senator Johnson, March 13, 1957, Pre-Presidential Memo File, Box 5, LBJ Library.

56. *New York Times* (November 10 and December 9, 1956).

57. Harry McPherson, *Oral History*, Tape 1, p. 10, LBJ Library.

58. Merle Miller, op. cit., p. 202.

59. Doris Kearns, *Lyndon Johnson and the American Dream* (New York: Harper & Row, 1976), p. 153.

60. Memo, George Reedy to LBJ, December 7, 1956, Pre-Presidential Memo File, Box 4, LBJ Library.

Chapter 12: The Civil Rights Act of 1957

1. Rowland Evans and Robert Novak, *Lyndon B. Johnson: The Exercise of Power* (New York: New American Library, 1966), p. 174.

2. Ibid., p. 176.

3. *New York Times* (January 8, 1957).

4. Ibid. (February 18, 1957).

5. Robert Dallek, *Lone Star Rising: Lyndon Johnson and His Times, 1908–1960* (New York: Oxford University Press, 1991), p. 512.

6. Harry McPherson, *Oral History*, LBJ Library, Interview 2, p. 33.

7. *New York Times* (January 17, 1957).

8. *New York Times* (January 25, 1957), news conference.

9. Dallek, op. cit., p. 514.

10. Alfred Steinberg, *Sam Johnson's Boy: A Close-up of the President from Texas* (New York: Macmillan, 1968), p. 475.

11. Dwight D. Eisenhower, *Waging Peace, 1956–1961* (Garden City, N.Y.: Doubleday, 1965), p. 129.

12. *New York Times* (January 11, 1957).

13. Ibid. (January 12, 1957).

14. Douglass Cater, "How the Senate Passed the Civil Rights Bill," *The Reporter* (September 5, 1957), pp. 9–10.

15. *New York Times* (January 13, 1957).

16. Harry McPherson, *A Political Education: A Washington Memoir* (Austin: University of Texas Press, 1995) p. 153.

17. *New York Times* (March 17, 1957).

18. Ibid. (July 8, 1957).

19. Robert Mann, *The Walls of Jericho: Lyndon Johnson, Hubert Humphrey, Richard Russell, and the Struggle for Civil Rights* (New York: Harcourt, Brace, 1996), p. 193.

20. Ibid., p. 195.

21. Merle Miller, *Lyndon: An Oral Biography* (New York: G. P. Putnam's Sons, 1980), p. 206.

22. *New York Times* (July 8, 1957).

23. Evans and Novak, op. cit., p. 127

24. Stephen E. Ambrose, *Eisenhower: Volume Two, The President* (New York: Simon & Schuster, 1984), p. 407.

25. *New York Times* (July 11, 1957).

26. Ibid. (July 17, 1957).

27. Miller, op. cit., p. 207.

28. Evans and Novak, op. cit., p. 133.

29. Steinberg, op. cit., p. 471.

30. Cater, loc. cit.

31. *New York Times* (July 28, 1957).

32. Cater, op. cit., p. 10.

33. Steinberg, op. cit., p. 473.

34. Mann, op. cit., p. 217.

35. Evans and Novak, op. cit., p. 139.

36. Mann, op. cit., p. 217.

37. Miller, op. cit., p. 211.

38. Letter, Lyndon Johnson to Bobby Baker, September 10, 1957, Pre-Presidential Confidential File, Box 1, LBJ Library.

39. *Congressional Record*, 85th Cong., 1st sess. (August 7, 1957), p. 13997.

40. Miller, op. cit., p. 212.

41. Lyndon Baines Johnson, *The Vantage Point: Perspectives of the Presidency, 1963–1969* (New York: Holt, Rinehart, & Winston, 1971), p. 272.

42. *Time* (October 21, 1957).

43. Ibid., p. 274.

44. George Reedy, *Lyndon B. Johnson: A Memoir* (New York: Andrews & McMeel, 1982), p. 13.

45. Dallek, op. cit., p. 535.

46. Evans and Novak, op. cit., p. 196.

Chapter 13: To Run or Not to Run

1. Harry McPherson, *Oral History*, Interview 1, Tape 1, p. 25, LBJ Library.

2. George Reedy, *Oral History*, Interview 16, p. 15, LBJ Library.

3. Ibid., Interview 14, p. 34.

4. Ibid., Interview 15, p. 28.

5. *Congressional Record*, 85th Cong., 2nd Sess. (November 12, 1958), p. 455.

6. *Congressional Record*, 86th Cong., 1st Sess. (February 23, 1959), p. 1294.

7. Robert Mann, *The Walls of Jericho: Lyndon Johnson, Hubert Humphrey, Richard Russell, and the Struggle for Civil Rights* (New York: Harcourt, Brace, 1996), p. 242.

8. *New York Times* (May 29, 1959).

9. Robert L. Riggs, "The South Could Rise Again: Lyndon Johnson and Others" in Eric Sevareid, ed., *Candidates 1960* (New York: Basic Books, 1959), p. 311.

10. Doris Kearns, *Lyndon Johnson and the American Dream* (New York: Harper & Row, 1976), p. 136.

11. Rowland Evans and Robert Novak, *Lyndon B. Johnson: The Exercise of Power* (New York: New American Library, 1966), p. 205.

12. Robert Dallek, *Lone Star Rising: Lyndon Johnson and His Times, 1908–1960* (New York: Oxford University Press, 1991), p. 550.

13. *New York Times* (April 4, 1959).

14. Ibid. (June 14, 1959).

15. Ibid. (June 23, 1959).

16. Ibid. (June 24, 1959).

17. Arthur Krock, "Butler Needs Allies in Democratic Battle," *New York Times* (July 19, 1959).

18. Dallek, op. cit., p. 553.

19. *New York Times* (June 25, 1959).

20. Dallek, op. cit., p. 554.

21. Merle Miller, *Lyndon: An Oral Biography* (New York: G. P. Putnam's Sons, 1980), p. 224.

22. *New York Times* (November 3, 1959).

23. Reedy, op. cit., Interview 15, p. 25, LBJ Library.

24. Herbert S. Parmet, *JFK: The Presidency of John F. Kennedy* (New York: Dial Press, 1983), p. 14.

25. *New York Times* (September 15, 1959).

26. Ibid.

27. Alfred Steinberg, *Sam Johnson's Boy: A Close-up of the President from Texas* (New York: Macmillan, 1968), p. 508.

28. Miller, op. cit., p. 237.

29. Dallek, op. cit., p. 561.

30. James Rowe, *Oral History*, Interview 2, Tape 1, pp. 11–12, LBJ Library.

31. Doris Kearns Goodwin, *The Fitzgeralds and the Kennedys* (New York: Simon & Schuster, 1987), p. 780.

32. Evans and Novak, op. cit., p. 257.

33. Ibid., p. 249.

34. Steinberg, op. cit., p. 511.

35. *New York Times* (January 12, 1960).

36. Reedy, op. cit., Interview 16, p. 25, LBJ Library.

37. Mann, op. cit., p. 243.

38. *New York Times* (February 16, 1960).

39. Steinberg, op. cit., p. 515.

40. *New York Times* (April 8, 1960).

41. *Newsweek* (March 14, 1960).

42. Miller, op. cit., p. 229.

43. *New York Times* (May 11, 1960).

44. Ibid. (May 23, 1960).

45. Connally's remarks at the 1990 symposiums in Robert Hardesty, ed., *The Johnson Years: The Difference He Made* (Austin: The LBJ Library, 1993), p. 150.

46. Miller, op. cit., p. 240.

47. *New York Times* (May 13, 1960).

48. Ibid. (June 2, 1960).

49. *Newsweek* (June 13, 1960).

50. *New York Times* (July 3, 1960).

51. Miller, op. cit., p. 231.

52. Clark Clifford, *Oral History*, Tape 1, p. 23, LBJ Library.

Chapter 14: Campaign Year 1960

1. *New York Times* (July 6, 1960).

2. Rowland Evans and Robert Novak, *Lyndon Johnson: The Exercise of Power* (New York: New American Library, 1969), p. 272.

3. Robert Dallek, *Lone Star Rising: Lyndon Johnson and His Times, 1908–1960* (New York: Oxford University Press, 1991), p. 572.

4. Thomas Reeves, *The Life and Times of Joe McCarthy: A Biography* (New York: Stein & Day, 1982), p. 170.

5. Rowland Evans and Robert Novak, *Lyndon B. Johnson: The Exercise of Power: A Political Biography* (New York: New American Library, 1966), p. 272.

6. *New York Times*, "News of the Week in Review" (July 10, 1960).

7. Jeff Shesol, *Mutual Contempt: Lyndon Johnson, Robert Kennedy, and the Feud That Defined a Decade* (New York: W. W. Norton, 1997), p. 40.

8. Evans and Novak, op. cit., p. 273.

9. Merle Miller, *Lyndon: An Oral Biography* (New York: G. P. Putnam's Sons, 1980), p. 249.

10. Ibid., p. 252.

11. Arthur Schlesinger Jr., *Robert Kennedy and His Times* (New York: Ballantine Books, 1979), p. 223.

12. James Rowe, *Oral History*, Interview 2, Tape 1, p. 22, LBJ Library.

13. James W. Hilty, *Robert Kennedy: Brother Protector* (Philadelphia: Temple University Press, 1997), p. 157.

14. Arthur Schlesinger Jr., *A Thousand Days: John F. Kennedy in the White House* (Boston: Houghton Mifflin, 1965), pp. 47–48, 58.

15. Bobby Baker and Larry King, *Wheeling and Dealing: Confessions of a Capital Hill Operator* (New York: W. W. Norton, 1978), pp. 124–125. The "darlin'" reflects the intimate relationship that Luce and LBJ once had.

16. Miller, op. cit., p. 257.

17. C. David Heymann, *RFK: A Candid Biography of Robert F. Kennedy* (New York: Dutton, 1998), p. 169.

18. *Newsweek* (July 25, 1960).

19. Robert Hardesty, ed., *The Johnson Years: The Difference He Made* (Austin: LBJ Library, 1993), p. 135.

20. Schlesinger, *Robert Kennedy and His Times*, p. 226.

21. Hilty, op. cit., p. 163.

22. *New York Times* (July 15, 16, 1960).

23. Ibid., July 31, 1960

24. Rowe, *Oral History*, op. cit., p. 24.

25. Miller, op. cit., p. 264.

26. Evelyn Lincoln, *Kennedy and Johnson* (New York: Holt, Rinehart & Winston, 1968), p. 110.

27. *New York Times* (September 7, 1960).

28. Ibid. (September 8, 1960).

29. Ibid. (September 11, 1960).

30. Ibid. (September 13, 1960).

31. Miller, op. cit., p. 265.

32. *New York Times* (September 13, 1960).

33. Ibid. (October 21, 1960).

34. Ibid. (September 30, 1960).

35. Ibid. (October 4, 5, and 6, 1960).

36. Miller, op. cit., p. 266.

37. *New York Times* (October 26, November 1, November 2, 1960).

38. Evans and Novak, op. cit., p. 303.

39. *New York Times Sunday Magazine* (October 23, 1960).

40. Dallek, op. cit., p. 589.

41. Alfred Steinberg, *Sam Johnson's Boy: A Close-up of the President from Texas* (New York: Macmillan, 1968), p. 341.

42. Ibid., p. 587.

43. George Reedy, *Lyndon Johnson: A Memoir* (New York: Andrews & McMeel, 1982), p. 54.

44. Steinberg, op. cit., p. 543.

45. Miller, op. cit., p. 271.

46. *New York Times* (November 6, 1960).

47. Ibid. (November 8, 1960).

48. Ibid. (November 10, 1960).

49. Ibid. (November 11, 1960).

Chapter 15: Vice President

1. Jacqueline Kennedy Onassis, *Oral History*, Interview 1, Tape 2, p. 2, LBJ Library.

2. Merle Miller, *Lyndon: An Oral Biography* (New York: G. P. Putnam's Sons, 1980), p. 277.

3. Ibid., p. 280.

4. Harry McPherson, *Oral History*, LBJ Library, Interview 1, Tape 2, p. 8.

5. Arthur Schlesinger Jr., *A Thousand Days: John Kennedy in the White House* (Boston: Houghton Mifflin, 1965), pp. 703–704.

6. Evelyn Lincoln, *Kennedy and Johnson* (New York: Holt, Rinehart, & Winston, 1968), p. 161.

7. Sam Houston Johnson, *My Brother Lyndon* (New York: Cowles, 1970), p. 108.

8. Jeff Shesol, *Mutual Contempt: Lyndon Johnson, Robert Kennedy, and the Feud That Defined a Decade* (New York: W. W. Norton, 1997), p. 104.

9. James Rowe, *Oral History*, Interview 2, Tape 1, p. 29, LBJ Library.

10. William S. White, *The Professional: Lyndon B. Johnson* (Boston: Houghton Mifflin, 1964), p. 227.

11. Robert Mann, *The Walls of Jericho: Lyndon Johnson, Hubert Humphrey, Richard Russell, and the Struggle for Civil Rights* (New York: Harcourt, Brace, 1996), p. 294.

12. Shesol, op. cit., pp. 94, 97.

13. Johnson, loc. cit.

14. Marie Smith, *The President's Lady: An Intimate Biography of Mrs. Lyndon B. Johnson* (New York: Random House, 1964), pp. 24–25, 74, 79.

15. Miller, op. cit., p. 278.

16. Authors' interview of Hyman Bookbinder, Washington, D.C., May 7, 1998.

17. Authors' interview of Harry McPherson, Washington, D.C., May 9, 1998.

18. Laura Kalman, *Abe Fortas: A Biography* (New Haven, Conn.: Yale University Press, 1990), p. 210.

19. Doris Kearns, *Lyndon Johnson and the American Dream* (New York: Harper & Row, 1976), p. 164.

20. Rowland Evans and Robert Novak, *Lyndon B. Johnson: The Exercise of Power: A Political Biography* (New York: New American Library, 1966), p. 330.

21. Bobby Baker and Larry King, *Wheeling and Dealing: Confessions of a Capitol Hill Operator* (New York: W. W. Norton, 1978), p. 27.

22. Ibid., p. 135.

23. Alfred Steinberg, *Sam Johnson's Boy: A Close-up of the President from Texas* (New York: Macmillan, 1968), p. 548.

24. Evans and Novak, op. cit., p. 308.

25. Baker, op. cit., p. 28.

26. Steinberg, op. cit., p. 559.

27. White, op. cit., p. 228.

28. Ibid., p. 229.

29. Baker, op. cit., p. 151.

30. Ibid., pp. 151–152.

31. Evans and Novak, op. cit., p. 317.

32. *New York Times* (June 18, 1962).

33. Ibid.

34. Ibid. (June 20, 1962).

35. Mann, op. cit., p. 326.

36. Mark Stern, *Calculating Visions: Kennedy, Johnson, and Civil Rights* (New Brunswick, N.J.: Rutgers University Press, 1992), p. 79.

37. Mann, op. cit., p. 343.

38. Ibid., pp. 356–357.

39. Stern, op. cit., pp. 85–86.

40. Johnson, op. cit., pp. 109–110.

41. Schlesinger, op. cit., p. 707.

42. Shesol, op. cit., p. 99.

43. Steinberg, op. cit., p. 564.

44. Miller, op. cit., p. 281.

45. George Reedy, *Lyndon B. Johnson: A Memoir* (New York: Andrews & McMeel, 1982), p. 25.

46. Booth Mooney, *The Lyndon Johnson Story* (New York: Farrar, Straus, 1964), p. 170.

47. Miller, op. cit., pp. 281–282.

48. Ibid., p. 286.
49. Lloyd C. Gardner, *Pay Any Price: Lyndon Johnson and the Wars for Vietnam* (Chicago: Ivan R. Dee, 1995), p. 52.
50. White, op. cit., p. 241.
51. Ibid., p. 240.
52. Evans and Novak, op. cit., p. 322.
53. White, op. cit., pp. 243–244.
54. Ibid., p. 244.
55. Harry McPherson, *A Political Education: A Washington Memoir* (Austin: University of Texas Press, 1995), p. 184.
56. Harry McPherson, *Oral History*, Tape 2, p. 13, LBJ Library.
57. Steinberg, op. cit., p. 589.
58. Lincoln, op. cit., p. 205.
59. McPherson, *Oral History*, Tape 2, p. 14, LBJ Library.
60. Lyndon Johnson to Robert Baker, January 5, 1962, Pre-Presidential Confidential File, Box 1, LBJ Library.
61. Kenneth P. O'Donnell and David F. Powers with Joe McCarthy, *Johnny, We Hardly Knew Ye: Memories of John Fitzgerald Kennedy* (Boston: Little, Brown, 1972), p. 5.
62. Schlesinger, op. cit., p. 1020.
63. Miller, op. cit., p. 310.
64. Michael Beschloss, ed., *Taking Charge: The Johnson White House Tapes, 1963–1964* (New York: Simon & Schuster, 1997), pp. 12–13.
65. O'Donnell et al., op. cit., p. 23.
66. Lyndon B. Johnson, *The Vantage Point: Perspectives of the Presidency, 1963–1969* (New York: Holt, Rinehart, & Winston, 1971), p. 2.
67. O'Donnell et al., op. cit., p. 25.
68. James Reston Jr., *Lone Star: The Life of John Connally* (New York: Harper & Row, 1989), p. 276.
69. Schlesinger, op. cit., p. 1025.
70. Johnson, op. cit., pp. 10–11.
71. Jack Valenti, *Oral History*, Interview 2, p. 15, LBJ Library.

Chapter 16: "Let Us Continue"

1. Merle Miller, *Lyndon: An Oral Biography* (New York: G. P. Putnam's Sons, 1980), p. 322.
2. Ibid.
3. Michael Beschloss, ed., *Taking Charge: The White House Tapes, 1963–1964* (New York: Simon & Schuster, 1997), p. 21.
4. Jack Valenti, *Oral History*, Interview 2, p. 22, LBJ Library.
5. Harry McPherson, *Oral History*, Interview 1, Tape 2, p. 24, LBJ Library.
6. Miller, op. cit., p. 335.
7. Jacqueline Kennedy Onassis, *Oral History*, Interview 1, Tape 2, p. 6, LBJ Library.
8. Doris Kearns, *Lyndon Johnson and the American Dream* (New York: Harper & Row, 1976), p. 170.
9. Lady Bird Johnson, *A White House Diary* (New York: Holt, Rinehart, & Winston, 1970), p. 725.
10. Lyndon Johnson, *The Vantage Point: Perspectives of the Presidency, 1963–1969* (New York: Holt, Rinehart, & Winston, 1971), p. 19.
11. *New York Times* (November 26, 1963).
12. Ibid. (November 27, 1963).
13. Joseph Rauh, *Oral History*, Interview 3, p. 2, LBJ Library.
14. James L. Sundquist, *Politics and Policy: The Eisenhower, Kennedy, and Johnson Years* (Washington, D.C.: Brookings Institution, 1968), p. 136.
15. Irwin Unger, *The Best of Intentions: The Triumphs and Failures of the Great Society Under Kennedy, Johnson, and Nixon* (New York: Doubleday, 1996), pp. 75–76.
16. *New York Times* (November 28, 1963).

17. *New York Times* (November 29, 1963).

18. Paul R. Henggeler, *In His Steps: Lyndon Johnson and the Kennedy Mystique* (Chicago: Ivan R. Dee, 1991), p. 109.

19. Richard Goodwin, *Remembering America: A Voice from the Sixties* (Boston: Little, Brown, 1988), p. 257.

20. *New York Times* (December 15, 1963).

21. Vaughn Davis Bornet, *The Presidency of Lyndon B. Johnson* (Lawrence, Kans.: University Press of Kansas, 1983), p. 51.

22. Jack Bell, *The Johnson Treatment: How Lyndon B. Johnson Took Over the Presidency and Made It His Own* (New York: Harper & Row, 1965), p. 63.

23. Lyndon Johnson, op. cit., p. 74.

24. *Newsweek* (January 6, 1964).

25. Russell Baker, *New York Times Magazine* (December 1, 1963); James Reston, *New York Times* (December 4, 1963).

26. *New York Times* (March 16, 1964).

27. Valenti, op. cit., pp. 31–32, LBJ Library.

28. Alfred Steinberg, *Sam Johnson's Boy: A Close-up of the President from Texas* (New York: Macmillan, 1968), p. 669.

29. *New York Times* (February 27, 1964).

30. Irving Bernstein, *Guns or Butter: The Presidency of Lyndon Johnson* (New York: Oxford University Press, 1996), p. 105.

31. Miller, op. cit., p. 363.

32. Kearns, op. cit., p. 190.

33. Beschloss, op. cit., pp. 185–186.

34. Rowland Evans and Robert Novak, *Lyndon B. Johnson: The Exercise of Power: A Political Biography* (New York: New American Library, 1966), p. 430.

35. Bernstein, op. cit., p. 98.

36. *New York Times* (March 17, 1964).

37. *The War on Poverty*, Senate Document 86, U.S. Senate, 88th Cong., 2nd sess. (Washington, D.C.: U.S. Government Printing Office, 1964), passim.

38. Bruce E. Altschuler, *LBJ and the Polls* (Gainesville, Fla.: University of Florida Press, 1990), pp. 32–33.

39. *New York Times* (March 17, 1964).

40. Bell, op. cit., p. 98.

41. Philip Rulon, *Compassionate Samaritan: The Life of Lyndon Baines Johnson* (Chicago: Nelson-Hall, 1981), p. 191.

42. *New York Times*, "News of the Week in Review" (April 22, 1964).

43. Bell, op. cit., p. 96.

44. Eric Goldman, *The Tragedy of Lyndon Johnson* (New York: Alfred A. Knopf, 1969), p. 184.

45. Bernstein, op. cit., p. 111.

46. Goldman, op. cit., pp. 188–189.

47. *New York Times* (August 29, 1963).

48. Ramsey Clark in Bernard J. Firestone and Robert C. Vogt, eds., *Lyndon Baines Johnson and the Uses of Power* (New York: Greenwood Press, 1988), p. 174.

49. Lyndon Johnson, op. cit., pp. 37–38.

50. Tom Wicker, "The Johnson Way with Congress," *New York Times Magazine* (March 8, 1964).

51. Robert Dallek, *Flawed Giant: Lyndon Johnson and His Times, 1961–1973* (New York: Oxford University Press, 1998), p. 116.

52. Bernstein, op. cit., p. 47.

53. Kearns, op. cit., p. 191.

54. *New York Times* (March 10, 1964).

55. Goodwin, op. cit., p. 314.

56. Valenti, op. cit., Interview 5, p. 12, LBJ Library.

57. Lyndon Johnson, op. cit., p. 158.

58. Bornet, op. cit., p. 98.

59. Miller, op. cit., p. 370.

60. *New York Times* (May 20, 1964).

61. Goodwin, op. cit., p. 315.

62. Ralph Ellison, "The Myth of the Flawed White Southerner," in James MacGregor Burns, ed., *To Heal and to Build: The Programs of President Lyndon Johnson* (New York: McGraw-Hill, 1968), p. 216.

63. Robert L. Hardesty, ed., *The Johnson Years: The Difference He Has Made* (Austin: LBJ Library, 1993), p. 32.

64. Goldman, op. cit., pp. 87–88.

65. Richard Harwood and Haynes Johnson, *Lyndon* (New York: Praeger, 1973), p. 52.

66. Ibid.

67. Arthur M. Schlesinger Jr., "The Challenge of Abundance," *The Reporter* (May 3, 1956) pp. 8–11.

68. Goldman, op. cit., p. 139.

69. Goodwin, op. cit., pp. 269–271.

70. *Public Papers of the Presidents of the United States: Lyndon B. Johnson, 1963–1964* (Washington, D.C.: U.S. Government Printing Office, 1965), pp. 704–707.

71. Arthur M. Schlesinger Jr., *Robert Kennedy and His Times* (New York: Ballantine Books, 1979), pp. 474–476.

72. Clark Clifford, *Oral History*, Tape 2, p. 16, LBJ Library.

73. George Reedy, *Lyndon B. Johnson: A Memoir* (New York: Andrews & McMeel, 1982), pp. 146–147. Jack Valenti later echoed Reedy's view. George Ball excepted, at least until mid-1966, Valenti claimed in a 1990s statement, "not a single member of the White House staff, not a single member of the administration . . . in any meeting or by any written memorandum, ever urged the president to get out of there. Not one." See Hardesty, op. cit., p. 163.

74. *New York Times*, transcript of Johnson news conference (June 3, 1964).

75. Lloyd Gardner, *Pay Any Price: Lyndon Johnson and the Wars for Vietnam* (Chicago: Ivan R. Dee, 1995), pp. 187ff.

76. Kearns, op. cit., pp. 251–252.

77. Beschloss, op. cit., pp. 362–364, *passim*.

78. James S. Olson and Randy Roberts, *Where the Domino Fell: America and Vietnam, 1945 to 1995* (New York: St. Martin's Press, 1996), p. 117.

79. Miller, op. cit., p. 382.

80. Stanley Karnow, *Vietnam: A History* (New York: Viking Press, 1983), p. 371

81. Beschloss, op. cit., p. 494.

82. *New York Times* (August 12, 1964).

83. Beschloss, op. cit., p. 507.

84. Bobby Baker and Larry King, *Wheeling and Dealing: Confessions of a Capitol Hill Operator* (New York: W. W. Norton, 1978), p. 195.

85. Booth Mooney, *LBJ: An Irreverent Chronicle* (New York: Thomas Y. Crowell, 1976), p. 153.

86. *New York Times* (July 30, 1964).

87. Rowland Evans and Robert Novak, *Lyndon B. Johnson: The Exercise of Power: A Political Biography* (New York: New American Library, 1966), p. 426.

88. Schlesinger, *Robert Kennedy and His Times*, p. 698.

89. *Newsweek* (August 10, 1964).

90. Lyndon Johnson, op. cit., Appendix A, p. 576.

91. Goldman, op. cit., p. 199.

92. Schlesinger, *Robert Kennedy and His Times*, p. 714.

93. Hardesty, op. cit., p. 153.

94. Beschloss, op. cit., p. 510.

95. Ibid., pp. 514–515.

96. Cartha DeLoach, *Hoover's FBI: The Inside Story by Hoover's Trusted Lieutenant* (Washington, D.C.: Regnery, 1995), p. 9.

97. Rauh, op cit., p. 17, LBJ Library.

98. Beschloss, op. cit., p. 530.

99. Ibid., pp. 484–487.

100. Goldman, op. cit., p. 218.

101. Valenti, op cit., Interview 4, p. 4, LBJ Library.

102. Goldman, op. cit., pp. 232–233.

103. Harry McPherson, *Oral History*, Interview 1, Tape 2, p. 33.

104. *New York Times* (July 16, 1964).

105. Paul F. Boller, *Presidential Campaigns* (New York: Oxford University Press, 1996), p. 311.

106. Staff of The New York Times, *The Road to the White House: The Story of the 1964 Election* (New York: McGraw-Hill, 1965), p. 174.

107. Steinberg, op. cit., p. 676.

108. Allen Matusow, *The Unraveling of America: A History of Liberalism in the 1960s* (New York: Harper & Row, 1984), p. 147.

109. *New York Times* (August 21, 1964).

110. *Time* (September 25, 1964), p. 20.

111. Michael Beschloss, "Evesdropping at the Highest Levels," *Newsweek* (October 5, 1998), p. 40.

112. Staff of the *New York Times*, op. cit., pp. 237–238.

113. *Public Papers of the Presidents of the United States. Lyndon B. Johnson, 1963–1964*, Book II (Washington, D.C.: U.S. Government Printing Office, 1965), pp. 1285–1286. The official document changed Johnson's "nigra" to "Negro." Observers reported the dialect version, "nigra," but Johnson himself records the racist expletive. See Lyndon Johnson, op cit., p. 110.

114. Milton C. Cummings, *The National Election of 1964* (Washington, D.C.: Brookings Institution, 1964), p. 55.

115. Ted Gittinger, ed., *The Johnson Years: A Vietnam Roundtable* (Austin: LBJ Library, 1993), p. 41.

116. Goldman, op. cit., p. 253.

117. Kearns, op. cit., p. 209.

Chapter 17: High Water

1. *Washington Post* (December 19, 1964).

2. Wilbur Cohen, *Oral History*, Interview 3, p. 16, LBJ Library.

3. Ibid.

4. Lawrence O'Brien, *Oral History*, LBJ, Interview 6, p. 840, LBJ Library.

5. Lee White in Robert Hardesty, ed., *The Johnson Years: The Difference He Made* (Austin: LBJ Library, 1993), p. 84.

6. Wilbur Cohen, *Oral History*, Tape 3, p. 17, LBJ Library.

7. Authors' interview with Harry McPherson, Washington, D.C. (May 7, 1998).

8. Hardesty, op. cit., p. 130.

9. Telephone interview with George Reedy (September 2, 1998).

10. O'Brien's remarks in Hardesty, op. cit., p. 76.

11. *New York Times* (January 5, 1965).

12. *New York Times* (January 5, 1965).

13. *Washington Post* (January 5, 1965).

14. Chalmers M. Roberts, "Domestic Front First," *Washington Post* (January 18, 1965).

15. *Washington Post* (January 18, 1965).

16. Merle Miller, *Lyndon: An Oral Biography* (New York: G. P. Putnam's Sons, 1980), p. 407.

17. R. H. McMaster, *Dereliction of Duty: Lyndon Johnson, Robert McNamara, the Joint Chiefs of Staff, and the Lies That Led to Vietnam* (New York: HarperCollins, 1997), p. 52.

18. George C. Herring, "The Reluctant Warrior: Lyndon Johnson as Commander in Chief," in David L. Anderson, ed., *Shadow on the White House: Presidents and the Vietnam War, 1945–1975* (Lawrence, Kans.: University Press of Kansas, 1993), p. 89.

19. Quoted by Barry Zorthian, an official in the Saigon embassy from 1964 to 1968. See Ted Gittinger, ed., *The Johnson Years: A Vietnam Roundtable* (Austin: LBJ Library, 1993), p. 42.

20. Robert S. McNamara, *In Retrospect: The Tragedy and Lessons of Vietnam* (New York: Times Books, 1995), p. 168.

21. Gittinger, op. cit., Appendix III, pp. 155–158.

22. Gittinger, op. cit., p. 59.

23. Rowland Evans and Robert Novak, *Lyndon B. Johnson: The Exercise of Power: A Political Biography* (New York: New American Library, 1966), p. 536.

24. *Washington Post* (February 9, 1965).

25. Ibid. (March 3, 1965).

26. Miller, op. cit., p. 407.

27. Lyndon Johnson, *The Vantage Point: Perspectives of the Presidency, 1963–1969* (New York: Holt, Rinehart, & Winston, 1971), p. 207.

28. Julie Roy Jeffrey, *Education for Children of the Poor: A Study of the Origins and Implementation of the Elementary and Secondary Education Act of 1965* (Columbus: Ohio State University Press, 1978), p. 74

29. Irving Bernstein, *Guns or Butter: The Presidency of Lyndon Johnson* (New York: Oxford University Press, 1996), p. 196.

30. *New York Times* (April 10, 1965).

31. Ibid. (April 10, 1965).

32. *Public Papers of the Presidents of the United States: Lyndon B. Johnson, 1965*, vol. I (Washington, D.C.: U.S. Government Printing Office, 1966), pp. 415–417.

33. *New York Times* (April 12, 1965).

34. McMaster, op. cit., p. 231.

35. *Washington Post* (June 2, 1965).

36. Ibid. (April 8, 1965).

37. Kathleen J. Turner, *Lyndon Johnson's Dual War: Vietnam and the Press* (Chicago: University of Chicago Press, 1987), p. 130.

38. Ibid., p. 132.

39. *Washington Post* (April 9, 1965).

40. Irwin Unger and Debi Unger, *Turning Point: 1968* (New York: Charles Scribner's Sons, 1988), p. 238.

41. James Olson and Randy Roberts, *Where the Domino Fell: America and Vietnam, 1945 to 1995* (New York: St. Martin's Press, 1996), p. 128.

42. *New York Times* (May 1, 1965).

43. Johnson, op. cit., p. 195.

44. *The New Republic* (May 15, 1965).

45. *New York Times*, May 7, 1965.

46. Olson and Roberts, op. cit., p. 136.

47. McNamara, op. cit., p. 194.

48. Lloyd Gardner, *Pay Any Price: Lyndon Johnson and the Wars for Vietnam* (Chicago: Ivan R. Dee, 1995), p. 240.

49. Brian VanDeMark, *Quagmire: Lyndon Johnson and the Escalation of the Vietnam War* (New York: Oxford University Press, 1991), p. 175.

50. Ibid., p. 176.

51. Miller, op. cit., p. 417.

52. Robert Dallek, *Flawed Giant: Lyndon Johnson and His Times, 1961–1973* (New York: Oxford University Press, 1998), pp. 282–283.

53. Ibid., p. 275.

54. *Washington Post* (July 29, 1965).

55. Johnson, op. cit., p. 383.

56. Gittinger, op. cit., p. 101.

57. In Gittinger, op. cit., p. 91.

58. *New York Times* (June 15, 1965).

59. Bernstein, op. cit., p. 218.

60. Harvard Sitkoff, *The Struggle for Black Equality, 1954–1980* (New York: Hill & Wang, 1981), p. 188.

61. Bernstein, op. cit., p. 221.

62. Johnson, op. cit., p. 161.

63. Richard Goodwin, *Remembering America: A Voice from the Sixties* (Boston: Little, Brown, 1988), pp. 322–323.

64. Ibid., pp. 333–334.

65. Sitkoff, op. cit., p. 194.

66. Robert Mann, *The Walls of Jericho: Lyndon Johnson, Hubert Humphrey, Richard Russell, and the Struggle for Civil Rights* (New York: Harcourt, Brace, 1996), p. 464.

67. *Washington Post* (March 27, 1965).

68. Miller, op. cit., p. 434.

69. *Newsweek* (May 10, 1965).

70. *New York Times* (August 7, 1965).

71. *Public Papers of the Presidents*, pp. 635–640.

72. *Washington Post* (August 16, 1965).

73. Harry McPherson, *Oral History*, Interview 5, Tape 1, p. 1, LBJ Library.

74. Bernstein, op. cit., p. 386.

75. *Washington Post* (July 27, 1965).

76. *Washington Post* (August 10, 1965).

77. Bernstein, op. cit., p. 159.

78. Eric Goldman, *The Tragedy of Lyndon Johnson* (New York: Alfred A. Knopf, 1969), p. 290.

79. Ibid., pp. 290–291.

80. Bernstein, op. cit., p. 179.

81. Ibid.

82. *Washington Post* (July 31, 1965).

83. *Washington Post* (April 9, 1965).

84. *New York Times* (August 10, 1965).

85. Wilbur Cohen, *Oral History*, Tape 3, p. 18, LBJ Library.

86. Johnson, op. cit., pp. 323–324.

87. Mrs. William Clark to President Johnson, Caseyville, Illinois, December 1, 1965. Mr. Walter Hormell to President Johnson, Beverly Hills, California, December 1, 1965. Jean Gettle to President Johnson, Tillamook, Oregon, December 7, 1965. All letters from White House Central Files, Box 10, LBJ Library.

88. *New York Times* (June 1, 1965).

89. Edward Zigler and Karen Anderson, "A Idea Whose Time Had Come: The Intellectual and Political Climate for Head Start," in Edward Zigler and Jeanette Valentine, eds., *Project Head Start: A Legacy of the War on Poverty* (New York: The Free Press, 1979), p. 52.

90. *New York Times* (September 1, 1965).

91. James Gaither, *Oral History*, Tape 1, p. 10, LBJ Library.

92. Cohen, op. cit., Tape 2, p. 10.

93. John Chamberlain in the *Washington Post* (August 24, 1965).

94. *Newsweek* (October 25, 1965).

95. Ronnie Dugger, *The Politician: The Life and Times of Lyndon Johnson: The Drive for Power from the Frontier to Master of the Senate* (New York: W. W. Norton, 1982), p. 21.

96. *Washington Post* (December 5, 1965).

97. Jack Valenti, *Oral History*, Interview 5, p. 24, LBJ Library.

98. George Reedy, *Lyndon B. Johnson: A Memoir* (New York: Andrews & McMeel, 1982), p. 5.

99. John Tebbel and Sarah Miles Watts, *The Press and the Presidency: From George Washington to Ronald Reagan* (New York: Oxford University Press, 1985), p. 493.

100. Memo, Robert Kintner to the president (June 21, 1966), Confidential File, Box 16, LBJ Library.

101. *Washington Post* (January 1, 1966).

102. Ibid. (January 2, 1966).

103. Unger, op. cit., p. 142.

104. *Washington Post* (September 30, 1965).

105. Bernstein, op. cit., p. 267.

106. *Public Papers of the Presidents*, pp. 155–165.

107. Bernstein, op. cit., pp. 291–293.

108. *New York Times* (October 21, 1965).

109. *Public Papers of the Presidents: Lyndon B. Johnson, 1963–1964*, p. 116.

110. *Washington Post* (November 8, 1965).

111. *New York Times* (October 21, 1965).

112. Joseph Califano, *The Triumph and Tragedy of Lyndon Johnson: The White House Years* (New York: Simon & Schuster, 1991), p. 84.

113. Larry O'Brien, memo to the president (September 18, 1965). Aides Files/Wilson, Box 8, LBJ Library.

114. Califano, op. cit., p. 85.

115. James L. Sundquist, *Politics and Policy: The Eisenhower, Kennedy, and Johnson Years* (Washington, D.C.: Brookings Institution, 1968), p. 379.

116. *New York Times* (November 9, 1965).

117. Ibid. (December 30, 1965).

Chapter 18: Guns vs. Butter

1. *Washington Post*, January 13, 1966.

2. Robert Dallek, *Flawed Giant: Lyndon Johnson and His Times, 1961–1973* (New York: Oxford University Press, 1998), p. 342.

3. Robert S. McNamara, *In Retrospect: The Tragedy and Lessons of Vietnam* (New York: Times Books, 1995), p. 222.

4. Ibid., p. 225.

5. *Washington Post* (January 13, 1966).

6. *New York Times* (January 3, 1966).

7. Clark Clifford, *Oral History*, Tape 2, p. 20, LBJ Library.

8. *Washington Post* (March 14, 1966).

9. Ibid. (January 28, 1966).

10. Irving Bernstein, *Guns or Butter: The Presidency of Lyndon Johnson* (New York: Oxford University Press, 1996), p. 360.

11. Louis Heren, *No Hail, No Farewell* (New York: Harper & Row, 1970), pp. 100–101.

12. William C. Westmoreland, *A Soldier Reports* (New York: Dell, 1980), p. 207.

13. Larry Berman, *Lyndon Johnson's War: The Road to Stalemate in Vietnam* (New York: W. W. Norton, 1989), p. 10.

14. Westmoreland, op. cit., p. 208.

15. *Washington Post* (February 8, 1966).

16. *New York Times* (April 26, 1966).

17. Joseph Califano, *The Triumph and Tragedy of Lyndon Johnson: The White House Years* (New York: Simon & Schuster, 1991), p. 180.

18. Ralph Nader, *Unsafe at Any Speed* (New York: Grossman Publishers, 1965), p. x.

19. Mark V. Nadel, *The Politics of Consumer Protection* (Indianapolis: Bobbs-Merrill, 1971), p. 140.

20. *Facts on File* (May 5–May 11, 1966)

21. Ibid., September 29–October 5, 1966.

22. *Washington Post* (March 27, 1966).

23. Fred Halstead, *Out Now! A Participant's Account of the American Movement Against the Vietnam War* (New York: Monad Press, 1978), p. 144.

24. Ibid., p. 141.

25. *Washington Post* (April 15, 1966).

26. Ibid. (April 18, 1966).

27. Ibid. (April 29, 1966).

28. *Facts on File* (May 12–18, 1966).

29. Alfred Steinberg, *Sam Johnson's Boy: A Close-up of the President from Texas* (New York: Macmillan, 1968), p. 788.

30. *Washington Post* (May 12, 1966).

31. Dallek, op. cit., p. 367.

32. Stokely Carmichael, "What We Want," *New York Review of Books* (September 22, 1966), p. 6.

33. *Facts on File* (June 2–8, 1966).

34. Harry McPherson, *A Political Education: A Washington Memoir* (Austin: University of Texas Press, 1995), p. 349.

35. *New York Times* (June 4, 1966).

36. *Washington Post* (June 19, 1966).

37. Jack Valenti in Ted Gittinger, ed., *The Johnson Years: A Vietnam Roundtable* (Austin: LBJ Library, 1993), p. 78.

38. Steinberg, op. cit., p. 791.

39. *Facts on File* (June 30–July 6, 1966).

40. The description is by historian Richard Wade, who headed RFK's campaign. See Arthur M. Schlesinger Jr., *Robert Kennedy and His Times* (New York: Ballantine Books, 1979), p. 727.

41. Ibid., p. 742.

42. Ibid., p. 784.

43. Ibid., p. 787.

44. *Facts on File* (July 28–August 5, 1966).

45. Lady Bird Johnson, *A White House Diary* (New York: Holt, Rinehart, & Winston, 1970), p. 407.

46. *Facts on File* (August 25–31, 1966).

47. *Facts on File* (September 1–7, 1966).

48. Steinberg, op. cit., p. 795.

49. Berman, op. cit., pp. 18–19.

50. *Facts on File* (October 27–November 2 and November 3–November 9, 1966).

51. Hugh Sidey, *A Very Personal President: Lyndon Johnson in the White House* (New York: Athenaeum, 1968), p. 150.

52. *Facts on File* (October 27–November 2, 1966, and November 3–November 9, 1966).

53. Califano, op. cit., p. 147.

54. *Washington Post* (October 16, 1966).

55. Ibid.

56. Charles M. Haar, *Between the Idea and the Reality: A Study in the Origin, Fate and Legacy of the Model Cities Program* (Boston: Little, Brown, 1975), Appendix 1, pp. 289–290.

57. *New York Times* (May 15, 1966).

58. *Washington Post* (June 1, 1966).

59. Califano, op. cit., p. 134.

60. *New York Times* (October 11, 1966).

61. Califano, op. cit., p. 134.

62. *New York Times*, "News of the Week in Review" (November 6, 1966).

63. *New York Times* (November 10, 1966).

64. Ibid.

65. *Facts on File* (November 10–November 16, 1966).

66. *Newsweek* (November 21, 1966).

67. Doris Kearns, *Lyndon Johnson and the American Dream* (New York: Harper & Row, 1976), p. 285.

Chapter 19: Retreat

1. Robert Dallek, *Flawed Giant: Lyndon Johnson and His Times, 1961–1973* (New York: Oxford University Press, 1998), p. 391.

2. Reston's remarks are from Emmette S. Redford and Marlan Blissett, *Organizing the Executive Branch: The Johnson Presidency* (Chicago: University of Chicago Press, 1981), p. 186. Members of the administration acknowledged the problems and in September 1966 Joseph Califano recommended creation of a task force to look into them. Soon after, Johnson authorized such a body, led by Ben Heineman, president of the Chicago and Northwestern, a liberal businessman who had supported him in 1964. In a series of reports in mid-1967 the Heineman group concluded that the "organizational criticism [of the administration] is merited." Johnson never allowed the task force's critical conclusions to be made public. See Redford and Blissett, p. 195.

3. *Washington Post* (December 29, 1966).

4. Ibid. (January 3, 1967).

5. Ibid. (January 1, 1967).

6. Joseph Califano, *The Triumph and Tragedy of Lyndon Johnson: The White House Years* (New York: Simon & Schuster, 1991), pp. 182–183.

7. Harry McPherson, *Oral History*, Interview 1, Tape 1, p. 16, and Interview 5, Tape 1, p. 12, LBJ Library.

8. *Washington Post* (January 11, 1967).

9. Ibid. (January 13, 1967).

10. *New York Times* (January 11, 1967).

11. *Washington Post* (February 12, 1967).

12. Johnson to Fortas (December 17, 1966), telephone tapes, LBJ Library.

13. Jeff Shesol, *Mutual Contempt: Lyndon Johnson, Robert Kennedy and the Feud that Defined a Decade* (New York: W. W. Norton, 1997), p. 366.

14. *Newsweek* (February 27, 1967).

15. Arthur M. Schlesinger Jr., *Robert Kennedy and His Times* (New York: Ballantine Books, 1978), p. 827.

16. *Washington Post* (February 13, 1967).

17. Paul R. Henggeler, *In His Steps: Lyndon Johnson and the Kennedy Mystique* (Chicago: Ivan R. Dee, 1991), p. 217.

18. Ibid.

19. *Washington Post* (February 3, 1967).

20. Lyndon Johnson, *The Vantage Point: Perspectives of the Presidency, 1963–1969* (New York: Holt, Rinehart, & Winston, 1971), pp. 592–593.

21. Ibid., pp. 594–595.

22. *Washington Post* (March 10, 1967).

23. *Washington Post* (April 5, 1967).

24. Ibid. (March 16, 1967).

25. David Lilienthal, *The Journals of David Lilienthal*, vol. 6: *Creativity and Conflict, 1964–1967* (New York: Harper & Row, 1976), pp. 418–419.

26. *Washington Post* (March 22, 1967).

27. Alfred Steinberg, *Sam Johnson's Boy: A Close-up of the President from Texas* (New York: Macmillan, 1968), p. 814.

28. Charles DeBenedetti, *An American Ordeal: The Antiwar Movement of the Vietnam Era* (Syracuse, NY: Syracuse University Press, 1990), p. 182.

29. Nancy Zaroulis and Gerald Sullivan, *Who Spoke Up?: American Protest Against the War in Vietnam, 1963–1975* (Garden City, N.Y.: Doubleday, 1984), p. 82.

30. *Washington Post* (April 15,1967).

31. Ibid. (April 29, 1967).

32. David M. Barrett, *Uncertain Warriors: Lyndon Johnson and His Vietnam Advisers* (Lawrence, Kans.: University Press of Kansas, 1993), p. 80.

33. Steinberg, op. cit., p. 816.

34. Barrett, op. cit., pp. 80–81.

35. Robert D. Schulzinger, *A Time for War: The United States and Vietnam, 1941–1975* (New York: Oxford University Press, 1997), p. 183.

36. *Washington Post* (May 4, 1967).

37. Richard Gid Powers, *Secrecy and Power: The Life of J. Edgar Hoover* (New York: The Free Press, 1987), pp. 427–428.

38. Dallek, op. cit., p. 489.

39. *Washington Post* (May 18, 1967).

40. Johnson, op. cit., pp. 290–291.

41. *Washington Post* (May 24, 1967).

42. Merle Miller, *Lyndon: An Oral Biography* (New York: G. P. Putnam's Sons, 1980), p. 477.

43. Johnson, op. cit., p. 297.

44. H. W. Brands, *The Wages of Globalism: Lyndon Johnson and the Limits of American Power* (New York: Oxford University Press, 1995), p. 209.

45. Ibid., p. 216.

46. Paul Warnke interview with authors, Washington, D.C. (April 15, 1998).

47. Brands, op. cit., p. 218.

48. *Newsweek* (July 10, 1967).

49. George Herring, *America's Longest War: The United States and Vietnam, 1950–1975* (New York: McGraw-Hill, 1979), p. 177.

50. Johnson, op. cit., p. 369.

51. Lloyd Gardner, *Pay Any Price: Lyndon Johnson and the Wars for Vietnam* (Chicago: Ivan R. Dee, 1995), p. 375.

52. *Washington Post* (July 15, 1967).

53. Ibid. (July 25, 1967).

54. Harvard Sitkoff, *The Struggle for Black Equality, 1954–1980* (New York: Hill & Wang, 1981), p. 217.

55. Memo, Robert Kintner to the president (August 1, 1967), Confidential File, Box 16, LBJ Library.

56. *Washington Post* (July 28, 1967).

57. Califano, op. cit., p. 220.

58. Ibid., p. 244.

59. Donald F. Kettl, "The Economic Education of Lyndon Johnson: Guns, Butter, and Taxes," in Robert Divine, ed., *The Johnson Years, vol. 2, Vietnam, the Environment, and Science* (Lawrence, Kans.: University Press of Kansas, 1987), p. 69.

60. *Washington Post* (August 6, 1967).

61. Johnson, op. cit., p. 84.

62. *Newsweek* (August 21, 1967).

63. Ibid. (August 24, 1967).

64. *Washington Post* (August 19, 1967).

65. Ibid. (September 1, 1967).

66. Johnson, op. cit., p. 267.

67. Ibid.

68. *New York Times* (September 30, 1967).

69. *New York Review of Books* (October 12, 1967).

70. *Washington Post* (October 24, 1967).

71. Robert McNamara, *In Retrospect: The Tragedy and Lessons of Vietnam* (New York: Times Books, 1995), pp. 304–309.

72. Schulzinger, op. cit., pp. 257–258.

73. Ted Gittinger, ed., *The Johnson Years: A Vietnam Roundtable* (Austin: LBJ Library, 1993), p. 112.

74. McNamara, op. cit., p. 311.

75. Ibid.

76. Booth Mooney, *LBJ: An Irreverent Chronicle* (New York: Thomas Y. Crowell, 1976), p. 172.

77. Dallek, op. cit., p. 186.

78. Carl T. Rowan, "Power's a Potent Aphrodisiac," *New York Post* (January 26, 1998).

79. Miller, op. cit., p. 445.

80. Nancy Dickerson, *Among Those Present: A Reporter's View of Twenty-five Years in Washington* (New York: Random House, 1976), pp. 138–140.

81. Mooney, op. cit., p. 255.

82. Taped interview with Diane Sawyer, "The Whole World Was Watching," American Broadcasting Company (December 10, 1998).

83. Patricia G. Zelman, *Women, Work and National Policy: The Kennedy-Johnson Years* (Ann Arbor: University of Michigan Research Press, 1982), p. 47.

84. *Nation* (April 3, 1967), p. 421.

85. Miller, op. cit., p. 449.

86. *Facts on File* (November 9–15, 1967).

87. Ibid. (November 16–22, 1967).

88. *Washington Post* (November 11, 1967).

89. Ibid. (November 18, 1967).

90. Miller, op. cit., p. 506.

91. *Washington Post* (November 18, 1967).

92. *Facts on File* (November 23–29, 1967).

93. *Washington Post* (November 21, 1967).

94. Leon Shull to LBJ, Washington, D.C. (December 21, 1967), White House Central Files, Box 164, LBJ Library.

95. Larry R. Jackson and William A. Johnson, *Protest by the Poor: The Welfare Rights Movement in New York City* (Lexington, Mass: Lexington Books, 1974), p. 32.

96. *Washington Post* (June 25, 1967).

97. Lady Bird Johnson, *A White House Diary* (New York: Holt, Rinehart, & Winston, 1970), pp. 599–600.

98. *New York Times* (December 17, 1967).

99. Califano, op. cit., p. 250.

Chapter 20: Renunciation

1. Larry Berman, *Lyndon Johnson's War: The Road to Stalemate in Vietnam* (New York: W. W. Norton, 1989), p. 123.

2. Lyndon Johnson, *Vantage Point: Perspectives of the Presidency, 1963–1969* (New York: Holt, Rinehart, & Winston, 1971), p. 433.

3. Merle Miller, *Lyndon: An Oral Biography* (New York: G. P. Putnam's Sons, 1980), pp. 495–496.

4. Lady Bird Johnson, *A White House Diary* (New York: Holt, Rinehart, & Winston, 1970), p. 643.

5. Miller, op. cit., p. 498.

6. He told Leo Janos: "My daddy was only sixty-two when he died and I figured that with my history of heart trouble I'd never live through another four years." See Janos, "The Last Days of the President: LBJ in Retirement," *Atlantic* (July 1973), pp. 35–41.

7. Miller, op. cit., p. 499.

8. Robert M. Collins, "The Economic Crisis of 1968 and the Waning of the 'American Century,'" *The American Historical Review* (April 1996), p. 401.

9. *Washington Post* (January 2, 1968).

10. Collins, op. cit., p. 396.

11. Joseph Califano, *The Triumph and Tragedy of Lyndon Johnson: The White House Years* (New York: Simon & Schuster, 1991), p. 253.

12. Ibid., p. 254.

13. *Washington Post* (January 18, 1968).

14. Califano, op. cit., p. 256.

15. *Washington Post* (January 18, 1968).

16. Ibid. (January 21, 1968).

17. Ibid. (January 25, 1968).

18. Ibid. (February 28, 1968).

19. Ibid. (January 30, 1968).

20. Johnson, op. cit., p. 533.

21. Irving Bernstein, *Guns or Butter: The Presidency of Lyndon Johnson* (New York: Oxford University Press, 1996), p. 471.

22. Don Oberdorfer, *TET! The Turning Point in the Vietnam War* (New York: Da Capo Press, 1983), p. 54.

23. Marilyn Young, *The Vietnam Wars: 1945–1990* (New York: Harper Perennial, 1991), p. 216.

24. Herbert Y. Schandler, *The Unmaking of a President: Lyndon Johnson and Vietnam* (Princeton, N.J.: Princeton University Press, 1977), p. 75.

25. George C. Herring, *America's Longest War: The United States and Vietnam, 1950–1975* (New York: McGraw-Hill, 1986), p. 190.

26. Schandler, op. cit., p. 82.

27. Walter Cronkite, *A Reporter's Life* (New York: Alfred A. Knopf, 1996), p. 258.

28. *Washington Post* (February 3, 1968).

29. Berman, op. cit., p. 152.

30. Schandler, op. cit., p. 85.

31. Robert Schulzinger, *A Time for War: The United States and Vietnam, 1941–1975* (New York: Oxford University Press, 1997), p. 259.

32. Johnson, op. cit., p. 383.

33. *Washington Post* (February 17, 1968).

34. Herring, op. cit., p. 194.

35. Lloyd Gardner, *Pay Any Price: Lyndon Johnson and the Wars for Vietnam* (Chicago: Ivan R. Dee, 1995), p. 436.

36. Califano, op. cit., p. 264.

37. Clark Clifford, *Counsel to the President: A Memoir* (New York: Random House, 1991), p. 486.

38. David M. Barrett, *Uncertain Warriors: Lyndon Johnson and His Vietnam Advisers* (Lawrence, Kans.: University Press of Kansas, 1993), p. 129.

39. Stanley Karnow, *Vietnam: A History* (New York: Viking Press, 1983), p. 552.

40. Clifford, op. cit., p. 493; Schandler, op. cit., pp. 167–169.

41. Clifford, op. cit., p. 495.

42. *Washington Post* (March 3, 1968).

43. *New York Times* (March 10, 1968).

44. *Washington Post* (March 12, 1968).

45. Walter Isaacson and Evan Thomas, *The Wise Men: Six Friends and the World They Made: Acheson, Bohlen, Harriman, Kennan, Lovett, McCloy* (New York: Simon & Schuster, 1986), p. 700.

46. *Report of the National Advisory Commission on Civil Disorders* (Washington, D.C.: U.S. Government Printing Office, 1968), p. 1.

47. *Facts on File* (March 14–20, 1968), p. 103.

48. *Washington Post* (March 17, 1968).

49. Ibid. (March 22, 1968).

50. Johnson, op. cit., p. 416.

51. Barrett, op. cit., p. 149.

52. Clark Clifford, *Oral History*, Tape 3, p. 5, LBJ Library.

53. Johnson, op. cit., pp. 422–423.

54. Ted Gittinger, ed., *The Johnson Years: A Vietnam Roundtable* (Austin: LBJ Library, 1993), p. 137.

55. Harry McPherson, *Oral History*, Interview 4, Tape 1, p. 20, LBJ Library.

56. Clifford, op. cit., p. 520.

57. Ibid., p. 521.

58. Theodore H. White, *The Making of the President, 1968* (New York: Athenaeum, 1969), p. 114.

59. Califano, op. cit., p. 269.

60. Clifford, op. cit., p. 523.

61. *Public Papers of the Presidents of the United States: Lyndon B. Johnson*, vol. 1 (Washington, D.C.: U.S. Government Printing Office, 1963–64) pp. 469–476.

62. Miller, op. cit., p. 513.

63. *Washington Post* (April 4, 1968).

64. Ibid. (editorial page) (April 1, 1968).

65. Irwin Unger and Debi Unger, *Turning Point: 1968* (New York: Charles Scribner's Sons, 1988), p. 131.

66. *Washington Post* (April 2, 1968).

67. Ibid.

68. Johnson, op. cit., p. 174.

69. Califano, op. cit., p. 274.

70. *Washington Post* (April 6, 1968).

71. Califano, op. cit., p. 279.

72. *Washington Post* (May 4, 1968).

73. Gardner, op. cit., p. 469.

74. Letter, Lyndon Johnson to Pope Paul VI, June 15, 1968, Confidential Papers of the President, Box 78, LBJ Library.

75. Califano, op. cit., pp. 291–292.

76. *Washington Post* (April 27, 1968).

77. Doris Kearns, *Lyndon Johnson and the American Dream* (New York: Harper & Row, 1976), p. 133.

78. *Facts on File* (May 2–8, 1968).

79. Ibid.

80. Johnson, op. cit., p. 455.
81. Ibid., p. 456.
82. Bernstein, op. cit., p. 376.
83. *Facts on File* (May 9–15, 1968).
84. Miller, op. cit., p. 516.
85. *Facts on File* (May 16–22, 1968).
86. *Washington Post* (May 30, 1968).
87. Califano, op. cit., p. 297.
88. *Facts on File* (June 6–12, 1968).
89. *Washington Post* (June 11, 1968).
90. Lady Bird Johnson, op. cit., p. 684.
91. Harry McPherson, *A Political Education: A Washington Memoir* (Austin: University of Texas Press, 1995), p. 381.
92. *Washington Post* (June 11, 1968).
93. Ibid. (June 13, 1968).
94. Ibid. (July 2, 1968).
95. *Facts on File* (June 20–26, 1968).
96. *Washington Post* (June 16, 1968).
97. Johnson, op. cit., p. 545.
98. Ibid., p. 546.
99. *Washington Post* (June 29, 1968).
100. Laura Kalman, *Abe Fortas: A Biography* (New Haven, Conn.: Yale University Press, 1990), p. 330.
101. Miller, op. cit., p. 485.
102. Bruce Allen Murphy, *Fortas: The Rise and Ruin of a Supreme Court Justice* (New York: William Morrow, 1988), p. 299.
103. Califano, op. cit., pp. 309–310.
104. Kalman, op. cit., p. 357.
105. Johnson, op. cit., pp. 546–547.
106. Murphy, op. cit., p. 1.
107. Gardner, op. cit., p. 476.
108. *Washington Post* (August 2, 1968).
109. Lewis Gould, *Lady Bird Johnson and the Environment* (Lawrence: University Press of Kansas, 1988), p. 186.
110. Ibid., p. 193.
111. *Washington Post* (August 20, 1968).
112. Johnson, op. cit., p. 488.
113. *Washington Post* (August 22, 1968).
114. *Facts on File* August 22–28, 1968).

Chapter 21: Winding Down

1. Robert L. Hardesty, ed., *The Johnson Years: The Difference He Made* (Austin: LBJ Library, 1993), p. 157.
2. Telegram, Richard Daley to President, August 17, 1968, Confidential Papers of the President, Box 78, LBJ Library.
3. Statement by Senator Lyndon B. Johnson of Texas at the Senate Democratic Conference (January 2, 1953), Pre-Presidential Confidential File, Box 1, LBJ Library.
4. Abe Peck, *Uncovering the Sixties: The Life and Times of the Underground Press* (New York: Pantheon, 1985), p. 118.
5. Joseph Califano Jr., *The Triumph and Tragedy of Lyndon Johnson* (New York: Simon & Schuster, 1991), p. 318.
6. Theodore H. White, *The Making of the President, 1968* (New York: Pocket Books, 1970), p. 344.
7. *Facts on File* (August 29–September 4, 1968).
8. *New York Times* (August 29, 1968).
9. Califano, op. cit., p. 323.
10. White, op. cit., p. 347.

11. *Washington Post* (August 22, 1968).

12. *New York Times* (August 29, 1968).

13. Lewis Chester, *An American Melodrama: The Presidential Campaign of 1968* (New York: Viking Press, 1969), p. 578.

14. Califano, op. cit., p. 322.

15. *Washington Post* (August 30, 1968).

16. White, op. cit., p. 303.

17. Kenneth Crawford, "Sore Losers," *Newsweek* (September 9, 1968).

18. *New York Times* (August 30, 1968).

19. Califano, op. cit., p. 322.

20. Edgar Berman, *Hubert: The Triumph and Tragedy of the Humphrey I Knew* (New York: G. P. Putnam's Sons, 1978), p. 272.

21. *Washington Post* (September 15, 1968).

22. Lloyd Gardner, *Pay Any Price: Lyndon Johnson and the Wars for Vietnam* (Chicago: Ivan R. Dee, 1995), p. 488.

23. Berman, op. cit., p. 218.

24. *Washington Post* (September 11, 1968).

25. Ibid. (September 13, 1968).

26. Carl Solberg, *Hubert Humphrey: A Biography* (New York: W. W. Norton, 1984), p. 376.

27. Berman, op. cit., p. 211.

28. Solberg, op. cit., p. 377.

29. White, op. cit., p. 439.

30. Humphrey obituary (*New York Times*), January 14, 1978.

31. *Washington Post* (October 1, 1968).

32. Gardner, op. cit., p. 491.

33. Solberg, op. cit., p. 386.

34. *Facts on File* (October 17–October 23, 1968).

35. *Washington Post* (October 26, 1968).

36. Ibid. (October 6, 1968).

37. Lady Bird Johnson, *White House Diary* (New York: Holt, Rinehart, & Winston, 1970), p. 717.

38. *New York Times* (October 11, 1968).

39. Lyndon B. Johnson, *The Vantage Point: Perspectives of the Presidency, 1963–1969* (New York: Holt, Rinehart & Winston, 1971), p. 515.

40. George Christian, *The President Steps Down: A Personal Memoir of the Transfer of Power* (New York: Macmillan, 1970), pp. 51–52.

41. Johnson, op. cit., p. 516.

42. Christian, op. cit., p. 59.

43. *Washington Post* (October 17, 1968).

44. Johnson, op. cit., pp. 517–518.

45. Douglas Frantz and David McKean, *Friends in High Places: The Rise and Fall of Clark Clifford* (Boston: Little, Brown, 1995), p. 247.

46. *Washington Post* (October 27, 1968).

47. Ibid. (October 28, 1968).

48. Gardner, op. cit., p. 510.

49. *New York Times* (November 1, 1968).

50. Solberg, op. cit., p. 398.

51. Califano, op. cit., p. 328.

52. *Washington Post* (November 4, 1968).

53. Ibid. (November 6, 1968).

54. Ibid. (November 7, 1968).

55. Solberg, op. cit., p. 406.

56. Christian, op. cit., p. 181.

57. Lady Bird Johnson, op. cit., p. 728.

58. Ibid., p. 243.

59. *Washington Post* (November 12, 1968).

60. Ibid. (November 12 and 16, 1968).

61. *Public Papers of the Presidents of the United States: Lyndon Baines Johnson, 1968–1969*, vol. 2 (Washington, D.C.: U.S. Government Printing Office, 1970), pp. 1140–1143.

62. Christian, op. cit., pp. 247–48.

63. *Washington Post* (December 29, 1968).

64. Christian, op. cit., pp. 247–248.

65. *Washington Post* (December 14, 1968).

66. Ibid. (December 15, 1968).

67. Ibid. (December 27, 1968).

68. Ibid. (December 28, 1968).

69. Ibid. (January 10, 1969).

70. Ibid. (December 25, 1968).

71. Ibid. (January 7, 1969).

72. Ibid.

73. Ibid. (January 14, 1969); Style Section by Dorothy McCardle.

74. *New York Times* (January 14, 1969).

75. *Washington Post* (January 15, 1969).

76. Clark Clifford, *Counsel to the President: A Memoir* (New York: Random House, 1991), p. 604.

77. Johnson, op. cit., p. 529.

78. *Washington Post* (January 18, 1969).

79. Califano, op. cit., p. 338.

80. Johnson, op. cit., p. 560.

81. Clark Clifford, *Oral History*, Tape 4, p. 34, LBJ Library.

82. Clifford, *Counsel to the President*, p. 606.

83. Lady Bird Johnson, op. cit., p. 785.

84. Ibid.

85. Johnson, op. cit., p. 567.

86. *Washington Post* (January 21, 1969).

Chapter 22: Last Days

1. *Houston Post* (January 24, 1973).

2. Robert Dallek, *Flawed Giant: Lyndon Johnson and His Times, 1961–1973* (New York: Oxford University Press, 1998), p. 601.

3. *Time* (January 31, 1969).

4. *Houston Post* (January 23, 1969).

5. *New York Times* (January 24, 1969).

6. Bill Porterfield, "Back Home Again in Johnson City," *New York Times Magazine* (March 2, 1969).

7. Ibid.

8. Ibid.

9. *Time* (January 31, 1969).

10. Porterfield, op. cit.

11. *New York Times* (January 27, 1969).

12. *Houston Post* (February 21, 1969).

13. *Time* (January 31, 1969).

14. *New York Times* (June 21, 1969).

15. Doris Kearns, *Lyndon Johnson and the American Dream* (New York: Harper & Row, 1976), pp. 358–359.

16. *New York Times* (August 28, 1969).

17. Jack Anderson, "What Five Years in the White House Have Done to Lyndon Johnson," *Parade Magazine* (January 12, 1969).

18. Kearns, op. cit., pp. 356–357.

19. Ibid. (June 21, 1969).

20. Merle Miller, *Lyndon: An Oral Biography* (New York: G. P. Putnam's Sons, 1980), p. 545.

21. Clark Clifford, *Oral History*, Tape 7, p. 5, LBJ Library.

22. Kearns, op. cit., p. 360.

23. Bernard Weisberger, personal letter, "Dear Kids," New York, N.Y. (November 11, 1970), with the permission of the author.

24. Miller, op. cit., p. 546.

25. *New York Times* (June 6, 1971).

26. Ibid. (November 9, 1969).

27. *New York Times* (December 12, 1969).

28. Walter Cronkite, *A Reporter's Life* (New York: Alfred A. Knopf, 1996), pp. 232–236.

29. Transcript of CBS News Special "LBJ: Why I Chose Not to Run," as broadcast over the CBS Television Network (December 27, 1969).

30. Transcript of CBS News Special "LBJ: The Decision to Halt the Bombing," as broadcast over the CBS Television Network (February 6, 1970).

31. Transcript of CBS News Special "LBJ: Tragedy and Transition," as broadcast over the CBS Television Network (May 2, 1970).

32. *Washington Post* (April 7, 1970).

33. Katharine Graham, *Personal History* (New York: Alfred A. Knopf, 1997), p. 438.

34. *New York Times* (May 2, 1970).

35. *Houston Post* (August 16, 1970).

36. *New York Times* (August 29, 1970).

37. *New York Times Book Review* (October 25, 1970).

38. *Washington Post* (May 23 and May 24, 1971); *Newsweek* (May 24, 1971).

39. Leo Janos, "The Last Days of the President: LBJ in Retirement," *Atlantic Monthly* (July 1973), p. 39.

40. Ibid.

41. *New York Times* (August 2, 1971).

42. Ibid. (October 27, 1971).

43. Ibid. (December 12, 1971).

44. Ibid. (October 10, 1971).

45. Janos, op. cit., p. 38.

46. *Austin American Statesman* (January 26, 1972).

47. *Washington Post* (January 26, 1972).

48. Transcript of CBS News Special "LBJ: Lyndon Johnson Talks Politics," as broadcast over the CBS Television Network (January 27, 1972).

49. Jan Jarboe, "Lady Bird Looks Back," *Texas Monthly* (December 1994).

50. Janos, op. cit., p. 40.

51. *New York Times* (January 31, 1973).

52. *Chicago Tribune* (July 14, 1972).

53. Janos, op. cit., p. 41.

54. *Washington Post* (August 17, 1972).

55. David Maraniss, *First in His Class: A Biography of Bill Clinton* (New York: Simon & Schuster, 1995), pp. 271–272.

56. *Washington Post* (August 23, 1972).

57. Miller, op. cit., p. 552.

58. George McGovern letter to authors (September 10, 1998).

59. *New York Times* (September 21, 1972).

60. *New York Times* (October 13, 1972).

61. Janos, op. cit., p. 40

62. " 'The Country Isn't Over the Hill' . . . Then LBJ Was Gone," *Los Angeles Times* (January 28, 1973).

63. *New York Times* (November 18, 1972).

64. Janos, op. cit., p. 40.

65. *Austin American Statesman* (December 12, 1972).

66. Miller, op. cit., p. 560.

67. *Newsweek* (December 25, 1972).

68. Miller, op. cit., p. 561.

69. *Austin American Statesman* (December 13, 1972).
70. Miller, op. cit., p. 562.
71. CBS transcript, "LBJ: The Last Interview," with Walter Cronkite (February 1, 1973).
72. Hugh Sidey, "One More Call to Reason Together," *Life* (December 29, 1972).
73. Jarboe, op. cit.
74. Miller, op. cit., p. 555.
75. "LBJ: The Last Interview."
76. *Los Angeles Times* (January 23, 1973).
77. *Austin American Statesman* (January 23, 1973).
78. Jack Valenti, *A Very Human President* (New York: W. W. Norton, 1975), pp. 391–392.
79. *Austin American Statesman* (January 24, 1973).
80. Ibid. (January 25, 1973).
81. *Newsweek* (February 5, 1973).
82. Miller, op. cit., p. 557.
83. *Newsweek* (February 5, 1973).
84. Miller, op. cit., p. 558.
85. *Austin American Statesman* (January 26, 1973).
86. Miller, op. cit., p. 558.
87. *New York Times* (February 4, 1973).

Index